The Role of the Father in Child Development *edited by Michael E. Lamb*

Handbook of Behavioral Assessment *edited by Anthony R. Ciminero, Karen S. Calhoun, and Henry E*

Counseling ... ach *by E. Lakin Phillips*

Dimension ... *and John E. Exner, Jr.*

The Ment ... non *by Peter A. Magaro, Robert Gripp, David M*

Nonverbal Communication: The State of the Art *by Robert G. Harper, Arthur N. Wiens, and Joseph D. Matarazzo*

Alcoholism and Treatment *by David J. Armor, J. Michael Polich, and Harriet B. Stambul*

A Biodevelopmental Approach to Clinical Child Psychology: Cognitive Controls and Cognitive Control Theory *by Sebastiano Santostefano*

Handbook of Infant Development *edited by Joy D. Osofsky*

Understanding the Rape Victim: A Synthesis of Research Findings *by Sedelle Katz and Mary Ann Mazur*

Childhood Pathology and Later Adjustment: The Question of Prediction *by Loretta K. Cass and Carolyn B. Thomas*

Intelligent Testing with the WISC-R *by Alan S. Kaufman*

Adaptation in Schizophrenia: The Theory of Segmental Set *by David Shakow*

Psychotherapy: An Eclectic Approach *by Sol L. Garfield*

Handbook of Minimal Brain Dysfunctions *edited by Herbert E. Rie and Ellen D. Rie*

Handbook of Behavioral Interventions: A Clinical Guide *edited by Alan Goldstein and Edna B. Foa*

Art Psychotherapy *by Harriet Wadeson*

Handbook of Adolescent Psychology *edited by Joseph Adelson*

Psychotherapy Supervision: Theory, Research and Practice *edited by Allen K. Hess*

Psychology and Psychiatry in Courts and Corrections: Controversy and Change *by Ellsworth A. Fersch, Jr.*

Restricted Environmental Stimulation: Research and Clinical Applications *by Peter Suedfeld*

Personal Construct Psychology: Psychotherapy and Personality *edited by Alvin W. Landfield and Larry M. Leitner*

Mothers, Grandmothers, and Daughters: Personality and Child Care in Three-Generation Families *by Bertram J. Cohler and Henry U. Grunebaum*

Further Explorations in Personality *edited by A.I. Rabin, Joel Aronoff, Andrew M. Barclay, and Robert A. Zucker*

Hypnosis and Relaxation: Modern Verification of an Old Equation *by William E. Edmonston, Jr.*

Handbook of Clinical Behavior Therapy *edited by Samuel M. Turner, Karen S. Calhoun, and Henry E. Adams*

Handbook of Clinical Neuropsychology *edited by Susan B. Filskov and Thomas J. Boll*

The Course of Alcoholism: Four Years After Treatment *by J. Michael Polich, David J. Armor, and Harriet B. Braiker*

Handbook of Innovative Psychotherapies *edited by Raymond J. Corsini*

The Role of the Father in Child Development (Second Edition) *edited by Michael E. Lamb*

Behavioral Medicine: Clinical Applications *by Susan S. Pinkerton, Howard Hughes, and W.W. Wenrich*

Handbook for the Practice of Pediatric Psychology *edited by June M. Tuma*

Change Through Interaction: Social Psychological Processes of Counseling and Psychotherapy *by Stanley R. Strong and Charles D. Claiborn*

Drugs and Behavior (Second Edition) *by Fred Leavitt*

(*continued on back*)

CONTEMPORARY TOPICS IN
DEVELOPMENTAL PSYCHOLOGY

Contemporary Topics in Developmental Psychology

Edited by

NANCY EISENBERG

Arizona State University

A WILEY-INTERSCIENCE PUBLICATION

JOHN WILEY & SONS

New York • Chichester • Brisbane • Toronto • Singapore

Library of Congress Cataloging in Publication Data

Contemporary topics in developmental psychology.

(Wiley series on personality processes)
"A Wiley-Interscience publication."
Includes bibliographies.
1. Child psychology. 2. Child development.
I. Eisenberg, Nancy. II. Series. [DNLM: 1. Child Development. 2. Human Development. 3. Socialization. WS 105 C7615]
BF721.C624 1987 155 86-34026
ISBN 0-471-82913-7

Printed in the United States of America

10 9 8 7 6 5 4 3 2 1

Contributors

Phyllis W. Berman, PhD
Guest Researcher
Laboratory of Comparative Ethology
National Institute of Child Health and Human Development
Bethesda, Maryland

James E. Birren, PhD
Professor
Andrus Gerontology Center
University of Southern California
Los Angeles, California

Sanford L. Braver, PhD
Associate Professor
Department of Psychology
Arizona State University
Tempe, Arizona

Laurie Chassin, PhD
Associate Professor
Department of Psychology
Arizona State University
Tempe, Arizona

Alison Clarke-Stewart, PhD
Professor
Department of Social Ecology
University of California, Irvine
Irvine, California

Philip R. Costanzo, PhD
Professor
Department of Psychology
Duke University
Durham, North Carolina

Nancy Eisenberg, PhD
Professor
Department of Psychology
Arizona State University
Tempe, Arizona

Peter Fraenkel, MA
Doctoral Candidate
Department of Psychology
Duke University
Durham, North Carolina

Susan Harter, PhD
Professor
Department of Psychology
University of Denver
Denver, Colorado

Bonnie Hedlund, PhD
Research Assistant
Andrus Gerontology Center
University of Southern California
Los Angeles, California

Claire B. Kopp, PhD
Professor
Department of Psychology
University of California, Los Angeles
Los Angeles, California

Paul Mussen, PhD
Professor Emeritus
Department of Psychology
University of California, Berkeley

Herbert L. Pick, Jr., PhD
Professor
Institute for Child Development
University of Minnesota
Minneapolis, Minnesota

Clark C. Presson, PhD
Associate Professor
Department of Psychology
Arizona State University
Tempe, Arizona

Diane N. Ruble, PhD
Professor
Department of Psychology
New York University
New York, New York

Arnold J. Sameroff, PhD
Director
Bradley Developmental Psychopathology Research Center
Bradley Hospital
Brown University
East Providence, Rhode Island

Irwin N. Sandler, PhD
Professor
Department of Psychology
Arizona State University
Tempe, Arizona

Steven J. Sherman, PhD
Professor
Department of Psychology
Indiana University
Bloomington, Indiana

Susan C. Somerville, PhD
Professor
Department of Psychology
Arizona State University
Tempe, Arizona

Esther Thelen, PhD
Professor
Department of Psychology
Indiana University
Bloomington, Indiana

Henry M. Wellman, PhD
Associate Professor
Department of Psychology
University of Michigan
Ann Arbor, Michigan

Sharlene A. Wolchik, PhD
Associate Professor
Department of Psychology
Arizona State University
Tempe, Arizona

Series Preface

This series of books is addressed to behavioral scientists interested in the nature of human personality. Its scope should prove pertinent to personality theorists and researchers as well as to clinicians concerned with applying an understanding of personality processes to the amelioration of emotional difficulties in living. To this end, the series provides a scholarly integration of theoretical formulations, empirical data, and practical recommendations.

Six major aspects of studying and learning about human personality can be designated: personality theory, personality structure and dynamics, personality development, personality assessment, personality change, and personality adjustment. In exploring these aspects of personality, the books in the series discuss a number of distinct but related subject areas: the nature and implications of various theories of personality; personality characteristics that account for consistencies and variations in human behavior; the emergence of personality processes in children and adolescents; the use of interviewing and testing procedures to evaluate individual differences in personality; efforts to modify personality styles through psychotherapy, counseling, behavior, therapy, and other methods of influence; and patterns of abnormal personality functioning that impair individual competence.

IRVING B. WEINER

University of Denver
Denver, Colorado

Preface

The purpose of this volume is to provide a current overview of important and interesting findings and viewpoints in developmental psychology. This is not an easy task, given both the breadth of the field and its interface with a variety of other disciplines and subdisciplines within psychology. Indeed, due to the diversity of topics studied by those with developmental perspectives, it is impossible for any single volume to contain an inclusive overview of the field.

The diversity of interests among developmentalists reflects both historical and current influences on the field. Until fairly recently, developmental psychology was fairly synonymous with the study of child development. The study of child development emerged, in large part, due to practitioners' (e.g., social workers, educators, physicians) desire to understand development so that they could better accomplish applied goals (cf. Sears, 1975). Thus, there always has been, and still is, an applied side to the field (see, e.g., the relatively new journal, *Journal of Applied Developmental Psychology*). Indeed, contemporary developmental theory and research are of interest to many clinicians and practitioners (e.g., research concerning children's learning and the effects of day care, divorce, and other life-style factors on social, emotional, and cognitive development); in addition, a substantial number of clinical psychologists, experimental psychologists, educational psychologists, anthropologists, and physicians are conducting research related to developmental issues.

There also is a strong basic science focus to much developmental work. Conceptual issues related to the "how" and "why" of development are central foci in many researchers' agenda. The content about which such questions are asked is quite diverse. Because developmentalists are concerned with change in regard to nearly all areas of psychological functioning, they examine issues also studied by clinical, social, educational, community, and experimental psychologists, as well as by other groups of social scientists. Thus, the content of contemporary developmental psychology ranges from perception to psychopathology, learning and cognition to social development, and growth and motor development to changes in personality structure (cf. Mussen, 1983).

A recent emphasis in the field has further broadened the scope of developmental psychology. Although there has always been some interest among developmentalists in change after adolescence (e.g., as evidenced by the interest in longitudinal research), the focus upon life span psychology, aging, and stages in adult development in recent years, by both developmentalists and other psychologists (e.g., Baltes, Reese, & Lipsitt, 1980; Baltes & Brim, 1979, 1980, 1982, 1983; Eichorn, Clausen, Haan, Honzik, & Mussen, 1981; Kohlberg & Higgins, 1984; Levinson, Darrow, Klein, Levinson, & McKee, 1978), has enriched and enlarged the domain of developmental psychology. Moreover, the focus on life span development by numerous developmentalists has served to highlight the relation of developmental psychology to social psychology, anthropology, sociology, and other disciplines within the social sciences that involve a focus on the social context of development (cf. Baltes et al., 1980).

ORGANIZATION OF THE VOLUME

The richness and diversity of topics and approaches currently evidenced in investigations of development are reflected, at least to some degree, in the contents of this volume. Contributors include developmental psychologists and those trained as biologists, social psychologists, and clinical psychologists. Yet all are studying development. The topics they have addressed include many of the major foci in developmental psychology today and span the life cycle. The chapters vary in the degree to which they are concerned with applied issues and in the degree to which they deal with an area of interface between developmental psychology and other areas of study.

The volume is divided into six sections. In the first, the issues of motor development (Esther Thelen) and self-regulation in the early years (Claire Kopp) are examined. Clearly, the development of motor skills and self-regulation of behavior are central to much of later development in a variety of domains. In the second section, the focus is cognitive and perceptual development during childhood, with an emphasis on the role of experience in perceptual development (Herbert Pick), spatial cognition (Clark Presson), and logical thinking (in the context of search behaviors) (Susan Somerville & Henry Wellman). The topic of the third section is social development. Within this section, issues related to the development of caretaking behaviors (Phyllis Berman), moral behavior (Nancy Eisenberg), and the role of socialization in social and personality development (Philip Costanzo and Peter Fraenkel) are explored by contributors. The focus of the chapters in the fourth section is the development of self-worth and self-related knowledge. In specific, topics of concern include the development, antecedents, and correlates of self-worth (Susan Harter) as well as processes related to obtaining and utilizing self-related knowledge (Diane Ruble). The latter chapter, and those by Costanzo, Eisenberg, and Chassin and colleagues are examples of research on the interface of social and developmental psychology, an area that is receiving increased attention in recent years (e.g., Masters & Yarkin-Levin, 1984).

In the fifth section of the volume, the interface between developmental conceptions and application is most evident. In this section, called "The Social Context: Its Role in Development," development is examined in the context of social interactions (Arnold Sameroff) and various child-care alternatives (Alison Clarke-Stewart), and in relation to social support, especially in the wake of parental divorce (Sharlene Wolchik, Irwin Sandler, & Sanford Braver). All chapters have relevance for prevention and/or intervention programs, especially if one is concerned with promoting healthy psychological and social development as well as with preventing or ameliorating negative developmental outcomes.

In the sixth and final section, contributors discuss issues relevant to a life span conception of development. In the first chapter, Laurie Chassin, Clark Presson, and S. J. Sherman demonstrate ways in which social psychological principles can be used to understand adolescents' health-related behaviors and cognitions. In the context of discussing longitudinal research, Paul Mussen presents some of the findings of the longitudinal studies housed at the University of California, Berkeley. In contrast, James Birren outlines a different method for studying development in adulthood—the use of autobiography.

As was noted previously, not all of the many exciting issues currently being examined from a developmental perspective are covered in the book. Nonetheless, the book includes a wide sampling of current theory and research with regard to a number of important issues, presented by major contributors to their respective areas of study. It is our hope that this volume is useful both for updating professionals already in the field or in related areas of study and for stimulating interest among those who might choose (or have recently chosen) to explore the multifaceted and intriguing topic of development.

NANCY EISENBERG

Tempe, Arizona
April 1987

REFERENCES

Baltes, P. B., Reese, H. W., & Lipsitt, L. P. (1980). Life-span developmental psychology. *Annual Review of Psychology, 31,* 65–110.

Baltes, P. B., & Brim, O. G., Jr. (Eds.). (1979, 1980, 1982, 1983). *Life-span development and behavior* (Vols. 2–5). New York: Academic.

Eichorn, D. H., Clausen, J. A., Haan, N., Honzik, M. J., & Mussen, P. H. (Eds.). (1981). *Present and past in middle life.* New York: Academic.

Kohlberg, L., & Higgins, A. (1984). Continuities and discontinuities in childhood and adult development revisited—again. In L. Kohlberg (Ed.), *Essays on moral development.* (Vol. 2). *The psychology of moral development.* San Francisco: Harper & Row.

Levinson, D. J., Darrow, C. N., Klein, E. B., Levinson, M. H., & McKee, B. (1978). *The seasons of a man's life.* New York: Knopf.

Masters, J. C., & Yarkin-Levin, K. (Eds.). (1984). *Boundary areas in social and developmental psychology.* New York: Academic.

Mussen, P. H. (Ed.) (1983). *Manual of child psychology* (Vols. 1–4). New York: Wiley.

Sears, R. R. (1975). Your ancients revisited: A history of child development. In E. M. Hetherington (Ed.), *Review of child development research* (Vol. 5). Chicago: University of Chicago Press.

Acknowledgments

This volume is the product of many individuals and groups, and I am indebted to them all. I cannot name everyone involved without some review of the book's history.

All of the contributors to this volume either were part of a special series of speakers who came to visit the Department of Psychology at Arizona State University, are faculty members in the department, or are persons who have collaborated with individuals in the department. The speakers were chosen because of their major contributions to our understanding of a wide variety of topics relevant to developmental concerns. This special program of speakers, entitled "Contemporary Issues in Developmental Psychology," was funded by monies paid to the Psychology Department by the Honors Program within the College of Liberal Arts. The Department of Psychology and I gratefully acknowledge the contribution of the Honors Program.

The speakers came to Arizona State University for 1½–2 days, during which time they engaged in a variety of activities and discussions. Their contributions to this volume were, in part, an outcome of their visit. Without their willingness to share their expertise, both in person and through their chapters, this volume would not have been possible.

Four of the chapters were written by my colleagues and their collaborators at other universities. Their help sponsoring the series of speakers and their contribution to this volume also are gratefully acknowledged. Moreover, the assistance of Clark Presson and Susan Somerville in reviewing some chapters was and is appreciated.

My participation in this project was funded not only by the Honors Program at Arizona State University but also by a research grant from the National Institute of Child Health and Development (I R0I HD17909) and by a Career Development Award from the same institute (I K04 HD00717). I am grateful for this support.

Thanks also are due to Sally Carney, who helped with the typing of parts of the manuscript, and to Herb Reich at Wiley for his support of this project. Finally, I want to thank my husband, Jerry Harris, for his support and patience throughout all.

Tempe, Arizona
April 1987

N.E.

Contents

CONTEMPORARY TOPICS IN
DEVELOPMENTAL PSYCHOLOGY

PART ONE

Motor Development and Self-Regulation in the Early Years

It is fitting that the chapters in the first section of this volume concern early motor development and self-regulation. These aspects of development not only are salient in the first years of life, but also provide a foundation for further development in a variety of domains.

The most rapid changes in behavior in the early months of life obviously are in the domain of motor development. Change is evident on a weekly or even daily basis, as a child learns to grasp objects, turn over, walk, or perform other motor tasks. These motor developments must have profound effects both on the nature of the infant's interactions with others and on his or her cognitive and perceptual experiences and development.

Despite the significance of motor advances for development in general, and despite the fact that early developmentalists were very interested in motor development, the topic has received relatively little attention in recent years. However, Esther Thelen, through her creative approach, has revitalized this area of research. In her chapter, Thelen reviews the history of ideas concerning motor development and then provides an overview of her own work and perspectives. She also presents a strong case regarding the importance of movement for understanding other developmental domains.

The development of self-regulatory processes is also a major achievement in the early years, one that is of obvious significance to the weary parent of a toddler or young child. The ability to control one's impulses and affect; modulate motor, linguistic, and other activities; and comply with commands and norms has to have a profound effect upon the quality of the child's social interactions, as well as his or her growth in nonsocial domains. Moreover, it is likely that later development with regard to self-regulatory processes is dependent on the nature of early accomplishments.

Despite the layperson's interest in young children's negativism and noncompliance, few psychologists have taken an in-depth look at the early development of self-regulatory processes and their connection to early cognitive development and social relationships. In her chapter concerning the growth of self-regulation, Claire Kopp tackles this task. In specific, she outlines the roles of both child and socializer in the emergence of socially appropriate, self-regulated behavior, and the role of key cognitive capabilities in the process. Finally, Kopp presents a working model for understanding the development of self-regulatory behavior in the second and third years of life.

CHAPTER 1

The Role of Motor Development in Developmental Psychology: A View of the Past and an Agenda for the Future

ESTHER THELEN

If you ask new parents what their baby is doing, you will most often hear about a motor milestone. "Oh, she just learned to roll over." "He's crawling around and getting into everything." "She pulls herself up in the crib, but she can't sit down." Likewise, the developmental screening done by the pediatrician will consist of many motor items, ranging from reflex evaluation in young infants to fine motor skills tasks for older babies.

The motor repertoire is highly salient for parents and pediatricians for good reasons. On one level, motor progress is the most easily observed marker of developmental progress in infancy. For parents, the obvious delight in seeing new accomplishments may also carry the less explicit message of relief that the infant is intact. For pediatricians, motor skills not only tag neuromuscular integrity, but also reflect perceptual and cognitive development. On a second level, the more subtle and seemingly gradual changes in perception and cognition do not seem to have the dramatic and immediate effect on everyday life that the acquisition of motor milestones does. Families must act very differently toward an infant who can roll off a table, or who can crawl or sit alone, than toward an infant without these skills.

What of our understanding of the development of motor skills in early life? As is well known, movement and its patterning were the dominant interests of some of the pioneers of developmental research, especially Myrtle McGraw and Arnold Gesell. In the decades since these early workers, the study of posture and movement had become largely dormant in the mainstream of devel-

---

I have collaborated with Alan Fogel and Scott Kelso on aspects of the theoretical position presented in this chapter, and I acknowledge their contributions with thanks. Research reported here was supported by grants from the National Science Foundation and the National Institute of Child Health and Human Development.

opmental psychology. Despite Piaget's emphasis on action as an essential organizer of the sensorimotor period, neither his nor subsequent theories of action or skill devote much attention to *movement;* rather, most are theories of cognition or perception (e.g., Bruner, 1970; Fischer, 1980; Forman, 1982; Frese & Stewart, 1984). Motor development per se has been the domain of pediatric neurology, physical education, and physical and occupational therapy, with a largely descriptive or clinical focus.

We are in the midst of a reawakening of interest in the motor side of the equation (see, e.g., Fentress, 1984; von Hofsten, 1984; Kelso & Clark, 1982; Reed, 1982; Thelen & Fogel, in press; Trevarthan, 1984). And with this reawakening is a sense of excitement as we come to realize the potential of movement studies to go beyond the traditional description and developmental norms to be an essential variable in our understanding of development. The purpose of this chapter is to suggest an agenda to reintegrate movement into our accounts of early development.

I have several reasons for this appeal. First, it is important and interesting in and of itself to understand how the nervous system controls the muscles and joints of the body so that we may act in our worlds. This has been the concern of adult motor psychology, neurophysiology, kinesiology, and biomechanics, and yet most of the insights from these fields have not filtered into the developmental sphere. But I make an even stronger case: that the study of other domains of infant development cannot ignore posture and movement. In preverbal infants, our understanding of perception, cognition, affect, and social relationships is necessarily movement mediated. The usual view is that because the periphery—the neuromuscular and skeletal apparatus—is driven by central processes, psychologists should study those more "interesting" central domains such as perception, cognition, and affect. I suggest here that the periphery can act as much more: as both a source of behavior and a constraint on it, such that a full understanding warrants a more holistic approach. In turn, movement itself acts as a powerful organizer and motivator of other developmental events, compelling us to look at posture and movement as part of the ecology of the infant.

Because the field of motor development has been dormant for so long, it would be easy to forget the enormous legacy of the towering giants of the field, McGraw and Gesell. Therefore, I begin this chapter with a critical discussion of their contributions to developmental psychology, with the suggestion that our new synthesis both incorporate and go beyond their work. Following this, I review several emerging action-based approaches and their implications for a more holistic developmental psychology. Finally, I outline several active areas of infant research that involve some aspect of movement but have not been commonly interpreted from a movement-based framework, and I suggest how such a framework can be and is being used to resolve some long-standing puzzles.

THE LEGACY OF MOTOR DEVELOPMENT: MCGRAW AND GESELL

The Embryology of Behavior

What are best remembered from the monumental works of Myrtle McGraw and Arnold Gesell—at least what have filtered into textbooks and introductory lectures—are *milestones* and *stages* of motor development. While this descriptive and normative work has been of enormous value, I would like to resurrect for discussion these authors' explicit theoretical underpinnings. Why did they choose to study motor development? What did they hope to learn from the study of movement and its changes of form over time? What can we learn from their work? While the exquisite descriptions are part and parcel of the work, neither author, I believe, meant them to be ends in themselves.

Our recognition of the contributions of McGraw and Gesell is enhanced when we understand something about the scientific context in which they worked and their orientation, which was thoroughly biological. Both were profoundly influenced by embryologists working largely in the second quarter of the twentieth century. This was a lively time in vertebrate embryology, with the appearance of the now classic works of Windle, Tilney, Coghill, Langworthy, and later, Waddington, Conel, Carmichael, and Humphrey. It was also a time of lively debate—the perennial debate in ontogeny—on whether the sources of developmental change were intrinsic (maturational) or extrinsic (experiential).

In a very explicit way, both McGraw and Gesell, in their studies of human infants, sought to answer this fundamental question of the relation between structure and function in generating developmental change. Both used the emergence of posture and movement to do this, and although their theoretical conclusions are somewhat different, their mutual reliance on the concepts, methods, and visions of the great embryologists cannot be underestimated.

McGraw and the Maturation of the Nervous System

McGraw used as her scientific paradigm the studies of G. E. Coghill and other experimental embryologists who sought to correlate observable changes in the nervous system, usually through histological studies with overt changes in behavior. If these relations could be demonstrated, McGraw believed, then it could be shown that human behavior emerged in a lawful manner from the structural growth and maturation of the nervous system. The specific steps involved, first, an understanding of neurogenesis—the general and specific course of development of the nervous system. Second, McGraw believed the researcher must observe the onset and form of the overt behavior. Finally, these two phenomena must be correlated so that a behavioral event can be related to its anatomical and physiological substrate (McGraw, 1943, 1946).

In a similar way, McGraw sought to elucidate structure–function relations in human infants. From the studies of Langworthy, Tilney, Conel, and others on the histology of the fetal and infant brains, McGraw could construct a general picture of brain maturation. Her own detailed studies provided the behavioral data. But how did she come to choose the motor repertoire—emergent posture and locomotion—for this purpose? Why not emergent perception or language or other cognitive or social skills? McGraw's thoroughly comparative perspective may provide part of the answer. When embryologists described behavior of the bird and reptile embryos and mammalian fetuses, they most often described *movement* (although there was an important literature on fetal sensory development). In the salamander, for example, Coghill traced the ontogeny of locomotion—from the first swimming movements of the early larva to the coordinated terrestrial locomotion of the adult, with a particular emphasis on the movement *form,* that is, the position of the body limbs and segments in space. McGraw similarly saw the clues to developmental processes in the unfolding patterning of motor actions. Compare McGraw's drawings of three phases of swimming behavior, taken from movie film, to those of Coghill (1929) on the early swimming movements of *Amblystoma* (Fig. 1.1). McGraw's analogy was explicit: "One who has observed the development of prone progression in infants cannot fail to be struck by the similarity in the infant's development of progression and the progression of the salamander as described by Coghill (1929)" (McGraw, 1946, p. 360).

Thus, by observing the patterning of prone progression, sitting, swimming, erect progression, adjustment to inversion, and grasping in infants and correlating the changes to her understanding of human neurogenesis, McGraw concluded that "certain qualities of movement signify grossly the level of neural maturation involved," (p. 359). In particular, each of these behaviors could be traced through a four-phase process of increasing cortical control in infancy.

Although McGraw studied primarily the motor domain, she saw the unfolding patterning of motor actions unlocking the secrets of the developmental process in general. In her study of erect locomotion, for instance, she envisioned her precise quantification of emergent walking as not just describing the "sequential features themselves," but rather determining "the dynamic element of change which leads one form of behavior to give way to the next" (McGraw & Breeze, 1941, p. 267).

McGraw attributed the driving force of developmental change to nervous maturation, and specifically, the increasing role of the cerebral cortex. As the brain matures, functions improve. The immediate causes of new forms of behavior—the identifiable phases of motor development—were "reorganizations" in the nervous system as it matured in a systematic and predictable fashion. In short, function emerged from structure and not the reverse.

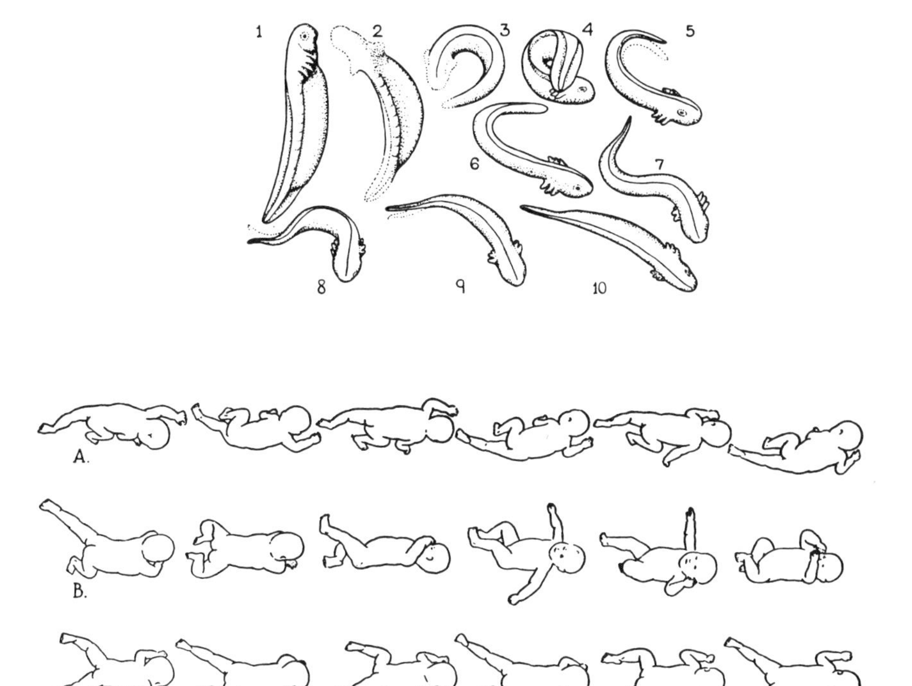

Figure 1.1. (*a*) Enlarged tracings of motion pictures of the early swimming movements of *Amblystoma tigrinum* (axolotl). Sequence lasted approximately 0.6 sec. From Coghill (1929). (*b*) Three phases in the development of aquatic behavior of the human infant. Drawings obtained from successive tracings from motion pictures. From McGraw (1946).

Gesell and the Morphology of Development

Like McGraw, Arnold Gesell used the patterning of posture and movement as his primary data. He was far bolder than McGraw, however, in his generalizations from the motor behavior of the infant to a larger developmental theory. It is unfortunate that Gesell is best remembered for his popular writings and widely used developmental norms, because his developmental theory is also a highly rich and generative one.

Although Gesell studied and wrote about human infants and children, his scientific foundations, like those of McGraw, were thoroughly comparative: "The study of infancy in its broadest sense must therefore be a comparative science. The most general laws of development will prove to be applicable to all vertebrates, not excluding either fish or man" (Gesell, 1946, p. 295).

More than any other developmentalist, Gesell saw human ontogeny, including the development of the mind, as a specific application of the very general laws of embryology. In remarking on the work of Coghill, Gesell stated: "The primitive vertebrate in the hands of Coghill (1929) has become a touchstone for elucidating problems of human behavior" (1946, p. 295). Although species-specific characteristics emerged during infancy through the selective agencies of evolution, the matrix of change occurred within "a general physiology of development" (1946, p. 296).

Fundamental to Gesell's theory and to his research program was his conviction that development was a *morphological* process. Morphology is the science of form and conventionally has been applied to the study of physical structures. But Gesell envisioned behavior as having *shape* just as the physical body has shape, and therefore behavior could be studied as the ontogenetic progressions and comparative features of a series of topographies of forms. Figure 1.2 reproduces photographs from his book, *The Embryology of Behavior,* illustrating the movement patterns of a premature ("fetal") infant, which should be compared to Coghill's salamanders in Figure 1.1. As Gesell

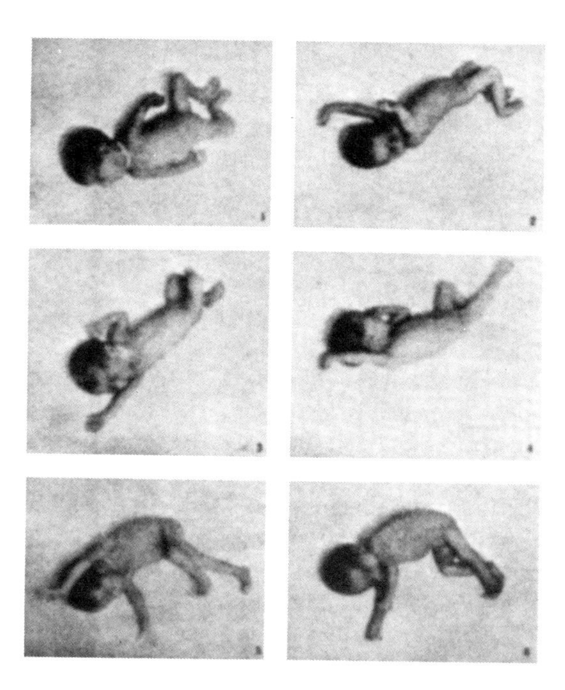

Figure 1.2. Supine postures and movements of premature infants at 33 weeks of gestational age. Sequence of movements lasting about 15 sec, illustrating slow tonic writhing. From Gesell (1945).

believed that mental processes were manifested in motor behavior, even the mind could be understood through these morphological processes.

For Gesell, the mechanisms of pattern formation were universal and applied just as well to the fertilized egg as to the development of the infant and child.

> The action systems of embryo, fetus, infant, and child undergo pattern changes which are so sequential and orderly that we may be certain that the patterning process is governed by mechanisms of form regulation—the same mechanisms which are being established by the science of embryology. (1946, p. 297)

Gesell saw his mass of descriptive data on the stages of motor, adaptive, language, and social behavior of children as much more, therefore, than a catalog of expected age norms. These patterns and sequences were the essential forms of developmental change and were as orderly and self-contained as the first cleavages of the fertilized egg. For example, Gesell introduced his study on the organization of prone behavior in infants as bringing "into panoramic view the total sweep of development" (Gesell & Ames, 1940, p. 247). The lawful trends evident in the progression of forms of the actions of prone infants were manifestations of powerful and universal principles of vertebrate development.

Gesell identified a number of developmental principles that emerged from the study of behavioral forms. One was the principle of *developmental direction:* that maturation proceeds in a head-to-toe, proximal-to-distal progression. The underlying mechanisms of developmental direction are the phenomena of *gradients and polarities* in embryology. It is useful to note that the 1930s saw remarkable advances in experimental embryology, especially toward an understanding of how the egg, a seemingly homogeneous structure, could differentiate into a complex organism without invoking a homunculus. From elegant transplantation experiments, embryologists showed that the determinants of fated organs were their relative *positions* in the egg and early embryo, and thus arose the notions of embryonic fields and gradients, induction, polarity, and regional determination. Gesell said there was "more than vague analogy" between these embryological concepts and human mental development (1946, p. 297).

Gesell's principle of *individuating maturation* was another analogy arising directly from embryology. In his studies of salamander embryos, Coghill (1929) discovered that organized movements for locomotion were established before the animal was responsive to sensory stimulation; movement was spontaneous in origin. During development, functional movements emerged from a pattern of total involvement of both the trunk and limb to more specific and individual actions of the limb segments. The organism is organized first as a perfectly integrated whole, and from this are carved discrete behaviors.

According to Gesell, this principle governed human development as well.

The human, too, begins life "as a perfectly integrated organism" (Gesell, 1946, p. 314). It is the process of growth itself, with the continuous reconfiguration of form, that drives developmental change. Because change is morphogenetic, this drive is entirely intrinsic to the organism and is not dependent on experience. Even the zygote is perfectly formed and adapted; behavior is not assembled from isolated pieces. As in the salamander, actions become more individualized and discrete within this matrix of organic unity. Any learning or conditioning is superimposed on, and constrained by, the fundamental impulse of maturation (Gesell, 1946).

Finally, Gesell invoked the principle of *self-regulating fluctuations.* Because of the inherently cyclical nature of biological systems, growth could be seen not as a linear process, but as a succession of states of "formation instability combined with a progressive movement toward stability" (1946, p. 317). This spiraling course whereby structure and function jointly mature leads to apparent retreats in organization. These are to be interpreted not as true involutions, but as times of reconsolidation resulting in a higher level of organization. Instability is a necessary correlate of stability, and these are both instantiations of the inherent self-regulating capabilities of biological systems.

Gesell's complex model of the *dynamic morphology of behavior* is summarized by Figure 1.3. Gesell advised us to read the model as a "timeflow map of morphogenetic movements which take place in a growing action system and which determine both the visible and concealed aspects of behavior organization" (1945, p. 175). In this time–space map, the small letters *a, b, c,* and *d* represent traits or components of traits, which over time coalesce into a developed complex of traits *D.* Some of the traits are manifest in the behavior of the infants, some are latent, and some are dormant. As traits combine, diverge, interweave, and are finally woven together, the pattern becomes both more complex and more synergistic.

Two Views of Development

Although Gesell and McGraw drew upon the same corpus of data—the patterning of movement—and while both assign the impulse of developmental change to growth, Gesell's *time–space* conceptions of development stand in contrast to McGraw's more prescriptive *neural-maturationist* model. This contrast, I believe, is a reflection of two very distinct traditions in biology in general—the more commonly accepted *reductionist* view, which posits that biological organization can be understood in terms of a central directing agency, and the perhaps less well-known *systems* view, which holds that the living organisms are characterized by the time–space dimensions of their interrelated parts. I argue in this section that, while McGraw's legacy is apparent in both a direct and a more subtle form, Gesell's ideas are worthy of serious reconsideration, and indeed, foreshadow a number of contemporary, action-based views of development.

The trend of twentieth century biology has been, and continues to be, reductionist. That is, biologists seek to understand the organism in terms of

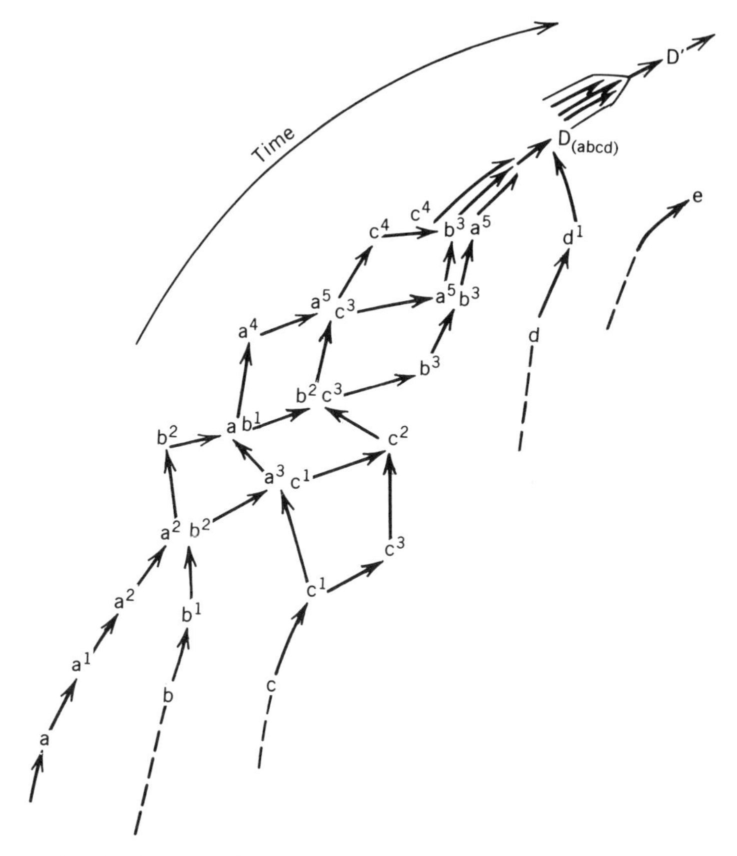

Figure 1.3. Gesell's time-space diagram of the morphogenetic processes which underlie the patterning of behavior. *a, b, c, d* = behavior traits or components. *D* = a developed complex of these components. Broken lines indicate latency. From Gesell (1945).

smaller and smaller units—and ultimately by molecular materials and molecular events of the genetic material. The rationale is, of course, that as we can know about the codes that direct all life we will know about living things. Despite the importance and, in many ways, success of this approach in contemporary biology, a second strand—complementary, but equally important—has continued to survive along with large-scale molecular biology and genetics. This stream, in which Gesell is clearly a participant, is a descendant more of morphologists—those who study form in the whole organism—than of geneticists. A systems view thus holds that knowing composition alone, be it nucleotides or amino acid sequences, is not sufficient. Atomistic conceptions of the organism are untenable, because they do not specify *form,* and it is the specific structure of chemicals that distinguishes a random soup from a living organism. In their review essay, Webster and Goodwin (1981) characterize a systems view as having three key concepts: wholeness, transformation, and self-regulation.

First, systems are *wholes* in the sense that they have the property of maintaining themselves while the elements change. The system defines the elements and not vice versa, but these interrelations are rule governed and not mystical. The generative laws of a system also define a finite and coherent set of *transformations* that the organism may undergo as a result of internal or external perturbations. Finally, as a consequence of their lawfulness or stability resulting from their organic relations, systems are *self-regulating,* which means they have the ability to maintain themselves despite perturbations. Systems in contemporary biology are exemplified by the modeling of *pattern formation* in embryogenesis and limb regeneration, which seeks to explain how spatial order can arise during development or regeneration (see, e.g., models proposed by French, Bryant, & Bryant, 1976; Gierer, 1981; Mittenthal, 1981).

While the details of embryogenesis and regeneration need not concern us here, the underlying principles guiding morphogenetic approaches to development have several important implications. First is the crucial emphasis on spatial and temporal *context* for determining developmental change. An isolated cell is an isolated cell; these models show that it is only a cell in context of a sheet of cells in a particular orientation in time and space that is the catalyst for the emergence of new forms. The elements and their instructions are meaningless without the relations between them. Second is that the nature of such complex relations leads to autocatalytic and self-regulating reactions. That is, small perturbations in the continual cellular field can lead to the emergence of highly discrete morphological forms such as limb segments or the neural tube. It is important to note that the genes need not specify the precise details of the emergent anatomical form. Contemporary embryological models have shown that, if the genetic material directs only the gradients and polarities in the cells and the timing of their appearance, specific structures will develop.

McGraw and Gesell Reconsidered

In the sense that she believed that the nervous system held the codes for developmental change, McGraw is more in the reductionist/prescriptive tradition in biology than in the systems mode. This prescriptive tradition has continued from McGraw, however, to be a very strong one in developmental psychology. First, there is an important segment of developmental research, especially in infancy studies, that seeks to understand ontogeny in terms of the maturation of the nervous system. This has been evident in direct anatomical studies (reviewed by Parmelee & Sigman, 1983), comparative studies that relate structural and behavioral development by both analogy and homology (see Gibson, 1981; Goldman-Rakic, Isseroff, Schwartz, & Bugbee, 1983), research in perception (Banks & Salapatek, 1983; Bronson, 1974; Clifton, Morrongiello, & Dowd, 1984), issues of laterality and brain development (Young, Corter, Segalowitz, & Trehub, 1983), organization of sleep and waking states (Prechtl, 1974), and direct measurements of brain activity (e.g., Hoffman, 1978).

These neurogenic accounts of behavioral development are an essential component of our understanding of ontogenetic processes. Nonetheless, while knowing the anatomical substrate of behavior is a desirable goal, I argue here that, just as knowing the genome alone will not tell us about the dynamics of developmental change, so neural maturation alone is an impoverished basis for a developmental theory. In many ways, the promise of Coghill's correlative paradigm remains unfulfilled. Why is this so? In the first place, even with our explosion of knowledge about the nervous system and its development, structure–function relationships in the nervous system are still poorly understood even in adult functioning. This is especially true when considering the complex activities that are of traditional concern to psychologists. It is not only the methodological restrictions that make such correlative studies fall short of a real understanding, but also the very nature of the nervous system. As an intricate biological system, the brain is coming increasingly to be viewed as a dynamic and self-organizing system, with highly plastic neural networks able to coalesce and regroup with time and task, in contrast to a hard-wired and static structure. As in embryology, these biological systems, by definition, are characterized by the *relations* among their elements, and thus cannot be explained by an isolated element. Studies of recovery from lesions in both adult and developing organisms are testaments to the fluidity, plasticity, and dynamic interrelations among the structural elements of the central nervous system (Edelman & Finkel, 1984; Goldman-Rakic et al., 1983). In short, a reductionist approach is not answering our questions about complex behavior.

Second, neural maturation alone is not a satisfactory explanation for the dynamics of developmental *change*. Since it is a given that the nervous system is maturing, correlations of structural changes such as myelinization with emergent behaviors are by necessity post hoc. Similarly, a neural "cause" can be invoked for any of the dips, regressions, spurts, asymmetries, and general surprises of the developmental course of any behavioral system by calling upon facilitation, inhibition, and reorganization, but we have not gained an explanation. What is missing is the process. If behavior changes because the instructions change, it is still unknown what causes the instructions to change.

The more subtle legacy of a neural–maturationist perspective is just this view that the sole sources of behavior are the instructions, usually seen as cognitive in nature. Such "top-down" explanations ignore the systems nature of the behaving organism, whose actions in context reflect contributions of many interrelated subsystems organized for functional tasks. Concepts like *cognitive metamorphosis* (Zelazo, 1983, p. 125) or *revolutionary periods* (Mounoud, 1982), by implying a single causal event for a variety of unrelated tasks, may mask the underlying and perhaps exceedingly convoluted dynamics of change.

In many ways, Gesell overcame the apparent linearity of McGraw's conceptualization and incorporated into his theory the contextual, time–space basis of more systems approaches to biological organization. Gesell built his model to deal with the multidetermined, interwoven subsystems he saw in the ontogeny of posture and movement. Rather than a linear progression of improving cortical function, Gesell explicitly invokes waxing and waning components or *traits* that intermesh in myriad ways in a spiral course. For instance, both authors describe an essentially similar sequence in the acquisition of fine prehension (Gesell, 1946; McGraw, 1946). But while McGraw assigns the course of developmental change to increasingly cortical control of vision combined with increasing cortical control of the neuromuscular apparatus, Gesell saw each stage as a merging and replacing of elements, whose combination induces a new maturational transformation.

The assumption of a nonlinear developmental progression and a time–space interaction of contributing subsystems or traits casts Gesell's model in surprisingly contemporary terms and provides, as Gierer (1981) and others have shown, a means to account for pattern *generation* without invoking infinite regress. No homunculus is necessary, but a code, be it genetic or neural, that can provide a minimal set of instructions sufficient to set the autocatalytic process in action.

In sum, I see two important implications of the legacies of McGraw and Gesell for the present and future study of motor development and development in general. First is the refocusing of attention to the relevance of movement patterning or form as a means to understand development. And second, Gesell, who is more clearly in the tradition of *organic* theories of development (see Overton & Reese, 1973; Reese & Overton, 1970), emphasized the multidetermined, multilevel nature of behavioral outcome and the autocatalytic or self-organizing properties of developing systems. As I suggest in the following section, this systems viewpoint is especially compatible with certain contemporary views of motor control and coordination, and provides the basis for an agenda for a revitalized look at the motor sphere.

Current Theories of Motor Control and the Developmental Implications

As we evaluate what we know and what we ought to know about the development of motor skill, it seems logical to ask about the contributions of contemporary work on adult motor control and coordination. Can we apply what is known about adults to infants and children? Is it possible to reconstruct developmental sequences from the principles and paradigms of adult functioning?

In the last several decades, studies of motor skill in adults have been conducted predominantly from an *information processing* perspective (see Schmidt, 1982, for a review). Major concerns were how movement information is coded and stored, how actions are represented in memory, and how information about errors is processed. Because the basic premise in such a cognitive approach is that more complex actions take more time to process, time was often the variable from which underlying cognitive processes were inferred. Within this overall perspective, there was considerable debate over whether movement is acquired and executed in a *closed-loop* (feedback) or an *open-loop* (feedforward) manner.

When age is used as a dependent variable in an information processing approach to skill, we are not surprised to learn that children become better information processors as they get older (Thomas, 1980). (They also become stronger, more fit, more accurate in tasks, have longer attention spans, and generally better in all aspects of skill; see, e.g., Connolly, 1970; Hay, 1981; Rothstein, 1977; Schmidt, 1982; Wallace, Newell, & Wade, 1978.) Generalizations beyond this are, as yet, difficult to make, although fine-grained movement analysis combined with more traditional information processing measures may offer more explanatory power. For example, using such a technique, Schellekens, Kalverboer, and Scholten (1984) discovered that improvements in speed between 5 and 9 years in a two-handed tapping task were more in the second or homing phase of the movement than in the first or distance-covering phase. This suggests that younger children are more deficient in their aiming or in their information processing than in their ability to move quickly per se. But despite this and other useful dissections of motor skill, no comprehensive account of skill development has emerged from this overall perspective.

One fundamental reason that information processing models have not been successful in explaining motor development is that they are deficient as models even of adult motor behavior. Like strict neurological accounts of movement, these top-down or prescriptive theories assume that actions arise solely from the coded instructions. But what is the nature of those instructions? Movements are changes over both space and time. Naturally occurring tasks involve the coordinated effort of many, and perhaps all, of the muscles of the body, which in combination can produce a nearly limitless number of unique configurations. At the same time, the contexts for each movement are different, depending on the particular state, posture, and motivation of the mover in a specific physical setting. It is a daunting task to envision how the brain or the cognitive structures could store and retrieve the instructions for movement in the face of so many individual and contextual degrees of freedom, and as the effectors themselves are continually moving in time and space. The analogy of humans as information processing devices ignores that humans have real body segments and computers do not (Bernstein, 1967).

One solution has been to propose that the instructions—the motor program—must be very general. Schmidt (1975, 1982), for example, has proposed that action plans are coded as relatively nonspecific schemata, which are then adjusted ad hoc to the particular demands of the task. Thus throwing might be encoded in outline form, so to speak, with the particular force and orientation varied as the context requires. The best evidence for schema theory is studies showing that adults learn a new motor skill as well when given practice on variations of the task as when given repeated trials on the criterion task itself. The few studies of children addressing this issue show that children do even better on varied practice, suggesting that they are building a general representation of the skill (Shapiro & Schmidt, 1982). Nonetheless, although schema theory addresses some of the problems of a strict information processing approach, it has not been entirely successful (Frohlich & Elliot, 1984; van Rossum, 1980; Shapiro & Schmidt, 1982). One problem is the theory's difficulty in explaining the accuracy of limb movements in the absence of knowledge of initial position (Shapiro & Schmidt, 1982). Second, the varied practice effect is largely lost when practice trials are blocked together, an effect not predicted by the theory (Lee, Magill, & Weeks, 1985). Finally, the developmental implications are, as yet, largely unexplored. The few studies in this paradigm have involved older children in discrete laboratory tasks, and it is unknown whether the notion of a generalized motor program can be applied to infant motor development, for example.

On a logical basis, however, information processing models of skill, like neurological correlations, are themselves insufficient for understanding developmental change. Like neurological models, information processing accounts provide no mechanisms for generating new forms, although they help us understand improvements in already existing forms. Where do new skills come from? What are the sources of change over time? Again, these accounts cannot escape the problem of infinite regress. Because they are essentially top-down or prescriptive accounts of behavior, the only "explanation" for development is a change in the instructions—cognitively or neurologically defined—and the homunculus rears its head again.

In the last few years, a more radical alternative to information processing approaches to movement has been proposed in the form of *dynamic motor theory,* and this approach may offer a more satisfactory understanding of both action in "real time" and the generation of new forms over developmental time. Major theoretical statements of the theory can be found in Bernstein (1967), Greene (1972), Kelso, Holt, Kugler, and Turvey (1980), Kelso and Tuller (1984), Kugler, Kelso, and Turvey (1980), and Turvey (1977). For a more extended discussion of the developmental implications of dynamic motor theory, the reader is referred to Kugler, Kelso, and Turvey (1982), Thelen and Fogel (in press), and Thelen, Kelso, and Fogel (1987).

In brief, the fundamental difference between a dynamic account of motor behavior and previous models is the nature of the instructions to move. Remember that the logical problem of understanding motor control is the "degrees of freedom" afforded by the skeletomuscular system in interaction with the ecological demands of the task, and thus how central commands can be stored, retrieved, and transduced into movement topographies. Invoking a central "representation" of a movement begs the question of the dynamic processes of moving bodies: the physical properties of the effectors—their mass, stiffness, and inertia, and their changes as they move through time and space. If only the command to move is stored, how does the segment "know" to apply the right force, deceleration, orientation, and so on?

A better solution to the problem of control is to *use* the dynamics of moving systems as sources of information in themselves, rather than just as recipients of higher-order commands. The theoretical underpinning for such a view arises, not surprisingly, from the nonreductionist or systems theoretical formulations in contemporary physics (e.g., Haken, 1977; Iberall, 1972; Prigogine, 1980) and biology (Rosen, 1978; Winfree, 1980). The basic premise for these mathematical formulations is that when elements of a system act cooperatively certain properties emerge that are not knowable from the behavior of the elements alone. (A commonplace example is the behavior of water molecules under pressure, where increasing the pressure leads to turbulent or laminar flow patterns, patterns not inherent in a water molecule acting in isolation.) Because such systems use energy in a nonlinear manner, higher-order organization is generated that is not apparent in the single elements.

Human motor systems are such cooperative systems. When humans are faced with a task, be it the repetitive movement of walking, or the complex and highly learned sequences of a dance, they recruit their muscles as coalitions that span many, and perhaps all, the segments of the body. Just as water molecules in a stream never act alone, muscles never enter into an action as isolated elements (Bernstein, 1967). Such muscle synergies are assembled not as abstractions but in response to specific task demands. Dynamic motor theorists propose that, when the individual elements of the body—the muscles, bones, and joints—work together under the control of the nervous system, these coalitions, or cooperative ensembles, assume certain autonomous properties. That is, order and regularity emerge from the unique relationships among the elements that are not apparent from the instructions alone. Although it is beyond the scope of this chapter to document in detail the theoretical and empirical bases of a dynamic, systems model of motor control, studies of both voluntary and skilled movements such as reaching, speech, and locomotion and of spontaneous movements such as leg kicks in young and premature infants offer compelling support for this model (Abbs, Gracco, & Cole, 1984; Kelso & Holt, 1980; Kelso, Tuller, V.-Bateson, & Fowler, 1984; Polit & Bizzi, 1978; Thelen, Kelso, & Fogel, 1987). The adjustments to preserve these target positions are made too rapidly for traditional feedback corrections. The maintenance of a desired position without ongoing corrections suggests that the structures involved in the movement act both synergistically and autonomously rather than as recipients of on-line instructions.

How can this be? How can coalitions of muscles and joints generate patterns in space and time without highly specific neural representations? Instead of envisioning the control system as a servomechanism, that is, providing continual on-line corrections, dynamic models utilize the self-organizing properties inherent in the skeletomuscular system. One such attractive model is the spring with a mass attached. When such a spring is stretched, it produces a stable trajectory and predictable final position without reference to a control center. Rather, these dynamic characteristics are a function of the parameters of the spring, specifically its stiffness and the amount of mass. Once these are specified, properties such as cycle time and target position "fall out." In a similar manner, muscle coalitions are thought to have properties of mass springs. Once the tension in the spring is parameterized by the nervous system to the demands of the task, trajectory and timing need not be continuously monitored, although in some circumstances, feedback corrections can surely be used. Information is generated, so to speak, by the periphery itself (Saltzman & Kelso, 1983).

An important corollary of these dynamic analogies is the role of nonneurological components of the system. When people act, the movement outcome is not a product of muscle activation patterns alone, but a result of both muscular and nonmuscular forces, including the inertial and reactive forces from the moving body, elastic properties of muscles, and forces associated with contact with the supporting surface and medium. There is much evidence to suggest, in addition, that the motor system in its entirety uses and indeed optimizes these forces to lessen the demands for active muscle contraction (Hinton, 1984). In short, the motor system is adapted to act as a cooperative unit to harmonize both the instructions from the brain and the biomechanical properties of the body (Hasan, Enoka, & Stuart, 1985).

The self-organizing properties of cooperative systems mean that these systems can maintain goal targets or states despite perturbations. But another property of such systems is that, if they are perturbed beyond certain limits, they respond in a nonlinear manner, that is, with a qualitative shift of topographies. For example, within a range of speeds (or power delivered to the muscles) four-legged animals show a stable gait pattern. As the power is scaled up, however, some critical dimension is reached where the animal shifts, discontinuously, into another gait style. There is no stable intermediate state between a walk and a trot in a horse, for example, even though the power may have been scaled in a continuous manner. Over a longer time scale, growth can be considered a scalar quantity, with developing organisms increasing gradually in size in all body organs and systems. The systemwide effects of growth have been documented by morphologists, who have shown how small scalar changes can have reverberations to produce large-scale morphological phase shifts. Here we raise the question of growth-related phase shifts on behavioral outcome.

Toward a Systems Synthesis of Action and Development

I have contrasted two approaches to early motor development and two approaches to real-time motor control as being either prescriptive or generative. Clearly, there is considerable correspondence between the organic–systems account of early development elaborated by Gesell based on his observations of motor patterning and the principles of embryology and the dynamic systems model of motor control. In this section, I suggest a synthesis of the two models as a source of a new agenda for understanding early motor development. A more detailed exposition of the transition from real-time principles to developmental organization can be found in Thelen and Fogel (in press).

What, then, are some principles that span both real and developmental time?

1. Action is a systems property not just of the code of formal representations or sets of anatomical constraints, but of the dynamic interactions of all the contributing subsystems and levels. At any point in time, the observable behavior cannot be reduced to the instructions alone, but must include considerations of the maturational status of the perceptual apparatus, postural control mechanisms, skeletomuscular apparatus, and motivational or affective state. Similarly, the generation of new forms in ontogeny is a systems product of the development of the components (Sameroff, 1983). The lesson from embryology is that time–space configurations of elements or traits can themselves be the catalysts for the emergence of new forms.
2. Complex biological systems are nonlinear in both real and developmental time. Just as a one-to-one mapping of muscle activation patterns will not uniquely determine the movement outcome, so there can be no prediction of behavior from knowledge of only one element in the system at one time. Over developmental time, these contributing subsystems may not mature either synchronously or linearly, but may act, as in Gesell's model, in an intricate waxing and waning, with each coalescence producing a unique configuration of behavioral outcome.
3. Movement outcome, like developmental outcome, is *task,* not instruction, specific. Constraints on action include not only the maturational status of the anatomical, neurological, and skeletomuscular apparatus, but the nature of the task itself. Thus tasks may be accomplished with a variety of muscle patterns, depending on the precise context. Similarly, particular muscle coalitions may be recruited for a variety of tasks. As Newell (1984) has argued, an important element in motor learning may be gaining knowledge about the task structure in a manner analogous to Gibson's (1969) mechanisms of perceptual development. That is, the infant must learn to recognize the salient features of the task upon which to act. Improvement in skill may be a result not solely of increases in processing speed or capacity, but of the ability to discriminate the affordances for skill. The concepts of embryonic fields and induction can thus be extended to include the task context, so that the task, as well as the internal maturational processes, can induce developmental change.
4. Cooperative systems exhibit self-organizing or autonomous properties. Because both moving and developing organisms exhibit systems characteristics, strict iconic representations are not necessary. The genetic code or the neural code need only contain the *minimally sufficient* instructions to assemble and regulate the inherent capabilities of the system.
5. Small, continuous changes in one sensitive element of the system can shift the entire configuration into a new form. At the same time, within certain ranges, dynamic systems are buffered to maintain stable configurations.

Ontogenetic Regressions: Puzzles of Development

Understanding regressive epochs in normal development has been a persistent, and fascinating, challenge to developmental theorists (see, e.g., Bever, 1982). How can infants and children, in the general progression toward competence, display seeming losses of motor, perceptual, or cognitive abilities? What causes these behaviors to disappear and then reappear, often in new and more complex forms? In this section, I use the principles outlined above to suggest explanations for developmental regressions that differ from conventional notions. Although my discussion will focus particularly on the coordinated behavior of early infancy, I show later how the same analytic perspective can be applied to other domains.

Some of the most dramatic "losses" of behavioral organization occur in the period of 1–4 months, where many striking capabilities of the newborn, including coordinated stepping and swimming, prereaching, head turning to localized sound, and facial imitation, seem to disappear, only to reappear a few or several months later in similar or more elaborated form. Several explanations have been offered for these "dips" in development. It is commonly believed, for example, that as the cortex matures it exerts an inhibitory influence on early behavior under subcortical control. A second possibility suggested by Prechtl (1982) is that developmental regressions are a function of transient phases in neural morphology. It is well known, for example, that during development neurons are overproduced and then eliminated, as are axonal and dendritic connections. Finally, some theorists have proposed major reorganizations in cognitive structures, suggesting that there are cognitive metamorphoses (Zelazo, 1982) or revolutionary periods (Mounoud, 1982) that reorient the child's entire processing or representations of the world. In these views, then, regressive periods result as transient deficits during these reorganizations.

There exists little, if any, direct evidence for these prevailing interpretations, however. Several studies have demonstrated that early reflexes need not be inhibited for more mature behavior to appear. On the contrary, both earlier and later behaviors tended to coexist (Sheppard & Mysak, 1984; Touwen, 1976). Similarly, there is no direct evidence that neurological remodelings—believed to occur largely in embryonic and fetal life—are the bases for the behavioral transformations observed postnatally. Finally, while there are times in infancy, at about 2 months or about 12 months, when whole constellations of new abilities appear, we cannot know or even test that a single psychological structure "causes" these diverse shifts of performance.

A dynamic systems approach can, I suggest, offer insight into the process of developmental regressions beyond these more global neurological or cognitive explanations. I use as a first example the disappearance of neonatal "stepping" and "swimming." At any point in time, the performance of these motor activities must be considered as a systems product of many contributing subsystems, or traits, as Gesell called them (see Thelen, 1986b). First, we might postulate some pattern-generating mechanism, that is, an ability to activate a specific combination of muscles in a defined time sequence resulting in coordinated action. But pattern generation does not occur in a vacuum. Infants make stepping or swimming movements also because of what they perceive through their senses—visual, tactile, vestibular—they "step" when held upright on a table, and "swim" when placed prone in water. Infants only perform certain behaviors when in particular "moods," or levels of behavioral activation; no one would expect these movements in a sleepy baby or one who is crying hard. Finally, the movement outcome must include considerations of the biodynamics of the effectors themselves—the muscle linkages, the segment weights, centers of gravity, and intrinsic "tone" or muscle stiffness. In this model, any of these systems can limit the behavioral expression. If the infant is not in an appropriate posture, or if he or she is asleep, stepping or swimming will not be performed, despite the integrity of the other subsystems.

Although this may seem to be trivial reasoning for real-time behavior, such an analysis can be powerful for ontogenetic processes. Remember that in a Gesellian model traits develop in nonlinear, asynchronous, and asymmetric fashion. At the same time, the effects of one contributing trait may be amplified, through system effects, to shift an entire topography. This makes it important to identify which of the contributing subsystems becomes *rate limiting* (Soll, 1979); the appearance of the outcome behavior may await maturation of a nonobvious element. Similarly, the nonperformance of a behavior may result from the contribution of an asynchronously maturing trait.

My colleagues and I have proposed such a systems explanation for the disappearance of newborn stepping. We reasoned that it was unlikely that the pattern generation was cortically inhibited for two reasons. First, when infants were given specific practice in stepping the activity did not disappear (Super, 1980; Zelazo, Zelazo, & Kolb, 1972), and second, infants continued to perform steplike movements when placed supine even after they no longer stepped in the upright position (Thelen & Fisher, 1982). One effect of the supine position is to lessen the effort demands of lifting the legs against gravity, suggesting that postural context was important. But what about the upright posture led to the decline and eventual disappearance of the movement? By looking at subsystems other than pattern generation, we discovered that there was a disproportionate and very rapid increase in nonmuscle (fat) tissue in infants during the first few months. Rapid weight gain without concomitant muscle strength might make it difficult to lift the legs against gravity. This hypothesis was supported in several studies: Infants who gained weight most rapidly showed the most rapid decline in stepping. In addition, experimental manipulations of leg mass by adding weights inhibited stepping while submersion in water facilitated stepping (Thelen, Fisher, & Ridley-Johnson, 1984). Further evidence that the pattern generation was available but suppressed because of dynamic and postural considerations was obtained when 7-month-old infants were held upright on a small, motorized treadmill (Thelen, 1986b). All of the 12 infants tested showed dramatic increases in step rate over a stationary treadmill baseline when the treadmill was moving. I proposed that the treadmill provided a biomechanical energy boost by stretching the stance leg sufficient to overcome the inertia of the legs. This is normally accomplished during development when the supporting leg becomes strong enough to allow the swing leg to extend backward. In short, pattern generation spontaneously "emerged" when the biomechanical context was manipulated.

Similar reasoning can be invoked to understand the disappearance of coordinated swimming movements seen when infants are placed prone in water. As McGraw (1939) reported, at about 4–5 months of age, the coordination of the limbs is disrupted, as infants thrash about and roll over. Is there a loss of the instructions or pattern generation? By looking at other sensory or neuromotor events, it is possible to suggest a more parsimonious explanation. At about the time the swimming pattern is lost, infants gain a rapid increase in strength in extensor muscles (Gesell, 1939; Thelen, 1985). This is especially noticeable in the extensors of the trunk and limbs, so that prone infants at this age will often assume a hyperextended back-arched and arms-extended position. Such a posture will naturally disrupt the flexed position needed by humans to float when prone. (This extensor strength is also important in rolling over.) Again, a change in one less obvious parameter may be the catalyst for a dramatic shift in movement topography, in this case leading to an apparent regression.

Other early regressions are amenable to similar reasoning. Both Trevarthan (1984) and von Hofsten (1984) have reported that during the second and third months the fluid total extension pattern of "reaching" of the newborn period was replaced by fewer and more jerky movements, characterized by fractionated movements of hand and arm. One possible cause for the dissolution of the early pattern proposed by Trevarthan (1984) is the unequal developmental course of control of proximal and distal arm segments, suggesting "successive waves of differentiation in a hierarchy of control systems" (p. 237). Additionally, increasing mass of the arm segments may affect the infant's abilities to lift the segments against gravity in a smooth trajectory (Trevarthan, 1982), while uneven development of agonist–antagonist muscle pairs could act to inhibit goal-directed movement (Gatev, 1972; von Hofsten, 1984). Such a component-by-component analysis of visually guided reaching reveals subsystems with differing developmental pathways. Any one subsystem may enhance, complement, or mask the effects of the other elements, leading to retarded or qualitatively different reaching performance.

Discontinuous Phase Shifts of Behavior in Infancy

One of the important characteristics of self-organizing systems is the nonlinearity of change over time. Earlier I offered the example of quadrupedal gait as showing discontinuous *phase shifts* as energy delivered to the system was scaled up or down. Here I illustrate how two aspects of infant neuromuscular organization—newborn states and later rhythmical stereotypies—may be interpreted as similar phase shift phenomena.

State appears to be a powerful behavioral organizer in the newborn period. State is reflected not only in autonomic functions such as respiration and heart rate, but also in observable motor output, attention levels, and perceptual sensitivities in all domains. State is especially intriguing from a dynamic systems perspective because the so-called states are qualitatively discrete and identifiable entities with little evidence of intermediate stages. Observers using behavioral criteria can very reliably assign an infant to a state designation (Anders, Emde, & Parmelee, 1971; Brazelton, 1973; Prechtl, 1974). What makes it possible for observers to identify states is that the constellation of behaviors is relatively discrete for each stage. That is, one never sees the alert, focused gaze and attention of state 4 at the same time as the staccato, rapid limb movements of state 6.

Just as new gait topographies emerge as power is increased, it is intriguing to speculate that qualitative behavioral changes seen in newborn states may be a product of an energy-related scalar. That is, as the system becomes more activated, discrete topographies of movement, as well as autonomic functions and perceptual sensitivities, may "fall out" as qualitatively distinguishable behaviors at different ranges of activation. The constellations of behaviors categorized as sleep states, for instance, may be associated with the lowest levels of activation, while loud, rhythmic vocalizations, particular facial configurations, high muscle tension (Casaer, 1979), staccato movements, and a rapid heart beat and respiration may be the result of the highest activation levels.

Discontinuities in activation-related movements continue after the newborn period. Bouts of rhythmical stereotypies provide a striking example. Thelen (1981) found that, while maturational status determined the particular forms of rhythmical movement performed in infancy, the moment-to-moment elicitation of the movement was highly arousal related. For rhythmical kicking, for example, infants only kicked when in moderately to highly aroused states. No kicking was seen when infants were sleepy or drowsy, and at the very highest activation level, infants shifted to a rigid, tonic immobility. It is important to note that within the first year the context for eliciting rhythmicities varied with the age-dependent salience of the stimulus, that is, what situations appeared to cause changes in activation level. At the earliest ages, these movements appeared to be related to internally driven state changes. At 3–5 months, infants performed the most stereotypies when in social situations, and later in the first year, rhythmicities were more often associated with object manipulation. Just as the topographies matured and waned, so the eliciting context changed with development. Nonetheless, I suggest that an activation metric mediated these context-specific reactions.

The Role of the Task in the Emergence of Form in Real and Developmental Time

In the previous sections, I suggested that for the predominantly involuntary movements of early infancy activation level was a common mediator of behavioral outcome by tuning the motor system so that certain topographies might emerge. This is not to suggest, however, that even in the early months behavior is task or context irrelevant. Infants can and do respond to functionally specific situations.

In this section, I further emphasize the importance of the *task* environment in eliciting movement topographies, in both real and developmental time. In this sense, I depart from a Gesellian model, which incorporates the dynamic concepts of parallel maturation and interweaving of subsystems and processes, but ignores factors extrinsic to the organism as organizers of change. Rather, I adopt the position elaborated by Reed (1982) for a *function-specific* rather than *instruction-specific* analysis of action. The lesson from contemporary motor theory is the exquisite variability and adaptability of every motor act, even simple reflex actions in relatively simple animals (e.g., Fukson, Berkenblit, & Feldman, 1980). What organizes behavior is its functional goals, as there are many ways of performing every action, be it sitting, eating, or climbing a tree. It is useless, Reed (1982) argues, thus to separate the affector functions, which actively sense and recognize the possibilities for action from those postures and movements that are the instantiations of the functions. Rather, these must be merged into *action systems* that construct, coordinate, and adjust the animal's movements to be adaptive in its environment. Actions are controlled by the environment, but not by instructions imposed upon the animal and triggered by stimulation. Rather the organism–environment must be considered as a single system, with self-stabilizing control processes actually inherent in the response itself, as I documented in an earlier section.

One way to conceptualize the organism–environment system is to envision action in real and developmental time as arising from nested constraints, or "boundaries or features that restrict or limit . . . the possible configurations of a system" (Newell, 1985, p. 25). According to Newell, these constraints exist at several levels. I have already discussed the level of *organismic constraints,* or those limits on movement presented by the biology of the animal itself. The system reverberations of changes in growth and form, for example, have been little explored in developmental psychology, but I illustrated earlier how disproportionate, accelerated, and retarded growth patterns of various physical systems may have acute behavioral outcomes (see Thelen, 1984, for an account of organismic constraints on learning to walk). Neurological or orthopedic handicaps that retard or limit motor development are yet another category of organismic constraints.

Newell suggests a second level of *environmental constraints,* or those general factors in the external world not related to a specific task. One of the most pervasive environmental constraints on infants is gravity. Newborn infants are prisoners of gravity as both control of antigravity muscles and requisite strength develop slowly over the first year. The significance of posture as a matrix for all actions has been less appreciated in North American infancy research, but a considerable French literature emphasizes the organizing dynamics of both posture and tone (see, e.g., Amiel-Tison, 1985; Bullinger, 1982; Mounoud & Hauert, 1982; Stamback, 1963). Postural control may indeed act as a *rate-limiting* element in the performance of many motor acts during the first year. That is, when postural support or facilitation is provided, capabilities characteristic of later maturational states may emerge. Postural constraints have been suggested for early reaching (von Hofsten, 1984) and for the emergence of walking (Thelen, 1984). Dramatic improvement in visuomotor coordination in the upper limbs of a 17-day-old infant was reported by Amiel-Tison (1985) when the head was held fixed in an upright position for about half an hour. The underlying coordinations are apparently available, but are not performed if the infant cannot maintain stability in the head. These authors speculated that lack of head control alone may underlie many of the reflex responses of infants under 2 months old. The maturation of the subsystem of supporting the head against gravity at about 6–8 weeks allows for the emergence of more controlled and adaptive coordination.

Newell's third level, the *task constraints,* concerns the coordinative patterns used to accomplish functional goals. In some skilled actions such as sports, constraints are imposed by actual rules of how the body may be used. In most everyday activities, however, the performer is free to use whatever muscle coordinations he or she desires. Nonetheless, the number of response configurations to a particular task, although variable both between and within performers, is not infinite. This is because in meeting tasks humans act to optimize certain parameters of the structure of the motor system and its biomechanical constraints. Although there is considerable debate on the nature of these optimizing parameters (see Hogan, 1984; Nashner & McCollum, 1985), they act as constraints on the available motor forms. When objects are to be used in the action, which is common for most everyday activities, the properties of those objects themselves constrain the choice of movements.

An elegant illustration of a task constraint approach to a common behavior is Van Summers's (1984) recent study of drawing. Van Summers begins by exploring what features of the execution of a drawing are "traceable to the anatomy of the drawer in interaction with the furniture and materials of drawing" (p. 2). By understanding the domains of these noncognitive constraints, the investigator is then able to comment upon the cognitive, self-expressive, and social content of drawing. But these higher-order considerations are layered upon the task constraints. Striking commonalities in the stroke production of adults and children in various different drawing contexts attest to the enormous influence of the task itself on its execution. For example, the forearm and hand are mechanically constrained such that movements in the up and down direction are freer than lateral movements, leading right-handed subjects consistently to prefer a lower left to upper right stroke direction regardless of the representational content of the drawing.

A few developmental studies have begun to adopt this approach. Palmer (1984) has demonstrated how infants adjust their manual exploration behaviors to the textural, size, weight, and "squeezability" qualities of the toys presented to them. Crawling and walking infants are sensitive to the constraints of the surfaces to be traversed. Walking infants, for example, were hesitant to step onto a water bed, whereas crawling infants were not hampered by that surface (Gibson, 1985). Inabilities to perform certain actions may reside as much in the task structure as in inherent wiring in the infant.

Thus a dynamic systems approach suggests that we determine the *interaction* between the maturational status of the infant and the external task constraints for understanding why certain activities are performed at particular times, and in particular, the "mobility" of some coordinative structures among functions. Leg kicks, for example, can be used as expressions of joy or temper, as means to act upon the environment or to propel the infant toward a desired goal. Babbling and other vocalizations may indeed be prelinguistic exercises, but while infants babble, babbling assumes an expressive and communicative function. The pointing gesture assumes both orientation and linguistic functions during infancy (Thelen & Fogel, in press).

Motor Activity as a Catalyst for Developmental Change

In a multidetermined, dynamic systems model of development, any of the intrinsic or extrinsic elements can act as the rate-limiting component or the trigger for a phase shift into a new behavioral topography. I have particularly emphasized the neuromotor and biomechanical contributions. In contemporary views of motor organization, these are essential, information-producing elements in the system rather than passive recipients of commands.

The model will similarly predict that the attainment of the new topography itself will be fed back as an element in the system contributing to the next level of topography shift. Such a dynamic is, of course, the essence of Piaget's equilibration theory. Despite the theoretical importance of the circularity of action and knowledge, many cognitive theorists have only looked at the knowledge-to-action half of the circle. Much less is known about how motor skills are themselves catalysts for developmental change in other spheres.

In a recent essay Bertenthal, Campos, and Barrett (1984) have cogently argued for reevaluation of the feedback of movement to other developmental domains, especially in the relation between self-produced locomotion and emotional, cognitive, and social development. The onset of crawling, they propose, acts as an organizer or setting event for the development of other skills, largely by increasing the probability that the infant will encounter "skill-enhancing experiences" (p. 178).

Active exploration of the environment may account for the onset of wariness of heights, as measured by reluctance to cross the visual cliff; for the change from egocentric (body-centered) coding of objects to stable, landmark coding; for new forms of social communication, especially the onset of social referencing; and generalized concept formation. Bertenthal and colleagues suggest that locomotion in all these cases acts as a *mediator* of development, in which one skill facilitates the development of another without becoming part of that skill; in other words, that locomotion is perhaps neither necessary nor sufficient but enhances or facilitates ongoing processes.

In the terminology introduced here, the ability to crawl may indeed be an organismic task constraint, or a rate-limiting component for many other developmental outcomes. The use of the terms *shifts* and *developmental reorganizations* in the literature on the onset of wariness or spatial coding suggests that a phase shift, or new topography, does arise with the catalysis of such a rate-limiting component. Nonetheless, the behavioral outcome must result from the systems interplay of many contributing subsystems, as Bertenthal and colleagues suggest, including improved selection of relevant task information, better visual motor calibration, and more emotional communication with the mother over the consequences of the action. None of these contributions can be considered a single, triggering event (in contrast with prescriptive cognitive theories), but the final behavioral outcome must result from their dynamic interplay. What is important in this systems approach is the inclusion of movement as an equal factor in the developmental equation.

Conclusion: New Roles for Motor Development

Just as the infant begins with action, the study of development has had a strong basis in the understanding of movement. The purpose of this paper has been a plea for a reintegration of the role of movement in development, both as a theoretical necessity and as an empirical strategy. The theoretical rationale comes from two sources. First, as in other systems, holistic, or organismic worldviews, I see developing humans as a class of complex, biological systems, and I rely especially on the embryological metaphors of morphology or form and the self-regulating and self-stabilizing properties of these systems. Such a view compels us to reject strict cognitive or neurological accounts of behavior as insufficient by themselves, since behavioral outcome is an emergent systems property not predictable by iconic instructions alone. The second theoretical justification for new roles for movement in development comes from convergent views on the organization of the motor system itself. These theories similarly echo the dynamic, emergent characteristics of behavior in real time.

In such a systems approach, the motor system and its functioning cannot be separated from other developmental domains, just as we cannot consider the infant as an information or visual processing device or social being in isolation from these complementary processes or from the contexts in which infants act. I have presented examples in the areas of developmental regressions, the organization of state, and the relevance of task identification where such a systems approach offers new ways of interpreting common and/or puzzling events in infancy.

Within this view of behavior as an emergent systems property of multilevel parallel developmental processes, no single developmental event in itself need be defined as *causal*. A more helpful perspective may be to think of the subsystems as essential, but as constraining or facilitating the emergence of the target behavior, much as in Gesell's dynamic model. Then, an empirical strategy is to identify the constraints and catalysts that account for the development shifts. By providing infants with weights, treadmills, or walkers, by offering postural support or practice on a task, we supply the "missing" element (or simulate a constraint) that occurs naturally during development. Muscle strength alone does not *cause* walking, just as crawling alone does not *cause* a fear of heights (but it may be equally inaccurate to invoke cognitive or neurological single causes). Nonetheless, these movement or peripheral factors are as much of the infant as those usually considered more psychologically central.

REFERENCES

Abbs, J. H., Gracco, V. L., & Cole, K. J. (1984). Control of multimovement coordination: Sensorimotor mechanisms in speech motor programming. *Journal of Motor Behavior, 16,* 195–231.

Amiel-Tison, C. (1985). Pediatric contribution to the present knowledge on the neurobehavioral status of infants at birth. In J. Mehler & R. Fox (Eds.), *Neonate cognition: Beyond the blooming, buzzing confusion.* Hillsdale, NJ: Erlbaum.

Anders, T., Emde, R., & Parmelee, A. (Eds.). (1971). *A manual of standardized terminology. Techniques and criteria for scoring of states of sleep and wakefulness in newborn infants.* UCLA Brain Information Service, NINDS Neurological Information Network.

Banks, M. S. & Salapatek, P. (1983). Infant visual perception. In P. H. Mussen (Gen. Ed.); M. M. Haith & J. J. Campos (Vol. Eds.), *Handbook of child psychology: Vol. II. Infancy and developmental psychobiology* (4th ed.). New York: Wiley.

Bernstein, N. (1967). *Co-ordination and regulation of movements.* New York: Pergamon.

Bertenthal, B. I., Campos, J. J., & Barrett, K. C. (1984). Self-produced locomotion: An organizer of emotional, cognitive, and social development in infancy. In R. N. Emde & R. J. Harmon (Eds.), *Continuities and discontinuities in development.* New York: Plenum.

Bever, T. G. (Ed.). (1982). *Regressions in mental development: Basic phenomena and theories.* Hillsdale, NJ: Erlbaum.

Brazelton, T. B. (1973). *Neonatal Behavioral Assessment Scale.* London: Spastics International Medical Publishing and Heinemann.

Bronson, G. (1974). The postnatal growth of visual capacity. *Child Development, 45,* 873–890.

Bruner, J. S. (1970). The growth and structure of skill. In K. Connolly (Ed.), *Mechanisms of motor skill development.* New York: Academic.

Bullinger, A. (1982). Cognitive elaboration of sensorimotor behaviour. In G. Butterworth (Ed.), *Infancy and epistemology: An evaluation of Piaget's theory.* New York: St. Martin's.

Casaer, P. (1979). *Postural behaviour in newborn infants.* London: Spastics International Medical Publishing and Heinemann.

Clifton, R. K., Morrongiello, B. A., & Dowd, J. M. (1984). A developmental look at an auditory illusion: The precedence effect. *Developmental Psychobiology, 17,* 519–536.

Coghill, G. E. (1929). *Anatomy and the problem of behaviour.* Cambridge: Cambridge University Press.

Connolly, K. (1970). Response speed, temporal sequencing and information processing in children. In K. Connolly (Ed.), *Mechanisms of motor skill development.* New York: Academic.

Edelman, G. M., & Finkel, L. H. (1984). Neuronal group selection in the cerebral cortex. In G. M. Edelman, W. E. Gall, & W. M. Cowan (Eds.), *Dynamic aspects of neocortical function.* New York: Wiley.

Fentress, J. C. (1984). The development of coordination. *Journal of Motor Behavior, 16,* 99–134.

Fischer, K. W. (1980). A theory of cognitive development: The control and construction of hierarchies of skills. *Psychological Review, 87,* 477–531.

Forman, G. E. (Ed.). (1982). *Action and thought: From sensorimotor schemes to symbolic operations.* New York: Academic.

French, V., Bryant, P. J., & Bryant, S. V. (1976). Pattern regulation in epimorphic fields. *Science, 193,* 969–981.

Frese, M., & Stewart, J. (1984). Skill learning as a concept in life-span developmental psychology: An action theoretic analysis. *Human Development, 27,* 145–162.

Frohlich, D. M., & Elliot, J. M. (1984). The schematic representation of effector function underlying perceptual-motor skill. *Journal of Motor Behavior, 16,* 40–60.

Fukson, O. I., Berkenblit, M. B., & Feldman, A. G. (1980). The spinal frog takes into account the scheme of its body during the wiping reflex. *Science, 209,* 1261–1263.

Gatev, V. (1972). Role of inhibition in the development of motor co-ordination in early childhood. *Developmental Medicine & Child Neurology, 14,* 336–341.

Gesell, A. (1939). Reciprocal interweaving in neuromotor development. *Journal of Comparative Neurology, 70,* 161–180.

Gesell, A. (1945). *The embryology of behavior.* New York: Harper.

Gesell, A. (1946). The ontogenesis of infant behavior. In L. Carmichael (Ed.), *Manual of child psychology.* New York: Wiley.

Gesell, A., & Ames, L. B. (1940). The ontogenetic organization of prone behavior in human infancy. *The Journal of Genetic Psychology, 56,* 247–263.

Gibson, E. J. (1969). *Principles of perceptual learning and development.* Englewood Cliffs, NJ: Prentice-Hall.

Gibson, E. J. (1985). *The concept of affordances in comparative development.* Paper presented at the biennial meeting of the Society for Research in Child Development, Toronto.

Gibson, K. R. (1981). Comparative neuro-ontogeny; its implications for the development of human intelligence. In G. Butterworth (Ed.), *Infancy and epistemology.* Brighton, England: Harvester.

Gierer, A. (1981). Generation of biological patterns and form: Some physical, mathematical, and logical aspsects. *Progress in Biophysics & Molecular Biology, 37,* 1–47.

Goldman-Rakic, P. S., Isseroff, A., Schwartz, M. L., & Bugbee, N. M. (1983). The neurobiology of cognitive development. In P. H. Mussen (Gen. Ed.); M. M. Haith & J. J. Campos (Vol. Eds.), *Handbook of child psychology: Vol. II. Infancy and developmental psychobiology* (4th ed.). New York: Wiley.

Greene, P. H. (1972). Problems of organization of motor systems. In R. Rosen & F. Snell (Eds.), *Progress in theoretical biology.* New York: Academic.

Haken, H. (1977). *Synergetics: An introduction.* Heidelberg: Springer-Verlag.

Hasan, Z., Enoka, R. M., & Stuart, D. G. (1985). The interface between biomechanics and neurophysiology in the study of movement: Some recent approaches. In R. L. Terjung (Ed.), *Exercise and sport sciences reviews* (Vol. 13). Lexington, MA: D. C. Heath.

Hay, L. (1981). The effect of amplitude and accuracy requirements on movement time in children. *Journal of Motor Behavior, 13,* 177-186.

Hinton, G. (1984). Some computational solutions to Bernstein's problems. In H. T. A. Whiting (Ed.), *Human motor actions: Bernstein reassessed.* Amsterdam: North-Holland.

Hoffman, R. F. (1978). Developmental changes in human infant visual-evoked potentials to patterned stimuli recorded at different scalp locations. *Child Development, 49,* 110-118.

Hofsten, C. von (1984). Developmental changes in the organization of prereaching movements. *Developmental Psychology, 20,* 378-388.

Hogan, N. (1984). An organising principle for a class of voluntary movements. *Journal of Neuroscience, 4,* 2745-2754.

Iberall, A. S. (1972). *Toward a general science of viable systems.* New York: McGraw-Hill.

Kelso, J. A. S., & Clark, J. (Eds.). (1982). *The development of movement control and coordination.* New York: Wiley.

Kelso, J. A. S., & Holt, K. G. (1980). Exploring a vibratory systems analysis of human movement production. *Journal of Neurophysiology, 43,* 183-1196.

Kelso, J. A. S., Holt, K. G., Kugler, P. N., & Turvey, M. T. (1980). On the concept of coordinative structures as dissipative structures: Vol. II. Empirical lines of convergence. In G. E. Stelmach & J. Requin (Eds.), *Tutorials in motor behavior.* New York: North-Holland.

Kelso, J. A. S., & Tuller, B. (1984). A dynamical basis for action systems. In M. S. Gazzaniga (Ed.), *Handbook of cognitive neuroscience.* New York: Plenum.

Kelso, J. A. S., Tuller, B., V.-Bateson, E., & Fowler, C. A. (1984). Functionally specific articulatory cooperation adaptation to jaw perturbations during speech: Evidence for coordinative structures. *Journal of Experimental Psychology: Human Perception & Performance, 10,* 812-832.

Kugler, P. N., Kelson, J. A. S., & Turvey, M. T. (1980). On the concept of coordinative structures as dissipative structures: Vol. I. Theoretical lines of convergence. In G. E. Stelmach & J. Requin (Eds.), *Tutorials in motor behavior.* New York: North-Holland.

Kugler, P., Kelso, J. A. S., & Turvey, M. T. (1982). On the control and co-ordination of naturally developing systems. In J. A. S. Kelso & J. E. Clark (Eds.), *The development of movement control and co-ordination.* New York: Wiley.

Lee, T. D., Magill, R. A., & Weeks, D. J. (1985). Influence of practice schedule on testing schema theory predictions in adults. *Journal of Motor Behavior*, 17, 283-299.

McGraw, M. B. (1939). Swimming behavior of the human infant. *Journal of Pediatrics, 15,* 485-490.

McGraw, M. B. (1943). *The neuromuscular maturation of the human infant.* New York: Columbia University Press.

McGraw, M. B. (1946). Maturation of behavior. In L. Carmichael (Ed.), *Manual of child psychology.* New York: Wiley.

McGraw, M. B., & Breeze, K. W. (1941). Quantitative studies in the development of erect locomotion. *Child Development, 12,* 267-303.

Mittenthal, J. E. (1981). The rule of normal neighbors: A hypothesis for morphogenetic pattern regulation. *Developmental Biology, 88,* 15-26.

Mounoud, P. (1982). Revolutionary periods in early development. In T. G. Bever (Ed.), *Regressions in mental development: Basic phenomena and theories.* Hillsdale, NJ: Erlbaum.

Mounoud, P., & Hauert, C. (1982). Development of sensorimotor organization in young children: grasping and lifting objects. In G. E. Forman (Ed.), *Action and thought: From sensorimotor schemes to symbolic operations.* New York: Academic.

Nashner, L. M., & McCollum, G. (1985). The organization of human postural movements: A formal basis and experimental synthesis. *The Behavioral & Brain Sciences, 8,* 135-172.

Newell, K. M. (1984). *The development of coordination: The significance of task constraints.* Paper presented at the annual meeting of the American Association for the Advancement of Science, New York.

Overton, W., & Reese, H. (1973). Models of development: Methodological implications. In J. Nesselroade & H. Reese (Eds.), *Life-span developmental psychology: methodological issues.* New York: Academic.

Palmer, C. F. (1984). Infants' knowledge of objects: Relations between perceiving and acting. Paper presented at the annual meeting of the American Psychological Association, Toronto.

Parmelee, A. H., & Sigman, M. D. (1983). Perinatal brain development and behavior. In P. H. Mussen (Gen. Ed.); M. M. Haith & J. J. Campos (Vol. Eds.), *Handbook of child psychology: Vol. II. Infancy and developmental psychobiology* (4th ed.). New York: Wiley.

Polit, A., & Bizzi, E. (1978). Processes controlling arm movements in monkeys. *Science, 201,* 1235-1237.

Prechtl, H. F. R. (1974). The behavioural states of the newborn infant (a review). *Brain Research, 76,* 185-212.

Prechtl, H. F. R. (1982). Regressions and transformations during neurological development. In T. G. Bever (Ed.), *Regressions in mental development: Basic phenomena and theories.* Hillsdale, NJ: Erlbaum.

Prigogine, I. (1980). *From being to becoming.* San Francisco: W. H. Freeman.

Reed, E. S. (1982). An outline of a theory of action systems. *Journal of Motor Behavior, 14,* 98-134.

Reese, H. W., & Overton, W. F. (1970). Models of development and theories of development. In L. R. Goulet & P. B. Baltes (Eds.), *Life-span development psychology: Research and theory.* New York: Academic.

Rosen, R. (1978). *Fundamentals of measurement and representation of natural systems.* New York: North-Holland.

Rossum, J. H. A. van. (1980). The schema notion in motor learning theory: Some persistent problems in research. *Journal of Human Movement Studies, 6,* 269-279.

Rothstein, A. L. (1977). Information processing in children's skill acquisition. In

R. W. Christina & D. M. Landers (Eds.), *Psychology of motor behavior and sport (1976)*. Champaign, IL: Human Kinetics Publishers.

Saltzman, E. L., & Kelso, J. A. S. (1983). Skilled actions: A task dynamic approach. *Haskins Laboratories Status Report on Speech Research, SR-76,* 3–50.

Sameroff, A. J. (1983). Developmental systems: Contexts and evolution. In P. H. Mussen (Gen. Ed.), *Handbook of child psychology: Vol. I. History, theory, and methods* (4th ed.). New York: Wiley.

Schellekens, J. M. H., Kalverboer, A. F., & Scholten, C. A. (1984). The microstructure of tapping movements in children. *Journal of Motor Behavior, 16,* 20–39.

Schmidt, R. A. (1975). A schema theory of discrete motor skill learning. *Psychological Review, 82,* 225–260.

Schmidt, R. A. (1982). *Motor control and learning: A behavioral emphasis.* Champaign, IL: Human Kinetics Publishers.

Shapiro, D. C., & Schmidt, R. A. (1982). The schema theory: Recent evidence and developmental implications. In J. A. S. Kelso & J. E. Clark (Eds.), *The development of movement control and co-ordination.* New York: Wiley.

Sheppard, J. J., & Mysak, E. D. (1984). Ontogeny of infantile oral reflexes and emerging chewing. *Child Development, 55,* 831–843.

Soll, D. R. (1979). Timers in developing systems. *Science, 203,* 841–849.

Stamback, M. (1963). *Tonus et psychomotricite dans la premiere enfance.* Neuchatel, Switzerland: Editions Delachaux & Niestle.

Super, C. M. (1980). Behavioral development in infancy. In R. H. Monroe, R. L. Monroe, & B. B. Whiting (Eds.), *Handbook of cross-cultural human development.* New York: Garland.

Thelen, E. (1981). Kicking, rocking, and waving: Contextual analysis of rhythmical stereotypies in normal human infants. *Animal Behaviour, 29,* 3–11.

Thelen, E. (1984). Learning to walk: Ecological demands and phylogenetic constraints. In L. P. Lipsitt (Ed.), *Advances in infancy research* (Vol. 3). Norwood, NJ: Ablex.

Thelen, E. (1985). Developmental origins of motor coordination: Leg movements in human infants. *Developmental Psychobiology, 18,* 1–22.

Thelen, E. (1986a). Treadmill-elicited stepping in seven-month-old infants. *Child Development, 57,* 1498–1506.

Thelen, E. (1986b). Development of coordinated movement: Implications for early human development. In H. T. A. Whiting & M. G. Wade (Eds.), *Motor skills acquisition.* Amsterdam: North-Holland.

Thelen, E., & Fisher, D. M. (1982). Newborn stepping: An explanation for a "disappearing reflex." *Developmental Psychology, 18,* 760–775.

Thelen, E., Fisher, D. M., & Ridley-Johnson, R. (1984). The relationship between physical growth and a newborn reflex. *Infant Behavior & Development, 7,* 479–493.

Thelen, E., & Fogel, A. (in press). Toward an action-based theory of infant development. In J. Lockman & N. Hazen (Eds.), *Action in social context.* New York: Plenum.

Thelen, E., Kelso, J. A. S., & Fogel, A. (1987). Self-organizing systems and infant motor development. *Developmental Review, 7,* 39–65.

Thomas, J. R. (1980). Acquisition of motor skills: Information processing differences between children and adults. *Research Quarterly for Exercise & Sport, 51,* 158–173.

Trevarthan, C. (1982). Basic patterns of psychogenic change in infancy. In T. G. Bever (Ed.), *Regressions in mental development: Basic phenomena and theories.* Hillsdale, NJ: Erlbaum.

Trevarthan, C. (1984). How control of movement develops. In H. T. A. Whiting (Ed.), *Human motor actions: Bernstein reassessed.* Amsterdam: North-Holland.

Touwen, B. (1976). *Neurological development in infancy.* London: Spastics International Medical Publishing and Heinemann.

Turvey, M. T. (1977). Preliminaries to a theory of action with a reference to vision. In R. Shaw & J. Bransford (Eds.), *Perceiving, acting, and knowing: Toward an ecological psychology.* Hillsdale, NJ: Erlbaum.

van Summers, P. (1984). *Drawing and cognition.* Cambridge: Cambridge University Press.

Wallace, S. A., Newell, K. M., & Wade, M. G. (1978). Decision and response times as a function of movement difficulty in preschool children. *Child Development, 49,* 509–512.

Webster, G., & Goodwin, B. (1981). History and structure in biology. *Perspectives in Biology & Medicine, 25,* 39–62.

Winfree, A. T. (1980). *The geometry of biological time.* New York: Springer-Verlag.

Young, G., Corter, C. M., Segalowitz, S. J., & Trehub, S. E. (1983). *Manual specialization and the developing brain.* New York: Academic.

Zelazo, P. R. (1982). The year-old infant: A period of major cognitive change. In T. G. Bever (Ed.), *Regressions in mental development: Basic phenomena and theories.* Hillsdale, NJ: Erlbaum.

Zelazo, P. R. (1983). The development of walking: New findings and old assumptions. *Journal of Motor Behavior, 15,* 99–137.

Zelazo, P. R., Zelazo, N. A., & Kolb, S. (1972). ''Walking'' in the newborn. *Science, 177,* 1058–1059.

CHAPTER 2

The Growth of Self-Regulation: Caregivers and Children

CLAIRE B. KOPP
University of California, Los Angeles

One of the most demanding aspects of the socialization process requires children to become aware of and to conform to standards of socially appropriate behavior and to assume responsibility for their own behavior. The term used to designate this competency is *self-regulation* (Flavell, 1977; Kopp, 1982).

Self-regulation is an abstraction that subsumes behaviors as diverse as compliance, delay of gratification, control of impulses and affect, modulation of motor and linguistic activities, and ability to act in accordance with social norms in the absence of external monitors. A common feature that unifies this diversity is adaptation to situations that have standards for conduct associated with them. Thus it is permissible to shout in a playground but not in a classroom, to run across a meadow but not a street, and to respect another's possessions whether the person is present or absent. During childhood and later, self-regulation assumes increasing importance as children are exposed to numerous educational and social situations. Their success in meeting situational demands will, in part, be measured by their ability to monitor effectively and adapt their own behaviors accordingly.

Despite the significance of self-regulation, relatively little is known of its early developmental course. Thus in the recent past, developmental and theoretical perspectives about self-regulation have been analyzed, summarized, and restated (e.g., Flavell, 1977, 1985; Kopp, 1982). To some extent, these discussions have focused upon the factors underlying and contributing to self-regulation, the nature of changes in early self-monitoring activities, and the usefulness of theoretical approaches for understanding self-regulation. Yet much remains unexplained. Hence this chapter continues in a reflective mode. Here the goal is to extend our view of caregiver and child as attempts are made to move the child toward self-regulation. This broader perspective is necessary

Appreciation is extended to Kim Johnson for initially integrating the literature on caregivers and compliance, and to Kathleen Brown and Sandra Kaler for critiquing this chapter.

because of numerous issues that have yet to be addressed in existing frameworks.

The chapter opens with a brief recap of theory and data concerning the role of caregivers in early forms of self-regulation, and then moves to a similar summary with respect to the child. Following, a working model of self-regulation is presented. The model primarily focuses upon the child who is in the second and third years of life, and is explicitly directed to early forms of self-regulation that pertain to standards for conduct. These include standards that involve teaching the child about safety (e.g., electrical outlets), introducing the child into ongoing family routines, protecting personal property from child destructiveness, and inculcating family values. The particular child behavior of interest (with reference to self-regulation) is compliance, because this is what caregivers initially demand.

The model first suggests that there are behavioral trends in caregivers' responses; these start from the time infants begin to display annoying actions to the point when they comply relatively regularly to caregiver requests for standards for conduct. A point of emphasis is that the caregiver's attempts to gain child compliance are a function of both infant capability and situational factors. Second, it is proposed that infant compliance grows in increments that reflect both quantitative and qualitative developments that are in part linked to the growth of cognitive processing abilities.

In a final section, two of the cognitive mediators that underlie child compliance during the second year of life are delineated. The goal here is to clarify how these cognitive processes are implicated in this socialization task.

SUMMARY OF THEMES

Caregivers

The caregiver's role in fostering self-regulation has in the main been discussed in relation to infants and very young children. This emphasis seemingly suggests that the caregiver's input becomes less important the older the child. However, as Maccoby (1984) has noted, it is unlikely that caregivers directly relinquish control to the school-aged child. Instead, there is probably a time of *co-regulation* in which "parents continue to exercise general supervisory control, while children begin to exercise moment-to-moment self-regulation" (p. 191).

Individual Differences Among Caregivers

One of the emphases found in the literature deals with characteristics of caregivers perceived to be vital in the transmission of standards. For example, sensitivity is thought to be crucial for facilitating self-regulation, especially compliance (Arend, Gove, & Sroufe, 1979; Londerville & Main, 1981; Rexford, 1978; Stayton, Hogan, & Ainsworth, 1971). Parental sensitivity, or tolerance as it is also referred to, is considered essential when dealing with toddlers and young preschoolers whose rapid maturation of motor and language skills makes them especially tuned to the environment and particularly vulnerable to repressive restrictions (Rexford, 1978). Going along with this theme, attachment as an indication of the child's response to sensitivity has been linked to child compliance in two studies (Londerville & Main, 1981; Matas, Arend, & Sroufe, 1978).

The link between sensitivity and compliance inherent in the work of Ainsworth and Sroufe and their colleagues has an analogue in the studies of Baumrind (1979) and Block and Block (1980). As one example, these researchers have noted that involved and responsive parenting is associated with the school-aged child's assumption of behavioral responsibility.

Imparting Knowledge via Social Interactions

In contrast to perspectives that focus upon variability in caregiving behaviors, the views of Vygotsky, Luria, and their followers emphasize caregiver behavior that seems to imply a species universal. In this view, self-regulation grows out of the pivotal role of the caregiver's structure and organization of child activities. These adult activities are inherent in communication patterns of parent and child (Luria, 1961; Rogoff & Wertsch, 1984; Vygotsky, 1978; Wertsch, 1979, 1984). Further, the child's process of thinking evolves from these shared social activities.

Recent research using Vygotskian theory has emphasized the *zone of proximal development* in which the child has partially mastered a task but can participate in its successful completion only with caregiver participation. Findings indicate that caregivers tailor their speech and actions both to a child's current level of functioning and to a perceived next step (Wertsch, 1979). Caregivers appear to provide a structured agenda for the child, taking into account the child's age and level of self-monitoring behavior that is displayed (Rogoff, Malkin, & Gilbride, 1984; Saxe, Gearhart, & Guberman, 1984). It is interesting to note that research in other domains suggests that caregivers' activities are not consciously thought through—whatever mothers bring to interactive situations with young children (e.g., methods of attention getting, Schaffer & Crook, 1979) appears intuitive and reflects an implicit teaching agenda (DeLoache, 1984).

Note that Vygotsky and his contemporary followers bring a developmental view to both caregiver and child activities. That is, both change as the transmission of self-regulation occurs. Although few details are provided about the processes of change and the transmission process per se, details about communication patterns of parent and child are often given (e.g., Wertsch, 1979).

Specific Caregiver Activities

Still another view holds that the child's self-regulatory activities grow out of specific types of control techniques used by caregivers (Holden, 1983; Johnson, 1982; Kopp, 1985; Kuczynski, 1984; Lytton, 1979; McLaughlin, 1983;

Minton, Kagan, & Levine, 1971; Schaffer, 1984; Schaffer & Crook, 1978, 1979, 1980). Many of these studies contain good descriptions of maternal behaviors evoked in compliance situations involving 2- and 3-year-old children. Attention-getting procedures, use of indirect commands, task structuring, and concomitant use of verbal and nonverbal messages are common strategies employed by caregivers of 2-year-olds. Caregiver behaviors specifically associated with child compliance with 2-year-old boys include suggestive verbal controls that are enhanced by nonverbal signals appropriately timed (e.g., Lytton, 1979, 1980). Caregiver consistency, encouragement of mature behavior, and use of positive rewards also predict compliance (Lytton, 1980).

In Kopp (1985), findings were reported about specifics of caregiver behaviors during a child cleanup task involving children 18–30 months old. Principal components analyses revealed that almost half of the common variance in maternal behaviors could be accounted for by three factors. These were labeled *mother as definer and organizer, mother as helper,* and *mother as partner.* A developmental trend, indicating significantly less defining and organizing, was found as a function of increasing child age and compliance. The factor scores and results also suggest that there are two primary aspects to the maternal role; one involves teaching and the other helping and sharing, or in other words, responsivity.

An Integration

In sum, a synthesis of the caregiver literature suggests that sensitive caregivers tuned to children's characteristics who use a variety of attention-getting mechanisms and are consistent stand the most chance of obtaining compliance from the young child. Despite this important information, the literature is strangely silent on the specifics of the process. Questions that have yet to be addressed include: What characteristics of the child do caregivers rely upon when they seek compliance? What situations cause them to require compliance? Is there an age trend for their demands?

The Child

Although caregivers provide the basis for standards of behavior, they cannot make the child adopt them. Children must have some understanding of caregiver expectations and have some desire to act upon them. Attempts to get at these issues have been addressed in two primary ways. These are described below.

A Developmental Formulation

Kopp's (1982) theoretical article was an attempt to develop premises about developmental trends in the emergence of self-regulation, and she specifically linked the growth of cognitive skills to the growth of self-regulation.

In order to call attention to the various kinds of cognitive skills that are characteristic of young children and associated with self-monitoring abilities,

Kopp defined phases leading to self-regulation. *Control* is the phase when children show awareness of social and task demands that have been defined by caregivers, and initiate, maintain, modulate, or cease acts accordingly upon demand. Kopp suggested that *control* subsumes intent, appraisal of differential features of the environment, and an elementary awareness of what is and is not acceptable. In the control phase, children are highly dependent upon the caregiver for reminder signals about acceptable behaviors.

Although it is not immediately obvious, Kopp's control phase covers the age period (12 to about 18 months) which is often the age of focus in the caregiver literature on self-regulation and compliance. Of importance, there is clear documentation that some forms of compliance are obtained by caregivers during this age (see Schaffer, 1984 for summary; Stayton et al., 1971).

In the next postulated phase (Kopp, 1982), *self-control,* it was suggested that a distinguishing feature was the child's ability to go along with caregiver expectations in the absence of external monitors. This was linked to cognitive growths of representational thinking and recall memory that let the child be aware of and remember the network of conventions that govern behavior in familiar routines such as eating, playing, dressing, and so forth. The child's ability to recall information means that fewer externally mediated cues and reminders should be needed for self-monitoring behaviors.

A final phase labeled *self-regulation* involves flexible and adaptive control processes that can meet quickly changing situational demands. The use of self-generated strategic behaviors and plans is implicated. Even though self-regulation is presumed to emerge during the preschool years, Kopp suggested that its consolidation and refinement continue for many, many years thereafter.

In the first research directed to the study of self-control, Vaughn, Kopp, and Krakow (1984) examined the compliance and delay abilities of children 18–30 months of age. Compliance and delay were evidenced only sporadically among the youngest children, were clearly demonstrated by 24 months, and showed across-task consistency by 30 months. In addition to these developmental trends, the coherence of behavior that was seen at 30 months represents a significant advance. In a very practical sense, this means that a degree of predictability begins to exist for child competencies around self-monitoring.

Although this research has provided thought-provoking data, self-control and its associated cognitive processes are still poorly understood with respect to the young child. In contrast, there are an extensive literature and a reasonable knowledge base devoted to older children. Of interest, this literature is so child focused that caregiver and other environmental factors are essentially ignored (e.g., Humphrey, 1984).

The Child Research

In essence there are two major themes, language and cognition. Spoken language is at the core of the Vygotskian (1962) view of the child's internalization of caregiver standards for behavior, and is also a component of the psychoanalytic perspective (Rexford, 1978). The former stresses that self-regulation is tied to the development of internalized speech that occurs about 4–6 years of age, having its origins first in social interactions where the caregiver is the external monitor, and then in the child's overt speech as he or she takes over the monitoring process. The latter emphasizes the development of language that functions to inhibit actions (Greenacre, 1950), along with control processes that arise out of the development of an executive function such as the ego.

The role ascribed to language in self-regulation is not generally supported by empirical findings. In a major review, Fuson (1979) found that spontaneous use of self-regulation speech is not characteristic of all children. Moreover, certain variables, such as age, task difficulty, communication level, intelligence, degree of impulsivity, and possibly gender, influence its use. Fuson's conclusions are not surprising in view of recent research that shows that young children who are limited in productive language have some self-regulatory capabilities. Thus processes either in addition to or other than language drive aspects of self-monitoring. Cognitive variables would seem to be implicated (Kagan, 1981; Kopp, 1982; Mischel, 1983).

The importance of cognition to self-regulation has been acknowledged in studies of processes such as attention, use of conceptual categories, strategies and plans, and individual goal setting (e.g., Bandura & Schunk, 1981; Kendall & Wilcox, 1980; Mischel, 1983) and is exemplified in Mischel's research on delay of gratification (e.g., Mischel & Baker, 1975; Mischel & Ebbesen, 1970; Mischel & Patterson, 1978). This behavior is presumed to represent the individual's ability to cope with a variety of situations. Attention and strategy production are the cognitive mechanisms identified by Mischel as important to delay. In order to delay, one must turn attention away from a desired object or event and generate appropriate distracting strategies.

Not surprisingly, Mischel has documented developmental trends both in the ability to delay and in the cognitive processes associated with that ability. Young preschoolers, for example, are not as successful as school-age children in generating strategies because they do not appear to understand what they are doing and why (Mischel & Mischel, 1977).

An Integration

Mischel's research is impressive, but the findings probably represent only a limited view of the cognitive and other processes that must be implicated in self-regulatory activities. To date, there is no documentation or analysis of the varied approaches that very young children spontaneously generate in challenging situations that call for self-monitoring. This information is critical for understanding and elucidating factors that are associated with functional and dysfunctional self-regulation, and for understanding additional components of social development including codification of one's own standards.

A PRELIMINARY MODEL OF THE TRANSMISSION PROCESS

In the most general sense, there are two major characters in the initial process of defining expectations for behavior—the caregiver and the child. The caregiver determines what behaviors are important, when and where the expectations will be met, and how to move the child toward accepting and meeting these expectations on his or her own. The child's role is to make sense of the demands for behavior as best he or she can, to determine that it is in his or her best interests to accept demands, and to carry them out accordingly.

As noted above, typically the behaviors demanded by caregivers involve some kind of child compliance. However, considerable diversity is subsumed by the term *compliance*. The child may be asked to cease an activity, change an ongoing act, initiate a new behavior, or to refrain from an activity whether another person is around or not. Given the participants and the behavioral goal of compliance, it is likely that developmental trends occur in caregiver and in child behaviors. The goal of this section is to describe these trends. Behaviors of the caregivers are focused upon first; it is presumed that what and how they demand standards for conduct are very much a function of the child's actions.

The Caregiver

Initial Input About Standards for Conduct

Initial input probably begins when infants begin to display *annoying* habits such as thumb sucking, throwing, hair pulling, pinching, and messiness as a function of attempts at self-feeding. These often surface at about 8–9 months of age, and are a derivative of the infant's ability to exercise good control of reach and grasp movements and to discriminate effectively an object's characteristics. Infants explore and try out their myriad skills, but not always with the approval of their caregivers.

Caregivers appear to give infants of this age two kinds of messages about standards for conduct. One is said matter-of-factly and conveys annoyance but also suggests there is no expectation of response. "Oh, you are so messy" is an example. The situations that elicit this type of response are not highly salient or important to the caregiver in ongoing day-to-day interactions. The other type of response occurs because of perceived intrusions into one's beliefs, values, and possessions. The message given is meant to be listened to and is told in the form of imperative commands such as "No!" or "Stop that!" Negative affect and changes in tone of voice accompany the message. In an observational study of his own infants, Myers (1922) recounted that destruction of his personal papers by his infant provoked very high levels of his own negative affect. He also noted that his own or his wife's negative affect and loud voice were initially powerful deterrents to unwanted infant behaviors.

In all probability, the extent and level of caregiver demands for infants of this age are limited and highly situation specific. There are, after all, a finite number of ways that crawling (or even walking) infants can get into trouble, although the trouble may be dangerous for themselves both literally and figuratively. It is also likely that an asynchrony exists between the number of caregiver expectations for infant behavior and the child's response—simply because the infant's understanding is very restricted.

Escalation of Caregiver Demands

Early in the second year of life, children's upright locomotion dramatically improves. They not only walk, they run, and they walk and run holding objects in their hands. The potential for trouble increases almost exponentially because children desire to explore and their exploration often appears to be mindless.

The very fact that children are more capable motorically means caregivers have more to respond to. Therefore it is likely that an increase in standards for conduct behaviors will occur with respect to number of demands made upon the child and the types of situations that elicit demands. Concerns around child safety will surely loom large, as will attempts to keep the child from interfering with household possessions such as telephones, television sets, and the like.

Active Organization and Direction of Child Activities in Standards for Conduct Situations

It is probable that a different quality of caregiver behavior emerges when children's motor activities become less frenetic and their language comprehension and production rapidly expand. Both of these occur around 16–19 months of age (Goldin-Meadow, Seligman, & Gelman, 1976; Wenar, 1971). The change in caregivers' behavior seems to involve use of organizational techniques in directing certain activities and the use of specific teaching modes.

Presumably these come about because the caregiver interprets the changes in child behavior as a sign that the child is more tractable and influenceable, and thus more teachable. In our self-control studies we found that mothers used very specific organizational techniques to get their children to respond to a toy cleanup task (Kopp, 1985). Frequently observed examples included touching the child for attention, other verbal and nonverbal attention-getting approaches, pointing toward and patting toys to be put away, and showing the shelf that was the toy repository. Caregivers also organized the cleanup by telling the child the sequence of cleanup (e.g., "Pick up the truck, take it over to the shelf"). At 18 months these organizational activities were significantly more common than at 24 and 30 months. Although no data currently exist about younger-aged children, it appears that this degree of specificity of direct teaching is not characteristic of the interactions of caregivers of children below 15–16 months.

A similar form of structuring is revealed in one mother's account of how she handles a situation that involves her child's learning to wait. Her 17-month-old invariably became fatigued and upset during long car rides. Accordingly, the mother waited until the child began to show a degree of impatience, and then she introduced distractions that utilized a series of participation songs. After each song, mother and child talked about a character in the song or about the song plot. Then they moved on to the next song. This example also nicely illustrates the Vygotskian (1978) principle of zone of proximal development in that the caregiver's participation led to a success for the child.

Beginning Disengagement in Specific Tasks

At age 2 years, Vaughn and colleagues (1984) reported that children begin to show high levels of compliance in a toy cleanup task. Not surprisingly, data on maternal acts complemented the child findings (Kopp, 1985). Mothers began to decrease their participation and direction of the cleanup task as the children exhibited more cooperation. Although in general, caregivers' active physical involvement may decrease over time in particular tasks, it is virtually certain that they will provide considerable input when the child engages in negativism and autonomous acts that jeopardize safety, possessions, or important plans.

During the third year, it also seems probable that caregivers continue to be involved in direct teaching of the child, particularly concerning value systems and behavioral conventions around politeness routines (e.g., "Say *please,*" "Say *thank you*"). This probably continues for many years (Maccoby, 1984).

Expanding Expectations

There is good evidence that caregivers in many cultures make very concerted efforts to get children to adhere to family and social standards by 3–4 years of age (e.g., Rogoff, Sellers, Pirrotta, Fox, & White, 1975; Whiting & Whiting, 1975) and continue to engage in direct tuition about manners (Grief & Gleason, 1980). However, interestingly, caregivers also appear to be somewhat inconsistent in what and when they demand (Grusec & Kuczynski, 1980; Whiting & Whiting, 1975).

It may be that for young children caregivers show more consistency than inconsistency in matters that pertain to family standards (safety, possessions) but less consistency around value systems that have less immediacy than survival or protecting the antique vase that belonged to Aunt Anna. Beyond that, sometimes caregivers may find it less effortful and more expedient to let an infraction go by or to complete a task by themselves. After all, high levels of psychic energy are required of caregivers from toddlers and young preschoolers, and there may be a feeling that some demands can be put off for another time.

The Young Child

Compliance to Standards of Conduct

In the following paragraphs, compliance is discussed from a developmental perspective. This approach differs both in formulation and degree of specificity from that used previously. The developmental approach calls attention to the complex nature of the construct *compliance,* and suggests that some kinds of compliance demand more active cognitive involvement on the part of the young child than other forms.

In the recent past, some investigators have measured compliance by recording the presence or absence of a child's response to a caregiver's demand, or in Schaffer's (1984) coding scheme, noted whether the child visually oriented, tactually contacted, or precisely carried out an object-related command given by the caregiver (labeled *task compliance*). In the developmental formulation presented here, compliance with respect to social standards consists of the following: inhibition of activity; production of an active response to a request given by the caregiver; self-initiated compliance; and modulation of an ongoing activity.

Inhibition

The cessation of an ongoing activity in response to a caregiver prohibition is referred to as inhibition. It is cognitively the least demanding form of compliance. Myers (1922) documented a first occurrence of infant inhibition to a command at around 8–9 months of age. In all probability, this was a response due to infant fear or surprise at the intensity of the caregiver's negative affect rather than an actual encoding of caregiver message. An example from Myers concerns his infant's thumb sucking. The child's mother noticed it and called out in a loud voice: "Take that thumb out of your mouth!" The thumb dropped from the infant's mouth. In another instance, Myers sharply chastised his son for touching important papers, at which the infant immediately withdrew his hand.

Myers felt the response occurred because of fear. Months later, Myers suggests inhibition comes about, and is routinely observed, because the child *understands* what is expected. Recent studies of infant comprehension tend to support Myers's thesis, at least with respect to understanding caregiver commands. There is good evidence that shows comprehension of specific words is minimal until the child is about a year of age. The issue of expectations and comprehension will be discussed more fully in a later section of this chapter.

Production Compliance

In this form of compliance, a response is produced by the child to a caregiver request around standards for conduct. Stated another way, the child initiates an activity that is expressly linked to caregiver request. From maternal reports, production compliance occurs initially around 12 or so months to simple situation-specific demands. As one example, caregivers often tell children to remove their shoes before sitting on a sofa or stuffed chair. Other common requests include "Sit down" (before eating), "Wave bye-bye," "Stand up" (for dressing). By implication, comprehension is involved, as is the ability to select the appropriate action from one's repertoire of behaviors.

It is likely that children of this age begin to generalize a response given in one specific situation to other similar contexts. A primitive form of categorizing may be involved. Thus a child who takes off her shoes in her own home before sitting on the sofa may attempt to do so when visiting at her grandmother's house. It is also reasonable to presume that once a child understands a phrase such as "Give me . . . " the command will be acted upon irrespective of the exact particulars of context. Going along with this, "Give me . . . " is understood and complied with by most 15-month-olds (Bühler, 1933).

Self-Initiated Compliance

Here the child acts on his or her own either to produce or to inhibit a response that is expected by the caregiver, whether the caregiver is present or not. Self-initiated compliance emerges at about 13–15 months of age to very specific situations (Kopp, 1982; Krakow, 1981; Stayton et al., 1971). An example reported by Krakow (personal communication, 1981) involved forcefully telling her daughter not to touch a particular bush in the back yard (the berries from the bush are poisonous if eaten). At a later date, the child took her teddy bear to the bush and said, "No! No!" Indeed, responses of children of this age to caregiver prohibitions often include reaching out and withdrawing or saying "no" to themselves when they are in the vicinity of a desired object.

Self-initiated compliance represents a remarkable growth in compliance, and is cognitively more advanced than inhibition or production compliance (Kopp, 1982). It signals understanding of caregivers' expectations and some notion of consequences. Self-initiated compliance involves recognition that an object has an association with a prohibition, an instruction to the self about that prohibition, and an action that is consonant with the instruction. This form of compliance with its emphasis on a desired action and the negation of that desire must be singularly important in helping children consolidate whatever understanding they have of caregiver prohibitions.

Modulation of an Ongoing Response as a Form of Compliance

In this type of compliance, the child changes the intensity of an ongoing behavior in response to a caregiver request. This form of compliance has not been discussed in the literature, but is clearly demanded by caregivers of younger and older children. Typically the request to an older child is to lower his or her voice, to slow down, and so forth. However, one mother of a little girl recently reported that she used the phrase, "Lower your voice, daddy's sleeping" when her child was slightly younger than 2 years. When the child was close to 24 months, she started to modulate the level of her speech.

This is also a challenging form of compliance for the young child because it requires interpretation of the request, an estimate of just how much modulation is required in order to meet the demand of the caregiver, and coordination of his or her action to the estimate.

In sum, this view of compliance is multidimensional and developmental. It is premised that the components described above emerge no later than the third year of life for normally developing children who are reared in supportive environments. The significant changes in compliance that come about in subsequent years probably relate to the amount that *each* aspect of compliance is displayed by the child, how compliance is linked to family and social demands, and the strategies the child produces in order to make compliance less onerous to his or her own particular wants and needs. Presumably, too, the child's ability to comply will show coherence with other aspects of self-regulation. Verification of these ideas awaits empirical research.

Cognitive Processes Linked to the Growth of Compliance

As noted above, research with older children clearly implicates cognitive processing mechanisms in self-regulatory activities. For example, Mischel (1983) showed that the child's abilities to turn attention away from a desired object and to generate strategies were related to delay of gratification. In research with young children, Kopp and colleagues (Johnson & Kopp, 1981; Vaughn, Kopp, Krakow, Johnson, & Schwartz, 1986) extended these findings to children as young as 2 years. The data unequivocally demonstrated that, even at this age, when given the command "Don't touch," children turned away from the prohibited object and began to engage in activities that seemed to serve as distractors (e.g., sitting on hands, engaging mother in conversation, turning around in chair). These behaviors looked very much like primitive strategies although they probably lacked elements of planfulness and evaluation that are common to mature forms of strategy production (e.g., Brown, Bransford, Ferrara, & Campione, 1983).

However, as important as strategic behaviors are to self-regulation, there are other behaviors that must come into play because they are fundamental to the child's responses to caregivers' messages. As one example, the young, immature child who is just learning about the social world has to be particularly *attentive* to caregivers and to the nuances of social situations in order to become knowledgeable about approved conduct. As another, in order to be able to respond adequately to a variety of standards for conduct demands, young children eventually require some way to *represent* and to *recall* expectations for behavior. These cognitive processes permit them to generalize from one event to another and to build a corpus of understanding. Without these processes, each event would stand as an isolated unit demanding an effort after meaning and a determination of possible solutions. In the long run, these isolated efforts would be ineffective, inefficient, and inflexible.

In the paragraphs that follow, the ideas of Kopp (1982) are extended with the goal of specifying more fully two of the cognitive mechanisms that are used in the service of compliance during the second year. The emphasis is on attention and comprehension as two important cognitive processing variables that are particularly relevant as young children begin to grapple with their caregivers' demands for conduct. In a very real sense, these cognitive processes are intrinsic to the antecedent phase of self-regulation that Kopp labeled *control* (1982).

Attention

The social world is one of challenges for children; important cues are not always salient and events can be unpredictable and complex. Attention to one's social surroundings is essential in order to learn what is expected in the way of behavior.

As noted earlier, attention and its role in self-regulation have been discussed for years; however, typically the focus is in terms of attention directed away from objects (e.g., Mischel, 1983). However, the attention under discussion here is *attention to* an object or an individual as a way of obtaining information. Of course attention turned away is important, but as children are initially exposed to standards for conduct, they first have to learn how to be attentive to social cues.

Attention is defined in a number of different ways (e.g., Parasuraman & Davies, 1984), but for the purposes of this discussion the view of Gibson and Rader (1979) is adopted—*attention* refers to "a search for information that is necessary for performance" (p. 7). Although Gibson and Rader's description is seemingly focused upon the individual in the physical world, their definition applies as well to the social world. The infant and young child, though apparently primed to respond to social stimuli from the beginning of life, do have to learn when and how to respond to relevant social inputs. The term *relevant* as used here refers to a form of selective attention in which the child focuses upon a social stimulus instead of something else.

Selectivity is the means by which individuals respond to certain features of the environment by their own choice, or involuntarily respond as a function of the strength of a stimulus that captures their attention, or because someone else has laid out a task such as an educational exercise that requires comparisons (Gibson & Spelke, 1983). Selectivity becomes more specific and systematic with increasing age although it is active and purposeful from the earliest days of life. With mature individuals, there is a bias toward attention to sensory input over attention to internal body sensations or to one's images and associations (Pope & Singer, 1978).

At the risk of stating the obvious, selective attention is fundamental to self-regulation. How else can young children (or even older individuals) learn what is expected of them? Clearly the selective attention involved in self-regulation is to the verbal output and visual displays (e.g., face, gestures) of the caregiver who is conveying messages about standards.

Why should the infant and young child pay particular attention to these messages? Are the caregiver's cues particularly salient and stronger than other, possibly competing, cues? The answer to these questions is complicated, and probably involves several factors. At times, for example, a caregiver's loud voice or a pat on the child's rear serves as a forceful stimulus and captures the child's attention. But beyond that, there is probably a social motive that underlies the infant's propensity to begin to attend to the caregiver's dicta about standards.

This social motive must in part have its origins in behaviors that emerge around the end of the first year. At this age infants come to the understanding that a shared meaning system exists with their caregivers (Bretherton, McNew, & Beeghly-Smith, 1981) or said differently, an understanding that each can communicate feeling and intents with the other. This is demonstrated by the emergence of "showing" behaviors in which infants use objects to initiate interactions with their caregivers (Uzgiris, 1967), the emergence of social referencing, which involves using caregivers as a source of information when ambiguous situations arise (Campos & Stenberg, 1981; Feinman, 1982), and the emergence of intentional communications (Bretherton & Bates, 1979), many of which involve a goal of interacting with the caregiver. All of these behaviors seem to prime infants to value their caregivers increasingly for what they can do: Valuing an individual often goes hand in hand with being attentive, although the other's message may not always be to one's liking.

At the same time that infants are developing an appreciation of others' characteristics and capabilities, they are beginning to be more aware of their own. They come to understand their own independent existence (Lewis & Brooks-Gunn, 1979), perhaps as a function of their own consciousness. This has been inferred to happen at about 12 months of age (Collins & Hagen, 1979). With the development of consciousness, the infant can actively (voluntarily) screen the material to be attended to. A choice can be made about attending or not attending to the caregiver at any given time.

Consciousness about one's self and one's activities also means that decisions (albeit primitive) can be made about how long attention is maintained or sustained to a given person, object, or event. In Krakow, Kopp, and Vaughn (1981) sustained attention was operationalized with respect to the length of time toddlers engaged with objects of their own choosing. However, sustained attention can also refer to the ability to continue to look or listen to another.

Sustained attention is also important to self-regulation. Clearly, the child must stay around long enough to take in and encode (as best as possible) the message given by caregivers. Whether or not the child acts on the message is another matter. The ability to sustain attention probably improves with age as children become more planful. But sustained attention may also be a function of individual differences in constitutional factors such as activity level.

Caregivers seem to have an intuitive sense about the importance of attention for infants and young children. Very early in life when infants' arousal systems are quite immature, they change the pitch and intonation of their voices and modify their facial expressions in order to initiate and maintain a visual–vocal interaction (e.g., Brazelton, Koslowski, & Main 1974; Stern, MacKain, & Spieker, 1982; Sullivan & Horowitz, 1983). By the second year of life, caregivers add verbal instructions (and gestures) as they attempt to get the child to attend to instructions (see, e.g., summary in Schaffer, 1984). And when the task involves a standard for conduct, caregivers make very concerted efforts to capture the child's attention by modifying their speech, touching the child (even physically moving him or her to facilitate eye contact), and pointing very specifically to an object of interest (Kopp, 1985).

The attentional efforts of child and caregivers would have little payoff for fostering standards for conduct if the child were unable to pick up clues about caregiver intentions and expectations. Fortunately, at about the same time that caregivers forcefully begin to emphasize this socialization task, the child shows beginning understanding of "the message." This is the focus of the next section.

Comprehension

There is compelling reason to argue that comprehension is critical for self-regulation. If the child does not understand the caregiver's message, then self-regulation (e.g., compliance) can be little more than a chance occurrence. Evidence, albeit sketchy, suggests a major transition in comprehension occurs around the end of the first year, and at about that same time the child begins to respond to caregiver admonitions (e.g., Stayton et al., 1971).

What is known about the knowledge base and degree of understanding of year-old infants? They appear to remember routines around daily living activities that may be represented in the form of a sequence of events (Nelson, 1978, 1983). Nelson (1983) proposes that scripts guide the actions in similar routines that "are the child's first exposure to the surrounding culture, embedding notions of how to eat, how to play, and so forth" (p. 34). A single word said to the child may act as a signal that activates an entire sequence of behavior.

Nelson's perspective is congruent with some of Shatz's (1978) ideas; in discussing the processing heuristics of the young child, she suggests that young children know that words act referentially and are often a call for action. This is done, Shatz continues, with only minimal knowledge of rule systems. When an element in the context specifies otherwise, the child learns that an action is not acceptable. In all probability, unacceptable behavior is conveyed by caregiver affect and voice intonations.

Research on comprehension indicates that growth of understanding occurs rapidly after 12 months of age, with comprehension of nouns exceeding that of verbs, and encoding first directed to one's own actions before the encoding of another's actions (Clark, 1983; Goldin-Meadow et al., 1976; Huttenlocher, Smiley, & Charney, 1983; Oviatt, 1980, 1982). By 24 months, children understand words associated with body parts, clothing, animals, living quarters, and food, along with numerous transitive and intransitive verbs (Goldin-Meadow et al., 1976).

Going beyond these general trends, Oviatt (1980, 1982) has hypothesized a developmental trend in early comprehension. In brief, she proposes that infants younger than 10–12 months have little understanding of words. At about 12 months, the infant develops a *recognitory comprehension* in which there is both awareness of a spoken category system and an association of linguistic items with regularities in the environment (e.g., day-to-day family routines). Affective cues also play a role. The net result is a child who can give an appropriate response to some words and short phrases.

Recognitory comprehension may be a comprehension that is based on a simple association of word and act, resulting in behavior that may at times seem almost automatic (e.g., infant holding out arms when caregiver starts to place sweater on child). Recognitory comprehension may also be why year-old children show evidence of production compliance. The child, for example, may begin to understand a word such as *hands,* which the caregiver undoubtedly uses in a variety of contexts. The child does not understand all of the communication but begins to pick up meanings as a function of regularity in day-to-day activities. If the caregiver says something like "Wash your hands before eating" when standing by the sink, and then washes the child's hands prior to bringing the child to the table, an association with word and routine comes about.

At about 13 months, Oviatt suggests that a beginning form of *categorical comprehension* occurs in which the infant appreciates a meaning for a word even though the object of reference is not in sight. An active memory is implicated. Going along with this, there is recognition that names refer to general classes of events. This can be inferred on the basis of comprehension studies that show overgeneralization (Thomson & Chapman, 1977).

Categorical comprehension seems to refer to the child's effort to make sense of a word or an idea. It is analogous to an individual listening to a foreign tongue, isolating what seems to be a recurrent word, trying to decipher the meaning of same, and then applying the word to different contexts. Intuitively, it seems that something akin to categorical comprehension is at the root of the child's ability to do self-initiated compliance. Using the word *No* as an example, the child begins to develop a sense of what *No* means, and has to extrapolate that *no* applies not to a single situation, but to many. Each, however different, involves a prohibition about keeping one's hands off certain objects.

At about 15–18 months, Oviatt indicates a new type of comprehension occurs. *Cognitory comprehension* is associated with the child's beginning coordination of his or her own interpretation of words to the referential use intended by adult speakers. With this type of comprehension, there is a beginning common frame of reference about objects, possessions, people, and events. Expectations for behavior can be shared. This advance, Oviatt premises, involves recall, perceived similarities between novel and familiar stimuli, and an inference that novel stimuli can have a common object name.

From my perspective, cognitory comprehension implies cognitive construction. The child has to encode the other's idea, group the word into a simple category, and then take the definition of the other and make it part of his or her own repertoire of symbols.

What kinds of behaviors might reflect cognitory comprehension? Agency behaviors that can be exemplified by a child actively *making* a doll behave in a way that is similar to that previously obtained by the caregiver from the child. More direct reflections of cognitory comprehension may be inferred from child behaviors that mirror self-consciousness about a misdeed. These include running away, bowing one's head, or bursting into tears after an act has been noticed, and the child admonished. Still another example was demonstrated recently by a child of 18 months whose mother had repeatedly told her not to stand on furniture. When the child saw an adult stand on a table, she attempted to wipe the table clean by brushing her hand across the surface (after the adult stepped down), repeatedly said "table" to her mother after the incident, and also showed emotional perturbation (e.g., worried expression on her face, a brief episode of clinging to her mother). The mother's response is of interest; she spontaneously comforted her daughter while at the same time emphasizing the correctness of her interpretation (e.g., saying, "That was not a good thing for the lady to do").

This instance demonstrates that caregivers do make attempts to foster child comprehension. Other techniques that have been noted include use of short, simple sentences utilized with very concrete semantic content, and labels that are overgeneralized to similar objects in order to keep encoding demands at a reasonable level (Bretherton, McNew, Snyder, & Bates, 1983; Mervis & Mervis, 1982).

In sum, the point has been made that increasing comprehension is inextricably linked to the child's ability to comply with a myriad of caregiver dicta. Of course this does not imply that the child will invariably show compliance—the growth of autonomy in the second year of life precludes such consistency. But as our own data have shown (Vaughn et al., 1984), by the end of the second year children more often than not do respond to caregiver demands.

CONCLUDING COMMENTS

This chapter has focused on the developmental period when young children begin to respond to standards that are wholly defined and dictated by caregivers. In this context, caregivers at first carry all of the burden—they not only define standards, they also convey the standards and work toward getting the child to adopt them. The child's initial tasks are to attend to the messages and to understand and act on them appropriately.

There is thus an interrelationship of three major conditions: the caregiver and the rules for behavior, the child's growing comprehension, and increasing child compliance. But it must also be recognized that during the second year children are still sensorimotor organisms, very much tied to the present and to the things and events seen and heard in their everyday world. In Flavell's (1985) words, intelligence here is unreflective, practical, and a perceiving and doing sort. It is most probable, then, that early standards for conduct are acquired around highly specific routinized events where the signals given by caregivers are very evident.

In time, as children become capable of using socially derived symbols and develop some internalized notions of their own selves and *goodness,* they will need fewer cues and reminders from their caregivers. Then they will increasingly adopt many of the standards for conduct espoused by the caregivers—at least for a while.

This chapter has focused on compliance as one aspect of self-regulation. Though an important early developmental component, compliance is neither the sum total of self-regulation nor the only component to emerge during the early years. Perhaps this chapter will serve as a catalyst for additional attempts to elaborate and extend our understanding of developmental trends in self-regulation.

REFERENCES

Arend, R. A., Gove, F. L., & Sroufe, L. A. (1979). Continuity of individual adaptation from infancy to kindergarten: A predictive study of ego resiliency and curiosity in preschoolers. *Child Development, 50,* 950–959.

Bandura, A., & Schunk, D. H. (1981). Cultivating competence, self-efficacy and intrinsic interest through proximal self-motivation. *Journal of Personality & Social Psychology, 41,* 586–598.

Baumrind, D. (1979). Current patterns of parental authority. *Development Psychology Monograph, 41* [1,P+2].

Block, J. H., & Block, J. (1980). The role of ego control and ego resiliency in the organization of behavior. In W. A. Collins (Ed.), *Minnesota Symposium of Child Psychology.* Hillsdale, NJ: Erlbaum.

Brazelton, T. B., Koslowski, B., & Main, M. (1974). The origins of reciprocity: The early mother–infant interaction. In M. Lewis & L. A. Rosenblum (Eds.), *The child in the family.* New York: Plenum.

Bretherton, I., & Bates, E. (1979). The emergence of intentional communication. In I. Uzgiris (Ed.), *New directions in child development* (Vol. 4). San Francisco: Jossey-Bass.

Bretherton, I., McNew, S., & Beeghly-Smith, M. (1981). Early person knowledge as expressed in gestural and verbal communication: When do infants acquire a "theory of mind"? In M. E. Lamb & L. R. Sherrod (Eds.), *Infant social cognition: Empirical and theoretical considerations.* Hillsdale, NJ: Erlbaum.

Bretherton, I., McNew, S., Snyder, L., & Bates, E. (1983). Individual differences at 20 months; Analytic and holistic strategies in language acquisition. *Journal of Child Language, 10,* 293–313.

Brown, A. L., Bransford, J. D., Ferrara, R. A., & Campione, J. C. (1983). Learning, remembering, understanding. In P. H. Mussen (Gen. Ed.); J. H. Flavell & E. M. Markman (Vol. Eds.), *Handbook of child psychology: Vol. 3. Cognitive development.* New York: Wiley.

Bühler, C. (1933). The social behavior of children. In C. Murchison (Ed.), *Handbook of child psychology.* Worcester, MA: Clark University Press.

Campos, J. J., & Stenberg, C. (1981). Perception, appraisal, and emotion: The onset of social referencing. In M. E. Lamb & L. R. Sherrod (Eds.), *Infant social cognition: Empirical and theoretical considerations.* Hillsdale, NJ: Erlbaum.

Clark, E. V. (1983). Meanings and concepts. In J. H. Flavell & E. M. Markman (Eds.), *Cognitive Development Vol. III.* In P. Mussen (Ed.) Handbook of child psychology (4th ed.) New York: Wiley.

Collins, J. T., & Hagen, J. W. (1979). A constructive account of the development of perception, attention and memory. In G. A. Hale & M. Lewis (Eds.), *Attention and cognitive development.* New York: Plenum.

DeLoache, J. S. (1984). What's this? Maternal questions in joint picture book reading with toddlers. *Quarterly Newsletter of the Laboratory of Comparative Human Cognition, 6,* 87–95.

Feinman, S. (1982). Social referencing in infancy. *Merrill-Palmer Quarterly, 28,* 445–470.

Flavell, J. H. (1977). *Cognitive development.* Englewood Cliffs, NJ: Prentice-Hall.

Flavell, J. H. (1985). *Cognitive development* (2nd ed.). Englewood Cliffs, NJ: Prentice-Hall.

Fuson, K. C. (1979). The development of self-regulating aspects of speech: A review. In G. Zivin (Ed.), *The development of self-regulation through speech.* New York: Wiley.

Gibson, E. J., & Spelke, E. S. (1983). The development of perception. In P. H. Mussen (Gen. Ed.); J. H. Flavell & E. M. Markman (Vol. Eds.), *Handbook of Child Psychology: Vol. 3.* New York: Wiley.

Gibson, E., & Rader, E. (1979). Attention: The perceiver as performer. In G. A. Hall & M. Lewis (Eds.), *Attention and cognitive development.* New York: Plenum.

Goldin-Meadow, S., Seligman, M. E. P., & Gelman, R. (1976). Language in the two-year-old. *Cognition, 4,* 189–202.

Greenacre, P. (1950). General problems of acting out. *Psychoanalytic Quarterly, 19,* 455–467.

Grief, E. B., & Gleason, J. B. (1980). Hi, thanks, and goodbye: More routine information. *Language in Society, 9,* 159–166.

Grusec, J. E., & Kuczynski, L. (1980). Direction of effect in socialization: A comparison of the parent versus the child's behavior as determinants of disciplinary technique. *Developmental Psychology, 16, 1–9.*

Holden, G. W. (1983). Avoiding conflict: Mothers as facilitators in the supermarket. *Child Development, 54,* 233–240.

Humphrey, L. C. (1984). Children's self-control in relation to perceived social environment. *Journal of Personality & Social Psychology, 46,* 178–188.

Huttenlocher, J., Smiley, P., & Charney, R. (1983). Emergence of action categories in the child: Evidence from verb meanings. *Psychological Review, 90,* 72–93.

Johnson, K. L. (1982). *Maternal behavior and self-control in young children.* Unpublished doctoral dissertation, University of California, Los Angeles.

Johnson, K., & Kopp, C. B. (1980 August). *The emergence of strategy production in a delay task.* Paper presented at the American Psychological Association Meeting, Los Angeles.

Kagan, J. (1981). *The second year. The emergence of self-awareness.* Cambridge, MA: Harvard University Press.

Kendall, P. C., & Wilcox, L. F. (1980). A cognitive-behavioral treatment for impulsivity: Concrete versus conceptual training in non-self-controlled problem children. *Journal of Consulting & Clinical Psychology, 48,* 80–91.

Kopp, C. B. (1982). The antecedents of self-regulation. *Developmental Psychology, 18,* 199–214.

Kopp, C. B. (1985). *The maternal side of child compliance.* Paper presented at the meeting of the Society for Research in Child Development, Toronto.

Krakow, J. B., Kopp, C. B., Vaughn, B. E. (1981 April). Sustained attention in early life. Paper presented at the Biennial Meeting of the Society for Research in Child Development, Denver.

Kuczynski, L. (1984). Socialization goals and mother–child interaction: Strategies for long-term and short-term compliance. *Developmental Psychology, 20,* 1061–1073.

Lewis, M., & Brooks-Gunn, J. (1979). *Social cognition and the acquisition of self.* New York: Plenum.

Londerville, S., & Main, M. (1981). Security of attachment, compliance and maternal training methods in the second year of life. *Developmental Psychology, 17,* 289–299.

Luria, A. R. (1961). *The role of speech in the regulation of normal and abnormal behavior.* New York: Liveright.

Lytton, H. (1979). Disciplinary encounters between young boys and their mothers and fathers: Is there a contingency system? *Developmental Psychology, 15,* 256–268.

Lytton, H. (1980). *Parent–child interaction: The socialization process observed in twin and singleton families.* New York: Plenum.

Maccoby, E. E. (1984). Middle childhood in the context of the family. In W. A. Collins (Ed.), *Development during middle childhood. The years from six to twelve.* Washington, DC: National Academy Press.

Matas, L., Arend, R. A., & Sroufe, L. A. (1978). Continuity of adaptation in the second year: The relationship between quality of attachment and later competence. *Child Development, 49,* 547–556.

McLaughlin, B. (1983). Child compliance to parent control techniques. *Developmental Psychology, 19,* 667–673.

Mervis, C. B., & Mervis, C. A. (1982). Leopards are kitty-cats: Object labeling by mothers for their thirteen-month-olds. *Child Development, 53,* 267–273.

Minton, C., Kagan, J., & Levine, J. A. (1971). Maternal control and obedience in the two-year-old. *Child Development, 42,* 1873-1894.

Mischel, W. (1983). Delay of gratification as process and as person variables in development. In D. Magnusson & U. L. Allen (Eds.), *Human development: An interactional perspective.* New York: Academic.

Mischel, W., & Baker, U. (1975). Cognitive appraisals and transformations in delay behavior. *Journal of Personality & Social Psychology, 31,* 254-261.

Mischel, W., & Ebbesen, E. B. (1970). Attention in delay of gratification. *Journal of Personality & Social Psychology, 16,* 329-337.

Mischel, W., & Mischel, H. N. (1977). Self-control and the self. In W. Mischel (Ed.), *The self: Psychological and philosophical issues.* Totowa, NJ: Rowan & Littlefield.

Mischel, W., & Patterson, C. J. (1978). Effective plans for self-control in children. In W. A. Collins (Ed.), *Minnesota Symposium on Child Psychology* (Vol. II). Hillsdale, NJ: Erlbaum.

Myers, G. C. (1922). Infants' inhibition: A genetic study. *Pedagogical Seminary, 29,* 288-295.

Nelson, K. (1978). How children represent knowledge of their world in and out of language: A preliminary report. In R. S. Siegler (Ed.), *Children's thinking: What develops?* Hillsdale, NJ: Erlbaum.

Nelson, K. (1983). The derivation of concepts and categories from event representations. In E. K. Skolnick (Ed.), *New trends in conceptual representation: Challenge to Piaget's theory?* Hillsdale, NJ: Erlbaum.

Oviatt, S. L. (1980). The emerging ability to comprehend language: An experimental approach. *Child Development, 51,* 91-106.

Oviatt, S. L. (1982). Inferring what words mean: Early development in infants' comprehension of common object names. *Child Development, 53,* 274-277.

Parasuraman, R., & Davies, D. R. (1984). *Varieties of Attention.* New York: Academic Press.

Pope, K. S., & Singer, J. L. (1978). Regulation of the stream of consciousness: Toward a theory of ongoing thought. In G. E. Schwartz & D. Shapiro (Eds.), *Conscious & self-regulation* (Vol. II). New York: Plenum.

Rexford, E. N. (1978). *A developmental approach to problems of acting out* (rev. ed.). New York: International Universities Press.

Rogoff, B., Malkin, C., & Gilbride, K. (1984). Interaction with babies as guidance in development. In B. Rogoff & J. V. Wertsch (Eds.), *Children's learning in the "zone of proximal development."* In W. Damon (Ed.-in-Chief), *New directions for child development, No. 23.* San Francisco: Jossey-Bass.

Rogoff, B., Sellers, M. J., Pirrotta, S., Fox, N., & White, S. H. (1975). Age of assignment of roles and responsibilities to children. *Human Development, 18,* 353-369.

Saxe, G. B., Gearhart, M., & Guberman, S. R. (1984). The social organization of early number development. In B. Rogoff & J. V. Wertsch (Eds.), *Children's learning in the "zone of proximal development."* In W. Damon (Ed.-in-Chief), *New directions for child development, No. 23.* San Francisco: Jossey-Bass.

Schaffer, H. R. (1984). *The child's entry into a social world.* London: Academic.

Schaffer, H. R., & Crook, C. K. (1978). The role of the mother in early social development. In H. McGurk (Ed.), *Issues in childhood social development.* London: Methuen.

Schaffer, H. R., & Crook, C. (1979). Maternal control techniques in a directed play situation. *Child Development, 50,* 989–996.

Schaffer, H. R., & Crook, C. (1980). Child compliance and maternal control techniques. *Developmental Psychology, 16,* 54–61.

Shatz, M. (1978). On the development of communicative understandings: An early strategy for interpreting and responding to messages. *Cognitive Psychology, 10,* 271–301.

Stern, D. N., MacKain, K., & Spieker, S. (1982). Intonation contours as signals in maternal speech to prelinguistic infants. *Developmental Psychology, 18,* 727–735.

Stayton, D. J., Hogan, R., & Ainsworth, M. D. S. (1971). Infant obedience and maternal behavior: The origins of socialization reconsidered. *Child Development, 42,* 1057–1069.

Sullivan, J. W., & Horowitz, F. D. (1983). Infant intermodal perception and maternal multimodal stimulation: Implications for language development. In L. P. Lipsitt (Ed.), *Advances in infancy research* (Vol. II). Norwood, NJ: Ablex.

Thomson, J. R., & Chapman, R. S. (1977). Who is "Daddy"? The status of two-year-olds' over-extended words in use and comprehension. *Journal of Child Language, 4,* 359–375.

Uzgiris, I. C. (1967). Ordinality in the development of schemas for relating to objects. In J. Hellmuth (Ed.), *Exceptional Infant: Vol. I. The normal infant.* Seattle, WA: Special Child Publications.

Vaughn, B. E., Kopp, C. B., & Krakow, J. B. (1984). The emergence and consolidation of self-control from eighteen to thirty months of age: Normative trends and individual differences. *Child Development, 55,* 990–1004.

Vaughn, B. E., Kopp, C. B., Krakow, J. B., Johnson, K., & Schwartz, S. S. (1986). Process analyses of the behavior of very young children in delay tasks. *Developmental Psychology*, *22*, 752–759.

Vygotsky, L. S. (1962). *Thought and language.* Cambridge, MA: M.I.T. Press.

Vygotsky, L. S. (1978). Mind in society: The development of higher psychological processes. Edited by M. Cole, V. John-Steiner, S. Scribner, & E. Souherman. Cambridge, MA: Harvard University Press.

Wenar, C. (1971). Executive competence in toddlers. A prospective, observational study. *Genetic Psychology Monographs, 93,* 189–285.

Wertsch, J. V. (1979). From social interaction to higher psychological processes: A clarification and application of Vygotsky's theory. *Human Development, 22,* 1–22.

Wertsch, J. V. (1984). The zone of proximal development: Some conceptual issues. In B. Rogoff & J. B. Wertsch (Eds.), *Children's learning in the "zone of proximal development."* In W. Damon (Ed.-in-Chief), *New directions for child development, No. 23.* San Francisco: Jossey-Bass.

Whiting, B. B., & Whiting, J. W. M. (1975). *Children of six cultures: A psychocultural analysis.* Cambridge, MA: Harvard University Press.

PART TWO

Cognitive and Perceptual Development

In the chapters by Thelen and Kopp, the interrelations among early cognitive, motor, and social development are clear. However, it still is useful to focus separately on the cognitive, social, and sociocognitive domains of development during the childhood years.

In Part Two, issues related to cognitive and perceptual development are examined. There are many issues that could have been discussed within this domain of research, because cognitive and perceptual development are popular topics for research and theorizing. Those topics that are addressed by contributors to this section are ones that are both intriguing and current. Moreover, they are representative of issues currently being investigated by developmentalists.

In the first chapter, Herbert Pick focuses primarily on the issue of the role of early perceptual experience in subsequent perceptual development. The interaction of experiential and biological factors is emphasized, both in his review of theory and in his presentation of research. In specific, Pick argues that early experience may affect the development of perception in the realms of spatial orientation and picture perception. To illustrate his point, Pick presents research in which the effects of early perceptual handicaps or mode of cultural experience on perceptual development are examined. The results of this work support his view that early perceptual experiences influence later perceptual development, and the research itself is an excellent example of how to examine complex issues concerning perceptual development.

In the second chapter in this section, Clark Presson further examines the development of spatial cognition, but from a different perspective than Pick's. Presson focuses upon how humans use spatial information in both practical and abstract ways, and the role of cognitive processes and knowledge in the child's understanding of space, location, and spatial transformations. His major thesis is that in order to understand how people perform on tasks requiring abstract, symbolic spatial ability (e.g., map reading) it is necessary to understand how those abstract skills are affected by individuals' practical use of spatial information in everyday situations.

Presson reviews the conceptual bases for his thesis and then presents several lines of research related to the issue. His perspective is innovative and has important implications for future work on this topic.

In the third chapter in Part Two, Susan Somerville and Henry Wellman use their work in the area of children's search behavior to address a fundamental but unresolved issue—the age at which children can understand the concepts of possibility and probability. They challenge Piaget's assertion that an understanding of possibilities does not develop until preadolescence. In specific, Somerville and Wellman present data consistent with the view that the understanding of possibilities appears early and continues to develop through childhood. These findings have profound implications for an understanding of children's logical capabilities and provide a new lens through which to view early cognitive development.

CHAPTER 3

Information and the Effects of Early Perceptual Experience

HERBERT L. PICK, JR.

INTRODUCTION: EFFECTS OF EARLY EXPERIENCE

The effect of early perceptual experience on subsequent perception and perceptual development has always been a topic of great interest to psychologists. Indeed, philosophers posed the problem long before psychologists were on the scene. The formulation of Locke's friend, Mr. Molyneau, sounds strikingly modern: He posed the problem of whether a man born blind who had his sight restored might recognize an object visually that he had known previously by touch (Pastore, 1971). Philosophers were primarily concerned with the origin of knowledge. Does all knowledge come through the senses or are we born with some kinds of innate ideas or knowledge? In many cases the reasoning of philosophers focused around examples involving perception, perhaps because there the issues were clearer. For example, a problem of concern to many philosophers was how it was possible to perceive a three-dimensional world when the information coming from the external environment was essentially two-dimensional; that is, it was mediated by a two-dimensional surface such as the skin or the retina of the eye. Generally philosophers advocated one of two solutions. On the one hand, we were able to perceive a three-dimensional world on the basis of two-dimensional information because we learned through experience to associate certain kinds of three-dimensional properties with intrinsically meaningless two-dimensional sensations (e.g., Berkeley). On the other hand, we perceived a three-dimensional world because that was the way our mind organized information (e.g., Kant).

With philosophy these questions tended to remain at an analytic and/or speculative level. In contrast, psychology's claim to be an empirical science was partially based on its ability to approach such problems experimentally

---

The preparation of this paper was supported in part by the Program Project Grant No. HD05027-15 to the Institute of Child Development, University of Minnesota, and by the Center for Research in Human Learning. The author is indebted to Eleanor J. Gibson, Anne D. Pick, and Clark Presson for very helpful comments on an earlier draft of this paper.

or at least empirically. For example, around the turn of the century some experiments were undertaken to demonstrate that certain very fundamental aspects of our perception could be modified by experience. These were the classic experiments of Stratton (1897), which attempted to show that the very basis of our perception of the world as upright could be modified. The particular problem was suggested by the fact that due to the lens system of the eye the image on the retina was upside down in relation to its source. How was it that we saw the world as right side up? Was it due to associations based on experience or was it the way our mind organized information? In the experiments subjects wore spectacles that inverted the retinal image and were able to adapt to such distortion to some extent. However, the initial questions were probably pseudoproblems and the original interpretation of results is problematic (see Smith & Smith, 1962 and Harris, 1965 for general reviews and more recent interpretations of the results of these and related studies).

In the psychology of perception the question of why we see things the way we do was originally framed in terms of the nativism–empiricism dichotomy. Extreme proponents of these two positions have argued on the one hand that all our perception is based on innate processes and on the other that all our perception is built on prior experience. There are few psychologists today who would seriously argue such extreme positions. It has only been during approximately the last 35 years that empirical evidence about the effects of early perceptual experience on perceptual development has been systematically gathered. With the accumulation of such evidence the basic questions have changed. No longer is it asked whether perception is learned or innate or even how much of perception is learned or innate; rather the questions are: How do environmental and biological factors interact to determine perception? How do perceptual experience and biological constraints interact to produce mature perceptual functioning? With this change of orientation the issues have remained at least as interesting, and their study has probably become more complex and more intriguing. Along with the original philosophical–theoretical motivating interest, the question has gained a practical side. With modern medical and engineering technology it is possible to compensate for some kinds of congenital sensory deficits by providing augmented sensory information in the case of sensory handicap. For example, congenitally blind infants can be fitted with a sonic guide. This is a sonarlike device that a child (or adult) can wear on the head. It converts ultra-high-frequency sound echoes from objects in the environment into an audible frequency range in a form that encodes information about direction, distance, and texture quality. The effect of such substitute sensory information on the ordinary perceptual development of blind children is not known. What are the consequences of such manipulations, and when should they be undertaken?

Starting about 1950 a number of experimental psychologists realized that it would be possible to study empirically the effects of early perceptual experience. Donald Hebb (1949) was one of the early pioneers in this endeavor. In general, experimental research manipulating early perceptual experience was conducted with animal models rather than directly on humans for ethical reasons. That research took three major forms, which might be characterized as perceptual deprivation, perceptual biasing, and perceptual enrichment.

Early research of the perceptual deprivation variety often involved visual deprivation. A typical experiment might consist of examining the effects of rearing animals in the dark (e.g., Riesen, 1958, 1966). In experiments with biased perceptual experience, the perceptual input might be modified in a particular way, for example, rearing animals with distorting optical devices (e.g., Foley, 1940; Hess, 1956), or an environment might be artificially structured to include a preponderance of stimulation of a particular type such as vertical contours (e.g., Blakemore & Cooper, 1970; Hirsch & Spinelli, 1970; Stryker & Sherk, 1975). In enrichment studies investigators tried to provide subjects with unusually rich perceptual experience. For example Forgus (1955) raised rats in a large, spacious environment with a variety of "interesting" toys and structures to climb and play on (see also Rosenzweig, Krech, Bennett, & Diamond, 1968). Deprivation studies often had widespread diffuse deleterious effects on subsequent perception and other activities. Biased perceptual experience typically had very specific and usually negative consequences that often could be obviously related to the nature of the bias. Enriched experience conversely sometimes had fairly general facilitative effects on subsequent perceptual activity.

These typical results found in the classical research on early perceptual experience may be related to several features characteristic of the methodology of that research. First, the deprivation research at least initially usually involved massive deprivation. Thus animals were raised in total darkness, a condition that resulted in receptor degeneration in primates (Riesen, 1966). Such early experience led to decreased visual functioning later in their life, but this was a rather uninteresting consequence. In order to avoid this kind of obvious result from peripheral physiological changes, more selective kinds of rearing experiments were undertaken, for example, rearing animals with homogeneous diffuse light (e.g., Riesen, 1958). Modified deprivation studies are related to a second methodological characteristic of the traditional research on experiential effects on perceptual development, namely, that the so-called perceptual bias studies are really selective deprivation or enrichment studies. If an organism is reared in an environment heavily biased toward one kind of stimulation, it is almost by definition being deprived of some other kind of stimulation. A third characteristic of this research concerns the enrichment paradigm. The enrichment provided in these experiments was by and large only relative enrichment. Stimulation was rich in comparison with the ordinary deprivation of normally reared laboratory animals. It was in most cases still quite impoverished in relation to the normal habitat of the species. Even in the best known human perceptual enrichment study, that of Burton White (1971), the infants were only enriched relative to the homogeneous bland surroundings of a traditional institutional environment. Finally the focus of concern in most of the traditional studies was on within-modality effects of perceptual experience. Thus most investigators conducting visual deprivation studies looked for effects on subsequent visual perception. Will the visual deprivation involved in dark-rearing rats affect their subsequent depth discrimination on the visual cliff? Will rearing rats in the visual presence of triangles and circles on the sides of their cages affect the visual form perception of the mature animal?

The emphases in these studies on massive deprivation and on the intramodal effects lead to the thesis of this paper. When very global treatments are introduced, whether they are massive deprivation or enrichment, it is very difficult to know what accounts for any changes that occur. This is especially true when the effects are also very general. One strategy for constraining the kinds of intervention to examine and the kinds of effects to look for is to focus attention on the way the intervention affects the information available to an organism. Deprivation (massive or selective) or enrichment (massive or selective) affects certain aspects of the information available to an organism. This information would typically serve a function for some activity or action of an organism, and that activity might well be carried out with or without a particular sense modality. This point of view suggests that any experiential manipulation be considered in relation to how it affects the information used for guiding particular activities and that the effects of the manipulation be examined intermodally as well as intramodally.

Although much of the experimental evidence for the effects of early perceptual experience has been obtained using animals, most of us are primarily interested in the implications for humans. While experimental manipulation of early experience in humans generally is precluded, there are two situations that can provide a means of looking at such effects directly in humans. One is the experiential deficit produced by naturally occurring sensory handicaps. Here, for the most part, we are constrained to examining intermodal effects. What are the effects of deafness on subsequent nonauditory linguistic perception? What are the effects of blindness on subsequent nonvisual space perception? (In a few cases where recovery from sensory handicap occurs, it is also possible to study intramodal effects. In fact, where the sensory deficit within some modality is not total it is also possible to study within-modality effects. For example, it would be possible to study visual functioning among subjects with various degrees of visual handicap. There are some very interesting and practical problems here, such as why there are very large individual differences in visual functioning among persons with apparently similar degrees of visual impairment.)

The other situation for studying the effects of early perceptual experience is to take advantage of cultural differences in perceptual experience. Such differences are probably more like the biasing experimental studies with animals than the more extreme deprivation or enrichment studies. Both investigating the effects of early perceptual experience by examining sensory handicaps and doing so by examining cultural differences in experience are limited by the fact that they are correlational methods rather than experimental. If one finds that groups with particular kinds of sensory handicap or particular kinds of cultural experience show some unusual perceptual functioning, it does not necessarily mean that those particular perceptual experiences are responsible. However, by a close examination of the way the early experience affects the information available to a person, it may be possible to construct plausible hypotheses about the nature and mechanism of the effects. Suppose that because of a sensory handicap or the kind of cultural environment one is exposed to a particular kind of perceptual information is missing. Children growing up under such circumstances might not develop sensitivity to that information. It might be difficult to respond to that kind of information if it is suddenly provided as adults or it might be difficult to perform certain kinds of cognitive tasks that are rather easy or automatic when one has developed sensitivity to such information.

I would like to illustrate in some detail how the application of such hypotheses might work with two examples. The first is a review and interpretation of some of the work John Rieser, Jeff Lockman, and I have done investigating the spatial orientation of visually handicapped subjects. This work has been continued, especially by John Rieser at Vanderbilt University. The other example is a way of thinking about some of the cross-cultural differences that have been reported in the perception of pictures and in susceptibility to illusions. The analysis of this problem will incorporate some intriguing ideas and experiments from the dissertation of a recent University of Minnesota student, Rebecca Jones (1982).

THE OPTIC ARRAY: INVARIANT AND PERSPECTIVE STRUCTURE

Both the example concerned with visually handicapped subjects and the example of cross-cultural perceptual differences involve a distinction James Gibson made regarding the information for perceivers available in the optic array. Gibson (1979) argued very cogently that the information underlying our visual perception is provided by what he called the *optic array.* The optic array is the structured ambient light in the environment that exists at any point of observation. The light is structured as it is reflected from the various surfaces in the environment, and this structure normally consists of nested sets of solid angles from a given point of view. Thus at the observation point where my eye is, there is a solid angle corresponding to the back wall. Within that, there is a solid angle corresponding to a window, and within that, to a pane, and within that, to a spot on the pane. The optic array is dense in that as one scans around a point in any direction there always exist such nested solid angles of stimulation. Gibson pointed out that the transformation of this optic array as the observation point shifts is particularly informative. With any shift in observation point the various solid angles expand, contract, compress in various ways. However, across those changes there are invariants. Thus relations of inclusion remain the same, straight lines transform into straight lines, and so forth.

These invariants across change that Gibson referred to as the *invariant structure* specify the rigid layout of the environment. Paradoxically these invariants are more easily detectable in the changing optic array than if an observer remained static. On the other hand, there is structure that changes in an orderly patterned way as one moves about. This was referred to by Gibson as *perspective structure.* Examples of perspective structure include the orderly expansion of the visual angle corresponding to an object as one approaches it, the occluding of a more distant surface by a nearer one as one's point of view is laterally translated, and so forth. The perspective structure specifies where the point of observation is and how it is changing, that is, the path of locomotion. Thus both the invariant structure and the perspective structure are dynamic and exist simultaneously in the optic array, and from them we can be aware simultaneously of what the layout of the environment is and where we are in it. The two cases I will consider are intended to illustrate how early perceptual experience might influence a person's sensitivity to the perspective and invariant structure available in the optic array. In the first case research on the spatial orientation of visually handicapped subjects will be reviewed. It will be suggested that the absence of exposure to perspective structure during locomotion leads to impairment in keeping track of their position in space as they move about. In the second case cross-cultural research on picture perception and susceptibility to visual illusions will be examined. Differences in perception between subjects in different cultures may be simply due to lack of experience with pictures. Limited exposure to pictures may result in insensitivity to the *portrayal* of invariant and perspective structure.

EARLY EXPERIENCE AND SENSITIVITY TO PERSPECTIVE STRUCTURE DURING LOCOMOTION

Now let us consider the first example of how early perceptual experience in the form of visual deprivation might affect later spatial perception. There has been considerable research on the perceptual abilities of blind persons and how these differ from those of blindfolded sighted people. An early hypothesis that blind persons develop compensatory increased basic sensitivity in their remaining senses has received rather little support (Warren, 1978, 1984, p. 60). In a majority of sensory tactual tasks, blind subjects are only slightly superior to blindfolded sighted subjects. However, in a few cases the results are even the opposite. In some cases, such as facial vision (the ability to detect approaching surfaces by means of echo location), where blind persons seemed to have developed an unusual sensitivity it has been shown that with a rather short period of experience sighted subjects can come to perform just as well. Thus even with considerably more need to use and more experience with tactile discrimination, blind subjects are only slightly if any better than unpracticed blindfolded sighted subjects. (However, this is not meant to imply that blind subjects are not considerably better with tactual tasks involving very specific complex learned skills such as reading braille.)

One practical arena in which blind persons are said to experience particular difficulties is maintaining spatial orientation during travel. For example, blind mobility instructors report that many of their clients have difficulty in making detours in travel spaces with which they are becoming acquainted. There are a number of reasons why a person might have difficulty in making detours.

One reason is that the person's knowledge of the space might not be in a form that would permit the kind of inferences underlying detours. If one's knowledge of a space included the overall configurational properties of that space, detours should be relatively easily made. On the other hand we often learn about larger spatial layouts serially, that is, by traveling specific routes. In order to achieve configurational knowledge some kind of subsequent integration of this serial information may be necessary (see Siegel & White, 1975, for a discussion of the development of route- and surveylike representations). This integration may be particularly problematic for blind persons because they get very little sensory information during travel about distal information off their serial routes. The argument here then is that ability to make detours depends upon having one's knowledge of space organized configurationally rather than serially. If our information about spatial layout is provided serially as we locomote about a space, the information may have to be transformed into a configurational organization. Having visual information about one's surround, especially about objects and locations off one's route, may be especially useful in facilitating the necessary transformation of information. There is in the literature evidence that children attend to more distal information as they grow older (e.g., Acredolo, 1976). There is also evidence of a shift with increasing age in the organization of children's spatial knowledge from routelike to configurational (e.g., Hazen, Lockman, & Pick, 1978; Siegel & White, 1975). Congenitally blind persons who lack the distal visual information may experience difficulty in making the transformation of serially spatial information into a configurational organization.

This analysis suggested an investigation of possible differences between blind and sighted persons in the extent to which their spatial knowledge is organized in a configurational form (Rieser, Lockman, & Pick, 1980). Groups of blind and sighted persons were asked to make judgments about the relative distances among locations in a space with which they were very familiar. (The space was a rather complex floor layout in a large building. It had a number of corridors and turns with rooms of various sizes.) Ten well-known locations were identified. From these locations sets of triads were formed such as: main office, exit door, drinking fountain. For each triad a subject was asked to judge which two locations were closest together and which two were farthest apart. From such judgments an ordering of distances between pairs of locations could be formed. This ordering was correlated with the true ordering based on the actual functional or walking distance, which was assumed to reflect the serial route information one initially obtains about a space. The ordering from the judgments was also correlated with a true ordering based on the actual Euclidean distances from a blueprint (i.e., the straight line distances even passing through walls and objects), which presumably reflect configurational information. The correlation of the judgments of the sighted subjects with the functional distances was .64 and with the Euclidean distances was only .26. For the group of congenitally blind subjects the correlations were very similar: The correlation between their judgments and the functional distances was .54, and between their judgments and the Euclidean distances, .31. It seems that the judgments of both groups of subjects indicated a serial routelike organization of spatial information rather than a configurational organization.

It should be kept in mind that instructions to the subjects in making their judgments had not specifically asked for functional or Euclidean distances. Under such neutral instructions, both groups either interpreted the instructions to mean functional distance or had the functional distances most readily available. If specifically asked, could the subjects bring their judgments more closely into correspondence with the Euclidean organization? If specifically asked to make functional judgments would they have shown an even higher correlation with the true functional distances? The same subjects were asked to repeat their judgments a second and third time, once responding in terms of the straight line or Euclidean distances between the locations and once in terms of the functional or walking distances between the locations. The results of the three sets of judgments are presented in Table 3.1. It is apparent from Table 3.1 that there is little difference between the correlations under functional instructions and those under the original neutral instructions. The subjects seem to have responded originally in as functional a way as they were able to. On the other hand, under Euclidean instructions the sighted subjects, but not the blind subjects, were able to shift the basis of their judgments and bring them more closely into correspondence with the actual Euclidean distances. Even though initially they did not respond in terms of the Euclidean distances, which reflect configurational knowledge, either they had this information available or they could generate it from their functional knowledge.

Why should sighted and blind subjects differ in the availability of configurational knowledge? One way subjects might build up configurational knowledge of spatial layout is if they kept track of where things were in relation to

TABLE 3.1. Correlations Between Orderings of Subjects' Distance Judgments and Actual Distance in Space

Instructed Baseline	Actual Baseline	Group	
		Sighted	Congenital Blind
Neutral	Functional	.64	.54
	Euclidean	.26	.31
Functional	Functional	.68	.53
Euclidean	Euclidean	.68	.31

themselves as they moved around. That is, they might update where things were in relation to themselves. Rieser, Guth, and Hill (1982) explored whether sighted and blind subjects were equally likely to do such updating of locations in their environment in relation to their own position as they moved about.

In their study blind and blindfolded sighted subjects were taught a simple spatial layout. Specifically they were taught to go from a home base to each of three locations, for example, A, B, and C, but they were never given any experience going directly from one of these labeled locations to another. After learning the initial distance and direction of the locations from home base, they were tested on their ability to point from home base to the three locations. As might be expected, since this task was directly related to their training, all the subjects pointed quickly and accurately at these learned locations. They were then asked to imagine themselves at each of the labeled locations facing in a specified way. From this imaginary station point the subjects were asked to point to the other two locations. All the subjects were rather slow at doing this and generally not as accurate as from home base. When asked how they figured out how to point in the latter condition, they tended to respond in terms of imagining themselves in the new position and performing some sort of mental calculation to come up with an answer. In another condition they were walked over to each *labeled* location in turn (the sighted subjects still blindfolded) and asked to point to the other locations. The blind subjects still were hesitant and relatively inaccurate in this condition but the blindfolded sighted subjects responded relatively quickly and accurately. Now when asked how they knew where to point the blind subjects responded, as before, in terms of mental calculations; the sighted subjects, on the other hand, almost did not understand the question because the answer seemed so obvious to them. They said they knew where they were and simply responded directly. Although the sighted subjects received no more specific information about the relative direction of the other locations, the very act of walking to the new position (or the actual change of station point) enabled them to point more quickly and accurately than if they simply imagined moving there. It seemed that they kept track of where they were in the space if they actually moved. The blind subjects did not do this. Moreover, the sighted subjects apparently accomplished this tracking without conscious effort.

What is different about the experience of the blind and sighted subjects which would account for this difference in awareness of where they are in relation to other locations? During most of the entire lifetime of sighted subjects, every movement of the head or body is accompanied by an optical flow pattern of the structured optical array. There is always perspective structure in this flow pattern providing information about how one is moving and how the relative direction of objects in the world is changing in relation to oneself. Even when objects are out of sight the extant optical flow pattern provides information about how their relative direction is changing. This pervasive visual information that is almost always available to sighted people as they move about may result in continuous updating of the relative direction of both the in-sight and out-of-sight objects in the world. When all objects are out of sight by virtue of darkness or closed eyes, sighted people nevertheless continue to register their position on the basis of other information about movement. Sighted people automatically register the perspective transformation of a kind of *virtual* optical array. Blind subjects without this experience of a structured optical array are not so sensitive to perspective structure and do not keep track of their position in the world as they move.

EARLY EXPERIENCE AND PERSPECTIVE STRUCTURE IN PICTURES

My second example of experimental studies concerning the effects on perception provides a way of thinking about cross-cultural differences in picture perception. There has been a long tradition of interest in cultural effects on the perception of pictures and susceptibility to visual illusions. That area has not been characterized by very rigorous methodology (Hagen & Jones, 1978; Pick & Pick, 1978). Nevertheless the accumulated evidence seems to suggest that there is rather little difference in difficulty across cultures in at least *identifying* objects depicted in pictures. This result fits in with experimental studies that show that young children with very little exposure to pictures can identify depicted objects (e.g., Hochberg & Brooks, 1962). On the other hand, some researchers have claimed there are real difficulties for persons in some cultures in perceiving depth relations in pictures. With the relatively poor quality of the research it is at present not clear how much of that difficulty stems from the poor quality of the pictures used and other methodological problems. For example, in one of the more widely quoted studies (Hudson, 1960), participants were shown an outline drawing of an arrangement of objects for which the information for relative distance was provided in some cases only by size differences. Poor perception of depth relationships in such pictures was taken to imply two-dimensional picture perceiving. In such tests subjects from western cultures typically show greater three-dimensional perceiving than the nonwestern cultures tested, for whatever reasons.

Susceptibility to illusions has also been reported to differ across cultures. For example, persons in a number of nonwestern cultures have been found to be less subject to the Muller-Lyer, horizontal–vertical, and Ponzo illusions than individuals from western cultures; that is, their perception is more veridical than ours. One example of such a result with the Ponzo illusion (depicted in Figure 3.1) shows that Ugandan village dwellers seem not to be subject to the Ponzo illusion at all (Leibowitz & Pick, 1972). It is important to note that these differences are more educational than cultural. The Ugandan college students show almost exactly the same pattern of susceptibility as the American (Pennsylvanian) college students. One interpretation of the Ponzo illusion is that it depends on seeing the illusory longer bar as further away. That is, it depends on seeing depth in this arrangement of lines. If some subjects perceive the lines more veridically than others, perhaps it is that they are not seeing as

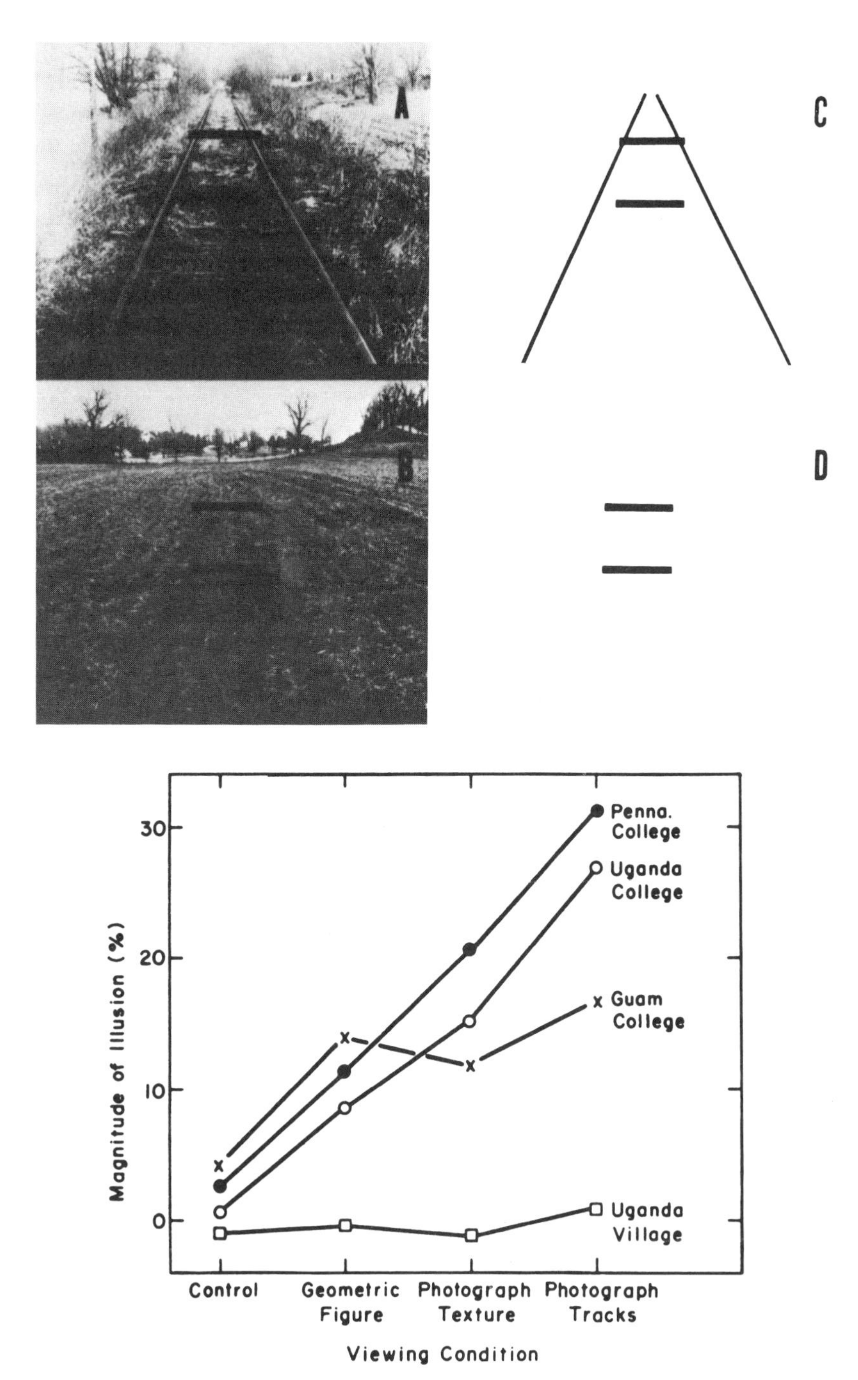

Figure 3.1. Upper half includes four examples of Ponzo illusion with different degrees of depicted depth information with panel D a control condition. Lower half indicates magnitude of illusion for these different degrees of depth information with different subject groups.

much depth in the display. Thus not being deceived by some illusory displays may also be correlated with lower sensitivity to depth information in pictures.

What could account for such cultural differences in picture perception and susceptibility to illusions? A number of hypotheses have been suggested. Some of these directly implicate the influence of early experience on perceptual development. The idea is that something within one's cultural environment provides a particular kind of experience that affects mature perception. According to one hypothesis, culture might affect a person's experience by altering the physical ecology. A strong proponent of this possibility was Marshall Segall (Segall, Campbell, & Herskovitz, 1966). That hypothesis, sometimes termed the "carpentered world" hypothesis, holds that westerners are so used to seeing carpentered right angles in their environment that they interpret oblique angles in visual displays as oblique projections of right angles. With this interpretation it is possible to predict illusions like the Muller-Lyer and Sander parallelogram illusions. Segall, Campbell, and Herskovitz gathered a fair amount of supportive correlational data that showed that persons from less carpentered cultures tended to be less susceptible to these illusions. However, the hypothesis has been severely weakened by subsequently accumulated evidence (e.g., Jahoda & McGurk, 1974). That evidence, of little relation between degree of carpenteredness and susceptibility to illusions, was gathered from cultures preselected to be similar in other aspects of environment but to have differences in carpenteredness. The carpentered world hypothesis also does not account for the fact that susceptibility to such illusions decreases with age in most cultures where one might expect exposure to the carpenteredness of the environment to increase with age, especially in western cultures. An alternative hypothesis was suggested by Robert Pollack (1969) to account for differences in susceptibility to illusions. He suggested that they were due to anatomical differences in pigmentation within the visual system. The magnitude of some illusions such as the Muller-Lyer is reduced when the inducing stimuli are generated with lines of low contrast. Pollack suggested that more pigmented visual systems correlated with racial differences (or more intense exposure to the sun) might reduce the effective contrast when viewing visual displays. Such a genetic (or environmental) hypothesis might account for degree of susceptibility to some illusions but does not encompass possible differences in picture perception.

A third hypothesis that I would like to discuss suggests that both the differences in picture perception and susceptibility to illusions are due to a lack of experience with pictures. The hypothesis is that perceiving the spatial arrangement of depicted scenes requires at least some level of exposure to pictures. The susceptibility to some illusions, in particular, the Ponzo illusion, is a by-product of the perception of spatial arrangement in pictures. This hypothesis is based on the view of James Gibson that perception of scenes depicted in pictures is something special. We are more adapted to perceiving the natural information-rich world. Perceiving via pictures rather than being the prototype mode of perceiving, in fact, involves something special. Some experience with the pictorial medium may be required in order to perceive proficiently by such artificial representation.

What is it about pictures that poses problems in their perception, above and beyond perception of real-world scenes? When viewing a scene in the real world, as discussed above, the observer's movements distinguish the invariant structure from the perspective structure in optic array. When viewing a picture, one's movements do not distinguish the invariant and perspective structure with respect to the depicted scene (but, of course, they do so with respect to the picture as an object in itself). Suppose a naive person, for example, a young girl with little experience viewing pictorial representations, looks at a picture. She might or might not identify the kind of object portrayed in a picture on the basis of distinctive features used to identify objects in the world. Even if she did identify an object correctly, she would probably move her head and eyes as anyone might when viewing something. The movement would not change any of the distinguishing features of the identified object, but neither would it provide the ordinary kind of disambiguating of perspective and invariant structure in the optical array specifying the depicted object. Movement would provide such information for the picture as an object in itself. Without experience with pictures there would be very little reason for an observer to ignore the very reliable motion parallax information that indicates the picture is a flat two-dimensional surface with lines on that surface.

What might experience with pictures contribute to their perception? Experience with pictures might lead to the realization or understanding that pictures are indeed an ambiguous stimulus, that there is information in the picture both for the depicted scene and for the picture as an object in itself. There are some reports that babies treat depicted objects as real and tangible. For example, Field (1976) found that babies 15–24 weeks old reach as often for a depicted as for a real object. On the other hand, there is evidence that babies can at least discriminate between solid geometric forms and two-dimensional projections of these forms (Jones-Molfese, 1972). It is not known how experience with pictures leads to the realization of their ambiguity. One way that this might occur is through conflict created when one identifies a depicted familiar three-dimensional object on the basis of detection of its distinctive features and then is confronted with the motion parallax and stereoscopic information indicating that it is flat.

Jones (1982) has pointed out that pictures are ambiguous in another but related way. The fact that a picture presents just one view makes the perception of a depicted object problematic. There are surfaces of the depicted object that are hidden, and the normal procedure of looking around the object will not work for revealing the nature of the occluded part of the object. This ambiguity becomes especially evident when the picture of an object is from a perspective that shows, for example, a single surface. This is illustrated in the right panel of Figure 3.2. In her study Jones showed that children even as old as 8 years of age did not seem to notice the ambiguity of such poorly depicted objects. In Jones's study participants tried to identify, by touch (with their

Figure 3.2. Left panel indicates an oblique view of cube with much invariant structure and little perspective structure. Right panel indicates a face-on view of cube with little invariant structure and much perspective structure (adapted from Jones, 1982).

hands out of sight under a curtain), objects depicted in photographs. The decision time for adults was much longer for such poorly depicted objects than for those with better perspective, for example, the left panel of Figure 3.2, whereas there was no difference in the decision times of young children.

Of course just registering the fact that a picture is ambiguous does not indicate how that ambiguity should be resolved. But at least noting the ambiguity makes it possible to start treating a picture differently with respect to perception. In particular, it makes it possible to start attending to a picture in a different way than we attend to real objects. In an intriguing analysis of the information in pictures, Jones (1982) emphasized the point that one source of ambiguity in pictures is that the ordinary means of separating invariant and perspective structure does not work. In viewing a real scene even very small exploratory movements differentiate the invariant and perspective structure. Jones goes on to argue that a good picture from the point of view of object recognition is one that presents a view that maximizes invariant structure. This would be a view that would show the least change with movement if it were a real scene. As Jones puts it, "a viewpoint that reveals edges in unique correspondence with hidden surfaces should be most informative about the object's solid shape" (p. 26).

The two pictures in Figure 3.2 exemplify a "good" picture and a "bad" picture of a cube. The one on the right, which portrays the square face of the cube as a square in the picture plane, is a poor picture of a cube because if it were a real scene any slight movement would bring into view new surfaces and edges. The one on the left is a good picture because any slight movement would not yield views of new surfaces and all the visible edges of occluded surfaces specify what those surfaces are like. It is interesting to note that in the good picture no projection of any surface of the cube is an actual square. Jones demonstrated the informativeness of such pictures for both children and adults. Objects could be recognized tactually on the basis of such pictures much more accurately than on the basis of pictures such as those on the right, which preserved the actual form of a prototypical surface.

An extension of Jones's analysis might be directed toward the question of how to depict an object or scene to emphasize the perspective structure as opposed to the invariant structure. As noted before, the perspective structure provides information about where the viewer is. In the case of pictures interest is usually focused, as in the preceding discussion, on what is best for object recognition or identification. However, pictures can also portray information normally provided by perspective structure concerning the location from which the scene is being viewed. Moreover, perspective structure may be critical for answering such questions as how far away different depicted objects are from the viewer. That is, questions related to depth in pictures, which have raised the most interesting cross-cultural comparisons, may involve sensitivity to the portrayal of perspective structure in pictures. Similarly, cultural differences in the susceptibility to illusions, some of which have been attributed to pictorial depth perception, may also depend on sensitivity to perspective structure.

Little is known about development of sensitivity to perspective structure in pictures. Piaget's three mountain problem depends on such sensitivity, but the judgments called for in that task are usually very crude.* It would be very interesting to develop a fine-grained analysis of sensitivity to the point of view from which a picture is taken. It may be that the very aspects of pictures that emphasize invariant structure tend to deemphasize perspective structure and vice versa. It seems clear in the case of Figure 3.2 that the picture on the right provides very precise information on the direction from which the object, if it is three-dimensional, is being viewed. The line of sight must be one in which only one surface is visible and persons could position themselves very accurately on that line of sight. Conversely, the picture on the left, precisely because small movements would not cause significant changes if the scene were real, does not provide very easily usable perspective information.

CONCLUDING REMARKS

An argument has been made that early experience may affect the development of perception in the realm of spatial orientation and picture perception. In the case of spatial orientation, the effect of prior experience was inferred by comparison of sighted and blind subjects. In the case of picture perception, the effect of experience was inferred on the basis of cross-cultural comparisons. Although these two domains are widely different, it is interesting that they converge on early experience affecting sensitivity to perspective structure.

In making the argument about how such sensitivity develops, one kind of evidence common to both domains was ignored. This is evidence of precocious sensitivity or at least surprising ability of young subjects to perfrom certain

*In an interesting series of experiments Light and his colleagues (Light & Humphreys, 1981; Light & MacIntosh, 1980; Light & Simmons, 1983) address the question of how perspective structure and invariant structure are represented in children's drawing. There appears to be a developmental trend in children's representations from being *array specific* to being *view specific,* which roughly corresponds to the distinction between invariant and perspective structure.

tasks that seem to involve such sensitivity. In the case of orientation this is manifest in a fascinating report by Landau, Gleitman, and Spelke (1981) of a blind toddler's behavior in solving a variety of detour and spatial inference problems. How can evidence of this early ability be reconciled with the data described above showing adult blind persons' deficiencies in this area? In the case of sensitivity to perspective structure in pictures, Yonas and Granrud (1985) provide very intriguing evidence that sensitivity to pictorial depth cues appears in infants 5–7 months of age. They showed that 7-month-old infants would reach for the nearer of two objects when nearer was specified by one of several pictorial depth cues (e.g., linear perspective, interposition, familiar size) whereas 5-month-olds responded at chance level. How can evidence of this early ability to respond to pictorial information about where an object is in relation to the viewer be reconciled with the thesis outlined above that it is just with respect to this ability that people without experience are deficient?

There would seem to be two related possible resolutions of the paradox. The first is that abilities in both these domains are present full-blown at birth but without use they atrophy and are less available at maturity. The other is that the abilities are present in primitive form at an early age but have to be exercised in order to develop to mature form (see Aslin, 1981, for a general discussion of related issues). The evidence cited above both for early nonvisual spatial orientation and for early pictorial depth perception only indicates the presence of a relatively gross level of capacity. It is not that a precise level of capacity does not exist; we just cannot yet specify the degree of the capacity.

Thus the question of when and how early experience affects the development of sensitivity to perspective structure has considerable theoretical import. There are also some intriguing practical implications. In the case of perspective structure and early visual experience, blind mobility training procedures might be developed as a substitute for exposure to the perspective structure of the optical array. Such a substitute could lead to greater facility by blind persons in keeping track of their relative position during locomotion. In the case of perspective structure and pictures, it might be of practical value to know the best way to portray pictorial information about the viewer's vantage point. This would be helpful for using pictures in a maplike way to guide locomotion or travel, and it could be used again for training of people who, for whatever reason, grow up with little experience with pictures if they have difficulty in picture perception.

REFERENCES

Acredolo, L. P. (1976). Frames of reference used by children for orientation in unfamiliar spaces. In G. Moore & R. Golledge (Eds.), *Environmental knowing*. Stroudsburg, PA: Dowden, Hutchinson & Ross.

Aslin, R. N. (1981). Experiential influences and sensitive periods in perceptual development: A unified model. In R. N. Aslin (Ed.), *Development of perception* (Vol. 2). New York: Academic.

Blakemore, C., & Cooper, G. F. (1970). Development of the brain depends on the visual environment. *Nature, 228,* 277–478.

Field, J. (1976). Relation of young infants' reaching behavior to stimulus distance and solidity. *Developmental Psychology, 12,* 444–448.

Foley, J. P. (1940). An experimental investigation of the effect of prolonged invision of the visual field in the rhesus monkey (macaca mulatta). *Journal of Genetic Psychology, 56,* 21–51.

Forgus, R. H. (1955). Early visual and motor experience as determiners of complex image learning ability under rich and reduced stimulation. *Journal of Cooperative & Physiological Psychology, 48,* 215–220.

Gibson, J. J. (1979). *The ecological approach to visual perception.* Boston: Houghton Mifflin.

Hagen, M. A., & Jones, R. K. (1978) Cultural effects on perception: How many words is one picture really worth? In R. D. Walk & H. L. Pick, Jr. (Eds.), *Perception and experience.* New York: Plenum.

Harris, C. S. (1965). Perceptual adaptation to inverted, revised, and displaced vision. *Psychological Review, 72,* 419–444.

Hazen, N. L., Lockman, J. J., & Pick, H. L., Jr. (1978). The development of children's representations of large-scale environments. *Child Development, 48,* 623–636.

Hebb, D. O. (1949). *The organization of behavior.* New York: Wiley.

Hess, E. H. (1956). Space perception in the chicks. *Scientific American, 195*(1), 71–80.

Hirsch, H. V. B., & Spinelli, D. N. (1970). Visual experience modifies distribution of horizontally and vertically oriented reception fields in cats. *Science, 168,* 869–871.

Hochberg, J., & Brooks, V. (1962). Pictorial recognition as an unlearned ability: A study of one's child's performance. *American Journal of Psychology, 75,* 624–628.

Hudson, W. (1960). Pictorial depth perception in sub-cultural groups in Africa. *Journal of Social Psychology, 52,* 183–208.

Jahoda, G., & McGurk, H. (1974). Pictorial depth perception in Scottish and Ghanian children: A critique of some findings with the Hudson test. *International Journal of Psychology, 9,* 255–267.

Jones-Molfese, V. (1972). Individual differences in neonatal preferences for planometric and stereometric visual patterns. *Child Development, 43,* 1289–1296.

Jones, R. K. (1982). *An ecological approach to the development of picture perception.* Unpublished doctoral dissertation, University of Minnesota.

Landau, B., Gleitman, H., & Spelke, E. (1981). Spatial knowledge and geometric representation in a child blind from birth. *Science, 213,* 1275–1278.

Leibowitz, H. W., & Pick, H. L., Jr. (1972). Cross-cultural and educational aspects of the Ponzo perspective illusion. *Perception & Psychophysics, 12,* 430–432.

Light, P., & Simmons, B. (1983). The effects of a communication task upon the representation of depth relationships in young children's drawings. *Journal of Experimental Child Psychology, 35,* 81–92.

Light, P. H., & Humphreys, J. (1981). Internal spatial relationships in young children's drawings. *Journal of Experimental Child Psychology, 31,* 521–530.

Light, P. H., & MacIntosh, E. (1980). Depth relationships in young children's drawings. *Journal of Experimental Child Psychology, 30,* 79–87.

Pick, A. D., & Pick, H. L., Jr. (1978). Culture and perception. In E. C. Carterette & M. P. Friedman (Eds.), *Handbook of perception.* New York: Academic.

Pastore, N. (1971). *Selective history of theories of visual perception: 1650–1950.* New York: Oxford University Press.

Pollack, R. H. (1969). Some implications of ontogenetic changes in perception. In D. Elkind & J. H. Flavell (Eds.), *Studies in cognitive development: Essays in honor of Jean Piaget.* New York: Oxford University Press.

Riesen, A. H. (1966). Sensory deprivation. In E. Stellar & J. M. Sprague (Eds.), *Progress in physiological psychology* (Vol. 1). New York: Academic.

Riesen, A. H. (1958). Plasticity of behavior: Psychological aspects. In H. F. Harlow & C. N. Worlsey (Eds.), *Biological and biochemical basis of behavior.* Madison, WI: University of Wisconsin Press.

Rieser, J. J., Guth, D. A., & Hill, E. W. (1982). Mental processes mediating independent travel: Implications for orientation and mobility. *Journal of Visual Impairment & Blindness, 76,* 213–218.

Rieser, J. J., Lockman, J. J., & Pick, H. L., Jr. (1980). The role of visual experience in knowledge of spatial layout. *Perception & Psychophysics, 28,* 185–190.

Rosenzweig, M. R., Krech, D., Bennett, E. L., & Diamond, M. C. (1968). Modifying brain chemistry and anatomy by enrichment or impoverishment of experience. In G. Newton & S. Levine (Eds.), *Early experience and behavior: The psychology of development.* Springfield, IL: Thomas.

Segall, M. H., Campbell, D. T., & Herskovitz, M. J. (1966). *The influence of culture on visual perception.* Indianapolis: Bobbs-Merrill.

Siegel, A. W., & White, S. H. (1975). The development of spatial representations of large-scale environments. In H. W. Reese (Ed.), *Advances in child development and behavior* (Vol. 10). New York: Academic.

Smith, K. V., & Smith, W. M. (1962). *Perception and motion.* Philadelphia: Saunders.

Stratton, G. M. (1897). Vision without inversion of the retinal image. *Psychological Review, 4,* 341–360, 453–481.

Stryker, M. P., & Sherk, H. (1975). Modification of cortical orientation selectivity in the cat by restricted visual experience: A reexamination. *Science, 190,* 904–906.

Warren, D. H. (1984). *Blindness and early childhood development.* New York: American Foundation for the Blind.

Warren, D. H. (1978). Perception by the blind. In E. C. Carterette & M. P. Friedman (Eds.), *Handbook of perception: Vol. X. Perceptual ecology.* New York: Academic.

White, B. L. (1971). *Human infants: Experience and psychological development.* Englewood Cliffs, NJ: Prentice-Hall.

Yonas, A., & Granrud, C. E. (1985). The development of sensitivity to kinetic, binocular, and pictorial depth information in human infants. In D. Ingle, D. Lee, & M. Jeannerod (Eds.), *Brain mechanisms and spatial vision.* The Hague: Nijoff.

CHAPTER 4

The Development of Spatial Cognition: Secondary Uses of Spatial Information

CLARK C. PRESSON

The past decade has witnessed a tremendous growth of research on early spatial development, ranging from studies of the infant's ability to locate objects in rather simple hiding tasks to studies of school-aged children's reasoning about more abstract spatial transformations. As with much of the post-Piagetian work in cognitive development, this recent work on spatial development has gone far beyond Piaget and Inhelder's (1967) classic account. There have been two important directions in which this work has been taken.

First, there has been a quest to identify, during the preschool years, early precursors of spatial abilities. Piaget's research typically focused on the cognitive deficits of the younger child, particularly in complex, abstract tasks. For example, children's difficulty in the coordination of perspectives tasks which will be discussed in greater detail later in the chapter) was interpreted as indicating that children up to 8–9 years old did not understand that basic spatial relations (e.g., right–left, before–behind) were relative to an observer's position (Piaget & Inhelder, 1967). Such a broad claim of logical incompetence ignores the successes of the child in the practical, direct use of spatial information and overlooks how a practical, direct orientation to the spatial surrounds affects abstract as well as concrete spatial behavior. More recent work has recognized the important spatial competencies in everyday reasoning concerning object hiding and finding (e.g., DeLoache, 1984; Sophian, 1984; Wellman & Somerville, 1982). In practical, real-world contexts, an increasing level of spatial abilities has been demonstrated in infants and young children (Acredolo, 1982; Anooshian & Siegel, 1985; Bremner, 1978). Various aspects of this work have been reviewed in detail elsewhere (Liben, 1982; Presson & Somerville, 1985; Sophian, 1984; Wellman & Somerville, 1982). Although young children are by no means perfect, the consistent trend that emerges within this

Preparation of this chapter was supported in part by NICHD Grant RO1 HD 20666. The author thanks Herbert L. Pick, Jr., and Susan Somerville for helpful comments.

work is that they have a surprisingly high degree of practical spatial competence.

A second, related thrust of recent work has been to provide a more detailed analysis of processes of task solution in specific situations or patterns of performance across task variations. For example, Wellman and Somerville (1982) have examined in detail factors guiding children's behavior in serial search for a lost or hidden object. This work has provided a more thoroughgoing account of the cognitive processes involved in specific spatial tasks, and how such component processes work together in determining specific solution strategies or patterns of task difficulty. With such data, we are in a better position to draw inferences as to the underlying reasons for success or failure on spatial tasks.

As the conceptual focus of recent work has shifted in these two ways, many researchers also have shifted their work physically away from the laboratory and toward more practical tasks in real-world settings (Herman & Siegel, 1978; Siegel, 1981; Wellman & Somerville, 1982). This has been an important development, and we are gaining both empirical and theoretical insights into the practical spatial competence of children. However, a complete account of human spatial abilities and their development must include abstract, symbolic skills as well as more practical spatial behaviors. It is now appropriate to broaden the focus of research to reexamine the development of more abstract spatial abilities, and, in particular, to identify how practical spatial abilities interact with more abstract spatial knowledge. To achieve this broader understanding, it is necessary (1) to examine the ways in which humans use spatial information in *both* practical and abstract ways and (2) to consider how humans' more abstract reasoning abilities and knowledge are coordinated with our immediate orientation to space. The current chapter will begin to address these two goals. The major thesis is that to understand how children (or adults) perform on tasks requiring abstract, symbolic spatial ability it is necessary to understand how such abstract skills are affected by more immediate, practical uses of spatial information.

Presson and Somerville (1985) recently introduced the distinction between two major ways (primary and secondary) in which humans gather and use spatial information. The first way of using space, which is both conceptually and developmentally the *primary* one, guides our immediate orientation and action in space. Given the requirements of a mobile organism, humans (like other mobile animals) have evolved a variety of primary perceptual mechanisms that specify where we are, orient us to act in space, and help us anticipate what to expect as we move (Howard & Templeton, 1966).

The processes of primary spatial orientation focus attention on aspects of the surrounding spatial world, with respect to which direct action can occur without further processing. The extent of that information implicitly defines our sense of near space, which for practical purposes forms the *working spatial memory* for orientation and action (Howard & Templeton, 1966). The processes involved in registering and updating information about the immediate surrounds as we move are relatively automatic in adults. Our spatial perception and orientation are in part guided by expectations and higher-order units (*frames*) that structure the amount of and type of features to which we typically first attend (Minsky, 1975).

Humans also use spatial information in a *secondary* way to deal with information to which they are not necessarily directly oriented. Secondary uses of spatial information include symbolic representation and various aspects of spatial thought (e.g., drawing or reading maps, mental rotation, perspective problems). These secondary uses of space develop after infancy and provide additional, powerful means to manipulate spatial information cognitively in abstract, formal ways. However, the addition of these conceptual skills does not diminish the ongoing importance of primary spatial skills. In fact, as we will see, the secondary, symbolic skills depend on and must be coordinated with the primary ones.

To illustrate the distinction between primary and secondary uses of spatial information, consider an animal traversing a terrain (of relatively small or large scale). If it is well adapted, the animal will be able to keep track of where it is in the changing surrounds, and will construct a mental representation of features of that environment (e.g., Krebs, 1978; Menzel, 1973; O'Keefe & Nadel, 1978; Olton, 1977). In later encounters, the animal will use the represented information to guide its behavior in that environment, and thus show a very practical gain from the earlier experience (e.g., the animal might remember and locate a food source or a hiding place, or use a more efficient route through the space). In the rather special case of the animal being an adult human, there is a second sense in which the represented information might be used. In addition to using that information directly to guide orientation and action through the space, the adult might draw a map to represent the space symbolically. This later, secondary use of the spatial information might even occur when the adult was some distance from the actual environment.

The current thesis is that in order to account for the development of abstract, secondary uses of spatial information in humans it is necessary to consider the behaviors in relation to more immediate, primary spatial activity. Although humans do develop secondary spatial skills, even as adults the primary spatial abilities remain integral to organizing immediate orientation and action in space (Presson & Somerville, 1985). Primary spatial orientation also can have an important effect on abstract uses of spatial information because the immediate surrounds provide an important frame of reference for all spatial behavior.

Just as a location in space can only be defined relative to some frame of reference (Pick & Lockman, 1981), the *spatial* meaning of a behavior (whether practical goal-seeking behavior or rather abstract cognitive problem solving) depends on the frame of reference to which the problem or behavior is referred. A simple movement has a spatial component, but to define the spatial meaning of that movement clearly requires that a frame of reference be specified. The primary, immediate spatial meaning of any behavior is defined in terms of the animal's position within the immediate spatial surrounds. Typically, this presents no difficulty because most behavior is directly enacted in relation to the immediate surrounds (e.g., going to the nest), so that the primary meaning is the only relevant one.

However, the situation in an abstract, symbolic spatial task is not so simple, because the responses or spatial symbols used in the task can have multiple spatial meanings depending on the frame of reference. For example, if I point toward my right, that gesture has a direct, primary meaning in relation to the immediate surrounds and might indicate the direction to travel to get from here to the library. However, the spatial (directional) referent of the gesture might be quite different if the gesture was interpreted relative to an abstract frame of reference. This might occur if the gesture was made to indicate how I would proceed *if I was already* at some other place. Here the gesture's meaning must be determined in relation to an abstract frame of reference, separate from the gesture's direct relation to the surrounds. Similarly, a map as a spatial symbol has a (secondary) spatial meaning based on an abstract relation to the space, but it also has a direct, primary relation to the spatial surrounds as an object. A person's primary orientation to the immediate surrounds defines a concrete, primary frame of reference. Our orientation to the spatial field acts as a "backdrop" against which other spatial behaviors (including symbol use) are interpreted. If the abstract frame of reference is not well specified, then children (or even adults) may use the most immediate, concrete frame of reference as a default to interpret the symbol or behavioral response. Spatial symbols are, in this sense, like deictic expressions (such as *here*), which themselves have no specific referent. Deictic reference words may have varying meaning depending on the speaker's frame of reference (Klein, 1983).

The importance of alternative frames of reference in spatial behavior often has been ignored, although the importance of the larger context as a frame of reference for interpreting specific local information has been shown repeatedly in perceptual contexts (e.g., Navon, 1977; Palmer, 1980; Rock, 1973). The importance of the embedding spatial context is also a pivotal concept within the broader theory of James Gibson (1966, 1979) concerning how we perceive invariance in the world. Recently, Just and Carpenter (1985) have spelled out the importance of frames of reference in spatial problem solving, because multiple coordinate systems can be (and at times are) used in spatial tasks. The importance of spatial frames of reference has been shown in several contexts in defining children's spatial behavior (Acredolo, 1976; Pick & Lockman, 1981). The potential conflict between primary and secondary frames of reference in defining the spatial meaning of a behavior can limit the performance of children in abstract tasks. This conflict exists particularly when a person is asked to use spatial information in relation to an abstract frame of reference at the same time that the person is *directly* oriented to the information in the immediate surrounds. In a very real sense, the development of secondary spatial ability may be characterized as one of replacing a dependence on that primary, concrete frame of reference with the use of more abstract reference frames that are not directly tied to the immediate spatial surrounds.

Three areas of research on spatial abilities will be reviewed to support the basic thesis concerning the importance of primary spatial orientation for the emergence of more abstract, secondary uses of spatial information. First, the distinction between primary and secondary uses of spatial information will be applied to current studies of how children use maps, perhaps the most prototypic of spatial symbols. A map reader's primary relation to the world will limit his or her abstract understanding and use of maps. The developmental advances in map use and understanding can be interpreted as the growing ability to define the map's meaning in terms of abstract, secondary frames of reference. In addition, the primary–secondary distinction will be applied to comparative data to help account for chimpanzees' limited abstract understanding of maps despite the practical spatial competence that these animals display. Second, work on the classic perspective problem and children's spatial reasoning will be reviewed. The systematic "egocentric" errors that occur in standard versions of the perspective task will be interpreted as resulting from a conflict between primary and secondary frames of reference in defining the meaning of the response, rather than a general lack of understanding about spatial relations. Finally, the distinction between primary and secondary activity will be extended to look at different modes of spatial learning. Recent work with adults contrasting map learning with more direct, primary forms of spatial experience will be discussed. The differences between the two modes of learning about the spatial world imply that multimodal, even multistorage models of spatial representation must be devised.

COORDINATING PRIMARY AND SECONDARY MEANINGS OF SPATIAL SYMBOLS: USING MAPS

The foregoing analysis of spatial behavior in terms of primary and secondary spatial activity implies that abstract uses of spatial information in children develop out of, and are often limited by, primary orientation to space. This distinction between primary and secondary meanings of spatial behavior (and the need to coordinate them) can best be illustrated in the development of children's use of maps, which are perhaps the quintessential spatial symbols.

Children initially use maps as if the maps have only a very direct, primary relation to the immediate surrounds. That is, they rely on the immediate spatial surrounds to define the meaning of the maps, rather than establishing the abstract, secondary meaning. The practical result of this reliance on the primary frame of reference is that children demonstrate only limited understanding of the map as a spatial symbol. The ability to use complex map information in fully abstract ways is a relatively late development—one that requires that children separate the primary and secondary meanings of the symbol. To clarify this distinction between different meanings of a map, it is necessary to delineate the different senses in which a map can serve as a symbol for aspects of the world. If one asks the question "At what age do children understand a map?" the answer will largely depend on the type of understanding to which you refer.

For a map to serve as a spatial symbol, it must have information that *corresponds to* (symbolizes) aspects of some space. However, the symbolic correspondence between a map and the world is not unitary. There are several distinct aspects of this correspondence that must be taken into account to use the map successfully. At the most basic level, the map reader must understand that the map carries *some* information about a part of the world. If not, then the map could legitimately be ignored. Given this general understanding, there are at least three types of correspondence that are psychologically important to symbolic map use. First, the elements in the map must refer to elements in the space. This can be referred to as *identity* correspondence. The extent to which the map element resembles the world element can vary a great deal, from rather iconic to arbitrary and abstract. The basic idea that a map has some identity correspondence to the world appears rather early in children. Even prior to 18 months of age, infants can establish basic identity correspondence in pictures and words, exhibiting what Gardner and Wolf (1982) termed *mundane symbolization.* Young preschoolers are able to recognize elements in aerial photographs as showing houses, their school, trees, and so forth (Blaut, McCleary, & Blaut, 1970), even though they themselves have never seen such views. Further, preschoolers can establish the specific correspondence between map elements and parts of the world under simple conditions (Bluestein & Acredolo, 1979).

The spatial nature of a map entails more than the identity of single elements, however. A map also requires a *relational correspondence* to the world, such that the elements in the map have the same pattern of spatial relations as do the corresponding elements in the world. These relations are typically represented at reduced scale and from an aerial perspective, but they provide an analogue representation that preserves the spatial pattern. A good map will maintain the spatial relations that are critical for the particular use for which the map was designed. (Of course many maps, such as the New York City subway map, do distort "true" relations somewhat for clarity of use, but the important functional relations are maintained.)

The quality of represented relations among elements is what makes the map logically a good spatial symbol. However, just because a map is a "good" map in this logical sense does not imply that its information is easily used (Robinson & Petchenik, 1976). Some information can be read from a good map under almost all conditions. For example, the information that an object represented in the map exists in the space or even some relational information, such as "is next to" or "is near" another element, can be read directly (within scale constraints). However, in practical map-reading situations, the map information must be translated to guide practical action. The relations that specify specific directions or more complex relations, such as "to the right of," are not coded directly in a map. Instead, when a map is read, the relations in the map (as perceived by the map reader) must be translated to the immediate space (as the reader is oriented to it). This translation requires an additional type of correspondence—the *orientational correspondence* between the map and the space that it represents. The need to consider the specific orientational correspondence of a map at the time of its use makes spatial symbols somewhat unique. As was noted earlier, this contextual quality of spatial symbols makes them much more like deictic words than abstract symbols.

The fact that a map's physical relation to the space that it represents (orientational correspondence) can affect the difficulty of using the map information can be seen in studies of early map use. In the most widely used map-reading task, children attempt to use information in maps to locate a hidden target. Developmental work with preschool children (Bluestein & Acredolo, 1979) as well as with early school-aged children (Presson, 1982a) has consistently shown that children can establish both identity and relational correspondences of a map to a space when the map is aligned with the world. In this simplest case, when the map is fully aligned with the world, then the direct, primary relation of the map to the surrounds (as object) is identical to the abstract, secondary meaning of the map (as symbol). There is no conflict between the two frames of reference and children have little difficulty in using the map information to guide search for the target.

However, if the map is not physically aligned with the space when it is read, then the task is much more difficult for young children. For example, for kindergartners using maps with single landmarks, when the maps were read inside the space when aligned the proportion correct was .92 and when not aligned it was .40 overall (.30 for 180-degree misalignment and .50 for 90-degree misalignment—Presson, 1982a). When the map is not aligned, there is a conflict between primary and secondary frames of reference. Younger children tend to rely on the direct, realistic meaning of the map, which results in the typical egocentric error (see Fig. 4.1). To use the map successfully when

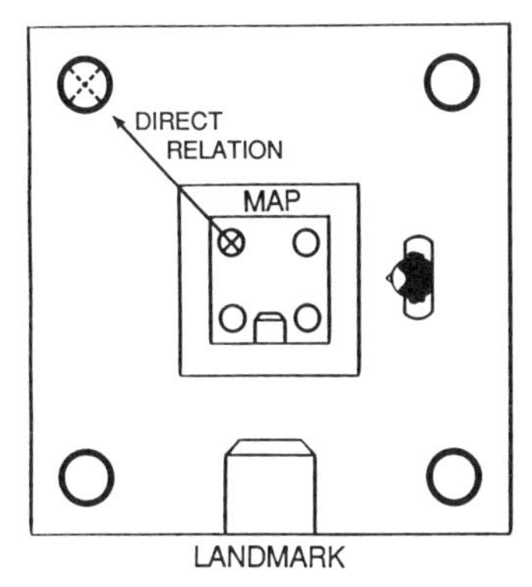

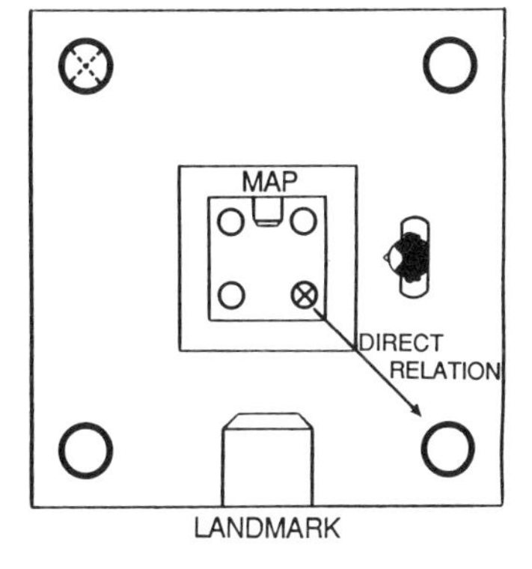

Figure 4.1. Examples of aligned and nonaligned map-reading trials. On aligned trial (left panel), the primary, direct meaning is correct. On nonaligned trial (right panel), the primary meaning is incorrect.

it is not aligned with the space requires some understanding of the alternative meanings that are possible for a spatial symbol, in relation to abstract, secondary, frames of reference. Young children find it difficult to coordinate the concrete, primary meaning with more abstract ones.

The detailed ways in which children come to establish abstract, secondary frames of reference and to achieve coordination between primary and secondary spatial frames of reference to use spatial symbols are still not well understood and require additional study. One promising direction may be suggested in the recent work by Howard Gardner and his colleagues at Project Zero (Gardner, 1983). They have launched an effort to examine some of these larger issues within the development of symbol use in a variety of domains. For example, they have focused on how children generate symbols, and have had children draw maps of a landscape over several years in a longitudinal study. Early maps were not different from drawings in that they contain specific perceptual detail, which suggests that young children treat a request to draw a map in the same way as a request to draw a picture (Davis & Fucigna, 1983). Children learned to differentiate the meaning of a map from that of a picture in the early grade-school years. In more mature maps, the appearance of individual items was no longer central. Children used abstract symbols (e.g., treating all trees alike) and constructed aerial views. The critical difference is that the map is an abstract symbolization, one that contains more formal, arbitrary rules of meaning translation, whereas a picture is closer to the direct perceptual experience. To the younger child, the map product was considered equivalent to a drawing in that they both had a very direct, immediate relation to what they represent. It was only at ages 8–9 that the spatial symbol was abstracted and disembedded from the immediate spatial field. This process of developing map understanding separates the meaning of the map (as an abstract symbol) from its direct relation to the space (as an object).

Comparative Data on the Use of Spatial Symbols by Chimpanzees

The data on children's map use suggest that an important dimension of spatial development in the child is the growing ability to treat spatial information in an abstract, secondary way. The ability to treat spatial information as separate from the immediate surrounds is added to the already existing primary spatial competence to act and orient directly in space. This distinction between primary and secondary uses of spatial information can also provide a context to examine comparative data about practical and abstract spatial abilities. In particular, it provides a useful framework to understand the relative strengths and weaknesses of chimpanzees' spatial abilities.

One implication of the proposed distinction between primary and secondary uses of spatial information is that both continuities and discontinuities can be identified when contrasting the spatial activities of humans and other animals. Primary spatial orientation abilities are essential to all mobile organisms, and many animals show extraordinary abilities to orient and navigate through familiar and unfamiliar spaces, locate and remember food sources, and so forth. Humans share a general need to orient and navigate in the immediate surrounds, and these uses of spatial information are all primary spatial abilities. Gardner (1983) refers to these shared practical demands in stating that the evolution of human spatial intelligence is more continuous with processes found in infrahumans. He points out that (primary) spatial intelligence "assumed pivotal importance" for the group life of many primates, which required returning to their homes after traversing wide spaces (p. 184).

In contrast to the practical, primary uses of space displayed by many animals, secondary uses of spatial information appear to be unique to human intelligence. The ability to break away from the effects of the immediate spatial surrounds in order to treat spatial information in arbitrary, fully symbolic ways develops fairly late in childhood. Such secondary uses of spatial information have not been clearly demonstrated in nonhuman species, despite the practical spatial competence and the sometimes quite impressive logical symbolic abilities that these animals display.

Even chimpanzees, who *can* represent spatial information and demonstrate very sophisticated spatial abilities in practical settings (e.g., Menzel, 1973, 1978), have not demonstrated the ability to use that information in fully arbitrary, secondary ways. For example, chimps in the laboratory of David Premack had great difficulty translating spatial information from one context to another. Even 5- and 6-year-old chimps had great difficulty with photo-object matching tasks that human infants can easily master at 18 months (Hochberg & Brooks, 1962). Further, even though chimps are very proficient at recovering hidden food from a complicated series of hiding places if they directly watch the hiding (and do so very efficiently—Menzel, 1973), the chimps fail at the recovery task if they watch the hiding on a television monitor (Premack & Premack, 1983). Such difficulties are perhaps all the more surprising in that some of these chimps have shown quite astonishing general symbolic skills in certain logical or communication tasks (e.g., Premack & Premack, 1983).

An effort was made to teach several chimps to use a "map" (Premack & Premack, 1983). Initially, two identical rooms were used. It turned out that after watching the baiting in the first room the chimps could locate the food in the second room (with additional controls to ensure that the chimps knew that there were two separate rooms). Gradually the interior of the first room was reduced in scale and placed on a canvas sheet to form a "map." After some extended experience with this situation, the chimps could use the scaled-down "map" information in the first room to locate the target in the second room. The use of the map in this situation shows the same concrete, direct use of spatial symbols that preschool children display, in that the chimps can establish identity correspondence and use the fixed relations of the two rooms to establish a direct relational correspondence. Even with extensive explicit training the chimps did not demonstrate abstract, secondary use of the map information. Their ability to use the map information was rather fragile, and they failed if the map was not aligned (requiring them to establish an orientational correspondence) or if the map was presented in a new context.

The finding that chimpanzees do not possess a general concept of a map, one that would allow for an abstract relation to the space (rotating the map or generalizing to a new setting), underscores the important discontinuity between primary, direct uses of spatial information and secondary, abstract ones. Using spatial information to which one is directly oriented differs from using the information in a model or map in an "as if," arbitrary manner. The former skills are basic to all mobile organisms, and chimps can easily demonstrate high levels of such practical skill. In contrast, to use spatial information in a manner distinct from one's direct orientation to it requires higher-level cognitive abilities.

Of course, it is important to recognize that the chimps *do* show the rudimentary level of concrete spatial symbol use (as do young children). Chimpanzees do display symbolic abilities (especially in logical, nonspatial tasks—Premack & Premack, 1983), but they show the same limitations in using spatial symbols as do young children. Chimps appear to utilize the information correctly from the symbol as long as the model and the target are *directly aligned* and simpler direct correspondence of the map to the surrounds will suffice.

In the discussion of how primary spatial orientation to the world provides a concrete frame of reference that conflicts with a spatial symbol's abstract relation to the space, the examples have focused on the map's direct relation to the *immediate surrounds.* However, in the Premacks' map training with chimpanzees, the actual target space was not immediately visible to the chimp when viewing the map. The chimpanzees still were successful only when the map had a fixed relation to the target space. Because the map and space were not simultaneously visible, this has implications concerning the range or extent of primary spatial orientation. It is likely that the chimps had a sense of their own relation (and hence the map's direct relation as well) to locations in the target space even when the maps were read in another room.

A person (or chimp) may well be able to be spatially oriented rather directly to parts of space that are beyond immediate perception. This notion is quite consonant with a Gibsonian theory of information uptake or the realization that mobile animals typically integrate information over separate, successive experiences to provide an interconnected world, even beyond the immediate perceived surrounds. Although the limits of such ability to be oriented to locations outside of immediate perception are not known, the spatial extent of primary orientation is likely to increase with development (Rieser, 1983). Kindergartners are able to point to landmarks in their neighborhood even from a distance, although accuracy increases with age (Anooshian & Young, 1981). Pick and Lockman (1981) have shown how the ability to point to objects out of sight increases with age, although preschoolers are quite good when the targets are on the same floor of the house. If the targets are on a different floor, then there are sharp developmental differences. One reason may be that the younger children can only anticipate positions that are at a limited distance from themselves based on practical action space. If their sense of near space is limited, they may point to the stairs instead of to the actual target if the stairs are part of the immediate surrounds and are an intermediate goal to get to the target.

When reading maps, young children also show evidence of using their knowledge of the target space even though that space is not visible. When maps are read at a distance from the space that they represent, then it could be argued that the specific orientation of the map vis-à-vis the world should not matter. The map reader must decode the critical information and carry it (in some mental representation) into the space. Although children do show much less of the realistic error when they read maps outside the space, such errors do not disappear entirely. Bluestein and Acredolo (1979) reported 65% of errors were of this type when the maps were read immediately outside the space (93% of errors were of this type when maps were read inside the space). If maps are read at a larger distance (15 m) from the target space, this tendency to make realistic errors among kindergartners and second graders does not occur (Presson, 1982a). This suggests that there are real limits to the spatial extent of primary orientation.

However, just as the chimps in Premack's lab could use the other model room or map to locate a target if the two were fully aligned, when children attempt to use map information near to but out of sight of the critical space, they also attempt to relate the map to the space rather directly. This has been shown both by Bluestein and Acredolo (1979) and also by recent evidence from my laboratory. This realistic error that occurs when maps are read out of sight of the target space is based on the map's relation to the target space, rather than a simple egocentric interpretation of the map (e.g., "The target is in the first hiding place on my right as I reenter the room"). It was possible to separate these two possible interpretations based on a study in which the children entered the hiding space in a different orientation than when they viewed the map (see Fig. 4.2). In this case, if the direct relation of the map to the space did not matter, then the orientation of the map would not have an effect or the critical orientation would be relative to the child as the map was read. In fact, the physical alignment of the map relative to the space was important. Trials for which the map was directly aligned with the space (which was not visible) were easier than those for which the maps were not aligned with the space. This effect of map alignment occurred both for kindergartners (52% vs. 40% correct on aligned and not-aligned trials) and for second graders (84% vs. 57%). Thus even when the target space was not in sight, the children did use the direct relation of the map to that space to help guide their search for the hidden target (at least when the point of reading is adjacent to the critical space). Such data suggest that the extent of "near space" may extend beyond

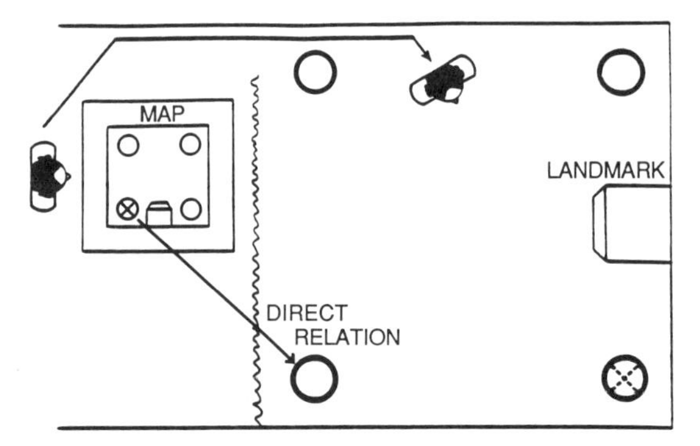

Figure 4.2. Map-reading trial for which primary, direct frame of reference is different from egocentric frame of reference.

the visual field. Extensions are likely to have limits, based on attentional factors or the salience of spatial features as well as physical distance, but the idea that near space extends beyond immediately visible space is fully consistent with Gibson's (1966) account of spatial perception.

In sum, this examination of the early development of map use has illustrated the distinction between primary and secondary uses of spatial information. Initial map use by children is limited by the conflict between the more direct primary meaning of the map in relation to the immediate surrounds and the more abstract secondary meaning in relation to an abstract frame of reference. Although children establish the basic symbolic correspondence between the map and the space (when the two are aligned), they rely on the primary, direct relation to space even when the map is not aligned. Developmentally, children show a growing ability to treat the spatial relations in the map as separate from the immediate surrounds, and thus coordinate the multiple "meanings" of the maps. This growing ability develops during the time that children are exhibiting a general increase in the cognitive ability to coordinate multiple aspects of specific task situations and to isolate the identity of and meaning of parts within a larger whole. The coordination of primary and secondary spatial meanings in spatial tasks may reflect this general trend in cognitive development. The abstract use of spatial symbols develops over the school years, although the need to coordinate abstract and concrete meanings of a symbol is necessary even for adults (Levine, 1982).

The distinction between primary and secondary meanings of a map as spatial symbol was also useful to help account for comparative data on map use with chimpanzees. Chimpanzees have only demonstrated map use based on the primary relation of the map to the surrounds, similar to the limitations shown by young children in initial map use. The ability to use spatial information in secondary ways—to utilize fully the abstract, arbitrary relation of a map to the world—may be a uniquely human ability.

DISTINGUISHING PRIMARY AND SECONDARY USES OF SPATIAL INFORMATION: EGOCENTRISM IN SPATIAL REASONING

The second example of the distinction between primary and secondary uses of spatial information comes from my own work on children's spatial reasoning (Huttenlocher & Presson, 1973, 1979; Presson, 1980, 1982b), which examined processes of imagined spatial transformation. A particular focus of this work was to understand how children solve the classic perspective, or three mountain, problem in which a child must anticipate how an array would appear relative to a viewer in some different vantage point (viewer-rotation task). Piaget and Inhelder (1967), as well as many other researchers who have followed up this work, have shown that the perspective problem is quite difficult in standard form until at least the middle elementary school years, and that children make a very specific type of error. With the standard questioning procedure (appearance questions), children select a picture or model to indicate what the entire array would look like to the viewer in a new position. When children pick pictures or models, they respond as if the observer would always see just what the child currently sees. Piaget and Inhelder labeled these errors *egocentric* and argued that the young child did not understand that spatial relations (left–right, before–behind) were relative to the position of the observer (Piaget & Inhelder, 1967). Figure 4.3 presents an example trial on a

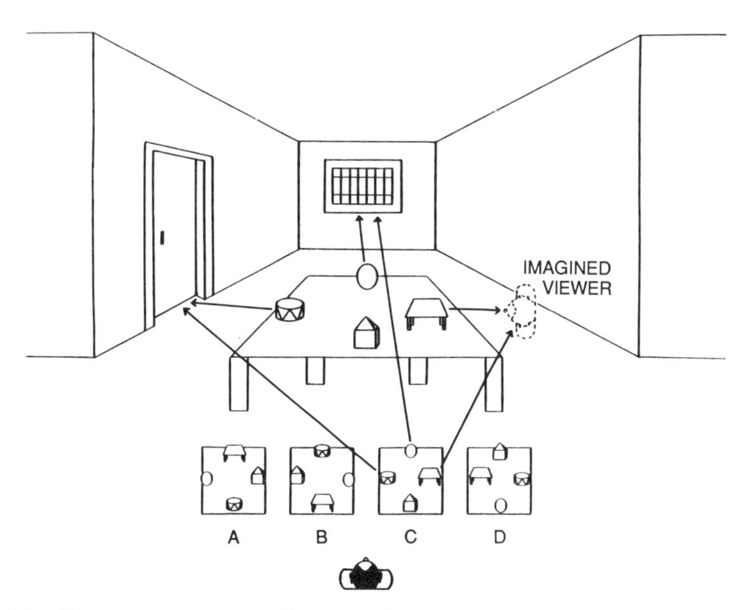

Figure 4.3. Viewer-rotation (perspective) task with appearance questions. Lines indicate the direct relation to the surrounds for the elements in the array and in the models. For the example shown, response alternative B is correct and alternative C is egocentric.

standard version of the viewer-rotation task using a four-object array (drum, table, house, ball). The four response alternatives for appearance questions are shown, with the correct response and the characteristic egocentric error identified.

Although the characteristic errors on the perspective task have provided one of the benchmarks of spatial developmental work, by examining children's performance in related tasks under varying response formats it is possible to account more fully for children's spatial reasoning performance. As we shall see, the pattern of egocentric errors does not mean that children fail to understand the practical changes in the observer–array relation as Piaget and Inhelder (1967) suggested. Children are able to anticipate the result of spatial changes in the surrounds as they would affect primary spatial orientation. However, they have difficulty when there is a conflict between primary and secondary meanings of the response, as described above for maps. To see how this is true, let us examine the typical viewer-rotation task along with several variants.

Some possible explanations of the egocentric error can be ruled out by contrasting children's performance on the viewer-rotation problem with their performance on logically equivalent problems in which children imagine the outcome of a physical rotation of the array relative to a stationary observer (array-rotation problem). When these two logically equivalent tasks are contrasted using the standard response procedures (appearance questions), grade-school children find the array-rotation task much easier than the viewer-rotation task (e.g., 85 vs. 44% correct with fourth graders—Huttenlocher & Presson, 1979). Further, children make the systematic egocentric error that Piaget described only on the viewer-rotation task. In that error, children pick a model that shows the array unchanged when asked for the viewer's perspective (see Fig. 4.3). For the viewer-rotation task with appearance questions, 80% of the errors that fourth graders made were of that one type. In contrast, only 25% of the errors that occurred in the array-rotation task were egocentric (in each case, 33% of errors would be of that type by chance). The children's success on the array-rotation task shows that the egocentric error is not due to a general inability to imagine concrete spatial transformations.

Other interpretations of the egocentric error pattern in standard viewer-rotation tasks also can be ruled out. For example, it is not the case that viewer rotation is always a more difficult task than array rotation, or that children always make systematic egocentric errors in viewer-rotation tasks. This can be seen by examining children's performance on these spatial transformation tasks using a different questioning procedure (item questions). With item questions, children are asked which of the array elements would be in a specified relation to the observer after the transformation (e.g., "What item in the array would be in front of [or on a side or furthest from] the viewer?"). These questions probe for all the logical information as to how the observer relates to each element in the array.

When the viewer-rotation and array-rotation tasks were contrasted using item questions, a dramatic shift in task difficulty and error patterns occurred. The relative task difficulty of the two tasks reversed (Huttenlocher & Presson, 1979; Presson, 1982b). For item questions, viewer rotation was much easier than array rotation (80 vs. 68% correct for fourth graders) and, more important, there was no systematic tendency overall for children to make egocentric errors in the viewer-rotation task (Huttenlocher & Presson, 1979). For 90- or 270-degree transformations, such egocentric errors were not more likely than expected by chance for viewer rotation (44%). Only for 180-degree transformations was the occurrence of egocentric errors (63%) above chance. Trials with 180-degree rotations introduce reversals and symmetries that are especially difficult, and these trials represent a special case (Pufall, 1975). Thus children who are egocentric with many errors with appearance questions in the viewer-rotation task can successfully answer item questions in that task, without systematic egocentric errors. This finding suggests that the children do know the logical information that underlies the viewer-rotation (perspective) task. However, they fail to use that information successfully when faced with appearance questions.

It was to account for this somewhat complex pattern of results (see Table 4.1) that the distinction between primary and secondary uses of spatial information was proposed (Huttenlocher & Presson, 1979; Presson, 1980, 1982b; Presson & Somerville, 1985). There are two principles that jointly can explain this pattern of results. First, subjects code the array information as a part of the immediate surrounds. They do not code the array as an abstract, single unit, but rather code each element separately in relation to the immediate surrounds. The second principle posits that when children imagine a transformation they anticipate how that transformation would actually change the immediate surrounds. In this view the children do understand the concrete implications of spatial changes and how their primary orientation to near space

TABLE 4.1. Task Difficulty and Egocentric Errors in the Spatial Reasoning Tasks as a Function of Conflict Between Frames of Reference

Response Type:	Appearance Questions	Item Questions	Position Questions
		Viewer-Rotation (Perspective) Task	
Conflict between primary and secondary frames of reference?	Yes	No	Yes
Relative difficulty	Hard	Easy	Hard
Egocentric errors?	Yes	No	Yes
		Array-Rotation Task	
Conflict between primary and secondary frames of reference?	No	No	No
Relative difficulty	Easy	Harder	Easy
Egocentric errors?	No	No	No

would be altered by those changes, although there would be limits on how much information could be transformed in imagination. If children focus on the changes in the actual surrounds in this way, it implies that they treat the two transformations (viewer rotation and array rotation) distinctly. They try to carry out the transformation instructions as described—to imagine the result of a viewer movement or an array movement.

If children do interpret the transformation instructions literally and concretely, then for array rotation they will imagine the array elements in new positions in the immediate spatial field. In this case, the relative difficulty of the two question types can be accounted for by the amount of information that the subject needs to transform. Appearance questions are relatively easy because if subjects can locate the new position of any one item then the correct model can be identified directly. In contrast, for item questions, because any item might be probed on a trial, to be consistently correct the subject must rotate all the items in the array. Thus these item questions are actually more logically demanding than are appearance questions (within a given transformation task), because more information needs to be transformed. As would be expected if the amount of information to be transformed determined difficulty, for the array-rotation tasks item questions were more difficult than were appearance questions.

For viewer-rotation (perspective) tasks, subjects are asked to imagine the viewer in a new position relative to a fixed array. To answer the item questions the child must locate the viewer in a new position and then determine the relation of the items in the array to that viewer. This task does *not* require the subject to recode the array in relation to the immediate spatial field at all. In fact, the movement of a viewer would not alter any of the array elements, only the position of the viewer. The fact that the array would not change helps the child with item questions. The item questions probe for the logical information about how the observer relates to the array elements. An item question might ask, for example, which object would be in front of the viewer in the new position (Fig. 4.3). This question is very much like asking which object is closest to the window. Both questions can be answered with direct reference to the actual relations among the elements in the spatial field (one of which is the imagined viewer). Because we have found that these item questions are actually rather easy, we can infer that the children *know* the logical information about how the array is related spatially to the observer. Perhaps more important for the current analysis, systematic egocentric errors do not occur overall with item questions. This is because there is no conflict between frames of reference in defining the meaning of the response.

For appearance questions, the viewer-rotation task is difficult and subjects make egocentric errors, even though choosing among models requires *less* logical information than answering a set of item questions. By the current framework, the appearance questions are difficult *not* because children do not understand the viewer–array relation (Piaget & Inhelder, 1967), but because they fail to understand how to use spatial symbols to represent what they do know about the viewer–array relation. That is, children rely on the immediate surrounds as a primary frame of reference to interpret the symbolic responses. This primary frame of reference conflicts with the abstract, secondary frame of reference that is necessary for the correct response.

In solving the viewer-rotation task, children are primarily concerned with the actual state of affairs in their immediate surrounds. The immediate spatial field as defined by primary spatial orientation is used as a frame of reference and a kind of "working memory" in solving these problems in a very concrete way. They know that the viewer's movement would not change the way the array elements relate to the immediate surrounds. Thus as shown in Figure 4.3 they know that wherever the viewer goes, the drum would still be near the door and so forth. When they are asked to pick the model that shows how the array would appear to the viewer, they know that the drum would be farthest from the viewer, but also that the viewer would see the drum near the door. Children tend to pick the egocentric choice because its direct, primary relation to the immediate surrounds (primary meaning) is the same as the array's. That is, it is the response that most directly shows the drum nearest the door. Thus when children attempt to interpret the response alternatives as symbols, instead of establishing the abstract, secondary meaning they relate the symbols to the surrounds in the simplest, one-to-one direct (primary) relational correspondence. They fail to separate the model as symbol (secondary meaning) from the model as object (primary meaning). Thus this error can be seen to result from a "naive realism" in reading the symbol (i.e., a conflict between the primary and secondary meanings of the symbol), rather than an inability to deduce how the observer–array relation would change (Liben & Belknap, 1981; Presson, 1980).

Presson (1980) found additional support for this explanation of the egocentric responses in the viewer-rotation problem with appearance questions. Children were presented with a small model of the actual experimental room. The model showed various room cues and other spatial features. On each trial, the model room was rotated to show how the immediate spatial field would look to the viewer. The model provided a concrete version of the alternate frame of reference (i.e., it was rotated), so that children did not have to imagine the secondary meaning of the response. The model could be used to establish directly the correct meaning of the symbolic response alternative. When the model was presented as an alternate frame of reference, children found the task easier, and did not show a general egocentric tendency (Presson, 1980). Thus children err with the standard appearance questions because they rely on the immediate framework of the surrounding room as an implicit frame of reference to provide (a primary) meaning to the symbol. The response is more of a "realistic" error than an egocentric one (see also Liben & Belknap, 1981).

It is important to note that the difficulty underlying children's egocentric errors with appearance questions is the result of a general conflict between a person's primary orientation to the spatial field and the hypothetical frame of reference that is necessary to treat the information in abstract, secondary ways.

Such a conflict between primary and secondary meanings of the spatial response is most evident when dealing with spatial symbols (e.g., pictures or models), but the problem is not limited to them. The generality of the conflict between primary and secondary frames of reference can be seen by examining a third type of question, termed *position question* (Presson, 1982b). For position questions in the viewer-rotation task, subjects point to "where the [named element] would be" relative to the viewer's new position. Position questions were used with children and adults in viewer-rotation and array-rotation tasks (Hardwick, McIntyre, & Pick, 1976; Presson, 1982b). In Hardwick and colleagues' (1976) version of the viewer-rotation task, subjects imagined themselves moving relative to an array that consisted of objects near the walls of a large room. On each trial, the subject pointed to the "new" position of the object. Errors for viewer rotation tended to be egocentric, which is predicted by the current analysis. In the example shown in Figure 4.4, with position questions children might be asked where the table would be relative to the viewer's imagined position. When responding, children tend to point directly to where the table is (and would still be) relative to the immediate surrounds. With respect to the primary frame of reference, the actual position of the array elements after any viewer movement would not change, and pointing directly to their current position makes sense. The correct pointing response has its secondary meaning defined relative to an abstract frame of reference ("as if" the child were in the alternative vantage point). This response is, of course, logically correct, but its *primary* meaning (considered with respect to the immediate spatial field as frame of reference) conflicts with what the child knows to be true about the immediate surrounds. This conflict be-

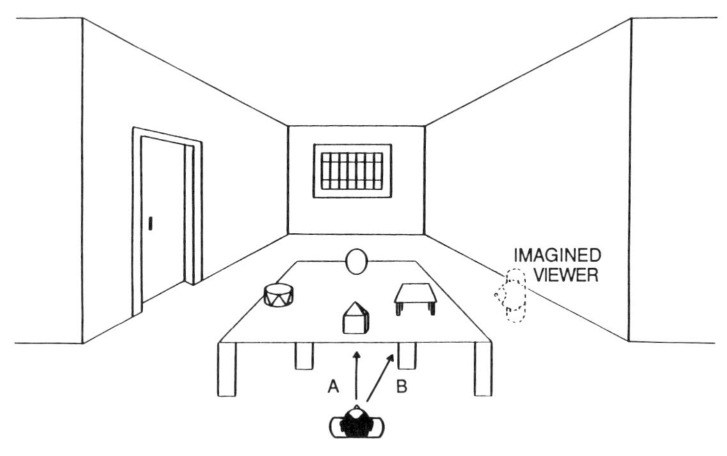

Figure 4.4. Viewer-rotation task with position questions. For the question "Where [relative to the imagined viewer] would the table be?" the arrows show the correct (A) and direct, egocentric (B) pointing responses.

tween the primary, direct meaning of the pointing response and secondary, abstract meaning makes these position questions difficult.

The data from these position questions are important because they demonstrate that children's difficulties in these tasks are not due simply to a general inability to use physical symbols. Position questions have subjects point and do not require them to use a symbolic representation to answer. The viewer-rotation task with position questions is difficult because the pointing response has two meanings. The direct, primary meaning indicates the (true) relative position of the target in the immediate spatial field. The abstract, secondary meaning (scored correct) requires an abstract frame of reference ("as if" you were there), which conflicts with the primary meaning. The fact that the position questions show the same pattern as do appearance questions (i.e., egocentric errors) suggests that the main factor in creating those errors is the conflict between the secondary meaning of the response with the primary meaning in relation to the immediate spatial surrounds (a conflict shared by both position and appearance questions) rather than a difficulty specifically involving the use of physical symbols.

Primary spatial orientation to the immediate spatial field creates an implicit frame of reference (Pick & Lockman, 1981) for solving spatial reasoning problems in a very practical way. This hypothesis successfully predicts which of the specific task situations show predominantly egocentric errors, and which do not. For tasks in which there is a conflict between primary and secondary meanings of the response, the errors will be egocentric. This is true of the standard perspective task with appearance or position questions. When the primary and secondary meanings of the response do not conflict, the errors will not be egocentric. When the elements in the correct response alternative stand in the same relation to the immediate spatial field as do the corresponding elements in the array *after* the transformation, there is no conflict. This is true for all versions of array-rotation tasks. It is also true for variants of the viewer-rotation tasks in which the subject actually moves to a new location (relative to a covered array). Although no additional logical information is provided by this movement, the inferences are much easier, and children do not make egocentric errors (Huttenlocher & Presson, 1973; Shantz & Watson, 1970; Schatzow, Kahane, & Youniss, 1980). In this case, once the viewer moves to a new location, there is no longer a conflict between the primary spatial context and the transformed appearance when making a response. Pick and Rieser (1982) suggest that this is part of the basic, automatic spatial updating that occurs when one moves through space. This focus on the importance of movement was also used in previous explanations of similar data (Huttenlocher & Presson, 1973; Shantz & Watson, 1970). In terms of the current conceptual framework, however, the critical factor is not movement per se but rather the interaction between primary and secondary uses of spatial information, and in particular the need to construct a hypothetical frame of reference to make the judgment without moving.

USING PRIMARY AND SECONDARY EXPERIENCES TO OBTAIN SPATIAL KNOWLEDGE

As we have seen, a person's direct spatial orientation to the surrounds can affect and even limit the more abstract, secondary uses of spatial information. This relation between primary and secondary uses of spatial information is evident in both tasks of map use and understanding and tasks of spatial reasoning. In each case there are clear patterns. Spatial symbols (or other behavior) are typically first interpreted directly with respect to the world as defined by a person's primary spatial orientation. The use of spatial information in fully abstract, secondary ways must be coordinated with this more immediate, direct frame of reference. The development of secondary uses of spatial information can be described as separating the interpretation of the information from its direct relation to the world, creating alternative frames of reference to provide abstract spatial meaning.

The examples used to exemplify the distinction between primary and secondary uses of spatial information have been situations in which people have used spatial symbols in known spaces. If there was an element of new information (e.g., where the target is hidden in the map studies), that information was an element within a known space. Additional questions can be raised concerning the generality of the distinction between primary and secondary uses of spatial information in other realms of spatial activity. In particular, are there important functional differences in how people treat new spatial information that is learned in either direct (primary) or symbolic (secondary) form?

Humans can obtain new spatial information from either direct, primary orientation to the information (especially through visual orientation and locomotion), or through symbolic, indirect encounters (e.g., from maps). Consistent with the contrast between primary and secondary uses of spatial information that has been proposed in this chapter, recent work on spatial learning has demonstrated functional differences between these two modes of gathering spatial information.

Relatively little is known about children's ability to gather systematic array information from map representations. In part, this lack of knowledge reflects the difficulty of abstract symbol use and the importance of primary orientation in establishing such information for children. The ability to use map information to learn about spatial relations in the world has been studied with adults.

Several investigators have shown that symbolic learning of spatial information by adults (maps displaying simple routes or configuration of objects) leads to a representation that is stored in an orientation-specific manner, like a picture or figural image. That is, later attempts to use that stored information are biased toward the specific orientation in which the information was learned. In later judgments, if the judgment is aligned with the stored orientation of the figure, the task is easy; if the judgment requires that the information be used in an orientation different from how it was learned, the task is very difficult (Evans & Pezdek, 1980; Levine, Jankovic, & Palij, 1982; Thorndyke & Hayes-Roth, 1982). For example, Levine and colleagues (1982) demonstrated that the information obtained from a map is stored in an orientation-specific manner. They argued that spatial representations are literally maplike and have a specific orientation just as a physical map does. The spatial information is retrieved in the specific orientation in which it was learned, which limits people's ability to use that information flexibly. Levine and colleagues (1982) made a much more general claim about spatial representation, proposing that all spatial information is stored in an orientation-specific way. However, it is not ecologically sound to suppose that all spatial information would be stored and used in such a fixed, inflexible manner. Humans, like all mobile organisms, have a need for more flexible knowledge representations to act and orient in space effectively, and our primary spatial senses may have evolved to provide them. In particular, information obtained when directly oriented to the space might well be stored in more flexible ways.

In contrast to map-learning studies (e.g., Levine et al., 1982), other studies have shown that if spatial information is learned through some form of *direct* experience (such as locomotion while blindfolded or sighted navigation) then the resulting representation is used much more flexibly. That is, later judgments were of equivalent difficulty regardless of whether they were made when aligned or not aligned with the initial orientation of learning (Evans & Pezdek, 1980; Thorndyke & Hayes-Roth, 1982).

Past explanations of the difference between learning from navigation and learning from a map have proposed that the critical factor distinguishing the navigation and the map conditions is that the former is successive whereas the latter is simultaneous (Thorndyke & Hayes-Roth, 1982) or that the former provides multiple vantage points for learning whereas the latter provides only a single vantage point for learning (Evans & Pezdek, 1980). Both of these distinctions have been proposed as important factors influencing current theories of spatial development (e.g., Shemyakin, 1962; Siegel & White, 1975), and both may play important roles in building spatial representations. However, they do not provide the critical factor to explain the difference between orientation-specific and orientation-free representations.

Recent work in my laboratory (Presson & Hazelrigg, 1984) contrasted these more classic factors with the distinction between primary and secondary spatial activity to see if the latter could better account for the different types of representation of spatial information. We first replicated Levine and colleagues' (1982) finding with maps. When subjects learned from a visual map, the alignment of the map display has a dramatic effect on the ease of making spatial judgments. We used Levine and colleagues' (1982) basic procedure with simple routes consisting of four locations and three connecting path segments. Subjects viewed a map of the route for 30 sec and then were blindfolded, wheeled to a point on the route, and asked to make a spatial judgment. The critical distinction was how the subject was oriented on the route when making a judgment. The two main types of judgment (aligned and contra-aligned) are shown in Figure 4.5. If when making a judgment the subject was oriented relative to the route the same way he or she was when initially viewing the map, the judgment was aligned. If the subject faced on the route the opposite way from how the map was learned, then the judgment was contra-aligned. For example, for the simple four location route shown in Figure 4.5, two subjects were shown the same map information in a specific orientation. The subject on the left was placed at location 4, told that location 3 was directly ahead of him, and then asked to indicate where location 1 would be. Thus the subject on the left was shown the map information in an orientation aligned with the judgment he was asked to make (aligned judgment). In contrast, the subject on the right was placed at location 4 and told that location 3 was directly behind him. Thus that subject was facing on the route opposite how he faced the map information, so the judgment was contra-aligned. As Levine and colleagues (1982) had reported, we found that subjects were much more accurate on aligned judgments than on contra-aligned ones (mean error in degrees: 20 vs. 58).

That finding replicated Levine and colleagues' finding concerning the orientation-specific nature of map learning. However, there was a striking contrast when subjects learned the same route information via primary spatial orientation. The route information was learned by one of two primary modes: looking directly at the route laid out on the floor or locomoting the route while blindfolded. The Look condition provides the clearest contrast between the primary and secondary input of information. In the Look condition, subjects viewed the route from a single vantage point for 30 sec. Thus with only minor exceptions, the route information that was provided to subjects in the Look and Map conditions was equivalent. The only difference was that the Look group viewed the route directly while oriented to it as an entity in space (primary learning), and the Map group viewed the route indirectly as part of a map (secondary learning).

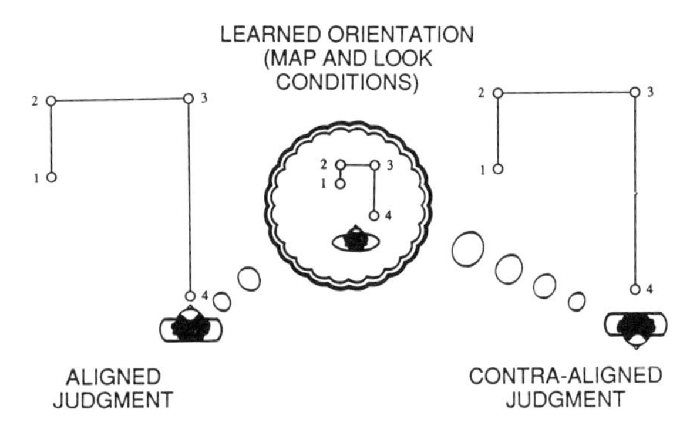

Figure 4.5. Aligned and contra-aligned judgments for the subjects learning the route by viewing a map or by viewing the route directly.

There was a large difference in the effect of alignment on subjects in the Look group compared to those in the Map group. In the Look group (as in the Walk group) there was virtually no difference in the subjects' ability to make judgments while aligned or contra-aligned with the initial viewing experience. The aligned and contra-aligned judgments had equivalent mean errors both for the Walk condition (50 vs. 54 degrees) and, more important, for the Look condition (40 vs. 40 degrees). Thus the route information was not stored in an orientation-specific manner when learned from a primary spatial experience. Spatial memory built from a direct, primary experience and memory built from a symbolic map experience result in important functional differences when that information is used in later judgments. Information obtained from a map is recalled and used in the specific orientation in which it was learned. When the information is gathered through primary spatial activity, the information can be used in a more flexible manner. This flexibility was shown for both conditions of primary spatial learning (Walk and Look conditions).

This marked difference between the orientation specificity of spatial information obtained from primary and that from secondary spatial learning experiences in adults has several important implications, which will be developed further as part of the general discussion. First, these data provide striking evidence of the importance of the primary–secondary distinction in spatial activity. Individuals deal with maps as abstract entities differently than they deal with the same information concretely as part of the immediate spatial surrounds. Second, although the different modes of spatial learning have not themselves been contrasted for children as they have for adults, it appears that the distinction between primary and secondary uses of spatial information can be important for spatial behavior in adults as well as in children.

Third, these data support the recognition that there are different types of spatial representation (or spatial storage—Liben, 1981), which are potentially related to the contextual demands involved in learning or using that information. A similar distinction between different frames of reference used to code spatial information was made by Joliecouer and Kosslyn (1983) in studies of how perceptual objects are represented. They provided evidence for object coding based on viewer-centered (and hence orientation-specific) versus object-centered (and hence orientation-free) frames of reference. Joliecouer and Kosslyn's distinction between different frames of reference for coding is consistent with several aspects of the distinction between primary and secondary spatial learning. A primary experience occurs when the information is encountered and learned as part of a world. Subjects report that when using information learned in a primary way they imagine themselves "inside" the information. In contrast, subjects report dealing with the information learned from a secondary experience as if they were at a distance from, and "outside," the information. Secondary spatial learning experiences (such as learning from a map) occur when the information does not have a specific embedding spatial framework. The learner treats the information as an abstract figure without being directly oriented to it as an integrated part of the spatial surrounds.

The distinction made here between primary and secondary spatial learning experiences is also similar to the distinction drawn by Gibson (1979) and others (e.g., Ittelson, 1973) between the perception of an object, which is observed from outside the information, and the perception of an environment, within which the perceiver participates. In the perceptual accounts, an important aspect of the contrast is that environments surround the perceiver. Discussions of how people represent spatial aspects of the world have also recognized that people store and use some world information as if they were within a surrounding "model" (e.g., Attneave, 1972). The data contrasting primary and secondary spatial learning experiences (Presson & Hazelrigg, 1984), as well as these other accounts of spatial perception and representation, suggest that multiple forms of spatial representation coexist, which is important for more general accounts of spatial development. Although developmental researchers have often sought to identify a single type of spatial representation, the structure of which might change over development (e.g., egocentric to allocentric), there is unlikely to be a single form and organization of all spatial knowledge.

DISCUSSION

The work reviewed in this chapter has shown the importance, in a variety of contexts, of the proposed distinction between primary and secondary uses of spatial information. To achieve a broad understanding of human spatial abilities and their development, it is necessary to consider how these abstract and practical spatial abilities interact. This is especially important to account for children's performance in spatial tasks that use spatial symbols or require abstract frames of reference. The typical difficulties that young children show are not the result of a general logical misunderstanding about the basic nature of space. Rather, the conflict between concrete and abstract frames of reference limits the ways in which the spatial information is used. Children appear to rely on their primary orientation to the immediate surrounds to define a direct, concrete frame of reference that is used instead of more abstract ones to define the meaning of spatial responses. These processes can account for the development of children's competence in both spatial reasoning and map tasks. This interpretation can account for the patterns of task difficulty and the presence of egocentric errors in spatial reasoning tasks (even though children know the logical information), as well as the limitations in interpreting maps when not aligned with the immediate surrounds.

The basic distinction between two ways of using spatial information—one more perceptual and direct, and the second more indirect and conceptual—is not new (e.g., Cassirer, 1955; Hart & Moore, 1973; Piaget & Inhelder, 1967; Shemyakin, 1962; Werner & Kaplan, 1963). Whenever theorists have considered taxonomies of spatial behavior, some similar distinction has been drawn.

There is even evidence that these two uses of spatial information may be mediated in distinct brain areas (O'Keefe & Nadel, 1978; Potegal, 1982).

However, although the theoretical distinction between primary and secondary uses of space has been made, it has not been consistently pursued in empirical work, and the ongoing role of primary orientation in all spatial tasks has been overlooked in the post-infancy years. The growing evidence that children do know more than traditional work had shown has led researchers to switch the focus of work on spatial development away from the laboratory, with its use of tabletop scale models and a dependence on symbolic skills, toward more practical tasks in real-world settings (e.g., Acredolo, 1981; Herman & Siegel, 1978; Siegel, Kirasic, & Kail 1978). Within the current analysis, the major thrust of these later studies has been to reduce the symbolic needs, which in turn removes the conflict between the primary and secondary uses of space. These studies have demonstrated the practical competencies of the child, and reinforced the observation that children's difficulties on more abstract, symbolic tasks do not mean that children lack practical spatial competence.

Within the current account, children's spatial development can be seen as reflecting several processes. One aspect of spatial development, which contributes to the greater general proficiency of older children in practical settings, is an increase in the extent of near space (as defined by primary spatial perception and orientation). This increase broadens the range of effectiveness of primary orientation and action and also increases the ability to integrate spatial information over multiple experiences into a single, coherent world knowledge (Rieser, 1983). The developmental change that is most important for understanding children's performance in abstract spatial tasks is the growing coordination of primary and secondary uses of spatial information. In particular, exhibiting abstract spatial skills requires that children recognize that primary and secondary meanings of symbols or behaviors can co-occur and can conflict. Here the major developmental advance is the ability to consider potential alternative, abstract frames of reference to define meaning to spatial symbols or spatial responses. This developmental ability to treat spatial information as isolated from its immediate surrounds allows for the successful abstract symbol use by adults, but this developmental advance is relative rather than complete. As will be discussed later, the potential conflict between primary and secondary spatial meanings is always present, and thus the underlying need to coordinate alternative frames of reference in abstract spatial tasks remains a potential conflict for adults as well as for children. This latter point will be discussed further after the implications of the primary–secondary distinction for comparative accounts of spatial behavior are discussed.

Primary Spatial Abilities in Mobile Animals

The spatial competence that has been the focus of much work in spatial development over the past decade is a reflection of practical, primary spatial abilities that are also important for other mobile organisms. The demands of establishing a stable representation of important spatial information (e.g., the location of sources of food and water, or of prey or predators) and the demands of updating that information to remain oriented while moving through space are shared by all mobile animals, including humans. Considering this biological commonality provides an ethological perspective on practical spatial abilities that is also important for the understanding of human spatial development (Hazen, 1983). Primary uses of spatial information in direct relation to the surrounds reflect basic properties of spatial perception that are part of the biological preparedness of mobile organisms. However, the secondary uses of spatial information in relation to more abstract frames of reference and the coordination of primary and secondary uses of information appear to be unique to human development.

Many perceptual and motor mechanisms have evolved in mobile animals to support the direct, immediate needs for spatial orientation and navigational skills. The spatial abilities of many animals are impressive, whether considering the homing or migrational abilities of birds over thousands of miles or relatively complex spatial memory in chimpanzees. For example, in Menzel's (1973) classic work, chimpanzees showed extraordinary (by human standards) ability to organize and represent spatial information about multiple food sources, and to use that information later in an extremely efficient manner when retrieving the food. Those chimps were able to demonstrate representation of not only the specific loci of hiding, but also the relative amounts and types of food that were hidden in the various locales (Menzel, 1973). Such practical displays of biologically meaningful spatial skill in animals have helped inspire the recent work on spatial search in infants (Cornell & Heth, 1979) and young children (Wellman & Somerville, 1982). These efforts have shown that young children, although far from perfect, are surprisingly competent at many practical skills in locating and retrieving spatial targets, organizing multitargeted search, and so on.

Whether one considers the behaviors of primary spatial orientation as displayed by Menzel's chimpanzees, homing and migration patterns of birds (Abel, 1980), or the behavior of wolves (Peters, 1973), it is clear that these perceptually based spatial skills are quite sophisticated. However, the spatial abilities of these animals have a common feature, which is shared with the spatial competencies of children. The spatial competence is very practical and immediate. These behaviors are directly goal oriented, such that the behavior is directly linked to the spatial locus of the goal. It is this quality that makes it a primary (direct) use of spatial information. Menzel's chimps were quite extraordinary in recovering hidden food in a very efficient manner. But they did so by searching directly the actual terrain that they saw being baited. Homing pigeons fly to distant home cages from unfamiliar release sites. But they do so by orienting to that home, based on their current relation to it.

Thus there are clear limits on what the chimp or pigeon can do. They have evolved several perceptual-motor mechanisms that allow them to solve important practical problems for their survival. But these abilities are limited to direct orientation and action (primary spatial activity). The current distinction between primary and secondary uses of spatial information would suggest that what the pigeon could *not* do is provide abstract directions to another pigeon as to its route and goal or consider that in the fall it would be taking a similar route in the opposite direction. Of course, making statements that an organism can *not* do something (even if framed with the tongue slightly in the cheek) has proven on many occasions to be a dangerous inclination. Yet there is no compelling evidence that animals can use spatial information in an abstract manner, divorced from the immediate surrounds as the mediating frame of reference. It is important to point out here that in these map tasks the goal of the behavior—to locate a specific target—is quite practical and concrete. However, to achieve that concrete goal in the map task the spatial information from the maps must be used in relation to an abstract frame of reference. The chimpanzees showed surprising failures to use maps in abstract ways (Premack & Premack, 1983). Thus the distinction between primary and secondary uses of spatial information is important to a comparative perspective on spatial ability to identify shared domains as well as to help account for the unique qualities of human spatial development.

The Primary–Secondary Distinction in Adults

The focus of this chapter has been on the development of the interplay between primary and secondary uses of spatial information. A major developmental advance occurs as children begin to coordinate primary and secondary spatial meanings of symbols and behaviors. This ability to consider the abstract spatial meaning of a spatial symbol allows older children to begin to demonstrate their logical spatial competence in tasks that require abstract frames of reference. It is important to recognize that the ability to use abstract frames of reference does not mean that primary uses of spatial information are no longer important for older children and adults, or that the potential conflict between primary and secondary spatial meanings disappears. For adults to orient and act in space requires the same primary spatial orientation skills as seen for any mobile animal (Sandstrom, 1951). Recently, there has been a growing interest in understanding some of the component processes that underlie such primary spatial orientation in adults. The ability of adults to register spatial information about the surrounds automatically and update spatially how their relation to the immediate surrounds changes as they move has been investigated in a variety of contexts (e.g., Gärling, 1980; Pick & Rieser, 1982; Smythe & Kennedy, 1982; see also Pick chapter in this volume).

The problem of coordinating primary and secondary frames of reference also affects adults in ways parallel to the ways it affects children, in that they are influenced by the immediate spatial framework when making abstract spatial responses. The conflict between primary and secondary uses of information is especially important at the time when early symbolic skills are evolving.

Yet although adults typically do overcome the conflict, adults show the same major patterns of relative task difficulty as children in solving the viewer-rotation and array-rotation tasks, across different types of questioning procedure (Presson, 1982b). The same relative task comparisons for adults were obtained for both errors and latencies for correct responses. Although adults did *not* show a preponderance of egocentric (realistic) errors in the viewer-rotation tasks, they did show the errors most often in viewer-rotation tasks with appearance and position questions.

Similarly, when adult map use is examined, the distinction between a direct, primary meaning of a map and the abstract, secondary meaning of the map remains important. Although adults do attain the ability to use spatial symbols in abstract ways, the importance of the immediate spatial surrounds can still influence map use. Levine (1982; Levine et al., 1982) has shown that when adults attempt to use maps to locate a target the orientation of the map to the space is very important. If the map is oriented so that there is a direct correspondence between the map and the space, the adults can easily use it effectively. However, if the map is misaligned with the space, then adults are occasionally misled. When they err with misaligned maps, adults tend to treat the map realistically, very much as do children.

Of course, in general adults are able to overcome these difficulties and successfully coordinate primary and secondary frames of reference in dealing with abstract spatial tasks. However, the basic distinction between primary and secondary uses of spatial information can help account for many aspects of adults' as well as children's spatial behavior.

Applying the Primary–Secondary Distinction

One of the important implications of the distinction between primary and secondary uses of spatial information is that the competence displayed in abstract spatial tasks may not apply to more practical settings. Thus attempts to build general theories or principles of spatial behavior based solely on tasks that depend on secondary uses of spatial information may well fail because of important functional differences between primary and secondary spatial activity. One example that has already been discussed is the proposal of Levine and colleagues (1982) that all spatial representations have a specific orientation. Although this principle of orientation specificity appears to describe accurately knowledge learned from maps, it does not account for the more orientation-free representations when information is learned through primary, direct experience (Evans & Pezdek, 1980; Presson & Hazelrigg, 1984).

Whenever tasks require a large component of abstract, secondary skills, some caution should apply in interpreting the generality of the findings. For example, Allen and his colleagues (Allen, 1981; Allen, Kirasic, Siegel, & Herman, 1978; Allen, Siegel, & Rosinski, 1979) developed an innovative procedure to study how people learn and represent route information. To provide realistic route information, but in a controlled laboratory setting, Allen developed a method using a slide presentation of views of a real-world walk, with slides taken at regular intervals along the route. This procedure has yielded the interesting finding that the integrated "route" can be learned, even if the slides are presented out of order (Allen et al., 1978). It has also been used to investigate hypotheses about landmark use and distance estimation by children and adults (Allen, 1981; Allen et al., 1979). Although these data have been very productive, it is important to recognize that they may not characterize landmark use and distance knowledge as seen in other contexts. The route task used by Allen requires subjects to imagine themselves at various points within a route that is never actually traveled. This requires secondary symbolic skills. Success on this task may reflect skills distinct from the ability to make direct distance estimates from "here." Thus there are two possible foci of development that could account for the developmental data in these studies. One possibility is the interpretation that the researchers have chosen, namely, that there are developmental changes in the way that landmarks are used to organize spatial knowledge about routes. An alternative and very real possibility is that the role of landmarks as organizers of spatial representations does not change developmentally. Instead, the change may occur in the ability to deal with the spatial information in the route in an abstract, secondary way as required in the task. In that case the developmental change would be in isolating and manipulating spatial information to which one is not directly oriented, rather than in the direct spatial abilities (route learning) for which the task provides an analogue.

Perhaps an even more important caution about the generality of abstract spatial behavior exists in the literature on adult spatial cognition. Many studies with adults have used abstract, figural arrays (such as maps without a specific real-world referent—Stevens & Coupe, 1978; Thorndyke & Stasz, 1980; Tversky, 1981) or spatial information presented in the highly controlled conditions of a tachistoscope (as in the mental rotation phenomenon—Shepard & Cooper, 1982). These studies have provided very powerful models of spatial cognition. The question here is whether the properties of spatial cognition in such abstract settings are also properties of practical spatial abilities. In more practical settings, the concrete nature of the immediate surrounds affects and even constrains the nature of spatial performance (Presson, 1982b). With a tachistoscope, there is no embedding spatial context, and the figures are "disconnected" from the world (Neisser, 1978). The current analysis of the distinction between primary and secondary uses of spatial information should lead researchers to show caution (and even to seek additional evidence) before assuming that the powerful cognitive mechanisms displayed in these abstract, controlled settings would occur in more concrete situations.

The Nature(s) of the Cognitive Map

A final implication of the distinction and the work reviewed above concerns the way in which we characterize spatial knowledge about aspects of the world.

Although there have been several attempts to provide a more neutral term (e.g., Liben, 1981—*spatial storage*), the term *cognitive map* is the one that has greatest currency and that is applied most broadly. Unfortunately, this notion has perhaps been as much of a bane as a boon (Allen, 1985). One of the largest problems with this term is the implication that there exists a single knowledge base concerning the world. This characterization seems wrong on several grounds. We have already discussed how spatial information may be registered differently when the information is obtained from primary (looking at a path) versus secondary (looking at a map of the path) learning. The finding that knowledge from maps was actually treated differently than direct knowledge makes the *cognitive map* metaphor all the more unfortunate. However, even if we consider only primary spatial experiences, the nature of spatial knowledge is likely to be multimodal and not unitary.

The primary spatial activities of direct action and orientation provide ample information to build sophisticated representations of the world (Presson & Somerville, 1985), as seen in the accomplishments of Menzel's chimpanzees. There are actually several categories of primary spatial orientation that have been identified as having ecological significance for mobile animals (Janders, 1975), and various sensory mechanisms or channels of information can be used to maintain meaningful spatial behaviors. All these channels of information may provide important knowledge bases for representing the spatial world. In fact, there is likely to be great selective pressure that favors redundancy in navigation and orientation systems in animals (Janders, 1975). The need to maintain awareness of and orientation to elements in the surrounds has led all mobile animals (humans included) to utilize multiple perceptual and cognitive systems to establish and maintain spatial orientation.

For example, no single cue system is likely to explain bird navigation (Abel, 1980). Birds have access to a variety of orientation information. Although much early work with homing pigeons was directed at finding the single mechanism underlying navigation (Hazen, 1983), those efforts have been replaced by studies of the conditions under which the various mechanisms are coordinated. Migratory birds are sensitive to information from sun and stars as well as the earth's magnetic field. For adult pigeons, the ability to orient is overdetermined, and either visual information from the sun or magnetic orientation will suffice to allow them to home. In young, inexperienced pigeons, *both* sorts of orienting information (visual and magnetic) appear necessary (Janders, 1975).

As evidence of early spatial abilities in young children has grown, it has become clearer that the mechanisms that underlie primary spatial orientation and practical spatial accomplishments in children are also multimodal. Research both in and out of the laboratory has become more sophisticated in demonstrating that even infants are sensitive to a broader range of spatial cues than the traditional, egocentric, view would seem to imply (Bremner, 1978; Cornell & Heth, 1979; McKenzie, Day, & Ihsen, 1984; Presson & Ihrig, 1982; Rieser, 1979). In fact, the study of the development of spatial knowledge and spatial orientation in children has at times been overly concerned with identifying a single spatial cue in a specific spatial task context. Such a search for *the* single type of spatial knowledge (or coding system) has impeded a broader understanding of spatial development. Children's difficulties in certain experimental situations were used as the basis to propose that the young child was limited to only a single type of coding for spatial information, typically egocentric. However, such a view is no longer tenable given the current evidence that even very young children are able to use nonegocentric information in many circumstances (see Presson & Somerville, 1985, for a review). It is likely that any mobile organism would possess multiple registration of some aspects of spatial information. Although there have been some accounts proposed of alternative organizations of spatial information (e.g., route information—Kuipers, 1982; maplike, survey representations—Levine et al., 1982) in the literature on adult spatial representations, there have not been any clearly integrative accounts to incorporate how multiple types of information are coordinated or how they interact. This remains an important challenge to accounts of spatial knowledge systems.

In summary, the distinction between primary and secondary uses of spatial information is central to understanding the development of early abstract, symbolic spatial skills. In this chapter the evidence for this distinction has been reviewed, and I have outlined some of the important issues in that development. The primary-secondary distinction also provides important links between the spatial abilities of humans and those of other mobile animals, as well as between accounts of children's and accounts of adults' spatial behavior.

The importance of the immediate surrounds as a primary frame of reference in spatial behavior is clear. The issues that remain unexplored concern how children develop the ability to use spatial symbols in more abstract ways, to begin to free themselves from the influence of the immediate spatial field. In both using maps to locate targets in a known space and using models or pictures to display relational information in spatial reasoning tasks, the major task (or problem) is to establish an abstract correspondence or an "as if" equivalence between the symbol and the immediate space. Children are able to deduce the logical relations of the observer to the array, and can name them, yet they fail when they attempt to convey that information in a symbolic response.

The developmental course described in this work is consistent with the proposed importance of primary spatial orientation in the early use of spatial symbols. The first use of spatial symbols is concretely tied to the immediate surrounds. Secondary uses of space form an integral part of human spatial development, and the ability to coordinate the more abstract use of symbols with the ongoing importance of primary spatial orientation is an important cognitive developmental process. Over the past decade we have demonstrated the practical spatial competence of young children. The challenge that remains is to turn our attention to the basic processes that underlie the emergence of abstract spatial competence, especially the coordination of the practical (primary) and abstract (secondary) aspects of human spatial abilities.

REFERENCES

Abel, K. P. (1980). Mechanisms of orientation, navigation, and homing. In S. A. Gauthreaux, Jr. (Ed.), *Animal migration, orientation, and navigation*. New York: Academic.

Acredolo, L. P. (1976). Frames of reference used by children for orientation in unfamiliar spaces. In G. Moore & R. Golledge (Eds.), *Environmental knowing*. Stroudsburg, PA: Dowden, Hutchinson, & Ross.

Acredolo, L. P. (1981). Small- and large-scale spatial concepts in infancy and childhood. In L. Liben, A. Patterson, & N. Newcombe (Eds.), *Spatial representation and behavior across the lifespan*. New York: Academic.

Acredolo, L. P. (1982). The familiarity factor in spatial research. In R. Cohen (Ed.), *New directions for child development: Children's conceptions of spatial relationships*. San Francisco: Jossey-Bass.

Allen, G. L. (1981). A developmental perspective on the effect of "subdividing" macrospatial experience. *Journal of Experimental Psychology: Human Learning & Memory, 7,* 120–132.

Allen, G. L. (1985). Strengthening weak links in the study of the development of macrospatial cognition. In R. Cohen (Ed.), *The development of spatial cognition*. Hillsdale, NJ: Erlbaum.

Allen, G. L., Kirasic, K. C., Siegel, A. W., & Herman, J. F. (1979). Developmental issues in cognitive mapping: The selection and utilization of environmental landmarks. *Child Development, 50,* 1062–1070.

Allen, G. L., Siegel, A. W., & Rosinski, R. R. (1978). The role of perceptual context in structuring spatial knowledge. *Journal of Experimental Psychology: Human Learning & Memory, 4,* 617–630.

Anooshian, L. J., & Young, D. (1981). Developmental changes in cognitive maps of a familiar neighborhood. *Child Development, 52,* 341–348.

Anooshian, L. J., & Siegel, A. W. (1985). From cognitive to procedural mapping. In C. J. Brainerd & M. Pressley (Eds.), *Basic processes in memory development*. New York: Springer-Verlag.

Attneave, F. (1972). Representation of physical space. In A. Melton & E. Martin (Eds.), *Coding processes in human memory*. New York: Winston.

Blaut, J. M., McCleary, G. F., & Blaut, A. S. (1970). Environmental mapping in young children. *Environment & Behavior, 2,* 335–349.

Bluestein, N., & Acredolo, L. P. (1979). Developmental changes in map-reading skills. *Child Development, 50,* 691–697.

Bremner, J. G. (1978). Egocentric versus allocentric spatial coding in nine-month-old infants: Factors influencing the choice of code. *Developmental Psychology, 14,* 346–355.

Cassirer, E. (1955). *The philosophy of symbolic forms: Vol. 2. Mythical thought*. New Haven: Yale University Press.

Cohen, R. (1982). The role of activity in the construction of spatial representations. In R. Cohen (Ed.), *New directions for child development: Children's conceptions of spatial relationships*. San Francisco: Jossey-Bass.

Cornell, E. H., & Heth, C. D. (1979). Response versus place learning by human infants. *Journal of Experimental Psychology: Human Learning & Memory, 5,* 188–196.

Davis, M., & Fucigna, C. (April, 1983). From drawing to mapping: Channeling symbolic activity. Paper presented in H. Gardner (Chair), *The development of early symbolic skills,* Symposium at the biennial meeting of the Society for Research in Child Development, Detroit.

DeLoache, J. (1984). *Rapid change in the representational capacity of very young children.* Paper presented at the meeting of the Psychonomic Society, San Antonio.

Evans, G., & Pezdek, K. (1980). Cognitive mapping: Knowledge of real-world distance and location information. *Journal of Experimental Psychology: Human Learning & Memory, 6,* 13–24.

Gardner, H. (1983). *Frames of mind.* New York: Basic Books.

Gardner, H., & Wolf, D. (1982). Waves and streams of symbolization: Notes on the development of symbolic capacities in young children. In D. Rogers & J. Sloboda (Eds.), *The acquisition of symbolic skills.* New York: Plenum.

Garling, T. (1980). *Environmental orientation during locomotion.* Stockholm: Swedish Council for Building Research.

Gibson, J. J. (1966). *The senses considered as perceptual systems.* Boston: Houghton Mifflin.

Gibson, James (1979). *The ecological approach to visual perception.* Boston: Houghton Mifflin.

Hardwick, D., McIntyre, C., & Pick, H. (1976). The content and manipulation of cognitive maps in children and adults. *Monographs of the Society for Research in Child Development, 41* (3, Serial No. 166).

Hart, R., & Moore, G. (1973). The development of spatial cognition: A review. In R. Downs & D. Stea (Eds.), *Image and environment: Cognitive mapping and spatial behavior.* Chicago: Aldine.

Hazen, N. L. (1982). Spatial exploration and spatial knowledge: Individual differences and developmental differences in very young children. *Child Development, 53,* 826–833.

Hazen, N. L. (1983). Spatial orientation: A comparative approach. In H. L. Pick, Jr., & L. P. Acredolo (Eds.), *Spatial orientation: Theory, research, and application.* New York: Plenum.

Herman, J. F., & Siegel, A. W. (1978). The development of cognitive mapping of the large scale environment. *Journal of Experimental Child Psychology, 26,* 389–406.

Hochberg, J., & Brooks, V. (1962). Pictorial recognition as an unlearned ability: A study of one child's performance. *American Journal of Psychology, 75,* 624–628.

Howard, I., & Templeton, W. (1966). *Human spatial orientation.* New York: Wiley.

Huttenlocher, J., & Presson, C. C. (1973). Mental rotation and the perspective problem. *Cognitive Psychology, 4,* 279–299.

Huttenlocher, J., & Presson, C. C. (1979). The coding and transformation of spatial information. *Cognitive Psychology, 11,* 375–394.

Ittelson, W. H. (1973). Environment perception and contemporary perceptual theory. In W. H. Ittelson (Ed.), *Environment and cognition.* New York: Seminar Press.

Janders, R. (1975). Ecological aspects of spatial orientation. *Annual Review of Ecology & Systematics, 6,* 171-181.

Just, M. A., & Carpenter, P. A. (1985). Cognitive coordinate systems: Accounts of mental rotation and individual differences in spatial ability. *Psychological Review, 92,* 137-172.

Joliecouer, P., & Kosslyn, S. (1983). Coordinate systems in the long-term memory representation of three-dimensional shapes. *Cognitive Psychology, 15,* 301-345.

Klein, W. (1983). Deixis and spatial orientation in route directions. In H. Pick & L. Acredolo (Eds.), *Spatial orientation: Theory, research, and application.* New York: Plenum.

Krebs, J. (1978). Optimal foraging: Decision rules for predators. In J. Krebs & N. Davies (Eds.), *Behavioral ecology: An evolutionary approach.* London: Blackwell.

Kuipers, K. (1982). The "map in the head" metaphor. *Environment & Behavior, 14,* 202-220.

Levine, M. (1982). YOU-ARE-HERE maps: Psychological considerations. *Environment & Behavior, 14,* 221-237.

Levine, M., Jankovic, I., & Palij, M. (1982). Principles of spatial problem solving. *Journal of Experimental Psychology: General, 111,* 157-175.

Liben, L., & Belknap, B. (1981). Intellectual realism: Implications for investigations of perspective-taking in young children. *Child Development, 52,* 921-924.

Liben, L. (1981). Spatial representation and behavior: Multiple perspectives. In L. Liben, A. Patterson, & N. Newcombe (Eds.), *Spatial representation and behavior across the lifespan.* New York: Academic.

Liben, L. (1982). Children's large-scale spatial cognition: Is the measure the message? In R. Cohen (Ed.), *New directions for child development: Children's conceptions of spatial relationships.* San Francisco: Jossey-Bass.

Mandler, J. M. (1983). Representation. In J. Flavell & E. Markman (Eds.), *Handbook of child psychology: Vol. 3. Cognitive development.* New York: Wiley.

McKenzie, B. E., Day, R. H., & Ihsen, E. (1984). Localization of events in space: Young infants are not always egocentric. *British Journal of Developmental Psychology, 2,* 1-9.

Menzel, E. (1973). Chimpanzee spatial memory organization. *Science, 192,* 943-945.

Menzel, E. (1978). Cognitive mapping in chimpanzees. In S. H. Hulse, H. Fowler, and W. K. Honig (Eds.), *Cognitive processes in animal behavior.* Hillsdale, NJ: Erlbaum.

Minsky, M. (1975). A framework for representing knowledge. In P. H. Winston (Ed.), *The psychology of computer vision.* New York: McGraw-Hill.

Navon, D. (1977). Forest before trees: The precedence of global features in visual perception. *Cognitive Psychology, 9,* 353-383.

Neisser, U. (1976). *Cognition and reality.* San Francisco: W. H. Freeman.

O'Keefe, J., & Nadel, L. (1978). *The hippocampus as cognitive map.* Oxford: Clarendon Press.

Olton, D. (1977). Spatial memory. *Scientific American, 236,* 82–98.

Olton, D. (1978). Characteristics of spatial memory. In S. H. Hulse, H. Fowler, & W. K. Honig (Eds.), *Cognitive processes in animal behavior.* Hillsdale, NJ: Erlbaum.

Palmer, S. (1980). What makes triangles point: Local and global effects in configurations of ambiguous triangles. *Cognitive Psychology, 12,* 285–305.

Peters, R. (1973). Cognitive maps in wolves and men. In W. P. Preiser (Ed.), *Environmental design research* (Vol. 2). Stroudsburg, PA: Dowden, Hutchinson, & Ross.

Piaget, J., & Inhelder, B. (1967). *The child's conception of space.* New York: Norton.

Pick, H. L., & Lockman, J. (1981). From frames of reference to spatial representation. In L. Liben, A. Patterson, & N. Newcombe (Eds.), *Spatial representation and behavior across the lifespan.* New York: Academic.

Pick, H. L., & Rieser, J. (1982). Children's cognitive mapping. In M. Potegal (Ed.), *Spatial abilities: Development and physiological foundations.* New York: Academic.

Potegal, M. (1982). Vestibular and neostriatal contributions to spatial orientation. In M. Potegal (Ed.), *Spatial abilities: Development and physiological foundations.* New York: Academic.

Premack, D., & Premack, A. J. (1983). *The mind of an ape.* New York: Norton.

Presson, C. (1980). Spatial egocentrism and the effect of an alternate frame of reference. *Journal of Experimental Child Psychology, 29,* 391–402.

Presson, C. (1982a). The development of map-reading skills. *Child Development, 53,* 196–199.

Presson, C. (1982b). Strategies in spatial reasoning. *Journal of Experimental Psychology: Learning, Memory, & Cognition, 8,* 243–251.

Presson, C., & Hazelrigg, M. (1984). Building spatial representations through primary and secondary learning. *Journal of Experimental Psychology: Learning, Memory, & Cognition, 10,* 716–722.

Presson, C., & Ihrig, L. (1982). Using mother as a spatial landmark: Evidence against egocentric coding in infancy. *Developmental Psychology, 18,* 699–703.

Presson, C., & Somerville, S. (1985). Beyond egocentrism: A new look at the beginnings of spatial representation. In H. Wellman (Ed.), *The development of children's spatial search.* Hillsdale, NJ: Erlbaum.

Pufall, P. (1975). Egocentrism in spatial thinking: It depends on your point of view. *Developmental Psychology, 11,* 297–303.

Rieser, J. (1979). Spatial orientation of six-month-old infants. *Child Development, 50,* 1078–1087.

Rieser, J. (1983). The generation and early development of spatial inferences. In H. Pick & L. Acredolo (Eds.), *Spatial orientation: Theory, research, and application.* New York: Plenum.

Robinson, A. H., & Petchenik, B. B. (1976). *The nature of maps.* Chicago: University of Chicago Press.

Rock, I. (1973). *Orientation and form.* New York: Academic.

Sandstrom, C. (1951). *Orientation in present space.* Upsala: Almqvist & Wiksell.

Schatzow, M., Kahane, D., & Youniss, J. (1980). The effects of movement on perspective taking and the coordination of perspectives. *Developmental Psychology, 16,* 582–587.

Shantz, C., & Watson, J. (1970). Spatial abilities and spatial egocentrism in the young child. *Child Development, 42,* 171–181.

Shemyakin, F. (1962). Orientation in space. In B. Ananyev, et al. (Eds.), *Psychological Science in the USSR.* Washington, DC: U.S. Office of Technical Reports (no. 11466), Vol. 1, Pt.1.

Shepard, R., & Cooper, L. (1982). *Mental images and their transformations.* Cambridge: M.I.T. Press.

Shepard, R., & Podgorny, P. (1978). Cognitive processes that resemble perceptual processes. In W. K. Estes (Ed.), *Handbook of learning and cognitive processes* (Vol. 5). Hillsdale, NJ: Erlbaum.

Siegel, A. (1981). The externalization of cognitive maps by children and adults: In search of ways to ask better questions. In L. Liben, A. Patterson, & N. Newcombe (Eds.), *Spatial representation and behavior across the lifespan.* New York: Academic.

Siegel, A., Kirasic, C., & Kail, R. (1978). Stalking the elusive cognitive map: The development of children's representations of geographic space. In J. Wohwill & I. Altman (Eds.), *Human behavior and environment: Children and the environment.* New York: Plenum.

Siegel, A., Herman, J., Allen, G., & Kirasic, C. (1979). The development of cognitive maps of large- and small-scale spaces. *Child Development, 50,* 582–585.

Siegel, A., & White, S. (1975). The development of spatial representation of large-scale environments. In H. Reese (Ed.), *Advances in child development and behavior* (Vol. 10). New York: Academic.

Smythe, M., & Kennedy, J. (1982). Orientation and spatial representation within multiple frames of reference. *British Journal of Psychology, 73,* 527–535.

Sophian, C. (1984). Developing search skills in infancy and early childhood. In C. Sophian (Ed.), *Origins of cognitive skills.* Hillsdale, NJ: Erlbaum.

Stevens, A., & Coupe, P. (1978). Distortions in judged spatial relations. *Cognitive Psychology, 10,* 422–437.

Thorndyke, P., & Hayes-Roth, B. (1982). Differences in spatial knowledge acquired from maps and navigation. *Cognitive Psychology, 14,* 560–581.

Thorndyke, P., & Stasz, C. (1980). Individual differences in procedures for knowledge acquisition from maps. *Cognitive Psychology, 12,* 137–175.

Tversky, B. (1981). Distortions in memory for maps. *Cognitive Psychology, 13,* 407–433.

Wellman, H., & Somerville, S. (1982). The development of human search ability. In M. Lamb & A. Brown (Eds.), *Advances in developmental psychology* (Vol. 2). Hillsdale, NJ: Erlbaum.

Werner, H., & Kaplan, B. (1963). *Symbol formation.* New York: Wiley.

CHAPTER 5

Where It Is and Where It Isn't: Children's Use of Possibilities and Probabilities to Guide Search

SUSAN C. SOMERVILLE
Arizona State University

HENRY M. WELLMAN
University of Michigan

We deal with two distinct but intertwined notions in this chapter. Both are fundamental to human cognition, and we argue that there are important connections between them in the course of development.

The first is the notion of searching for missing or hidden objects, the importance of which is obvious in our daily activities. We live in a three-dimensional world of objects in space. The things we need are seldom immediately at hand and so we invest considerable effort in searching for them or arranging circumstances ahead of time to reduce the searching.

The second notion is that of possibility. For our purposes, something is possible if both it might be so and it might not be so. For example, if, given the evidence available at the moment, *X* might occur or it might not, then *X* is only one possibility among others. Some event is possible, rather than certain or necessary, if it is one member of a set of mutually exclusive events or possibilities: The set might be simply *X* and not-*X*; or it might be *X* and *Y* and *Z*.

The ability to consider sets of possibilities has traditionally been thought of as a cornerstone of mature cognition (e.g., Inhelder & Piaget, 1958; Neimark & Lewis, 1967). It is also part and parcel of other fundamental notions such as choice, probability, chance, and necessity. A distinction can be made between considering sets of possibilities that are mutually exclusive, each one conceivably being true, and considering possibilities of a purely hypothetical

Preparation of this chapter was supported by NIH Grant HD 13317–06 to the authors. The authors are grateful to Joan Cultice for her help in conducting experiments, to Catherine Sophian for her collaboration, and to Clark Presson for his comments on an earlier version of this chapter.

nature, whose truth is not at issue. Both kinds of activities have been found to be important in the development of reasoning skills (e.g., Eimas, 1970; Inhelder & Piaget, 1958). However, in this chapter we will be concerned only with the first kind in which someone is considering more than one tangible possibility.

Considering a set of mutually exclusive, realizable possibilities is essential to everyday decision making, for example, to the task of choosing between several career paths. It is also essential to making inferences when information must be pieced together to reach one of several possible conclusions. Finally, it is essential to everyday as well as scientific theorizing, in the course of which competing predictions or explanations must be evaluated. As these examples suggest, entertaining different possibilities lies at the heart of processes that involve logical reasoning. Although this has been reflected in studies that have examined reasoning in middle childhood and adolescence, on the whole it has not been reflected in studies of the early emergence of logical skills (e.g., Adams, 1978; Bryant & Trabasso, 1971; Kuhn, 1977; Shultz, 1982), a notable exception being the work of Pieraut-Le Bonniec (1980). A central claim of our chapter is that preschoolers' logical reasoning is even more impressive than much of the recent research has suggested because it includes a nascent ability to consider possibilities.

The two notions of search and possibility are intimately interconnected. For example, in searching for objects one may need to examine several locations because each may possibly, but does not necessarily, contain the object. Our discussion depends on this interconnection. By examining children's developing ability to search for objects we propose to uncover developmental changes in their ability to conceive of and reason about possibilities.

SEARCH

Studying the ways that children search for and retrieve hidden objects has revealed information about three aspects of their cognition (Wellman, 1985a): spatial knowledge, strategic knowledge, and logical knowledge.

With regard to spatial knowledge, *if* a child consistently searches for objects, this suggests that he or she understands that they exist independently in space (Piaget, 1954). *Where* the child searches sheds light on how an object's perceived spatial position is represented, whether in terms of an egocentric or allocentric system of reference (e.g., Acredolo, 1979; Bremner & Bryant, 1977; Pick & Lockman, 1981; Presson & Somerville, 1985). With regard to strategic knowledge, children develop strategies that are tailored to different situations, for example, strategies for searching an array of locations either comprehensively or selectively (Wellman & Somerville, 1982). The study of searching also has revealed much about the child's more general strategies for solving problems (Wellman, 1985a).

The third type of knowledge, logical knowledge about where an object could and could not be, is the type most closely related to our concern with notions of possibility. By *logical knowledge* we mean the ability to solve problems in which two complementary reasoning processes are involved: the drawing of inferences and the consideration of more than one logical possibility.

Inferences about where to search must be drawn whenever there is no direct information about the location of an object, as is the case, for example, in the invisible displacement procedures used by Piaget (1954). However, indirect information can be specific to different degrees, and our concern is with situations where even the most logical of inferences will not lead to a conclusion that the object must be in one and only one place. This means that both before and after drawing an inference the searcher must generate or keep in mind a number of possibilities. Situations like this include, for example, problems that have been said to involve a critical search area consisting of more than one location (Drozdal & Flavell, 1975). These problems mimic the unpleasant everyday circumstance in which something becomes unexpectedly lost in the course of a journey. The critical area consists of places visited after the object is last seen up until the point where its absence is noticed. To solve such a problem without retracing the whole journey, the searcher must make an inference that rules out places where the object could not be and retains all those where it might be (i.e., those in the critical area).

In a variety of situations of this kind young children have been found to concentrate their searches in the critical area and to avoid locations visited before the object was last seen or after it was discovered missing (Anooshian, Hartman, & Scharf, 1982; Anooshian, Pascal, & McCreath, 1984; Haake, Somerville, & Wellman, 1980; Somerville & Capuani-Shumaker, 1984; Wellman, Somerville, & Haake, 1979). An intriguing aspect of young children's success on these tasks is that it seems to reflect some consideration of a number of search possibilities: The critical areas comprised two, three, or four locations in these studies. This aspect of the children's success is all the more striking because previous studies of reasoning about possibilities have dealt with much older children (e.g., Eimas, 1970; Inhelder & Piaget, 1958; Neimark & Lewis, 1967), and there has been an implicit assumption that young children are not inclined to consider multiple possibilities or to find ways of using evidence to decide between them. We propose to challenge this assumption, suggesting that a rudimentary ability of this kind can be found in preschoolers.

LOGIC AND POSSIBILITY

We begin by noting that from Piaget's (Inhelder & Piaget, 1958, 1964) point of view our proposal must be considered an unlikely one. He contended that notions of possibility and the ability to reason logically are completely outside the grasp of preschoolers. However, in his discussion Piaget did claim that the ability to use logical, scientific reasoning and the ability to conceive of possibilities go hand in hand. This part of his theory is consistent with our view of the connection between logical search and possibility.

Piaget

In Piaget's account (Inhelder & Piaget, 1958, 1964), it is presumed that any logical system specifies a set of statements that can be made and also specifies rules for combining statements to arrive at others. The statements may be propositions to which, for example, the rules of binary logic apply; or statements of asymmetrical relations, obeying transitive inferential rules; or statements of relations between classes, and so forth. In each case, the logical system is formal and abstract, having a structure that is independent of any specific statements or notions about the real world. Young children do not make inferences that could be said to stem from an understanding of such systems, reasoning instead on the basis of past experience or of idiosyncratic connections between particular instances. One aspect of their nonlogical reasoning is that, being focused on actual particulars, it does not take into account possibilities that do not happen to occur.

According to Piaget, the first kinds of logical reasoning appear in the stage of concrete operations, at the age of 7 or 8 years, when the child organizes his or her operations for classifying, ordering, and enumerating objects into coherent structures that have a semilogical form. However, these operations are derived from and in a sense limited to what has been or might be encountered in the real world. Inhelder and Piaget (1958) described the child's thought in this stage as "characterized by an extension of the *actual* in the direction of the *potential*" (p. 248, Inhelder and Piaget's emphasis). However, they insisted that this does not amount to an ability to consider hypothetical possibilities, arguing that, for the concrete operational child, "the role of *possibility* is reduced to a simple potential prolongation of the actions or operations applied to a given content" (p. 249).

In Inhelder and Piaget's view, it is only with the attainment of formal operational thinking, at 11–12 years of age, that the child considers hypothetical possibilities and can entertain notions of what might be the case that do not derive from empirical observations. "*Possibility* no longer appears merely as an extension of an empirical situation or of actions actually performed. Instead it is *reality* that is now secondary to *possibility*" (1958, p. 251, Inhelder and Piaget's emphasis). The changes in thinking that take place in early adolescence involve a dramatic change in the child's approach to discovering lawful relationships: Now "the given facts . . . are neither explained nor even regarded as facts until the subject undertakes verifying procedures that pertain to the entire set of possible hypotheses compatible with a given situation" (p. 251). Thus for Inhelder and Piaget (1958) the consideration of possibilities arises in connection with hypotheticodeductive reasoning and is part of a qualitative shift in the child's thinking that can be discerned in early adolescence.

In contrast with this view, our hypothesis is that the early logical skills of preschoolers embody a crucial ability to consider multiple possibilities. There are two main reasons for our contrary hypothesis. The first is an objection to Piaget's focus on abstract, formal logic to the exclusion of other more everyday forms of reasoning. There are many practical situations in which it is important to evaluate possibilities. It has long been recognized that such notions as necessity and consistency, certainty and uncertainty, possibility and impossibility, reticence, presupposition, certain knowledge, and true belief all play an important part in natural thought and in what is communicated in everyday language. Theoretical notions of this kind (frequently referred to as modal notions) have arisen because of an interest in the relations between thought, language, and the knowledge of truth. Philosophers since the time of Aristotle and more recently linguists have developed systems to describe these notions (Pieraut-Le Bonniec, 1980). However, our ability to examine what we think, say, and know, and to understand the relationship of these cognitive activities to what may or what must be true, is an ability that has received little attention from developmental psychologists.

Our second reason for thinking that young children have abilities of this sort is an empirical one. Children of preschool age give everyday indications that they are aware of uncertainties, possibilities, and the like, for example, when they use expressions such as "I think that I know," or "She might be in here, or she might be in there." And as we will see our studies of logical search skills show that young children can solve practical problems involving multiple possibilities, at least in some circumstances.

Whether or not young children are able to reason about possibilities is an important issue. If they are, this means that there is more continuity in the development of logical reasoning than, for example, Inhelder and Piaget's (1958) account would imply. And if logical skills of this kind are available to children at an early age, they must affect their thinking and acquisition of other sorts of knowledge. So the central question we consider is: Can young children deal with multiple possibilities?

CONSIDERING POSSIBILITIES IN LOGICAL SEARCH TASKS

Initial Studies

In the initial studies of critical area search skills (Anooshian et al., 1982; Anooshian et al., 1984; Haake et al., 1980; Wellman et al., 1979), the critical area consisted of three or four widely spaced locations in an indoor or outdoor preschool environment. Each child participated in a sequence of events in which an object that was initially being carried along was later discovered missing. The critical area was the subset of locations extending from the last place that the object was present to the first place it was known to be missing. The findings were that children 3–9 years of age chose to search in the correct subset of locations at levels substantially greater than would be expected by chance.

These studies demonstrate that young children can arrive logically at a place where the object may be, inferred from events surrounding its invisible movements. They do not, however, demonstrate that these children consider that the unfound object could equally well be in any one of *several* locations. The critical areas in these studies did comprise several locations, and children were much more likely to search those areas than elsewhere, but they may have done so believing (at any given moment) that the object was in a *single* location. A conception of where the object might be that involved only one (logically derived) location at a time could account for the fact that children's first searches were in the critical area. In addition, such a conception coupled with mere search persistence could account for the fact that many of their second searches were also correct. The child could search persistently in the critical area by inferring first that the object was in a single (critical) location and then, upon discovering that it was not there, searching again (and again) on the basis of further inferences or other rules. Persistent logical searching (rather than extended searching guided all along by considering multiple possibilities) may account for preschoolers' performance in the original critical area studies for two reasons.

First, in the only one of these early studies with sufficient numbers of children to analyze extended search sequences in detail (Wellman et al., 1979), children's first searches were typically at the place where they had last seen the item. Persistence beyond this first search, by simply repeating the earlier sequence of movements from this place onward (see Somerville & Haake, 1985), would have ensured that the children's second searches were in the critical area as well. Second, the youngest children in this study, 3-year-olds, showed a tendency to search repeatedly at a single location. This suggests that some children at least were quite literally conceiving of the object as being in just a single (logically derived) hiding place and not in one of several possible places. In short, we are left with at least two plausible interpretations of children's logical behavior: (1) that it is based on entertaining several possibilities; or (2) that it is based on an initial derivation of just a single place for the object to be (coupled with some form of search persistence in the face of failure to find the object).

Current Research

One step toward deciding between these interpretations is to obtain more extensive evidence about children's searches beyond the first one. Somerville and Capuani-Shumaker (1984) did this using problems that were laboratory analogues of the naturalistic situations. A set of different problems, each one defining a critical area comprising two locations, was given to each child. To rule out the possibility of success through persistent repetition of movements, there were two types of sequences: in one type (*hiding* sequences) children could cover the critical area by noting where the object was last seen and then repeating the sequence of movements used earlier by the experimenter from that point on, but in the other type (*finding* sequences) they could not. The hiding sequences represented the traditional situation: An object was moved invisibly between several places and was seen to be still present at one (or two) early point, then absent at two (or one) later points (see Fig. 5.1). Specifically, an object was first shown to the child, then enclosed in a hand, and in the

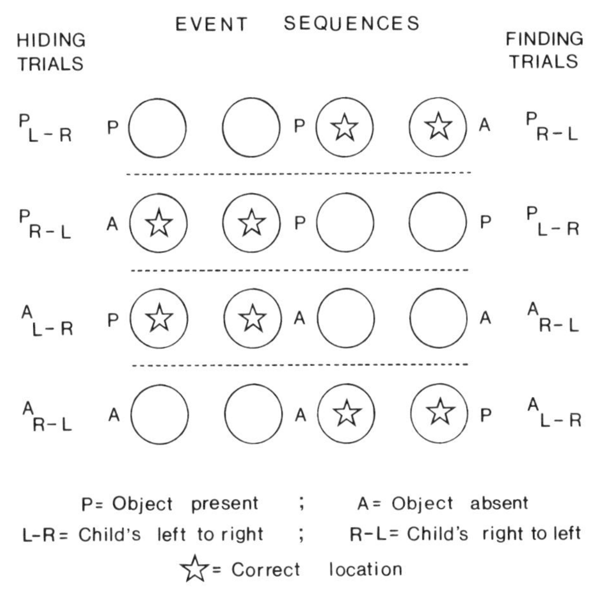

Figure 5.1. Sequences of events in the hiding and finding tasks in Somerville and Capuani-Shumaker's (1984) study. (Reprinted from the *British Journal of Developmental Psychology, 2,* p. 318.)

course of a sequence of movements hidden invisibly by being placed under one of a number of cloths without the child seeing this displacement directly. The displacement could, however, be inferred from the fact that the hand no longer contained the object after emerging from under some of the cloths. The finding sequences were essentially the reverse of the hiding ones. The hand did not initially contain an object, but after being closed and passed under some cloths it did, the implication being that the object must have been found under one of them. The child's task in this case was to look for a duplicate of the object that had been found, on the understanding that two objects were always concealed in exactly the same place and that the experimenter always removed only one.

The hiding and finding sequences in this study all involved a total of four locations and were all such that two of the four locations possibly contained the toy that the child had to find, whereas the other two definitely did not. The child could be certain about the elimination of two locations but could not be certain which of the two that remained contained the toy. In other words, there were two equally likely possibilities that should be kept in mind. Did young children understand this?

Children 3–5 years old showed little evidence that they did recognize the two possibilities. Their first choices were correct at levels significantly above chance in both the hiding and the finding sequences, that is, were in the critical search area. This corroborates the earlier evidence that young children reason logically from the information given. However, on the occasions when their first choice, although logical, did not locate the object, the children were at a loss as to where to go next.

However, there are reasons to believe that this evidence of not considering more than one possibility underestimates young children's ability. Specifically, there are at least two other explanations for the children's unsuccessful second searches. First, memory demands may have contributed to their failures. The children may have conceived of both critical locations as possible before choosing one but then have forgotten the second possibility by the time a second search was required. Second, because all of the four locations were visited in any given sequence, some of the hiding and some of the finding sequences ended with redundant repetitions of previous events (see Fig. 5.1: the final events in the top two finding trials and the bottom two hiding trials). For example, the child sometimes knew that the object had been hidden midway through the sequence and gained no new information about where it was after that. These were the sequences in which children did less well, even in making a *first* choice of where to search, and it seems possible this was due to the difficulty of processing superfluous information. On the other hand, it is also conceivable that these young children were genuinely unable to understand that there were two indistinguishable logical possibilities, and that they tended to use various strategies in order to arrive at what they thought of as a necessarily correct location for the object.

Somerville and Sophian (1984) set out to evaluate these differing interpretations of children's second search failures, in a study of 4½-year-olds. First, in order to reduce memory problems they devised procedures in which children could choose two places to search before finding out whether either choice was correct. Second, by visiting only two instead of all four locations they eliminated the redundancy problem referred to earlier, and at the same time they were able to avoid the problem of introducing (in an uncounterbalanced way) locations that were unvisited and that were never correct. This was done using sequences (illustrated in Fig. 5.2) in half of which the visited and half the unvisited locations were correct.

For every sequence of events used in this study there was something hidden in one location within an array of four, out of the child's view, before the sequence began.* The experimenter always began at one end of the array of

*Full details of the event sequences and procedures can be obtained from the first author. The procedures for the finding condition were essentially the same as in the Somerville and Capuani-Shumaker (1984) study except that the sequences stopped after two locations had been visited (see Fig. 5.2). However, the hiding condition differed from its counterpart in the previous study. In the new procedure, one toy (a fictional character such as Minnie Mouse) was already hidden and the experimenter's role was to take a second character to look for the first one. The child was told that the two characters wanted to hide together in the same place, so that if the second one came to the place where the first was hiding he or she would hide there too, but if not then the second one would stay in the experimenter's hand. The two kinds of sequences were (1) ones in which the second toy was gone from the hand after visits to two locations, implying that both toys were now in one or the other of the visited places, and (2) ones in which the second toy was still in the hand after two visits, implying that the first toy was in one or the other of the unvisited places.

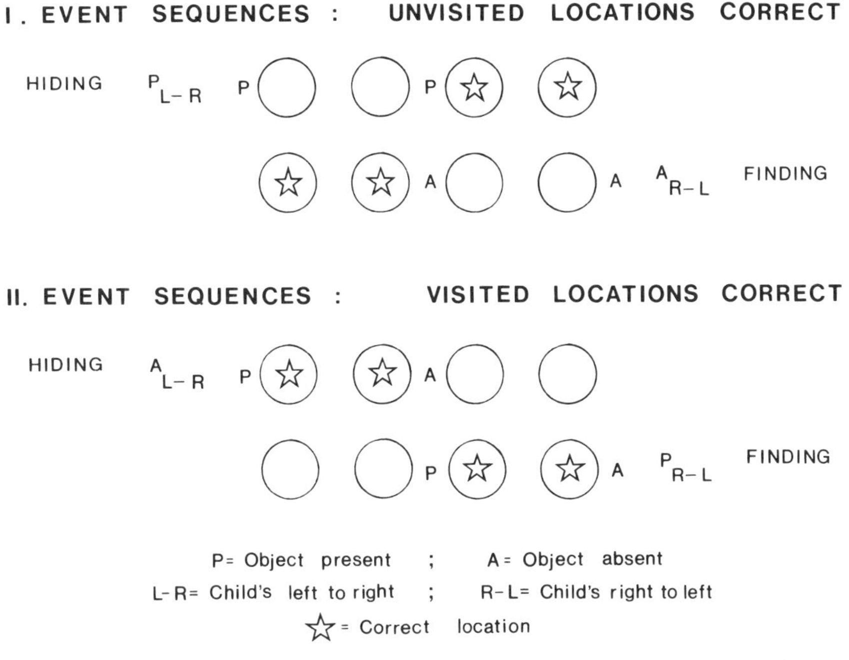

Figure 5.2. Illustrative sequences of events in the hiding and finding tasks in Somerville and Sophian's (1984) study. For convenience, hiding sequences are shown left to right, finding sequences right to left, but in practice each type of sequence was conducted half of the time in each direction.

four locations and showed the child whether or not there was an object (a miniature cartoon character) in her hand after visiting two adjacent ones (i.e., in the center of the array). The child's task was to work out both of the possible places where a toy or toys might be hiding. This method of prior choosing was achieved by using as hiding places a row of four cups, suspended above the table in a rack that could be tilted so that the contents of all four cups would tumble out at the same time. The child was asked to place two cushions, consecutively, on the table, one under each of the places where the toy(s) might fall.

Under the conditions of this experiment, in which the child was left in no doubt that more than one place should be chosen, in which both choices could be made before knowing whether either was correct, and in which the sequence of events ceased as soon as there was sufficient information to choose between two halves of the array, it was initially surprising that children still did not seem to reveal a conception of multiple possibilities in their second choices.**

**Sixteen 4½-year-olds were given eight hiding and eight finding trials each. They were consistently accurate in their first choices. In the hiding and finding conditions, respectively, 12 and 11 children made significantly more correct first choices (i.e., 7 or 8) than would be expected by chance (binomial theorem, $p < .05$). The overall proportions of correct first choices were .87

However, the children's apparent lack of success in this regard is not so surprising when we see that it was accounted for largely by the occurrence of one particular type of error. Essentially, children were sensitive to multiple possibilities when considering the location of an event that had yet to occur, but not when considering an event that had occurred by the time the sequence ended. For example, in a finding sequence, if the experimenter had *not* found a toy by the time she had searched two locations and arrived at the middle of the array, the children understood that either of the remaining two might contain it. If, on the other hand, a toy *had* been found before the middle point, they were less able to understand that it might have been found in either one of the two visited places. We can see this in two kinds of analyses. First, if we disregard whether the child's first choice was correct or not and simply examine the numbers of correct second choices, a clear pattern emerges. When the two *unvisited* locations were correct (i.e., in hiding, the experimenter had not hidden the toy that was initially in her hand; in finding, she had not found a toy by the time the sequence ended), the children's second choices were correct on 77% of trials, on average. By contrast, when the *visited* locations were correct the children were correct on only 35% of trials.*

Secondly, we can consider just the second choices that followed a correct first choice, on the grounds that in these instances we have reason to believe that the child interpreted the sequence of events appropriately, up to a point. The question is whether children who can follow the implications of the events are able to understand that the information they have does not specify a single correct location (although, at the same time, they know that only one contains the toy). Second choices following a first correct one at an endpoint of the array are not really informative: They were correct on 84 percent of trials overall, but this may have been due to a tendency always to move to the location adjacent to the endpoint chosen first. When the first correct search was at an inner location, however, there was the same clear pattern of second

---

and .81 for the hiding and finding conditions, respectively, compared with .80 and .74 for 4½-year-olds in the corresponding conditions of the study by Somerville and Capuani-Shumaker (1984).

When a second search was necessary (because the first correct search failed to locate the object) Somerville and Sophian's 4½-year-olds chose correctly on .84 of occasions following a first correct search at an endpoint (.83 for hiding, .85 for finding), but on only .49 of occasions following a first correct search at an inner location (.55 for hiding, .42 for finding). These figures are roughly comparable with those for the 4½-year-olds in the earlier study, whose second choices were correct on .97 of occasions when the first was at an endpoint (.94 for hiding, 1.00 for finding), but on only .61 of occasions when the first was at an inner location (.58 for hiding, .63 for finding). In both studies the high success rates following endpoint searches can be disregarded, since children tended to search adjacently to an endpoint search whether or not that first endpoint search was correct.

*A 2 (condition: hiding vs. finding) × 2 (type of sequence: visited correct vs. unvisited correct) × 16 (subjects) analysis of variance conducted on the numbers of correct second choices showed that there was a significant effect of the type of sequence ($F(1,15) = 54.90$; $p < .001$), but no effect of condition and no interaction between condition and the type of sequence.

choices as when we considered second searches overall. Again the vast majority of errors in these choices occurred when the visited locations were correct.

Further, the exact pattern of first and (erroneous) second choices that the children made* showed that they were incorrectly ruling out a particular one of the two possibilities when the correct location lay among the two visited ones. The one that they tended to rule out was the location that the experimenter had visited first. It was as if they could assume that she would not continue on to a second location if she had already hidden or found a toy at the first one. This is in many ways a reasonable assumption. In many hiding and retrieval games that young children play, a sequence of actions may conventionally be stopped as soon as the goal has been accomplished. But it is important to realize that this convention does not hold for these experimental procedures and it is not the case that all hiding and finding games that are played with young children share this convention. In fact the children did not see inside the experimenter's hand between the first and second locations, so it was perfectly possible for the hiding or finding to have occurred at the first one. What is remarkable is that children essentially ignored or overruled this possibility and, when asked to choose a second location, chose one in which the toy could not conceivably have been hidden, given the sequence of events. It is equally remarkable, however, that children at this young age did consider both possibilities in other types of sequences.

Our interpretation of these findings is that young children have more difficulty accepting that they have uncertain knowledge about the location of an event when that event is known to have occurred than when they are still waiting for it to occur. If someone has already hidden or found a toy, albeit out of their direct view, they know full well that the hiding or finding did occur at *one* place, not several. Given this, they fail to realize that although the object is in one place their own knowledge of where it is must include two possible places. Under these circumstances they are inclined to make use of whatever conventions or notions are available in order to arrive at a specific conclusion, so much so, in fact, that they will make erroneous second choices that they would not make under other conditions.

By contrast, when young children have to consider instead an event that might happen but has not happened yet, they are able to treat the remaining possibilities as equally likely. They are also able to accept, ahead of time, the

*In the hiding (finding) condition, children made a total of 40 (44) errors in their second choices following a correct choice at an inner location. Thirty-four (i.e., .85) of the errors in hiding (37, i.e., .84 in finding) were made when the visited locations were correct and 27 of those 34 hiding errors (30 of 37 finding errors) consisted of choosing the other (incorrect) inner location instead of the correct end location. By contrast, following a first correct inner choice when the two unvisited locations were correct, a second (incorrect) choice of the other inner location occurred only 6 times in the hiding condition and 7 times in the finding condition. In these circumstances it was the correct end location that was chosen most often: 30 out of 36 times in hiding, 26 out of 34 times in finding.

fact that their own knowledge of where an event is about to occur is not completely specific. This is shown by the fact that the children's choices of a second location were quite accurate when the *unvisited* locations were correct.

This interpretation of the results of Somerville and Sophian's (1984) study suggests some possible early steps in children's understanding of uncertainty. Specifically, it suggests a developmental progression from a younger child, who knows before a hiding occurs that there are several places to which the object might go, to an older child, who knows *after* a hiding occurs that, whereas the object has to be in just one place, there are several possibilities. (Note that for simplicity here and elsewhere we are using *hiding* to refer to the crucial event of either depositing or retrieving an object in the hiding and finding procedures, respectively.) The 4-year-olds in Somerville and Sophian's (1984) study showed some legitimate understanding of possibilities (of the first sort) but not a complete understanding (of the second sort).

The interpretations we are suggesting for Somerville and Sophian's (1984) results, although intriguing, are in need of further confirmation. Sophian and Somerville (1985) conducted two subsequent studies that modified and extended the previous procedures in several ways. First, they added a group of older children (6-year-olds) to find out whether they would succeed in considering multiple possibilities in this type of task. Second, to avoid a possible bias toward choosing inner locations induced by the hand's movements, they conducted only half of the sequences from an endpoint to the center of the array (as in Somerville & Sophian's study), the other half from the center to an endpoint. Finally, they included in the warm-up procedures an explicit explanation and demonstration of the somewhat unconventional aspect of the procedures when the visited locations were correct (referred to earlier). Specifically, the child was shown that (in hiding) when the experimenter hid a toy in the first location she visited she would continue on to visit a second location (with her empty hand closed) before showing the child that the toy was gone. Similarly (in finding), when she found a toy in the first visited location she would continue with it concealed in her hand while visiting a second one. This warm-up might help the child overcome, in part, a tendency to decide on these trials that the location visited last must contain the object.

The older children, as expected, made very few errors in this study, and several of them made statements expressing the mixture of certainty and uncertainty in their conclusions about where the object(s) could and could not be, for instance, "I know it isn't in those [indicating the two places that could be eliminated], but I don't know which one of these it's in [indicating the other two places]." Furthermore, many of the 6-year-olds (but no 4-year-olds) volunteered the assessment that these problems were too easy for them, an assessment that is borne out by the fact that altogether the 6-year-olds made only 7 errors in their 256 first choices and only 21 errors in their 256 second choices.

The 4-year-olds also did well in this study, in both their first and second choices. They made only 15 errors in their 256 first choices and, more importantly, only 51 errors in their 256 second choices. Their overall proportion of correct second searches (.82 for hiding, .78 for finding) was much higher than that of 4½-year-olds in any previous study (e.g., .59 for hiding, .52 for finding in the study by Somerville & Sophian, 1984). We can conclude that the precautions that Sophian and Somerville (1985) took to simplify and clarify the task for the young children did help. Their results provide clear evidence that 4½-year-olds do consider more than one possibility. The results also show that by 6 years of age children can be reasonably explicit about the issue of certainty and uncertainty in their knowledge, an issue whose implications for searching they clearly understand.

These studies evolved from the initial naturalistic studies of logical search in an attempt to pin down more clearly whether young children are considering more than one possibility when they engage in this type of search. The conclusions that have emerged are at the same time less clear-cut and more intriguing than we imagined at the outset. The first is that 4-year-olds can consider more than one possibility, but for the most part only when it concerns the location of an event about to take place. Children who are 6 years old, on the other hand, understand that they may have uncertain knowledge about the location of an event that has already occurred just as much as about an event that has not yet occurred. In other words, the older but not the younger children seem able to separate the uncertainty in their knowledge from the uncertainty of the event itself.

The combined information from all of these studies shows that preschool children understand quite a bit about the possible places for an object to be. However, these same children have a tendency to disregard possibilities and instead to decide prematurely on a single place for the object to be if it has already been hidden. In the studies we have reviewed, children's conceptions of this sort were revealed by careful examination of their search behavior. However, the same conclusion is suggested by other research as well.

Other Studies

The first studies to consider are those that deal with children's understanding of their own mental states as revealed in their use of mental verbs. Our interest is specifically in their appreciation of the difference between knowing necessarily and only guessing (i.e., knowing possibly); thus the relevant investigations are those focusing on their understanding of the distinction between the verbs *know* and *guess*. Suppose an object is hidden and after the hiding but before it is found I choose one of a set of locations as the place where I think it is. I may know that the chosen location is necessarily the correct place—if, for example, I saw it hidden there—or I may know that it is only one of a number of possible places—if, for example, I did not see the hiding. In the former case I could say that I *know* where the object is, but in the latter case I should say something less definite, such as "I *think* it's there," or "I *guess* it's there."

Studies by Miscione, Marvin, O'Brien, and Greenberg (1978) and Johnson and Wellman (1980) have both shown that even 4-year-olds tend to say that they *know* where the item is if they have seen where it was placed, but are more likely to say that they are *guessing* where it is if they did not see this. Their findings corroborate the notion that young children are sensitive to the uncertainty that results when there are several possible places as opposed to a single necessary place for an object to be.

The same studies, however, suggest again that children at this age tend at times to think of the object's location as a single necessary place rather than as one of several possible places. At this point we need to distinguish three phases of a search task: (1) before the object is hidden; (2) after it is hidden but before it is found; and (3) after it is found. Suppose the child does not see the object hidden, but then is required to choose one of the locations as his or her guess, and then is shown that the guess was indeed correct. In this case, in which the child must evaluate the event and his or her state after the finding, he or she is likely to claim to have *known* where it was rather than to have guessed (correctly) (Johnson & Wellman, 1980; Miscione et al., 1978). Having happened (fortuitously) upon the place the object does occupy, the young child judges that the object could only have been there. *After the fact,* the child thinks of the possibility that turns out to be an actuality as being necessarily correct.

Additional evidence of young children's ability to think of several possibilities coupled with a tendency to think, after the fact, of possible events as necessary ones comes from children's use of hypothetical references—their ability to talk about possible or hypothetical events as opposed to actual ones (Cromer, 1974; Kuczaj, 1981; Kuczaj & Daly, 1979). References to hypothetical events are made from the age of about 3 years on but they appear first in connection with future events. Talking about hypothetical (nonactual) past events—what might have been—occurs very rarely throughout the preschool years. An inability to conceive of past, completed, known events as anything other than necessary (e.g., as only one of many possibilities) characterizes the preschool child, who nevertheless can think of unknown and future events in terms of multiple possibilities.

Summary

The central point of our discussion is that the young child's "unjustified" judgments and choices occur in particular circumstances. When children know either by inference (before they search) or by visual evidence (after the fact) that an object's place has been determined, the likelihood is that they will decide that the object is necessarily (or must necessarily have been) in some one place rather than, more appropriately, in an unknown one of several possibilities. Four-year-olds at times consider multiple possibilities but at other times draw conclusions to which they unjustifiably attach certainty. They are struggling with what it is to be *definitely uncertain.*

We can conclude from these studies that preschool children experience uncertainty and doubt. This is especially clear when the event in question is something that has not yet happened and also when the child is simply confused. In these circumstances the child knows that he or she doesn't know or that his or her conclusions are not clear-cut. The same child is just coming to grips, however, with a different sort of uncertainty; not uncertainty resulting from vague thinking or unforeseeable outcomes, but uncertainty resulting instead from perfectly precise thinking that leaves open several logical possibilities. It is as if the young child thinks that because the event is definite he or she can be definite, without understanding that a definite event combined with perfectly accurate reasoning can yield as its outcome several possibilities—that is, can yield definite *un*certainty. By 6 years of age children are quite competent to deal with this sort of undecidability, marking the culmination of an elementary knowledge of possibilities. This is an impressive achievement on their part. But it should also be acknowledged that throughout the preschool years children do entertain possibilities, albeit in a less accomplished and consolidated fashion. Their more limited ability is no small matter either.

TOWARD AN EXTENDED DEVELOPMENTAL DESCRIPTION

We have concentrated our discussion to this point on the preschool child, who seems to us to have a rudimentary grasp of possibilities. If our claim is correct it means that notions of possibility play a more important role in the young child's thinking than has been recognized in the past, and it also suggests that a more formal understanding of possibility may be acquired step by step rather than resulting from an abrupt change in adolescence. If the idea of a gradual, extended course of development in these notions is correct, it should be possible to sketch in more of the steps involved. We will do this looking first backward from the preschool years toward infancy and then forward from preschoolers to children who are older still.

Infants and Toddlers

Our claim that 4-year-olds have some understanding of possibilities raises the question of whether even younger children and infants might have such an understanding as well. The evidence seems to be, on the contrary, that infants and toddlers up to the age of about 2 years fail to conceive of several possible locations for an object to be, at least in search tasks of the sort we are considering.

Let us examine first what happens when infants are given tasks involving invisible displacements. The child watches as an object is hidden in the experimenter's hand and then sees the closed hand travel to several locations in succession. Then he or she is shown that the object is no longer in the hand. At an early age, about 9 months, infants will not search the containers at the various locations at all. Instead they search only in the experimenter's hand

(Piaget, 1954). This, of course, suggests that they only entertain a single possibility for the object's position.

Somewhat later, infants search the containers as well and even begin to do so systematically, in sequence. This systematic searching might be taken to suggest that the infant represents the object's invisible movements and thinks it may be in any of the relevant (possible) places. He or she then proceeds to examine them in turn. However, Bertenthal and Fischer (1983) have shown that systematic searches of this sort, at least on the part of infants 12–24 months old, can be accounted for by assuming that the infants search first at a single salient (end) location and only continue for reasons of persistence. Having failed to find the object initially, they simply try again. So it is distinctly possible that there is an age at which extended searches are based on sequences of single-location conceptions of where the object is.

In addition, Haake and Somerville (1985) have given infants 9–18 months old simplified versions of some of the critical area search tasks discussed earlier (Somerville & Capuani-Shumaker, 1984; Somerville & Sophian, 1984; Sophian & Somerville, 1985). Their tasks involved only two locations, one of which was the correct (or critical) place to search on a given trial. They found that 18-month-olds and, to a lesser extent, even 15-month-olds were able to search logically, meaning that they could infer the hidden object's location by simply viewing a sequence of object-present and object-absent events. However, it was apparently crucial to their success that the inference to be made always specified a *single* correct location. When Somerville and Haake (1985) gave a hiding task involving four locations to 2-year-old children they found that these children completely failed to infer the critical area. The task that they used was the same as the two-location task on which Haake and Somerville's (1985) infants succeeded, except that there were four locations altogether, two of which constituted the critical search area. It is at least suggestive of an early inability to consider multiple possibilities that infants solve the task requiring an inference of a single specific location, whereas the same task requiring an inference of two possible locations is not solved until 3–4 years of age.

In short, we believe there is preliminary evidence that infants and perhaps toddlers are constrained to thinking that a missing object is in a single location that can be specified. Theirs is quite a reasonable view since, in point of fact, a single object can only occupy a single position at any given time. At an early age the child's understanding of this fact may be a hindrance to thinking of multiple possible locations (as opposed to a single unique place) as a "description" of where the object must be. Somewhat older children, of preschool age, have a beginning grasp of sets of indistinguishable possibilities.

Children of School Age

The evidence from critical area search studies indicates that children by 6 years of age are quite adept at bearing in mind a number of possible locations for an object. Recall that Sophian and Somerville's (1985) 6-year-olds rarely erred in pointing out two equally plausible locations. So by the early school years children grasp the notion of possible rather than necessary places for an object to be.

At this point a further problem may confront the child, that of degrees of possibility, perhaps best expressed in terms of probabilities. Having mastered the distinction between what is possible and what is necessarily so, the question arises as to the extent of the possibility. The realm of possibilities includes those things that are very likely as well as those that are only moderately likely and those that are quite unlikely. Our hypothesis is that the older preschooler knows what it is for something possibly to be in several places but at the same time understands the possibilities in only a qualitative way, in terms of simple eligibility and ineligibility. Although this puts the child on the road to thinking quantitatively about possibility, in effect to thinking of *probabilities,* he or she at first does not approach it that way.

Adopting a mathematical approach, the correct way to consider possibilities in critical area search tasks can be expressed in quantitative terms. Some of the locations are ruled out—that is, the probability that they contain the object is zero; and some are retained—the sum of the probabilities that each contains the object is unity. Typically, although this need not be the case, the n locations that are retained are equiprobable, the probability that the object is in each being $1/n$. However, we have evidence to suggest that at first the child does not adopt a quantitative approach. He or she simply sees some locations as all being possibilities, in a qualitative way. His or her conception amounts to a simple listing of them, for example, as follows: possible, possible, possible. This conception involves no quantified notion of their equiprobability, expressible, for example, as $1/n = 1/n = 1/n$.

What does the child with a qualitative conception of possibilities do when faced with search tasks of a more probabilistic nature? We have begun to investigate this in some recent research (Somerville, Wellman, & Cultice, 1985). The situation we present to the child is a simple one. A small object is first hidden in a large quantity of effectively continuous material (dried peas), and this quantity is then divided in different ways between two containers, in view of the child. On some trials the division is equal, so that the hidden object is equally likely to be in each container. On others, the division is obviously unequal and in point of fact the object is twice as likely to be in one container—the bowl with twice as much material—as in the other.

We asked 4-, 8-, and 18-year-olds to search for objects concealed in this way. They did so in a somewhat constrained manner so that we could observe the progression of their search efforts in detail. Specifically, the subject used a small scoop and searched through the material by taking scoops from the bowls, examining and discarding those scoopfuls in succession. If a searcher is sensitive to the probabilities involved—not just aware that the object is in one of the two possible locations (bowls), but aware of the precise likelihoods attached to each location—he or she should divide the search effort roughly equally between the two bowls on equal probability trials, but should concentrate more effort in the more likely bowl on unequal probability trials.

Four-year-olds, when faced with these search problems, behave as if they know that the object might be in either place—that is, they understand the possibilities involved—but they do not appreciate the different probabilities of its placement. This is shown by the fact that their pattern of search was essentially the same on equal and unequal probability trials; in both cases, they concentrated about 80% of their search in a single bowl, whereas they should have concentrated it in this fashion only on the unequal probability trials. This pattern of performance raises the question, once again, as to whether they conceive of both bowls as possible places for the object to be, or simply conceive of the object as in a single bowl and search that bowl exclusively. Again, however, children to some extent managed to consider both possibilities at this age. Four-year-olds did not stay as much as possible in one bowl, with a deviation to the other bowl only when (and if) the first bowl chosen was exhausted before the end of the trial. The children tended to alternate searches between the bowls, moving back and forth about three times per trial. Alternation between the bowls occurred more often on trials where the object had been hidden—search trials of the type described above—than it did on comparison control trials where no object was hidden and the child or adult was simply told to scoop the materials out of the bowls ("for practice"). In summary, when searching for an object possibly hidden in either bowl, 4-year-olds alternated their searching between bowls, and they did this on both equal and unequal probability trials.

A further piece of evidence that children did understand the possibilities involved was obtained in a second study in which they were presented with a different type of search scenario. In the above task the problem was to find the object—this we term a *recovery problem*. The second study presented children and adults with what we term a *whereabouts problem*. The object was hidden as before, but now the task was not to find the object itself but to home in on its whereabouts. The children and adults were told that after searching through part of the material they must choose one of the bowls to be fed to the Cookie Monster, and that the monster must not be given the bowl with the hidden object (because he would choke on it). Without necessarily finding the object, the searcher's task was to eliminate one of the possibilities as unsafe to give to the monster. In this sort of task, although the object may be in either place, one's search effort should be concentrated in one place in order to eliminate it as a possibility (or at least reduce its likelihood). Even if exhausting that single bowl does not produce the object itself, it makes clear that the object is in the other bowl (that should not then be given to the monster).

Four-, 8-, and 18-year-olds did indeed concentrate their searches more in one bowl in the whereabouts study than they did in the original recovery study. For example, they alternated between bowls 3.2 times on the average in recovery searches but only 1.9 times in whereabouts searches, and there was no effect of age on these results.

We can conclude that even 4-year-olds understood something of the possibilities involved because they alternated between the two possible locations when required to find the object, but focused more on one when the implicit task was to eliminate one of the possibilities. These findings provide further evidence of preschoolers' initial but imperfect grasp of possible places for a hidden object to be. In spite of this demonstration that they comprehend the task and the quite subtle distinction between a recovery and a whereabouts problem, there was no indication that they considered the locations in terms of their *probabilities* of containing the object. They considered both places to be possible, but did not assess them as equally or unequally probable locations for the hidden object.

At the other extreme of the age range we investigated, 18-year-olds (like the 4-year-olds) understood the possibilities involved, but they were also sensitive to the probabilities, as appropriate. In the recovery task they essentially divided their effort equally between the two locations on equal probability trials but concentrated on the high probability one on the unequal probability trials. Specifically, they spent only about half of their time, on average, in one bowl during equal probability trials (57 percent in whichever bowl they happened to prefer over the other, as determined for each individual and then averaged), but spent 70 percent of their time in the most likely bowl on unequal probability trials. Eight-year-olds showed an intermediate understanding of probabilities, falling between the insensitivity of the 4-year-olds and the relative sophistication of the 18-year-olds.

The most important aspect of these results is the failure to assess probabilities shown by 4-year-olds, even in a situation in which their command of the possibilities was quite high. A more quantitative understanding of the differential probabilities applying to two possible locations was achieved much later, tenuously by 8 and clearly by 18 years of age.

GENERAL SUMMARY

The most definitive results we have are for children 4–6 years old. However, there is also sufficient evidence about younger and older children to allow us to sketch in an extended developmental progression. We outline this admittedly speculative progression for two reasons. First, an extended story is needed to anchor our findings about preschoolers within an overall description of development. Second, we argue that notions of possibility are acquired in a gradual fashion beginning quite early. This view should, at the very least, be capable of making adolescents' mastery of necessity and possibility at a formal level (Inhelder & Piaget, 1958) seem less abrupt and unheralded. In short, we hope to point out early conceptions that may pave the way for later understanding.

Our overview of the developmental progression is as follows. We begin with the very young infant who has no sense of objects, if invisible, or of their unseen positions in space. The next step takes us to the somewhat older infant who knows that a single object must occupy a single location and who can conceive of a hidden object as potentially residing (invisibly) only in some single *specified* place. Next we have the toddlers and young preschoolers, who probably know *before a hiding occurs* that several locations are all possible places for the object to go, but believe *after the (invisible) hiding occurs* that since the object must be in only one place they can choose a place where it must be. Later again, we find the older preschoolers who also know at least some of the time that *after hiding* (but before finding) the object could be in one of several places and can still bear in mind multiple possibilities at this point. The same children nonetheless may also, in some circumstances, judge *after a finding* is achieved that now, in retrospect, the object had to have been, of necessity, in that particular place. After the fact they apparently transform the actual place into a necessary one, no longer treating it as simply one of the possibilities. And indeed, like the toddlers and younger preschoolers, they tend in many situations to think of a hidden and as yet unfound item as necessarily being in one particular place rather than in an unknown one of several possibilities. These children are just beginning to understand what it is to be definitely uncertain about possible events.

Finally, by about 6 years of age, the ability to consider possibilities is well established, at least as it applies to the search tasks we have studied. However, it still remains for the child who has reached this kind of understanding to achieve a *quantified* notion of possibilities, coming to grips with the fact that alternatives that are all possible may nevertheless differ in the degree to which they are probable.

DISCUSSION AND CONCLUSIONS

We are not the first researchers to become interested in the development of an understanding of possibility and its place in the logical reasoning of the child. Inhelder and Piaget (1958) were interested in this question, and Pieraut-Le Bonniec (1980) has argued that Piaget's studies of reasoning should be extended so that they become capable of investigating concepts of possibility and necessity. Her arguments and ours are similar.

Pieraut-Le Bonniec's (1980) first point is that modal logic, encompassing concepts such as necessity and possibility, offers a way of describing reasoning that is closer to natural thought than is formal, two-valued logic. Her second point is that a model of logical development that is based on modal notions rather than on formal logic will exhibit more continuity and will avoid the problems associated with postulating abrupt qualitative changes at certain points, particularly in adolescence. She has suggested that "possibility plays a more important role than supposed by the Piagetian description and that a form of hypotheticodeductive thought may exist well before the age of adolescence" (p. 58). In her view, the younger child may acquire a sense of logical necessity through the "simultaneous consideration of *observable* cases of possibility and impossibility" (p. 59, Pieraut-Le Bonniec's emphasis), and she has shown that the young child's inferential abilities can be said to form a limited but logically coherent structure.

In addition to examining modal concepts on a theoretical level, Pieraut-Le Bonniec (1980) conducted a series of studies with children 3–10 years of age in order to chart the development of these concepts. Perhaps the most directly relevant of her studies for our discussion is one in which children 4–10 years old were shown two boxes whose lids had different slots cut in the top, one a squarish shape and one longer but thinner than the squarish slot. There was a marble that would fit only through the first slot and a stick that, somewhat paradoxically (because, overall, it seemed bigger to the children), would fit through either slot.

The children were familiarized, in a training phase, with these facts and relations and then tested on their understanding of the difference between two kinds of questions about events that happened out of their view—decidable questions and undecidable questions. When the child was told (without seeing directly) *either* that a marble had been placed in one of the boxes *or* that something had been placed in the box with the long thin slot, the questions "Which box is the marble in?" and "What object is in the box with the long thin slot?," respectively, were decidable ones. By contrast, there was no logical way to decide on the box into which the stick had been placed, or on the nature of the object (stick or marble) that had been placed in the box with the squarish slot, without looking.

Pieraut-Le Bonniec found that it was not until they were 9 years of age or older that a majority of children understood that they could not decide without looking in the boxes in the case of the latter questions. The decidable questions were answered correctly much earlier. She argued that the notion of *undecidability* is mastered only at this age. To account for children's answers prior to the attainment of this understanding, Pieraut-Le Bonniec described a developmental progression through two different ways of (mistakenly) making decisions in the undecidable cases. The earliest developmental level (comprising about 50 percent of 4- and 5-year-olds, about 35 percent of 6- and 7-year olds, and almost no children older than this) was characterized by choices based on stereotyped notions of correspondences, for example, that the stick and the long thin slot always went together. At a more advanced level (no 4-year-olds, about 25 percent of 5-year-olds, 40 percent of 6- and 7-year-olds, over 50 percent of 8-year-olds, about 40 percent of 9-year-olds, and very few 10-year-olds), children used factors external to the situation to make decisions about the undecidable questions. "For example, they thought that there was an alternation rule between sticks and marbles or small and large openings" (Pieraut-Le Bonniec, 1980, p. 85). These external grounds for making decisions are quite similar to the conventional notions about hiding actions (e.g., that someone would not proceed to a second location after hiding or finding a toy at a first one) that were invoked by 4-year-olds and (much less often) by 6-year-olds to decide between possibilities in the critical area search tasks, when they were considering an event that was known to have occurred.

Whereas there is a striking parallel between the developments in understanding of possibilities revealed by our studies of search skills and by the studies of Pieraut-Le Bonniec (1980), there is at the same time a very large discrepancy (3 years or more) in the ages at which the concepts are understood in the two types of studies. In our view, this discrepancy is probably due to the fact that our search tasks are more readily comprehensible to young children than tasks in which they are asked more explicitly to consider multiple possibilities. The responses required by our search tasks are overt searches rather than verbal decisions as to whether it is necessary to look inside some boxes to know the answer to a question. Further, in the critical area search tasks, the unseen events that have to be inferred and considered by the children are always implied by actions that they see directly, rather than being conveyed just in a verbal statement by the experimenter (e.g., "I have put something into the box with the long thin slot").

The essential step made by a child who masters in Pieraut-Le Bonniec's (1980) terms *undecidability* and in ours *definite uncertainty* is the step of knowing what possibilities are eligible for consideration within some system and what kinds of rules or information it is permissible to use to decide between them. If there is no way to decide, using the allowable rules, then the child understands that he or she definitely does not know, or in other words is definitely uncertain, about which one to choose. We have argued that this knowledge of what it means to be definitely uncertain can be discerned in the performance of 6-year-olds and even, at times, in that of 4-year-olds as well, on logical search tasks.

Two related conclusions stem from this work. The first is that the understanding of possibilities appears early in development and undergoes a progression of informative changes. Initially the child's understanding is quite limited, lacking in particular a tight grip on what it means to be definitely *un*certain. Young children think that they can be more certain about events that have occurred than they have a right to think. This is a serious limitation, but it should not be seen as completely undermining their ability to reason about possibilities. It is likely to be true that even adults do not completely overcome this tendency. For example, Fischhoff's (1975) research on hindsight bias in adults suggests that adults overestimate the obviousness and necessity of events if asked to judge them *after* the events have occurred.

The second conclusion concerns the wider implications of the young child's ability, albeit imperfect, to conceive of and reason about possibilities. Let us return to Piaget's claim that reasoning about possibilities goes hand in hand with scientific thinking and is required for formulating and testing theories about the world. That young children can entertain possibilities suggests that they may be able to evaluate and revise theories. Whether or not young children do hold theories is an important question for current approaches to cognitive development. It has been suggested that *all* conceptual knowledge is entrenched in theories (Murphy & Medin, 1985), that young children's knowledge of everyday domains consists of theories (Carey, in press; Karmiloff-Smith & Inhelder, 1975; Wellman, 1985b), and that cognitive development can be construed as being like the development of theories (Carey, 1985). This approach provides a promising new perspective on cognitive development, although it is still being forged and tested. Its validity rests at least in part on the issue of whether young children hold theories. Before we liken children's knowledge and its growth to the growth of theories, we need to be sure of our grounds for claiming that children have rudimentary theoretical abilities.

Preschoolers certainly have some of the skills prerequisite to theory construction. For example, they can make logical inferences and they have reasonable ideas about causal explanations (Bullock, Gelman, & Baillargeon, 1982; Haake et al., 1980; Shultz, 1982; Somerville, Hadkinson, & Greenberg, 1979; Sophian & Huber, 1984). However, as Inhelder and Piaget (1958) claimed, what is central to theoretical reasoning is an ability to combine logical arguments and causal explanations of a particular sort. In effect what is required is an approach that entertains all or many of the relevant possibilities, initially, and then attempts to reason logically with respect to them, ultimately ruling some of them out and retaining others. We have argued in this chapter that on a practical level this particular kind of reasoning is within the province of the preschooler, especially as applied to certain kinds of search problems. This suggests that it is plausible to think of young children's knowledge as theoretical and of their reasoning as theory driven, despite the fact that they do not operate within a formal, abstract logical system.

REFERENCES

Acredolo, L. P. (1979). Laboratory versus home: The effect of environment on the 9-month-old infant's choice of spatial reference system. *Developmental Psychology, 15,* 666–667.

Adams, M. J. (1978). Logical competence and transitive inference in young children. *Journal of Experimental Child Psychology, 25,* 477–489.

Anooshian, L. J., Hartman, S. R., & Scharf, J. S. (1982). Determinants of young children's search strategies in a large-scale environment. *Developmental Psychology, 18,* 608–616.

Anooshian, L. J., Pascal, V. U., & McCreath, H. (1984). Problem mapping before problem solving: Children's cognitive maps and search strategies in large-scale environments. *Child Development, 55,* 1820–1834.

Bertenthal, B. I., & Fischer, K. W. (1983). The development of representation in search: A social-cognitive analysis. *Child Development, 54,* 846–857.

Bremner, J. G., & Bryant, P. E. (1977). Place versus response as the basis of spatial errors made by young infants. *Journal of Experimental Child Psychology, 23,* 162–177.

Bryant, P. E., & Trabasso, T. (1971). Transitive inferences and memory in young children. *Nature, 232,* 456–458.

Bullock, M., Gelman, R., & Baillargeon, R. (1982). The development of causal reasoning. In W. Friedman (Ed.), *The developmental psychology of time.* New York: Academic.

Carey, S. (1985). *Conceptual change in childhood.* New York: Bradford.

Carey, S. (in press). Do children think differently from adults? In S. Chipman, J. Segal, & R. Glazer (Eds.), *Thinking and learning skills: Current research and open questions.* Hillsdale, NJ: Erlbaum.

Cromer, R. F. (1974). The developmetn of language and cognition: The cognition hypothesis. In B. Foss (Ed.), *New perspectives in child development.* Harmondsworth, Middlesex, England: Penguin.

Drozdal, J. G., & Flavell, J. H. (1975). A developmental study of logical search behavior. *Child Development, 46,* 389–393.

Eimas, P. D. (1970). Information processing in problem solving as a function of developmental level and stimulus saliency. *Developmental Psychology, 2,* 224–229.

Fischhoff, B. (1975). Hindsight =/= foresight: The effect of outcome knowledge on judgment under uncertainty. *Journal of Experimental Psychology: Human Perception & Performance, 1,* 288–299.

Haake, R. J., & Somerville, S. C. (1985). Development of logical search skills in infancy. *Developmental Psychology, 21,* 176–186.

Haake, R. J., Somerville, S. C., & Wellman, H. M. (1980). Logical ability of young children in searching a large-scale environment. *Child Development, 51,* 1299–1302.

Inhelder, B., & Piaget, J. (1958). *The growth of logical thinking: From childhood to adolescence.* London: Routledge & Kegan Paul.

Inhelder, B., & Piaget, J. (1964). *The early growth of logic in the child: Classification and seriation.* London: Routledge & Kegan Paul.

Johnson, C. N., & Wellman, H. M. (1980). Children's developing understanding of mental verbs: Remember, know, and guess. *Child Development, 51,* 1095–1102.

Karmiloff-Smith, A., & Inhelder, B. (1975). If you want to get ahead, get a theory. *Cognition, 3,* 195–212.

Kuczaj, S. A. (1981). Factors influencing children's hypothetical reference. *Journal of Child Language, 8,* 131–137.

Kuczaj, S. A., & Daly, M. J. (1979). The development of hypothetical reference in the speech of young children. *Journal of Child Language, 6,* 563–579.

Kuhn, D. (1977). Conditional reasoning in children. *Developmental Psychology, 13,* 342–353.

Miscione, J. L., Marvin, R. S., O'Brien, R. G., & Greenberg, M. T. (1978). A developmental study of preschool children's understanding of the words "know" and "guess." *Child Development, 49,* 1107–1113.

Murphy, G. L., & Medin, D. L. (1985). The role of theories in conceptual coherence. *Psychological Review, 92,* 289–316.

Neimark, E. D., & Lewis, N. (1967). The development of logical problem-solving strategies. *Child Development, 38,* 107–117.

Piaget, J. (1954). *The construction of reality in the child.* New York: Basic.

Pick, H. L., & Lockman, J. J. (1981). From frames of reference to spatial representation. In L. S. Liben, A. H. Patterson, & N. Newcombe (Eds.), *Spatial representation and behavior throughout the life-span.* New York: Academic.

Pieraut-Le Bonniec, G. (1980). *The development of modal reasoning.* New York: Academic.

Presson, C. C., & Somerville, S. C. (1985). Beyond egocentrism: A new look at the beginnings of spatial representation. In H. M. Wellman (Ed.), *Children's searching: The development of search skill and spatial representation.* Hillsdale, NJ: Erlbaum.

Shultz, T. R. (1982). Rules of causal attribution. *Monographs of the Society for Research in Child Development, 47* (No. 1).

Somerville, S. C., & Capuani-Shumaker, A. (1984). Logical searches of young children in hiding and finding tasks. *British Journal of Developmental Psychology, 2,* 315–328.

Somerville, S. C., & Haake, R. J. (1985). The logical search skills of infants and young children. In H. M. Wellman (Ed.), *Children's searching: The development of search skill and spatial representation.* Hillsdale, NJ: Erlbaum.

Somerville, S. C., Hadkinson, B. A., & Greenberg, C. (1979). Two levels of inferential behavior in young children. *Child Development, 50,* 119–131.

Somerville, S. C., & Sophian, C. (1984). *Four-year-olds' reasoning about possibilities in logical search tasks.* Unpublished study.

Somerville, S. C., Wellman, H. M., & Cultice, J. C. (1985). *The development of strategies for recovering objects and for determining their whereabouts.* Manuscript in preparation.

Sophian, C., & Huber, A. (1984). Early developments in children's causal judgments. *Child Development, 55,* 512–526.

Sophian, C., & Somerville, S. C. (1985). *Logical reasoning in early search: Understanding multiple possibilities.* Manuscript submitted for publication.

Wellman, H. M. (Ed.). (1985a). *Children's searching: The development of search skill and spatial representation.* Hillsdale, NJ: Erlbaum.

Wellman, H. M. (1985b). The child's theory of mind: The development of conceptions of cognition. In S. R. Yussen (Ed.), *The growth of reflection.* San Diego: Academic.

Wellman, H. M., & Somerville, S. C. (1982). The development of human search ability. In M. E. Lamb & A. L. Brown (Eds.), *Advances in developmental psychology* (Vol. 2). Hillsdale, NJ: Erlbaum.

Wellman, H. M., Somerville, S. C., & Haake, R. J. (1979). Development of search procedures in real-life spatial environments. *Developmental Psychology, 15,* 530–542.

PART THREE

Social Development

The domain of social development, like that of cognitive development, has been examined by many researchers in many different ways. Examples of current research concerning various aspects of social development are provided in this section.

An obvious difference in the social behavior of males and females is that females engage in more caretaking behavior with infants than do males. In Chapter 6, Phyllis Berman examines the emergence of gender differences in caregiving behavior and in responsiveness to infants, and considers various possible explanations for the development of caregiving behavior. Her conclusion is that children gradually develop cognitions and expectations about appropriate behavior with infants, and create scripts for various social situations involving babies. Her perspective contrasts with a predominantly biological viewpoint and has significant implications for the study of gender role behavior.

Gender roles are one major topic within the domain of social development; moral development is a second. In Chapter 7, Nancy Eisenberg examines the relation between individuals' level of moral reasoning and their moral behaviors. Conceptual issues to consider when examining this issue are discussed and methodological problems with the relevant empirical literature are delineated. Eisenberg's conclusion is that there is a positive relation between moral reasoning and moral behavior; however, such a relation can be expected only in certain situations.

In Chapter 8, Philip Costanzo and Peter Fraenkel also examine aspects of social cognition and morality, but from a different perspective. Costanzo and Fraenkel discuss the process of social influence, especially in the form of parenting, from a social-psychological as well as a developmental perspective. The effects of parental constraints on specific domains of children's functioning—internalization of moral and social conventional beliefs and deviant adjustment—are explored. The topic of this chapter has conceptual and applied implications for issues of relevance to social, developmental, and clinical psychologists.

CHAPTER 6

Children Caring for Babies: Age and Sex Differences in Response to Infant Signals and to the Social Context

PHYLLIS W. BERMAN

This chapter focuses on the developmental roots of caregiving and the origins of the familiar differences between men and women in the quality and quantity of their interactions with babies and young children. Considering what is known about the early development of behaviors in other domains, it is surprising that so little is known about the early antecedents of adults' responsiveness and caregiving to the young. Fortunately, during the last 10 years the topic has enjoyed new attention from researchers.

It is obvious that there are practical reasons for scientific knowledge about the existing sex differences in responsiveness to children. There are additional factors that give impetus to this field of inquiry. In our society child care is typically considered a feminine task, and the development of child-rearing behaviors seems to be a prototypic aspect of gender role development. Furthermore, it is evident that biological, social, and experiential variables all contribute in an important way to these behaviors. Biological and environmental theories are relevent, and our increasing knowledge of the functioning and interaction of these variables should enrich both types of theories.

The research program described in this chapter addresses several questions: Are the sex differences in adults' assumption of responsibility for caregiving to be found during childhood, and if so, at what age do these differences arise? Are some features of infant stimuli, for example, physical appearance or cries, compelling for very young children, and are they so for both males and fe-

This chapter was written with the support of the American Association of University Women Educational Foundation and the National Institute of Child Health and Human Development. Much of the research described was executed while the author was at Florida State University. The original research owes much to Vickie Goodman, Vicki L. Sloan (Smith), Stuart Weinstock, Lori D. Monda, and Richard P. Myerscough, who were graduate and undergraduate students at Florida State University. Thanks are also extended to Martha Zaslow and Beth Rabinovich for their helpful critique of early drafts of the chapter.

males? What do young children learn during the many years before parenthood that may be relevant to the demands of future parenting? Finally, how do sex differences arise in children's orientation toward and styles of interactions with younger children, toddlers, and infants?

It is particularly interesting to study the development of these sex differences in our children because children in our culture have so little responsibility for the care of younger siblings. There have been many societies in which young children played a major role in the care of infants and toddlers (Weisner & Gallimore, 1977; Whiting & Whiting, 1975). These children were usually assigned responsibility for caregiving very early, often as early as age 5 or before. Boys served as caregivers as well as girls, particularly when girls were unavailable. Clearly, young children are capable of many behaviors that are necessary to care for younger children and infants, but in modern America they are rarely asked to assume responsibility for this task. Several questions arise concerning the many children who have such minimal responsibility, and often, in fact, very little contact with younger children and babies.

The research has been guided by several assumptions. First, young children do learn patterns of interactions with babies, even when caregiving responsibilities are nonexistent. When children are given an opportunity to interact with babies, the nature of these interactions should vary with children's age as a result of this learning as well as cognitive maturation. It is also assumed that sex differences in responses to babies are embedded in larger, more general social role differences between men and women. Sex differences in responses to babies should, therefore, not be found among very young children, but they should arise with age as children learn the gender roles common to our culture.

Moreover, sex differences do not seem to be equally salient to all types of adult involvement with children. For example, a common finding is that fathers spend a greater proportion of their time in play with their babies than mothers do (cf. Parke, 1981). Sex differences emerge predominantly in responsibility for child care, degree of investment of time and energy, and style of interactions with children (Berman, 1980). It is also assumed that sex differences in children's behavior with babies should be differentially manifest in various contexts.

A helpful way to conceptualize children's interactions is that they develop "scripts" that guide their responses to babies. These scripts should be well differentiated for specific social situations, and the likelihood that a specific script will be used should vary from one situation to another. In this chapter illustrative data are presented on children's responses to babies in several situations, and the utility of two conceptual approaches is explored. One highlights the role of infant stimuli, and the other emphasizes the role of children's understanding of the social situation and the formation of social scripts. It is proposed that these two approaches are not mutually exclusive, but that both are necessary to learn more about the variables that determine the development of children's interactions with infants. Questions will be raised about when each approach is most appropriate and useful.

THEORETICAL APPROACHES TO THE DEVELOPMENT OF RESPONSIVENESS TO BABIES

Our lack of knowledge about the early antecedents of adults' responsiveness to the young is partly due to the fact that over many years human caregiving interactions with the young have been widely considered to be "natural." By the same token, sex differences in these behaviors have also been considered "natural" (Shields, 1975, 1984). Researchers are affected no less than laypeople by a heritage from folklore and early philosophers. Parents' interactions with babies simply appear "natural" to most of us.

During prescientific times the prevailing view of the development of caregiving was that these behaviors appear in full-blown form with little or no input from learning and experience (Shields, 1975, 1984). Although human parent–infant interactions later became a popular research topic, several factors in the evolution of the psychology of parenting may have operated so that comparatively little attention was paid to the developmental aspects of learning caregiving or to the impact of social contexts, except when cross-cultural settings or abnormal clinical conditions were studied.

In 1943 Lorenz formulated the first well-articulated theory of human caregiving, attributing attraction to babies to an innate mechanism. According to the theory, a unique emotional response and motor response (i.e., pressing the baby against the heart) are released by the sight of the distinctive physical characteristics that are typical of infants. These characteristics include a head that is large in proportion to body size; a forehead large in proportion to facial size; large eyes; short, heavy, large-footed limbs; round, protruding cheeks; and soft, elastic skin. Lorenz was not explicit about possible age or sex differences in the response to these physical characteristics. However, he described his own daughters' responses when they were less than 2 years old and compared their responses to dolls and in one case a soft round ball of woolen thread to mature women's responses to babies. Thus in Lorenz's formulation adultlike responsiveness to the young also appears in very young children in a manner that is independent of experience and learning.

Historically the roots of ethological theory have been in animal research. This work has moved far beyond simple concepts of fixed action patterns. At its best, animal research in the ethological tradition is designed so that an organism's behavior can be studied as a product of biological biases, individual developmental history, and the demands and potential of the immediate situation. Experimental animal studies have shown major effects on parental behavior of systematically rearranged elements of the immediate situation interacting with hormones (cf. Lehrman, 1961). It is quite possible to conduct comparable research with humans, studying the effects of small, ethically permissible but socially meaningful manipulations of the social context in which child care is given. Unfortunately, there have been few systematic research efforts of this sort. Similarly, Harlow's well-known work (cf. Arling & Harlow, 1967) showing the effects of rhesus monkeys' early experience on later maternal behavior to offspring is believed to be relevant to human parenting behavior. Yet except for information gleaned from clinical and anthropological studies, little is known about the contributions of humans' early experiences to the development of adult caregiving behaviors.

Ethological theory has made major contributions to the study of caregiving. However, it has tended to concentrate on the role of infant signals and the adequacy of the adult's response to ensure survival. The starting point for such research has very often been to ask what needs of the offspring caregiver behaviors serve, what infant signals the caregiver responds to, and what the functions of the infant's signals and the caregiver's behavior are. There have been many productive investigations into adults' responses to infant stimuli such as cries, vocalizations, looks and smiles, and also physical features. Despite the considerable advances resulting from this research, ethological work needs to be complemented by research on the contribution of the caregiver's history and the social situation to the caregiver's responsiveness to the baby.

Social learning theory, particularly in its extension to gender role learning theory, approaches the development of caregiving behavior in ways that contrast rather sharply with prescientific notions about the "natural" bases for caregiving. In contrast with ethological theorists, social learning theorists put less emphasis on the role of infant characteristics and signals in determining the nature of caregiving behaviors. Instead, reinforcement, cognitive approaches, and modeling have all been used to explain not only the course of acquisition of caregiving responses for males and females, but also the existence of sex, age, and stage of life differences in style and sheer amount of caregiving behavior (see, e.g., Berman, 1980; Berman & Goodman, 1984; Feldman & Nash, 1978, 1979a, 1979b; Feldman, Nash, & Cutrona, 1977; Melson & Fogel, 1982; Whiting, 1983).

The most intriguing questions concern how we learn what behaviors are appropriate when; that is, for whom to perform, and in which situations. Since males and females are expected eventually to assume different caregiving roles, young boys and girls may very well be learning to make fine discriminations about socially "appropriate" responses to a variety of somewhat different situations involving babies. These situations are at times distinctive in only very subtle ways (cf. Berman, 1986; Weinstock, 1979). That is, some of the most interesting but also most difficult questions are those that involve social discriminations, and those that involve performance rather than competence.

EARLY DEVELOPMENT OF CAREGIVING SCRIPTS

How then can we best conceptualize the operation of the many variables that determine the nature of human beings' interactions with their young? It is obvious that the physical and behavioral features of babies are important stimuli that may elicit caretaking responses from children and adults, although they do not do so reliably. The contributions of social and experiential variables are more difficult to understand. Elsewhere, the concept of *social script-*

ing has been used (Berman, 1980, in press) to characterize children's and adults' acquisition and performance of behaviors in the caregiving role. This term is not used to refer to prescriptions for overlearned rotely performed mundane behaviors. Rather, scripts for caregiving activities denote socially learned guides for highly motivated behaviors directed toward the young. These behaviors are often accompanied by emotional overtones that contribute to a sense of spontaneity, adding to the impression that the overt behaviors are "natural," that is, unlearned.

In the sphere of sexual behavior William Simon and John Gagnon (Gagnon, 1973; Gagnon & Simon, 1973; Simon & Gagnon, 1969) have used the term *scripting* to refer to social processes by which meanings are assigned to body sensations and by means of which loosely organized plans, fantasies, and cognitions give direction to interpersonal events. The concept seems equally appropriate when applied to social processes that give meaning and direction to human beings' interactions with the young. Caregiving and playful interactions with babies and young children are similar to sexual interactions in that both types of interactions often seem to be spontaneous and biologically programmed.

Sex differences in caregiving, as well as sex differences in sexual behavior, may appear to be attributable to anatomical and hormonal differences between males and females. Nonetheless, men and women come to parental caregiving, as they come to sexuality, with vastly differing social and experiential histories. Even naive adults with very little experience with children have had a history of learning the elements of culturally approved scenarios that include relationships with babies and young children. This is particularly true of females. That is, although many children in our society have relatively little direct experience with babies, there is a well-defined ideology concerning mothers' roles and behaviors with children. In contrast, there is considerable ambiguity at this time about fathers' roles with children. Children's experiences with their own parents as well as cognitions gleaned from other social models and the media may all contribute to a sense of what adult males and females can and should do in various situations.

It is likely that parenting or caregiving scripts are assembled in a gradual but discontinuous manner throughout childhood, and it is reasonable to believe that these early scripts may be precursors of and contributors to scripts generated in adulthood. Childhood scripts can function as flexible guidelines for behaviors with babies. Moreover, they depend not only upon child variables (such as age, sex, and experience) and infant variables (such as temperament, appearance, and behavior), but also on the child's understanding and perception of the social situation. Observations of children's interactions with toddlers and babies in varied semistructured situations offer valuable evidence about the functioning of these variables.

In this chapter three early studies are described. In the first two, which will be described briefly, the effects of children's age and sex were studied in various social situations in which children were about to interact with babies. A third study that involved many babies is described in greater detail, and attention is given to the role of infant stimuli, as well as the social situation and the older children's age and sex. Taken together these studies serve to illustrate the complex interactions to be expected between all of these variables. Children's behaviors may be predicted from our understanding of both gender role development and the effects of infant characteristics and signals.

TWO EARLY OBSERVATIONAL STUDIES

Our theoretical position leads to several testable predictions: Children of both sexes should be attracted to babies and should respond to infant signals. The extent and quality of such responses should depend, in large part, on the age and sex of the children and the demand qualities of the social situation, as well as the babies' behavior. Because children acquire caregiving scripts gradually, and in accord with their growing awareness of socially acceptable gender roles, we would expect little difference between very young boys' and girls' interactions with toddlers and babies. In contrast, sex differences should be found among older children. Older girls should have the highest and older boys the lowest levels of interaction with babies. Because in our society women have greater responsibility than men for care of the young, sex differences should be particularly pronounced in situations where there are heightened demands for children to take responsibility for caregiving.

The first study involved 86 boys and girls 32–63 months old in their regular day-care group situation (Berman, Monda, & Myerscough, 1977). Children were observed on 7 successive days during their daily free-play period. In a minimal alteration of the usual routine a visitors' area was marked off in a very large room that had areas for competing activities, such as art and nature study. During the observations the visitors' area contained a playpen with one side against the wall and an observer on each of the other three sides. Children wore identifying numbers. They were free to come and go as they pleased and individual children's presence in the area and behaviors were recorded. For the first 3 days of the study children were adapted to the procedures. Following this, a 13-month-old baby girl was placed in the playpen on "baby days" (days 5 and 6). A fish tank with a goldfish was placed in front of the empty playpen as a control for novelty on "fish days" (days 4 and 7).

As hypothesized, girls spent significantly more time in the area than boys did when the baby was present, but not on other days. Older boys in the group spent significantly less time in the area than younger boys did on baby days, but not on other days, a finding that might be expected if the older boys had acquired gender role attitudes that were incongruent with attraction to infants.

There were many limitations to this first study. Among the most obvious limitation was the fact that it was a group study of attraction and, as such, it was not possible to study individual children's behaviors in detail. The playpen severely restricted the baby's mobility and potential behavior, and because of the size of the group children were prohibited from touching the baby, a prohibition that was not always effective. Above all, children's behavior was very much affected by the presence of their peers. It was not at all unusual for a child to call to a friend or physically lead a friend into or out of the visitors' area. Indeed, effects of the presence and character of a peer group is a subject that deserves intensive and systematic attention.

A second study was planned in order to observe the behavior of individual children who were segregated with a baby within a small space through no choice of their own. The rather narrow age range of participants in the first study was expanded because it was thought that there might be a trend for older girls to be more responsive than younger girls to the baby. Most important, the second study was planned to test whether children's responses to babies could be manipulated by varying the social circumstances in which children are given the opportunity to interact with babies.

In the second observational study (cf. Berman, 1986; Berman, Smith, & Goodman, 1983), 38 children were enlisted from a different cohort of students at the same day-care center. On the basis of the previous study boys were expected to decrease in responsiveness to babies after approximately age 4½. Therefore, the available children were divided into a group of 10 boys and 10 girls 3½–4½ years old, and 9 boys and 9 girls 4½–5½ years old. Each child was brought individually to a room at the day-care center with a partitioned-off area occupied by a boy or girl baby 13–16 months old and many toys. For the first 6 min subjects were told that they could play as they wished. After this time each child was told that the "teachers" (observers) were busy, and was asked to help by "taking care of" the baby. Children were then observed for an additional 3 min.

The most frequent activity was solitary play (recorded on 82% of all 10-sec intervals). Children played with, touched, or vocalized to the baby during only 17 percent of the intervals. The amount of baby-directed activity during the period of spontaneous play was not significantly related to the children's age or sex, or to an Age × Sex interaction. However, as predicted, after an adult made a caretaking request there were large, significant differences between groups in the amount of interaction with the baby. Older girls interacted with the baby the most (on 43% of all intervals), older boys the least (on 2 percent of all intervals), and the younger boys and girls were at intermediate levels (26 and 13%, respectively).

Our major hypotheses about the expected Age × Sex interaction were supported. Not only were older boys *less* responsive to babies, as in the previous study, but also older girls were *more* responsive to babies than the younger children. Older girls were the only group of children who initiated interactions with the baby more often than they engaged in mutually initiated interactions. As predicted, the demand for caretaking was also effective in increasing the differences between the age–sex groups. In fact, it was only when children were asked to take responsibility for caregiving that the differences between groups were significant. The age–sex difference in children's behaviors appeared to be in response not only to the baby, but also to children's assignment to the role of caregiver.

CHILDREN'S RESPONSES TO VARIED BABIES AND SITUATIONS

Although our hypotheses about age and sex differences and the effects of demands for caretaking were verified, a third study was planned for several reasons. In order to determine the conditions that are associated with various types of responses to babies, it is necessary to vary the infant stimuli. That is, infant characteristics, as well as the social situations in which children meet, need to be explored. Children's interactions with toddlers are greatly affected by toddler's temperament and maturity, and we therefore enlisted a large number of toddlers in the study to eliminate sources of bias due to the idiosyncratic behavior of a particular baby. It was thus possible to analyze more accurately than in the previous studies several stimulus sources associated with babies' behaviors that were important determinants of children's caregiving.

We also hoped to be able to analyze in fine detail the stimulus conditions associated with children's baby-directed responses. To do this it was necessary to structure situations that might elicit fairly high rates of interactions with babies. In the previous study children engaged in solitary play during an average of 83% of all intervals, but they interacted with the baby, on the average, during only 17% of the intervals. In the third study (Berman & Goodman, 1984) a few simple toys were substituted for the many attractive toys available in the earlier experiments. It was hoped that with fewer attractive toys children would spend less time playing alone, and more time interacting with the baby.

Because young children in our culture rarely interact with babies without adult supervision and direction, we designed a study to replicate age and sex differences in children's interactions with a baby. Children were first observed after assignment to a caretaker role and then after an adult gave direct instructions concerning how the child could interact with the toddler. Four short scripts were developed, one for each of the sets of toys in the area. A male or female demonstrator showed the child how to use the toy to attract the toddler's attention and to entice the toddler to reach for the toy and join the child in mutual play.

Adults' instructions always followed a period of time when children were asked to assume the caretaker role without further instructions. In order to distinguish between the effects of the instructions and the effects of simply spending time with the baby, a double baseline design was used. Half of the 12 children in each of the four age–sex groups were asked to "take care of the baby" while the adults were "busy" for 6 min, and the remaining children were asked to do so for only 3 min before the adult demonstrator entered the area and showed the child how to "take care of" the baby. The length of the predemonstration period was not related to children's behavior before or after the demonstration and, therefore, data from both baseline conditions were combined for all subsequent analyses.

The setting for the study was a day-care center with a population of children similar to those in the previously described studies, but with a wider age range. In the younger group there were 12 boys and 12 girls between 2 years and six months old and 5 years and 3 months old, and in the older group there were 12 boys and 12 girls between 5 years and 9 months old and 7 years and 8 months old. These children and the 11 babies who were in the study were all regular attendees at the center.

Six male and 5 female babies 8–19 months old met the criteria to serve in the study; that is, they were mature enough to walk and approach children, but had not mastered more than a few words and were unlikely to be mature enough to be considered a peer, even by the youngest subjects. The baby for any particular session was chosen on a random basis from those of the group who were awake and available, with the restriction that close to half of the 12 subjects (5–7) in each of the four age–sex groups would be paired with girl babies, and the remaining subjects would be paired with boy babies.

A small area (approximately 100 sq ft) in the corner of a large, unoccupied playroom at the day-care center served as the research location. The area was blocked off from the rest of the room by low bookcase dividers, with the observers outside. Four sets of simple toys were provided: balls, a set of blocks, toy trucks and cars, and a beanbag toss game. After the baby began playing, the older child was brought to the area and told, "We really need someone to help us while we do some work. We're going to a room with some toys in it and a baby, and we'd like you to take care of the baby while we do some work. This is the baby we'd like you to take care of. We'll be doing some work right over here, and it's important that no one bother or interrupt us while we do our work, so we'd like you to stay right in this area with the baby. You take care of the baby now."

Half of the children in each of the four age–sex groups were randomly chosen to be in the baseline (uninstructed) caretaking condition for 6 min and the other half for 3 min before an adult entered the area for the demonstration. Toy interactions were chosen for the demonstration because our previous research had shown this to be the most likely type of interaction with the baby to occur for both sexes and both age groups.

The demonstrators each used one of the four toys saying, "I'd like to show you something. Watch me a minute." The demonstrator then used the randomly selected toy in a scripted manner, picking up the toy, showing the toy to the baby, and trying to induce the baby to reach for the toy. After the demonstration the experimenter left the area. The observation was continued for another 3 min. The sex of the demonstrator was balanced over the four age–sex groups.

The occurrence of each of several behaviors was recorded within 10-sec intervals: solitary play, toy interaction, accidental physical touch, all other physical touch, verbal or vocal interactions, verbalizations or vocalizations to the self, and any response to the observers. Separate observers recorded the child's behavior and the baby's behavior. The initiator and nature of each recorded behavior were noted. At the end of each session each observer also wrote a narrative account of activities and behaviors observed (see Berman & Goodman, 1984, for a detailed description of procedures).

Table 6.1 shows the mean percentage of all intervals before and after the demonstration when the children in each group engaged in particular activities. Total interaction scores were determined for each subject in order to assess the extent of his or her overall interactions with the baby. These scores were the sum of three percentage scores: toy interaction plus verbal or vocal interaction plus nonaccidental physical interaction. Two total interaction scores were determined for each subject, one for the period before and another for the period after the caretaking demonstration.

The data presented in Table 6.1 show that efforts to reduce the extent of solitary play were successful (from 82 percent of all intervals in the previous study to 54 percent in this study). Almost all of the children engaged in some interactions with the babies. However, solitary play was still the most common activity for all groups but the older girls. The most striking feature of the data is the contrast between the older girls' interactions with the toddlers and those of the other groups. In fact, the older girls' total interaction scores for the predemonstration period were almost three times higher than the younger boys' and girls', and more than seven times higher than the older boys'. The contrast between older girls' postdemonstration scores and the scores of other groups was even more striking.

Analyses (cf. Berman & Goodman, 1984) showed that children's sex and age were significantly associated with the extent of their interactions with the baby, but that the high scores of the older girls were responsible for these effects. There was a highly significant statistical interaction between age and sex. As predicted, there was little difference between the extent of younger boys' and girls' interactions with the baby, but there was a large significant difference between older boys' and girls'. Older boys interacted *less* with the baby than the younger boys did, but this effect was not significant. However, older girls interacted with the baby significantly *more* than younger girls did.

The demonstration was an effective way of stimulating interactions with toddlers, and male and female adults were equally effective as demonstrators. However, the demonstration was reliably effective only for the older groups. It should be noted, though, that not only was the demonstration a very brief and modest intervention, but also its effects were tested for only a very short period of time immediately following the demonstration. Its lack of effect for the younger children and the lack of differences due to demonstrators' sex need to be tested with a longer-term intervention.

TABLE 6.1. Mean Percentage of All Intervals Before and After the Demonstration When Subjects in Each Group Engaged in Particular Activities (n per group = 12)

Group:	Older Girls		Younger Girls		Older Boys		Younger Boys	
Before or After Demonstration	Before	After	Before	After	Before	After	Before	After
Interaction with toys	22.7	58.3	15.7	20.8	9.3	15.3	18.8	20.4
Verbal/vocal interaction	27.8	38.9	2.8	0.9	1.4	0.9	8.3	9.7
Physical interaction	25.2	15.7	8.6	7.4	0.0	0.0	0.0	0.0
Solitary play with toys	25.9	27.3	57.6	59.7	58.6	67.6	66.0	71.3
Vocalization to self	3.5	3.2	6.9	12.0	2.1	0.9	14.8	9.0
Accidental touch	1.4	0.5	0.7	0.5	0.0	0.0	0.0	0.0
Responses to observers	0.0	0.5	0.7	1.4	0.2	0.0	0.7	1.9

Source: From "Age and Sex Differences in Children's Responses to Babies: Effects of Adults' Caretaking Requests and Instructions" by P. W. Berman and V. Goodman, 1984, *Child Development, 55,* 1071–1077. Copyright 1984 by the Society for Research in Child Development, Inc.

Qualitative Aspects of Children's Interactions with Babies

In order to examine more closely the nature of children's interactions with babies, a system was devised to classify the observers' descriptions of the behaviors that were recorded (cf. Berman & Goodman, 1984). The classified behaviors are presented in Table 6.2. The numbers of children in each group who initiated specific types of interactions are listed. All activities initiated by at least 3 of the 48 subjects are included in the table. Baby-initiated interactions of the types listed were quite rare and were, therefore, excluded.

It can be seen from Table 6.2 that the older girls interacted with the baby not only more often than other children did, but also in many more different ways. For example, although most of the children in each group spent some time with the baby in interactions involving toys, these episodes were often brief and similar to young children's play with agemates. Occasionally toy play with the baby included showing, offering, or giving toys to the baby, but more often it involved only mutual play with the same toys. The older girls were the only group in which there were more children who offered, gave, or showed toys to the baby than those who merely engaged in mutual toy play with the baby.

Similarly, verbal interactions occurred among all groups but were common only for the older girls. Older girls often greeted or called to the babies, instructed them, and talked to them at some length. These verbal interactions were common before as well as after the demonstration. However, the extent and quality of older girls' physical interactions were most impressive, particularly when compared with the paucity of these behaviors in the other groups. Although none of the boys touched any of the babies, more than half of the older girls interacted physically with the baby in a variety of ways: lifting the baby, carrying or holding the baby, or taking the baby by the hand. A few of the younger girls also engaged in physical interactions with the baby, and these physical interactions resembled those of the older girls.

Children's Behavior as a Response to Baby Stimuli

The classification of children's behaviors reported in Table 6.2 was completed without the judges' awareness of the babies' behaviors that preceded them. Therefore, it is all the more interesting to speculate about how these behaviors might be related to the stimulus characteristics of the infants. Because many babies were enlisted in the third observational study, a wide range of infant characteristics and behaviors served as infant stimuli. We found no differences in any of the four age–sex groups' general responsiveness to babies based on babies' sex. That is, in no group were subjects' total interaction scores significantly different depending on whether the baby was a boy or a girl.

It might be that children's responsiveness to individual babies was influenced by the extent to which each baby possessed the type of infant features to which Lorenz has drawn our attention (1943), or by the baby's general

TABLE 6.2. Number of Children in Each Group Who Initiated Specific Types of Interactions with the Baby Before and After the Demonstration (*n* per group = 12)

Group:	Older Girls		Younger Girls		Older Boys		Younger Boys		All Ages	
Before (B) or After (A) the Demonstration	B	A	B	A	B	A	B	A	B	A
Interactions:										
Mutual play	6	12	5	7	4	6	7	5	22	30
Offer, give, show	8	8	2	3	4	4	4	3	18	18
Any toy interaction	10	12	7	10	5	8	8	8	30	38
Greet, call	7	0	0	2	1	2	2	1	10	5
Instruct, command	6	6	1	0	1	1	1	0	9	7
Reassure, reinforce	3	1	1	0	1	0	1	1	6	2
Other talk	8	8	1	0	0	0	2	2	11	10
Any verbal interaction	9	10	3	2	1	3	3	4	16	19
Pick up, hold	5	3	0	2	0	0	0	0	5	5
Touch, carry, lead	7	4	3	3	0	0	0	0	10	7
Any physical interaction	7	5	3	4	0	0	0	0	10	9

Source: From "Age and Sex Differences in Children's Responses to Babies: Effects of Adults' Caretaking Requests and Instructions" by P. W. Berman and V. Goodman, 1984, *Child Development, 55,* 1071–1077. Copyright 1984 by the Society for Research in Child Development, Inc.

physical attractiveness. Unfortunately, the babies' physical characteristics were not evaluated. Subjectively, all of the babies appeared to be at least moderately attractive and "cute." However, in future research it might be valuable to have ratings on the babies' physical appearance.

Babies did vary in their behavior, and these differences were documented by our data. Not only were there differences between babies, but there were also differences in individual babies' behavior from session to session. The tendency to cry was probably the most influential behavioral characteristic of the babies in our study. Crying is usually considered to be among the most powerful and compelling of all infant stimuli for adult caregivers (cf. Murray, 1979). It would be interesting to know whether a baby's cries are also compelling for young children who are placed in a position of responsibility for a baby. If so, what kind of responses might children be most likely to make to a baby's cries?

Although everything possible was done to avoid babies' crying, 7 of the 11 babies who served in Study 3 cried at some time during a session with an older child. In fact, the baby cried at least briefly during 11 of the 48 sessions. Data for these 11 sessions are presented in Table 6.3. In order to augment these data, additional data have been added to the table from C8, a pilot subject who also encountered a crying baby.

Conclusions that might be drawn from the data in Table 6.3 are obviously limited. Both the small number of sessions when babies cried and the variable timing and duration of baby cries across sessions precluded the possibility of comparing the responses of children in the four age-sex groups. For example, it can be seen that the 3 babies who were paired with older boys cried for only 20 sec whereas most of the remaining subjects listed in Table 6.3 were faced with babies who cried for much longer periods. It is not possible to know whether two of the three older boys failed to respond to crying babies because these babies cried for only a very short time, or because older boys were generally less responsive to babies.

Despite these limitations it is possible to make some observations about those children listed in Table 6.3 as a group, and to compare their behaviors with children who were in sessions with babies who did not cry. The data, though not extensive, are particularly valuable because they are unique. We have not been able to find in the existing literature any other reports of modern western children's responses to crying babies for whom they have caregiving responsibility.

Seven of the 11 babies who served in the study cried during the experimental sessions. Four of the babies were boys and 3 were girls. Three of the babies cried during only 1 session. The remaining 4 babies cried during 2 or 3 different sessions, that is, when paired with different subjects. Most often the baby seemed to cry when startled by some change, particularly the entry of a new person into the research area. Although children were brought to the area only after the baby was playing there contentedly, babies often cried soon after the child entered the area. In 8 of the 12 sessions listed in Table 6.3, the baby

TABLE 6.3. **Children's Behavior Following Onset of Baby Cries**

Pair	Age	Cry onset	Cry duration	Cry[a] (Stops)	Offer, Give Toy	Verbal Response	Touch Response	Vocal to Self	Vocal to Observers
C1[b] (F)[c]	2–9	Interval	6 min	67%	Gives toy[d]		Touch		
B1[b] (M)[c]	1–7	1		(9)	starts game	"Shhh"[d]	hand[d]		
C2 (F)	3–8	Demon-	50 sec	7%					
B2 (F)	1–1	stration		(2)	Offers toy[d]		Holds[d]	Yes	
C3 (F)	4–7	Interval	8 min,	93%			Touch		
B3 (F)	1–1	3	40 sec	(2)	Offers toy[d]		Caress[d]	Yes	
C4 (F)	6–10	Interval	40 sec	11%		"Shhh. Want			
B4 (F)	1–5	15		(1)	Offers toy	this?"			
C5 (F)	7–1	Interval	1 min,	13%			Picks up		
B5 (M)	1–0	2	10 sec	(1)		"Come here"	Cuddles		
C6 (F)	7–4	Interval	4 min,	33%	Offers toy[d]				
B3 (F)	0–10	2	50 sec	(6)	Mutual play[d]	Quiet talk[d]	Touch[d]		
C7 (F)	7–5	Interval	20 sec	4%					
B5 (M)	1–0	53		(0)		"It's okay"			
C8 (M)	4–3	Interval	7 min,	46%					
B6 (M)	0–7	5	20 sec	(6)				Sings	
C9 (M)	4–3	Interval	6 min	100%					
B3 (F)	0–10	1		(0)	Offers toy[d]	"Shhh"[d]			
C10(M)	6–8	Interval	20 sec	3%					
B7 (M)	0–10	17		(1)					
C11(M)	6–9	Interval	20 sec	3%		"Hi. It's okay.			
B4 (F)	1–4	1		(1)	Gives toy	Want the ball?"			
C12(M)	7–6	Interval	20 sec	4%					
B7 (M)	0–10	2		(1)					yes

[a]Percentage of all intervals during which the baby cried. Number of stops during crying are given in parentheses.
[b]C1 refers to the Child Number 1. B1 refers to Baby Number 1. C1 and B1 are paired together.
[c](M) = male, (F) = female.
[d]Behavior that is repeated during more than one interval.

began to cry within the first 50 sec after the child's entry, usually during the first 20 sec. In 1 of the sessions (Child 2 with Baby 2), the baby began to cry when the demonstrator entered the area, and in another, the baby (Baby 5) cried after a tower of blocks that the older child (Child 7) had built "for the baby" crashed to the floor. In the 2 remaining sessions the babies may have been responding to some sudden movement made by the older child.

The data in Table 6.3 clearly show that most of the children who were faced with the task of caring for a crying baby met that assignment with constructive and often persistent attempts to placate and calm the baby. Nine of the 12 children did so. Seven of the children offered or gave the baby a toy when the baby began to cry. An equal number of children offered verbal assurance to the babies when they cried, saying "Shhh," or "It's okay," or talking quietly to the baby while sitting close to the baby. In fact, it can be seen from a comparison of Tables 6.2 and 6.3 that children's verbal assurance to crying babies accounts for almost all of the behaviors that had been classified in Table 6.2 as "Reassure, reinforce." It should again be noted that the children's behaviors listed in Table 6.2 were classified earlier without knowledge of the infants' behaviors that preceded them.

Five of the girls also touched the baby, or caressed or cuddled the baby in an apparent attempt to comfort the distressed infant. Although older girls frequently touched babies whether they cried or not, the younger girls did so far less frequently. It is interesting that, although many of the older girls needed no such provocation, most of the younger girls who touched the baby did so only after the baby cried (cf. Tables 6.2 and 6.3).

In this study children's age seemed to be unrelated to responsiveness to crying babies. Even some of the youngest subjects responded amply to the babies' distress. For example, Baby 1 began to cry as Child 1 (a girl, 2 years and 9 months old) entered the research area. The baby continued to cry or whine intermittently throughout much of the session, stopping nine times for intervals of 10 sec or more. Although Child 1 was only 14 months older than the baby, Child 1 offered him toys and touched his hand several times, repeatedly saying "Shhhshhh" when he cried. She was finally able to engage the baby in a game, rolling a ball back and forth. This successful toy interaction with the baby occurred after an adult demonstrated the use of a toy other than the ball. Although the demonstration may have contributed to the child's ability to do so, considerable ingenuity was required for this young child to calm the baby and to initiate and sustain joint play activity.

Child 9 (a boy 4 years and 3 months old) was confronted by a 10-month-old baby who cried continuously, and often vigorously, throughout the session. Although his efforts met with no success, the 4-year old kept offering toys to the baby, moving close to her and saying "Shhhshhh" over and over. This pattern was typical of many children 2–7 years old. Their responses to the babies' cries were almost immediate, and were repeated often when babies continued to cry.

Most of the babies began to cry very early in the session before the children had witnessed an adult's demonstration of how one might "take care of" a baby. Therefore, it appeared as though these typical responses to crying babies were not dependent on formal instruction or modeling within the research situation. They may have been learned very early, perhaps from children's experiences with adults' attempts to relieve their own distress.

Not all of the children responded directly to the crying baby, although most of them did. Three of the children, all boys, made no effort to distract or comfort the distressed baby. Instead, some of the children may have directed their efforts toward self-distraction. For example, Child 12 was paired with a baby who cried briefly soon after the child entered the area. Although he had just been asked to take care of the baby, the child called to the observers, asking whether he could play with the toys. Child 8 was faced with a 7-month-old who cried during almost half of the intervals in the session. The 4-year-old boy did not respond directly to the crying baby. Instead, he vocalized to himself and sang the baby's name over and over. Behavior such as this might be considered peculiar unless it were interpreted as indicating that he was aware of the baby but sought to interfere with perception of the baby's cries.

To summarize, 9 of the 12 children who were with crying babies responded to the babies promptly, and often repeatedly. Although it was not possible to compare the responses of the four age–sex groups, even the youngest children responded appropriately and amply to the babies' distress. Boys and girls offered toys to the baby and offered verbal reassurance. Girls also touched, held, cuddled, or caressed the baby. Almost all the responses that previously had been classified as "Reassure, reinforce" were made to babies who were crying. Although older girls were likely to touch the baby whether or not the baby was crying, almost all of the younger girls' touch responses were to crying babies.

Older Girls' Responses to Crying and Noncrying Babies

Baby cries seemed to be potent elicitors of heightened responsiveness to babies for many of the children. However, except for the fact that they verbally reassured crying babies, the older girls appeared, as a group, to behave similarly to babies who cried and those who did not cry during the research sessions. Older girls generally had very high rates of interaction with babies. To what stimuli were they responding? What might have motivated their baby-directed behavior?

Table 6.4 presents data for the 12 older girls in the study. Latency data are given for each girl's initial verbal, physical, and toy interactions with the baby. The time of onset of crying is also given if the baby cried during the session. In 8 of the 12 sessions the baby did not cry at all. In 3 of the 4 sessions with crying babies, the crying began after the older girl had already interacted with the baby. Only one child, Subject 10, could possibly have been responding to cries in her initial interactions with the baby.

The most striking feature of these data is the very early onset of older girls'

TABLE 6.4. Latency of Older Girls' Initial Interactions with Babies and of Babies' Cries (latency is in seconds; $n = 12$)

Subject (age)	With Toy	Vocal	Physical	Onset of Baby Cry
1 (6–2)	AD[e]	10	20	No cry
2 (6–3)	140			No cry
3 (6–3)	10		10	No cry
4 (6–5)	60	AD[e]		No cry
5[a] (6–10)	90	100		140
6 (6–10)	20	10	50	No cry
7 (7–0)	110	50	10	No cry
8 (7–0)	40	20	130	No cry
9[b] (7–1)	160	10	60	10
10[c] (7–4)	30			10
11[d] (7–5)	40	110		520
12 (7–5)	110	10	20	No cry

[a]Subject C4, Table 6.3.
[b]Subject C5, Table 6.3.
[c]Subject C6, Table 6.3.
[d]Subject C7, Table 6.3.
[e]After the demonstration.

responses to the babies. Six girls, that is, fully half of the group, interacted with the baby in the first 10 sec of the session. In fact, all but two of the older girls responded to the baby within the first minute. Not only did the older girls interact with the babies very early during the sessions, but many of the girls' behaviors seemed to follow a particular pattern. We might think of this behavioral pattern as an expression of a script, common to girls this age for use in caregiving situations. Two-thirds of the older girls talked to the baby, usually during the first minute, often greeting or calling to the toddler, then later showing a toy or instructing the baby about its use. More than half of the girls touched the baby during the first minute or two; five of them picked up, held, or carried the baby, led the baby by the hand, or assumed a position that maintained continuing physical contact with the baby.

These children gave the appearance of taking the babies physically in hand. Some of the older girls were successful in initiating and maintaining playful and often nurturant interactions with the babies. These girls combined close physical contact with much quiet talk to the babies, and the sharing of toys. The babies in these sessions were content to remain in physical contact. They exchanged toys, entered into joint play, and sometimes vocalized. For example, Subject 8, a 7-year-old, talked quietly to the baby throughout the 6 min before an adult entered the situation to demonstrate how to "take care of" a baby. She talked to the baby beginning in the first 10 sec that she was with her, all the while offering several different types of toys. During the second minute the baby accepted a ball. The child and the baby then sat close together in continuous physical contact. After 3 min the child was able to engage the baby in a game wherein the children rolled the car to each other repeatedly, with the baby vocalizing to the child.

Subject 9 was confronted with a more difficult situation, a baby who began to cry after 10 sec and persisted for more than 1 min. She held and cuddled the baby, talked to him, and then offered toys that he accepted and later threw back to her. In the sixth minute (before the adult's demonstration) she "sat him down" and showed him how to stack blocks, guiding his hand with her hand on his arm.

Not all the older girls' interactions were this successful. Occasionally a baby was startled by a child's overtures. For instance, the baby cried when Subject 5 gave her a ball after rolling the ball to her and unsuccessfully exhorting her, "Get it." Sometimes a baby appeared to find physical contact with an older girl too confining and moved away. More frequently babies simply remained passive despite the older girls' ministrations. For example, Subject 7 picked up the baby during the first 10 sec of the session, holding him in her lap for 1.5 min. She talked quietly to him, telling him, "Look," and "Give it to me." Despite the fact that he followed her instructions, the baby did not initiate any activities.

Whether their interactions with the babies were successful or not, the older girls apparently believed that they knew how to "take care of" babies and they went about doing so with very little hesitation soon after entering the experimental situation. They had obviously already acquired a "script" that few of the younger girls had acquired. Even after an adult demonstrated how to "take care of" a baby many of the older girls behaved in a manner that expressed elements of the original script. Although the adults' demonstrations did not include any physical contact with the baby, most of the older girls' scripts did. Despite the prestige and obvious expertise of the adults, and despite the fact that almost all of the older girls replicated the demonstrators' actions faithfully, five of them reverted to physical interactions after the demonstration. This usually happened after children's attempts to enlist the baby's cooperation by imitating the demonstrator failed.

As a group the older girls seemed to be quite different from the other children. Most of them responded promptly to the experimenters' requests for caregiving by talking to the baby and offering toys. Many of them also assumed physical control of the baby, a type of behavior not observed in the other children. Only a small proportion of their baby-directed behaviors seemed to be in direct response to the babies' cries. Instead they appeared to be responding with what they considered to be appropriate behavior to social cues denoting a general class of situations concerned with baby care.

SUMMARY AND FUTURE DIRECTIONS FOR RESEARCH

Despite the fact that parent–child interaction has been a thriving field of psychological research, relatively little is known about children's responses to babies or about the ways patterns of responsive, nurturant care develop in young girls or boys. In the modern western world the nature and extent of parental involvement with young children are obviously different for most men and women, but we know very little about the developmental course of sex differences in caregiving. Even less is known about how and why sex differences come about and the conditions that are necessary and sufficient for them to emerge.

Two different theoretical approaches have characterized research on development of caregiving in male and female children and adults. One has emphasized the importance of infant characteristics and signals, and the assumption is often made that there is a specieswide genetic bias to respond to infant stimuli. The other approach has emphasized the importance of experience, situational cues, changing roles during the life course, and the individual's cognitions and perceptions of appropriate gender roles. Both approaches are necessary to an understanding of the antecedents of various types of caregiving activities.

Much of what is known about the development of nurturance in young children comes from studies of traditional cultures where considerable child-care responsibility is allocated to older siblings (cf. Weisner & Gallimore, 1977; Whiting & Whiting, 1975). Whiting and Whiting have shown that infants elicited nurturant responses from children more than three times as often as their peers or elders did. It may even be the case that regular responsibility for infant care can influence children's behavioral repertoires, generally increasing the probability of habitual nurturant responses. Ember's (1973) observations of boys who were given responsibility for child care support this notion. Because children's tasks and responsibilities largely determine the social context within which they spend time, Whiting (1983) stresses the far-reaching consequences of the parents' role in task assignment. Boys as well as girls may respond with nurturance to infant signals when given an opportunity. However, cultural support is necessary for contact between children and infants to occur. Parents' cognitions, perceptions, and social attitudes, which usually differ for sons and daughters, determine the frequency of such contact.

Although much remains to be learned about the development of caregiving in traditional cultures, it is an even greater challenge to understand the origins of sex differences in societies such as ours, where boys and girls have little contact with infants, and even less responsibility for child care. Children in modern western societies presumably share with children in traditional societies any existing biases to respond nurturantly to infant signals. Our observations of the persistent and varied responses of even very young children to crying babies lend support to the theory that there may be specieswide biases to comfort distressed, crying infants (cf. Frodi & Lamb, 1978). It is important to keep in mind that any such biases do not guarantee that behavior will be nurturant. A few of our subjects either were unresponsive or appeared to be attempting to interfere with the focal perception of aversive baby cries. It is also possible that there are age or sex differences in responsiveness to infant cries, but our data are not adequate to test for group differences.

Though there has been an upsurge of research on responses to baby cries, most of the research has been with adults, not children, and has relied heavily on self-reports. Unfortunately, we cannot make assumptions about the way subjects might behave based on their ratings of cries and reports of how they might act in real-life situations. An even greater problem is that self-reports tend to be biased so that traditional sex differences are exaggerated (cf. Berman, 1980). In one study (Zahn-Waxler, Friedman, & Cummings, 1983), when children had an opportunity to "help a mother find a lost bottle" for a baby who had presumably been crying, there were no significant sex differences in the amount of help offered but, during an interview, girls verbalized significantly more empathy for the crying baby than boys did.

It is certainly time-consuming to observe children's direct responses to crying babies in ecologically valid situations. It is also difficult to deal with responses to naturally occurring cries, which are neither uniform nor under the experimenters' control. However, data such as these are essential for both theoretical and practical purposes. In addition, similar information is needed about children's responses to other naturally occurring baby behaviors such as smiles and vocalizations. It may also be profitable to compare children's behaviors toward infants who vary in the degree to which they possess "Lorenz-type" babyish physical characteristics.

Though children from both traditional and modern western societies share the tendency to respond to infant signals, western children must draw on different experiences to develop cognitions and expectations about appropriate baby-directed behaviors, and to create scripts for various social situations in which babies are encountered. Direct experience with babies may be minimal, but families, peers, the media, and many cultural institutions provide ample information to be used as guidelines for developing role behavior. Even preschool children seem to be aware of the various behavior patterns that are culturally approved in situations involving babies. Moreover, there is evidence (Weeks & Thornburg, 1977) that young children articulate acceptance of future family roles that are even more traditional than their parents'.

Perhaps most important, young children make fine distinctions about the various behaviors that are "appropriate" for males or for females in situations that seem on the surface to be only minimally different. For example, sex differences are most often found when there is a demand for caregiving responsibility, but there may be little difference between boys and girls in situations when a specific type of help is needed (Berman, in press; Weinstock, 1979), or when there is no demand for caregiving responsibility (Berman, 1986; Berman et al., 1983). Young children not only appear to understand that women typically bear major responsibility for child rearing in our society (Melson, Fogel, & Toda, 1985); they also know who usually assumes each role in a variety of situations.

A good example is the contrast between older boys' and girls' behavior in Experiment 3, following the experimenter's initial request that they "take care of" the baby. Four of the 12 older boys spent at least 1 min in the experimental situation without recordable behaviors. The observers noted that these children "watched" or "stared at" the baby. Berman and Goodman (1984, p. 1076) suggested that watching a baby may be a rather passive form of caregiving that is in accord with a young child's interpretation of the proper masculine role. They proposed that future research "be directed toward understanding the developing differences between males and females in the way they construe their 'proper' roles and responsibilities for child care" (p. 1076). These differences should be measured not only by interviews and children's self-reports but also by observations of children's behaviors in a variety of situations. Situations should be designed or selected because they vary with respect to the type of people present (i.e., age, sex, relationship with the child, and social status) and the explicit and implicit demands made on the child, as well as the babies' characteristics and behavior.

Observations of children's baby-directed behaviors are particularly valuable when behaviors can be related to infant variables and situational variables. However, there are also opportunities to explore subject variables beyond sex, age, life stage, and sibling status. The existing body of cross-cultural literature demonstrates that subject variables can also be a rich source of information about cultural variables that are important to the development of caregiving. The diversity of family forms and caregiving traditions provides contrasts that can be exploited in a selective fashion.

It has been suggested (Allen, 1985; Brookins, 1985) that black mothers' long tradition of employment in the United States has contributed to more egalitarian roles and more caregiving involvement for males in black families, compared with whites. Research is now under way comparing black boys' baby interactions with those of white boys (Reid, personal communication, 1985). Furthermore, rapid changes in certain areas of the world afford unique opportunities for research. One example is modern urban China where children from one-child families have no opportunities for experience with siblings. However, Chinese boys and girls are immersed in a family-oriented culture where young males and females are expected to be helpful and expressive toward their peers and younger children. These are only two of many populations with rich potential for research.

In summary, the early acquisition of ability to care for the young is a promising and important area for investigation. It is time to broaden our knowledge of not one but several classes of variables that interact to determine children's responsiveness to younger children and babies. Selective attention to particular situational variables, population variables, and variables associated with infant signals can greatly enhance our understanding of the processes that underlie the development of men's and women's emotional investment and competence to care for their young.

REFERENCES

Allen, W. R. (1985). Race, income and family dynamics: A study of adolescent male socialization processes and outcomes. In M. B. Spencer, G. K. Brookins, & W. R. Allen (Eds.), *Beginnings: Social and affective development of black children*. Hillsdale, NJ: Erlbaum.

Arling, G. L., & Harlow, H. F. (1967). Effects of social deprivation on maternal behavior of rhesus monkeys. *Journal of Comparative & Physiological Psychology, 64,* 371-377.

Berman, P. W. (1980). Are women more responsive than men to the young? A review of developmental and situational variables. *Psychological Bulletin, 88,* 668-695.

Berman, P. W. (1986). Young children's responses to babies: Do they foreshadow differences between maternal and paternal styles? In A. Fogel & G. F. Melson (Eds.), *Origins of nurturance*. Hillsdale, NJ: Erlbaum.

Berman, P. W., & Goodman, V. (1984). Age and sex differences in children's responses to babies: Effects of adults' caretaking requests and instructions. *Child Development, 55,* 1071-1077.

Berman, P. W., Monda, L. D., & Myerscough, R. P. (1977). Sex differences in young children's responses to an infant. An observation within a day-care setting. *Child Development, 48,* 711-715.

Berman, P. W., Smith, V. L., & Goodman, V. (1983). Development of sex differences in response to an infant and to the caretaker role. *Journal of Genetic Psychology, 143,* 283-284.

Brookins, G. K. (1985). Black children's sex-role ideologies and occupational choices in families of employed mothers. In M. B. Spencer, G. K. Brookins, & W. R. Allen (Eds.), *Beginnings: Social and affective development of black children*. Hillsdale, NJ: Erlbaum.

Ember, C. (1973). Female task assignment and the social behavior of boys. *Ethos, 1,* 424-439.

Feldman, S. S., & Nash, S. C. (1978). Interest in babies during young adulthood. *Child Development, 49,* 617-622.

Feldman, S. S., & Nash, S. C. (1979a). Changes in responsiveness to babies during adolescence. *Child Development, 50,* 942-949.

Feldman, S. S., & Nash, S. C. (1979b). Sex differences in responsiveness to babies among mature adults. *Developmental Psychology, 15,* 430-436.

Feldman, S. S., Nash, S. C., & Cutrona, C. (1977). The influence of age and sex on responsiveness to babies. *Developmental Psychology, 13,* 675-676.

Frodi, A., & Lamb, M. (1978). Sex differences in responsiveness to infants: A developmental study of psychophysiological and behavioral responses. *Child Development, 49,* 1182-1188.

Gagnon, J. H. (1973). Scripts and the coordination of sexual conduct. In J. K. Cole & R. Dienstbier (Eds.), *Nebraska symposium on motivation*. Lincoln, NE: University of Nebraska Press.

Gagnon, J. H., & Simon, W. (1973). *Sexual conduct*. Chicago: Aldine.

Lehrman, D. S. (1961). Gonadal hormones and parental behavior in birds and infrahuman mammals. In W. C. Young & G. W. Corner (Eds.), *Sex and internal secretions* (Vol. 2, 3rd ed.). Baltimore: Williams & Wilkins.

Lorenz, K. (1943). Die angebornen Formen moglicher Erfahrung. *Zeitschrift fur Tierpsychologie, 5,* 235-582.

Melson, G. F., & Fogel, A. (1982). Young children's interest in unfamiliar infants. *Child Development, 53,* 693-700.

Melson, G. F., Fogel, A., & Toda, S. (1985). *Children's ideas about infants and their care.* W. Lafayette, IN: Department of Family Studies, Purdue University.

Murray, A. D. (1979). Infant crying as an elicitor of parental behavior: An examination of two models. *Psychological Bulletin, 86,* 191-215.

Parke, R. D. (1981). *Fathers.* Cambridge, MA: Harvard University Press.

Shields, S. A. (1975). Functionalism, Darwinism, and the psychology of women. *American Psychologist, 30,* 739-754.

Shields, S. A. (1984). To pet, coddle, and "do for": Caretaking and the concept of maternal instinct. In M. Lewin (Ed.), *In the shadow of the past: Psychology examines the sexes, 1800-1900.* New York: Columbia Univesity Press.

Simon, W., & Gagnon, J. H. (1969). On psychosexual development. In D. A. Goslin (Ed.), *Handbook of socialization theory and research.* Chicago: Rand-McNally.

Weeks, M. O., & Thornburg, K. R. (1977). Marriage role expectations of five-year-old children and their parents. *Sex Roles, 3,* 189-191.

Weinstock, S. C. (1979). *Preschool children's sex differences in prosocial behaviors directed toward a younger child.* Unpublished honors thesis, Florida State University, Tallahassee, FL.

Weisner, T. S., & Gallimore, R. (1977). Child and sibling caretaking. *Current Anthropology, 18,* 169-180.

Whiting, B. B. (1983). The genesis of prosocial behavior. In D. Bridgeman (Ed.), *The nature of prosocial development: Interdisciplinary theories of strategy.* New York: Academic.

Whiting, B. B., & Whiting, J. W. (1975). *Children in six cultures.* Cambridge, MA: Harvard University Press.

Zahn-Waxler, C., Friedman, S. L., & Cummings, E. M. (1983). Children's emotions and behaviors in response to infants' cries. *Child Development, 54,* 1522-1528.

CHAPTER 7

The Relation of Altruism and Other Moral Behaviors to Moral Cognition: Methodological and Conceptual Issues

NANCY EISENBERG

For hundreds of years, philosophers have debated the role of moral cognition in moral action. Some philosophers such as Kant (1797/1964) have taken the position that behavior, to be classified as moral, must be motivated by rational cognitions related to issues such as duties and responsibilities. In contrast, other philosophers have argued that moral actions can have an affective (e.g., sympathetic) as well as cognitive basis (e.g., Blum, 1980; Hume, 1777/1966).

Until relatively recently, psychologists studying moral development formed two major camps. Psychologists adhering to a social learning perspective were concerned with the actual performance or nonperformance of behaviors labeled moral or immoral; those with a cognitive developmental viewpoint studied primarily moral cognitions. In recent years, however, researchers increasingly have examined the relation or links between the behavioral and cognition domains of morality.

In general, theorists and researchers concerned with the role of moral cognition in moral behavior have assumed implicitly or explicitly that rational processes, including conscious values and goals, are central to moral functioning. Moral cognitions are viewed not only as engendering some moral actions, but at a more basic level, as being essential for the classification of an action as moral. An action that is not motivated by moral cognitions is not deemed to be moral, regardless of the nature of the action itself (Bar-Tal, 1982; Blasi, 1983; Kohlberg & Candee, 1984).

Despite the centrality of moral cognitions for cognitive developmentalists and some philosophers interested in moral behavior, many writers (e.g., Blasi, 1980; Kohlberg, 1971) have pointed out that one cannot expect to find a one-

Research and time contributed to the chapter were funded, in part, by a grant from NICHD (1 RO1 HD17909-01A1).

to-one relation between level of moral cognition and the performance of moral actions. There are numerous reasons why this is so. The purpose of this chapter is to consider some of these reasons. In my discussion of moral action, prosocial behaviors (i.e., behaviors intended to benefit another) will be emphasized, although the issues addressed generally are relevant to a variety of moral behaviors. Prior to discussion of these issues, however, I will briefly review the pattern of relations found between moral cognitions and moral behavior in the empirical research.

THE EMPIRICAL ASSOCIATION BETWEEN MORAL COGNITIONS AND MORAL BEHAVIORS

In the past few years, there have been several reviews of the relation between moral cognitions and moral action (e.g., Blasi, 1980; Eisenberg, 1982, 1986; Underwood & Moore, 1982). Rather than duplicate these efforts, I will use these reviews to summarize the current state of the empirical research. This summary will provide the basis from which to move to the issues more central to this chapter—conceptual and methodological considerations with regard to the association between moral reasoning and behavior.

Blasi (1980) examined the relation of moral cognitions to a wide range of behaviors commonly considered to be moral or immoral, including delinquent acts, honesty, altruism, and resistance to conformity. Consistent with the cognitive developmental approach, Blasi focused on one type of moral cognition—moral reasoning—which he described as "characterized by the justification of a moral conclusion and by the general or specific criteria by which moral decisions are supported" (p. 7). Blasi did not examine moral knowledge (i.e., the recognition of moral norms) or moral attitudes and values (expressed as either a personal belief, an affective inclination, or a tendency to behave in a certain moral manner); the significance of these is viewed by cognitive developmentalists as being dependent on one's moral reasoning. Such an emphasis on moral reasoning is common in most of the literature on moral cognition, and will be adopted in this chapter.

Overall, Blasi obtained moderate support for the notion that there is a positive relation between moral reasoning and moral behavior. The strongest support was obtained for the hypotheses that (1) delinquents and nondelinquents differ in their moral reasoning and (2) at higher stages of moral reasoning there is greater resistance to pressure to conform one's own judgments to those of others. Clear but less consistent support was found for the hypothesis that higher-level moral reasoning is positively related to the enactment of altruistic and honest behavior. Finally, Blasi did not obtain support for the expectation that individuals reasoning at the abstract, postconventional level (Kohlberg's highest level, 1976) are more resistant than other persons to social pressure when choosing a moral or nonmoral course of action.

Other reviewers have come to conclusions similar to those of Blasi (1980). For example, Underwood and Moore (1982) computed a meta-analysis to examine the association of prosocial behavior and moral reasoning. They obtained a significant positive relation between the two aspects of moral functioning. Similarly, Eisenberg noted a positive association between prosocial actions and reasoning about moral conflicts involving potential altruistic behavior (Eisenberg, 1982, 1986).

Despite evidence of a link between moral reasoning and moral behavior in all the aforementioned reviews, the pattern of interassociation is not entirely consistent. Many factors may account for the uneven relation between the two aspects of moral functioning. Some of these factors will now be considered. Definitional and methodological issues will be examined first; discussion of conceptual issues will follow. The methodological issues that will be considered are procedures for operationalizing moral behavior, procedures for operationalizing moral reasoning, and the use of single indices rather than aggregate measures of behavior.

OPERATIONALIZATION AND DEFINITION OF MORAL BEHAVIOR

One of the most obvious explanations for the sometimes inconsistent relation between moral behavior and moral cognition is that not all behavior that appears moral is, in reality, motivated by moral considerations (e.g., internalized moral values, norms, and responsibilities or concern for others). Indeed, much behavior that appears to be moral may be motivated by nonmoral or immoral factors.

Let us consider in detail the case of prosocial behavior. It is clear that not all children's apparently altruistic behaviors are motivated by moral concerns. When directly asked why they performed previous acts of helping or sharing, children 4–5 years old (e.g., Eisenberg, Lundy, Shell, & Roth, 1985; Eisenberg-Berg & Neal, 1979) and elementary school children (e.g., Bar-Tal, 1982; Hertz-Lazarowitz, 1983; Raviv, Bar-Tal, & Lewis-Levin, 1980) frequently have said that they assisted for pragmatic or self-oriented reasons, or because they liked the recipient of aid. Moreover, preschoolers sometimes attribute their own adult-requested prosocial actions to fear of punishment and/or blind deference to authority (Eisenberg, Lundy, Shell, & Roth, 1985). In yet other situations, children say their prosocial behavior is motivated by the desire for social approval or avoidance of shame (e.g., Eisenberg-Berg, 1979a; Ugurel-Semin, 1952; see Eisenberg, 1986, for reviews of this literature).

Because so many apparently altruistic behaviors are not viewed even by the actor as altruistic, there is little reason to expect a strong positive association between level of moral judgment and merely any intentional behavior that results in benefits for others (i.e., any prosocial action). The psychological significance of the act must be considered.

Methods for Identifying Altruistic Behavior

Given that not all behaviors that appear to be moral really are motivated by moral concerns, one issue that needs to be addressed is how to identify those behaviors that are moral so that it is possible to examine the association between moral cognitions and these behaviors. One way to do this is to question individuals with regard to their motives after they have performed a specific potentially moral behavior. This technique is quite useful because it allows behavior to be viewed from the actor's rather than the experimenter's perspective (the two may differ considerably). However, it is possible that some persons, especially older children and adults, will intentionally or unintentionally distort their reported motives to enhance their public or private image. Moreover, in some situations, especially when a behavior is habitual or not of great personal significance, individuals may not have ready access to their own motives (Nisbett & Wilson, 1977; for discussion of this issue see Smith & Miller, 1978; von Cranach, Kalbermatten, Indermuhle, & Gugler, 1982). Thus the degree to which this strategy would be successful in isolating moral behaviors is unclear. Nonetheless, self-report of motives is probably a reasonable strategy for identifying actions that appear to be moral but are motivated by conscious nonmoral considerations (as reported by the actor), even if some behaviors are incorrectly labeled as moral.

An alternative strategy for identifying moral behavior involves differentiating among various behaviors that vary on characteristics likely to be relevant to the classification of an action as moral. Some of these critical characteristics may be inherent in the act itself; others may vary, in part, as a function of the situation. If one can identify modes of prosocial behavior that are more likely than others to be motivated by moral concerns, then the strength of the relation between these modes of behavior and moral reasoning could be examined.

Researchers frequently have implicitly or explicitly employed this strategy. For example, in many studies concerning altruism in children, investigators have assessed prosocial responding in a context in which there were no persons other than the child present (i.e., the behavior seemed to be anonymous). This strategy has been used to reduce the probability that assisting would be motivated by social approval concerns. Unfortunately, researchers rarely have determined whether children's motives are actually influenced by the presence of others. Nonetheless, the fact that elementary school children share more in public situations (e.g., Kenrick, Baumann, & Cialdini, 1979) suggests that the presence of others does elicit nonmoral motives for assisting.

Another example of a dimension that seems to be especially related to individuals' motives for a potentially moral act (especially a prosocial act) is the cost of the behavior for the actor. Clearly, people are more likely to assist another if the act of assisting is low in cost rather than high (Eisenberg & Shell, 1986; Weyant, 1978; see Staub, 1978). If a potential prosocial behavior is low in cost to the actor, circumstances involving the potential behavior should be relatively unlikely to elicit moral cognitions or moral conflict (i.e., internal conflict between various wants, needs, and values). In fact, low-cost behaviors such as helping to pick up spilled groceries or opening the door for another person may be performed somewhat automatically or habitually without much conscious thought, moral or otherwise (Langer, Blank, & Chanowitz, 1978; cf. Gerson & Damon, 1978). Such low-cost behavior frequently may be embedded in individuals' social scripts, that is, in knowledge structures consisting of coherent sequences of actions and events expected in a given situation. These scripts are stored in one's memory and are used to guide behavior with the minimum of cognitive functioning. Thus unless a social script was originally constructed as the consequence of careful consideration of moral issues, one would expect relatively little association between scripted prosocial behaviors and level of moral reasoning.

Eisenberg and Shell (1986) obtained some support for the notion that low-cost prosocial behaviors are less likely than high-cost behaviors to be related to children's typical level of moral judgment. Preschoolers and third graders were interviewed regarding their moral reasoning about hypothetical helping situations and then were given opportunities to donate, on two different occasions, valuable and less valuable commodities. Moreover, the children were given an opportunity to help another at either a cost to the self or no cost to the self. For both age groups, high-cost but not low-cost donating was positively related to developmentally mature moral judgment. Similarly, low-cost helping was unrelated to moral reasoning whereas high-cost helping was associated with preschoolers' mature reasoning.

Other findings in the research concerning prosocial behavior also are consistent with the view that costly prosocial action involves moral conflict, and thus is positively related to level of moral reasoning. For example, in studies of preschoolers' naturally occurring prosocial behaviors, peer-directed sharing behaviors (which by our definition involve a cost to the self) have been more highly related to moral reasoning than have low-cost prosocial behaviors (Eisenberg-Berg & Hand, 1979; Eisenberg, Pasternack, Cameron, & Tryon, 1984). This relation holds only for spontaneously offered sharing behaviors, not for sharing in reaction to a peer request. Moreover, in laboratory studies with older children, developmentally mature moral judgment has been more highly positively related to prosocial behaviors involving a cost (e.g., donating money) than to those low in cost (e.g., helping to pick up spilled paper clips; Eisenberg, Boehnke, Schuhler, & Silbereisen, 1985; Eisenberg, Pasternack, & Lennon, 1984; Eisenberg-Berg, 1979b).

The point of importance here is that investigators can take steps to identify specific behaviors that are more likely than others to involve moral cognitions. Of course, one cannot say for certain whether or not the actor perceives the prosocial action in the same terms as does the experimenter (cf. Zarbatany, Hartmann, Gelfand, & Ramsey, 1982). What constitutes a high cost for a child may be viewed as low cost by most adults. Nonetheless, there is a need for researchers to identify selectively those behaviors that are likely to involve moral cognitions if they wish to relate performance of purportedly moral acts with moral reasoning.

OPERATIONALIZATION OF MORAL REASONING

Procedures for assessing and scoring moral judgment differ considerably. Some of the differences in methods are likely to affect the magnitude of the association between reasoning and behavior.

Consider first the content and form of the various modes of moral cognitions that researchers have examined in relation to moral behavior. Among the various types of moral cognitions that have been studied in relation to prosocial behaviors are the following: (1) Piagetian (Piaget, 1932) hypothetical moral dilemmas concerning distributive justice (e.g., Emler & Rushton, 1974); (2) Piagetian hypothetical dilemmas concerning the understanding of the role of motives versus consequences in morality (e.g., Grant, Weiner, & Rushton, 1976); (3) Kohlberg's (1971, 1976, 1981) hypothetical moral dilemmas, which concern primarily prohibition-related issues (i.e., rules, laws, authorities and their dictates, violation of formal obligations) and principles of justice (e.g., Harris, Mussen, & Rutherford, 1976; Staub, 1974); (4) Rest's (1979) objective pencil-and-paper index of Kohlberg's levels involving selection of those issues critical to one's resolution of a moral conflict (e.g., Andreason, 1976; Brissett, 1977); (5) Damon's (1977) level of positive (distributive) justice reasoning (e.g., Blotner & Bearison, 1984; Damon, 1977); (6) Eisenberg's (Eisenberg, Lennon, & Roth, 1983; Eisenberg-Berg, 1979a) hypothetical moral dilemmas concerning prosocial moral conflicts in which an actor's needs or wants are in conflict with those of another in a context in which the role of prohibitions and authorities is minimal or irrelevant (e.g., Eisenberg-Berg & Hand, 1979; Eisenberg-Berg, 1979a); (7) other sets of hypothetical dilemmas used in only one or two studies (e.g., Levin & Bekerman-Greenberg, 1980); and (8) self-report of motives for previously performed prosocial behaviors (e.g., Bar-Tal, 1982; Eisenberg, Lundy, Shell, & Roth, 1985).

Content of Reasoning

The various aforementioned indices of moral cognition differ considerably in both content and form. With regard to content or focus, reasoning about all the various issues listed above is unlikely to be equally related to a given type of moral behavior (cf. Blasi, 1980). Consider again the case of altruistic behavior. The conceptual relation between altruism and the use of motives versus consequences as criteria in moral judgments is indirect at best, especially for children aged 7 and older, most of whom have a firm grasp of the concepts involved in the Piagetian dilemmas. The link between distributive justice reasoning and prosocial behavior is also very indirect. Some modes of prosocial behavior do not involve the distribution of goods. Moreover, the ways in which children who reason in terms of equality versus equity behave in various helping situations should depend on characteristics of the specific context (e.g., whether or not the child earned the commodity to be distributed). Similarly, altruism should be more closely related to reasoning about prosocial moral dilemmas than to reasoning about authorities and their dictates, rules, and such prohibition-related issues. This is because the issues that are relevant to the decision to engage in altruistic behavior are more likely to be similar to the issues central to prosocial dilemmas. Indeed, Levin and Bekerman-Greenberg (1980) found that the degree of positive association between sharing behavior and moral reasoning was a function of the degree to which a hypothetical moral dilemma was similar in situational details to the circumstance in which sharing was assessed. Whereas reasoning about sharing in a hypothetical situation quite similar to that in which actual sharing was assessed was positively related to prosocial behavior, reasoning on Damon's (1977) distributive justice interview was negatively related to sharing when the effects of age of child were statistically controlled.

Some proponents of Kohlberg's system appear to believe that Kohlberg's stages of reasoning should be related, at least to some degree, to all modes of moral behavior. For example, Kohlberg and Candee (1984) proposed a model for explaining the relation between moral judgment and moral behavior, one in which the class of moral behaviors was not limited to any subset of moral actions. Kohlberg apparently holds the aforementioned view because of his belief that his stages of reasoning are based on increasing maturity in *structure* of reasoning, not content; thus the stages are viewed as more or less content free. Structure is defined as the more formal and abstract features of moral judgment, and is viewed as reflecting advances in sociomoral role taking (Colby & Kohlberg, in press).

The view that Kohlberg's stages are based solely on structure is questionable. Numerous researchers have noted the strong influence of content at each of Kohlberg's stages, and the fact that specific content issues are coded at some stages but not others (cf. Rest, 1979). Indeed, some investigators have suggested that the contents of each of Kohlberg's stages (or levels) reflect different generalized value orientations (Berndt, 1981; Eisenberg, 1986; Nisan, 1984; Staub, 1982). If Kohlberg's stages each emphasize different content and values (e.g., the valuing of others' approval vs. hedonistic outcomes for the self), the level of Kohlbergian reasoning should be more closely related to some modes of moral behavior than others, and some stages should be especially relevant to certain moral behaviors.

In summary, conceptual simplicity is reflected in much of the research concerning the relation between moral reasoning and moral behaviors. There is often no compelling conceptual reason to expect an association between a given index of moral judgment and the mode of moral behavior in question.

Scoring of Moral Judgment

Another factor that no doubt affects the magnitude and perhaps even direction of the relation between moral reasoning and moral behavior is the manner in which moral judgment is indexed when correlated with moral action. As was noted by Blasi (1980), researchers frequently have dichotomized subjects' moral judgment into high and low levels or have assumed a monotonically increasing positive relation between higher-level moral judgment and moral behavior. Such procedures obscure curvilinear relations between reasoning and behavior, or may mask an association between reasoning at a specific level or stage and moral behavior. For example, reasoning reflecting the desire to obtain social approval for one's behaviors (a middle-level type of reasoning in both Kohlberg's and Eisenberg's schemes) might be expected to relate particularly to the performance of some public acts of assistance, especially at certain age levels. If this were the case, such a relation might well be masked if the moral reasoning data were dichotomized or treated as a single, unidimensional construct. In our own work, we often have obtained stronger and more consistent relations between reasoning and behavior when we have correlated behavior with specific modes of reasoning (e.g., hedonistic, needs oriented, approval oriented) rather than a summary index of level of reasoning (scored as a global "stage" score or a weighted composite score based on use of various modes of reasoning at different levels; e.g., Eisenberg, Lennon, & Roth, 1983).

Moral Reasoning versus Moral Attributions

Operationalizations of moral judgment differ not only in content, but also in their form. Differences among the various operationalizations of moral cognitions should be noted because they may be differentially related to moral behavior.

The well-known Piagetian (1932) moral dilemmas related to children's use of consequences versus motives as moral criteria (and derivations thereof) are examples of one type of moral cognition labeled moral judgments. With the Piagetian paradigm, the child is presented with stories of children who behaved in specific ways. The child is then asked to evaluate the story protagonist(s). Thus the child is asked to make attributions about others' morality or goodness after the others have already performed specified behaviors. Children are not asked to resolve moral dilemmas themselves. Moreover, in many cases, researchers have not weighted heavily the child's reasons for his or her decision.

In contrast, in the procedures used by Kohlberg (Colby et al., 1983), Eisenberg (Eisenberg et al., 1983), Damon (1977), and others, children are presented with hypothetical (or perhaps real) moral dilemmas that they are asked to resolve (the protagonist is usually someone else, but could be the self). Their reasons for resolving the dilemma in a specific manner are elicited and are the primary unit of analysis. Thus, with these procedures, respondents are not merely judging other actors; they are making and justifying their own decisions.

A third procedure for assessing moral cognitions has involved eliciting individuals' justifications for their own moral behaviors subsequent to their execution (e.g., Bar-Tal, 1982; Eisenberg, Lundy, Roth, & Shell, 1985). In this case, individuals' responses can be considered to be either self-reported motives (if one believes the actor has access to his or her own motives) or self-attributions (if one believes that individuals do not have access to their own motives and that actors merely attribute motives to the self upon observing their own behavior). In either case, the judgment is made post hoc to the behavior, and concerns one's own real-life behavior.

There are yet other procedures of assessing moral reasoning that differ somewhat from those already described (e.g., Rest, 1979). However, for our purposes, it is sufficient to contrast the three methods just described.

There is virtually no research in which the relative strength of the relation of these three types of moral cognition to behavior has been examined. However, some of the dimensions on which the three modes of moral cognition differ do appear to affect reasoning, and therefore should be considered when examining the link between moral cognitions and moral behavior. For example, the reasons children provide for the resolution of moral dilemmas in which they themselves are the actor seem to be lower in developmental level than the reasons they provide for hypothetical others (e.g., Damon, 1977; Eisenberg-Berg & Neal, 1981). Children may, however, attribute their own behaviors, once accomplished (either in real life or hypothetically), to more lofty motives than those to which they attribute others' behaviors (Gelfand & Hartmann, 1982; Keasey, 1977).

These two sets of findings seem somewhat contradictory, and point out the need for careful consideration of the differences among various modes of moral cognition. The explanation for these findings seems to be twofold. First, there is often a positive, self-enhancing bias in how people interpret their own prior behavior versus that of others (cf. Schlenker, Hallam, & McCown, 1983; Snyder, Stephan, & Rosenfield, 1978); such a bias would serve to elevate self-attributions. Second, when trying to decide how to *resolve* a dilemma, nonmoral (and often self-oriented) concerns seem to become more salient if the situation is viewed from one's own perspective rather than that of a hypothetical other (cf. Eisenberg-Berg & Neal, 1981). Often one's self-serving objectives can only be justified with the use of lower-level reasoning; thus people may revert to lower-level reasoning in order to justify an egoistic choice of behavior they select for themselves but not others ("reconciliation through rationalization"; cf. Gerson & Damon, 1978). This lower-level reasoning is probably more similar to the reasoning associated with decisions about real-life moral behaviors involving a cost than is the higher-level reasoning children use to resolve hypothetical dilemmas involving others.

The above analysis would suggest that moral *reasoning* about situations involving the self (especially real-life situations) should be more closely related to actual behavior than is reasoning about others. On the other hand, *attributions* about the self should not be more closely related to behavior than are attributions about others. Systematic research concerning this issue is lacking but would be useful for clarifying the relation between moral cognitions and moral behavior.

Another factor to consider when comparing the various modes of moral cognition is that attributions elicited post hoc to a behavior generally are limited in the sense that they justify only the chosen course of action. For example, if a person is explaining why he or she behaved in a prosocial manner, his or her reasoning probably will concern motives for helping, and not reasons for choosing not to assist. In contrast, when resolving a moral dilemma in which the choice of behavior is the focus of attention, the individual often will offer reasons both for and against a given course of action (e.g., for and against helping). Thus one might expect a clearer relation between moral reasoning and behavior, especially in situations in which the individual chooses to behave in a nonmoral or immoral fashion, than between post hoc attributions and moral behavior. Moreover, it is possible that in some situations post hoc self-attributions will be based on merely viewing one's own behavior and not on an awareness of one's own real motives (cf. Bem, 1972; Nisbett & Wilson, 1977); this would be most likely when the behavior was performed rather automatically (Eisenberg, Pasternack, Cameron, & Tryon, 1984; Smith & Miller, 1978) and internal cues are "weak, ambiguous, or uninterpretable" (Bem, 1972, p. 2). In contrast, when moral conflict is induced (e.g., the individual really has to think about his or her choice of behavior), self-report of motives is more likely to be based on knowledge of one's own motives (Eisenberg & Shell, 1986).

In summary, until now, moral cognitions of various sorts generally have been treated as a rather homogeneous group. Nonetheless, it is likely that various dimensions of moral cognitions, such as whether they concern real or hypothetical situations, the self or others, and are a priori versus post hoc, influence the degree of association between moral cognitions and moral behavior.

AGGREGATION OF MEASURES

Another methodological issue to consider when examining the relation of moral cognition to moral behavior concerns aggregation of indices. In general, researchers have measured a single moral behavior in a specific setting, often a laboratory situation, whereas moral judgment has been assessed with moral dilemmas concerning very different circumstances and behaviors.

There are now theoretical arguments as well as data consistent with the conclusion that the sum of a set of measurements of a characteristic or behavior is a more unbiased and stable estimator than is any single measurement from the larger set (Epstein, 1979; Rushton, Brainerd, & Pressley, 1983). By combining across measures, error due to the use of particular instruments may average out; in addition, the generality of the measure is enhanced. Thus it is not surprising that a single index of moral behavior sometimes has not been associated with indices of moral cognition. It is likely that some researchers have failed to obtain a relation between moral cognitions and behavior because their index of behavior (or reasoning) was unreliable or too situationally specific to be a powerful measure. If aggregate indices were used more frequently in empirical research concerning the association between moral cognition and moral behavior, it is likely that empirical evidence for a positive relation between the two would be stronger.

CONCEPTUAL ISSUES

Thus far, a number of methodological issues concerning the investigation of the relation between moral cognitions and behavior have been discussed. Of course, some of these considerations relate to some degree to conceptual issues. However, there are other issues that are predominantly conceptual that have not yet been adequately considered. These issues concern when an association between moral behavior and cognitions is to be expected, and the nature of this relation.

CAUSAL RELATIONS BETWEEN MORAL COGNITION AND BEHAVIOR

Decades ago, in his book *The Moral Judgment of the Child,* Piaget (1932) suggested that the child acquires morality on the plane of action prior to acquiring morality on the plane of conscious cognition. In Piaget's view, moral action spawns moral cognitions; indeed, moral cognitions are described as often lagging a year or two behind moral behavior in actual practice. Moreover, as was pointed out by Locke (1983b), it is likely that Piaget viewed the development of moral cognitions as a three-stage process; first in time should be "the behavior itself and its motivation, then the conscious realization of that motivation, and finally, through a second-order conscious realization, theorizing about the motivation and its application to unfamiliar or wholly hypothetical situations" (Locke, 1983b, p. 163).

Piaget's theorizing has profound implications for the understanding of the relation between moral thought and behavior. If Piaget is correct, causality flows from action to reasoning, at least early in development. This perspective is quite contrary to that of many researchers who seem to view moral behavior as being the product of moral reasoning (both in terms of development and in specific situations).

If abstract hypothetical moral judgment is derived from moral reasoning in real-life situations, which in turn is derived from action itself, one would expect reasoning about practical real-life situations to be more advanced than reasoning about hypothetical situations. However, the research related to this issue is inconsistent. Whereas Haan (1975) and Gilligan and Belenky (1980) found that people's reasoning tended to be higher for real-life than hypothetical situations, Arndt (1976) and Damon (1977) obtained findings in which hypothetical reasoning was higher than real-life reasoning. Moreover, Damon (1977), in another study dealing with children's understanding of authority, obtained no difference between the two types of reasons; nor did De Mersseman (1977) in another study. Thus the existing research does not clearly support Piaget's assertion that practical morality precedes morality on a hypothetical level.

Lack of clear empirical support for Piaget's ideas does not, of course, indicate that there is no truth in them. The kinds of moral conceptions that one would expect to emerge in action prior to thought are the simpler conceptions that are embedded in everyday interactions, not higher-level abstractions. Thus primitive concepts such as those concerning the need to care for others, cooperation, and reciprocity might be expected to emerge initially via action, whereas concepts related to the nature of society and abstract principles might be based as much (or more) on cognitive reflection as on action. If this were the case, action might be the basis of conscious moral reasoning primarily in the early years when the more rudimentary moral conceptions are emerging. In contrast, in later childhood and adulthood, action may be only one basis for the emergence of new, higher-level conscious moral reasoning.

Even if the causal relation between action and conscious abstract moral reasoning is not unidirectional in the manner proposed by Piaget, it is worthwhile to consider the idea that causality sometimes flows from actions to moral reasoning. Although this perspective is not predominant in the moral judgment literature, it has occasionally been discussed. For example, Locke (1983a) suggested that behavior can affect specific moral values or judgments, which, in turn, can influence the structure of the individual's moral reasoning. In his model, causality between action and formal reasoning goes both ways.

Similarly, I (Eisenberg, 1986) have suggested that moral behavior might both influence subsequent self-perceptions regarding one's own morality (one's self-image as a moral person) and shape new beliefs and values that are then reflected in moral reasoning and behavior. People appear to have a need to maintain consistency between their behaviors and beliefs (à la cognitive dissonance theory; Festinger, 1957; Wicklund & Brehm, 1976), and sometimes modify their moral values and moral reasoning to be consistent with prior behavior. Indeed, there is evidence that the performance of behavior inconsistent with prior reasoning (i.e., counterattitudinal behavior), when done voluntarily, promotes higher-level reasoning, especially if the counterattitudinal behavior is justified with reasoning higher than that of the individual (Rholes, Bailey, & McMillian, 1982; cf. Rholes & Lane, 1985). Inconsistency between one's actions and cognitions may serve as stimulus to further development in moral reasoning due to the need for dissonance reduction. Moreover, engaging in a given potentially moral behavior may provide the opportunity for learning via role-taking experiences (i.e., the individual may be provided with opportunities to learn about others' feelings and perspectives). Level of moral reasoning is viewed by Kohlberg as being highly influenced by one's sociomoral role-taking capabilities (Kohlberg, 1969, 1976), and has been shown to be somewhat (although not consistently) positively related to level of moral reasoning (Kurdek, 1978). Thus the role-taking opportunities provided by action may affect the individual's social cognitive processing and thereby influence his or her moral judgment.

In summary, a simple unidirectional model of the relation between behavior and moral cognition is likely to be inadequate to capture the true complexity of the link between the two. More complex models clearly are needed.

DEVELOPMENTAL CONSIDERATIONS

It was suggested previously that the relation between moral behavior and cognition may not be identical at all ages. Indeed, developmental factors may influence this association in a variety of ways.

As was already discussed, it is possible that the direction of causality between action and moral reasoning may shift somewhat with age. Moreover, there is some evidence to suggest that the relation between moral action and moral reasoning should become more consistent with age. Researchers have found that persons reasoning at higher levels demonstrate higher consistency between reasoning and behavior than persons reasoning at lower levels (cf. Kohlberg & Candee, 1984; McNamee, 1978; Rholes & Bailey, 1983). This pattern of findings seems to be due, in part, to the fact that people reasoning at higher levels seem to assign more responsibility to the self for acting in a manner consistent with their choice of behavior (Kohlberg & Candee, 1984). Thus, given that level of moral judgment is highly age related, one would expect consistency between action and moral reasoning to increase with age and sociocognitive development.

Gerson and Damon (1978) suggested another way in which developmental factors might influence the strength of the association between moral behavior and cognition. They pointed out that the child's sociocognitive capacities are very dynamic, and are constantly changing and being reorganized. Thus at a given point in development children may have a firm grasp of some moral conceptions and only a very tentative understanding of other, more sophisticated notions. If this is the case, we can expect uneven use of those capacities that are in the process of being acquired or consolidated.

DELIBERATE VERSUS HABITUAL OR SCRIPTED ACTION

As discussed previously, one cannot expect all types of apparently moral behavior to relate equally to moral cognition. This point bears reemphasizing.

Automatic or habitual moral behaviors should be expected to involve little conscious processing, moral or otherwise. Thus those behaviors that are habitual because they have been performed many times and/or are part of a social script should be unrelated to moral reasoning unless the pattern of behavior was originally established due to conscious moral concerns. Especially if the behavior in question is low in cost for the actor and the outcome is of relatively low moral significance, there is no reason to expect the behavior to have been based on moral considerations (cf. Gerson & Damon, 1978; Eisenberg & Shell, 1986). Moreover, even behaviors with moderate costs and outcomes may be habitual and unrelated to moral concerns; for example, a person may start giving to the United Appeal at the office without much thought (e.g., just because someone asked him or her to) and may continue to do so without really considering the moral significance of the behavior.

Another type of undeliberated moral action may be unrelated to conscious moral reasoning, but for different reasons. As was mentioned previously, Piaget (1932) and others (e.g., Gerson & Damon, 1978; Locke, 1983b) have discussed the possibility that people, especially children, act morally due to a primitive understanding of moral issues at the level of action prior to the point at which they acquire a conscious, reflective understanding of the relevant moral concern. If people sometimes act in ways that are motivated by action-based rather than reflective moral concerns, one would not expect a strong positive relation between such behavior and contemporaneous moral reasoning (although behavior might predict reasoning at a later age).

EMOTIONAL CONTRIBUTIONS TO MORAL BEHAVIOR

Another instance in which moral behavior may be intuitive rather than cognitive and deliberate is when it is emotionally driven. For many years, philosophers such as Hume (1777/1966) suggested that moral behaviors may sometimes be motivated by feelings such as sympathy. In recent years, investigators have noted that emotional reactions to another's state may reflect either other-oriented concern (sympathy), self-oriented anxiety or discomfort (personal distress), or perhaps merely emotional contagion (cf. Batson & Coke, 1981; Eisenberg, 1986; Eisenberg & Miller, 1987; Hoffman, 1984). Those apparently moral behaviors engendered primarily by sympathetic, other-oriented concern frequently are viewed as truly moral (e.g., Batson & Coke, 1981; Blum, 1980), whereas behavior motivated by self concern (personal distress) is not (Batson & Coke, 1981).

In some situations, emotional responsiveness to others may be the primary instigator of moral behavior; in others, moral cognitions also may be highly involved. As an example of the former case, Radke-Yarrow and Zahn-Waxler (1984) have noted many instances of prosocial behavior in children 1–2 years old that seem to be motivated, at least in part, by sympathy or empathy. In such young children, it is unlikely that conscious moral cognitions are major contributors to performance of these prosocial acts. Similarly, in crisis situations, such as when a young child falls in a swimming pool, many adults seem to respond immediately on the basis of a compelling emotional reaction; in such circumstances, the degree of conscious cognitive deliberation frequently may be minimal (cf. Piliavin, Dovidio, Gaertner, & Clark, 1981). Moreover, in everyday life, many moral behaviors may occur primarily as a consequence of sympathetic or empathic feelings without conscious cognitive consideration of these feelings. In all of these instances, one would not expect a strong relation between individuals' levels of moral cognition and their moral behavior.

It is important to note, however, that sympathetic or empathic reactions may influence the individual's goals in a specific situation, and consequently may be reflected in their moral reasoning. Primitive empathy (orienting to the other's need) is evident in the moral reasoning and self-reported motives of even many children 4–5 years old (e.g., Eisenberg-Berg & Hand, 1979; Eisenberg-Berg & Neal, 1979, 1981). Moreover, people of late elementary school age and older not infrequently mention self-reflective empathic/sympathetic concerns in their moral reasoning (e.g., Eisenberg, Pasternack, & Lennon, 1984; Eisenberg-Berg, 1979a; Gilligan, 1982). Although Kohlberg (1969, 1971) has argued that affect is shaped by moral judgments rather than vice versa, it is quite possible that emotional responses such as sympathy influence which level of reasoning, among those the individual is capable of using, is dominant in a given situation (cf. Eisenberg, 1986; Hoffman, in press). If moral reasoning is viewed as reflecting the individual's value hierarchy or goals in a specific situation (e.g., Berndt, 1981; Eisenberg, 1986; Staub, 1982), and values and goals can be based on or influenced by emotional reactions, then emotional reactions could influence the nature of one's moral cognition. In situations in which emotional reactions are reflected in both individuals' conscious moral cognitions and their moral behaviors, it is reasonable to expect a positive relation between the two. Of course, to detect accurately the strength of this relation, it would be imperative to differentiate between egoistic emotional responses such as personal distress and other-oriented responses such as sympathy.

MEDIATORS OF THE RELATION BETWEEN MORAL REASONING AND BEHAVIOR

The route from moral reasoning to behavior, even when one ignores the possible bidirectionality of this relation, is not direct or simple. There are intermediary "steps" on the way, and many factors that influence whether or not the causal influence of moral cognition is actualized. We will now consider some of the factors that appear to affect whether or not moral cognitions are translated into behavior.

Decision Making: An Intermediate Step

For decades psychologists have pondered and examined the relation between attitudes and behavior (e.g., Ajzen & Fishbein, 1977; Fishbein & Ajzen, 1975). Many have come to the conclusion that it is necessary to consider intention as an intermediate step between attitudes and behavior. For example, Fishbein and Ajzen (1975) presented a model in which intentions lead to behavior, and intentions are a function of a number of factors including attitudes. This type of model has proved useful for predicting prosocial behavior as well as other behaviors (e.g., Pomazal & Jaccard, 1976; Zuckerman & Reis, 1978).

Analogously, with regard to moral judgment, theorists have proposed an intermediate step between moral judgment and behavior—that of making a specific moral judgment or decision in a specific situation. More precisely, for Kohlberg, this intermediate step is making a judgment about what is right in the specific situation, what "should" be done, followed by a judgment of one's responsibility to perform the right action (Kohlberg & Candee, 1984). For Locke (1983a), the intermediate factor is the content of particular beliefs or judgments; for Eisenberg (1986), it is the decision to behave in a particular manner (i.e., the behavioral intention). In Eisenberg's view, this decision is a function of a variety of factors including one's general value hierarchy (as reflected in one's moral judgment), affective reactions, the subjective evaluation of costs and benefits of the action, attributions regarding other persons (e.g., the reason for their need), and a variety of personality factors (see Fig. 7.1).

In summary, it has been suggested by various persons that the relation between one's general level of moral reasoning and one's behavior in a specific situation is not direct. Decision-making processes intervene between the two. Moreover, a number of researchers have proposed that variables other than moral reasoning affect this decision-making process, as well as the execution of a decision once made (e.g., Blasi, 1983; Eisenberg, 1986; Locke, 1983a). Some of these other factors will now be considered.

Factors That Influence the Moral Reasoning–Moral Decision Relation

Researchers have suggested a variety of factors that potentially influence the relation between moral reasoning and the individual's choice of behavior (intended behavior) in a specific situation. Indeed, one could write several chapters just discussing these influences. At this time I will indicate what some of these factors might be and point to references concerning relevant theory and research.

A major reason for the fact that the relation between moral reasoning and moral action is not simple is that the individual has many needs, desires, and motives, many of which may be relevant to the decision whether or not to behave in a moral manner in a given situation (cf. Blasi, 1983; Eisenberg, 1986; Gerson & Damon, 1978; Haan, 1978; Staub, 1978). Moreover, these

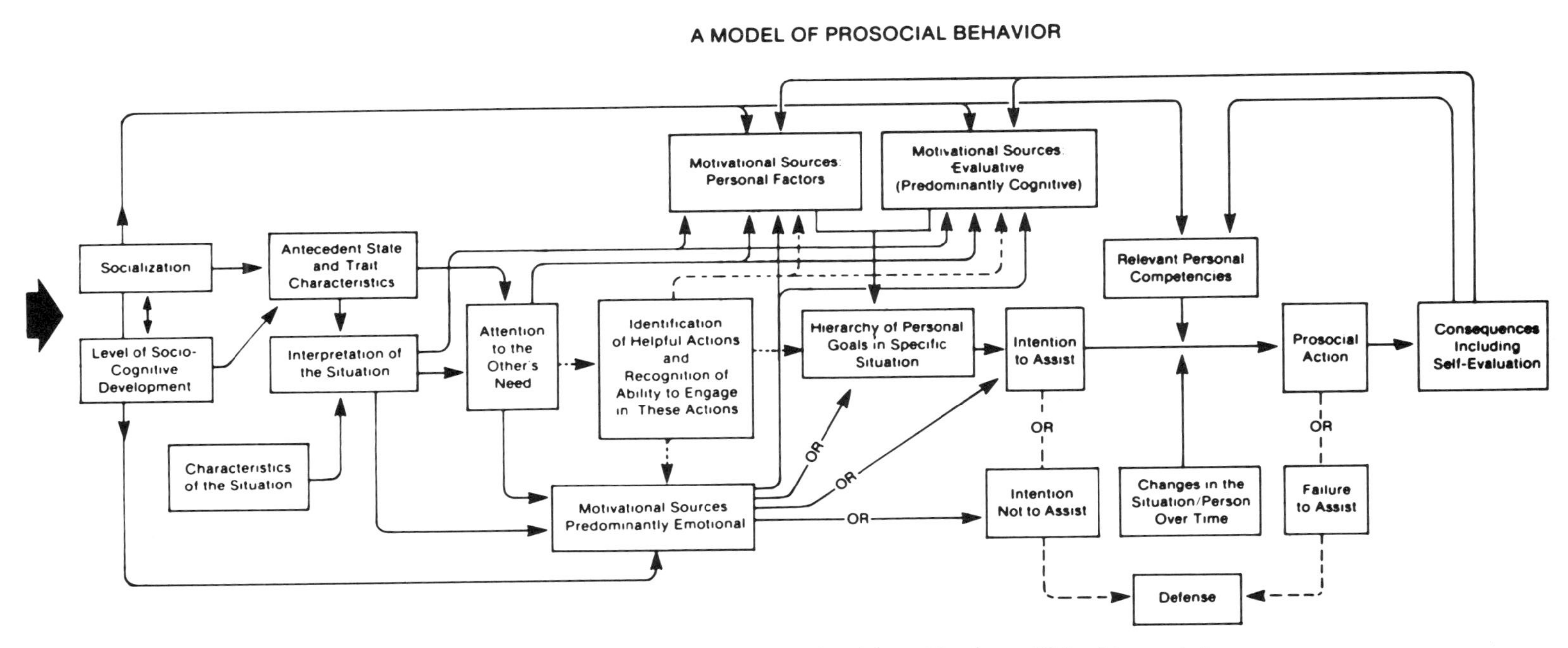

Figure 7.1. A model of prosocial behavior. (Reprinted from Eisenberg, 1986, with permission of Lawrence Erlbaum Associates.)

various needs and motives may be competing or conflicting. For example, costs and benefits to the self (concrete, social, and emotional) and one's self-identity with regard to relevant moral issues are factors that will enter into many moral decisions (for more discussion of these factors see Blasi, 1983; Eisenberg, 1986).

Even prior to confronting a moral conflict, the individual can be viewed as having a hierarchy of personal goals (i.e., motivational preferences for certain end states and aversions to others; Staub, 1978, 1982). Personal goals can be moral or nonmoral; moreover, the relative importance of various goals undoubtedly varies across people. For example, for one person social approval may be more important than upholding internalized principles related to justice; for another, it may not. One can view the individual's moral reasoning, when considered across a variety of dilemmas, as providing a rough index of the relative importance of various personal goals for a given individual. In other words, the individual's moral reasoning can be viewed as reflecting, to some degree, the individual's hierarchy of personal goals (e.g., Berndt, 1981; Eisenberg, 1986; Staub, 1982).

The values, needs, and preferences that underlie personal goals and their relative importance clearly change with development. These developmental shifts are reflected in age-related changes in the individual's typical hierarchy of personal goals, and, consequently, in level of moral judgment. Given that both other-oriented values based upon self-reflective role taking or sympathy and internalized moral principles are much more common with age, one would expect moral personal goals to rank higher in the hierarchies of older children and adults than in those of younger children (e.g., Colby et al., 1983; Eisenberg, 1982, 1986; Kohlberg, 1976).

In any given decision-making situation, certain personal goals will be highlighted whereas others will not. Thus in one situation the desire for approval or the need to achieve may be relevant whereas in other situations these goals may be irrelevant. Moreover, the relative ranking of various goals probably varies across contexts depending on the "pull" for specific goals in different contexts. Thus one's hierarchy of personal goals may vary across situations, depending on the specific characteristics of the situation, the individual's interpretation of the situation (which is, in part, a function of the person's personal goals), and the quality and quantity of affect (e.g., sympathy, personal distress) elicited by the situation. Moreover, personal factors such as one's coping and defense mechanisms may affect how the individual deals with the anxiety evoked by conflicts between moral and nonmoral concerns, for example, whether a person distorts the situation to justify action inconsistent with moral values (Haan, 1978). In the final analysis, however, the factors that emerge as highest in the individual's hierarchy of personal goals should directly determine the decision of what will be done.

The choice of a mode of action in a given situation is, therefore, the outcome of what can be a complex and conflicted decision-making process. Many factors besides moral judgment must be considered, including personality, cognitive (e.g., attributional processes), and affective variables. Only when models of the moral judgment–moral action link are more comprehensive will predictions regarding the interrelations be more accurate.

The Road from Intention or Choice of Behavior to Actual Behavior

Even after a person has decided what he or she plans to do with regard to a potential moral behavior (based, perhaps, in part on moral cognitions), the behavior in question may or may not be enacted. For example, numerous factors may prevent even the well-intentioned person from performing a moral act. These factors include lack of the specific skills required for the moral action or lack of knowledge of workable strategies (e.g., Peterson, 1983a, 1983b; Pomazal & Jaccard, 1976), insufficient self-regulatory capabilities to perform the intended behavior (Grim, Kohlberg, & White, 1968; cf. Kanfer, 1979), feelings of low self-efficacy, or deficits in interpersonal competence (e.g., insufficient assertiveness to carry out the behavior; cf. Barrett & Yarrow, 1977; Eisenberg et al., 1981; Larrieu, 1984; Midlarsky & Hannah, 1985). Moreover, if there is a gap in time between the formation of behavioral intentions and the opportunity to perform a given moral behavior, either the situation itself or aspects of the actor may change in ways that affect performance of the intended behavior. For example, situational factors may be altered in a manner that influences the individual's estimate of the utility of the act. Moreover, the relative salience of various norms, values, personal needs, and affective reactions related to the decision to behave in a given manner may shift if the situation is changed. In addition, the situation may be altered to the degree that the intended moral behavior is no longer relevant, needed, or appropriate.

In brief, behavioral intentions, once formulated, may not be reflected in actual behavior. In instances when this occurs, the association between moral cognitions and behavior should be relatively weak. Thus there is a need to consider factors that may undermine the translation of intentions into behavior when examining the association between moral cognitions and behavior.

SUMMARY

To summarize, the interrelations between moral cognitions and behavior appear to be bidirectional and influenced by a variety of factors. The complexity of this interassociation is not captured by current conceptual models; in addition, our methods of assessing moral cognitions and moral behaviors too frequently have been naive and crude. Indeed, given the conceptual and methodological shortcomings in the literature, it is somewhat surprising that positive relations generally have been obtained between the two domains of moral functioning. With increased conceptual and methodological sophistication, it is likely that researchers will find an even stronger, albeit complicated, relation between the cognitive and behavioral domains of morality.

REFERENCES

Ajzen, I., & Fishbein, M. (1977). Attitude–behavior relations: A theoretical analysis and review of empirical research. *Psychological Bulletin, 84,* 888–918.

Andreason, A. W. (1976). The effects of social responsibility, moral judgment, and conformity on helping behavior. (Doctoral dissertation, Brigham Young University, 1975.) *Dissertation Abstracts International, 36,* 5856B. (University Microfilms No. 76-9829)

Arndt, A. W. (1976). Maturity of moral reasoning about hypothetical dilemmas and behavior in an actual situation. (Doctoral dissertation, University of California, Berkeley, 1975). *Dissertation Abstracts International, 37,* 435B. (University Microfilms No. 76–15, 099)

Barrett, D. E., & Yarrow, M. R. (1977). Prosocial behavior, social inferential ability, and assertiveness in young children. *Child Development, 48,* 475–481.

Bar-Tal, D. (1982). Sequential development of helping behavior: A cognitive-learning approach. *Developmental Review, 2,* 101–124.

Batson, C. E., & Coke, J. S. (1981). Empathy: A source of altruistic motivation for helping? In J. P. Rushton & R. M. Sorrentino (Eds.), *Altruism and helping behavior: Social, personality, and developmental perspectives.* Hillsdale, NJ: Erlbaum.

Bem, D. J. (1972). Self perception theory. In L. Berkowitz (Ed.), *Advances in experimental social psychology* (Vol. 6). New York: Academic.

Berndt, T. J. (1981). Relations between social cognition, nonsocial cognition, and social behavior: The case of friendship. In J. H. Flavell & L. Ross (Eds.), *Social cognitive development.* Cambridge, England: Cambridge University Press.

Blasi, A. (1980). Bridging moral cognition and moral action: A critical review of the literature. *Psychological Bulletin, 88,* 1–45.

Blasi, A. (1983). Moral cognition and moral action: A theoretical perspective. *Developmental Review, 3,* 178–210.

Blotner, R., & Bearison, D. J. (1984). Developmental consistencies in socio-moral knowledge: Justice reasoning and altruistic behavior. *Merrill-Palmer Quarterly, 30,* 349–367.

Blum, L. A. (1980). *Friendship, altruism and morality.* London: Routledge & Kegan Paul.

Brissett, M. J., Jr. (1977). Moral judgment level, social context of commitment, monetary incentive, and altruistic behavior in college students. (Doctoral dissertation, Purdue University, 1976.) *Dissertation Abstracts International, 37,* 5317B. (University Microfilms No. 77-7422)

Colby, A., & Kohlberg, L. (Eds.). (in press). *The measurements of moral judgment* (Vol. 1). New York: Cambridge Press.

Colby, A., Kohlberg, L., Gibbs, J., & Lieberman, M. (1983). A longitudinal study of moral judgment. *Monographs of the Society for Research in Child Development, 48* (Serial No. 200), 1-124.

Damon, W. (1977). *The social world of the child.* San Francisco: Jossey-Bass.

De Mersseman, S. L. (1977). A developmental investigation of children's moral reasoning and behavior in hypothetical and practical situations. (Doctoral dissertation, University of California, Berkeley, 1976.) *Dissertation Abstracts International, 37,* 4643B (University Microfilms No. 77-4435)

Eisenberg, N. (1982). The development of reasoning regarding prosocial behavior. In N. Eisenberg (Ed.), *The development of prosocial behavior.* New York: Academic.

Eisenberg, N. (1986). *Altruistic emotion, cognition, and behavior.* Hillsdale, NJ: Erlbaum.

Eisenberg, N., Boehnke, K., Schuhler, P., & Silbereisen, R. K. (1985). *Journal of Cross-Cultural Psychology, 16,* 69–82.

Eisenberg, N., Cameron, E., Tryon, K., & Dodez, R. (1981). Socialization of prosocial behavior in the preschool classroom. *Developmental Psychology, 17,* 773–782.

Eisenberg, N., Lennon, R., & Roth, K. (1983). Prosocial development in childhood: A longitudinal study. *Developmental Psychology, 19,* 846–855.

Eisenberg, N., Lundy, T., Shell, R., & Roth, K. (1985). Children's justifications for their adult- and peer-directed compliant (prosocial and nonprosocial) behaviors. *Developmental Psychology, 21,* 325–331.

Eisenberg, N., & Miller, R. (1987). The relation of empathy to prosocial and related behaviors. *Psychological Bulletin, 101,* 91–119.

Eisenberg, N., Pasternack, J. F., Cameron, E., & Tryon, K. (1984). The relation of quantity and mode of prosocial to moral cognitions and social style. *Child Development, 55,* 1479–1485.

Eisenberg, N., Pasternack, J. F., & Lennon, R. (1984, March). *Prosocial development in middle childhood.* Paper presented at the biennial meeting of the Southwestern Society for Research in Human Development.

Eisenberg, N., & Shell, R. (1986). The relation of prosocial moral judgment and behavior in children: The mediating role of cost. *Personality & Social Psychology Bulletin, 12,* 426–433.

Eisenberg-Berg, N. (1979a). Development of children's prosocial moral judgment. *Developmental Psychology, 15,* 128–137.

Eisenberg-Berg, N. (1979b). The relationship of prosocial moral reasoning to altruism, political liberalism, and intelligence. *Developmental Psychology, 15,* 87–89.

Eisenberg-Berg, N., & Hand, M. (1979). The relationship of preschoolers' reasoning about prosocial moral conflicts to prosocial behavior. *Child Development, 50,* 356–363.

Eisenberg-Berg, N., & Neal, C. (1979). Children's moral reasoning about their spontaneous prosocial behavior. *Developmental Psychology, 15,* 228–229.

Eisenberg-Berg, N., & Neal, C. (1981). The effects of person of the protagonist and costs of helping on children's moral judgment. *Personality & Social Psychology Bulletin, 7,* 17–23.

Emler, N. P., & Rushton, J. P. (1974). Cognitive-developmental factors in children's generosity. *British Journal of Social & Clinical Psychology, 13,* 277–281.

Epstein, S. (1979). The stability of behavior: 1. On predicting most of the people most of the time. *Journal of Personality & Social Psychology, 37,* 1097–1126.

Festinger, L. (1957). *A theory of cognitive dissonance.* Stanford, CA: Stanford University Press.

Fishbein, M., & Ajzen, I. (1975). *Beliefs, attitudes, intentions and behavior: An introduction to theory and research.* Reading, MA: Addison-Wesley.

Gelfand, D. M., & Hartmann, D. P. (1982). Response consequences and attributions: Two contributors to prosocial behavior. In N. Eisenberg (Ed.), *The development of prosocial behavior.* New York: Academic.

Gerson, R. P., & Damon, W. (1978). Moral understanding and children's conduct. In W. Damon (Ed.), *New directions for child development: Moral development.* San Francisco: Jossey-Bass.

Gilligan, C. (1982). *In a different voice: Psychological theory and women's development.* Cambridge, MA: Harvard University Press.

Gilligan, C., & Belenky, M. F. (1980). A naturalistic study of abortion decisions. In R. Selman & R. Yando (Eds.), *Clinical-developmental psychology new directions in child development.* San Francisco: Jossey-Bass.

Grant, J. E., Weiner, A., & Rushton, J. P. (1976). Moral judgment and generosity in children. *Psychological Reports, 39,* 451–454.

Grim, P., Kohlberg, L., & White, S. (1968). Some relationships between conscience and attentional processes. *Journal of Personality & Social Psychology, 8,* 239–253.

Haan, N. (1975). Hypothetical and actual moral reasoning in a situation of civil disobedience. *Journal of Personality & Social Psychology, 32,* 255–269.

Haan, N. (1978). Two moralities: Reasoning, action, development and ego regulation in white and black adolescents. *Journal of Personality & Social Psychology, 36,* 286–305.

Harris, S., Mussen, P., & Rutherford, E. (1976). Some cognitive, behavioral, and personality correlates of maturity of moral judgment. *Journal of Genetic Psychology, 128,* 123–135.

Hertz-Lazarowitz, R. (1983). Prosocial behavior in the classroom. *Academic Psychology Bulletin, 2,* 319–338.

Hoffman, M. L. (1984). Interaction of affect and cognition in empathy. In C. E. Izard, J. Kagan, & R. B. Zajonc (Eds.), *Emotions, cognitions, and behavior.* Cambridge, England: Cambridge University Press.

Hoffman, M. L. (in press). The contribution of empathy to justice and moral judgment. In N. Eisenberg & J. Strayer (Eds.), *Empathy and its development.* Cambridge, England: Cambridge University Press.

Hume, D. (1966). *Enquiries concerning the human understanding and concerning the principles of morals.* Oxford: Clarendon Press. (Original work published 1777)

Kanfer, F. H. (1979). Personal control, social control, and altruism: Can society survive the age of individualism? *American Psychologist, 34,* 231–239.

Kant, I. (1964). *The doctrine of virtue.* New York: Harper & Row. (Original work published 1797)

Keasey, C. B. (1977). Young children's attributions of intentionality to themselves and others. *Child Development, 48,* 261–264.

Kenrick, D. T., Baumann, D. J., & Cialdini, R. B. (1979). A step in the socialization of altruism as hedonism: Effects of negative mood on children's generosity under public and private conditions. *Journal of Personality & Social Psychology, 37,* 747–755.

Kohlberg, L. (1969). Stage and sequence: The cognitive-developmental approach to socialization. In D. A. Goslin (Ed.), *Handbook of socialization theory and research.* New York: Rand-McNally.

Kohlberg, L. (1971). From is to ought: How to commit the naturalistic fallacy and get away with it in the study of moral development. In T. Mischel (Ed.), *Cognitive development and genetic epistemology.* New York: Academic.

Kohlberg, L. (1976). Moral stage and moralization: The cognitive-developmental approach. In T. Lickona (Ed.), *Moral development and behavior: Theory, research, and social issues.* New York: Holt, Rinehart, & Winston.

Kohlberg, L. (1981). *The philosophy of moral development: Moral stages and the idea of justice.* San Francisco: Harper & Row.

Kohlberg, L., & Candee, D. (1984). The relationship of moral judgment to moral action. In W. M. Kurtines & J. L. Gewirtz (Eds.), *Morality, moral behavior, and moral development.* New York: Wiley.

Kurdek, L. (1978). Perspective taking as the cognitive basis of children's moral development: A review of the literature. *Merrill-Palmer Quarterly, 24,* 3–28.

Langer, E. J., Blank, A., & Chanowitz, B. (1978). The mindlessness of ostensibly thoughtful action. *Journal of Personality & Social Psychology, 36,* 635–642.

Larrieu, J. A. (1984, March). *Prosocial values, assertiveness and sex: Predictors of children's naturalistic helping.* Paper presented at the biennial meeting of the Southwestern Society for Research in Human Development, Denver.

Levin, I., & Bekerman-Greenberg, R. (1980). Moral judgment and moral behavior in sharing: A developmental analysis. *Genetic Psychology Monographs, 101,* 215–230.

Locke, D. (1983a). Doing what comes morally: The relation between behavior and stages of moral reasoning. *Human Development, 26,* 11–25.

Locke, D. (1983b). Theory and practice in thought and action. In H. Weinreich-Haste & D. Locke (Eds.), *Morality in the making.* London: Wiley.

McNamee, S. (1978). Moral behavior, moral development and motivation. *Journal of Moral Education, 7,* 27–31.

Midlarsky, E., & Hannah, M. R. (1985). Competence, reticence, and helping by children and adults. *Developmental Psychology, 21,* 534–541.

Nisan, M. (1984). Content and structure in moral judgment: An integrative view. In W. M. Kurtines & J. L. Gewirtz (Eds.), *Morality, moral behavior and moral development.* New York: Wiley.

Nisbett, R. E., & Wilson, T. D. (1977). Telling more than we can know: Verbal reports on mental processes. *Psychological Review, 84,* 231–259.

Peterson, L. (1983a). Influence of age, task competence, and responsibility focus on children's altruism. *Developmental Psychology, 19,* 141–148.

Peterson, L. (1983b). Role of donor competence, donor age, and peer presence on helping in an emergency. *Developmental Psychology, 19,* 873–880.

Piaget, J. (1932). *The moral judgment of the child.* London: Routledge & Kegan Paul.

Piliavin, J. A., Dovidio, J. F., Gaertner, S. L., & Clark, R. D., III. (1981). *Emergency intervention.* New York: Academic.

Pomazal, R. J., & Jaccard, J. J. (1976). An informational approach to altruistic behavior. *Journal of Personality & Social Psychology, 33,* 317-326.

Radke-Yarrow, M., & Zahn-Waxler, C. (1984). Roots, motives, and patterns in children's prosocial behavior. In E. Staub, D. Bar-Tal, J. Karylowski, & J. Reykowski (Eds.), *Development and maintenance of prosocial behavior: International perspectives.* New York: Plenum.

Raviv, A., Bar-Tal, D., & Lewis-Levin, T. (1980). Motivations for donation behavior by boys of three different ages. *Child Development, 51,* 610-613.

Rest, J. R. (1979). *Development in judging moral issues.* Minneapolis: University of Minnesota Press.

Rholes, W. S., & Bailey, S. (1983). The effects of level of moral reasoning on consistency between moral attitudes and related behaviors. *Social Cognition, 2,* 32-48.

Rholes, W. S., Bailey, S., & McMillian, L. (1982). Experiences that motivate moral development: The role of cognitive dissonance. *Journal of Experimental Social Psychology, 18,* 524-526.

Rholes, W. S., & Lane, J. W. (1985). Consistency between cognitions and behavior: Cause and consequence of cognitive development. In J. B. Pryor & J. D. Day (Eds.), *The development of social cognition.* New York: Springer-Verlag.

Rushton, J. P., Brainerd, C. J., & Pressley, M. (1983). Behavioral development and construct validity: The principle of aggregation. *Psychological Bulletin, 94,* 18-38.

Schlenker, B. R., Hallam, J. R., & McCown, N. E. (1983). Motives and social evaluation: Actor-observer differences in the delineation of motives for a beneficial act. *Journal of Experimental Social Psychology, 19,* 254-273.

Smith, E. R., & Miller, F. D. (1978). Limits on perception of cognitive processes: A reply to Nisbett and Wilson. *Psychological Review, 83,* 355-362.

Snyder, M. L., Stephan, W. G., Rosenfield, D. (1978). Attributional egotism. In J. H. Harvey, W. Ickes, & R. F. Kidd (Eds.), *New directions in attribution research* (Vol. 2). New York: Wiley.

Staub, E. (1974). Helping a distressed person: Social, personality, and stimulus determinants. In L. Berkowitz (Ed.), *Advances in experimental social psychology.* New York: Academic.

Staub, E. (1978). *Positive social behavior and morality: Social and personal influences* (Vol. 1). New York: Academic.

Staub, E. (1982, September). *Toward a theory of moral conduct: Goal orientations, moral judgment, and behavior.* Paper presented at the annual meeting of the American Psychological Association, Washington, DC.

Ugurel-Semin, R. (1952). Moral behavior and moral judgment of children. *Journal of Abnormal & Social Psychology, 47,* 463-474.

Underwood, B., & Moore, B. (1982). Perspective-taking and altruism. *Psychological Bulletin, 91,* 143-173.

von Cranach, M., Kalbermatten, U., Indermuhle, K., & Gugler, B. (1982). *Goal-directed action.* London: Academic.

Weyant, J. M. (1978). Effect of mood states, costs, and benefits on helping. *Journal of Personality & Social Psychology, 36,* 1169–1176.

Wicklund, R. A., & Brehm, J. W. (1976). *Perspectives on cognitive dissonance.* Hillsdale, NJ: Erlbaum.

Zarbatany, L., Hartmann, D. P., Gelfand, D. M., & Ramsey, C. (1982, August). *Ecological validity of experiments on children's charitable behavior.* Paper presented at the annual meeting of the American Psychological Association, Washington, DC.

Zuckerman, M., & Reis, H. T. (1978). Comparison of three models for predicting altruistic behavior. *Journal of Personality & Social Psychology, 36,* 498–510.

CHAPTER 8

Social Influence, Socialization, and the Development of Social Cognition: The Heart of the Matter

PHILIP R. COSTANZO
PETER FRAENKEL

Over the past two decades, both social and developmental psychologists have independently devoted an enormous amount of attention to the relationships that prevail between strategies and processes of causal thinking and the phenomena of social adaptation. An article of faith buttressing much of this theory and research from both fields is the supposition that our actions and adaptations in the social world are mediated by our contemporary understandings of ongoing social events and the people who produce those events. Whether we approach or avoid others, help or hinder them, retaliate or turn the other cheek in the face of their aggression, for example, is purportedly dependent upon how we label the meaning of their behavior and whether we attribute behavior we observe to one or another stable property of the actor or to accidental or constraining environmental factors.

The intellectual heritage of this perspective on social relations owes much to the seminal ideas of Piaget (1932/1965) for developmental psychologists and Heider (1944) for social psychologists. Both of these celebrated theorists centered their respective analyses upon the unique properties of human *causal* thought as it guides the social analysis of action and meaning. The ideological descendants of Piaget and Heider have explicated a wide variety of models to account for the relationships among cognitive processes, social perception, and social adaptation. These models, such as attribution theory and moral judgment theory, have contributed a great deal to our understanding of both social development and social cognition. Nevertheless, the notion that social behavior and social judgment largely proceed from the perceiver's cognitive processes and structures is one that ignores a wide array of the interpersonal–dynamic factors that phenomenally pervade social relations. To use a perhaps corny and indirect idiom, our social behavior and understanding are guided not only by our minds, but also by our "hearts."

In the course of psychological development, we most certainly mature in both cognitive processing capacity and the differentiatedness of our cognitive structures and schemes. Further, given much of the research on developing social cognition, this maturation in cognitive–adaptive phenomena contributes much to our discernment of the social and moral meaning of the behaviors and situations we confront. However, another clear legacy of development is the contribution it makes to the person's chronic beliefs, values, attitudes, and prescriptions for action. The child's transactions with important socializers play a distinct role in differentiating regions of social space bearing disparate meaning for different observers. For example, for those of us attaching special significance to truth telling, the behavior of lying carries different weight in our evaluation of others than it does for those of us who attach less special significance to such an action. Similarly the acquired differentiation of the prescriptivity of transactions in a wide variety of interpersonal domains is a crucial element in our interpretation of our own and others' actions in those separate domains.

At the outset of this chapter, we propose that a full understanding of developing social cognition can be approached only through concerted inquiries into the relationships between socially transmitted, acquired beliefs and developing cognitive processes and structures. While there has been much empirical attention to each of these developmentally unfolding phenomena in both social and developmental psychology, little effort has been put to understanding their connections and coimplications for social development. There exists extensive literature on social influence processes in social psychology and on socialization or child-rearing phenomena in developmental psychology. Yet we have failed to relate what is understood about these processes to our contemporary understandings of social cognition and its development. In our corny idiom, are our "minds" and our "hearts" separately employed in our transactions and perceptions in the social world? We begin this chapter with the presumption that it is conceptually (and perhaps empirically) implausible that such is the case.

In order to consider the relationships implied above, this chapter is organized to consider several issues. First, some consideration will be given to the ideological basis for the separation of inquiry traditions in the study of social influence and social cognition in developmental and social psychology. Next, we will present some of our research on social cognition and its development that casts doubt on an exclusively cognitive–causal model of such phenomena. Finally, we will propose a beginning perspective that considers the conjunction between socialization–social influence and social cognition.

THE CAPACITY OF THE INDIVIDUAL VERSUS THE POWER OF THE COLLECTIVE: THE IDEOLOGICAL RUB

The conception of human beings as autonomous, rational, and self-generative organisms was never more prominently advanced as a model for developmental theory and research than it began to be in the 1960s. From this vantage point, if we are "driven" at all, we are driven to make sense of reality, to seek truth, and to understand the environments we confront. Through the collusion of experience and maturation the developing human becomes increasingly more effective in generating the epistemological processes that give rise to such understanding. Experience with objects results in schemes or plans for further engaging those objects and associated structures for apprehending and accommodating to them. When a structure or scheme fails to result in adaptive consequence we alter it in the direction of a more adequate structure. Across development we move from the trial-and-error sensorimotor schemes of the infant to the abstract schematizing of the formally operational adolescent in which direct exposure to the objects of understanding is not required and symbolic representation and syllogistic thought become sufficient for engaging in prodigious feats of understanding.

While this vision of the developing child had existed for over three decades through the work of Piaget, it was "rediscovered" by American psychologists in the early 1960s. Aided by the masterful summary of Piaget's thought by Flavell (1963), American developmental psychologists enthusiastically embraced his and other optimistic cognitive models of developmental acquisition.

For our purposes, a major feature of these cognitively driven models was the implicit insistence on locating the child as the central force in his or her own development. Social partners, be they parents, siblings, or peers, carry their influence by virtue of their role-related capacity to facilitate or inhibit particular forms of reasoning in the child. The effects of such social mediation were implicitly viewed as temporary. Longer-term influence was seen as interfering with endogenously driven processes of intellectual adaptive growth. This was particularly true of the impact of parental injunctions and constraints. The constraining force of parental socialization could serve to imprison a child in his or her own perspective and forestall the development of subjectivism or relativism in social thought. However, as the conditions of social life changed with development, the child would be cognitively freed of such constraints by the relations of negotiated mutual respect emanating from peer-centered interaction. This Rousseaulike vision of the role of socializers in the emergence of the child's thought has had as a by-product the idea that parents or authority serve the role of "minding the store" until the child's experience and emergent skill lead it to self-defined principles, ideas, and adequate cognitive–adaptive strategies. Little in the way of substantive legacy of parental socialization was proffered in these models. Such conventionally viewed "stable" products of socialization as beliefs, attitudes, values, behavioral dispositions, self-regulatory processes, and the like were not afforded serious theoretical nor empirical status as determinants or mediators of developing social cognition.

This prevailing constructivist ideology in the study of emergent social cognition is quite incompatible with many of the deterministic assumptions evident in models of thought-probing social influence and socialization. From the perspective of the constructivist, it is inappropriate to view the child's dispositions as molded like "so much clay" by parents and other socially important partners. In a sense, an antinomy was posed between the autonomy and self-generativity of the developing child on the one hand and his or her social dependence and influencibility on the other. It is important to note here that such a dichotomy has been an unfortunate one. Any model of social development must simultaneously account for the social susceptibility of the developing child *and* his or her growing competencies, skills, and adaptations. In fact, we would quite prematurely offer that *the dynamic working-through of the dialectic between self-determination and social determination is the critical struggle of social development.*

As we shall see later on in this chapter, there is a paradox that lies at the heart of this struggle. This paradox is perhaps one of the factors that renders conflict in the social world a developmentally pervasive phenomenon. To state this paradox simply, it would hold that, as our cognitive capacities and processing and reasoning skills become more advanced and complex, our beliefs, moral standards, and affective tendencies simultaneously become more "fixed." In short, we do not engage in social cognitive processes de novo with each new circumstance, but we come to be increasingly obdurate in our belief structures. This relative fixity of beliefs, norms, values, and the like affects the level of cognitive analysis, information search, and reasoning processes employed in understanding contemporary social and moral issues and circumstances.

It is in the instance of fixed beliefs and content-based principles that social influence and socialization can be conceptualized as exerting their primary effects. The developmental and interpersonal processes that give rise to the internalization of principles during socialization must be considered jointly with the developmental transitions in self-generative cognitive processes for the emergence of social and moral cognition to be understood. The supposed dichotomy between individual self-generative capacities and human social susceptibility is not a dichotomy at all but rather a joint index of the complexity of human nature and the reality of conflict-driven development.

Since the 1960s and early 1970s, there have been rapid advances in our understanding of the child's developing cognitive processes. These advances have taken us well beyond the seminal derivatives of Piaget's thought so prominent in the early portion of those two decades. Unfortunately little of this research and theory concerning social cognitive development has easily incorporated variables indexing socialization-based phenomena.

The remainder of this chapter will represent an attempt to search for an understanding of developing social cognition that includes consideration of phenomena of social influence and socialization-based transmission of beliefs. In doing so we will explore some perceived connections between social and developmental psychology's visions of social cognition and reconstruct the findings from several of our investigations into a formulation on the impact of social influence on developing social thought.

DEVELOPING MORAL THOUGHT AND THE PROCESS OF ATTRIBUTION

While the abbreviated analysis of the self-generative view as it initially penetrated developmental models is provided above, it should also be clear that a similarly timed and quite compatible "cognitive revolution" in perspective had permeated the social psychology of the mid-1960s and beyond as well. Attribution theory as originally cast by Heider (1958) and modified by the important treatises of Jones and Davis (1965) and Kelley (1967) moved to center stage in social psychological research. Nearly every phenomenon known to social psychologists became explicated through one or another attributional model. As with the developmental models of social cognition, social psychology's counterparts proceeded from the assumption that rationally based understanding of social events is the antecedent governing social adaptations of all kinds. Our putative means of accomplishing such understanding involves the deployment of a variety of cognitive processing strategies and principles. "Mistakes" or biases in social inference derive either from our developmentally given incapacities to employ various processes and principles or from a variety of universal illusions or incomplete heuristic shortcuts of the social perceiver and thinker (cf. Kahneman & Tversky, 1973; Ross, 1977). In a sense, then, various processing models such as attribution theory were viewed as rational baselines (cf. Jones & McGillis, 1976). Deviation from these baseline models was viewed not as an indicator of the inappropriateness of the models but as an instance for considering either the variance in the capacities of different perceivers or the inherently ambiguous nature of social event perception and perceivers' chronic adaptations to such pervasive ambiguity.

As we began our own search for the factors giving rise to "mature" social perception in the developing person, we were compelled by the compatibilities in the constructivist foci on social perception from both developmental and social psychology. In the early 1970s we too were intrigued by the proposition that the child's discovery of order and stability in the social world is a developmentally emergent consequence of both experience and the maturation of cognitive structures. It struck us that the formulations of Piaget (1932/1965) and Kohlberg (1969) concerning the child's developing moral thought paralleled the implications of the attribution theories that were becoming central to social psychological inquiry. In retrospect, our search for compatibility in these disparate perspectives was a bit primitive and heavy-handed. Nevertheless, there was a clear conceptual and developmental fit in the perspectives. If one takes the adult attribution models as a portrayal of the product of social cognitive development, this fit or compatibility is clearly evident.

In this respect, Jones and Davis (1965) proposed that one important element in coming to terms with the social world was the person's interpretation of the causes of the observed acts of others. The primary category of "cause" that their analysis addressed was the likelihood that an observed act could be attributed to an underlying stable disposition of the actor. Their model of correspondent inference was proposed as one that could explain the information-gathering steps that a perceiver would take in order to arrive at a determination of whether an observed act was caused by an underlying disposition of the actor or by the demands inherent in the situation. The centerpiece of this information analysis was proposed to be the perceiver's inference that the actor *intended* his or her actions. Such inferences of intention are made through the use of cues indexing the actor's volition and/or effort and the degree of external physical, normative, or social constraint impinging upon the actor. When external constraint is perceived to be minimal and volition perceived to be evident, an inference of intention was proposed as a product. The inference of dispositional cause follows upon this intention inference. In the terms of correspondent inference theory, the act and the actor's underlying disposition would be judged as *correspondent*—and thus the act and the actor could be described by the same inferential term (e.g., *hostile, aggressive, smart, introverted,* etc.).

With this brief introduction to the skeletal structure of the developing attribution framework of mid-1960s social psychology, we can now portray our perception of the parallels with developmental psychology's models of sociomoral thought. In particular, we were struck by the parallel implications of correspondent inference theory's portrayal of adult social inference and Piaget's perspective on the emergence of moral judgment in development. Piaget (1932/1965) proposed that the bases for the child's judgments of moral fault underwent change with maturation. Young, preoperational and early operational children were viewed as unswervingly "objective" in their moral evaluations. Judgments of moral fault or dispositional naughtiness were viewed as being made on the basis of the consequences of another's acts. Two bases for this anchoring on consequences were noted. On the one hand, young children's cognitive "limitations" including their egocentrism and lack of subjective perspectivism centered them on the most objectively available cues to an actor's fault or naughtiness. In addition, young children are aided and abetted in this objective focus by the authority-mediated social conditions under which they live. In this latter sense, adult social regulation or constraint serves the role of facilitating the realistic moral judgment tendencies of children by centering them upon the phenomena relating to rule or norm violation.

In contrast, developmentally advanced children in Piaget's model were theorized to have developed perspectival subjectivity in their cognitive accommodations and to have become freer of adult-constraining relationships. Accordingly, their judgments and explanations of rule-violating actors would depend upon the antecedent *intentions* of those actors. In short, in moral judgment the child is portrayed as proceeding from an objective and consequence-based evaluation of others to a relativistic and intersubjective one in which moral fault or naughtiness would hinge upon the malevolence or benignness of the intentions underlying observed action and its consequences.

The compatibility of correspondent inference theory and Piaget's moral judgment perspective inheres in their shared emphasis on the intention-based relativism of social evaluation. For Jones and Davis the evaluation of an act as intended mediates a perceiver's inference about the correspondence between that act and an underlying and stable attribute of the actor. Similarly for Piaget, mature moral judgment issues from the child's capacity to employ intention cues in discerning the "stable" moral status of rule violators. Each of these perspectives follows a different line from this point of commonality. Piaget sought to understand the developmentally relevant shifts in cognitive process, cognitive structure, and social conditions that permit and mediate intention-based moral judgment. The adult attribution researchers focused most heavily on the data-gathering strategies and social cues most likely to be used in intention attribution. Nevertheless, in 1970 we were most impressed by their conjunctive implications. If correspondent inference models describe processes relevant to adult social judgment baselines, it seemed likely that Piagetianlike inquiries into moral development processes might depict the path of their acquisition. In a sense, we were intrigued by the possibility that the rational baselines of adult social reasoning were emergent products of the development of social–cognitive structures. The early 1970s research program at Duke that followed upon this intriguing inference has been detailed elsewhere (Costanzo & Dix, 1983; Kassin & Pryor, 1985). Nevertheless, we will briefly recapitulate these studies and their implications for the emergence of social reasoning. Our intent in reviewing this work is to detail the primary empirical sources of our current perspective on the relationships between socialization and the emergence of social cognition.

MORAL THOUGHT, CONSTRAINT, AND ATTRIBUTIONAL DEVELOPMENT: BEGINNING RESEARCH

The first study (Costanzo, Coie, Grumet, & Farnill, 1973) to follow upon the conjunction perceived between correspondent inference theory and the Piagetian moral judgment perspective sought to reexamine and replicate the developmental sequence of moral thought posited by Piaget (1932/1965) and described above. Such a reexamination was necessary because the classic Piagetian moral comparison paradigm had some serious limitations that rendered the generalization to broad trait attribution phenomena somewhat difficult. In the original paradigm, Piaget asked children to make a vignette-based moral comparison between two actors. It was invariable in Piaget's model that one of the actors produced large negative consequences even though his or her intentions were quite benign, while a second actor produced small negative consequences with antecedent malevolent or negative intentions. The children Piaget interviewed were asked to judge which of the two portrayed actors was the naughtier and then to explain the basis for their choice. There were three primary problems with this paradigm. First, in the stories, the actors' outcomes were incidental to their intentions. That is, Piaget's vignette performers always produced *accidental* outcomes while intending some other good or bad act. Second, the vignettes were restricted to negative, damage-related outcomes. And, third, because of the invariant comparison format, outcomes and intentions were confounded (i.e., positively intended actors always produced large negative outcomes while negatively intended actors always produced small negative outcomes). These limitations made it questionable as to whether the findings that Piaget and others (e.g., Boehm, 1962; Johnson, 1962) had reported were restricted to the particular moral comparison circumstances portrayed by the paradigm or whether these findings had implications for the general emergence of the kinds of social judgment processes addressed in attribution theory.

In Costanzo and colleagues' (1973) study, we elicited children's moral evaluations of vignette characters who produced either negative or positive outcomes and whose intentions were either negative *or* positive. This 2 × 2 breakdown of intention and consequence conditions allowed us to examine in an unconfounded way the relative prominence of intention and consequence cues in the moral judgments of children of different ages. Furthermore, our story constructions portrayed actors whose outcomes were direct rather than accidental consequences of their intentions. Finally, judgments of naughtiness were elicited separately for each actor rather than comparatively. This last feature of our study allowed for the examination of whether, with age, there is an incremental use of intention cues in moral evaluation.

The primary findings of this study are presented in Figure 8.1. As can be seen from this illustration, our findings in the case of negative consequences were quite similar to the implications of Piaget's model. Young, kindergarten-age children failed to differentiate the naughtiness of positively and negatively intended actors producing negative consequences. Furthermore, the degree of intent differentiation of these actors increased with age. Thus in the conditions that most closely mirrored Piaget's original paradigm we largely replicated the age effects found in studies employing that paradigm. However, in the case of the positive-consequence vignettes, we discovered a surprising lack of age-related differences in intention use. Kindergarten children were as likely as second- and fourth-grade children to differentiate the positive evaluations given to vignette actors on the basis of the valence of their intentions.

This consequence-based difference in age changes in intent use initially puzzled us. Surely, both judgments of moral fault and moral adequacy should

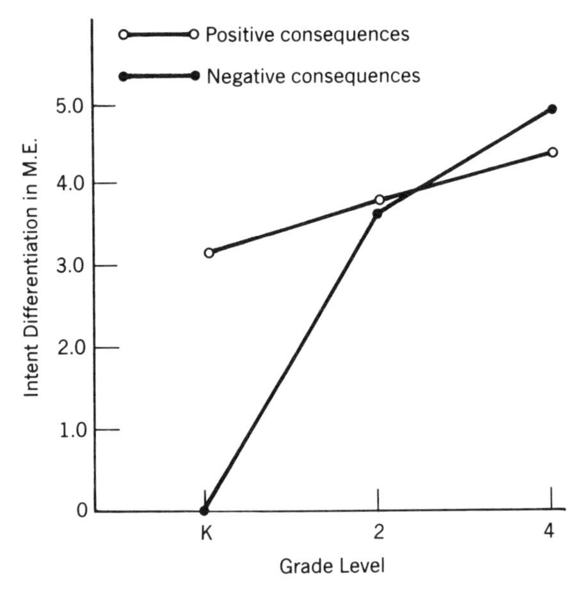

Figure 8.1. Intent differentiation in moral evaluation (M.E.) as a function of age and consequence. (From Costanzo, Coie, Grumet, & Farnill, 1973.)

follow the same formal model. If the developmental shift from objectivity to subjectivity in moral evaluation was presumed to be based upon a broader underlying shift in cognitive capacity, then the valence of the outcomes of the actors evaluated should not matter greatly. The fact that the valence of outcomes was critical to age effects in intention use suggested to us that the social constraint evident in early child–adult socialization encounters might be an especially important source of moral cognition. It struck us that a child's direct encounters with parental constraint would differ for instances of rule violation and rule conformity. On the most mundane level one could consider the kinds of interpersonal transactions that accompany a child's production of damage or rule violation and those accompanying the child's production of positive outcomes. In the latter case, parents are likely to be quite attentive to intentional considerations in both their affective expression and their direct statements. Thus parents would probably not reward children or express warm affect toward children who accidentally or malevolently happen to produce a positive outcome. It is likely that the rewards contingent upon positive outcomes are based upon the child's antecedent intentions and efforts. In the case of negative outcomes, it is reasonable to suppose that parents would deliver quite confusing messages to the child concerning the importance of underlying intentions. On the one hand, they might overtly not hold the child accountable for unintended bad outcomes; on the other hand, their affect arousal is likely to be mediated by the magnitude of bad outcome. For example, while a parent might not hold a child accountable for accidentally knocking a younger sibling down a flight of stairs while intending to help him out the door, this is probably obscured by covertly expressed parent affect in instances when the outcomes of such actions are high in negative magnitude (e.g., younger brother breaks his leg).

Such a formulation suggests that in direct transactions parental influences over a child's developing evaluation predilections have both overt and covert properties. In instances in which children produce unintended negative outcomes, an overt parental message that acknowledges the child's innocent intentions might be undermined by the parent's covert communication of concern derived from the magnitude of the bad outcome. Such covert messages of concern in the case of "real-life" negative outcomes may serve to center a child's moral evaluations on the consequences of one's own or another's acts and render intentions less relevant to evaluation.

Proceeding from this provisional perspective, Farnill (1974) sought to discern whether the developmental lag in intention use in the case of negative outcomes is particular to moral evaluations or is more pervasively characteristic of social attributions of all kinds. In other terms, Farnill was probing whether the moral significance of others' acts to children diverges from their trait significance. For example, a child might view a helpfully intended actor who accidentally causes damage as simultaneously "helpful" and "bad." The social constraint propositions described above might serve to infuse certain parentally sanctioned outcomes with an "ought" quality thus resulting in legalistic judgments of naughtiness for the young child. On the other hand, the young child might be quite capable (as he or she is in the case of positive outcomes) to use intentions for judgments that are not moral nor strictly evaluative—even when the actors' outcomes are negative.

In order to test this proposition, Farnill presented 5-, 7-, and 9-year-old children with videotapes of a boy moving flowerpots at his mother's request. The target child ends up breaking one or four flowerpots either because of maliciousness, ineptness, or the occurrence of unavoidable accident. The observer children were asked to evaluate both the naughtiness of the actor they observed and his helpfulness. For moral or naughtiness judgments, the standard Piagetian findings were once again found. The youngest children rated the multiple pot breaker as naughtier than the single pot breaker irrespective of the maliciousness of the displayed intentions. With age there was increasing intent-based discrimination of naughtiness ratings. With regard to ratings of helpfulness, however, Farnill found that even the youngest children rated the well-intentioned accident victim as significantly more helpful than the maliciously intended child in both consequence conditions.

Combining Farnill's findings with those of Costanzo and colleagues, we concluded that the young child's failure to deploy intention cues in person evaluation is a quite situation-specific phenomenon. Apparently from a rather tender age children evidence a sensitivity to actor intentions in making inferences about their actions and traits. Nevertheless, the particular instance in which young children seem to ignore the intentions of actors in their evaluations is a quite important one. Specifically, when an actor produces negative outcomes and the young child is asked to evaluate his or her degree of naughtiness, their moral evaluations largely depend upon the magnitude of the consequences irrespective of intentions. Since young kindergarten-age children were found to make intention-based moral judgments of actors producing positive consequences and intention-based trait judgments of actors producing negative consequences, it was difficult to argue that their single failure to do so derived from a general cognitive deficit. Instead, we were once again compelled by the implication that the particular conditions of social constraint governing children's real-life negative outcomes served to *preempt* their nascent capacities to deploy subjective cues in moral evaluation. It became clear to us at this point that our rather neat conceptual conjunction of Piaget's moral judgment theory and correspondent inference theory would not tell the story of developing social cognition. While these two studies did not directly address the specific impact of adult constraint on children's social attributions, the situational differences in the young child's evaluation behavior in formally similar circumstances suggested to us that social forces in the child's world are strong determinants of the manner in which children engage in social reasoning.

The first direct test of the impact of adult constraint on the child's social attributions that followed upon our developing formulation was a rather paradigmatic one (Costanzo, Grumet, & Brehm, 1974). We reasoned that, since young children seem capable of deploying subjective cues in making attributions to others, they should indeed be capable of using the simple heuristics of correspondent inference. Furthermore, we conjectured that this capacity to infer others' attributes on the basis of their wishes or intentions would be interfered with in young children when adult constraints partially governed the behavior of the actor. To test these propositions, we adopted a paradigm with children that was derived from adult research on the attribution of attitudes to others (cf. Jones & Harris, 1967). In the study, first-, third-, and sixth-grade children observed a videotape of a child making a choice between two equally attractive toys and subsequently playing with either the chosen or unchosen toy. When the actor played with the chosen toy, choice was either freely made or adult approved. When the actor was denied play with the chosen toy, such play was prohibited by an adult sanction or by an environmental constraint (i.e., the toy was out of reach). Observer children in each condition were asked to evaluate the degree to which the actor liked each of the toys. Use of correspondent inference in these liking evaluations would be reflected by the child inferring that chosen toys were liked better than unchosen toys irrespective of play behavior. Our results showed that children in all age groups made exactly such inferences when there was no adult mediation of toy play. First graders were as likely as third or sixth graders to rate actors as liking freely chosen and played-with toys more than toys that were played with because the preferred toy was out of reach. Age differences emerged, however, when adults mediated the play behavior of the target child. In such circumstances, first-grade children inferred that the target child's liking for the toys was in line with the adult approval or prohibition *irrespective* of initial choice.

Older children, on the other hand, conserved and even enhanced their deployment of choice cues in evaluating liking when adults mediated behavior. Sixth graders, in particular, not only viewed initial choices as important to liking but also saw adult constraint as reducing the desirability of the played-with toy. In short, in this investigation we found that, while children employ the relativistic and subjective heuristics of correspondent inference from a quite early age, such precocity is undermined when adults constrain behavioral options.

It should be noted that Grumet (1975) replicated and extended the findings of Costanzo and colleagues (1974). She reasoned that, if the presence of adult norms restricted the young child's use of information about the internal state preferences of others, then perhaps older children might show this same preemptive effect if actor behavior was constrained by norms that they perceived as particularly meaningful. In addressing this question, Grumet repeated the complete design of Costanzo and colleagues' (1974) study and in addition included a peer constraint condition. Since the relevance of peers as sources of social norms increases from early to middle childhood (cf. Costanzo, 1970; Costanzo, Coie, & Dorval, 1985), peer norms might be seen as particularly valid by older children and, like adult norms for younger children, restrict the use of information about internal preferences in their social judgments. This is indeed what was found. In addition to replicating the results of the original study, Grumet found that, when peers constrained the play behavior of the target, younger children did *not* attribute toy preference on the basis of actor play behavior as they did when adults were the source of constraint. In fact, peer constraint tended to *enhance* their use of the initial preferences of the targets. Sixth graders, on the other hand, evaluated the target's toy preferences to be congruent with peer constraint even when such constraint was opposed to the target's initial choice. In short, while all age groups of children displayed the capacity to employ subjective volitional cues in inferring another's "attitude," norm-relevant social constraint preempted this discriminative capacity. For younger children, such normative constraints issued from adults and for older children from peers. What is critical here is the demonstration that the conditions of social influence have clear and decided effects on social cognitive processes.

On the basis of this series of studies conducted at Duke in the mid-1970s, Costanzo and Dix (1983) proposed a two-process model of developing social cognition. The first of these processes inheres in the child's developing formal reasoning capacities and relates to the self-generative and cognitive–adaptive perspective on the development of social understanding. The child's capacity to reason soundly in the face of multiple social cues is the developmental task indexed by such formal acquisitions. A variety of studies had clearly documented that children not only are more flexible in their use of subjective data in reasoning about others, but also seem increasingly capable, with age, in deploying a variety of heuristic reasoning principles and schemes to infer another's traits and to infer causes for another's behavior (cf. DiVitto & McArthur, 1978; Herzberger & Dix, 1980; Karniol & Ross, 1976; Shultz & Butkowsky, 1977). Also in our own work described above both Costanzo and colleagues (1973) and Farnill found that older children deploy intention cues in reasoning about moral attributes in a wider range of circumstances than did younger children.

Nevertheless, it was apparent to us from the studies just described that the maturation of reasoning capacity was not a sufficient determinant of the age variations observed in social and moral judgment. For example, our rather simple formulation linking the descent from moral realism with the development of correspondent inference was not sustained by these studies. What is "correct" or logical in the moral or social world is an inherently relativistic matter. To this extent, norms governing behavior constitute clear guides emergent from the social world for evaluating social actions and the actors who perform them. When norms are particularly constraining they mandate that some behavioral end states are preferred to others *regardless* of the antecedent wishes, choices, or intentions of an actor. In these cases, subjective information about an actor's internal desires might not be employed in judging that actor's traits despite the child's capacity to reason with multiple cues. Thus norms emanating from the social world can *preempt* complete information search and center the perceiver on issues of an actor's conformity to or violation of norms in his or her behavior and consequences. It is this normatively bound social inference that Costanzo and Dix proposed as the second process in their two-process model. In order to understand the development of such normatively constrained judgment tendencies, the changing social identifications and the particular normative internalizations of the developing child would need to be linked to his or her developing social–cognitive skills.

In the research just described, we did not begin with the intent of exploring norm-relevant moral and social reasoning. Instead we were compelled by the attempt to examine the developmental underpinnings of adult attributional models. As noted throughout our report on this research, we became increasingly convinced that our unexpected results were a function of the differential impact of real-life social constraint on different-aged children. Yet it was only in the investigations of Costanzo and colleagues (1974) and Grumet (1975) that we were able to document some of these effects of adult constraint.

In order to pursue more fully an understanding of norm-constrained and socially influenced social cognition in our subsequent research, we sought to examine directly the impact of norms, values, and beliefs on the social cognitions of adults and children. This took us to two related lines of inquiry. The first of these lines employed adult college students as subjects. It was our assumption that, at least as a first step, more or less stable and persistent domains of social constraint would be more accessible to measurement in adult subjects. Furthermore, while it is clear that the conditions of active social constraint vary with developmental group, the *consequences* of the socialization of particular norms are likely to transcend epochs of development through processes of internalization. By looking at the manner in which adult norms and values preempt social information processing and social attribution we thought we would be able to further our general understanding of norm-constrained, socially influenced social cognition.

The second line of inquiry we pursued involved us in a direct exploration of the impact of parental belief and parental rearing strategy in different value-relevant domains on their children's social perceptions and judgments in those domains. It is this last rather comprehensive study that provides the clearest evidence for the importance of the connection between socialization and social cognition. Below, we briefly report on the results of each of these lines of inquiry.

THE IMPACT OF CULTURALLY SHARED AND INDIVIDUAL VALUES ON THE SOCIAL INFERENCES OF ADULTS

An individual's beliefs, values, and behavioral norms are derivative of a variety of social influence processes. In some instances, these influences issue from transitory pressure from reference persons or groups. In still other instances such beliefs, values, and norms are internalized derivatives of extended socialization experience. In the Grumet (1975) investigation we saw that transitory directive norming of behavior by adults and peers greatly affected the kind of social reasoning engaged in by children. The agents of such social influence effects would be expected to change with developmental shifts in social life phases (cf. Higgins & Parsons, 1983). With such changes one would expect episodic shifts in the norms that might preempt contemporary social reasoning. It is this sense of adult constraint that is most congruent with cognitive portrayals of the impact of social influence on social cognition. In Piaget's model, for example, the morality of adult constraint is a phenomenon of early development, with later cognitions being mediated by negotiations with peers.

As we pointed out earlier in this chapter, such a limited portrayal of social influence effects on moral and social cognition provides for little in the way of a relatively stable legacy of beliefs derivative from an individual's experience with significant socializers. Surely, our transactions with socializers in development tell us something about the structure of the social world. They help define preferences, norms, and values of a more durable variety—ones carried forward from developmental era to era by processes of internalization. In our research with adults we hoped to approach the impact of social constraints of this second kind.

In our first study (Costanzo & Archer, 1979) with college-aged adults, we chose to examine the impact of a presumably pervasive and early-appearing set of shared internalized norms. Specifically, we examined the impact of shared and typical gender role beliefs on the perceptions and attributions that adults made to actors who violated and exemplified such implicit role strictures. The study was constructed to be quite similar in cast to the moral judgment research described earlier. College-aged adults read vignettes in which a male or female actor behaved rather aggressively or rather submissively in a complex social interaction. Actors were portrayed as expressing either their aggressive or their submissive behavior following a provocation by another or where no apparent provocation preceded the behavior. The implications we drew from our earlier research led us to expect that, when the actor's behavior was congruent with gender role norms, observers would employ the provocation cue as a discriminative one in attributing a behavior-congruent trait to the actor and in rating how positively they evaluated the actor. However, when the actor's behavior violated sex role norms, we expected that provocation would be irrelevant to observers' assignments of behavior-congruent traits to the actor and to their ratings of the actor's likability. In short, we presumed that internalized sex role norms would preempt an observer's deployment of mitigating cues in the instance of role violation in the same manner that adult constraints seemed to preempt a young child's deployment of intention cues in judging negative consequence situations. The results of the study bore out our expectations. When females behaved submissively and males aggressively, they were rated as significantly more trait submissive or trait aggressive when unprovoked than when provoked. In addition, they were liked significantly less when unprovoked than when provoked. However, when actors behaved "out of role" (i.e., males submissively and females aggressively) ratings made of both their behavior-relevant traits and likability *did not differ* as a function of provocation).

From this study we concluded that it was quite plausible to propose that for adults as well as children, normative constraints serve to preempt the use of mitigating cues in the case of norm violation. Obdurate and culturally loaded beliefs derived from socialization experience tend therefore to play a directive role in our processing of information in the social world.

The second study with adults (Woody, 1981; Woody & Costanzo, 1985) constituted a further probe of our internal constraint hypothesis. While sex role beliefs derive from culturally shared assumptions, many of our value-laden beliefs about social behavior are the products of unique experiences. For example, some of us most strongly value ambition and achievement, while others of us place greater importance on behaving kindly or helpfully. It is our assumption that such differentiated value schemes are products of socialization influence. With regard to the kinds of hypotheses offered and tested in the above-reported research, we assumed that the preemption of information use in social cognition would depend upon the relative importance an individual attached to the values expressed in an actor's behavior. In short, in this study we examined whether persistent individual values operate as constraints on social perceptual processes. In the study, college students were administered the Rokeach (1973) value survey early in the academic term. On this survey individuals are asked to rank 18 positive social values in order of personal importance. The values on the portion of the survey we employed were instrumental in character and thus were relevant to social action. It includes values such as honesty, cheerfulness, ambition, responsibility, and the like. At a later point in the term subjects were administered a story situation questionnaire. The questionnaire contained nine vignettelike descriptions of actors. For half of the subjects each vignette depicted the violation of a value selected from Rokeach's survey. For the other half of the subjects the vignettes portrayed nine value-exemplifying actors. Furthermore, half the subjects were administered stories in which the value-relevant consequences of the actors were constrained by situational demands, while half of the subjects were administered stories in which the value-relevant behaviors were freely chosen by the actors and unconstrained by situational demand. Finally, the selection of the particular value vignettes administered to each subject was dependent on his or her Rokeach survey ratings. Each subject rated actors in three value domains of high importance to him or her, three of moderate importance, and three of low importance. Subjects were asked to rate these actors on several measures. Two of the more important of these were the degree to which actors possessed traits congruent with their value-relevant behavior and the degree of liking they had for the actors. The findings obtained were quite concordant with the sex role preemption data. In subjects' high importance value domains trait and liking ratings of value-exemplifying actors significantly differed as a function of choice or situational constraint information. Similarly, in subjects' low important value domains the trait and liking ratings of both value-exemplifying and value-violating actors differed significantly as a function of choice information. However, in high importance value domains subjects' ratings of value-violating actors were uniformly negative and did not differ as a function of actor choice or situational constraint.

The results of this study once again are illustrative of the degree to which the important beliefs and values of adult perceivers preempt their use of "logically necessary" information in proffering social judgments. Apparently, the absolutism and objectivism that characterize the moral thought of the young child are similarly evident in the social cognitions of adults when shared or individual beliefs are violated.

There are two implications of these studies of adult social perception:

1. An individual's most important beliefs and values tend to guide a perceiver's inferences about the social acts of others. The baseline models such as correspondent inference tend to be descriptive of dispassionate or uninvolved social reasoning processes. However, in areas in which the individual holds clear implicit *and* explicit standards for behavior, adult perceivers evidence a rule-matching or consequence-based perspective on violations that bears similarity to the moral objectivity found in the cognitions of the young child.
2. The kinds of values and beliefs (e.g., sex role standards) that serve as internal constraints on social cognition are likely products of developmental

processes of value acquisition and internalization. In this sense, we would propose that the development of social perception and person evaluation is as much a product of content-specific socialization as it is one of the maturation of cognitive processes.

In the last study to be reported on, we offer a beginning cross-sectional test of the role of socialization influences on developing moral attribution.

THE IMPACT OF DOMAIN-SPECIFIC PARENT SOCIALIZATION ON AGE DIFFERENCES IN THE MORAL JUDGMENTS OF CHILDREN

In this study we addressed the role of within-parent differences in value socialization on the pattern of children's moral judgments in differing value domains. While Hoffman (1975, 1979; see also Hoffman & Salzstein, 1967) has pursued similar questions, his specific approach to the understanding of the relationship between parent socialization strategy and children's moral judgment was not geared to assess content-specific effects. That is, Hoffman explored the relation between the general manner in which parents exerted disciplinary power and children's associated tendencies to be external (consequence based) or internal (intention based) in their moral judgments. He has generally found that the children of power-assertive mothers are external in their moral judgments while the children of mothers who employ inductive discipline approaches tend to be internal in their moral judgments. Hoffman links his results to the underlying relationships that exist between the controllingness of a parent's disciplinary approach and the child's internalization of a moral stance. Put simply, Hoffman's work implies that parental control undermines the child's development of internal or subjective guides to moral evaluation. While Hoffman's careful work is quite important and while his general hypothesis concerning the relationship between parent socialization control and children's developing moral predilections is generally concordant with the perspective we have offered in this chapter, his perspective differs from ours in two critical and related ways. First, Hoffman, like many researchers and theorists in the study of parenting, implicitly conceives of parents as monolithic in their child-rearing ideology. That is, parents are categorized in general terms (e.g., as warm or hostile; controlling or permissive, etc.). While parents certainly differ from one another in their global socialization approaches, we do not believe that such differences are easily linked to the specific content of a child's internalized value or belief systems. Furthermore, it is most likely the case that parents are relatively variable in their rearing ideologies. They likely deal with some domains of a child's behavior with great concern or powerful control and others with benign neglect or permissiveness. We are offering that it is this differentiation of social domains that typifies a parent's complex ideology that is most important to the child's differential internalization of moral standards. Accordingly, in our research we sought to assess a parent's rearing ideology as it varies from one value domain to the next rather than to index parenting in terms of a single average.

A second difference in our perspective and Hoffman's research inheres in our view that a child's moral judgment tendencies are not exclusively *either* "internal" or "external" in caste. Rather, whether children employ a subjective and relativistic moral reasoning process or an objective and consequence-based one is viewed as dependent upon the particular domain of social action they observe. In those value domains in which parental concern and/or control is high, we expect that children internalize strong constraints and thus are quite objective in focus. In domains of lesser importance to parents, children are proposed to be subjective in their reasoning.

In order to explore these notions, we (Costanzo & Fraenkel, 1985) conducted a study in which mothers' rearing ideologies were first assessed in multiple value domains. Kindergartners and first graders, second and third graders, and fourth- through sixth-grade children were then read moral vignettes that were individually selected differentially to represent value domains of high and low importance to their very own mothers. As with the general moral judgment paradigm used in our past studies, children were asked to rate the naughtiness or goodness of actors who evidenced value-violating or value-exemplifying behaviors that were either intended or not intended.

The measurement of parent rearing ideology in specific value domains was somewhat unique. While we generally employed the rather typical two-dimensional typology of parenting that has been often employed in child-rearing research, we did recast the dimensions. More specifically, much theory and research on parenting has employed some variant of a warmth–hostility dimension and a restrictive–permissive dimension jointly to characterize parental rearing approach (cf. Maccoby & Martin, 1983). We translated these two dimensions into *concern* (or the amount of worry or pride a parent reports experiencing in the face of his or her child's value violation or value exemplification in a wide variety of value domains) and *constraint* (or the degree of power assertion and external inducement parents employ indirectly disciplining and/or rewarding their children for different value violations and exemplifications). We assessed these two dimensions in parents in 13 separate value domains that were quite similar to the Rokeach domains described earlier (e.g., achievement, helpfulness, responsibility, obedience, etc.). The assessment device employed was a story situation device. Parents read vignette descriptions of children's violations and exemplifications of values in the 13 separate domains. They were asked to imagine that the story described the actions of their own child. After each vignette they endorsed several scales to rate their positive (pride, warmth, happiness, etc.) and negative (worry, disappointment, anxiety, anger, etc.) concerns about the value-relevant behaviors depicted. In addition, on a set of separate scales they reported on the ways in which they would directly deal with the behavior in question (e.g., give maternal rewards, pat the child on the head, punish the child physically or by love withdrawal, etc.). Their concern and constraint in response to each of the 13 value-relevant dimensions were then compiled. For each parent, four value domains were then selected to be used for the solicitation of his or her child's moral judgment ratings. These four domains comprised the 2 × 2 partition of high versus low concern domains and high versus low constraint domains for each parent. Children were then read four stories derived from their own parents' ratings in each of the four domains. Two of the stories portrayed value violation in that domain (one in which the actor was negatively intended) and two value exemplification. For each story they were asked to evaluate the goodness or naughtiness of actors on visually aided continuum scales.

The primary results of the study are depicted by Figures 8.2 and 8.3.

As can be seen from these figures, the age differences in intent differentiation varied as a function of both parent concern and actor consequences. The results for the low concern domains are quite reminiscent of the results of Costanzo and colleagues (1973). Specifically (compare Figs. 8.1 and 8.2), for negative outcomes there is a significant increase in intent differentiation with age. While there is an increase in intent differentiation with age for positive consequences, it is not nearly as steep. In essence, for value domains of low parent concern, we find the same pattern of results originally found in Costanzo and colleagues' study. This is quite reasonable since the kinds of rule violations employed in much of the earlier moral judgment research were probably ones of lower overall concern to parents. These outcomes typically

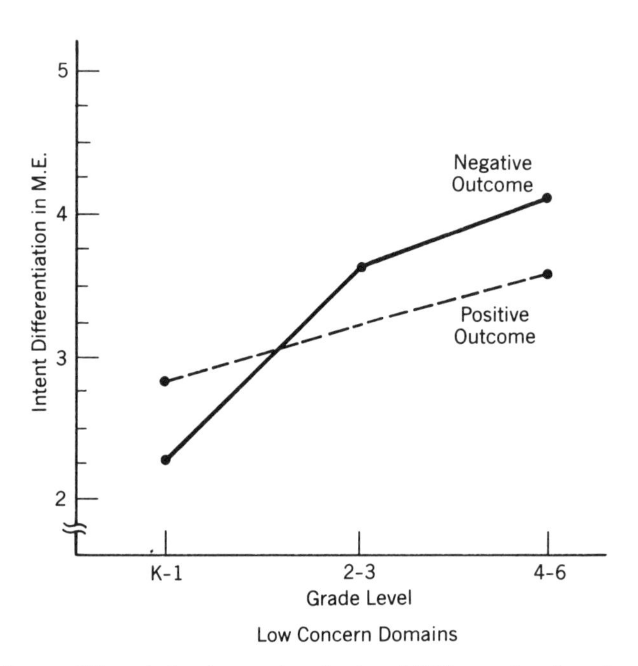

Figure 8.2. Intent differentiation in moral evaluation (M.E.) as a function of age and consequence in parent low concern domains.

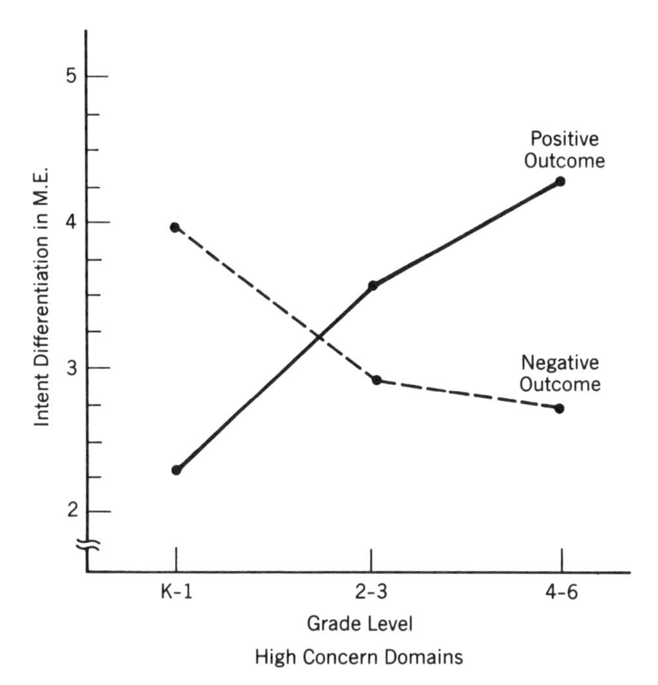

Figure 8.3. Intent differentiation in moral evaluation (M.E.) as a function of age and consequence in parent high concern domains.

included acts of maternal damage or sloppiness, for example, rather than strongly value-laden social acts.

In high concern domains (see Fig. 8.3) we find a rather striking pattern in the case of negative outcomes. There is a significant *decrease* in intent use with age for high parental concern value violations. For positive outcome–high concern circumstances we find a significant increase in intent differentiation with age. The trends in these two figures are supported by a significant Age × Parent Concern × Intention × Consequence interaction. While there were also some effects of parental constraint on children's moral evaluations, they were not ones that implicated intent use. Put most simply, parental constraint served to have children make larger distinctions between value violators and value exemplifiers with age. In short, high and low parental constraint appears only to affect a child's sense of the degree to which a behavior is good or bad, not his or her ability or willingness to take account of intentions when evaluating that behavior.

The results of this study are quite revealing with regard to the impact of parent rearing concerns on the child's internalization of values. It appears that the subtle force of a parent's worry or pride in response to particular value-relevant acts has a significant impact on rendering the child a moral absolutist in that domain. The age decrement in intent use in the case of these high concern value violations could be interpreted as representative of the child's internalization of the parent's affective perspective. It should be noted (see Fig. 8.3) that young kindergarten children are quite sensitized to issues of intention in these high concern domains. It is likely that, in their most important domains of social value, parents are initially quite "inductive" and discriminant in their social approach to the young child. In essence, these are the domains in which parents are most motivated to engage in moral instruction. Such efforts, however, further connote to the child the absolute importance of exemplifying the values in that domain. As a consequence, the child eventually internalizes rather harsh norms for evaluating behaviors in such domains.

In summary, we concluded from these data that parent affective variation in different value domains is a critical force in instilling rather invariant principles for action and evaluation in the child. Moral realism is not the sole purview of the young child, but is a product of the internalization of valent principles in older children and (if our data on adults are considered) in adults.

SUMMARY, CONCLUSIONS, AND SIDESTEPS TOWARD A FORMULATION

This chapter began by considering the ideological origins of prevailing, contemporary views on the development of cognitions about the social world. In the course of this beginning, we conjectured that it was implausible that researchers and theorists could provide a compelling portrayal of developing sociomoral perspective on the basis of an understanding of changes in the solitary, self-mediated cognitive processes of the developing child. On the premise that the evaluation of social acts is an inherently value-guided process, we sought to explore the impact of social development of a purely interpersonal variety on social cognition. If you will, we were interested in the simultaneous and conjoint application of perspectives of the "heart" and processes of the mind in the social world. We proposed that the self-determining and developmentally advancing processes of thought bore a dialectic relationship to the socially determined, value-punctuated guides of the developing "heart." Put most simply, we proposed that, as our processes of thought become more formally flexible, our social principles and values tend to become more fixed. As a consequence, our base of formal reasoning skills may not always be represented in our social evaluations. We did not believe this variance to be capricious, nor explicable by simple heuristic vulnerabilities of the beleaguered social perceiver. Instead, we implicitly proposed that social influence and socialization allow the developing child to partition an otherwise relativistic social world into domains of invariant inherent importance and domains whose importance would vary with context and situation. In the former domains the evaluation of acts is self-evident to a perceiver and inheres in an actor's conformance with externally or internally salient standards. In the latter case, the evaluation of acts is not self-evident and must be reasoned by a consideration of available disambiguating evidence (such as actor intention and situational constraints).

The various and sundry studies that informed this dualistic view of developing social cognition were then reviewed. In this work, we saw several rather repetitive phenomena:

1. From early development, violations of implicit rule constraints on the part of actors are morally appraised by young children in a rather direct and unmitigated fashion. In short, such violations carry with them an evaluative injunction that is rather self-evident to the perceiver. Instances of rule conformity, since they represent the exemplifications of "oughts," require additional evidence for purposes of evaluation. Thus in the former case young children do not even use obvious actor intentions in judging them, while in the latter case they constitute a critical feature contributing to actor evaluation.
2. External constraints of a referentially relevant kind operate similarly for children in nonmoral, social evaluation (cf. Costanzo et al., 1974; Grumet, 1975).
3. The assumed internalized principles of adult perceivers, whether ones of shared cultural presumption (e.g., sex-types) or of individual value ideology, also result in the rather "self-evident" evaluation of violating actors. In instances of nonviolation of prescription or the evaluation of less prescriptive domains of the perceiver, balanced and informationally guided evaluations of actors ensue.
4. Finally, we attempted to discover whether parental rearing concerns provide for at least one source of the emergence of the kinds of fixed social principles that guide moral and social appraisal. Setting aside the limits of cross-sectional methods, we found a rather strong implication that children become *more* absolutistic in their evaluation of negative behavior with age in domains for which parents report strong emotional involvement or concern. However, in domains of lower parent concern and with the exemplification of a parent's perspectives of high concern, we find an enhanced relativism in sociomoral judgment with development. What is most compelling about these last bits of data is that, as the domains of high and low concern varied across parents, differences in absolutism varied within their children. Thus two children viewing the *same vignette* would differ in intent–use depending upon the level of self-reported domain-specific concern of their parents.

A succinct reformulation of a perspective on developing social cognition founded upon this data base would take as a point of departure the differential developmental tasks a child confronts in the physical and social world. Hartup, Brady, and Newcomb (1983) compellingly point out that, while "predictability and stability may characterize the physical world, the social world seems to be less certain and more sensitive to a variety of factors defining the context of social experience" (p. 84). They go on to note that such disparities in physical and social phenomena render perspectives viewing the deployment of social reasoning as an analogic companion to physical reasoning somewhat misguided. They cite Berndt (1981) in noting that, while different children may grow up in a physical world whose laws are rather static, their conceptions of social relations are defined and constrained by the nature and meaning of these relations within a given cultural context. To this we would add that different children grow up in a world in which the meaning of social relations is also more narrowly centered within a given family socialization context.

We would offer that the primacy of the deductive cognitive strategies used to discern order in the physical world is not terribly evident in the social world. What characterizes developing individuals in the physical and social world commonly is their *search* for invariance. That is, through development individuals seek static invariance of principle. They deploy their capacities to distinguish how things appear from how they in essence "are." In the physical world, deduction and logical reasoning serve this end well, for one is likely to evaluate "meaning" successfully when such cognitive strategies are deployed. The inherent relativism of the social and moral world, however, requires that, with development, principles bearing the *illusion of stability* be arrived at by individuals. Given that our direct and individual encounters with relativistic social phenomena do not allow for the extraction of self-determined principles and "law," we became dependent upon significant and salient others in order to frame such principles. It is in this sense that socialization and the processes of life-course-relevant social influence became most compelling. We are not indeed molded like so much clay by parents and other socializers. Instead we actively seek out definition and meaning in a complex social world. In such active encounters we become susceptible to the injunctions of relevant and powerful others in arriving at differentiated principles of action. Parents and other primary socializers, then, serve to differentiate a complex social world into domains of importance in which invariant end states are to be pursued and domains of "variability" in which the end state pursued depends upon one's purpose at any given moment and the context one finds oneself within. To presume that such socialized principles are overturned by the advance of cognitive flexibility and processing ability is to assume that somehow the social world is ordered by true invariant principles that every participant might discover if he or she only thought and reasoned enough. Instead, we propose that social cognition is inherently a process that develops through important and largely constraining interpersonal encounters. The principles we arrive at developmentally are not necessarily obdurately invariant "forever" but their transformation requires "resocialization" and they are thus not readily overturned by dint of a skillful mind.

It seems mundane to state that the way we evaluate self and others in the social world depends upon what we believe is important and compelling about behavior in that world. Nevertheless, it needs saying at this point given that our beliefs are primed by our significant socialization transactions and the contemporary view is that such transactions are incidental to the development of social cognition.

We do hope that subsequent research probes more directly than our own research the kinds of socialization transactions that give rise to fixed beliefs and principle-based reasoning in the social world. Indeed, to understand the development of capacities of the mind in social life we must comprehend the underlying thumps of individual "hearts."

REFERENCES

Berndt, T. J. (1981). Relations between social cognition, non-social cognition and social behavior: The case of friendship. In J. Flavell & L. Ross (Eds.), *Social cognitive development.* Cambridge: Cambridge University Press.

Boehm, L. (1962). The development of conscience: A comparison of American children of different mental and socioeconomic levels. *Child Development, 33,* 575–590.

Costanzo, P. R. (1970). Conformity development as a function of self-blame. *Journal of Personality & Social Psychology, 14,* 366–374.

Costanzo, P. R., & Archer, E. (1978). *Sex-typing and attribution: The preemption of information use by gender norms.* Unpublished manuscript.

Costanzo, P. R., Coie, J. D., & Dorval, B. (1985). Age transitions in susceptibility to adult and peer opinion pressure. *Society for Research in Child Development.* Toronto, Canada.

Costanzo, P. R., Coie, J. D., Grumet, J., & Farnill, D. (1973). A reexamination of the effects of intent and consequence on children's moral judgments. *Child Development, 45,* 799–802.

Costanzo, P. R., & Dix, T. H. (1983). Beyond the information processed: Socialization in the development of attributional processes. In E. T. Higgins, D. N. Ruble, & W. W. Hartup (Eds.), *Social cognition and social development: A sociocultural perspective.* Cambridge: Cambridge University Press.

Costanzo, P. R., & Fraenkel, P. (1985). The role of parent concern and constraint in the development of value mediated moral judgment. A domain-specific perspective. *Society for Research in Child Development.* Toronto, Canada.

Costanzo, P. R., Grumet, J., & Brehm, S. (1974). The effects of choice and source of constraint on children's attributions of preference. *Journal of Experimental Social Psychology, 10,* 352–364.

DiVitto, B., & McArthur, L. (1978). Developmental differences in the use of distinctiveness, consensus, and consistency information for making causal attributions. *Developmental Psychology, 14,* 474–482.

Farnill, D. (1974). The effects of social judgment set on children's use of intent information. *Journal of Personality, 42,* 276–289.

Flavell, J. (1963). *The developmental psychology of Jean Piaget.* New York: Van Nostrand.

Grumet, J. (1975). *Effects of adult and peer sanctions on children's attributions of preference.* Unpublished doctoral dissertation, Duke University.

Hartup, W. W., Brady, J. E., & Newcomb, A. F. (1983). Social cognition and social interaction in childhood. In E. T. Higgins, D. N. Ruble, & W. W. Hartup (Eds.), *Social cognition and social development: A sociocultural perspective.* Cambridge: Cambridge University Press.

Heider, F. (1944). Social perception and phenomenal causality. *Psychological Review, 51,* 358–374.

Heider, F. (1958). *The psychology of interpersonal relations.* New York: Wiley.

Herzberger, S. D., & Dix, T. H. (1980). *The development of integrated impressions of others.* Unpublished manuscript, Northwestern University.

Higgins, E. T., & Parsons, J. E. (1983). Social cognition and the social life of the child: Stages as subcultures. In E. T. Higgins, D. N. Ruble, & W. W. Hartup (Eds.), *Social cognition and social development: A sociocultural perspective.* Cambridge: Cambridge University Press.

Hoffman, M. L. (1975). Moral internalization, parental power and the nature of parent–child interaction. *Developmental Psychology, 11,* 228–239.

Hoffman, M. L. (1979). Development of moral thought, feeling and behavior. *American Psychologist, 10,* 958–966.

Hoffman, M. L., & Salzstein, H. D. (1967). Parent discipline and the child's moral development. *Journal of Personality & Social Psychology, 5,* 45–57.

Johnson, R. C. (1962). A study of children's moral judgment. *Child Development, 33,* 327–354.

Jones, E. E., & Davis, K. E. (1965). From acts to dispositions: The attribution process in person perception. In L. Berkowitz (Ed.), *Advances in experimental social psychology* (Vol. 2). New York: Academic.

Jones, E. E., & Harris, V. A. (1967). The attribution of attitudes. *Journal of Experimental Social Psychology, 3,* 1–24.

Jones, E. E., & McGillis, D. (1976). Correspondent inference and the attribution cube: A comparative reappraisal. In J. H. Harvey, W. J. Ickes, & R. F. Kidd (Eds.), *New directions in attribution research* (Vol. 1). Hillsdale, NJ: Erlbaum.

Kahneman, D., & Tversky, A. (1973). On the psychology of prediction. *Psychological Review, 80,* 237–251.

Karniol, R., & Ross, M. (1976). The development of causal attributions in social perception. *Journal of Personality & Social Psychology, 34,* 455–464.

Kassin, S. M., & Pryor, J. B. (1985). The development of attribution processes. In J. B. Pryor & J. D. Day (Eds.), *The development of social cognition.* New York: Springer-Verlag.

Kelley, H. H. (1967). Attribution theory in social psychology. In D. Leving (Ed.), *Nebraska Symposium on Motivation* (Vol. 1). Lincoln: University of Nebraska Press.

Kohlberg, L. (1969). Stage and sequence: The cognitive developmental approach to socialization. In D. A. Goslin (Ed.), *Handbook of socialization theory and research.* New York: Rand-McNally.

Maccoby, E. E., & Martin, J. A. (1983). Socialization in the context of the family: Parent–child interaction. In P. H. Mussen (Ed.), *Handbook of child psychology* (Vol. 4). New York: Wiley.

Piaget, J. (1965). *The moral judgment of the child.* New York: Free Press. (Original work published 1932)

Rokeach, M. (1973). *The nature of human values.* New York: Free Press.

Ross, L. (1977). The intuitive psychologist and his shortcomings: Distortions in the attribution process. In L. Berkowitz (Ed.), *Advances in experimental social psychology* (Vol. 10). New York: Academic.

Shultz, T., & Butkowsky, I. (1977). Young children's use of the scheme for multiple sufficient causes in the attribution of real and hypothetical behavior. *Child Development, 48,* 464–469.

Woody, E. Z. (1981). *Personal values and social perception.* Unpublished doctoral dissertation, Duke University.

Woody, E. Z., & Costanzo, P. R. (1985). *The place of facts in a world of values: Value moderated person perception.* Unpublished manuscript.

PART FOUR

The Development of Self-Worth and Self-Related Knowledge

The infant probably is born with only the most primitive sense of the self. Thus the development of self-related cognitions and affects is an important aspect of early personality development, one that can be expected to influence social behavior and psychological well-being.

In Part Four of this volume, issues related to the self are examined. In Chapter 9, Susan Harter reviews major theoretical issues regarding the self-concept and presents a theoretical model of the determinants of self-worth. In her model, both others' positive regard and the discrepancy between one's self-perceived competence and one's pretensions are factors contributing to the development of self-worth. Moreover, self-worth is viewed as a mediator of both affect and motivation. Harter presents several lines of research related to her model and examines developmental change in self-worth. Her findings generally are consistent with her model and have clear implications both for understanding the effects of variations in self-worth on behavior and affect and for enhancing children's self-esteem.

In Chapter 10, Diane Ruble examines a somewhat different issue, self-socialization aspects of self-knowledge. In her view, the process of self-definition often is self-initiated, and individuals use the information they acquire to monitor their own behavior. In other words, children socialize themselves with the aid of self-constructed, self-relevant theories and information. In support of her views, Ruble presents research regarding the development of self-knowledge in several domains of functioning. Her conceptualization of the process of self-socialization is a fruitful blending of several lines of thought in the developmental literature, and is a promising mode of analysis that can be used to understand many facets of social and personality development.

CHAPTER 9

The Determinants and Mediational Role of Global Self-Worth in Children

SUSAN HARTER

INTRODUCTION

In recent years, there has been controversy over whether the self-concept is best viewed as a global entity, captured by a single score, or whether it is more fruitful to adopt a domain-specific approach in which a profile of scores reflecting self-evaluations across a number of domains best depicts one's sense of self (see Harter, 1985a). Rather than polarize the issue, our own orientation has involved an integration of these two approaches. Our research has clearly demonstrated that children's self-evaluations vary depending on the particular domain. This is evidenced by the many saw-toothed profiles we have identified across five domains: scholastic competence, athletic competence, social acceptance, physical appearance, and behavioral conduct. Moreover, these five subscales define distinct clusters when subjected to factor-analytic procedures (Harter, 1985b).

However, we have demonstrated that children 8 and older are also capable of making global judgments about their worth as people. These global judgments are tapped by general items asking the extent to which they like themselves as people, like the way they are leading their lives, are happy the way they are, and so forth. It is important to appreciate the fact that global self-worth is tapped by an independent set of items, questions that address the construct of global self-worth *directly*. It is *not*, in our approach, assessed by taking an average of those items tapping specific domains. Certain investigators have defined general self-esteem or self-concept as such an aggregate (Coopersmith, 1967; Piers & Harris, 1969). In contrast, we have sought to assess global self-worth directly and independently of self-evaluations in specific domains, an approach very similar to Rosenberg's (1979). One goal,

The research reported in this chapter was facilitated by Grant #HD 09613 from the National Institutes of Child Health and Human Development. I would especially like to thank Nancy Whitesell and Wanda Mayberry for their assistance in the preparation of this chapter.

therefore, becomes an examination of the relationship that global self-worth might bear to the child's domain-specific evaluations.

Most recently, an understanding of the self-worth construct has been paramount in our efforts to elucidate various facets of children's self-concept. Thus we have directed these efforts toward the test of a general model of the determinants and mediational role of self-worth (Harter, 1985a; Harter & Hogan, 1985). For theoretical guidance, we turned to two historical scholars of the self, James (1892) and Cooley (1902). Each of these theorists was explicit on the point that one possesses a global concept of self, over and above more specific self-evaluations in the different domains of one's life. However, their theoretical formulations put forth very different determinants of this global sense of self.

For James, global self-esteem was captured by the ratio of one's successes to one's pretensions. One's level of self-esteem hinged on the extent to which one considered oneself successful in those domains where one had aspirations of success. If one's successes are viewed as equal to or greater than these pretensions, high self-esteem would result. Conversely, if one's pretensions toward success vastly exceed one's actual level of success, the outcome would be low self-esteem. It should be noted that to operate according to such a model one must possess more than a modicum of cognitive–evaluative skills. One must first have the ability to construct a hierarchy of perceived competencies or successes across several domains, as well as a hierarchy of the importance of these domains. One must then be able to compare these two hierarchies, simultaneously attending to the relative position of every domain within each hierarchy. Out of these complex comparisons must come a summary score or statement about the relationship of one's competencies to one's aspirations, a judgment that for James directly affects one's global sense of self-worth.

In contrast to this type of cognitive–analytic model, Cooley (1902) postulated that the origins of our sense of self lie in our perceptions of what significant others think of us. According to Cooley, therefore, the self is a social construction, based on our appraisal of others' opinions about the self. Mead (1934) elaborated on this theme in his concept of the *generalized other,* which represented the pooled or collective judgments of the significant others in one's life. Implicit in these formulations is a modeling process wherein we imitate the attitudes that others hold toward us, and these reflected appraisals come to define what Cooley termed the *looking-glass self.*

In our previous research, we have attempted to assess the contribution of each of these potential determinants of self-worth. We began with the assumption that these two positions, the cognitive–analytical model of James and the looking-glass self model postulated by Cooley, were not necessarily antithetical. Both types of processes may well be operative in that each may account for a significant portion of one's sense of self-worth.

Our initial target group consisted of children in sixth through eighth grade. In operationalizing James's formulation, perceived successes were defined as the perceived competence or adequacy scores across the five domains of our

Self-Perception Profile for Children (Harter, 1985b). These include: scholastic competence, athletic competence, social acceptance, physical appearance, and behavioral conduct.

The construct of pretensions, in James' parlance, was operationalized as the *importance of success* in each of these same five domains. Each child was given a separate rating scale asking about how important it was to do well in each domain, in order to feel good about oneself as a person. Thus we obtained five competence/adequacy judgments, five importance ratings, and a global self-worth score, tapped by a separate subscale asking children how much they liked themselves as people. Both competence judgments and importance ratings utilized a 4-point scale.

In order to capture the essence of James's ratio between successes (competence) and pretensions (importance of success), we obtained a discrepancy score (competence minus importance) averaged across just those domains that the child considered *important*. (In James's formulation, competence, high or low, in domains deemed unimportant, should not affect one's global self-esteem.) The bigger this discrepancy score in a negative direction, that is, the more one's importance scores exceed one's competence–adequacy judgments, the lower one's self-worth should be. High self-worth should be associated with scores close to zero indicating that one's hierarchy of perceived competencies and one's hierarchy of importance ratings are very congruent (see Harter, 1985a, for a complete description of these procedures).

In operationalizing Cooley's formulation, we defined the construct of others' opinions toward the self as the degree to which children felt that significant others acknowledged their worth. Subjects rated the extent to which others treat them as a person, feel that they are important, like them the way they are, and so on. Two classes of significant others were identified, parents and peers. Given such a measure, tapping perceived regard from others, it was possible to examine the relationship between perceived regard from others and perceived regard for the self, namely, global self-worth.

Our findings provided clear support for the formulations of both James and Cooley. In support of James, we found that across several samples the correlations between the (competence minus importance) discrepancy score and self-worth ranged from .55 to .72. Thus the larger the negative discrepancy score, that is, the more one's importance ratings exceed one's perceived competence, the lower one's self-worth. The smaller this discrepancy score, the closer it moves to zero, the higher the child's sense of worth. More direct evidence (see Harter, 1985a) has revealed that the child with low self-worth is one who is unable to discount the importance of areas in which he or she is not competent. In contrast, the child with high self-worth appears to be able to discount the importance of domains in which his or her competence is relatively low, while touting the importance of those areas in which he or she is successful.

In support of Cooley, we found that the correlations between perceived parental and peer regard and the self-worth score ranged from .50 to .65, across three separate samples of middle school children. Thus the more one feels that significant others have regard for the self, the higher one's self-worth, that is, the more one has regard for oneself. Interestingly, these two sources of self-worth, regard from others as well as the discrepancy between one's competence and the importance of success, are relatively independent of each other. We will explore the implications for an additive model in a subsequent section.

The Larger Theoretical Model

In our earlier work, an important goal was to identify the determinants of self-worth, specifically those postulated by James and Cooley. However, equally important was an examination of the degree to which self-worth influences other behaviors within the larger self-system. That is, we were particularly interested in whether self-worth has a particular function in mediating other constructs of interest or whether it is merely epiphenomenal in nature.

The constructs we selected represented two general systems, *affect* and *motivation.* The choice of these constructs was partially guided by recent sequential models that have demonstrated that self-judgments elicit in affective reaction, which in turn motivates the individual to engage in a particular behavior (e.g., Bandura, 1978; Harter & Connell, 1984; Kanfer, 1980; Wicklund, 1975). Our interest in affect and motivation was also sparked by our efforts to devise an instrument sensitive to a variety of components that have been implicated in the study of depression, a topic to which we will return in a later section. The affect scale of this self-report instrument, entitled the Dimensions of Depression Scale for Children (Harter & Polesovsky, 1985), provides a general index of perceived happiness or cheerfulness versus sadness or depression. The motivation subscale provides an index of the energy, interest, and desire children have to engage in age-appropriate activities. Judgments of affect and motivation were *not* domain specific, but required subjects to provide a general assessment of both constructs, just as they were required, on the self-worth subscale, to make a global judgment about their worth as a person.

Figure 9.1 depicts the larger theoretical model we sought to test in Model A. There are two determinants of global self-worth, the Jamesian competence–importance discrepancy score and the social support–positive regard construct derived from Cooley's formulation. Self-worth is placed in the middle of the model, as a potential mediator of affect, primarily, and motivation, secondarily. That is, we hypothesized that the effect of self-worth on motivation should largely be mediated by the affective component. Based on previous findings within the domain of scholastic performance (Harter & Connell, 1984), as well as on the general sequential models mentioned, we predicted that there would also be a strong path from affect to motivation.

Employing path-analytic or causal modeling techniques, we compared this model (A) to an alternative in which the mediational role of self-worth was removed (Model B). In this alternative model, the paths from the discrepancy

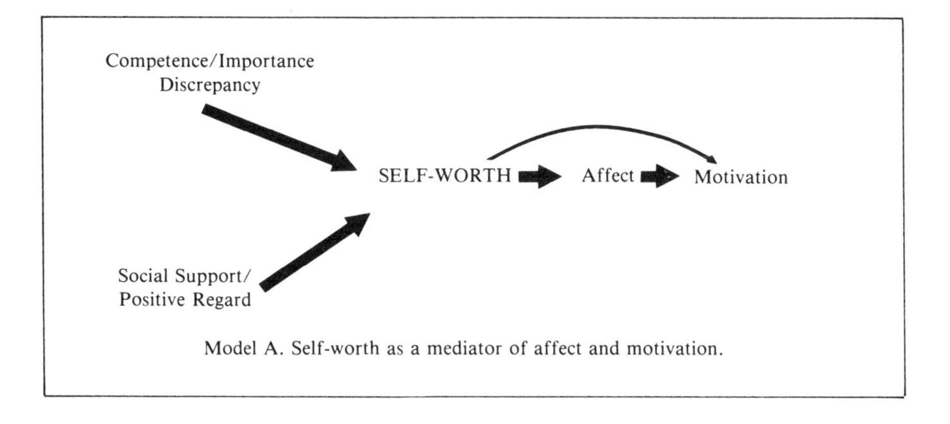

Model A. Self-worth as a mediator of affect and motivation.

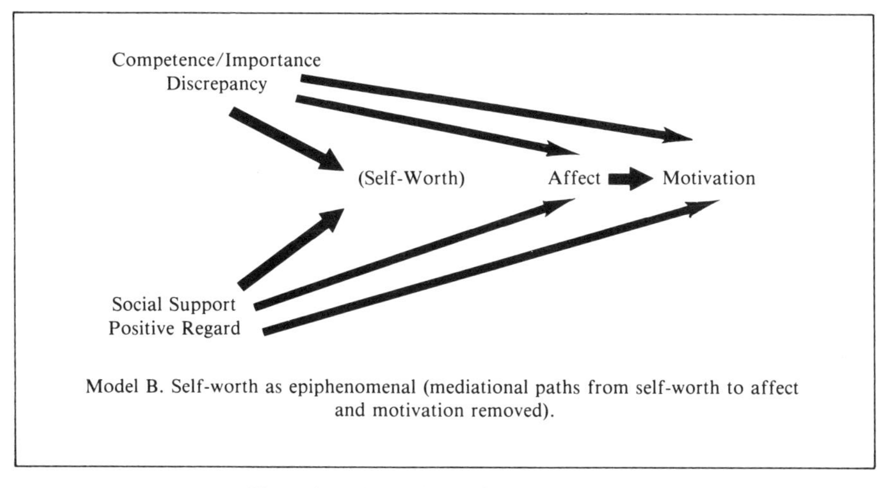

Model B. Self-worth as epiphenomenal (mediational paths from self-worth to affect and motivation removed).

Figure 9.1. Two alternative models tested.

score and the positive regard index bypassed self-worth and influenced affect and motivation directly, allowing us to address the question of whether we need to invoke self-worth as a mediator. Model B, then, was an attempt to determine whether self-worth is best viewed as epiphenomenal.

The findings overwhelmingly supported a refinement of Model A that provides a vastly better fit than Model B (see Harter, 1985a). Overall, the model provides strong support for the mediational function of self-worth. The path from self-worth to affect is the largest in the model. Although self-worth has a small direct effect on motivation, its influence is primarily mediated through affect, which is represented by a strong path from affect to motivation.

These modeling efforts have led us to several conclusions, although they have also raised further questions to be explored in the present chapter. With regard to the determinants of self-worth, there is strong support for both

James's and Cooley's formulations. Older (sixth–eighth grade) children appear to be weighing their competencies against the importance of success in the domains we tapped. In addition, their perceptions of the regard by others, specifically parents and peers, also directly affect their sense of self-worth. The findings also allow us to conclude that we cannot treat global self-worth as epiphenomenal. It has a definite function within the network of constructs examined, the most important of which is its direct impact on the general affective state or mood of the individual. Middle school children who like themselves as people are the happiest, whereas those who have a more negative sense of their overall worth are more apt to feel sad and depressed. The particular affect state of the individual, in turn, has a powerful effect on his or her motivation. The child who tends toward sadness or depression has little energy or desire to engage in age-appropriate activities, whereas the child who is cheerful is highly motivated to engage in such behaviors. The evidence, therefore, indicates that this type of sequential model does account for relationships among children's general perceptions of their self-worth, affect, and motivation.

QUESTIONS TO BE ADDRESSED IN THE PRESENT CHAPTER

The findings just summarized have provided support for a general model of the determinants of self-worth as well as for its function in mediating affect and motivation (Harter, 1985a; Harter & Hogan, 1985). However, there are numerous questions still to be addressed. The present chapter will describe our programmatic effort to pursue a number of issues raised by the initial model.

1. In our prior efforts we have only employed middle school children in our tests of the model. Given our concern with developmental issues, we will first examine the applicability of this model to somewhat younger children, in grades three through six. Third grade is the youngest age at which we can address this model, since prior to this age the child does not have an integrated sense of self, as a person, as reflected in our global self-worth score. Thus we sought to test the robustness of the model among older elementary school children.

2. We will then explore the additive nature of this model, examining the scores of children at low, medium, and high levels of discrepancy as well as positive regard, for both elementary and middle school children. In so doing, we will be able to provide more complete cameos of actual children with high and low self-worth, and to describe the contributions of the discrepancy construct and positive regard more concretely.

3. With our original model, we merely examined the impact of an overall competence/importance discrepancy score, as well as the impact of positive regard, averaged across peer and parental sources of support. It will be instructive, therefore, to determine which *particular* competence domains, and

which *particular* sources of positive regard, are the more powerful predictors of self-worth. Thus we will examine the relative influence of each of the five specific domains: scholastic competence, athletic competence, social acceptance, physical appearance, and behavioral conduct. We will also compare the relative importance of parental support with two sources of peer support, close friends versus classmates, and with teacher support.

4. The strong, positive relationship between self-worth and affect (r = .70–.80), a path that is central to the model, also requires further elucidation. Do these highly correlated variables really represent two separate constructs that are meaningfully related within the child's self-system? Or is it possible that the items defining each subscale are actually tapping the same construct, which accounts for their high correlation? Findings bearing on these two alternatives will be presented. We will also address the issue of the relationships among self-worth, affect, and motivation within the context of childhood depression.

5. Finally, we will explore the network of relationships among social support, perceived competence, affect or mood, and energy or interest among young children for whom the global concept of self-worth does not yet exist. In the absence of such a global self-perception, do domain-specific self-perceptions provide the mediating link between social support and mood and energy? Or might the link between social support and affect be very direct? Additional questions concerning the content and structure of young children's judgments about mood and energy will also be addressed.

DOWNWARD EXTENSION: PATTERN OF RELATIONSHIPS AMONG CHILDREN IN THIRD THROUGH SIXTH GRADES

Our initial modeling efforts were restricted to older children and young adolescents, primarily middle school children in grades six through eight. Thus we were interested in determining whether the same pattern of relationships was obtained in a group of elementary school children, grades three through six. Third grade was our lower limit for this particular network of constructs since we have determined that a child below this age level does not yet appear to have an integrated concept of his or her global worth as a person (see Harter & Pike, 1984). We will return to a discussion of the particular nature of the young child's network of perceptions in a subsequent section.

Our findings, in the form of correlations among the constructs of interest, indicate that the patterns obtained for middle school children replicate those found among older elementary school children. The primary correlations of interest are presented in Table 9.1. There it can be seen that the relationships between the two determinants of self-worth, the competence–importance discrepancy and social support, are very similar in the two samples. The contributions of the competence–importance discrepancy score and the social support score are comparable for both age groups. In addition, self-worth was found to bear an equally strong relationship to affect at both age levels. More-

TABLE 9.1. Relationships Among Variables for Elementary and Middle School Children

	Global Self-Worth	
	Elementary School (grades three–six)	Middle School (grades six–eight)
Competence–importance discrepancy	.50	.51
Social support–positive regard	.55	.50
Affect–mood	.68	.66
Motivation–interest	.50	.49

over, the relationship between self-worth and motivation was similar in both samples. Finally, the link between affect and motivation was comparable in both groups, .60 among the elementary school group and .58 among the middle school students. Thus the findings indicate that the same basic pattern of relationships is obtained across the age range from third to eighth grades, suggesting the robustness of this model for the period of middle childhood and early adolescence. We are currently addressing these issues among older adolescents, college students, and older adults to determine its applicability or the need for modification at older age levels.

THE IMPACT OF PARTICULAR LEVELS OF DISCREPANCY AND SOCIAL SUPPORT ON SELF-WORTH

The structural modeling efforts, as well as the pattern of correlations, provide one route to an examination of the relationship between self-worth and the discrepancy construct as well as social support. However, it is also instructive to examine how particular levels of discrepancy and social support combine to produce different self-worth scores.

In order to address this issue, we first created a 3 × 3 matrix, dividing children into high, medium, and low discrepancy intersecting with high, medium, and low social support. Children in the high groups were more than .5 standard deviations above the mean, low children were more than .5 standard deviations below the mean, and medium children were within .5 standard deviation. This procedure is analogous to dividing the sample into thirds. Using these criteria, there were sufficient numbers of children in all nine cells to warrant an examination of their self-worth scores. In our initial analysis of these groups, we employed the same social support composite that we utilized in the earlier modeling efforts, namely, a combination of parent and peer support.

Figure 9.2 presents the mean self-worth scores for all nine subgroups, separately for the elementary and middle school samples. As the figure reveals, the impact of both the competence–importance discrepancy and social support is very systematic across the three levels for each variable. Moreover, the ef-

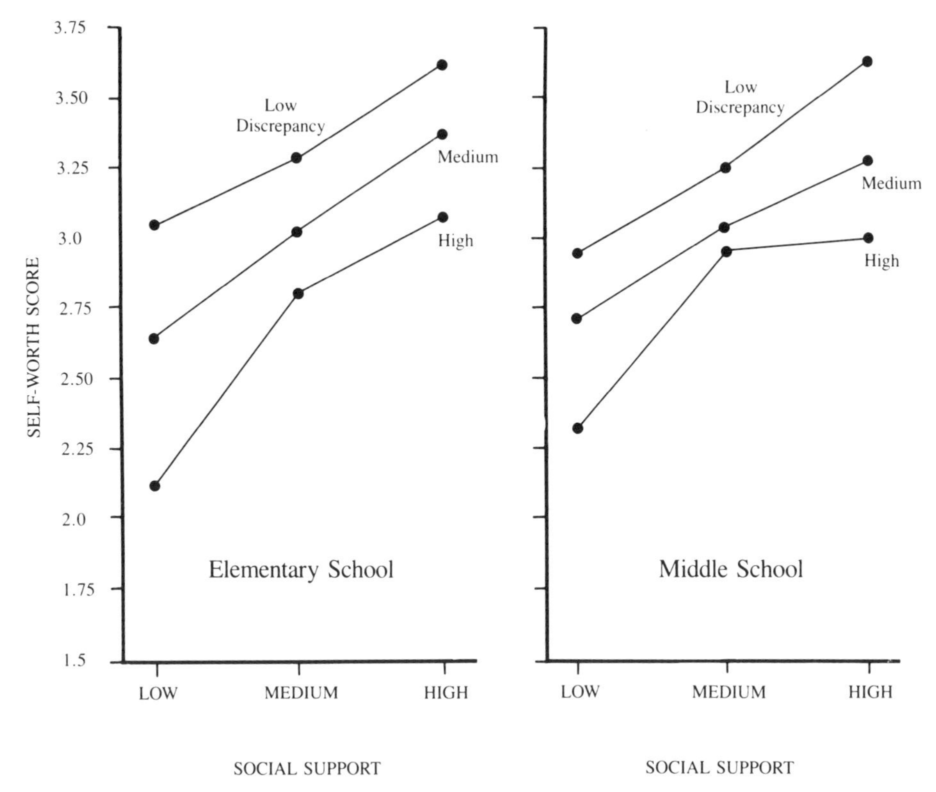

Figure 9.2. Self-worth as a function of levels of social support and competence–importance discrepancy among elementary and middle school children.

fects of these two variables are additive. They do not interact with one another. (This was borne out in analyses of variance indicating highly significant main effects for both variables, but no interactions.)

The implications of these findings, presented in this manner, are that both variables combine to produce a child's level of self-worth. One variable does not appear to offset or compensate for the other. For example, the self-worth of a child with very little discrepancy between competence judgments and importance ratings, a child who is doing well in domains deemed important, will suffer if social support is also not forthcoming. That is, the congruence between one's competence and importance hierarchies does not totally insulate the child against the impact of low social support from significant others. The self-worth of such a child, with little discrepancy but *low* social support, will be about 3, on a 4-point scale, in contrast to the self-worth of a child with little discrepancy coupled with *high* social support, which will be about 3.5.

Similarly, the support of significant others does not totally protect one against the impact of a high discrepancy score. Despite the fact that a child has high social support, a large discrepancy between competence and the importance of success will take its toll and lower self-worth. As the figure indicates, the child with the highest self-worth is one who possesses a combination of high social support and a low discrepancy score. These are the children scoring in the 3.5 range on self-worth. The child with the lowest self-worth is one who displays the opposite pattern, low social support in combination with a high discrepancy score. These are the children scoring slightly above 2 in self-worth. Thus the difference between these extreme groups is marked, indicating the impact that both of these determinants, combined, have on the child's global sense of worth as a person. These findings suggest that in our attempts to influence a child's self-worth we need to attend to the competence-importance discrepancy construct as well as the support provided by the child's social environment in order maximally to enhance a child's sense of worth.

In concluding that the impacts of social support and the competence-importance discrepancy construct are *independent,* one must be clear that we are addressing only one form of social input, namely, the general regard that social agents manifest toward children. However, there are other social influences that one could well address, for example, the impact social agents have on the particular importance hierarchies children develop. The values of the adult culture (e.g., parents and teachers) may well determine the importance of such domains as scholastic performance and behavioral conduct, whereas the peer culture may have more of an impact on the importance of social acceptance and appearance. To date, we have not addressed this source of potential social input; however, it would be important to pursue this issue in the future.

WHICH PARTICULAR DOMAINS HAVE THE MOST IMPACT ON SELF-WORTH?

In presenting a general model supporting the Jamesian notion that the discrepancy between one's competence or adequacy and the importance attached to success affects self-worth, we operationalized this construct averaging discrepancies across five domains. However, this procedure does not allow us to determine whether there are systematic effects associated with particular domains. That is, do the group findings indicate that some domains contribute more than others, or are children's importance hierarchies so individualized, so idiosyncratic, that overall effects for particular domains do not emerge? We examined this question by looking at the correlations of discrepancy scores, calculated separately by domain, and self-worth, for both the elementary and middle school samples. These correlations are presented in Table 9.2.

As can be seen in Table 9.2, there are systematic effects indicating that certain domains do make more of a contribution than others. Moreover, the ordering of domains is similar for both the elementary and middle school students. Physical appearance heads the list for both groups, making the biggest

TABLE 9.2. Correlations Between Domain-Specific Discrepancy Scores and Self-Worth

	Elementary School (grades three–six)	Middle School (grades six–eight)
Physical appearance	.66	.57
Social acceptance	.36	.45
Scholastic competence	.35	.36
Athletic competence	.33	.24
Behavioral conduct	.30	.26

contribution to self-worth. Thus the discrepancy between the importance of being good-looking and one's actual evaluation of one's appearance would appear to be a major concern for children in this age range, as judged by its impact on their overall sense of worth as a person. Social acceptance is the second most critical concern with regard to the influence of discrepancies of self-worth. For the middle school children, this is followed by scholastic competence, and then by athletic competence and behavioral conduct, which have the least impact. The differences between social acceptance, scholastic competence, and athletic competence are negligible for the elementary school children, although athletics and conduct appear to be the least salient domains, just as with the middle school sample.

This pattern of domain differences is illuminating with regard to the factors most likely to influence children's self-worth. Although one cannot generalize to the individual child, nevertheless, the overall pattern suggests that the most critical domains involve children's social selves, how they feel they look and act in relation to their peers. Domains perhaps deemed more relevant by parents, for example, scholastic competence and behavioral conduct, appear less relevant to children's sense of worth. This is not to say that children consider the domains of scholastic competence and behavioral conduct *unimportant.* To the contrary, they judge both of these domains as extremely important. However, the discrepancy score construct, namely, the level of their competence–adequacy in these domains in relation to the importance score, does not affect self-worth very significantly. For example, consider the pupil who feels school is important but admits that he isn't doing that well and thus has a large discrepancy. Or the child who feels that it is very important to behave even though she admits that she is not well behaved, creating a large discrepancy. Discrepancies in these two domains appear not to have much impact on the child's overall sense of worth, in contrast to discrepancies in the domains of physical appearance and social acceptance.

These findings raise intriguing questions with regard to how the values of attractiveness and popularity come to dominate, as determinants of a child's sense of global worth as a person. One can speculate on the impact of the peer group, and the emphasis the media place on appearance and its relationship to acceptance. Movies, television, rock videos, teen magazines, and pop culture paperback novels all tout the importance of attractiveness, designer fashions, and romance, glamourizing the famous role models whom one should emulate. Preteens and teenagers should seem to be the biggest consumers of the products conveying these messages. Moreover, as Elkind (1984) has pointed out, the importance of physical appearance among young people, as manifested by looks as well as dress codes, has escalated in recent years, and is also apparent at increasingly younger ages. Our own findings would certainly support this contention, and further suggest that children's and young adolescents' judgments of their attractiveness are highly predictive of the global worth they see in themselves as persons.

Specific Sources of Social Support and Self-Worth

In exploring the explanatory power of Cooley's formulation regarding the impact of the perceived attitudes of others on one's sense of self-esteem, our initial modeling efforts revealed that a single score, representing a composite of perceived support across several significant others, was predictive of self-worth. However, in testing this general model we did not determine the relative contribution of each source of support. More recently we have examined this issue, looking separately at the relationships between four different sources of support (parent, classmate, close friend, and teacher) and self-worth. These correlations are presented in Table 9.3.

It can be seen from the table that for both elementary school children and middle school young adolescents support from parents and classmates is more predictive of self-worth than is support from a close friend or a teacher. Two points are of interest in this pattern. First, the general support of one's peers or classmates has a greater impact on self-worth than does the regard that one receives from one's closest friend(s). This finding is consistent with Rosenberg's (1979) results indicating that in later childhood and early adolescence the general peer group is the more critical source of information concerning one's self-esteem, whereas when one moves to later adolescence one's best friends become the primary source of feedback concerning the self. It will be interesting, therefore, to pursue this issue in our own work, examining the pattern of relationships among high school students.

The strength of the parent influence is also noteworthy. Although it has

TABLE 9.3. Relationships Among Self-Worth and Four Sources of Social Support

Source of Support	Elementary School (grades three–six)	Middle School (grades six–eight)
Parent	.42	.45
Classmate	.46	.42
Friend	.38	.30
Teacher	.36	.27

been common in general textbook treatments of development to assume that the impact of parental attitudes declines as one moves into adolescence, our findings do not support such a claim among middle school students, for whom parental regard is as important as general support from classmates. Damon (1982) has also suggested that parental influence does not wane during adolescence to the extent that many others have claimed. In our own work we plan to pursue this issue, extending our investigation into the period of later adolescence. One possibility is that the *magnitude* of parental influence may not change with development, whereas the *nature* of parental social support may manifest developmental differences. Anecdotal observations with our middle school students led us to suspect that during this early period of adolescence parents act as a buffer with regard to their children's interactions with peers. That is, parents provide support in terms of their display of sympathy and suggestions around issues involving peer relationships; they provide a secure base that allows the young adolescent to refuel psychologically before reentering the all-important world of the peer culture. The analogy to the processes involved in Mahler's (1963) descriptions of the individuation of the toddler is intentional.

In future studies we hope to address this issue systematically, across the entire span of adolescence, employing interview techniques that will probe into the reasons adolescents give for their responses on our social support scale. The items on this scale yield judgments concerning the degree to which one's parents treat one as a person, care about one's feelings, and feel that what one does is important. That is, they elicit evaluations of the parents' general regard for their child. However, we do not know precisely what form parental support may take at various periods during adolescence, nor whether it changes with development. Thus we will be pursuing this issue in our continuing research on the specific role social support plays in influencing one's self-worth.

ON THE RELATIONSHIP BETWEEN GLOBAL SELF-WORTH AND MOOD

In our general model (Model A in Fig. 9.1), the path between global self-worth and mood is the strongest of any in magnitude. Across a number of samples, the correlation between self-worth and mood ranges from .67 to .82. Moreover, when we factor the Dimensions of Depression Scale for Children (Harter & Polesovsky, 1985) with separate subscales designed to tap self-worth, mood, energy, and self-blame, the self-worth and mood subscales combine to form one factor. (Energy and self-blame define the second and third factors.) Thus the pattern of findings indicates an extremely strong relationship between self-worth, how much one likes oneself as a person, and mood, the degree to which one is cheerful or depressed.

There are two possible explanations for this strong correlation. The first is specified by the model, namely, that there is a direct relationship between these two constructs, such that if one likes oneself as a person this will affect the degree to which one is happy. That is, we have proposed that these are two distinct constructs that are intimately and functionally related in the lives of children and adolescents.

The second interpretation is that these constructs are not distinct from one another; rather, we are tapping but one construct, defined by two sets of very similar items. Thus although our theorizing and instrumentation have identified these as differentiated constructs, such a distinction may simply be arbitrary in that it exists in our minds as theorists but not in the minds of our child and adolescent subjects. We felt, therefore, that it was essential to design a procedure that would allow us to determine which of these two alternative explanations for the strong relationship between self-worth and mood was correct.

The procedure we devised consisted of having middle school children sort the statements from the Dimensions of Depression Scale into clusters. That is, we presented subjects with a list of the key content of the items, for example, Like the kind of person I am, Feel like smiling a lot, Have lots of energy, Don't blame myself for things that go wrong, Am happy with myself, Am pretty cheerful about things, Have energy to do things, Don't think things that go wrong are my fault, and so on. We first asked subjects to put the items into clusters, and then requested that they give each cluster of items a name or descriptive label. We employed two different procedures here, each with a different group of subjects. In one group we did not specify the number of clusters. In a second group, we specifically requested that they group the items into four clusters, in order to determine the accuracy with which they placed designated items (from our subscales) into their respective clusters. If the constructs of self-worth and mood were not differentiated in the minds of our subjects, this would be manifested by their grouping both sets of items together in the first procedure where they could decide on the number of clusters. In the second procedure requiring four clusters, errors would be made in the placement of mood and self-worth items, if these did not represent cognitively distinct categories. If these constructs *were* differentiated by subjects, we would expect them to generate four clusters, to assign items correctly to each cluster corresponding to the four subscales we had designated, and to label them accordingly.

The findings clearly indicated that these constructs are quite distinct in the minds of middle school children. For the procedure in which children determined the number of clusters these items would require, the large majority of subjects placed them into four groups. When we specifically asked the second group of subjects to sort the items into four clusters, they recreated the intended structure of our instrument. With regard to the most critical discrimination, over 85% of the self-worth and mood items were correctly assigned to separate clusters.

Moreover, the descriptive labels these middle-school children attached to the four categories closely corresponded to the constructs they were designed to tap. Typical labels for the mood cluster included the following: My feelings, How I feel, Happiness, Being happy or sad, My emotions. In contrast, typical labels for the self-worth cluster were: Myself, Being me, Liking myself, The way I look at myself, How I think I am, The person I am. The differentiated labeling of these two clusters, in particular, was central to our hypothesis. In addition, energy items were clustered separately under such rubrics as: My energy, Energy to do things, How I do things, Having fun and energy, Being energetic. Self-blame clusters were labeled: Not blaming myself, Problems not being my fault, Not taking the blame, About blaming yourself.

The most critical findings involve the distinction between self-worth and mood. They reveal that children of this age definitely view these as distinguishable systems within the self, separating their feelings or emotional reactions from their sense of self as a person. They do not combine or confuse the two sets of items. Thus these results bolstered our faith in the initial interpretation of our model with regard to the strong correlation between these two sets of items. That is, this relationship would appear to exist because these two distinct constructs are intimately linked in reality, in the lives of children. The evaluative judgment that one does or does not like oneself as a person has a powerful effect on one's general mood. Liking oneself provokes personal happiness. Disliking the self engenders sadness and feelings of depression. Thus self-worth is best viewed as a *mediator* of affect in our model, and not a construct synonymous with mood.

Implications for Childhood Depression

The literature on childhood depression has been equivocal with regard to the issue of whether *negative self-perceptions* should be considered a primary, that is, cardinal, symptom of depression. *Depressed affect* is generally agreed upon as a primary symptom. However, in certain diagnostic schemes, negative self-evaluations are viewed as critical to the definition of depression, whereas in other systems poor self-image is relegated to the status of a potential secondary symptom, one not necessary for the diagnosis.

Our normative findings suggest that among children *8 and older,* feelings of low self-worth are highly correlated with depressive affect, as assessed through self-report measures. Moreover, the general relationship between self-worth (positive–negative) and mood (cheerful–depressed) can be found to exist at every point along the distributions of these two variables. Figure 9.3 presents this relationship, for three different age periods, indicating the self-worth scores associated with five levels of mood. There it can be seen that depressed affect is associated with very low self-worth scores, and that there is a highly systematic increase in self-worth scores as the mood scores shift from depressed to cheerful affect. These findings strongly imply that since self-perceptions are so intimately related to mood they should be considered a primary symptom in the diagnosis of depression during middle childhood. In future work, we plan to pursue this issue in clinical samples.

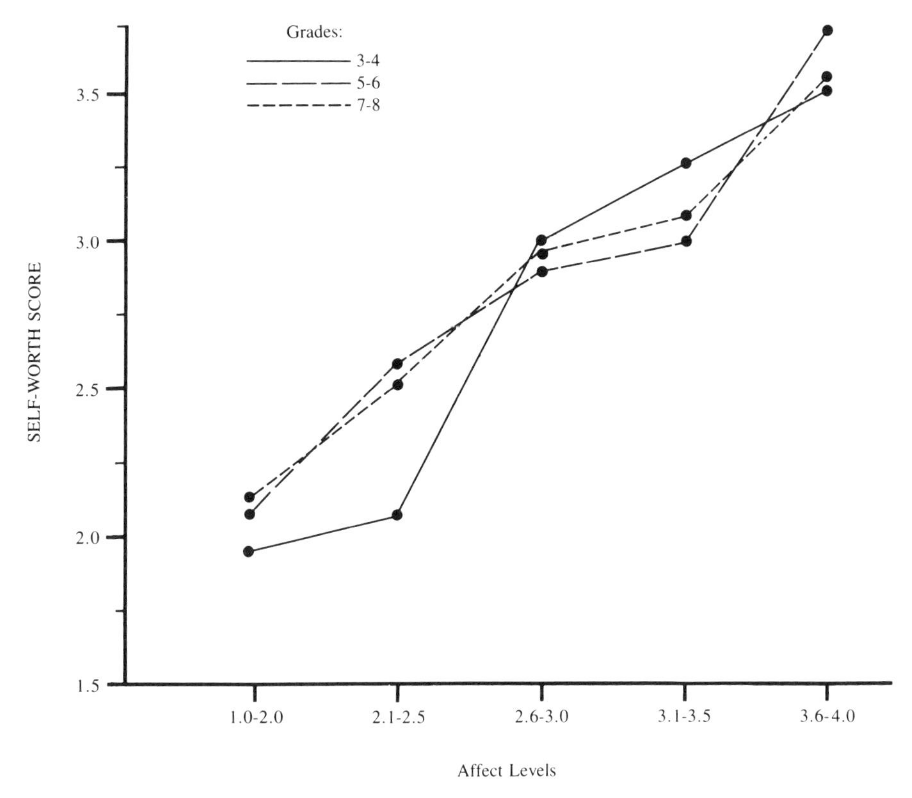

Figure 9.3. Self-worth scores associated with five levels of affect among elementary and middle school children.

THE NETWORK OF SOCIAL SUPPORT, SELF-PERCEPTIONS, MOOD, AND ENERGY AMONG YOUNG CHILDREN

Having established a working model of the determinants and correlates of self-worth among older elementary and middle school children, we next sought to explore certain relationships in the network of constructs among young children. The components of such a network will necessarily vary, however, given the cognitive limitations of the young child. Our previous work (Harter, 1985a; Harter & Pike, 1984) has revealed that a child below the age of 8 does not have a consolidated concept of one's worth as a person, as tapped by global self-worth items. The concept of oneself as a person, to which some level of general worth is attached, is a cognitive construction not possible until middle childhood. Such cognitive limitations carry with them several implications for the network of relationships among young children.

It may well be, extrapolating from this observation, that young children are also unable to make global or generalized judgments about their mood or affect. Rather, their judgments may be restricted to domain-specific perceptions of mood, analogous to their domain-specific perceptions of competence (Harter & Pike, 1984). It may also be the case that, unlike older children, who differentiate between the constructs of mood and energy (Harter & Polesovsky, 1985), young children do not distinguish between these psychological constructs. Although the young child may be able to differentiate between the specific observable *contexts* in which such feelings arise, for example, home versus classroom versus playground, the distinction between internal states such as feeling happy and interested is cognitively blurred, rendering them one undifferentiated judgment.

In a recent study (see Wright, 1985) we sought to investigate these issues, focusing first on the content and structure of young children's judgments concerning their mood and interest level. We were particularly interested in whether the young child can even make reliable judgments about these states, since many have questioned the utility of self-report measures at the younger ages. However, given the success of our Pictorial Scale of Perceived Competence and Social Acceptance for Young Children (Harter & Pike, 1984), we were optimistic about the possibility of constructing a reliable measure of perceptions of mood and interest level for children 4–7.

We selected three specific contexts in which such feelings might be experienced: home with family, the school classroom, and interactions with peers. Within each context we devised an equal number of mood items (focusing on the degree to which one is happy or sad) and interest items (tapping the degree to which one liked or wanted to engage in each context-specific activity). Examples of *home* items included helping Mom and Dad get ready for dinner, being with the family, and having meals with the family. *School* items focused primarily on cognitive tasks, for example, looking at books, working on papers, and learning from the teacher. Examples of *peer* items included being with other kids, talking with other kids, and doing things with other kids.

As a test of whether or not young children had the ability to make generalized or global judgments about their mood or interest level, we included a fourth subscale tapping general feelings of happiness or sadness, as well as interest and lack of interest, independent of any particular context. All items were presented in pictorial form. For each item, there were two pictures on each page; for the mood items, one picture depicted a same-gender child who was happy in the situation or with the activity whereas the second picture depicted the child as sad. For the interest items, one picture depicted a child appearing very interested whereas the second picture depicted a child who was not interested in the activity.

Initially, in order to ascertain the structure of children's judgments in these areas, we factor-analyzed the items. An interpretable three-factor solution emerged. Each of the three specific contexts, family, classroom, and peer interaction, defined a separate factor. The mood and interest items were not differentiated from each other, as anticipated. Moreover, the general items did not form a factor, nor did the items systematically cross-load on the other factors. The internal consistency of the three context-specific clusters of items was acceptable, whereas the general items were not internally consistent. Thus these findings revealed that young children can make reliable, and somewhat independent, judgments about their mood and interest in three distinct contexts, though mood is not distinguishable from interest. Moreover, generalized, context-free judgments about these constructs do not emerge as reliable, consistent with our findings regarding the construct of global self-worth among young children.

Having established that children could make mood–interest judgments within the context of family, classroom, and peer interactions, we could then examine the relationships these judgments bore to their perceptions of social support, as well as their perceived competence. Perceptions of competence and support were obtained from our Pictorial Scale of Perceived Competence and Social Acceptance (Harter & Pike, 1984). This instrument taps young children's perceptions of cognitive competence and physical competence, as well as their perceived acceptance by their mothers, fathers, and peers.

Given that these young children possess no reliable concept of self-worth, we could not examine a model in which self-worth serves as a mediator of mood–interest. Thus we sought to determine whether there was a direct link between perceived social acceptance and mood–interest, or whether self-perceptions in the form of domain-specific perceived competence might represent the mediating link between social support or acceptance and mood–interest. Moreover, we could determine whether or not these links occurred primarily within a given context; for instance, parental acceptance is related to positive mood–energy within the family setting, and perceptions of cognitive competence are related to positive mood–energy within the classroom context. Findings in support of a *direct* link between social support and mood–interest would be suggested by a positive correlation between social support and mood–affect and would be interpreted as indicating that if one feels one's parents engage in positive behaviors toward the self this directly affects one's mood and interest. A mediational model would be supported by a strong relationship between social support and perceived competence, as well as a strong relationship between perceived competence and mood–interest, with a weak relationship between social support and mood–interest.

The findings support an interpretation focusing on the direct link between social support and mood–interest, particularly among the 6- and 7-year-olds for whom the relationships were stronger. This network is presented in Figure 9.4. There it can be seen that the perceived support from both mother and father correlates with mood–interest within the family context. Perceived peer support predicts mood–interest in peer interactions to about the same degree. Interestingly, peer support also predicts mood–interest within the classroom, a finding that makes sense given that most peer interactions occur at school. At the time of this study we did not have teacher support items; however, such a subscale has now been created, and it will be interesting in future research to test the hypothesis that teacher support also predicts classroom mood–interest. (The remaining cross-context relationships between social support and

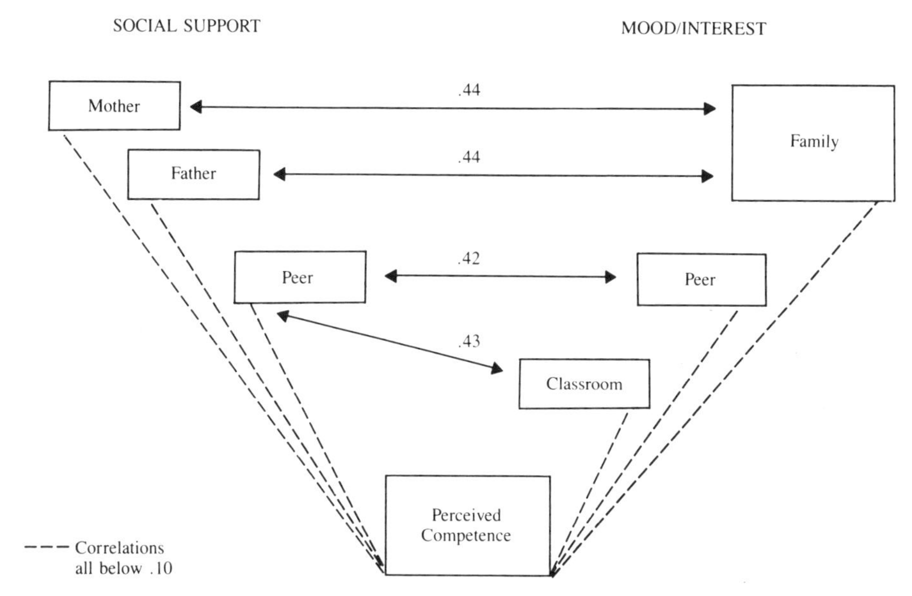

Figure 9.4. Relationships among social acceptance, mood-interest, and perceived competence for children 6–7 years old.

mood-interest, e.g., mother support and mood in the peer context or father support and mood in the classroom, were all negligible.)

The overall pattern, therefore, suggests that social support and mood-interest are directly related in a context-specific manner for young children. At this point, since our approach has been correlational in nature, we cannot specify the directionality of these effects (and thus the double arrows in Fig. 9.4). There is no support for a model in which self-perceptions in the form of perceived competence act as a mediator between social support and mood-interest. The correlations of perceived competence and both social support and mood-interest were negligible.

These findings raise intriguing questions with regard to developmental shifts in the determinants of mood and interest. Among young children within the age range of 4–7, social factors in the form of acceptance by significant others appear to be primarily responsible for their level of happiness and interest. Although this link continues at older ages, self-worth comes to mediate the impact of social support on affect and interest or energy. We know little, however, about the specific processes underlying the evolution of a sense of one's worth as a person. The developmental findings, taken together, imply that social support may be an important factor in determining the level of self-worth when it emerges. For example, one would predict that the young child with a sense of social acceptance by significant others would develop a positive sense of self-worth when this generalized concept emerges in middle childhood, whereas the child who lacks social support would be more likely to develop a sense of low self-worth. In fact, earlier theorists (e.g., Hales, 1979; White, 1963) have proposed such a link. Longitudinal research would be welcome here, a project in which we are currently involved.

However, the documentation of a relationship between perceived acceptance from significant others during the early years and high self-worth in middle childhood does not speak to the psychological processes governing this link. The demonstration of the effects of particular child-rearing styles and parental attitudes toward the child certainly provides some insight into causal mechanisms (e.g., Block & Block, 1980; Coopersmith, 1967; Maccoby & Martin, 1983; Waters, Noyes, Vaughn, & Ricks, 1985). However, investigators have yet to unravel the mechanisms through which the messages of significant others lead to a conception of self, as reflected in either global judgments of worth or domain-specific self-perceptions.

Thus there is much yet to be learned about the specific developmental processes underlying the formation of the looking-glass self. Certain theorists, for example, Rosenberg (1979), have emphasized the role of perspective taking, proposing that the child must have the ability to appreciate another's perspective toward the self in order to adopt that attitude and transform it into his or her self-concept. There is certainly historical precedent for such a position in the works of Baldwin (1897) and Mead (1934). However, given the complexity of the perspective-taking skills proposed, this would place the impact of the opinions of others on the child's sense of self at middle childhood, when such processes seem to emerge (Selman, 1980).

Theorists such as White (1963), however, would argue that the impact of parental opinions toward the child occurs much earlier, as the toddler (and even the infant) develops some rudimentary sense of parental attitudes toward the self. He noted that the esteem in which we are held by others begins to assume importance as soon as the very young child can sense that others are a source of attitudes. There is much to be learned, however, about the nature of this "sense," and how it manifests itself in the young child. For example, we may need to postulate more rudimentary forms of perspective taking. Moreover, the perception of parental attitudes may lead to observable behaviors from which one can *infer* the very young child's sense of self, long before the child has an articulated concept he or she can verbalize.

This line of reasoning suggests two fruitful avenues to pursue. One involves a thoughtful examination of the processes through which the young child may adopt the attitudes of significant others toward the self, processes that do not involve those more complex skills of perspective taking that emerge during middle childhood. That is, it may be necessary to take a developmental approach to the looking-glass self, postulating different mechanisms at different developmental levels.

Second, we feel that it is important to identify the *behavioral* manifestations of self-worth in the very young child. There may well be observable dimensions such as *confidence* that will predict later self-worth in the form of a verbally expressed, cognitive construction about the self. That is, although one's verbalized concept of global self-worth does not emerge until middle childhood, the young child appears to display behaviors indicative of a rudimentary sense of self-esteem. Some progress has been made toward specifying these behaviors by Waters and his colleagues (Waters et al., 1985). It will be interesting to pursue this avenue of research longitudinally in order to identify the behavioral precursors of the concept of global self-worth that emerge in middle childhood. Such efforts would begin to illuminate the developmental origins of a pattern of fascinating relationships that we have documented within the self-system of children.

SUMMARY

In the present chapter we sought to extend and refine our model of the determinants and mediational role of self-worth. The initial model sought to apply the formulations of both James (1892) and Cooley (1902) to the periods of late childhood and early adolescence. General support for both formulations was obtained. The evidence indicated that self-worth is determined by the extent to which one is competent in domains deemed important, the theory that James put forth at the turn of the century. There was also evidence for Cooley's contention that our global sense of self-worth represents the incorporation of the attitudes that significant others hold toward the self. Moreover, our initial model demonstrated that self-worth is not epiphenomenal, but plays an important mediational role in its influence on one's general affective state, which in turn affects one's general level of motivation and interest in age-appropriate activities.

The findings presented in this chapter have revealed that this model is quite robust across the ages of 8–15, the ages we have examined to date. We have also demonstrated the additive nature of the model with regard to the determinants of self-worth. Success in areas of importance and the influence of the attitudes of significant others appear to be independent sources of self-worth.

We have also determined that certain competence domains, as well as certain sources of support, are particularly critical during this age period. The domain of physical appearance is the most powerful predictor of self-worth, followed by peer acceptance, suggesting that judgments concerning the physical and social self that one manifests to the world, particularly within the peer culture, strongly affect one's global sense of worth as a person.

Social support in the form of positive regard from both peers and one's parents is also an important determinant of self-worth. Although the salience of peer support was to be expected, the finding that parent support was equally critical runs counter to the claims of some concerning the waning impact of parental influence in adolescence. We have speculated that, although the magnitude of the effect of parental support on one's self-worth may not change across the periods we have examined, the nature or function of positive regard from one's parents may differ as one moves into adolescence. We hope to explore this hypothesis in our future research.

Another issue of concern in the present chapter involved the question of whether the constructs of self-worth and general mood state, which are highly correlated with each other, actually constitute differentiated constructs in the minds of our subjects. An alternative explanation for their strong correlation would be that they represent the same construct, for example, happiness with self. Our findings revealed that middle school children clearly distinguish between the two constructs, discriminating between the items on the two subscales as well as assigning different descriptive labels to each cluster. Thus it would appear that self-worth has a definite mediational role in our model in that it influences one's mood state, rather than being synonymous with one's general level of affect. The implications of this relationship for our understanding of childhood depression were also explored, since it would appear that, beginning in middle childhood, depressed affect and low self-worth are very strongly associated with one another.

Finally, we examined the network of domain-specific constructs among very young children, for whom the more global concepts of self-worth and mood state are not yet present. These findings revealed a strong relationship between perceived social acceptance of parents and peers and context-specific mood levels. Thus acceptance by parents determines one's mood and interest within the family context, whereas peer support is a critical determinant of mood and interest within the realm of peer interaction. These effects are direct; that is, they are not mediated by self-perceptions of competence. In presenting these findings, we urged that more attention be devoted to the mechanisms through which social acceptance influences one's emerging sense of self, since it is apparent that different developmental processes characterize the network of relationships among these constructs at different developmental levels.

REFERENCES

Baldwin, J. M. 1897. *Social and ethical interpretations in mental development.* New York: Macmillian.

Bandura, A. (1978). The self-system in reciprocal determinism. *American Psychologist, 33,* 344–358.

Block, J. H., & Block, J. (1980). The role of ego-control and ego-resiliency in the organization of behavior. In W. A. Collins (Ed.), *Minnesota Symposium on Child Psychology* (Vol. 13). Hillsdale, NJ: Erlbaum.

Connell, J. P. (1980). *A multidimensional measure of children's perceptions of control.* Unpublished master's thesis.

Cooley, C. H. (1902). *Human nature and the social order.* New York: Charles Scribner's Sons.

Coopersmith, S. (1967). *The antecedents of self-esteem.* San Francisco: W. H. Freeman.

Damon, W. (1982). *Social and personality development.* New York: Norton.

Elkind, D. (1984). Growing up faster. *Psychology Today, 12,* 38–45.

Hales, S. (1979). *Developmental processes of self-esteem.* Paper presented at the Society for Research in Child Development, San Francisco, CA. March 15–18.

Harter, S. (1982). The perceived competence scale for children. *Child Development, 53,* 87–97.

Harter, S. (1983). The development of the self-system. In M. Hetherington (Ed.), *Handbook of child psychology: Social and personality development* (Vol. 4). New York: Wiley.

Harter, S. (1985a). Processes underlying the construct, maintenance and enhancement of the self-concept in children. In J. Suls & A. Greenwald (Eds.), *Psychological perspectives on the self* (Vol. 3). Hillsdale, NJ: Erlbaum.

Harter, S. (1985b). *The Self-Perception Profile for Children: Revision of the Perceived Competence Scale for Children.* Manual, University of Denver.

Harter, S., & Connell, J. P. (1984). A comparison of alternative models of the relationships between academic achievement and children's perceptions of competence, control, and motivational orientation. In J. Nicholls (Ed.), *The development of achievement-related cognitions and behaviors.* Greenwich, CT: JAI.

Harter, S., & Hogan, A. (1985). *A causal model of the determinants of self-worth and the affective and motivational systems which it mediates.* Paper presented at the meeting of the Society for Research in Child Development, Toronto.

Harter, S., & Pike, R. (1984). The Pictorial Perceived Competence Scale for Young Children. *Child Development, 55,* 1969–1982.

Harter, S., & Polesovsky, M. (1985). *Components and correlates of childhood depression.* Unpublished manuscript, University of Denver.

James W. (1892). *Psychology: The briefer course.* New York: Henry Holt & Co.

Kanfer, F. H. (1980). Self-management methods. In F. H. Kanfer & A. P. Goldstein (Eds.), *Helping people change: A textbook of methods* (2nd ed.). New York: Pergamon.

Maccoby, E., & Martin, J. (1983). Socialization in the context of the family: Parent–chid interaction. In E. M. Hetherington (Ed.), *Handbook of child psychology: Vol. 4. Socialization, personality and social development.* New York: Wiley.

Mahler, M. S. (1963). Thoughts about development and individuation. *Psychoanalytic study of the child* (Vol. 18). New York: International Universities Press.

Mead, G. H. (1934). *Mind, self, and society.* Chicago: University of Chicago Press.

Piers, E., & Harris, D. (1969). *The Piers-Harris Children's Self-Concept Scale.* Nashville, TN: Counselor Recordings and Tests.

Rosenberg, M. (1979). *Conceiving the self.* New York: Basic.

Selman, R. (1980). *The growth of interpersonal understanding.* New York: Academic Press.

Waters, E., Noyes, D. M., Vaughn, B. E., & Ricks, M. (1985). *Q*-sort definitions of social competence and self-esteem: Discriminant validity of related constructs in theory and data. *Developmental Psychology, 21,* 508–522.

White, R. W. (1963). Ego and reality in psychoanalytic theory. *Psychological Issues,* Monograph 3.

Wicklund, R. A. (1975). Objective self-awareness. In L. Berkowitz (Ed.), *Advances in experimental social psychology* (Vol. 8). New York: Academic.

Wright, K. (1985). *Self-reported mood in young children and its relationship to perceived social acceptance.* Unpublished master's thesis, University of Denver.

CHAPTER 10

The Acquisition of Self-Knowledge: A Self-Socialization Perspective

DIANE N. RUBLE

The acquisition of knowledge about one's self strongly shapes and affects human personality and behavior throughout the life span. It has an especially powerful impact, however, on the developing child. The focus of my research over the past 10 years has been on how children form judgments at various points in development about their abilities, values, and personal characteristics and on how such judgments affect self-evaluation and behavior.

The research described in the present chapter is concerned with self-socialization aspects of self-knowledge. That is, the process of self-definition is viewed as active and self-initiated and the conclusions drawn allow the child to monitor his or her own behavior. The present emphasis on self-socialization differs from traditional notions of socialization in which the child is viewed as a relatively passive recipient of information from socializing agents (for reviews see Bandura, 1969; Mischel, 1970). That is, the dominant approach to research in social-personality development has been social learning theory, which, until recent reformulations (e.g., Bandura, 1977), has been primarily a theory of how socializing agents "shape" children through reinforcement and modeling (Maccoby & Martin, 1983). Applied to self-knowledge, for example, research based on traditional approaches to socialization has examined how the actions of socializing agents, such as setting limits, affect children's self-concept and self-esteem (Coopersmith, 1967; Wylie, 1979).

The self-socialization perspective represents an alternative, though complementary, view of social-personality development in general and the acquisition of self-knowledge in particular. The focus is on processes internal to the child, such as the child's interpretation of or susceptibility to the messages conveyed by socializing agents.

Preparation of this chapter and some of the research were supported, in part, by grant No. 37215 and a Research Scientist Development Award, No. 00484, both from the National Institute of Mental Health. I would like to thank Jennifer Altshuler, Shelly Chaiken, Karin Frey, Tory Higgins, and Peggy Thoits for reading and commenting on an earlier draft of this chapter.

This emphasis on the child represents a convergence of several different trends in the socialization literature. One is an increasing application of cognitive-developmental principles (e.g., Kohlberg, 1966) to social-personality development, including the acquisition of self-knowledge (e.g., Damon & Hart, 1982). This approach emphasizes the active, constructive processes during development, such as how a child constructs a theory of the self (Harter, 1983; Lewis & Brooks-Gunn, 1979). A second trend is the recognition of the reciprocity of influence among participants in social interaction; that is, characteristics of the child, such as temperament or state, influence socializing agents as well as the reverse (Bell & Harper, 1977; Maccoby & Martin, 1983). A third trend is the study of *anticipatory socialization* in the sociology literature, such as Lazarus and Folkman's (1984) research on anticipatory coping. A final trend is the recognition that the motivation to act in accordance with social conventions or to view oneself in particular ways may be internally based, on competence or mastery motivation, for example (Bandura, 1982; Berlyne, 1960; Deci, 1975; Harter, 1978; White, 1959), rather than externally based, on, for example, rewards from parents. Taken together, these trends contribute to the view that children, in part, socialize themselves—that they are motivated to construct rules or theories about themselves and their social environments and that such constructions influence their behavior and, in turn, how others respond toward them.

In my research self-socialization has been conceptualized as a series of self-definitional episodes in which different goals become salient in response to changing conditions. Differing goals may be made salient in a variety of ways—through biological, cognitive, or social changes—such as when the social pressures of high school or the advent of first pregnancy makes salient information relevant to attractiveness and parenting self-definitions, respectively. A major implication of this approach to socialization is that individuals may be viewed as maximally susceptible to certain kinds of information during relatively circumscribed time periods. Thus the consequences of these self-socialization processes may be quite significant. Once conclusions are drawn, they may be difficult to change because the individual's interpretations of additional information and his or her subsequent behavior are influenced by the concepts and distinctions already formed (Bartlett, 1932; Nisbett & Ross, 1980). If, for example, a girl concludes that she is poor at math, she may distort discrepant information (e.g., attribute a high score to luck), or stop trying. In either case, her negative self-perception is maintained, and feelings of discouragement and low self-esteem are a likely consequence. It is important, therefore, to understand exactly how changing conditions influence information gathering, because information available at the time individuals initially become highly motivated to engage in self-assessment may have long-lasting consequences.

The present chapter is concerned with self-socialization processes involved in three different aspects of self-knowledge: (1) the acquisition of gender-related self-knowledge during early childhood; (2) the acquisition of competence-related self-knowledge during the early school years; and (3) self-definitional processes related to female puberty. Although these three areas of self-knowledge are quite diverse, they share a fundamental similarity in that each concerns self-socialization processes in response to one or more changing conditions: (1) changes in social cognitions (e.g., level of understanding about gender); (2) changes in social pressures or norms (e.g., changing emphasis on achievement during the early years of school); and (3) biological changes (e.g., menarche). In the detailed discussion of each of these changes in the following sections, we are concerned primarily with two issues: changes in self-relevant information seeking accompanying changing conditions, and the impact on self-perception and behavior of self-definitional processes occurring at a particular developmental period.

GENDER-RELATED SELF-KNOWLEDGE

Early in development, girls and boys begin to manifest different interests and behaviors, and such sex role differentiation remains strong throughout the life span. A long tradition of developmental research has been concerned with how sex role differentiation occurs (e.g., Huston, 1983; Maccoby & Jacklin, 1974; Mischel, 1970). Most research concerned with nonbiological explanations has focused on social learning mechanisms. Certainly it is well established that the culture provides clear messages about normative differences between the sexes that children can emulate. Moreover, boys and girls are clearly treated differently; they receive differential encouragement to engage in physical activity, to be independent, to play with cars or dolls, and so on (for reviews see Huston, 1983; Ruble, 1984).

The question we have been addressing is what role the child plays in this process. Does a child's knowledge of being a boy or girl influence what information is responded to? Is there a point during development where children are particularly interested in and/or sensitive to gender-related information?

Gender Constancy and Responsiveness to Gender-Related Information

According to cognitive–developmental theory predictions (Kohlberg, 1966; Kohlberg & Ullian, 1974), structural cognitive changes that allow children to perceive constancy of gender serve as organizers of sex role behaviors. Our research has been concerned with the self-socialization implications of the acquisition of gender constancy. Briefly, gender constancy refers to the consistent labeling of oneself and others as male and female in spite of superficial transformations, such as changes in clothing or toy interest. This concept is typically measured by a series of questions addressing three aspects of constancy: (1) identity (e.g., "Is this a woman or a man?"); (2) stability (e.g., "When you grow up, will you be a mommy or a daddy?"); and (3) consistency (e.g., "If you played [opposite sex of subject] games, would you be a boy or a girl?"). Identity is the easiest and is mastered by 4 years of age; stability and consistency are usually understood by 4–5 years of age (e.g., Marcus & Overton, 1978; Slaby & Frey, 1975).*

The logic underlying our research is that, once children become aware of the inevitability of the gender, they become motivated to seek information relevant to defining themselves as males or females and to regulate their behavior accordingly. Thus children at advanced stages of gender constancy would be expected to show greater attention to gender-related information (particularly information available from same-sex models who can direct them to appropriate activities) and to be more responsive behaviorally to such information. Indeed, consistent with the first part of this hypothesis, Slaby and Frey (1975) showed that children, especially boys, at advanced stages of gender constancy spent more time selectively attending to a same-sex model in a movie than did children at less advanced stages of gender constancy.

The purpose of our research has been to examine whether the apparent heightened attention to same-sex models during later stages of gender constancy translates into heightened behavioral responsiveness at that time. In one study (Ruble, Balaban, & Cooper, 1981), preschool and kindergarten children were shown a toy commercial in the middle of a cartoon in which either two boys or two girls played with a toy pretested to be perceived as equally appropriate for girls and boys. The subjects then had an opportunity to play with the target toy, as well as with other toys of interest. An analysis of the time spent playing with the target toy revealed that only children at advanced levels of gender constancy were affected by the gender of model manipulation. For this group, children who viewed same-sex children in the commercial subsequently played with that toy significantly longer than children who had seen opposite-sex children in the commercial. In contrast, children at less advanced levels of gender constancy showed no effect of the sex of the models. In addition, the children's verbal labeling of the toy as appropriate for girls versus boys was influenced by the sex of the model for high but not low gender constant children in this study. These effects remained significant even when age was covaried out of the analyses.

Other studies have also shown a relation between gender constancy and gender-related behavior. Perloff (1982) found that, when given a choice between imitating a same-sex model performing a relatively unpleasant task and an opposite-sex model performing a pleasant task, children at more advanced levels of gender constancy were more likely to prefer to imitate the same-sex model than were children at less advanced levels of constancy. Similarly, Eaton, Von Bargen, and Keats (1981) found that when children were asked to choose between toys varying on two dimensions—activity level involved in playing with the toy as well as sex appropriateness—children who had achieved

*There is some debate about when gender constancy develops. Different ways to operationalize the construct result in different ages of development (see Aboud & Ruble, in press, for a review). Research using one set of criteria for gender understanding, for example, reports that gender constancy is not achieved even by most 7-year-olds (Emmerich, Goldman, Kirsh, & Sharabany, 1977).

gender constancy were more likely to base their choice on sex appropriateness than those who had not. Thus there is support for the idea that the development of gender constancy is related to children's responsiveness to gender-related information. Moreover, the findings that children at advanced stages of constancy base choices on gender rather than attractiveness suggest that this change in responsiveness represents a choice to behave appropriately rather than a passive orientation toward gender based on a history of reinforcement contingencies.

This conclusion should not be taken to mean that sex role differentiated behavior emerges only after the understanding of gender constancy has occurred. Indeed, there is ample evidence to the contrary. By at least the ages of 3–4 years, many aspects of sex typing are evident, such as preferences for sex-stereotypic toys or sex differentiation in play (for reviews see Huston, 1983; Ruble, 1984). Such differences are probably determined by a number of external factors, such as reinforcement from socializing agents, what playthings are available, and other characteristics of toys (Eisenberg, Murray, & Hite, 1982). As such, then, these early differences may be viewed as outcomes of passive socialization processes and do not contradict the basic suggestion that attainment of gender constancy may be a special point in sex role development. That is, it may represent a shift in the role of the child from being passively influenced by sex role reinforcement and information to actively seeking it out.

Additional results from our television study further illustrate this point. In contrast to the results for the toy showed in the commercial, age but not gender stage was significantly related to children's ability to label correctly highly sex-stereotypic toys, such as trucks and dolls. This pattern of results supports the suggestion that different processes are likely to be involved in different aspects of sex role development. Perhaps age represents changes primarily associated with increasing understanding of and experience with sex-typed labels and reinforcement for "proper" behavior, whereas the tendency to regulate one's own behavior in terms of such labels may depend upon motivational changes associated with gender stages. Thus for example a boy at an early gender stage may label a dish set as "female" but then decide to play with the toy, having little motivation to regulate his own behavior in terms of the sex-typed label of the dish set.

Contradictory Evidence Regarding Gender Constancy

Some contradictory evidence suggests the need to be cautious about conclusions regarding the impact of attaining gender constancy on responsiveness to gender-related information. For example, in contrast to the findings of Slaby and Frey (1975), Bryan and Luria (1978) failed to find differential attention to slides of males and females in children 5–6 and 9–10 years old. It is not clear, however, that their results seriously question the validity of the hypothesis. Their stimuli were relatively simple and only a single model was presented at a time. Thus there was no need to attend selectively as there was in the Slaby and Frey study, in which male and female models were presented simultaneously. This interpretation is consistent with Taylor and Thompson's (1982) analysis of contradictory findings regarding "vividness" effects. They suggest that such effects may be more likely when two or more types of information compete for subjects' attention.

Similarly, one recent study failed to find any evidence of a relation between gender constancy and behavioral responsiveness to gender-related information—that is, same-sex modeling (Bussey & Bandura, 1984). The reasons for these discrepant results remain to be resolved, although one possibility is that the children in the Bussey and Bandura (1984) study were quite young (MA = 44.5 months). Thus a tertiary split on gender constancy scores may have led to a different operationalization of a high level of gender constancy than in previous studies, because advanced stages of gender constancy are generally not achieved until at least 50 months of age (e.g., Slaby & Frey, 1975).

In our own research, we have also found contradictory evidence with respect to gender constancy (Frey & Ruble, 1981). In this study, children aged 5–6 years, varying in level of gender understanding, viewed TV commercials of two boys or two girls playing with gender-inconsistent toys, or they saw no commercial (control). When asked, as a manipulation check to identify the sex of the target, a high percent of the subjects (52%) made an error. Surprisingly, however, memory for gender was not significantly affected by level of gender constancy. Moreover, in contrast to our predictions, children who had attained gender constancy did not show differential preference for the activity of the same-sex model during subsequent free play. Instead, children at the high gender levels played with both target toys more if they had seen the commercial than if they had not.

Thus the commercial stimulated play with the cross-sex toy shown with same-sex models, as expected, but also stimulated play with the same-sex toy, shown with cross-sex models. In the absence of other control conditions (e.g., neutral toys), it is difficult to interpret this finding clearly. It may be that gender-constant children showed heightened responsiveness to same-sex information—be it toy or model—and were not dissuaded by the inconsistencies in the situation nor did they feel the need to distort them to make them appear consistent (see Ruble & Stangor, 1986, for a review of distortion effects at this age). Alternatively, other research suggests that toy attractiveness may be enhanced when it is *in*consistent with the sex of the model (Masters, Ford, Arend, Grotevant, & Clark, 1979), perhaps because the toy must seem unusually desirable to elicit behavior that violates sex role norms. Finally, the children's toy behavior may have been mediated by changes in the perceived sex appropriateness of the toy. In this study as well as our earlier study (Ruble et al., 1981), labeling the toy as appropriate for males versus females was influenced by the sex of the models, but only for children at higher gender stages. Thus children who had attained gender constancy may have played with the toy more than other children, because they saw it in a commercial *and* because after viewing the commercial they perceived the toy as appropriate for both boys and girls.

Conclusions

Although the exact nature of the relation between gender constancy development and self-definitional processes related to gender remains to be specified, there is considerable evidence that children at advanced stages of gender constancy are more likely to seek and utilize gender-related information than children at less advanced stages. The effects in some studies are quite striking in that a single exposure to subtle cues about the sex appropriateness of an activity can have powerful effects on children's subsequent choices and perceptions of the activity (e.g., Ruble et al., 1981). These data are consistent with the hypothesis that children show heightened sensitivity to gender information at particular points during development. We are currently examining the time parameters delimiting this kind of "sensitive period."

SELF-DEFINITION OF COMPETENCE

The second area to which we have applied a self-socialization analysis concerns changes in young school children's understanding of achievement-related performance. Our early work described age-related changes in self-evaluation, focusing mostly on what kinds of information are used. More recently, and more directly relevant to the concept of self-socialization, we have been examining the reciprocal relation between information seeking and social cognitions about one's own competence and about the concept of competence more generally.

In this domain, 7–8 years of age seems to represent an important time of change, a potentially "sensitive period" in self-knowledge about competence. Let me first illustrate this point anecdotally. Several years ago, a colleague relayed a story about his 8-year-old son (call him Gary). Gary was in a school heavily populated by faculty children and was beginning to have a great deal of trouble. Not only did he become anxious about going to school, but he did not want to do anything remotely school related, such as reading, while at home. His father consulted a learning disability specialist, who indicated there was no problem; Gary, if anything, tested above grade level. Why, then, was Gary responding this way? Our research has been examining issues related to this question.

There is considerable experimental evidence consistent with the behaviors shown by Gary. Specifically, children show a dramatic drop in positive self-evaluations during the early years of school (Benenson & Dweck, 1986; Eccles, Midgley, & Adler, 1984; Stipek, 1984). Younger children view their abilities more positively (e.g., Nicholls, 1978; Ruble, 1975) and their chances of success more optimistically (e.g., Yussen & Berman, 1981) than do older children. Interestingly, such age differences even emerged in a study of spontaneous verbal exchanges in the classroom. Younger children were more likely to make positive rather than critical self-evaluative statements than were older children (Frey & Ruble, in press).

Developmental Changes in Conceptions of Competence

We believe these age-related changes in self-evaluation are related to social-cognitive changes related to the meaning of ability, similar to the changes in gender understanding, described earlier. Specifically, we have focused on self-definitions of competence that incorporate notions of stability (perceptions that a particular strength or weakness is enduring across time and situation) and comparison (achievement relative to peers).

A number of studies suggest that during the early years of school children increasingly view abilities (and other traits) as involving a sense of stability and predictability. With respect to self-perceptions, for example, several studies suggest that younger (under 6–7 years) children's predictions about performance and ratings of ability show relatively little effect of prior performance feedback, especially failure (e.g., Clifford, 1978; Parsons & Ruble, 1977; Ruble, Parsons, & Ross, 1976; Stipek & Hoffman, 1980). Thus younger children apparently do not view poor performance, even multiple failures, as having implications for their subsequent performance.

Perceptions of another's competence also show a developmental increase with regard to perception of stability, but in a different way. In this case, children younger than 7 years do seem to view capabilities as stable over time in that they make predictions about future performance based on previous outcomes at the same task (Rholes & Ruble, 1984; Stipek & Hoffman, 1980). Younger children do not, however, typically conceptualize others in terms of underlying dispositional characteristics that generalize across situations (Barenboim, 1981; Rholes & Ruble, 1984). For example, younger children are less likely than older children to predict that a child who is clumsy in one situation will be clumsy in another, even though they can accurately label the behavior. Thus even though young children can label themselves and others as good or able at a task, these terms seem to imply different things at different ages.

In addition to changes in the perceived stability of competence, there appear to be developmental changes in the incorporation of comparative standards in performance evaluation. Surprisingly, children often do not seem to be greatly affected by comparative standards until about 7–9 years of age (Aboud, 1985; Boggiano & Ruble, 1979; Harter & Pike, 1984; Stipek & Tannatt, 1984). Instead, their assessment of their performance or of themselves seems to depend on more absolute kinds of information—how many they got right or whether they were told they succeeded or failed—rather than on comparative standards (Ruble, 1983; Veroff, 1969). In one study, for example, kindergarten and second- and fourth-grade children were provided with specific incentives to assess themselves accurately (Ruble, Boggiano, Feldman, & Loebl, 1980), and the only way they could be accurate was by basing their assessment on comparative standards. Kindergartners made virtually no use of social comparison information on any of the measures of perceived competence. In contrast, by fourth grade there was a clear incorporation of the comparative information in their self-evaluations.

Such findings occur in spite of manipulation checks showing that even kindergartners are capable of indicating who got more right. They know how many they got and how many someone else got. Also, children younger than 7 years do evaluate others on the basis of social comparison standards (Feldman & Ruble, 1980), and do sometimes make relative judgments, at least when the differences in outcome are concrete and highly salient (Levine, Snyder, & Mendez-Caratini, 1982; Smith, Davidson, & France-Kaatrude, in press). Thus it is clear that young children *can* compare socially, but social comparison does not seem to be natural or of high priority in young children's self-evaluation of ability.

In summary, most laboratory research suggests that the incorporation of comparative standards into self-evaluation emerges at 6–9 years of age. This conclusion does not mean that preschool children never engage in social comparison. Indeed, preschool children seem to want to make sure that they are getting their fair share of rewards (Masters, 1971), readily engage in competition (Heckhausen, 1982), and make overt comparative statements (Mosatche & Bragonier, 1981). Thus young children do make comparisons, but such comparisons may not be particularly important to their own self-assessment in the sense of an evaluation of the self with significant implications for general ability levels or future performance on related tasks.

It is this kind of change—perceiving the comparative and relatively enduring character of competence—that may have affected Gary once he perceived that he was a relative failure in a class of high-achieving others. Indeed, there is empirical evidence that such changes do have behavioral consequences. In one study, older children (9–10 years) avoided a task when they had previously received comparative information indicating incompetence at the task. In contrast, younger children (5–6 years) were negatively affected only by direct information indicating incompetence but not by social comparison information (Boggiano & Ruble, 1979). Similarly, in other research, only children who had attained a concept of traits as stable and dispositional showed learned helplessness responses (i.e., gave up trying) to repeated failure experiences at a task (Rholes, Blackwell, Jordan, & Walters, 1980; Rholes & Jones, 1985). Thus the particular point in time that changes in information seeking occur, in relation to changes in self-definition of competence, may be quite important. The point that children realize the relative permanence and evaluative significance of achievement performance may be quite painful for some children and may have long-term consequences for their subsequent achievement potential.

Performance-Related Information Seeking

Our most recent research, therefore, has examined more directly the process of actively gathering information about competence and the factors that affect such information seeking. The goals of this research have been to examine the following: (1) the effects of age-related changes (e.g., experience with school and conceptions of ability) on interest in performance-related information; and (2) the relation between emerging self-definition of competence and level of interest in information seeking.

Classroom Observations

One approach to these issues has been to observe children's spontaneous interactions in the classroom and relate these to aspects of social cognitions and self-definition, as assessed through interviews (Frey & Ruble, 1985, in press; Ruble & Frey, in press). In this research, kindergarten, first-, second-, and fourth-grade children were observed during independent work times in their classrooms. Observers coded everything children said during a series of 4-min focal child observations. The verbal categories used included a range of performance and information-seeking statements. After each 4-min focal observation, the observer scanned the room to record what activity each of a group of five or six children was engaged in at that time in order to assess focus of attention. Subsequently, the subjects were interviewed individually about their knowledge of performance differences and their self-perceptions of ability level.

One specific question in this research concerned the focus of comparison at different ages. If, as previous research suggests (Damon & Hart, 1982; Dweck & Elliott, 1983; Ruble, 1983), children's conceptualizations of their abilities shift to include comparative and dispositional qualities at around second grade, then earlier forms of social comparison may represent functions other than self-evaluation. For example, comparisons among children first entering school may be more likely to involve nonacademic aspects of behavior, because the need to learn school routines and ensure the appropriateness of behavior is likely to be greater at this time than when children have had more experiences with school routines (Blumenfeld, Hamilton, Bossert, Wessels, & Meece, 1983).

This issue was addressed by comparing the frequencies of different forms of comparison: (1) those reflecting an interest in *achievement* (e.g., peer progress checks—"What page are you on?"); and (2) those reflecting an interest in comparison of a nonachievement nature (e.g., the frequency of looking at peers themselves as opposed to peers' work in the scan observations). Consistent with our expectations, achievement-related comparisons *increased,* whereas nonachievement comparisons *decreased* between kindergarten and first grade. Moreover, as expected, nonachievement comparisons continued to decrease after first grade. Although age trends observed after first grade differed across measures of achievement comparison (attention to peers' work decreased whereas peer progress checks increased), these differences also suggested an age-related shift in comparison goals. Looking at another's work is probably the best way to determine *how* to perform an assignment, whereas peer performance checks are probably the most efficient way to determine *how well* one is performing. These data thus provide behavioral support for findings based on verbal responses in our previous research (Feldman & Ruble, 1977).

Taken together, the findings suggest that there are differences in the kind of social comparison that children at different ages engage in. Younger children are more likely to compare the appearance and behavior of peers, whereas older children are more likely to compare rates of progress on specific tasks. Thus the nature of performance-related information that children seek changes qualitatively during the early years of school. Children at different ages, therefore, are likely to have very different kinds of information on which to base inferences about performance.

Another major goal of our observational research was to examine the ecological validity of previous findings in the laboratory concerning the late-developing use of social comparison for self-evaluation. Although it was not possible to collect direct information about this issue from children's spontaneous statements in the classroom, we were able to collect indirect evidence in a number of ways.

First, children's "knowledge" of comparative standing, as assessed in the interviews, showed a clear progression in accuracy from kindergarten to second grade. Interestingly, relevant to self-socialization processes, knowledge of relative standing was related to frequency of social comparison behavior in the kindergarten and first-grade classrooms only, presumably because this is when self-conceptions are in the formative stages.

A second type of indirect evidence related to the developmental timing of comparison-based self-evaluations concerns age-related changes in the relation between children's spontaneous verbal exchanges and their concepts of ability. Once children recognize that abilities are relative, performance on any given task has implications beyond feelings about that particular performance. Such changes seem likely to lead to increased concern or anxiety over evaluation. Indeed, dramatic changes in knowledge about and orientation toward performance seemed to occur between first and second grade in ways that were consistent with the above line of reasoning. Results from the interview showed a significant qualitative shift in references to dispositional abilities of peers. At the same time, verbalizations about performance decreased after a peak in first grade.

The curvilinear relation in performance verbalizations probably represents two converging processes. The first is that the heightened interest in performance and comparison shown by first graders may represent the primacy of competence assessment goals during a period of transition. The second process concerns a growing recognition of the potentially sensitive nature of performance-related exchanges (Brickman & Bulman, 1977). Children's increasing appreciation of the comparative basis and long-range significance of performance has implications for self-esteem. Indeed, we found that children who more frequently engaged in performance-related information seeking evaluated themselves more negatively. The decrease in performance-related exchanges may also represent a growing desire to maintain social harmony by avoiding exchanges that may disrupt friendships (Levine, 1983). Thus the growing interest children exhibit in performance information in first grade may, for some children, turn into anxiety or concern by second grade. Although there seem to be strong social pressures to avoid performance-related verbalizations, not all measures decreased after first grade. In particular, although overt and blatant forms of performance concern decreased, interest in information seeking revealed in more subtle measures (peer progress checks) continued to increase.

In summary, shifts observed in spontaneous verbal exchanges and knowledge are consistent with previous laboratory findings that the impact of social comparison on self-evaluation shifts at approximately seven years of age. We are currently attempting to specify the nature of the mechanisms linking these age-related changes in performance-related knowledge and information seeking in a longitudinal study.

Laboratory Study of Information Seeking

The observational study (Frey & Ruble, 1985) provided data consistent with a basic process of self-socialization: that changes in cognitions (e.g., conceptions of ability) were related to changes in information exchange (e.g., reduced frequency of overt self-evaluative statements). The suggested explanation for this relation concerned goal conflict between self-assessment needs (Festinger, 1954) and emerging goals to minimize self-consciousness and threats to social harmony or self-esteem. In order to examine this hypothesis more directly, we examined information seeking in a more controlled setting, using subjects who were expected to vary in the likelihood of having negative concerns about self-evaluation—namely, those experiencing classroom failure as opposed to success (Ruble & Flett, in press).

There is little direct evidence relevant to the relation between evaluative concern and information seeking. Intuitively it would seem that anxiety about and/or anticipation of negative feedback would lead to a relative avoidance of evaluation-related information, and some research with adults supports this hypothesis (see Trope, 1986). Although there are no comparable developmental data, our previous research and that of others suggest that evaluative concern emerges at around 7–8 years of age, as children's conceptualization of performance factors becomes increasingly differentiated, and the concept of ability becomes invested with a sense of stability, with implications for future behavior (Frey & Ruble, 1985; Nicholls & Miller, 1985; Rubles & Rholes, 1981). Thus the effect of goal conflict on information seeking should begin to become evident at around this age. That is, on the one hand, changes in the meaning of performance and ability should lead to increased interest in self-assessment during the early years of school. For children receiving relatively negative feedback, however, an approach–avoidance conflict is likely to emerge, such that low-ability children would show less interest in evaluative feedback than high-ability children.

To test these predictions, children 7, 9, and 11 years old (classified as high, medium, and low in mathematics ability) performed a series of arithmetic tasks, on which they were given ambiguous outcome information. During "rest" periods they had a chance to look at information relevant to evaluating their performance. Specifically, folders containing two types of information were available to be examined: (1) folders containing the outcomes on the same tasks of other children their age (social comparison information); and (2) folders containing information about their own outcome on previous tests at the same level of difficulty and answer keys (autonomous evaluation information). The room also contained a set of age-appropriate toys.

Consistent with predictions, children low in ability showed the *least* interest in obtaining any information relevant to evaluating their performance. Overall, interest in obtaining self-evaluative information increased with age, as expected, but the relative "avoidance" behavior of the low-ability children was generally consistent across ages. These data suggest that evaluation concern was present even in children as young as 7 years of age. Low-ability children at this age were less interested than high-ability children in obtaining information they presumably expected to have negative implications for self-esteem.

Although the effect of ability level on overall interest did not interact with age, there were significant interactions with the kind of information sought. For high-ability children, interest in social comparison information remained relatively constant across age, whereas interest in autonomous evaluation increased dramatically. Medium-ability children preferred social to autonomous evaluation folders at all age levels, with little change in evaluation interest across age. Low-ability children preferred social to autonomous evaluation information at the oldest two age levels. At 7 years, however, they showed equal interest (lack of interest?) in both.

Although we can only speculate about the meaning of these trends, they are consistent with our prediction that information seeking would increase with age and that high- and low-ability children would show differential interest. The shift of high-ability children toward autonomous evaluation is quite striking. One interpretation is that reaching a conclusion that one possesses high ability renders further self-assessment unnecessary. Thus it becomes possible to turn attention toward mastering the task, and information available in the answer keys and evidence of progress in relation to previous performance (autonomous folders) would be more relevant than social comparison.

Conclusions

The results of these two large studies have led to several tentative conclusions regarding self-socialization processes in performance assessment. First, the studies showed dramatic age-related differences in the general motivation to seek competence-related information, and such differences were related to social cognitions about competence. Second, the studies showed differences in specific information-seeking goals and strategies, as a function of age, social–cognitive differences, and self-perceptions of competence. In answer to one of the specific questions guiding the research, children younger than 7 years do engage in social comparison, but their goals appear to emphasize learning guidelines for appropriate behavior rather than self-evaluation. Finally, some of these information-seeking differences may have long-term personal consequences. A self-definition of high ability, for example, apparently allowed older children to shift toward emphasizing mastery rather than self-assessment goals, a shift with major implications for subsequent performance and self-esteem.

SELF-DEFINITION AT MENARCHE

Puberty constitutes another developmental phase in which new aspects of self-knowledge must be acquired. For girls, one important aspect of self-definition at this time concerns what it means to be a menstruating woman. Certainly, the culture conveys clear messages. Mass media articles and advertisements portray menstruation solely in negative terms—as a taboo topic and as an event that causes physical and emotional disruption (Delaney, Lupton, & Toth, 1976). Moreover, retrospective self-report studies suggest that women typically associate negative psychological and behavioral changes with menstruation, even though prospective studies often fail to support such beliefs (Ruble & Brooks-Gunn, in press).

Girls experience menarche within this cultural context, and we have been examining how such cultural beliefs are translated into girls' self-definitions as menstruating women. Another self-socialization aspect of this process that we have been examining concerns how the initial self-definition affects subsequent experience. The definition of the menstrual experience established at this time may be resistant to later change because subsequent experiences are perceived in terms of and may be distorted by this definition (Ruble & Brooks-Gunn, 1979). Thus perceptions of and information received about menstruation during menarche and shortly after may have long-lasting impact.

We have examined self-definitional processes related to menstruation in two ways. The first involves changes that occur at menarche in girls' perceptions of the menstrual experience. The second concerns how the positive–negative features of the context in which menarche is experienced affect subsequent perceptions of menstruation. In both cases, our analysis involved how psychological processes influenced menstrual attitudes and symptom reports.

Previous studies of menarche have not addressed these aspects of the development of girls' understanding of menstruation. Instead, previous research has examined how pre- and postmenarcheal girls differ psychologically, for example, in self-image or sexual differentiation (see Greif & Ulman, 1982, for a review). Studies concerned with perceptions of menstruation per se have been primarily clinical in nature, with small samples and nonquantitative analyses (e.g., Kestenberg, 1967; Whisnant & Zegans, 1975). Thus conclusions regarding self-definitional processes at menarche in the present chapter rely heavily on research we have recently completed, using a large sample and a combination of longitudinal and cross-sectional designs (for additional details of the investigation see Brooks-Gunn & Ruble, 1982; Ruble & Brooks-Gunn, 1982).

The cross-sectional sample consisted of 639 public school girls in fifth to eighth and eleventh to twelfth grades. The longitudinal sample consisted of an initial group of 120 fifth and sixth graders who were premenarcheal at the time of first testing. The longitudinal design employed a matching procedure to control for repeated testing: For the second testing, each girl who had reached menarche was matched, based on age and school, with a girl who had not. Using this procedure, 92 girls (46 pairs) completed both phases of testing. At each testing, the girls completed a lengthy questionnaire that included sections on incidence and severity of menstrual and premenstrual symptoms, attitudes about menstruation, and sources of menstrual-related information. In addition, girls from the longitudinal sample were interviewed at the second testing.

Anecdotal evidence that anticipation of menarche was significant for these girls comes from the premenarcheal girls' responses to our phone calls every few months. We would ask them a standard set of questions concerning changes in height, weight, school, and so on; and in each of these cases the responses were quick and straightforward. When we asked, however, if they had gotten their periods, many girls would hesitate before answering "no," with a clear indication of disappointment and/or embarrassment in their voices. Our research was concerned with how this interest or sensitivity was reflected in information-gathering and self-definitional processes.

Girls' Perceptions of the Menstrual Experience at Menarche

What are girls' beliefs as they approach their first experience with menstruation? Our data show that even the youngest premenarcheal girls we studied expected to experience the symptom cluster commonly associated with the menstrual cycle. Thus when girls enter menarche, they expect to experience premenstrual and menstrual distress.

What impact do these early expectations have? If girls define their experience at menarche in terms of these expectations, then there should be few differences between the reports of pre- and postmenarcheal girls. Indeed, in the cross-sectional sample, the only difference in symptom reports is that postmenarcheal girls reported experiencing *less* pain than premenarcheal girls expected. Similarly, in the longitudinal sample, girls' reports of symptoms were either the same or less severe after menarche than what they had expected premenarcheally and what their premenarcheal counterparts expected at the second testing. Similar results were obtained for the attitude and feeling measures; menarcheal status affected responses on only two of nine scales. Consistent with differences in symptom reports, postmenarcheal girls viewed menstruation as *less* debilitating than premenarcheal girls.

In general, then, girls' perceptions of menstruation appear to show little change as a function of initial direct experience. Moreover, direct experience, if anything, seems to result in perceptions of fewer symptoms and less debilitation. Perhaps the premenarcheal girls receive or attend to more negative information about menstrual symptoms than postmenarcheal girls. Alternatively, premenarcheal girls may adhere to the same information more strongly because they do not have any contrary evidence.

These findings appear to conflict with previous reports that postmenarcheal girls are more negative than premenarcheal girls (Clarke & Ruble, 1978; Koff, Rierdan, & Jacobson, 1981). This apparent discrepancy, however, may indicate little more than the complexity of defining the experience. Girls' responses seem to be sensitive to the timing of the interview in relation to age and menarcheal status. In cross-sectional studies, age or grade and menarcheal status are almost inevitably confounded. Thus the greater negativity of postmenarcheal girls in previous research may be due to age-related factors rather than to the direct experience of menstruation. Indeed, there is a considerable amount of research suggesting increasingly negative reactions to menstruation with age among postmenarcheal girls and women (Golub & Harrington, 1981; Ruble & Brooks-Gunn, 1982; Widholm & Kantero, 1971). Moreover, in our longitudinal study in which age effects could be examined separately from menarcheal status, the results of other measures suggested that negative evaluations (e.g., "Menstruation is something I would prefer not to have") and perceptions that it is bothersome (e.g., "Menstruation is something I just have to put up with") increased as a function of age only, not menarcheal status.

Another important factor to consider in interpreting the results is that girls appear to be particularly sensitive or secretive about menstruation immediately after menarche, the time that we interviewed girls in our longitudinal study. This sensitivity is indicated, in part, by our findings of decreased comfort talking to others about menstruation reported by postmenarcheal compared to premenarcheal girls. It is also indicated by responses during a telephone interview within 2 months after each girl's first period. Although most girls reported telling someone soon after the event, almost all of these initial discussions were with their mothers. Only 18% said they told a friend. By the time girls had had two to three periods, however, most were no longer extremely secretive. Indeed, about half of the girls appear to discuss menstruation regularly with a friend. It is noteworthy, in the context of reports of increasing symptoms during the first few years after menarche (Ruble & Brooks-Gunn, 1982), that the most frequent topic of discussion was symptomatology. To the extent that discussing symptoms represents a social comparison process, a form of oneupsmanship or undirectional drive upward (Festinger, 1954) may exacerbate the frequency or severity of psychosomatic complaints (Mechanic, 1972; Ruble & Brooks-Gunn, 1979). Of course, such age-related increases in reported symptoms may reflect physiological changes, such as increased frequency of ovulation occurring within the first few years after menarche (Vollman, 1977). Interestingly, however, cross-cultural differences in symptom reports during these years suggest that socialization processes must be considered as well (Ruble & Brooks-Gunn, 1982).

In summary, the literature suggests that by the time girls reach menarche they have negative expectations regarding somatic and emotional effects of menstruation and mixed feelings and attitudes. The actual experience of menstruation changes little except that girls appear to find the event less debilitating than they expected. These data suggest that, relative to direct, physical sensations, girls' social construction of the menstrual experience at menarche represents an important influence on their subsequent reports of symptoms. Additional analyses of our longitudinal data support this conclusion. Symptom reports of postmenarcheal girls at the second testing were significantly correlated with their premenarcheal expectations at the first testing. The fact that no significant relations were found between expectations at time 1 and at time 2 for the girls who remained premenarcheal seems to rule out response bias explanations of this relation. Instead, it is as if expectations present at the time a girl begins to menstruate provide the definition of that experience, whereas expectations of premenarcheal girls continually change. Indeed, the expectations of premenarcheal girls became more negative between time 1 and time 2, presumably in response to age-related changes in the nature or amount of information available.

We cannot, of course, argue from these data that the self-definitions formed at menarche necessarily represent an active search for information; girls' initial expectations may result from more passive socialization processes. Instead, we would argue that these data illustrate the second aspect of self-socialization described earlier: the continuing impact of a self-definition formed at a particular developmental period. The self-socialization interpretation is that the biological event (menarche) stimulated an application of the available information to the self, such that subsequent experiences were perceived in terms of the self-definition already formed.

Effects of the Context in Which Menarche Is Experienced

Because a girl's construction of her menstrual experience at menarche may have long-lasting implications, it is important to examine factors that influence how positive or negative the experience is. Negative menarcheal experiences may have detrimental consequences for a girl's subsequent experience of the menstrual cycle; and, because of the intimate link between menstruation, womanhood, and sexuality, menarcheal experiences also may affect more general aspects of a girl's self-concept. We have examined this issue by relating girls' reports or recollections of contextual factors affecting the experience of menarche to subsequent self-perceptions and symptoms.

Adequacy of preparation is one such factor that is believed by many to be necessary for later menstrual adjustment (e.g., Deutsch, 1944; Rees, 1953). Relevant studies, however, have relied on retrospective reports and are inconsistent and difficult to interpret (May, 1976; Paige, 1973; Rierdan, 1983; Shainess, 1961; Woods, Dery, & Most, 1983).

A related contextual factor is timing of menarche. An important source of information during a period of self-definitional change is social comparison, and the values and norms that peers provide may be particularly significant because of heightened conformity pressures at that time (Costanzo & Shaw, 1966). Reaching menarche at about the same age as her peers can provide a girl with a sense of sharing and closeness. Reaching menarche earlier than most peers, however, may generate insecurity about being different from the group and make the experience more negative than it is for average-maturing girls. Previous data on age of maturation are consistent with this analysis (e.g., Brooks-Gunn, Petersen, & Eichorn, in press; Faust, 1983; Jones & Mussen, 1958), although these studies did not focus on the effects of timing of menarche on symptoms per se.

Our examination of the effects of timing and preparation differed from previous studies in several ways: (1) The girls were younger and thus recollections were based on more recent experiences; (2) the sample was very large and thus we could look at more extreme variations; and (3) a longitudinal sample reporting on immediate experiences was included. Although many of the differences failed to reach statistical significance, effects that did emerge were generally in the predicted direction. Girls who were unprepared or who matured earlier than average reported more current negative reactions and symptoms, and (in the seventh grade) their self-image ratings were more negative. Interestingly, some of these effects on current experiences were evident for girls as old as eleventh and twelfth graders, in that there was no interaction with grade level. Thus the data are, at least, indirectly supportive of the idea of long-lasting effects of these aspects of the menarcheal experiences.

Of course, the effects of feeling prepared may represent a response bias, because if girls feel negatively about the experience generally, they may respond negatively to all relevant items, including reports of preparation. It is noteworthy, therefore, that not all relevant variables showed similar effects. The lack of first period symptom effects is particularly important because it rules out the alternative explanation that girls felt totally unprepared *because* they had severe symptoms.

A third factor likely to affect positive–negative experiences at menarche is girls' perceptions of the reactions of significant others. Since overall, female and health sources are viewed as having positive attitudes and male sources as having negative attitudes, we would expect positive attitudes to be related to more learning from female and health sources. The correlations were generally consistent with these predictions. Perceiving menstruation as a natural event and comfort with talking about it were positively correlated with amount learned from female sources and parents and doctor. The importance of sources of information was also indicated in the longitudinal data. Girls who reported learning more from male sources premenarcheally reported greater menstrual and premenstrual distress postmenarcheally. Similar significant correlations were found for perceptions of symptoms menarcheally and perceptions of male sources as having negative feelings about menstruation menarcheally. Thus receiving information premenarcheally from sources perceived to be negative appears to be associated with more negative perceptions of symptoms after menarche. Alternatively, perhaps girls who learn more from male sources have mothers who are less willing to discuss the event, and it is this latter "avoidant" behavior that contributes to the girls' negative perceptions.

In summary, several context variables have been identified that affect how positively or negatively menarche is experienced. Alternative explanations for each individual relation may, of course, be offered. Taken together, however, they are consistent with a self-definitional perspective in suggesting that positive–negative context influences menstrual attitudes and symptoms at menarche or shortly after, and may even influence symptom reports as late as senior high school.

Conclusions

We have argued that around the time of menarche girls construct a definition of the menstrual experience from various sources of information, of which direct knowledge of symptoms is only one. Our data suggest that adolescent girls' symptom reports are correlated with their own premenarcheal expectations, suggesting that the direct experience of menstruation is interpreted in terms of expectations previously formed. Moreover, individual differences in symptom reports can be predicted from the context in which self-definitions are initially formed. Current negative reports of symptoms in postmenarcheal girls from seventh to twelfth grades are related to being unprepared for menarche, being early to mature, or receiving information from sources perceived as negative. Thus menarche may be viewed as a sensitive period with respect to menstrual-related self-perceptions. Adolescent experiences may create a foundation for an association between menstruation and negative experiences, particularly if premenarcheal expectations are based on informational sources that emphasize this association.

GENERAL CONCLUSIONS AND IMPLICATIONS

Although the areas of research described in the present chapter concern several diverse aspects of social development (sex roles, achievement, menarche), they share a fundamental similarity in that each involves self-socialization processes in response to transitions of various sorts. With respect to sex roles, for example, our research suggests that, as children begin to recognize that gender is stable and consistent in spite of superficial transformations, they become actively involved in seeking gender-relevant information and behaving in accordance with it—that is, they begin to socialize themselves.

Similarly, with respect to achievement, our studies suggest that children's experiences with performance during the early years of school affect both their information-seeking behavior and self-definition relevant to competence. Data from both naturalistic observations in the classroom and laboratory studies support this conclusion. First, changes associated with grade level influence both the amount and nature of performance-related information seeking and information exchange. Second, these information-gathering processes affect self-evaluation and behavior such that, for example, comparative standards become more closely associated with conclusions children draw about competence and the activities they choose.

Finally, with respect to self-definitional processes at menarche, our studies suggest that, when girls experience the biological changes associated with menarche, cultural attitudes become specifically relevant to the self, and a self-definition is formed in terms of these attitudes. Specifically, converging evidence from our cross-sectional and longitudinal analyses indicates that variation in the context in which menarche occurs (e.g., who they receive information from; whether they are early or late maturers) affects girls' subsequent menstrual-related experiences.

We have attempted to highlight two major aspects of self-socialization processes in our research to date. One has been information seeking as central to an *active,* constructive self-definition. Clearly the idea that the child is more than a passive recipient of external forces is not new to the socialization literature. An emphasis on active and reciprocal processes is now commonly incorporated into descriptions of socialization (e.g., Bandura, 1982; Huston, 1983; Maccoby & Martin, 1983). Yet there has been little attempt empirically to specify what creates a motivation toward active information seeking or to indicate how such a motivation is reflected in behavior. Our efforts along these lines have involved several approaches. In the area of sex roles, we have made inferences about active information seeking from the behaviors children exhibit after being exposed to gender-related information. In the area of achievement, we observed the frequency and focus of information seeking in situations involving relatively free choice. Finally, in the area of menarche, we have questioned girls about the kinds of information they have received and from whom.

One problem with this research, however, is that it is often very difficult to demonstrate conclusively that any particular measure represents an active rather than a passive process. The survey methodology in the menarche research, for example, makes it impossible to know whether girls are simply reacting to information they receive or whether they are actively seeking it out.

In current survey research, we are attempting to address this problem, at least in part. Specifically, in extending our analysis to self-definitional processes during pregnancy (Deutsch, Ruble, Fleming, Brooks-Gunn, & Stangor, 1986), we are including information sources that represent primarily an active search—that is, books. It will be necessary in future research as well to supplement these correlational methods with experimental manipulations of goals, so that the behavioral manifestations of the resulting motivations can be examined directly.

The second major aspect of self-socialization that we have attempted to highlight in our research concerns the implications of initial self-definitional processes for self-perception and behavior. Our operating assumption is that the kind of information available at the time of heightened interest in or susceptibility to relevant information is important because once a conclusion about the self is formed (e.g., as incompetent at school), subsequent information processing is likely to be selective and behavioral choices restricted. Although we have not examined selective processes directly in our own research, there is considerable evidence that prior beliefs influence every stage of information processing (Fiske & Taylor, 1984; Markus & Zajonc, 1985). Attention, perception, and memory are selective and often distorted, such that preexisting beliefs are maintained or strengthened, even in the face of contradictory evidence (Nisbett & Ross, 1980; Ross, 1977).

With respect to gender, there are secondary effects of children's beginning to monitor their own behaviors on the basis of perceived appropriateness for their own sex. Girls' and boys' toys differ in very fundamental ways that may affect the development of skills. Boys' toys, for example, tend to have the feature of "take-apartedness" thought by many to be important to the development of spatial skills; and, indeed, "masculine" play does seem to predict performance at spatial tasks (Huston, 1983). Thus the conclusion of a 5-year-old girl that she should not play with mechanical toys may affect her options on a continuing basis.

With respect to implications of self-definitions of competence, previous research has shown that, once the child has reached a certain level of social–cognitive understanding, a conclusion about incompetence can lead to avoidance or lack of effort on related activities (e.g., Boggiano & Ruble, 1979; Rholes et al., 1980). Moreover, application of findings from the attribution literature to this area would suggest that, once children have labeled themselves as incompetent, they may interpret feedback in a way that reinforces this conclusion, such as by attributing success to effort and failure to lack of ability (Ross & Fletcher, 1985). It is interesting to note in this context, then, that an analysis of spontaneous attributions in early elementary school classrooms suggests that girls are more likely to refer to lack of ability as a reason for failure than are boys (Frey & Ruble, in press).

Finally, with respect to girls' self-definitions at menarche, our research indicates that conclusions about the menstrual experience formed near the time of the first menstruation are related to subsequent perceptions of menstruation, possibly even as late as senior high school. Given the significant health problem that menstrual distress or premenstrual syndrome represents, further exploration of the influence of these early self-definitional processes on perceptions of menstrual symptoms seems warranted.

Although our own analysis to date has focused on self-socialization processes during transitions in childhood, the approach need not be restricted to children. Important transitions occur throughout the life span that may lead to the initiation of a search to define or redefine a dimension of the self. Self-definitional processes in women having their first child are one such example. Consistent with our approach to the studies with children, we are examining information seeking in relation to women's definitions of themselves as mothers (Deutsch et al., 1986) and associated mood, self-esteem, and role relationship changes (Fleming, Ruble, & Flett, in preparation; Ruble, Fleming, Hackel, & Stangor, 1986). Of course, the suggestion that developmental processes continue beyond childhood is hardly new (Baltes & Brim, 1980; Dion, 1985; Erikson, 1963). Previous analyses, however, have not systematically and empirically identified *when* these changes occur (e.g., what sets a self-definitional process in motion), *what* steps are critical, nor *how* they proceed. By means of comparisons across different points in the life span, we hope to be able to identify underlying commonalities in self-definitional processes and thus to begin these tasks.

REFERENCES

Aboud, F. E. (1985). Children's application of attribution principles to social comparisons. *Child Development, 56,* 682–688.

Aboud, F., & Ruble, D. N. (in press). Identity constancy in children: Developmental processes and implications. In T. M. Honess & K. M. Yardley (Eds.), *Self and identity: Individual change and development.* London: Routledge & Kegan Paul.

Baltes, P. B., & Brim, O. G., Jr. (Eds.). (1980). *Life-span development and behavior.* New York: Academic.

Bandura, A. (1969). Social learning theory of identificatory processes. In D. A. Goslin (Ed.), *Handbook of socialization theory and research.* New York: Rand-McNally.

Bandura, A. (1977). *Social learning theory.* Englewood Cliffs, NJ: Prentice-Hall.

Bandura, A. (1982). Self-efficacy mechanism in human agency. *American Psychologist, 37,* 122–147.

Barenboim, C. (1981). The development of person perception in childhood and adolescence: From behavioral comparisons to psychological constructs to psychological comparisons. *Child Development, 52,* 129–144.

Bartlett, F. C. (1932). *Remembering: A study in experimental and social psychology.* New York: Cambridge University Press.

Bell, R. Q., & Harper, L. V. (Eds.). (1977). *Child effects on adults.* Hillsdale, NJ: Erlbaum.

Benenson, J. F., & Dweck, C. S. (1986). The development of trait explanations and self-evaluations in the academic and social domains. *Child Development, 57,* 1179–1187.

Berlyne, D. E. (1960). *Conflict, arousal and curiosity.* New York: McGraw-Hill.

Blumenfeld, P. C., Hamilton, V. L., Bossert, S. T., Wessels, K., & Meece, J. (1983). Teacher talk and student thought: Socialization into the student role. In J. M. Levine & M. C. Wang (Eds.), *Teacher and student perceptions: Implications for learning.* Hillsdale, NJ: Erlbaum.

Boggiano, A. K., & Ruble, D. N. (1979). Competence and the overjustification effect: A developmental study. *Journal of Personality & Social Psychology, 37,* 1462–1468.

Brickman, P., & Bulman, R. J. (1977). Pleasure and pain in social comparison. In J. M. Suls & R. L. Miller (Eds.), *Social comparison processes: Theoretical and empirical perspectives.* New York: Wiley.

Brooks-Gunn, J., & Ruble, D. N. (1982). The development of menstrual-related beliefs and behaviors during early adolescence. *Child Development, 53,* 1567–1577.

Brooks-Gunn, J., Petersen, A. C., & Eichorn, D. (Eds.). (in press). Timing of maturation and psychosocial functioning in adolescence. *Journal of Youth & Adolescence* (special issue).

Bryan, J. W., & Luria, Z. (1978). Sex-role learning: A test of the selective attention hypothesis. *Child Development, 49,* 13–23.

Bussey, K., & Bandura, A. (1984). Influence of gender constancy and social power on sex-linked modeling. *Journal of Personality & Social Psychology, 47,* 1292–1302.

Clarke, A. E., & Ruble, D. N. (1978). Young adolescents' beliefs concerning menstruation. *Child Development, 49,* 231–234.

Clifford, M. (1978). The effects of quantitative feedback on children's expectations of success. *British Journal of Educational Psychology, 48,* 220–226.

Coopersmith, S. (1967). *The antecedents of self-esteem.* San Francisco: Freeman.

Cordua, G. D., McGraw, K. O., & Drabman, R. S. (1979). Doctor or nurse: Children's perceptions of sex-typed occupations. *Child Development, 50,* 590–593.

Costanzo, P. R., & Shaw, M. E. (1966). Conformity as a function of age level. *Child Development, 37,* 967–975.

Damon, W., & Hart, D. (1982). The development of self-understanding from infancy through adolescence. *Child Development, 53,* 841–864.

Deci, E. L. (1975). *Intrinsic motivation.* New York: Plenum.

Delaney, J., Lupton, M. J., & Toth, E. (1976). *The curse: A cultural history of menstruation.* New York: Dutton.

Deutsch, F., Ruble, D. N., Fleming, A. S., Brooks-Gunn, J., & Stangor, C. (1986). *Becoming a mother: Information-seeking and self-definitional processes.* Paper presented at Eastern Psychological Association meeting, New York.

Deutsch, H. (1944). *The psychology of women.* New York: Grune & Stratton.

Dion, K. K. (1985). Socialization in adulthood. In G. Lindzey & E. Aronson (Eds.), *The handbook of social psychology* (Vol. II, 3rd ed.). New York: Random House.

Dweck, C. S., & Elliott, E. S. (1983). Achievement motivation. In P. H. Mussen (Gen. Ed.); E. M. Hetherington (Vol. Ed.), *Handbook of child psychology: Vol. IV. Socialization, personality, and social development* (4th ed.). New York: Wiley.

Eaton, W. O., Von Bargen, D., & Keats, J. G. (1981). Gender understanding and dimensions of preschooler toy choice: Sex stereotypes versus activity level. *Canadian Journal of Behavioral Science, 13,* 203–209.

Eccles, J., Midgley, C., & Adler, T. F. (1984). Age-related changes in the school environment: Effects on achievement motivation. In J. H. Nicholls (Ed.), *The development of achievement motivation.* Greenwich, CT: JAI.

Eisenberg, N., Murray, E., & Hite, T. (1982). Children's reasoning regarding sex-typed choices. *Child Development, 53,* 81–86.

Emmerich, W., Goldman, K. S., Kirsh, B., & Sharabany, R. (1977). Evidence for a transitional phase in the development of gender constancy. *Child Development, 48,* 930–936.

Erikson, E. (1963). *Childhood and society.* New York: Norton.

Faust, M. S. (1983). Alternative constructions of adolescent growth. In J. Brooks-Gunn & A. C. Petersen (Eds.), *Girls at puberty.* New York: Plenum.

Feldman, N. S., & Ruble, D. N. (1977). Awareness of social comparison interest and motivation: A developmental study. *Journal of Educational Psychology, 69,* 579–585.

Feldman, N. S., & Ruble, D. N. (1980, April). A developmental study of actor/observer differences in the use of social comparison information. Paper presented at the annual meeting of the Eastern Psychological Association, Hartford, Connecticut.

Festinger, L. (1954). A theory of social comparison. *Human Relations, 7,* 117–140.

Fiske, S. T., & Taylor, S. E. (1984). *Social cognition.* Menlo Park, CA: Addison-Wesley.

Fleming, A. S., Ruble, D. N., & Flett, G. L. (in preparation). *Postpartum adjustment in the first time mother. I. Changes in mood during the postpartum period.*

Frey, K. S., & Ruble, D. N. (1981, April). *Concepts of gender constancy as mediators of behavior.* Paper presented at the biennial meeting of the Society for Research in Child Development, Boston.

Frey, K. S., & Ruble, D. N. (1985). What children say when the teacher's not around: Conflicting goals in social comparisons and performance assessment in the classroom. *Journal of Personality & Social Psychology, 48,* 18–30.

Frey, K. S., & Ruble, D. N. (in press). What children say when the teacher is not around: II. Age and sex differences in self-evaluation. *Child Development.*

Golub, S., & Harrington, D. M. (1981). Premenstrual and menstrual mood changes in adolescent women. *Journal of Personality & Social Psychology, 4*(5), 961–965.

Greif, E. B., & Ulman, K. J. (1982). The psychological impact of menarche on early adolescent females: A review of the literature. *Child Development, 53,* 1413–1430.

Harter, S. (1978). Effectance motivation reconsidered: Toward a developmental model. *Human Development, 1,* 34–64.

Harter, S. (1983). Developmental perspectives on the self-esteem. In P. H. Mussen (Gen. Ed.); E. M. Hetherington (Vol. Ed.), *Handbook of child psychology: Vol. IV. Socialization, personality and social development* (4th ed.). New York: Wiley.

Harter, S., & Pike, R. (1984). The pictorial scale of perceived competence and social acceptance for young children. *Child Development, 55,* 1969–1982.

Heckhausen, H. (1982). The development of achievement motivation. In W. W. Hartup (Ed.), *Review of child development research.* (Vol. 6). Chicago: University of Chicago Press.

Huston, A. C. (1983). Sex typing. In P. H. Mussen (Gen. Ed.); E. M. Hetherington (Vol. Ed.), *Handbook of child psychology: Vol. IV. Socialization, personality, and social development* (4th ed.). New York: Wiley.

Jones, M. C., & Mussen, P. H. (1958). Self-conceptions, motivations, and interpersonal attitudes of early and late-maturing girls. *Child Development, 29,* 491–501.

Kestenberg, J. (1967), Phases of adolescence with suggestions for correlations of psychic and hormonal organizations: II. Prepuberty, diffusion, and reintegration. *Journal of the American Academy of Child Psychiatry, 6,* 577–614.

Koff, E., Rierdan, J., & Jacobson, S. (1981). The personal and interpersonal significance of menarche. *Journal of the American Academy of Child Psychiatry, 20,* 148–158.

Kohlberg, L. (1966). A cognitive-developmental analysis of children's sex-role concepts and attitudes. In E. E. Maccoby (Ed.), *The development of sex differences.* Stanford: Stanford University Press.

Kohlberg, L., & Ullian, D. Z. (1974). Stages in the development of psychosexual concepts and attitudes. In R. C. Friedman, R. M. Richart, & R. L. Vande Wiele (Eds.), *Sex differences in behavior.* New York: Wiley.

Lazarus, R. S., & Folkman, S. (1984). *Stress, appraisal, and coping.* New York: Springer.

Levine, J. M. (1983). Social comparison and education. In J. M. Levine & M. C. Wang (Eds.), *Teacher and student perceptions: Implications for learning.* Hillsdale, NJ: Erlbaum.

Levine, J. M., Snyder, H. N., & Mendez-Caratini, G. (1982). Task performance and interpersonal attraction in children. *Child Development, 53,* 359–371.

Lewis, M., & Brooks-Gunn, J. (1979). *Social cognition and the acquisition of self.* New York: Plenum.

Maccoby, E. E., & Jacklin, C. N. (1974). *The psychology of sex differences.* Stanford, CA: Stanford University Press.

Maccoby, E. E., & Martin, J. A. (1983). Socialization in the context of the family: Parent–child interaction. In P. H. Mussen (Gen. Ed.); E. M. Hetherington (Vol. Ed.), *Handbook of child psychology: Vol. IV. Socialization, personality, and social development* (4th ed.). New York: Wiley.

Marcus, D. E., & Overton, W. F. (1978). The development of cognitive gender constancy and sex role preferences. *Child Development, 49,* 434–444.

Markus, H., & Smith, J. (1981). The influence of self-schemas on the perception of others. In N. Cantor & J. Kihlstrom (Eds.), *Personality, cognition and social interaction.* Hillsdale, NJ: Erlbaum.

Markus, H., & Zajonc, R. B. (1985). The cognitive perspective in social psychology. In G. Lindzey & E. Aronson (Eds.), *The handbook of social psychology* (Vol. I, 3rd ed.). New York: Random House.

Martin, C. L., & Halverson, C. F., Jr. (1981). Schematic processing model of sex typing and stereotyping in children. *Child Development, 52,* 1119–1134.

Masters, J. C. (1971). Social comparison by young children. *Young Children, 27,* 37–60.

Masters, J. C., Ford, M. E., Arend, R., Grotevant, H. D., & Clark, L. V. (1979). Modeling and labeling as integrated determinants of children's sex-typed imitative behavior. *Child Development, 50,* 364–371.

May, R. R. (1976). Mood shifts and the menstrual cycle. *Journal of Psychosomatic Research, 20,* 125–130.

Mechanic, D. (1972). Social psychological factors affecting the presentation of bodily complaints. *New England Journal of Medicine, 286,* 1132–1139.

Mischel, W. (1970). Sex-typing and socialization. In P. H. Mussen (Ed.), *Carmichael's manual of child psychology.* New York: Wiley.

Mosatche, H. S., & Bragonier, P. (1981). An observational study of social comparison in preschoolers. *Child Development, 52,* 376–378.

Nicholls, J. G. (1978). The development of the concepts of effort and ability, perception of academic attainment, and the understanding that difficult tasks require more ability. *Child Development, 49,* 800–814.

Nicholls, J. G., & Miller, A. T. (1985). Development and its discontents: The differentiation of the concept of ability. In J. G. Nicholls (Ed.), *The development of achievement motivation.* Greenwich, CT: JAI.

Nisbett, R., & Ross, L. (1980). *Human inference: Strategies and shortcomings of social judgment.* Englewood Cliffs, NJ: Prentice-Hall.

Paige, K. E. (1973, September). *Determinants of menstrual distress: Stress, femininity, and religion.* Paper presented at the American Sociological Association meeting.

Parsons, J. E., & Ruble, D. N. (1977). The development of achievement-related expectancies. *Child Development, 48,* 1075–1079.

Perloff, R. M. (1982). Gender constancy and same-sex imitation: A developmental study. *The Journal of Psychology, 111,* 81–86.

Rees, L. (1953). The premenstrual tension syndrome and its treatment. *British Medical Journal, 1,* 1014–1016.

Rholes, W. S., Blackwell, J., Jordan, C., & Walters, C. (1980). A developmental study of learned helplessness. *Developmental Psychology, 16,* 616–624.

Rholes, W. S., & Jones, M. L. (1985). *Developmental trends in vulnerability to learned helplessness as related to the acquisition of stable dispositions concept.* Manuscript submitted for publication.

Rholes, W. S., & Ruble, D. N. (1984). Children's understanding of dispositional characteristics of others. *Child Development, 55,* 550–560.

Rierdan, J. (1983). Variations in the experience of menarche as a function of preparedness. In S. Golub (Ed.), *Menarche.* Lexington, MA: Lexington Books.

Ross, L. D. (1977). The intuitive psychologist and his shortcomings: Distortions in the attribution process. In L. Berkowitz (Ed.), *Advances in experimental social psychology.* New York: Academic.

Ross, M., & Fletcher, G. O. (1985). Attribution and social perception. In G. Lindzey & E. Aronson (Eds.), *The handbook of social psychology* (Vol. II, 3rd ed.). New York: Random House.

Ruble, D. N. (1975). Visual orientation and self-perceptions of children in an external cue relevant or irrelevant task situation. *Child Development, 46,* 669–676.

Ruble, D. N. (1983). The development of social comparison processes and their role in achievement-related self-socialization. In E. T. Higgins, D. N. Ruble, & W. W. Hartup (Eds.), *Social cognition and social development: A sociocultural perspective.* New York: Cambridge University Press.

Ruble, D. N. (1984). Sex-role development. In M. H. Bornstein & M. E. Lamb (Eds.), *Developmental psychology: An advanced textbook.* Hillsdale, NJ: Erlbaum.

Ruble, D. N., Balaban, T., & Cooper, J. (1981). Gender constancy and the effects of sex-typed televised toy commercials. *Child Development, 52,* 667–673.

Ruble, D. N., Boggiano, A. K., Feldman, N. S., & Loebl, J. H. (1980). A developmental analysis of the role of social comparison in self-evaluation. *Developmental Psychology, 16,* 105–115.

Ruble, D. N., & Brooks-Gunn, J. (1979). Menstrual symptoms: A social cognition analysis. *Journal of Behavioral Medicine, 2,* 171–194.

Ruble, D. N., & Brooks-Gunn, J. (1982). The experience of menarche. *Child Development, 53,* 1557–1566.

Ruble, D. N., & Brooks-Gunn, J. (in press). Perceptions of menstrual and premenstrual symptoms: Self-definitional processes at menarche. In B. F. Carter & B. E. Ginsburg (Eds.), *Legal and ethical implications of the biobehavioral sciences: Premenstrual syndrome.* New York: Plenum.

Ruble, D. N., Fleming, A. S., Hackel, L., & Stangor, C. S. (1986). *Division of household labor and the marital relationship during the transition to parenthood.* Manuscript submitted for publication.

Ruble, D. N., & Flett, G. (in press). Conflicting goals in self-evaluative information-seeking: developmental and ability level analyses. *Child Development.*

Ruble, D. N., & Frey, K. S. (in press). Self-evaluation and social comparison in children: Developmental changes in knowledge and function. In J. C. Masters & W. P. Smith (Eds.), *Social comparison and social justice: Theoretical, empirical, and policy perspectives.* Hillsdale, NJ: Erlbaum.

Ruble, D. N., Parsons, J. E., & Ross, J. (1976). Self-evaluative responses of children in an achievement setting. *Child Development, 47,* 990–997.

Ruble, D. N., & Rholes, W. S. (1981). The development of children's perceptions and attributions about their social world. In J. H. Harvey, W. Ickes, & R. Kidd (Eds.), *New directions in attribution research* (Vol. 3). Hillsdale, NJ: Erlbaum.

Ruble, D. N., & Stangor, C. (1986). Stalking the elusive schema: Insights from developmental and social analyses of gender schemas. *Social Cognition, 4,* 227–261.

Saltz, E., & Medow, M. L. (1971). Concept conservation in children: The dependence of belief systems on semantic representation. *Child Development, 42,* 1533–1542.

Shainess, N. (1961). A re-evaluation of some aspects of femininity through a study of menstruation: A preliminary report. *Comparative Psychiatry, 2,* 20–26.

Slaby, R. G., & Frey, K. S. (1975). Development of gender constancy and selective attention to same-sex models. *Child Development, 46,* 849–856.

Smith, W. P., Davidson, E. S., & France-Kaatrude, A. C. (in press). Social comparison and achievement evaluation in children. In J. C. Masters & W. P. Smith (Eds.),

Social comparison and social justice: Theoretical, empirical, and policy perspectives. Hillsdale, NJ: Erlbaum.

Stipek, D. J. (1984). Young children's performance expectations: Logical analysis or wishful thinking? In J. Nicholls (Ed.), *The development of achievement motivation.* Greenwich, CT: JAI.

Stipek, D., & Hoffman, I. (1980). Development of children's performance-related judgments. *Child Development, 51,* 912–914.

Stipek, D., & Tannatt, L. (1984). Children's judgments of their own and their peers' academic competence. *Journal of Educational Psychology, 76,* 75–84.

Taylor, S. E., & Thompson, S. C. (1982). Stalking the elusive "vividness" effect. *Psychological Review, 89,* 155–181.

Trope, Y. (1986). Self-enhancement and self-assessment in achievement behavior. In R. M. Sorrentino & E. T. Higgins (Eds.), *Handbook of motivation and cognition: Foundations of social behavior.* New York: Guilford.

Veroff, J. (1969). Social comparison and the development of achievement motivation. In C. P. Smith (Ed.), *Achievement-related motives in children.* New York: Russell Sage Foundation.

Vollman, R. F. (1977). *The menstrual cycle.* Toronto: Saunders.

Whisnant, L., & Zegans, L. A. (1975). A study of attitudes toward menarche in white middle-class American girls. *American Journal of Psychiatry, 132,* 809–814.

White, R. W. (1959). Motivation reconsidered: The concept of competence. *Psychological Review, 66,* 297–333.

Widholm, O., & Kantero, R. C., III. (1971). Menstrual pattern of adolescent girls according to chronological and gynecological ages. *Acta Obstetrica et Gynecologica Scandinavia, 1* (Suppl. 14), 19–29.

Woods, N. F., Dery, G. K., & Most, A. (1983). Recollections of menarche, current menstrual attitudes, and premenstrual symptoms. In S. Golub (Ed.), *Menarche.* Lexington, MA: Lexington Books.

Wylie, R. (1979). *The self-concept: Vol. 2. Theory and research on selected topics.* Lincoln: University of Nebraska Press.

Yussen, S., & Berman, L. (1981). Memory predictions for recall and recognition in third-, fourth-, and fifth-grade children. *Developmental Psychology, 17,* 224–229.

PART FIVE

The Social Context: Its Role in Development

In recent years, there has been a growing awareness among developmentalists of the often subtle yet powerful effects that the social context can have on individuals' development. We now realize that various families, social networks, schools, or communities are not equivalent in their effects on the developing person. Moreover, current models of the ways in which characteristics of the environment and those of the individual interact and influence development are more complex and reciprocal than in the past. No longer is it assumed either that the individual is passively molded by his or her environment or that an individual's environment is unaffected by the individual.

The chapter contributors to Part Five of this volume all have been concerned with the role of social context, or features of the context, in individual development. In Chapter 11, Arnold Sameroff reviews various theories and models of development and the differences among them with regard to the way in which the contributions of the environment and the individual are depicted. He then presents his transactional model and discusses the relevance of this model both to understanding development and to conceptualizing the intervention process. The implications of Sameroff's model are far-reaching and of importance to psychologists interested in all aspects of psychological development.

In Chapter 12, Allison Clarke-Stewart analyzes the effects of a specific feature of the child's social ecology—the child-care setting—on children's development. She reports findings from her study in which she compared the effects of care in the child's own home, in day-care homes, and in day-care centers on social, sociocognitive, and cognitive development. In addition, Clarke-Stewart examined differences in the features of these three child-rearing contexts and in the type of interactions associated with them so that she could better understand the ways in which the social context actually affects developmental outcomes. This research is some of the best in existence concerning the child-rearing context and is a model of how to investigate complex issues concerning individuals' social ecologies.

In Chapter 13, Sharlene Wolchik, Irwin Sandler, and Sanford Braver discuss an important aspect of the individual's social context: the nature of his or her social support system. They review definitional and conceptual issues related to this topic and then present research in which social and psychological outcomes are linked to the individual's social support. In addition, the association of gender and age to the receipt of social support is considered. The research in this chapter will be of particular interest to those who wish better to understand factors that affect individuals' coping in stressful environments (e.g., in the wake of a divorce). Moreover, it is an excellent example of the fruitful melding of clinical and developmental approaches and concerns.

CHAPTER 11

The Social Context of Development

ARNOLD J. SAMEROFF

Theories of development have varied in the emphasis they place on contributions the characteristics of the person and characteristics of the environment make to later behavior. While this debate can be treated as merely an academic discussion, it has important ramifications for the utilization of vast amounts of social resources. From intervention efforts that cost millions of dollars to the educational system that costs billions, practitioners rationalize their efforts on the basis of scientific knowledge. One of the major flaws in such knowledge is an inadequate conceptualization of the environment. Bronfenbrenner and Crouter (1983) have traced the history of empirical investigations of the environment and shown how theoretical limitations have placed limits on the sophistication of research paradigms. The goal of this presentation is to expand upon our understanding of the environment in order to lay a basis for more complex paradigms in both research and practice.

The significance of nature and nurture for development can be viewed from two perspectives. The first is whether they make a contribution at all and the second is whether these contributions are active ones or passive ones. Riegel (1978) placed models of development into four categories reflecting various combinations of passive and active persons and environments. In the passive person–passive environment category he placed mechanistic theories that arose from the empiricist philosophy of Locke and Hume in which combinations of events that occur in the environment in the presence of observers are imprinted into their minds. This view has been the basis for learning theories in which factors such as the continuity, frequency, or recency of stimuli determine how they will be coded into the receiving mind.

In a second category the passive person is combined with an active environment. In this category are Skinnerian approaches to behavior modification in which the conditioner actively structures the input to alter the person's behavior in particular directions, but in which the person is assumed to make no contribution to the outcome independent of experience.

The third category contains the concept of the active person but retains the passive environment. In this grouping fall the cognitive theories of Piaget and the linguistic views of Chomsky. Piaget sees the person as an active constructor of knowledge based on experience with the environment. The environment is a necessary part of development, but has no active role in structuring thought or action. Similarly, Chomsky sees language development as the person's application of innate linguistic categories to linguistic experience. The organization of that experience is not a determinant of language competence.

In the fourth category are models that combine an active person and an active environment. Riegel sees these models as deriving from Marx's interpretations of the dialectical nature of development in which the actions of the individual change reality, and then, in turn, the changes in reality affect the behavior of the individual. Sameroff and Chandler (1975) captured this process in their transactional model of development. In this view developmental outcomes are not a product of the initial characteristics of the child or the context or even their combination. Outcomes are the result of the interplay between child and context across time, in which the state of one affects the next state of the other in a continuous dynamic process.

Arguments over appropriate theories have important implications for both research and clinical strategies. Unless one understands how development proceeds, there is little basis for attempts to alter it, through either prevention or intervention programs. The conclusion that I will work toward is that both nature and nurture are necessary for any developmental process and that the contributions of both are not only active, but interactive and transactive as well.

Attempts to intervene in development have been based on stable models of child development. In these views, if a child is doing well or poorly early in life, he or she would be expected to continue to do well or poorly later on. As an example, children who were identified early in life as being at developmental risk from biological circumstances, such as birth complications, were thought to have generally negative behavioral outcomes later in life. On the contrary, longitudinal research in this area has demonstrated that the majority of children suffering from such biological conditions did not have intellectual or social problems later in life (Sameroff & Chandler, 1975). On the other hand, early interventionists believed that getting children to perform well early in life would lead to them performing well throughout childhood. The early childhood education movement as exemplified in the Head Start program was designed to improve the learning and social competence of children during the preschool years with the expectation that these improvements would be maintained into later life. However, follow-up research of such children has found only minimal intellectual gains being maintained into adolescence (Zigler & Trickett, 1978), although there were reduced rates of grade retention and need for participation in special education programs and improved maternal attitudes toward school performance (Lazar & Darlington, 1982).

In both domains early characteristics of the child are frequently overpowered by factors in the environmental context of development. Where family and cultural variables have fostered development, children with severe perinatal complications have been indistinguishable from children without complications. When these variables have hindered development, children from excellent preschool intervention programs developed severe social and cognitive deficits. Thus while a continuous view of developmental functioning makes intuitive sense, it has not been borne out by empirical investigations.

As will be seen, all development seems to follow a similar model. In this view outcomes are never a function of the individual taken alone or the experiential context taken alone. Behavioral competencies are a product of the combination of an individual and his or her experience. To predict outcome, a singular focus on the characteristics of the individual, in this case the child, will frequently be misleading. What needs to be added is an analysis and assessment of the experiences available to the child.

DEVELOPMENTAL MODELS

Ancient theorists interpreted development as an unfolding of intrinsic characteristics that were either preformed or interacted epigenetically (Sameroff, 1983; see Fig. 11.1). This model was countered by an environmental model of discontinuity in which each stage of development was determined by the contemporary context analogous to Riegel's (1978) passive person–active environment category. If the context remained the same the child remained the same. If the context changed, the child changed (see Fig. 11.2).

An interactionist position combined these two as in Figure 11.3. Her continuity is carried by the child but moderated by possible discontinuities in experience. Anastasi (1958) is credited with the important interactionist conceptual breakthrough in pointing out that development could not occur without an environment. There is no logical possibility of considering development of an individual independent of the environment. Continuity could not be explained as a characteristic of the child because each new achievement was an amalgam of characteristics of the child and his or her experience. Neither alone would be predictive of later levels of functioning. If continuities were found, it was because there was a continuity in the relation between the child and the environment, not because of continuities in either taken alone.

More recent conceptualizations of the developmental model have incorporated effects of the child on the environment posited by Rheingold (1966) and Bell (1968). These dynamic interactionist (Thomas, Chess, & Birch, 1968) or transactional models (Sameroff & Chandler, 1975) add to the independent contributions of child and environment, characteristics of the environment that are conditioned by the nature of the child. Different characteristics of the child will trigger different responses from the environment (see Fig. 11.4).

$$C_1 \longrightarrow C_2 \longrightarrow C_3 \longrightarrow C_4$$

Figure 11.1. Deterministic constitutional model of development. (C1 to C4 represent state of the child at successive points in time.)

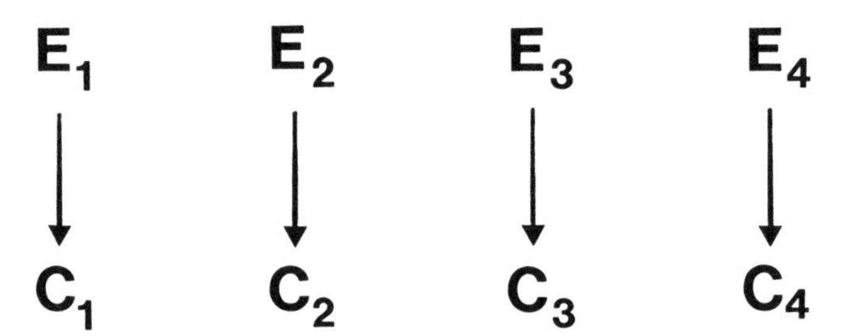

Figure 11.2. Deterministic environmental model of development. (E1 to E4 represent experiential influences at successive points in time.)

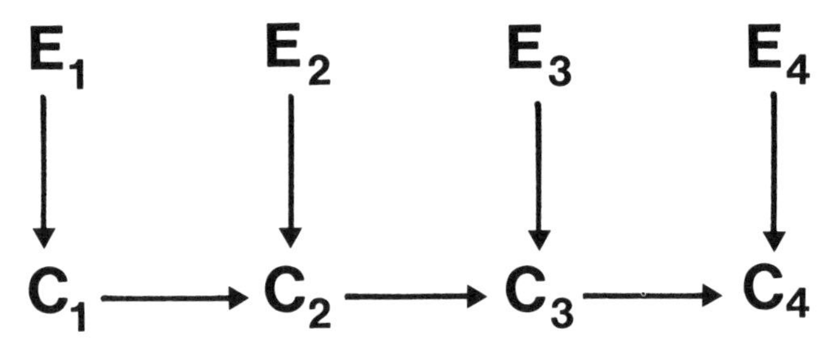

Figure 11.3. Interactionist model of development.

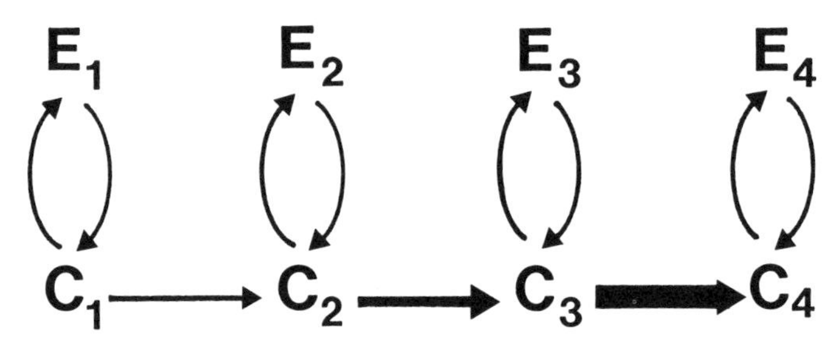

Figure 11.4. Reciprocal interaction model of development.

In Figure 11.4 there is a continuity implied in the organization of the child's behavior by the series of arrows from C1 to C2 to C3. What is still missing from this model is a sense of continuity in the organization of the environment that would be indicated by a series of arrows from E1 to E2 to E3. The characterization of this organization will be contained in what follows.

Recently, I reviewed at length the dynamic, dialectical interplay between individual and context in not only development, but evolution as well (Sameroff, 1983). Two points from this review are pertinent to this discussion. The first is that no organism ever existed outside of an environment. The classic chicken-and-egg paradox is a dialectical truism. The fertilized egg contains the genotype but also an organized biochemical environment with which the genotype interacts. This cytoplasmic environment was not produced by the genome it contains. Each species evolved in intimate relationship to some environment. The second point is that environments are organized. In evolution there was an organization of existing forms into which each new species had to fit. The organization may have been a biological one in terms of the food sources or predators available or a physical one related to the geographic context or a temporal one related to the seasons of the year. On the other hand, species can play an active role in selecting among niches within that environment to reduce the variance in life attributable to the environment. In summer, an animal can search for relatively cool locales, while in winter it can seek out relatively warm ones.

In human development, as well, there is an organized environment. Someone needs to feed, protect, and provide warmth to infants. There is a cultural code in each society that provides an agenda of experiences for the developing child aimed at producing an adult suitable to fill a role in that society. Behavioral development is regulated by the interplay between the individual and the cultural system. Neither can be said to dominate the other. We have paid a lot of attention to the organization of one control system, the genetic one, but relatively little to the organization of the other, the cultural one.

The environment takes an active role in regulating development. Most individuals can only grow up to fill existing roles in a culture. There are vast periods of human existence when the number of roles were highly limited, either in absolute number or in the number available to certain parts of society. Feudal society was not a meritocracy. Serfs, no matter what their talents, could not fill intellectual or political roles in their societies.

To the extent that roles are open to individuals, there are usually selection systems to determine who would be most appropriate for available positions in the existing social organization. Academic tests allow certain children to enter or prevent certain children from entering certain tracks, but so may discrimination. The same may be true for athletic or artistic efforts. In these situations the contributions of the genotype to the selection process may be large, but it is the environment that decides which developmental tracks are permissible for a given individual. In a society in which artistic achievement is proscribed, that aspect of the genotype will have little positive effect on developmental outcomes. Within our own culture there are still major restrictions the environment places on individual development based on characteristics other than talent. Race, social status, and sex are examples of such restrictive criteria. Bronfenbrenner (1977) has cogently argued that a much more sophisticated analysis of the ecological environment is necessary. In his view the understanding of human development requires the examination of multiperson systems of interaction that go beyond the immediate setting into larger social contexts.

Extending the work of Lewin (1936) on the individual's participation in multiple contexts, Bronfenbrenner (1977) proposed a hierarchical model of environmental organization encompassing microsystems, mesosystems, exosystems, and macrosystems. This model has been productive in permitting empirical investigations in a variety of cognitive and personality domains (Bronfenbrenner & Crouter, 1983). The *microsystem* is the immediate setting of a child in an environment with particular features, activities, and roles. The *mesosystem* comprises the relationships between major settings at a particular point in an individual's development. The *exosystem* is the next higher level in which the mesosystem settings are embedded, including, for example, the world of work and neighborhoods. The *macrosystem* comprises the overarching institutional patterns of the culture including the economic, social, and political systems of which the micro-, meso-, and exosystems are concrete expressions.

Bronfenbrenner's model reflects the complexity of the human context at any point in time. For the purposes of this discussion, the focus will be on the lifelong coherence of environmental influences rather than an analysis of the multiple influences within a single period of development.

TRANSACTIONAL MODEL

A model of development that included both the child and the child's experiences extended through time was suggested by Sameroff and Chandler (1975). Within this "transactional model," the development of the child was seen as a product of the continuous dynamic interactions of the child and the experience provided by his or her family and social context. What was innovative in the transactional model was the emphasis placed on the effect of the child on the environment, so that experiences provided by the environment were not independent of the child. The child by its previous behavior may have been a strong determinant of current experiences. In Figure 11.5 one can see a con-

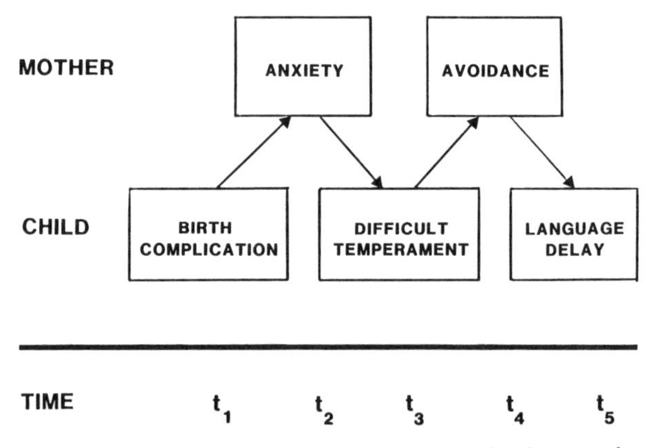

Figure 11.5. Example of transactions leading to poor developmental outcome.

crete example of such a transactional outcome. The arrows implying continuities in child and environment have been eliminated in this figure in order to emphasize the interplay between child and caregiver.

A complicated childbirth may have made an otherwise calm mother somewhat anxious. The mother's anxiety during the first months of the child's life may have caused her to be uncertain and inappropriate in her interactions with the child. In response to such inconsistency the infant may have developed some irregularities in feeding and sleeping patterns that give the appearance of a difficult temperament. This difficult temperament decreases the pleasure that the mother obtains from the child and so she tends to spend less time with the child. If there are no adults interacting with the child, and especially speaking to the child, the child may not meet the norms for language development and score poorly on preschool language tests. In this case the outcome was not determined by the complicated birth nor by the mother's consequent emotional response. If one needed to pick a cause it would be the mother's avoidance of the child, yet one can see that such a view would be a gross oversimplification of a complex developmental sequence.

When attempts are made to operationalize transactional processes within a specific research design the data are rarely as simple as the figure would indicate. Crockenberg and Smith (1982) examined the relation of infant and mother characteristics to the development of infant temperament and mother–infant interaction during the first 3 months of life. Mothers' responsive attitudes and infant behavior were measured during the newborn period. Mothers with responsive and flexible attitudes responded more quickly when their 3-month-old infants cried, and their infants spent less time fussing and crying. There was no significant contribution of neonatal irritability to the amount of child crying at 3 months. On the other hand, time required to calm down was not related to maternal attitudes and was related to newborn irritability. In other words, crying at 3 months was not a consequence of the initial characteristics of the child, but time to calm down was. Amount of time crying was a function of the subsequent caregiving experiences, and time to calm down was not. From the infant's side a transaction had occurred: the state of the child was changed as a function of the environment. There was also evidence in this study that the behavior of the mother was changed by the specific characteristics of the child. Alert infants had mothers who spent more time in contact with them, and mothers of irritable females responded more quickly to fussing and crying than mothers of irritable males. The mother's behavior was sensitive to both the behavioral and physical characteristics of the child. The evidence for transactional processes in this study is an example of the multidimensional nature of both maternal and child behavior. Depending on the antecedent and outcome measures and the ages of assessment, different relations will be found, some giving strong evidence for transactions and others not.

Observations of families in natural settings provide insights into possible causal sequences in development, but definitive evidence can only be produced by attempts to manipulate developmental variables (Bronfenbrenner, 1977). Experimental manipulations designed to illuminate transactional processes have not been frequent as yet. Bugental and Shennum (1984) assessed beliefs about causes of caregiving outcomes for a group of mothers who were then placed in interaction situations with children who had been trained to be more or less responsive and assertive. Short-term transactions were identified in some conditions where mothers responded differently as a function of the combination of their attributions and the actual behavior of the child. Other research projects have been directed at long-term transactions resulting from massive intervention programs.

Zeskind and Ramey (1978, 1981) examined the effects of an intensive early intervention program on the development of a group of fetally malnourished infants. Intervention began at 3 months and included social work, medical and nutritional services, and an educational curriculum. Children attended the program approximately 8 hr a day, 5 days per week, during the whole year. A control group received similar social work and medical and nutritional services but did not participate in the educational program. Comparisons were made in the later functioning of lower-SES underweight (i.e., low ponderal index) infants, half of whom participated in the educational program and half of whom did not. As a group, the infants without educational intervention declined in DQ from 3 to 18 months of age and continued to score lower on tests at 36 months of age. However, within that group the low ponderal index babies showed a much greater decline into the retarded range. These lower DQs were associated with lower levels of maternal involvement. In contrast, in the group of families that received educational intervention, the malnourished infants who had scored significantly lower than the rest of the group at 3 months were doing as well as the others by 18 months. Zeskind and Ramey (1981) concluded that the educational program had interrupted the negative transaction found in the control group. Where low social status mothers would usually be put off by the characteristics of a fetally malnourished infant, contributing to a worsening developmental outcome, intervention fostered the relationship between mother and child, thereby leading to an above-average outcome within this sample.

Biological Basis of Developmental Models

The transactional model despite its novel name is in reality not a novel model. It is merely a new emphasis on some very old traditions in developmental theory, especially theories of the dialectic in history and philosophy. A more cogent referent is theory and research in biology where transactions are a recognized essential part of any developmental process.

In the study of embryological development, for example, there are continuous transactions between the phenotype and the genotype (Ebert & Sussex, 1970; Waddington, 1957). A simple view of the action of genes is that they produce the parts that make up the organism. A brown eye gene may be thought to produce a brown eye. In reality there is a much more complex process of mutual determinism. The material in the fertilized egg cell will turn on or off specific genes in the chromosomes. The turned-on genes will initiate changes in the biochemicals in the cell. These changed biochemicals will then act back on the genetic material turning on or off more genes in a continuous process usually producing an adult organism.

In certain circumstances one has the illusion of a linear relationship between a particular gene and a particular feature of the phenotype as in the case of eye color. In reality, however, there is never a linear determinism because of the complexity of biological processes. What then creates the illusion? The answer is in the regulatory system that buffers development, what Waddington (1957) described as canalization. Within all the complex interactions between genotype and phenotype is a regulatory system that monitors the developmental changes to ensure that they stay within defined bounds. This regulatory system and the bounds are the result of an evolutionary process that occurred across myriad generations, that now ensures a particular outcome.

With eye color the system is hidden since it is so tightly buffered (i.e., regulated) that if one knows the structural genes one can predict the outcome. However, there are some simple examples where the regulatory system is quite evident. In the case of identical twins, a single fertilized cell splits in two. Shouldn't the result be two half-sized children? The genetic regulatory system ensures that this is not the outcome. Compensations are made so that the resulting infants will all be of normal size. In the case of genetic dominance the result for a homozygous individual is the same as for a heterozygous one. If there are two brown eye genes, the eyes are no browner than if there were only one. A regulation has occurred.

A more complex example is the result of the translocation in Down's syndrome. Here in the meiotic process of forming a germ cell there is a breakage in a chromosome such that in one of the resulting germ cells there is too much genetic material and in the other there is too little. In the cell with too much, the Trisomy 21 condition, regulations can occur that compensate for much of the anomalous genetic condition. A child is born that looks in large part like other human infants. In the case of the germ cell in which there is too little, regulation fails and the zygote is aborted. Another perspective is that regulation succeeded in the aborted cell and failed in the trisomy cell, but that issue will not be dealt with in this presentation.

Regulatory Systems

When thinking in terms of the biological model, one has to think about a system with two levels, the developing organism and a superordinate regulatory system. In biology the regulatory system for physical outcomes is found in the genetic code. For behavioral outcomes there is also a system that regulates the way human beings fit into their society. This cultural code is directed at the regulation of cognitive and social-emotional processes so that the individual will be able to fill some social role defined by society including the reproduction of that society.

The genetic code has two properties that permit it to maintain its superordinate regulatory role. It is transmitted as an organized system through time from one individual to another, and it is not affected by the individual action of those that carry it. The cultural code has the same two properties. It is transmitted through time as an organized system from one individual to another (Berger & Luckmann, 1966), and it is not affected by the individual action of those that carry it. The cultural code can be changed by groups of individuals who combine to produce formal changes in legislation or informal changes in customs. The banding together of parents of handicapped children to alter laws about segregated educational systems is an example of a formal change, whereas the greater role of men in modern child rearing in conjunction with the liberation of women from the home is an example of an informal change.

The cultural code can be broken down into sets of regulatory functions that operate across different magnitudes of time. The longest cycle is associated with *macro-regulations* that are a culture's "developmental agenda." The developmental agenda is a series of points in time when the environment is restructured to provide different experiences to the child. Age of weaning, toilet training, schooling, initiation rites, and marriage are coded differently in each culture, but provide the basis for socialization in each culture. The validity of such agendas is not in their details but in the fact that the culture is successfully reproduced in generation after generation of offspring.

On a shorter time base are *mini-regulations* that refer to the caregiving activities of the child's family. Such activities are feeding children when they awaken, changing diapers when they are wet, and keeping children warm. Both the mini- and macro-regulations are known to acculturated members of society and can be transmitted from member to member and generation to generation.

On the shortest time base are *micro-regulations,* which refer to the momentary interactions between child and character that others have referred to as *behavioral synchrony* or *attunement* (Field, 1979; Stern, 1977). Micro-regulations are a blend between the cultural and biological codes because many of these activities appear naturally and even without awareness. These include the caregiver's smiling responses to an infant's smile or possibly the matching of vocal and movement patterns between caregiver and child (Condon & Sander, 1974).

Although the cultural code can be conceptualized independently of the child, changes in the abilities of the child are major triggers for regulatory changes and in all likelihood were major contributors to the evolution of the code. In most cultures formal education begins between the ages of 6 and 8 (Rogoff, 1981) when most children have attained the cognitive ability to learn from such formalized experiences. On the other hand, informal education can begin at many different ages depending on the culture's attributions to the child. The Digo and Kikuyu are two East African cultures that have different beliefs about infant capacities (deVries & Sameroff, 1984). The Digo believe that infants can learn within a few months after birth and begin socialization at that time. The Kikuyu wait until the second year of life before they believe serious education is possible. During the first year they keep their infants swaddled.

Given this understanding of the regulatory system for psychological development, what implications will it have? The primary application will be in the analysis of problems of deviant development. On the caregiver's side one must analyze the factors that caused regulation to fail. These would include such factors as parents not knowing the cultural code or knowing the code but being unable to use it because of other demands for their time and resources. Such other demands may include the need to be away from the home to make a living, life event stresses that interfere with their caregiving, or mental illness that diverts their attention from their children's needs to their own.

On the child's side the parents may know the cultural code and even have the time and resources to use it but be confronted by a child who does not fit the code. A child with a handicap, one born prematurely, or one with a difficult temperament would present such problems. Within this model deviancy will be the outcome of a stress on the regulatory system. The prevention of deviancy will be a function of the identification of that stress, whether it comes from the child, the parents, or perhaps the larger social context.

The caregiving environment has evolved to provide normative experiences for the normative child. Should a child be born who does not fit the normative pattern, then new regulations must be made to restore the child to the appropriate developmental trajectory. The activation of these new regulations requires transactions in which the environment is sensitive to individual differences in the children raised in that environment.

APPLYING THE TRANSACTIONAL MODEL

At the outset I raised the issue of the importance of developmental models for targeting interventions in children's lives. At this point we can examine how an understanding of development in terms of regulatory systems would affect intervention strategies.

When one begins to assess the effect of environments on child development, a wide variety of risk factors are apparent. The most obvious of these is social status. Socioeconomic factors have been consistently related to cognitive (Broman, Nichols, & Kennedy, 1975; Golden & Birns, 1976) and social-emotional competence (Hollingshead & Redlich, 1957; Sameroff, Seifer, & Zax, 1982). Social status is only a summary variable that incorporates a variety of risk factors that exert both independent and interactive influences on outcomes. We (Sameroff and Seifer, 1983; Sameroff, Seifer, Zax, Barocas & Greenspan, 1987) have shown that the developmental outcomes for young children are multiply determined. No single factor was always present or always absent in cases where high levels of social-emotional and intellectual incompetency were found. When one searches for factors that can be easily altered to improve the outcome for such children the list is short. Certain of these variables are enduring characteristics of the family, for instance, minority status and family size, whereas others are not in the usual domain of intervention, for example, stressful life events and marital status. Another set is highly unlikely to change, for example, occupation and educational level. What is left is the coping skills of the parents. These include the psychological variables of mental health, parental perspectives, and parent–child interaction patterns. These coping skills are what we have described above as the cultural code, the social regulatory system that guides children through their development and buffers them from those aspects of the broader environment with which they are not yet able to cope by themselves.

The basic developmental model in which transactional processes between child and environment are combined with continuities in each can be seen in Figure 11.6. There is a set of arrows leading from the child's initial state (C1) to the child's state at succeeding points in time. This dimension refers to the continuity of competency within the child. As children increase in age the line gets thicker as they learn more and more skills for taking care of themselves and buffering themselves from stressful experiences. There is another set of arrows leading from the environment's initial state (E1) to the environment's state at succeeding points in time. The relevant environmental factors for the present discussion are the parents' understanding of the cultural code and their competency at regulating their child's development. The sets of vertical arrows refer to the actions of parents on children and conversely of children on parents.

Intervention strategies must focus on the vertical arrows that mediate the transactional regulatory functions. These strategies fall into two categories affecting, respectively, the upward and downward arrows. The upward arrows reflect the effect of the child on the parents. Their effects can be moderated by either changing the child or changing the parents' interpretation of the child. The downward arrows reflect the effect of the parents on the child. Parent effects can be similarly altered by either changing the parents or changing the child's interpretation of the parents. In early childhood this last cat-

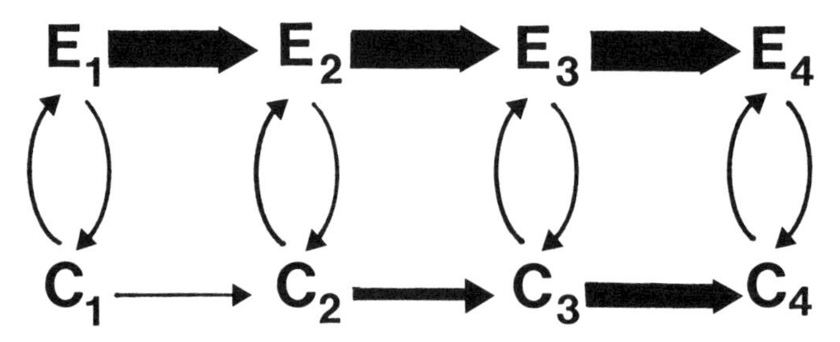

Figure 11.6. Social regulatory model of development.

egory is not feasible given the limited cognitive abilities of the child, so the following analysis will be based on the first three possibilities. For simplicity I have labeled these the "three R's" of intervention—remediation, redefinition, and reeducation.

Remediation

The strategy of remediation is the traditional prevention mechanism aimed at repairing or changing the child. Within the traditional medical model (Engel, 1977), this strategy is based on the idea that the psychological development of the child is determined by the child's biological state. Thus by repairing biology, one can normalize psychological functioning. Although there are many physical conditions for which such an approach may be valid, for example, intestinal or cardiac anomalies, the vast majority of behaviorally disordered children are the result of transactional processes. In such cases the intervention strategy is to change the child's effect on the parental regulating system.

Malnutrition in infancy may be a good example of how this strategy operates. Although there was an early assumption that malnutrition in infancy affected later intelligence adversely because of reductions in the number of brain cells, longitudinal studies with appropriate control groups have shown that lower later intelligence in malnourished infants is the consequence of their poor environments, not their poor biology (Read, 1982). Cravioto and DeLicardie (1979) found that the behavioral effects of malnutrition were most prevalent in families in which the mothers were passively traditional in their child care and provided little stimulation to their children. In a naturalistic study Winick, Meyer, and Harris (1975) compared two groups of Korean children who had suffered severe malnutrition as infants. One group was raised by their parents in Korea and scored very poorly on psychological tests given during adolescence. The second group was adopted by middle-class U.S. parents who had no knowledge that the children had suffered from malnutrition as infants. The adopted group scored as well as or better than their U.S. contemporaries when tested.

Transactional effects of infant malnutrition were hypothesized to be the result of impaired attentional processes, reduced social responsiveness, heightened irritability, inability to tolerate frustration, low activity level, reduced independence, and diminished affect (Barrett, Radke-Yarrow, & Klein, 1982). Lester (1979) is cited by Barrett and colleagues (1982) as suggesting that

> such effects may occur within a synergistic system where the malnourished infant is less successful at engaging caretakers in interaction and, in turn, is responded to less often and with less sensitivity, resulting in a failure to develop normal patterns of social interaction. If so, we should suspect that insufficient nutrition early in life would be associated with poor interpersonal skills and general lack of responsiveness in later childhood. (p. 542)

Based on these hypotheses, Barrett and colleagues (1982) compared a group of children who had received caloric supplementation during infancy with a group that did not. The results were that better nutrition was associated with greater social responsiveness, more expression of affect, greater interest in the environment, and higher activity level at school age.

Food supplementation of young infants interrupted the transaction by which their low energy levels failed to stimulate their parents to engage in adequate socialization. The failure to develop normal patterns of social interaction, especially with peers, found for the malnourished control group was prevented in the supplemented group.

Remediation as an intervention does not tamper with the cultural code, that is, the parental regulatory system. It changes the child to fit better whatever the normative code is. For older children both biochemical and behavioral approaches to remediation have been used. Hyperactive children who disturb their parents and teachers are very frequently given medication to quiet them down. Such children as well as those with conduct disorders can be given behavior therapies to modify their behavior so that they will be less likely to elicit negative responses from others in their social context. Such positive changes may be possible for some behavioral problems but are less successful with other problems such as handicaps or difficult temperaments. One cannot easily make a blind child see or a spina bifida child walk. One cannot easily stop some babies from having irregular sleeping and eating habits or from having high levels of endogenously determined crying. In these cases another strategy must be used to prevent later disabilities—redefinition.

Redefinition

In order for a transactional regulation to occur the parent must define the child as being deviant. In the case of a child with a severe motor problem the parent identifies the child as abnormal and may decide that the usual regulatory function, that is, normal child rearing, is not possible. In some such cases the parent may try to convince society that the child cannot be maintained in the family and must be reared in a completely different setting, that is, an institution, with an appropriate abnormal child-rearing program for their abnormal child. In other cases the parents may accept the responsibility for the physical care of their child but expect little in the way of a satisfactory psychological relationship with the child (Roskies, 1972).

The prevention effort with such families is directed at a *redefinition* of the situation, at identifying for the parents the possibilities for normal child rearing within what appears to be a deviant situation. In the case of a child with motor handicaps the redefinition may involve a refocus on the possibility of normal cognitive and social-emotional development. In the case of a retarded child, such as one with Down's syndrome, the redefinition may involve a focus on the normal sequencing of development, albeit at a slower pace.

These redefinitions allow the family to admit the child to their caregiving system. They allow the parents to see that they can indeed raise the child within the caregiving system they already know. They may need to learn some special skills for feeding or positioning the child, but these are only variations of what they would have done with a nonhandicapped child. In the case of temperamental problems, the redefinitions may be simpler. When a colicky child who cries most of the time may be perceived as emotionally deviant, the redefinition takes the form of indicating that colic is only an extreme on a normal dimension of individual differences (Chess, 1966). Crying babies need not become mentally ill adults or even crying adults. Admittedly, it is a greater strain on the regulatory system to raise a handicapped or colicky infant, but this does not mean that the regulatory system is not adequate for this purpose.

The strategy of redefinition is to intervene so that the parents will use their existing regulatory system to guide the child toward normative developmental outcomes. It prevents the initial biological deficit from being converted into a later behavioral abnormality. In systems terminology, it prevents a cycle of positive feedback that would have amplified the deviation by placing the child in an abnormal child-rearing context such as an institution.

Redefinition is a reasonable strategy when the parents have a normal child-rearing capacity, when they know the cultural code. But if the parents don't know this code, if they are not aware of how to raise a child at all, then redefinition would be an insufficient prevention strategy.

Reeducation

The third strategy, reeducation, simply refers to teaching parents how to raise children. Its purpose is to teach the cultural code that regulates the child's development from birth to maturity. The most obvious target for such prevention efforts is adolescent mothers. An increasing proportion of children are being born to teenage, unmarried mothers who have few intellectual, social, or economic resources for raising their children. In these cases the intervention is aimed at training them how to be mothers and in some cases fathers. There are few normative strategies among these parents, and the child's survival is more a function of the child's resiliency or the supporting social network than the parents' abilities (McDonough, 1985).

Other populations include parents of children at high risk because of either psychosocial or biological factors. One technique that has proven fruitful for such interventions is the demonstration of how to elicit infant behaviors by an expert. Widmayer and Field (1981) compared three groups of low-income teenage mothers with preterm infants. Mothers in one group watched the administration of the Brazelton Neonatal Behavioral Assessment Scales and were trained to administer an adaptation of the scales during their babies' first month. Mothers in another group were only trained to administer the adaptation. Mothers in the third group did neither. Observations of later mother-child interactions saw improvements in the intervention groups, and the infants scored higher on developmental assessments at 12 months of age. These very needy parents seemed to benefit greatly from a targeted 1-month intervention program. An interesting question was whether such interventions would also benefit less needy mothers.

The effects of similar interventions were examined in several studies of middle-class mothers of healthy full-term babies. One study compared three groups of mothers who either watched a demonstration of the Brazelton examination, watched a standard physical examination of their baby, or were routinely discharged (Liptak, Keller, Feldman, & Chamberlin, 1983). Three months later the group that saw the Brazelton demonstration spent more time playing with, looking at, and talking to their infants, but the authors felt that these were not highly significant differences. In all three groups over 90% of the parents were married, living together, had attended childbirth education classes, and the father had been present during delivery. The power of the procedure is evident in the fact that any differences were found at all in this low-risk sample.

While adolescent parents may be an easily identified target for education efforts, there is a similar problem even among middle-class professional parents. There are many fathers and mothers who have had no experience taking care of siblings when growing up and who are separated from their own parents who provide the child-rearing training in more traditional societies. The difference between these two kinds of parents is that the middle-class professionals usually will seek out the information to educate themselves in how to raise a child whereas teenage mothers usually will not. In both cases information and training are necessary to equip the parents with the cultural code. For some parents having the information available will be sufficient; for others, more intrusive educational efforts are necessary to prevent developmental deviancies.

UNDERSTANDING ENVIRONMENTS

The preceding discussion has been aimed at understanding the complexity of contextual influences on development. A case was made that the environment is an active force in shaping outcomes. However, the shaping force is constrained by the state and potentialities of the individual (Sameroff, 1983). In an attempt to incorporate both aspects in a coherent model of development, the utility of the transactional model for designing programs to prevent cognitive and social-emotional problems was explored. The development of these problems has been interpreted as deviations in a child-rearing regulatory system. The prevention of these problems has been defined as the adjustment of the child better to fit the regulatory system or the adjustment of the regulatory system better to fit the child. Within this regulatory framework transactions are ubiquitous. Wherever parents change their way of thinking about or behaving toward the child as a result of something the child does, a transaction has occurred. Most of these transactions are normative within the existing cultural code and facilitate development. Intervention only becomes necessary where these transactions are nonnormative. A normative event for which society is prepared is the family's registering the child in school. Society responds by changing a large part of the child's environment by the provision of a new physical environment, the school, new regulators of socialization, the teachers, and a new social network, the classmates. A nonnormative event for which society may or may not be prepared is when the parent seeks a professional for help with a deviant child. The degree of help that can be provided is a function of society's awareness of how development is regulated and the availability of resources for intervening.

In sum, models that focus on singular causal factors are inadequate for either the study or manipulation of developmental outcomes. The evolution of living systems has provided a regulatory model that incorporates feedback mechanisms between the individual and regulatory codes. These cultural and genetic codes are the context of development. By appreciating the workings of this regulatory system, we can obtain a better grasp of the process of development.

REFERENCES

Anastasi, A. (1958). Heredity, environment, and the question, "How?" *Psychological Review, 65,* 81–95.

Barrett, D. E., Radke-Yarrow, M., & Klein, R. E. (1982). Chronic malnutrition and child behavior: Effects of early caloric supplementation on social and emotional functioning at school age. *Child Development, 18,* 541–556.

Bell, R. Q. (1968). A reinterpretation of the direction of effects in studies of socialization. *Psychological Review, 75,* 81–95.

Berger, P. L., & Luckmann, T. (1966). *The social construction of reality.* Garden City, NY: Doubleday.

Broman, S. H., Nichols, P. L., & Kennedy, W. A. (1975). *Preschool IQ: Prenatal and early developmental correlates.* Hillsdale, NJ: Erlbaum.

Bronfenbrenner, U. (1977). Toward an experimental ecology of human development. *American Psychologist, 32,* 513–531.

Bronfenbrenner, U., & Crouter, A. C. (1983). The evolution of environmental models in developmental research. In P. H. Mussen (Gen. Ed.); W. Kessen (Vol. Ed.), *Handbook of Child Psychology: Vol. 1. History, theories, and methods.* New York: Wiley.

Bugental, D. P., & Shennum, W. A. (1984). "Difficult" children as elicitors and targets of adult communication patterns: An attributional-behavioral transactional analysis. *Monographs of the Society for Research in Child Development, 49* (Whole No. 205).

Chess, S. (1966). Individuality in children: Its importance to the pediatrician. *Journal of Pediatrics, 69,* 676–684.

Condon, W. S., & Sander, L. W. (1974). Synchrony demonstrated between movements of the neonate and adult speech. *Child Development, 45,* 456–462.

Cravioto, J., & DeLicardie, E. R. (1979). Nutrition, mental development, and learning. In F. Falhner & J. M. Turner (Eds.), *Human Growth: Vol. 3. Neurobiology and nutrition.* New York: Plenum.

Crockenberg, S. B., & Smith, P. (1982). Antecedents of mother–infant interaction and infant irritability in the first three months of life. *Infant Behavior & Development, 5,* 105–119.

deVries, M. W., & Sameroff, A. J. (1984). Culture and temperament: Influences on temperament in three East African societies. *American Journal of Orthopsychiatry, 54,* 83–96.

Ebert, J. D., & Sussex, I. M. (1970). *Interacting systems in development* (2nd ed.). New York: Holt, Rinehart & Winston.

Engel, G. L. (1977). The need for a new medical model: A challenge for biomedicine. *Science, 196,* 129–136.

Field, T. M. (1979). Interaction patterns of preterm and term infants. In T. M. Field, A. M. Sostek, and H. H. Schuman (Eds.), *Infants born at risk: Behavior and development.* New York: SP Medical and Scientific Books.

Golden, M., & Birns, B. (1976). Social class and infant intelligence. In M. Lewis (Ed.), *Origins of intelligence: Infancy and early childhood.* New York: Plenum.

Hollingshead, A. B., & Redlich, F. C. (1957). *Social class and mental illness: A community study.* New York: Wiley.

Lazar, I., & Darlington, R. (1982). Lasting effects of early education: A report from the consortium for longitudinal studies. *Monographs of the Society for Research in Child Development, 47* (Whole No. 195).

Lester, B. M. (1979). A synergistic process approach to the study of prenatal malnutrition. *International Journal of Behavioral Development, 2,* 377–394.

Lewin, K. (1936). Problems of topological psychology. New York: McGraw-Hill.

Liptak, G. S., Keller, B. B., Feldman, A. W., & Chamberlin, R. W. (1983). Enhancing infant development and parent–practitioner interaction with the Brazelton Neonatal Assessment Scales. *Pediatrics, 72,* 71–78.

McDonough, S. C. (1985). Intervention program for adolescent mothers and their offspring. *Journal of Children in Contemporary Society, 17,* 67–76.

Read, M. S. (1982). Malnutrition and behavior. *Applied Research in Mental Retardation, 3,* 279–291.

Rheingold, H. L. (1966). The development of social behavior in the human infant. In H. W. Stevenson (Ed.), Concept of development. *Monographs of the Society for Research in Child Development, 31,* 5 (Whole No. 107).

Riegel, K. F. (1978). *Psychology, mon amour: A countertext.* Boston: Houghton Mifflin.

Rogoff, B. (1981). Schooling and the development of cognitive skills. In H. C. Triandis & A. Heron (Eds.), *Handbook of cross-cultural psychology: Developmental psychology* (Vol. 4). Boston: Allyn & Bacon.

Roskies, E. (1972). *Abnormality and normality: The mothering of thalidomide children.* Ithaca, NY: Cornell University Press.

Sameroff, A. J. (1983). Developmental systems: Contexts and evolution. In P. H. Mussen (Gen. Ed.); W. Kessen (Vol. Ed.), *Handbook of Child Psychology: Vol. 1. History, theories, and methods.* New York: Wiley.

Sameroff, A. J., & Chandler, M. J. (1975). Reproductive risk and the continuum of caretaking casualty. In F. D. Horowitz, M. Hetherington, S. Scarr-Salapatek, & G. Siegel (Eds.), *Review of child development research* (Vol. 4). Chicago: University of Chicago Press.

Sameroff, A. J., & Seifer, R. (1983, April). *Sources of continuity in parent-child relationships.* Paper presented at the meeting of the Society for Research in Child Development, Detroit.

Sameroff, A. J., Seifer, R., Barocas, B., Zax, M., & Greenspan, S. IQ scores of 4-year-old children: Social-environmental risk factors. *Pediatrics,* in press.

Sameroff, A. J., Seifer, R., & Zax, M. (1982). Early development of children at risk for emotional disorder. *Monographs of the Society for Research in Child Development, 47* (7, Serial No. 199).

Stern, D. (1977). *The first relationship: Infant and mother.* Cambridge: Harvard University Press.

Thomas, A., Chess, S., & Birch, H. (1968). *Temperament and behavior disorders in children.* New York: New York University.

Waddington, C. H. (1957). *The strategy of the genes.* London: Allen & Unwin.

Widmayer, S. M., & Field, T. M. (1981). Effects of Brazelton demonstrations for mothers on the development of preterm infants. *Pediatrics, 72,* 711–714.

Winick, M., Meyer, K., & Harris, R. (1975). Malnutrition and environmental enrichment by early adoption. *Science, 190,* 1173–1175.

Zeskind, P. S., & Ramey, C. T. (1978). Fetal malnutrition: An experimental study of its consequences for infant development in two caregiving environments. *Child Development, 49,* 1155–1162.

Zeskind, P. S., & Ramey, C. T. (1981). Preventing intellectual and interactional sequelae of fetal malnutrition: A longitudinal, transactional, and synergistic approach to development. *Child Development, 52,* 213–218.

Zigler, E., & Trickett, P. K. (1978). IQ, social competence, and evaluation of early childhood intervention programs. *American Psychologist, 33,* 789–799.

CHAPTER 12

The Social Ecology of Early Childhood

ALISON CLARKE-STEWART

When Sandy wakes up in the morning the first thing she hears is the doorbell ringing. It's Mrs. Dunn. Sandy bounces out of bed and runs to answer the door. In comes Mrs. Dunn, who, after a quick "Hi, doll!" to Sandy, bustles about the kitchen making breakfast for Sandy and her younger brother, Ben. A few minutes later Mommy and Daddy give Sandy and Ben big hugs and leave for work. Mrs. Dunn feeds the children breakfast, puts Ben in his playpen, cleans up the kitchen, takes out her knitting, and sits down. Sandy plays on the floor near her, chatting occasionally about her dolly and the Care Bears. After an hour or so Ben starts fussing. It's time to change him. Sandy helps Mrs. Dunn. That done, the three go outside and play in the backyard until lunchtime. Mrs. Dunn makes cheese sandwiches for lunch while Sandy sets the table. After lunch it's time for a couple of quick songs and then a nap. Sandy settles down to sleep. Ben needs more attention and keeps Mrs. Dunn busy until Sandy wakes up at 3:30. When Sandy does wake up, Mrs. Dunn sits her in front of the TV cutting up cheese cubes for dinner with a plastic knife. Ben continues to demand Mrs. Dunn's attention, as Sandy dutifully cuts and watches. At 5:30 Mother arrives, laden with groceries. Sandy is glad to see her and cuddles up on her lap while Mother watches the evening news. Mrs. Dunn stays to watch the news, too, and tells Mother about the problems she's had with Ben all afternoon. After Mrs. Dunn leaves, Sandy and Ben play with their Legos while Mother cooks up something to go with the cheese. Daddy arrives just in time to join the rest of the family for dinner. They eat quickly so there will be time for Daddy to give the children their baths and a quick playtime before bed. Sandy falls asleep dreaming of Care Bears and cheese.

Alex stumbles out of bed after his mother calls him three times. "Is it a school day?" he asks. "Yes it is, so hurry up or we'll be late." "I don't want to go to school," Alex grumbles, but he pulls on the clothes his mother has put out for him. "I don't want cereal for breakfast. I want pancakes." "Sorry, no time for pancakes. Come on slowpoke, move that spoon." Mother rushes Alex along through breakfast and into the car. As she drops him at the gate of Merry Montessori Alex is still scowling. He cheers up when he sees his friend Brandon, and the other kids, though. "Time to come in," calls Miss Kelly and rings the bell. The children file in and take their places in the circle. "This afternoon we're going to have a special treat—a puppet show—so I want everyone to work especially hard this morning," says Miss Kelly. Alex knows what that means, and spends the morning working diligently with the counting rods, the modeling clay, and the map puzzles. Brandon helps him with the puzzles. He also helps him cut up cheese for snack. After lunch he and Brandon and the other boys play He-Man in the playyard. And then it's time for the puppet show. Alex is fascinated and sits attentively with all the other children. He can hardly wait to tell his mother when she appears at the gate to pick him up. "Mommy, Mommy, we had a puppet!" "That's nice, dear. Was that how you got so dirty?" Alex's mother waves to Mrs. Turpitz from the gate as she signs Alex out. On the way home they pick up chicken from the Colonel and are already munching when Dad arrives. A new book for Alex has come in the mail from the Junior Book Club, so after dinner Dad reads it to him—three times. Alex gets to play a fast game of Chutes and Ladders with Mom, before she tucks him into bed. "Is tomorrow a school day?" "No—it's Saturday. Want to come to the office with me? You can play on the computer." "Yippie!" And Alex goes to sleep to dream of puppets and 'puters.

Sandy and Alex are modern American 3-year-olds. Their lives reflect common patterns in the contemporary ecology of early childhood. Now, for the first time in the history of the United States, it is just as likely as not that a preschool child will live in a household in which the mother works. Now for the first time it is just as likely as not that a preschooler will be in some kind of group program—a nursery school, day-care center, day-care home, or early intervention program. We have turned a corner in this society as the traditional arrangement for preschool children of care provided exclusively by parents at home, relieved occasionally by visits to friends or relatives, has become the arrangement of a minority of families. In this chapter we begin to explore the implications of this shift in the social ecology of early childhood in this country by describing the various patterns of preschool child care that are common today and how they are related to children's development.

THE STUDY OF CONTEMPORARY CHILD CARE

It is difficult to get exact statistical estimates of the parameters of contemporary child care. For one thing the U.S. Bureau of the Census has not made this a high-priority goal. For another, more important thing, even if the census bureau did make collecting statistics on child-care arrangements a priority, the table necessary to cover the variety of existing arrangements would be exceedingly large. Child care is not simply a question of mother versus "other."

To describe any child's care arrangement it is necessary to specify who the caregiver is (mother, father, grandmother, other relative, neighbor, child-care professional), where the care is provided (child's home, someone else's home, church basement, day-care center, etc.), whether there are other children present (how many, of what ages, etc.), and for how many hours a day the child is there. Because it is common for parents to have put together a complicated package of relatives, neighbors, nursery school, and lessons to cover the time that they are not themselves available to provide child care, it is also necessary in describing a child's care arrangement to consider all the caregivers, settings, and children the child is with over the course of a week. To describe the dynamics of child care in the United States, moreover, it is also necessary to reflect changes from month to month and year to year, because as children get older and as family or child-care circumstances change, any child is likely to experience a number of different arrangements.

Given the complexity of the total child-care picture, it is not surprising that available information about contemporary child care falls far short of reflecting the ecology of early childhood. The information that surveyors have collected is about just three broad categories of child care: care in the child's own home by someone other than mother; care in someone else's home; and care in a center. As a first step in describing the ecology of early childhood, therefore, we in this chapter, too, focus on these three major categories of child care—realizing that such a focus is incomplete and preliminary, and anticipating more complex descriptions in the future.

Our description of the three child-care categories is based not only on data collected by census takers but on observations of the quality of life for preschool children at home, in day-care homes, and in centers made by other researchers and by my students and me. Since 1976, my students and I have observed 150 children 2–4 years old in Chicago, for 10–12 hr each. We recorded their activities and experiences in 2½-hr blocks, twice each in the morning, the afternoon, and at dinnertime—wherever the children were at the time. The observers kept continuous records of the children's ongoing activities in 15-min segments with breaks to fill out checklists at the ends of the segments and of the 2½-hr period. The continuous records included (1) every utterance directed to or made by the child, coded on the spot into the following categories: teaching–explaining, demanding–directing, offering a choice, scolding–reprimanding–criticizing, and responding to a previous utterance or behavior; (2) the occurrence of every incident involving the child of physical contact, physical affection, help, play (cooperative, sociodramatic, with toys), lessons, reading or singing, responding appropriately to a request or demand, exchanging objects, imitation, negative affect, positive affect, and aggression; and (3) the time the child was alone, watching TV, and watching other people. The checklists assessed qualities of the physical environment (messiness, dangerousness, adult decoration, toys and educational equipment and materials) and the social environment (number and kinds of children and adults present).

In addition, background information about each child's mother, father, and caregiver was collected in a number of interviews.

The study was limited to two-parent English-speaking families who were not on welfare and who did not live in areas of Chicago in which it was dangerous for observers to travel at night. They were recruited primarily through churches, doctors, a mailing list (for the *Read-About-Me* books), and a child-care referral network. As a result of our selection, these sources of names, and subjects' willingness to participate, the final sample consisted of families who were predominantly of middle- and professional-class status (about one-quarter were of lower social status) and white (12% were black, 2% Asian, and 1% Hispanic). Approximately one-third of the mothers worked full-time, one-third part time, and one-third were not in the labor force. At the beginning of the study, there were 46 children in the sample who were cared for at home by their mothers, 27 who had a regular daily babysitter in their own homes, 20 who were cared for in someone else's home during the day, and 57 who were in center programs. The children in day care had been in these, their first, child-care arrangements for 3–8 months.

The numbers of children in the sample in different child-care categories reflected our particular interest in variations in center programs rather than in any way representing the usage of various types of child care. In fact, for working mothers, the most common kind of supplementary care for their children is home care (in either their own homes or someone else's). The most recent figures available (U.S. Bureau of the Census, 1982; Kamerman, 1983) indicate that for working mothers of children 2–4 years old, approximately one-third have a sitter who looks after the child in the child's own home, another third use child care in someone else's home, and one-sixth send the child to a center. (The rest juggle their work schedules and conditions so that nonparental child care is not necessary.) In addition, some 10% of mothers who are not in the labor force use some form of child care—while they are in school, doing volunteer or recreational activities, or looking for work. Home child care is relatively more popular for children under 3, from working-class backgrounds, and in intact families; center care is more widely used for children over 3, from middle-class backgrounds, and in single-parent families.

QUALITY OF LIFE IN CHILD-CARE SETTINGS

In-Home Care

On the face of it, in-home care offers many advantages. The hours are flexible; there is no need for the child to travel; the child remains in a familiar, secure place; and the parents are able, to some extent, to monitor the behavior of a caregiver who becomes increasingly well known to them. In-home care keeps siblings together, and the caregiver can provide each child with individual attention.

The in-home caregiver may be the grandmother, an aunt, neighbor, friend, paid sitter, nanny, housekeeper, maid, live-in student, or *au pair.* Most often, particularly if there is an adult female living in the household, it is a relative who provides in-home care. More than half the in-home sitters nationwide are relatives; in our study in Chicago one-fourth of the sitters were unpaid relatives. The sitters we observed were typically older women; about half were over 55. They did not have professional training or high levels of education. They were unlikely to have graduated from high school; only two had taken a course in child development. The physical settings—the children's own homes—were predominantly adult oriented. They had, for example, more different kinds of adult decorative items like plants, musical instruments, television sets, stereos, and vases (19) than different kinds of toys and educational materials for the child (12). They did not usually have specific areas set aside for children's play activities, and there were quite often (7 on the average) dirty, messy, and even potentially dangerous objects accessible—overflowing ashtrays, peeling paint, dirty dishes, broken objects, cleaning supplies, medicines, knives, and so on.

In in-home care the sitters supervised, at most, two children. This offered the children frequent opportunities for one-to-one interaction with an adult, and indeed the amount of caregiver–child interaction (social, verbal, physical, helpful, affectionate, playful, directive, and responsive) in in-home care was significantly greater than was observed in day-care homes or centers (see Table 12.1). It was just as frequent, in fact, as adult–child interaction observed in homes where children were being cared for by their own mothers. The only difference we found between mothers' and sitters' behavior was that mothers did more teaching and sitters did more playing.

Although adult–child interaction was frequent, in-home care offered children limited opportunities to interact with other children. When there was another child present it was usually a younger sibling, offering the child only exchanges with an unskilled playmate with whom he or she would have been able to play anyway. No child in our study was with another youngster who was more than a year older than the child himself. Nor did visits with other children when with the sitter—at home, in the park, at a neighbor's—greatly augment this contact. Children with in-home sitters, on the average, interacted with fewer than two other children during an observation, and they spent significantly less time playing with other children than children in day-care homes, centers, or at home with their mothers.

In in-home settings, the activities the children engaged in were homey rather than schoollike. Activities were likely to be woven around the normal loose routines of a household—infants needing to be fed and changed, lunches prepared, toys cleaned up, and so on. With only one or two children and few real deadlines, sitters had little need to create the structural support that routines and organized activities provide. Indeed it is this homey informality and flexibility, combined with a greater sense of their own control over their child's environment, that makes this child-care arrangement attractive and reassuring

TABLE 12.1. Multivariate Analyses of Variance for Different Child-Care Settings

	Group Means						F Values				
	1		2	3	4	5					
	Dinner										
Observation Variables	Both Parents	Mother	Home with Mother	Home with Sitter	Day-Care Home	Day-Care Center	Overall	1 vs 2	2 vs 3	3 vs 4	4 vs 5
Adult-child social	503	290	391	388	179	168	66.9***	33.4***	<1	23.8***	<1
Adult-group social	7	4	9	5	26	80	131.1***	<1	<1	9.3**	73.3***
Child-child social	49		87	93	153	119	13.8***	16.2**	<1	8.1**	3.1+
Child-group social	2		3	3	9	7	15.5***	<1	<1	15.7***	1.7
Infant-child social	.5		3	.8	2	0	2.7+	10.5***	3.6*	<1	2.9+
Total social	562		493	491	371	375	28.5***	16.0***	<1	10.0***	<1
Adult-child verbal	440	255	345	329	180	233	35.4***	30.2***	<1	15.3***	2.3
Peer-child verbal	42		77	73	130	91	8.9***	16.3***	<1	9.3***	5.0*
Adult-child physical	26	10	16	18	8	13	21.2***	41.1***	<1	11.7***	4.0*
Adult-child help	9	5	7	8	4	6	6.9***	11.0***	<1	7.5**	1.5
Peer-child help	.4		.5	.2	.5	.9	<1				
Adult-child teach	33	20	30	19	9	12	14.6***	1.4	6.1**	2.4	<1
Adult-group teach	2		5	3	4	8	3.6**	1.3	<1	<1	3.7*
Adult-child lesson	17		15	14	26	17	<1				
Adult-group lesson	0		0	0	0	15	8.2***	<1	<1	<1	11.6***
Adult-child read	12	5	9	10	4	43	30.2***	<1	<1	<1	44.4***
Adult-child verbal demand	68	40	51	50	36	48	7.4***	21.0***	<1	3.1+	3.0+
Adult directiveness	.16	.16	.17	.17	.23	.22	16.4***	<1	<1	9.3**	<1
Adult-child control	48	28	36	38	29	39	5.2***	17.6***	<1	1.7	2.9*
Adult-child choice	19	10	17	15	14	6	24.5***	2.1	<1	<1	8.5**
Adult-child verbal response	233		185	159	65	96	41.3***	20.2***	2.7+	16.1***	2.1
Adult responsiveness	.54	.54	.51	.46	.37	.41	25.8***	<1	8.2**	8.3**	1.8

(continued)

TABLE 12.1. (*continued*)

Observation Variables	Group Means						F Values				
	1		2	3	4	5					
	Dinner										
	Both Parents	Mother	Home with Mother	Home with Sitter	Day-Care Home	Day-Care Center	Overall	1 vs 2	2 vs 3	3 vs 4	4 vs 5
Peer responsiveness	.16		.22	.26	.31	.32	16.2***	8.6**	1.9	1.6	<1
Peer–child verbal response	17		31	34	46	34	7.1***	12.5***	<1	2.0	2.2
Adult appropriateness	.47	.48	.51	.73	.58	.72	4.9***	<1	5.4*	1.1	<1
Positive affect	95		92	82	75	79	3.6***	<1	1.4	<1	<1
Negative affect	27		22	23	11	16	6.0***	3.4+	<1	5.1*	1.3
Adult–child play	30	10	27	65	28	6	9.9***	<1	16.9***	6.9**	2.7+
Child–child play	21		53	19	73	53	4.8***	12.7***	6.9**	7.6**	1.2
Group play	5		13	19	24	47	9.0***	2.0	<1	1.3	3.5*
Adult–child affection	3	2	2	2	0	1	9.1***	5.5*	<1	6.1**	2.3
Child alone in room	79		132	100	65	2	31.0***	30.7***	5.2*	2.9+	11.6***
Child watches peers	10		12	12	48	51	39.9***	<1	<1	19.1***	<1
Child alone with object	96		140	146	138	122	5.5***	19.9***	<1	<1	<1
Child–child aggression	1.2		1.8	2.1	2.8	3.4	10.1***	2.6+	<1	<1	<1
Child watches TV alone	58		65	79	50	0	14.8***	2.4	<1	2.4	9.0***
Child–child physical	3		4	2	11	11	24.6***	<1	1.5	22.2***	<1
Adult informativeness	.07	.08	.08	.05	.06	.08	3.8**	1.2	12.7***	<1	1.9

+$p < .10$
*$p < .05$
**$p < .01$
***$p < .001$

to parents. Unfortunately, no other studies are available with which to compare these results, since this form of care as a distinct category has not been assessed before.

Day-Care Homes

The second broad child-care category is care in someone else's home. This day-care home may be licensed or unlicensed; the caregiver may be related or unrelated, trained or untrained. The number of children may range from 1 to 6 in a family day-care home or 6 to 12 in a group day-care home. The arrangement may be based on an informal agreement between friends or, much less often, on a highly formal, supervised network of facilities that are satellites of a center.

Day-care homes, like in-home care, offer the child a high degree of continuity. The home is usually located near the child's home, in a familiar neighborhood, where people are likely to share the parents' values and circumstances. As she can with an in-home sitter, the mother can give the day-care home caregiver instructions about special care and individual attention for her child, especially when there are problems or illnesses at home. The homey setting is a familiar one for the child with few new rules and routines and without the difficulty of adapting to a large group of children.

The National Day Care Home Study (Fosburg et al., 1980), which included 305 day-care homes in 25 cities, presented the following picture of life in this form of care. Nearly all day-care homes provided full-day care, including lunch and snacks. Most had only one to three children in care at one time (most in the age range of 18–36 months); in nearly half, the children included one of the provider's own. The typical provider was married, in her thirties, a high school graduate with 6 years of home day-care experience. Her husband was stably employed and made a comfortable income. She was providing child care because she was fond of children as well as for the money. On the average, the provider spent about half her time involved with the children and the rest of the time on housework or personal activities.

In our study in Chicago, also, the women who provided child care in their homes were in their thirties (average age = 36). They were unlikely to have had professional experience in child care. They did have more education than the in-home sitters we observed (most had taken some college-level courses and half had taken at least one course in child development), but their level of education was still significantly below that of teachers in center programs. Although it is common for home day care to be provided by a relative, this was not the case in our study; only one day-care home provider was a relative and only two were unpaid.

The day-care homes we observed were identical to children's own homes in their messiness and dangerousness, variety of toys and materials, and predominance of adult decorations. At first glance this may be surprising; one might expect that a facility used for the *business* of providing child care would be more child centered than children's own homes. But a day-care home is fundamentally a home, even when it is stretched to take in more children or to provide a service for a fee. It functions as a home for the family who lives there, and most day-care providers, even those who are doing it for profit, strive to incorporate their young charges into their own families' routines, rather than making child care a career and their home an institution.

The main way in which day-care homes are different from children's own homes is in the social milieu they provide. In the typical day-care home in our study there were five children, and the child we were observing interacted with all of them. Thus day-care homes provide significantly more varied opportunities than in-home care for interaction with different children. These children represented a mix of racial, ethnic, and social-class backgrounds—but they were all young. None of the day-care homes in which we observed had children more than a year older than the child in the study, so children's encounters were, as in in-home care, limited to those with relatively unskilled playmates.

Children in day-care homes spent significantly more time interacting with peers than did children in in-home care with mothers or babysitters (see Table 12.1)—playing, touching, imitating, talking, or just watching—and less time interacting with adults—talking, touching, being helped or directed. In day-care homes, as was not the case for other settings, children interacted as much with other children as they did with adults. Children in day-care homes also were more likely than children in other settings to interact with the caregiver as part of a group of children, whereas children with in-home caregivers had more one-to-one exchanges with the adult. Verbalizations from the caregiver to the child in day-care homes were not only less frequent overall, they were more likely to be directive, whereas those from in-home caregivers were more likely to be responsive. Compared to the experience in day-care centers, children in day-care homes interacted more with infants, had more physical contact and play with the adult, were offered more choices by the caregiver, and spent more time alone and watching TV.

Few other observations have been made comparing the experiences of children in day-care homes with those of children at home with their mothers or in day-care centers. Two studies (Rubenstein, Pedersen, & Yarrow, 1977; Siegel-Gorelik, Everson, & Ambron, 1980) suggest that at-home mothers are more emotional and sociable with their infants and young children and their children are more sociable with them than is observed with caregivers in day-care homes. We, too, observed more adult sociability (physical, affectionate, verbal, helpful, informative, responsive) at home than in day-care homes—but we found this was true whether the home caregiver was a sitter or the mother. Two studies have compared children's experiences in day-care homes and in centers. With younger toddlers, Howes (1983) did not observe differences in the caregivers' or children's behavior. But Prescott (1973), as in our study, found day-care homes to provide preschoolers with more positive adult input, more time alone, and more opportunities to make choices than center programs.

Centers

Center child care—in nursery schools and day-care centers—is the most visible and easily identified form of supplementary child care today. A center may provide care for fewer than 15 children or more than 300, but, on the average, in the United States centers serve about 50 children. In our study the average center size was 70. The average class size was 17. The typical head teacher in the centers we observed, like the day-care home providers, was in her thirties (average age = 33), but there the similarity ended. These women were child-care professionals. All were college graduates and over 90% had had formal training in child development at college. They had been in their present jobs an average of 3 years. The physical settings in the centers we observed were neat and orderly, free of hazards, with only a couple of messy features per setting—significantly better than the home-care settings on these dimensions. Centers had more different toys and educational materials (19) than either day-care homes (12) or children's own homes (12) and more toys and educational materials than adult decorative items (12).

In centers, children were exposed to at least three different adults, and instead of a lone sibling or a handful of fellow toddlers to play with, there was a large group of children, 10 of whom our children were observed to interact with, on the average, during each 2-hr observation. Children in centers participated in one-to-one interaction with an adult as frequently as children in day-care homes did, but only half as frequently as children with sitters or mothers at home. On the other hand, they participated in group activities with the teacher—listening to the teacher read, talk, or teach—3 times as much as children in day-care homes and 10 times as much as children in their own homes. Despite the substantial amount of peer interaction, even in centers children interacted more with adults than they did with other children (see also Finkelstein, Dent, Gallacher, & Ramey, 1978). In centers, proportionately more of the teachers' interactions with the children were responsive and proportionately fewer offered the children choices than interactions with the day-care home providers, but otherwise no difference was observed in the quality or nature of adult–child interaction in the two settings. Center children had more frequent and varied interactions with other different children—playing, helping, watching, learning, fighting—than children with sitters at home, but in overall amount of time spent interacting with another child they did not differ from these children. The children with whom they interacted, however, included some who were older, who could offer them more socially mature playmates and models, and represented a wider range of ethnic and social-class backgrounds. Center programs were more likely than home care of any kind to have scheduled activities, clearly defined play areas with associated routines, and a specific curriculum like "traditional nursery school," "open education," "Piagetian," or "Montessori." Center programs were evaluated by our observers and by the caregivers themselves as offering children more opportunities for education, interaction, and socialization than home-care programs.

Other research (Golden et al., 1978; Howes, 1983) confirms the obvious finding that center programs are larger than home day-care programs (more children and adults), more child oriented (more spaces specifically designed for children), and more educational (more toys and equipment, caregivers better trained). As for the teachers' behavior, Howes's results parallel our finding that center teachers were more likely than home providers to respond to children's requests but otherwise were not discriminably different.

In comparing the behavior of center teachers and mothers of preschoolers, other researchers have found that mothers are more interactive, emotional, explicit, conversational, participative, controlling, and likely to offer children choices, whereas teachers are more cognitively demanding, indirect, flexible, responsive, and elaborative (Cochran, 1977; Gunnarsson, 1977; Hess, Price, Dickson, & Conroy, 1981; Prescott, 1973; Tizard, Carmichael, Hughes, & Pinkerton, 1980; Tizard, Pinkerton, & Carmichael, 1982). Our findings complement these showing that mothers were more emotional, playful, affectionate, sociable, and conversational with their children and gave them more directions and choices, whereas teachers were more likely to be responsive. Otherwise the only differences we observed between teachers and mothers were not qualitative but situational—teachers interacted relatively more with the children in groups.

Quality of Life at Home

Children in in-home care, day-care homes, and centers thus have distinctly different experiences during the day. But what about at night and on weekends? This is part of the children's ecology too. Often forgotten in discussions of child care is the fact that children in full-time alternative care for 40 hr a week spend an equal amount of awake time *not* in day care, presumably with their families. This time is important, too. What are preschool children's experiences during this part of their lives?

To answer this question we analyzed the observations made of all the children in our sample at home with their families at dinnertime. Compared to all other situations—at home with mother during the day or with a sitter, in a day-care home, or in a center—at home at night with their mothers, fathers, and siblings, children had the least one-to-one interaction with other children and the most interaction with adults, including talking, touching, hugging and kissing, helping, teaching, directing, giving choices, and responding. There was more positive and negative affect expressed and children were least likely to spend their time playing alone with objects. These differences held up even for the children who were home with their mothers during the day.

Why the increase in adult–child interaction at dinnertime? Did mothers, relieved by having another adult, the father, present, spring into action in the evening? Because there was likely to be another adult present during the daytime observation as well, it apparently was not just the presence of another adult. Was it that the emotional support the father offered energized the mother and she became more interactive? No—mothers did less reading, playing, talking, directing, and giving orders to the child in the evening observations than they did, if they were with the child, during the day. Was it, then, the fathers themselves who made the difference? Clearly this was an important contributor. Although for no kind of interaction was the father's level at night as high as the mother's during the day, and for only two (playing and reading) was it as high as hers during the evening, clearly the active participation by *both* parents in interactions at dinnertime added up to a grander total. Another contributor, however, was the presence—or lack of it—of other children. Highly significant differences in the dinnertime experiences were related to whether the child had siblings. Children with no siblings interacted with their parents significantly more than children with siblings (561 vs. 351); children with siblings interacted significantly more with other children (82 vs. 40). The general lack of peer companionship at home at night allowed, encouraged—or perhaps required—the adults to interact more with the children at dinnertime than during the day.

But were evening experiences the same for all children regardless of where they spent their days? It has been suggested that working mothers compensate for their time away from the child during the day with an extra dose of "quality" time at night. Does this happen? Certainly not according to our data. Differences at dinnertime between families in which mothers had been taking care of the children all day and families in which they had not were extremely few, and certainly did not support the belief that working mothers are more active. There were no significant differences favoring the mothers who used any form of day care. There was a hint that fathers in families with working mothers were more participative: Fathers of children in center programs full time were more likely to teach and read to their children than fathers whose wives were home all day. But these differences were not found consistently among all users of day care.

The major difference in preschool children's experiences then would seem to be what happens to them during the day—experiences ranging from solitary involvement with toys while a sitter does housework to participation in play with a group of rowdy peers. What implications do these differences in daily experience have for children's development?

CHILD CARE AND CHILD DEVELOPMENT

Measures of Child Development

Home day care has been touted as offering the child the advantages of mixed-age contacts, a homey environment, a caregiver with similar values to the mother's, and the opportunity to see an adult carry out multiple, real-life tasks, not just child-oriented activities (Belsky, Steinberg, & Walker, 1982). Are these really advantages? To answer this question, in our Chicago study, we invited each child and his or her mother to come to the university for a series of standard tests and observations, and we also observed each child in standard situations at home. When the data from all these tests and observations were compiled and analyzed a set of eight measures that seemed to reflect important developmental competencies resulted. These are summarized in Table 12.2. On all these measures (except negative behavior to the peer), we found that older children scored higher than younger children, suggesting that the measures did indeed index developmental competence. They were also related in reasonable ways to children's behavior in the natural observations. Children who scored high on cognitive and social-cognitive tests and in the encounters with adult strangers were more verbal and compliant and less demanding, aggressive, and physical in the observations at dinner and during the day. Children who stayed closer to their mothers in the laboratory were more demanding and compliant and initiated more physical contact with their mothers at home. Children who were high in social reciprocity with their mothers were verbal and demanding. Children high in social interaction with the unfamiliar peer (both positive and negative) were outgoing—in both positive (verbal) and negative (aggressive, demanding, noncompliant) ways at dinner and during the day.

Group Differences in Child Development

When we compared these measures for children in different forms of child care, there were strong differences related to the form of child care (details of these analyses and results can be found in Clarke-Stewart, 1984; Clarke-

TABLE 12.2. Measures of Child Development

Proximity to mother: How close the child stayed to mother in our testing sessions at the university.

Social reciprocity with mother: How positive, reciprocal, cooperative, and empathic the child's interactions with mother were in our testing sessions (which included periods of free play and specific tasks meant to measure mother–child interaction).

Social knowledge: How well the child could take the perspective of another person (e.g., knowing what the other person is thinking or what a picture looks like to another person), and how much the child knew about emotional words and situations and about what is gender-appropriate behavior for boys and girls.

Sociability with adult stranger: How friendly, cooperative, sympathetic, helpful, trusting, and likable the child was with an unfamiliar adult examiner.

Sociability with an unfamiliar peer: How much positive interaction—talking, playing, cooperating—the child engaged in with an unfamiliar child of the same age and sex and in the same form of day care, during the testing session at the university.

Negative behavior to the peer: How much the child engaged in negative behavior with this unfamiliar child—taking away toys, controlling his or her actions, offering insults, refusing to cooperate, withdrawing from or avoiding the other child. (Hitting did not occur.)

Social competence at home: How obedient, self-confident, sociable, autonomous, assertive, playful, and cheerful the child was at home during the dinnertime observation.

Cognitive ability: How well the child did on standard tests of language comprehension, verbal fluency, knowledge of concepts, and memory span.

Stewart & Gruber, 1984). Children attending center programs scored consistently higher across the board, but especially higher on assessments of cognitive ability, social knowledge, and sociability with the adult stranger. (In terms of developmental differences, these children were 6 to 9 months advanced over children in home care.) Children in day-care homes had the distinction of scoring highest on sociability with the unfamiliar peer and proximity to the mother. Least advanced were children with mothers or sitters in their own homes.

Thus we see that the general categories of child care we observed were associated with sensible patterns of competence in children: The educational orientation of the center programs was reflected in children's advanced cognition and adult-oriented competence. Children from day-care homes, who had less familiarity than center children with an "institutional" setting, stayed closer to their mothers in our university setting, but, going along with their opportunity for intimate social interaction with agemates, played more comfortably, cooperatively, and actively with an unfamiliar peer than children at home with mother or sitter. Children with untrained adults in their own home, with, at most, one other child, who was usually younger, and with no educational program, did not excel in any domain of competence. These associations between development and experience are supported by the results of other research (extensively reviewed by Clarke-Stewart & Fein, 1983) showing that the development of children in nursery schools and day-care centers is advanced over that of children who do not participate in such programs.

Individual Differences in Development

The associations between child care and development were tested in more detail, next, by analyzing correlationally how the development of individual children was related to features of their particular child-care settings. This was done separately for children in home and center programs (see Tables 12.3, 12.4, 12.5, and other analyses in Clarke-Stewart & Gruber, 1984).

Developmental Differences in Home Settings

In the home settings, significant differences in children's development were found to be related to what other people were present, what they did with the child, and how the physical environment was arranged. There was no relation between children's competence and the amount of formal training in child development the caregiver had, but children generally did better on our assessments when the caregiver was more highly educated, knew more about child development, and interacted more frequently with the child. In home-care settings with other children present, positive relations were found between children's intellectual and social competence with peers and adult strangers and the frequency of one-to-one conversation with the caregiver and how much she touched, read to, and gave directions to the child. Children were also more

TABLE 12.3. Correlations Between Measures of Child Development and Experience in Daytime Home Settings with Children Present

	Child Development Measures									
			Sociability to Stranger							
Observation Variables	Cognition	Social Cognition	Lab	Home	Proximity to Mother	Reciprocity with Mother	Positive to Peer	Negative to Peer	Positive to Friend	Dinner-time Compe-tence
Adult–child social				.25**			.21*			
Child–child social							−.20*	.19*		
Infant–child social		−.23*			.33**	−.35***				
Adult–group social				−.22**						
Adult–child verbal	.20*			.24**			.22*			
Child–child verbal								.21*		
Adult–child physical				.23*						
Child–child physical										
Adult–child affection										
Group social						−.27**	−.24*	.20	.20*	
Adult–child help	−.34**	−.28**								−.24*
Child–child help				−.19*					.18	−.26*
Adult–child play									−.20*	
Child–child play										
Adult–child teach							.25*	−.24*	−.25*	
Adult informativeness			.27	−.28	−.30***	−.20*				

Adult–child read	.34***									.22*
Adult–child verbal demand			.21*	−.18		.23*				
Adult–directiveness	−.22*									
Adult–child control				.20*	−.19*		.22*			
Adult–child choice										
Adult responsiveness	.36***					.31**		−.23*		
Peer responsiveness										
Adult appropriateness										.17
Positive affect						.26**		−.23*		
Negative affect		−.18								
Child alone in room			−.17							
Child watches TV alone										
Child watches peers	−.18			−.20*						−.17
Child–child aggression		−.21*		−.22*						
Child alone with object	−.21*			−.22	.17					
Group play					.17	−.37***			.24*	−.24*
Child imitates peer						−.18	−.20*			−.24*
Adult–child group lesson				−.27**						
Child–child cooperative play					−.19					
Child–child dramatic play									.20*	

All r's significant at $p < .10$ shown; analyses done with child's age controlled.
*$p < .05$
**$p < .01$
***$p < .001$

TABLE 12.4. Correlations Between Measures of Child Development and Experience in Daytime Home Settings with No Other Children Present

	Child Development Measures									
			Sociability to Stranger							
Observation Variables	Cognition	Social Cognition	Lab	Home	Proximity to Mother	Reciprocity with Mother	Positive to Peer	Negative to Peer	Positive to Friend	Dinner-time Competence
Adult–child social	−.26									
Adult–child verbal	−.20									
Adult–child physical							−.30*			
Adult–child affection										
Adult–child help	−.26	−.54***	−.40**				.29			
Adult–child play										
Adult–child teach	−.34*				−.25					
Adult informativeness			.27		−.27				−.30*	
Adult–child read										.33*
Adult directiveness		−.45**							−.47**	
Adult–child control	−.28	−.46**							−.38*	−.40**
Adult–child choice									.27	
Adult responsiveness		.26	.37*				.33*			
Adult appropriateness										.17
Positive affect	−.40**									
Negative affect	−.35*	−.41**			−.25					
Child alone in room										
Child watches TV alone										
Child alone with object										
Adult–child group lesson										

All r's significant at $p < .10$ shown; age controlled.
*$p < .05$
**$p < .01$
***$p < .001$

TABLE 12.5. Correlations Between Measures of Child Development and Experience in Day-Care Centers

	Child Development Measures									
			Sociability to Stranger							
Observation Variables	Cognition	Social Cognition	Lab	Home	Proximity to Mother	Reciprocity with Mother	Positive to Peer	Negative to Peer	Positive to Friend	Dinner-time Compe-tence
Adult–child social				−.23*				−.20		
Child–child social						.22*				
Child–group social	−.19			−.19	.19		−.22*			
Adult–group social										
Adult–child verbal						−.19		−.24*		
Child–child verbal										
Adult–child physical	−.34**	−.31**		−.40**		−.24*		−.18	−.22	
Child–child physical										
Adult–child affection	−.28**		−.28**	−.40**			.27**			
Group play						−.20				
Adult–child help		−.38**								
Child–child help			.19		−.21					
Adult–child play										
Child–child play					.20*		−.26*			.51***
Adult–child teach						−.26*		−.26*		
Adult informativeness					−.24*			−.24*		
Adult–child read	.18					−.21				
Adult–child verbal demand	−.19			−.21*	−.19		.20	−.27**	−.18	
Adult directiveness			−.19			.27**				

(continued)

TABLE 12.5 ***(continued)***

	Child Development Measures									
			Sociability to Stranger							
Observation Variables	Cognition	Social Cognition	Lab	Home	Proximity to Mother	Reciprocity with Mother	Positive to Peer	Negative to Peer	Positive to Friend	Dinner-time Compe-tence
Adult–child control	−.24*			−.23*			.20	−.19		
Adult–child choice	.20*		−.22*		.25*					
Adult responsiveness										
Peer responsiveness	.20				−.25*	.24*	.19			
Adult appropriateness	.41***					−.56**	−.28*			
Positive affect	−.19			−.25*		.32**				
Negative affect	−.23*		−.24*				−.27**			
Child alone in room	.18			.18			−.21		.35**	
Child watches TV alone										
Child watches peers						.28*	.24*			
Child–child aggression	−.23*	−.27*					.19	.21*		
Child alone with object	.34**	.26*	.18							
Child imitates peer		−.29**		−.19				−.27*	.27**	−.32**
Adult–child group lesson		−.29**						−.28**	.25*	
Child–child cooperative play							−.24*			.48***
Child–child dramatic play			.22*	.19		.28*	.19	.20		

All *r*'s significant at $p < .10$ shown; age controlled.
$^{*}p < .05$
$^{**}p < .01$
$^{***}p < .001$

competent when the quality of these interactions with the caregiver was more responsive, informative, and nondirective. The number and kinds of other children who were present in the home day-care setting also were related to how competent children were. Children generally did better on our assessments of social knowledge and social competence when neither too few (no other children) nor too many (more than five) children were present, when these children did not include infants and younger toddlers, and when interaction with the other children was not all the child spent his or her time on. Children who spent more time interacting with, imitating, or simply watching other children, especially groups of children, or whom the caregiver interacted with more as part of a group, did more poorly on our tests of competence in the laboratory, especially social competence with the unfamiliar peer (whom they treated less positively and more negatively).

Children's relationships with their mothers were also related to their child-care experiences. Children whose interactions with their mothers were positive, reciprocal, and cooperative spent less of their time playing with groups of other children, an infant, or toys, and the caregiver's interactions with them, although not more frequent, were more positive and responsive. These relations held up when children in the care of caregivers other than their own mothers during the day were analyzed separately. Children who stayed physically close to their mothers in our laboratory assessment played more with other children and objects and were the recipients of less teaching, directing, and controlling from their caregivers, particularly their mothers.

Finally, how the physical environment in the home was organized was related to our measures of children's competence. Children were developmentally advanced when the home was neat and orderly, was organized around their activities, and contained fewer adult-oriented decorative items (with perhaps less need for restrictions—"Stay away from that plant," "Don't touch that vase!"). Just providing more different toys was not in itself helpful, however, and, in fact, when children spent more time playing alone with toys and objects rather than interacting with the caregiver they did more *poorly* in our assessments of competence. The more time children spent alone in the room, also, the worse they did, but how much time children spent watching TV during our observations was not related to their competence.

These relations are generally supported by the handful of available studies of children in day-care homes. Such studies find that the quality of care and children's development are better in those day-care homes where the provider has a professional self-concept, is knowledgeable about child development, and is able to interact well with the children, where the number of children is small, and where the physical environment is suitable for children's activities (Espinosa, 1980; Fosburg et al., 1980; Howes, 1983; Howes & Rubenstein, 1981; Kagan, Fargo, Rauch, & Crowell, 1977). The research on home-reared children's development (reviewed by Clarke-Stewart, 1977, 1979; Wachs & Gruen, 1982), similarly, reveals relations between development and the following factors: mother's level of education and knowledge about children; verbal, responsive, informative, and nonauthoritarian interaction with parents; a smaller number of children in the family; and a physical environment that is not crowded, restrictive, or chaotic.

The associations between child care and development that we have just described appeared in the present study in analyses done for children in home settings where other children were present. Surprisingly, removing other children from the setting did not simply increase the correlation between the development of competence and the caregiver's behavior. Consistent with the observations in the multichild settings, the *quality* of the caregiver's interactions with more competent children was more responsive, informative and accepting. But the *quantity* of the caregiver's interaction—social, verbal, emotional, helping, teaching, directing, controlling—when no other children were around was related to less rather than more competence in the child. Because the overall amount of caregiver-child interaction when there was only one child present was higher than when there was more than one child, perhaps the high level of caregiver interaction got to the point of being too much. Or perhaps the difference in correlational patterns simply underscores the substantial differences between social situations in which there are pairs of people and those in which there are groups. Further studies and analyses are necessary to follow up this finding.

Not only were associations between children's competence and caregiver's behavior observed in the daytime observations, but the present study also revealed associations between children's developmental competence and their experiences at home at dinnertime (Table 12.6). More competent children (high on cognitive and social-cognitive tests and sociable in their interaction with adult strangers) experienced less interaction with their mothers at dinnertime than less competent children, but these interactions were more likely to be affectionate, positive, accepting, and responsive, to offer choices and songs and stories, not physical contact, and to involve the whole family, not just the mother-child dyad. Competent children spent more time alone, more time interacting with their fathers, and more time interacting with the whole family. Children who demonstrated socially reciprocal interactions with their mothers in our laboratory assessments spent more time interacting with them—and with their fathers—at dinnertime in playful, positive, sociable, nondirective, and physical ways. Children who were positive with a peer in the laboratory had mothers who at dinnertime talked, taught, and read, but were not physical with them. These children also had the opportunity to interact with other children; they spent more time interacting, watching, and even fighting with peers and less time with infants or toys. Children who were negative with the peer in the laboratory, too, spent more time playing with other children and their mothers at home at dinnertime and less time with toys, but their interactions with their fathers were more likely to be physical and directive, and although they played with other children they were less likely to touch them.

TABLE 12.6. Correlations Between Measures of Child Development and Experience at Home at Dinnertime

Observation Variables	Child Development Measures								
		Social Cognition							
	Cognition	Lab	Home	Sociability to Stranger	Proximity to Mother	Reciprocity with Mother	Positive to Peer	Negative to Peer	Positive to Friend
Mother–child social	−.23***		−.12*	−.11		.18**		.17**	
Father–child social	.10								
Child–child social							.13*		
Infant–child social					.18**		−.18**		
Mother–group social	.15**	.14*				.15*			
Father–group social	.15**		.12			.12		−.11	
Mother–child verbal	−.22***		−.11	−.11		.18**	.11	.17**	
Father–child verbal	.12*								
Child–child verbal			.10				.14*		.11
Mother–child physical	−.22***	−.14*							
Father–child physical									
Child–child physical					.14*			−.10	
Mother–child affection				.20**	.11			.19**	
Father–child affection									
Mother physicalness	−.16**	−.22**	−.16*		.22***	.13*	−.15*		
Father physicalness	−.13*							.15*	
Mother–child help	−.25***	−.20***		−.11				.19**	
Father–child help									
Child–child help						−.20**	.17**		
Mother–child play						.20***			
Father–child play						.10			
Child–child play		.14*	.10					.21**	
Mother–child teach	−.13*			−.11			.13*		
Father–child teach	.12					−.14*			−.16**
Mother informativeness							.13*		−.17**
Father informativeness						−.11	−.14*		
Mother–child read	.11	.11		.12		.13	.11	.24***	

(continued)

TABLE 12.6. ***(continued)***

Observation Variables	Child Development Measures								
		Social Cognition							
	Cognition	Lab	Home	Sociability to Stranger	Proximity to Mother	Reciprocity with Mother	Positive to Peer	Negative to Peer	Positive to Friend
Father–child read	.14*				−.14*				
Mother–child verbal demand	−.38***	−.20***	−.15*	−.14*	−.15*	−.14*		.12	
Father–child verbal demand				.14*		−.14*			−.13*
Mother directiveness	−.17**	−.18**				−.14*			
Father directiveness	−.13*	−.14*						.11	−.12*
Mother–child control	−.36***	−.23***	−.16*	−.13*	−.12			.14*	
Father–child control				.14*		−.12			
Mother–child choice		.12*				.14*			
Father–child choice									
Mother responsiveness	.18**					.19**	.12		
Father responsiveness									
Peer responsiveness									
Mother appropriateness					.18**	.15*	−.13*		
Father appropriateness									
Positive affect						.20**			
Negative affect	−.14*	−.15*		−.15*			.13*		
Child alone in room			.17**		−.13*				
Child watches TV alone									
Child watches peers				−.11			.13*		
Child–child aggression							.14*		
Child alone with object			−.16*	−.17**	−.14*	−.23***	−.11	−.14*	

All r's significant at $p < .10$ shown; age controlled.
$^{*}p < .05$
$^{**}p < .01$
$^{***}p < .001$

Developmental Differences in Center Settings

A salient theme that seems to emerge from the associations observed in home settings, during the daytime and at dinner, in the child's own home or another's, is that there are benefits for the preschool child to be gained from having more people around—be it father or other children—rather than just a solitary caregiving adult and a lone child. In centers there is never a solitary caregiver and a lone child. In centers the danger is having too many people, not too few. In general, in our study, children in large classes and in large centers with heterogeneous mixes of children, including larger numbers of younger children in their classes (like children in crowded day-care homes), did more poorly on the tests of competence. The only advantage of size was that these children were less likely to behave negatively toward the unfamiliar peer—perhaps because such behavior was not allowed in more crowded classrooms. A parallel advantage was related to having a large number of children per teacher: Children in classes with more children per teacher were more cooperative with peers and adults in our assessments. As in home care, children in center programs who spent more (too much) of their time playing with the classmates were less sociable with the unfamiliar peer. But if their classmates were responsive and older, and set a mature model that children could watch, or played with the child at a more sophisticated level (e.g., dramatic play), then children were advanced in cognitive and social competence. Not surprisingly, children whose interchanges with their classmates were more aggressive and negative were less competent in our tests.

As far as the qualifications and training of the caregivers went, results were mixed. When the teacher was older, had been in the center longer, was more highly trained in child development, and more knowledgeable about child development, children scored higher on tests of cognitive abilities. But they were less independent of their mothers and less sociable with peers, parents, and adult strangers. Being more socially competent was related to the teacher's having a higher level of overall education but less academic training specifically in child development—a provocative finding, suggesting that a narrowly focused academic training may be facilitative of youngsters' academic intellectual skills at the expense of their social skills. Children's cognitive skills were advanced in day-care centers in which the teacher read to the children, offered them choices, and encouraged them to manipulate materials on their own. The number of explanatory informative utterances and the time the teacher spent actually giving lessons were not related to children's cognitive skills, but children who heard more explanatory utterances and received more directions from the teacher were more competent with the peer. This suggests that perhaps the instruction the children got in their day-care classes was about how to get along with peers rather than about what comes before 7 or after C. The effects of teacher directiveness were not uniformly positive, however. The more the teacher directed, demanded, controlled, and punished children, the worse they performed on our tests of cognition and of cooperation with adult strangers. Children who were more competent in these tests attended programs where they were given freedom to learn in a safe, orderly environment, with stimulating toys, decorations, and educational materials, appropriately organized into activity areas, and where teachers did not spend as much time hugging, holding, or helping them.

The child's relationship with mother was also, to some extent, related to experiences in the center. Children with the best relationship with their mothers had less interaction with the teacher (touching, talking, teaching, or reading) but spent more time happily interacting with and watching other children.

Previous research has revealed positive associations between preschool children's cognitive competence and the following: caregivers' training in child development, moderately structured (i.e., teacher directed), intellectually demanding experiences in the program, and the presence of a relatively small group of children (Connolly & Smith, 1978; Johnson, Ershler, & Bell, 1980; McCartney, 1984; Miller & Dyer, 1975; Ruopp, Travers, Glantz, & Coelen, 1979; Rubenstein & Howes, 1983; Sylva, Roy, & Painter, 1980; Tizard et al., 1982; Tizard, Philips, & Plewis, 1976). Advantages for peer interaction have been associated with teacher direction, fantasy play, small groups, older children, and well-organized play spaces (Beller, Litwok, & Sullivan, undated; Field, 1980; Howes, 1983; Huston-Stein, Friedrich-Cofer, & Susman, 1977; Smith, Dalgleish, & Herzmark, 1981). These findings are consistent with ours. So is the finding from the National Day Care Study (Ruopp, Travers, Glantz, & Coelen, 1979) that a low adult-child ratio—that supposed sine qua non of "high-quality" child care—is not necessarily a predictor of better outcomes for preschool children.

LOOKING FORWARD

Even bolstered by these generally supportive findings from other studies, the present study and the analyses reported here are only a small step in the direction of describing—and someday understanding—the social ecology of early childhood. We have many studies and analyses to go before we can fit all the pieces of this very complex domain into a coherent picture. The effort, however, is not only necessary but well worth it, to provide a document of our life and times and an extension of our knowledge of the multitudinous, subtle, and complicated influences on children's development in the preschool years.

REFERENCES

Beller, E. K., Litwok, E., & Sullivan, K. (undated). *An observational study of interaction in day care.* Unpublished manuscript, Temple University.

Belsky, J., Steinberg, L. D., & Walker, A. (1982). The ecology of day care. In M. E. Lamb (Ed.), *Childrearing in nontraditional families.* Hillsdale, NJ: Erlbaum.

Clarke-Stewart, K. A. (1977). *Child care in the family: A review of research and some propositions for policy.* New York: Academic Press.

Clarke-Stewart, K. A. (1979). Evaluating parental effects on child development. In L. Shulman (Ed.), *Review of research in education* (Vol. 6). Itasca, IL: F. E. Peacock.

Clarke-Stewart, K. A. (1984). Day care: A new context for research and development. In M. Perlmutter (Ed.), *The Minnesota Symposium on Child Psychology* (Vol. 17). Hillsdale, NJ: Erlbaum.

Clarke-Stewart, K. A., & Fein, G. G. (1983). Early childhood programs. In P. H. Mussen (Ed.), *Handbook of child psychology: Vol. 2. Infancy and developmental psychobiology.* New York: Wiley.

Clarke-Stewart, K. A., & Gruber, C. (1984). Day care forms and features. In R. C. Ainslie (Ed.), *The child and the day care setting.* New York: Praeger Special Studies.

Cochran, M. M. (1977). A comparison of group day and family child-rearing patterns in Sweden. *Child Development, 48,* 702–707.

Connolly, K. J., & Smith, P. K. (1978). Experimental studies of the preschool environment. *International Journal of Early Childhood, 10,* 86–95.

Espinosa, L. (1980). *An ecological study of family day care.* Unpublished doctoral dissertation, University of Chicago.

Field, T. M. (1980). Preschool play: Effects of teacher/child ratios and organization of classroom space. *Child Study Journal, 10,* 191–205.

Finkelstein, N. W., Dent, C., Gallacher, K., & Ramey, C. T. (1978). Social behavior of infants and toddlers in a day-care environment. *Developmental Psychology, 14,* 257–262.

Fosburg, S., Hawkins, P. D., Singer, J. D., Goodson, B. D., Smith, J. M., & Brush, L. R. (1980). *National Day Care Home Study* (Contract No. HEW 105-77-1051). Cambridge, MA: Abt Associates.

Golden, M., Rosenbluth, L., Grossi, M. T., Policare, H. J., Freeman, H., Jr., & Brownlee, E. M. (1978). *The New York City Infant Day Care Study.* New York: Medical and Health Research Association of New York City.

Gunnarsson, L. (1977). *The Swedish childrearing study: A longitudinal study of children in different childrearing environments—First follow-up.* Paper prepared for the Conference on Research Perspectives in the Ecology of Human Development, Cornell University, Ithaca, NY.

Hess, R. D., Price, G. G., Dickson, W. P., & Conroy, M. (1981). Different roles for mothers and teachers: Contrasting styles of child care. In S. Kilmer (Ed.), *Advances in early education and day care.* Greenwich, CT: JAI.

Howes, C. (1983). Caregiver behavior in center and family day care. *Journal of Applied Developmental Psychology, 4,* 99–107.

Howes, C., & Rubenstein, J. L. (1981). Toddler peer behavior in two types of day care. *Infant Behavior & Development, 4,* 387–394.

Huston-Stein, A., Friedrich-Cofer, L. K., & Susman, E. J. (1977). The relation of classroom structure to social behavior, imaginative play, and self-regulation of economically disadvantaged children. *Child Development, 48,* 908–916.

Johnson, J. E., Ershler, J., & Bell, C. (1980). Play behavior in a discovery-based and a formal-education preschool program. *Child Development, 51,* 271–274.

Kagan, M., Fargo, J., Rauch, M. D., & Crowell, D. (1977). *Infant satellite nurseries: Family day care with a difference.* Report NIMH Grant: MH 21129.

Kamerman, S. B. (1983). Child care services: A national picture. *Monthly Labor Review,* pp. 35–39.

Miller, L. B., & Dyer, J. L. (1975). Four preschool programs: Their dimensions and effects. *Monographs of the Society for Research in Child Development, 40* (5–6, Serial No. 162).

McCartney, K. (1984). Effect of quality of day care environment on children's language development. *Developmental Psychology, 20,* 244–260.

Prescott, E. (1973). *A comparison of three types of day care and nursery school-home care.* ERIC ED 078910.

Rubenstein, J. L., & Howes, C. (1983). Social-emotional development of toddlers in day care: The role of peers and of individual differences. *Advances in Early Education and Day Care, 3,* 13–45.

Rubenstein, J. L., Pedersen, F. A., & Yarrow, L. J. (1977). What happens when mother is away: A comparison of mothers and substitute caregivers. *Developmental Psychology, 13,* 529–530.

Ruopp, R., Travers, J., Glantz, F., & Coelen, C. (1979). *Children at the center.* Cambridge, MA: Abt Associates.

Siegel-Gorelick, B., Everson, M. D., & Ambron, S. R. (1980). *Qualitative versus quantitative differences in caregivers in family day care and at home.* Paper presented at the International Conference on Infant Studies, New Haven, CT.

Smith, P. K., Dalgleish, M., & Herzmark, G. (1981). A comparison of the effects of fantasy play tutoring and skills tutoring in nursery classes. *International Journal of Behavioral Development, 4,* 421–441.

Sylva, K., Roy, C., & Painter, M. (1980). *Child watching at play group and nursery school.* London: Grant McIntyre.

Tizard, B., Carmichael, H., Hughes, M., & Pinkerton, G. (1980). Four year olds talking to mothers and teachers. In L. A. Hersoveval (Ed.), *Language and language disorders in childhood* (Supplement No. 2, *Journal of Child Psychology & Psychiatry*). London: Pergamon Press.

Tizard, B., Philips, J., & Plewis, I. (1976). Play in pre-school centres: II. Effects on play of the child's social class and of the educational orientation of the centre. *Journal of Child Psychology & Psychiatry, 17,* 265–274.

Tizard, B., Pinkerton, G., & Carmichael, H. (1982). Adults' cognitive demands at home and at a nursery school. *Journal of Child Psychology & Psychiatry, 23,* 105–116.

U.S. Bureau of the Census, Current Population Reports, Series P-23, No. 117 (1982). *Trends in Child Care Arrangements of Working Mothers,* U.S. Government Printing Office, Washington, DC.

Wachs, T. D., & Gruen, C. E. (1982). *Early experience and human development.* New York: Plenum.

CHAPTER 13

Social Support: Its Assessment and Relation to Children's Adjustment

SHARLENE A. WOLCHIK
IRWIN N. SANDLER
SANFORD L. BRAVER
Arizona State University

Over the past two decades many researchers have documented clear and consistent relations between maladjustment and children's exposure to environmental stressors such as parental divorce, parental death, and extreme poverty (Garmezy, 1983; Links, 1983; Sandler & Block, 1979). However, not all children who face these stressors experience psychological difficulties (Elder, 1974; Sandler, 1980; Werner & Smith, 1982). In an attempt to explain differences in resistance to stress, researchers recently have begun to explore the impact of personal, psychological, and environmental variables that may mediate reactions to stressful situations. The importance of this type of research has been well articulated by Rutter (1979):

> The exploration of protective factors in children's responses to stress and disadvantage has only just begun. We are nowhere near the stage when any kind of overall conclusions can be drawn. What is clear, though, is that there is an important issue to investigate. Many children do not succumb to deprivation, and it is important that we determine why this is so and what it is that protects them from the hazards they face. (p. 70)

The focus of this chapter is on one such protective factor, social support. Whereas there is a large body of research with adults that demonstrates that social support has a beneficial impact on both physical and psychological health (cf. Cohen & Wills, 1985; Kessler, Price, & Wortman, 1985), research examining children's social support is exceptionally limited. Researchers are just beginning to explore basic issues, such as how to operationalize the construct of social support, how to assess social support in a reliable and valid

Partial support for writing this chapter was provided by NIMH grant #MH39246-02 to establish the Program for Prevention Research at Arizona State University.

manner, what personal and environmental factors influence the amount and quality of support children receive, and what aspects of support are related to better adjustment. Studying children's social support processes not only may lead to a better understanding of the resilience some children display when faced with stressful situations but also may provide the empirical data base for the development of intervention and prevention programs designed to modify children's social support networks and, thus, enhance their psychological adjustment.

Although there is only a limited literature on children's social support processes, extensive attention has been given to related constructs such as parent–child relationships (cf. Maccoby & Martin, 1983), attachment (e.g., Arend, Gove, & Sroufe, 1979; Waters, Wippman, & Sroufe, 1979), peer interactions (cf. Asher & Gottman, 1981; Youniss, 1980), and family social climate (McCubbin & Patterson, 1981; Moos, 1974; Moos & Moos, 1981). The issue of how social support is related to these aspects of children's social worlds is important. However, because we feel that an understanding of the relations between social support and the above constructs will require empirical attention, this issue will not be addressed at length in this chapter. At this stage, it is most useful to articulate how children's social support processes differ from the above constructs on a conceptual level. First, the assessment of social support includes children's ties with the many people who constitute children's networks rather than just focusing on the most salient dyads (e.g., parent–child, friend–child). Second, social support usually refers to particular types of interpersonal transactions that are particularly salient to helping children when they are in need of assistance (e.g., emotional support, advice) whereas constructs such as parenting or family climate include interactions that are not particularly related to a child's need for help (e.g., discipline, transmission of societal norms, teaching religious and moral values).

In this chapter, we will first discuss conceptual issues in the definition and assessment of social support. We will then describe the inventories that are currently available for assessing children's social support and discuss ways to improve assessment approaches. Next, we will discuss the literature on relations between social support and adjustment. A discussion of our research on age and gender differences in the social support processes among children of divorce will follow. Finally, we will discuss directions for future research.

CONCEPTUALIZING SOCIAL SUPPORT

Social support has been conceptualized in many different ways, and currently little consensus exists regarding how best to define this construct. Recently, Gottlieb (1983) commented, "with each new study, a new definition of social support surfaces" (p. 50). These definitions are diverse and vary greatly in their degree of specificity and the breadth of transactions encompassed. For example, Caplan (1974) defined social support as consisting of "continuing social aggregates that provide individuals with opportunities for feedback about themselves and for validations of their expectations of others'' (pp. 4–5). More specifically, Caplan noted that, in times of need, information and cognitive guidance, tangible resources, and emotional sustenance are provided by these supportive others. In contrast, from Cobb's (1976) perspective, social support consists of information that leads a person to believe that she or he is cared for and loved, esteemed and valued, or belongs to a network of communication and mutual obligations. Yet other researchers have defined social support in more behavioral terms. For example, Barrera, Sandler, and Ramsay (1981) suggested that social support includes activities directed at helping others in mastering emotional distress, sharing tasks, giving advice, teaching skills, and providing material assistance. Similarly, House (1981) defined social support as an interpersonal transaction involving one or more of the following: emotional concern, instrumental aid, information about the environment, and information related to self-evaluation.

Recently, Barrera (in press) has argued that the term *social support* is not sufficiently specific to be a useful research construct. Similarly, Rook (1985) has cautioned that grouping ''diverse types of interpersonal exchanges under the common heading of social support is likely to create conceptual and methodological confusion'' (p. 245). Barrera proposed that instead of the global term *social support* researchers use the following more precise terms, which reflect important differences in how support is conceptualized: *social embeddedness* (connections with significant others); *perceived support* (quality of support); and *enacted support* (frequency of supportive behaviors). Support for the assertion that more refined definitions are needed is provided by research indicating that intercorrelations among measures of these three concepts for adults are low (cf. Barrera, in press; Cohen & Wills, 1985). Also, measures of these support constructs are differentially related to psychological and physical health in adults (cf. Barrera, in press; Cohen & Wills, 1985). Our research with children of divorce similarly indicates weak correlations between measures of social embeddedness and measures of perceived support (Sandler, Wolchik, & Braver, 1985). In the following discussion of the ways in which children's social support has been operationalized, we will use the conceptual categories suggested by Barrera (in press). However, we have renamed Barrera's category of *perceived support* as *perceived quality of support*. This more descriptive term was selected to highlight the unique aspect of social support represented by this construct. Whereas all three categories represent perceptions of an individual's social support processes, the perceived support measures refer to an individual's evaluation of the quality or adequacy of social support.

Social Embeddedness

This concept refers to the connections or linkages that individuals have to significant others in their environment. These connections indicate that a relationship exists but do not necessarily specify the content of the exchanges that occur between people. Measures of social embeddedness may be as simple as the presence or absence of a specific type of tie or may include more complex assessment of the structure of the overall pattern of social ties in an individual's network. Examples of social embeddedness measures include whether or not a child has an older sibling or a father in the household (Sandler, 1980), the frequency of contact with a specific network member (Berndt & Hawkins, 1984), and the total number of social ties or network size (Wolchik, Sandler & Braver, 1984).

More complex social network measures can be derived to assess other potentially important features of the social network. For example, the degree to which the network members interrelate with one another independently of their relationship with the subject has been referred to as *network density* (Wellman, 1981). The directionality of exchange of resources across network ties (reciprocity) is a second potentially interesting structural variable. Conflicted network size, or the number of supporters who are also sources of interpersonal conflict, is another structural measure that may have important implications for understanding the relations between characteristics of support networks and adjustment. Finally, the number of different types of supportive exchanges that are provided by network members (multiplexity) can be assessed. Although these types of social network measures generally have not been used in social support research with children, these structural variables may have important implications for children's adjustment. For example, a dense network in which members are more likely to know each other may be less likely to support an adolescent's experimentation with different social roles (Hirsch, 1979), whereas a network in which the flow of resources is reciprocal between the child and others may be more likely to foster a sense of personal competence.

It is important to remember that social embeddedness measures generally do not tell us much about the actual content of the transactions that occur or how they may be evaluated by the child (Barrera, in press; Wellman, 1981). Some recent measures, however, have added some content to the social embeddedness concept by assessing characteristics of the network for specific types of supportive functions. For example, some measures assess the social network that provides one kind of transaction, such as emotional support (Belle & Longfellow, 1983; Bryant, 1985), whereas others include several kinds of support, such as cognitive guidance, tangible assistance, positive feedback, and recreation (Barrera, 1981; Hirsch & Reischl, 1985; Wolchik et al., 1984; Zelkowitz, 1984). Like measures of enacted support, this type of social embeddedness measure focuses on supportive transactions. However, whereas enacted support measures assess the *frequency of supportive behaviors,* social embeddedness measures refer to the *number of individuals* who provide support.

Perceived Quality of Support

This type of measure reflects the subjective appraisal of support. For example, subjects may rate their satisfaction with support that was actually received or that may be available to them or they may rate their feelings toward particular network members. Ratings of the helpfulness of various kinds of supporters (Cauce, Felner, Primavera, & Ginter, 1982) and satisfaction with specific types of support received (Barrera, 1981; Wolchik et al., 1984) have been used in research with children and adolescents. Other measures of this type include satisfaction with particular relationships (Furman & Buhrmeister, 1985) and perceived closeness of relationships with network members (Zelkowitz, 1984).

These types of measures are most clearly cognitive and as such they are most directly tied to theoretical models of how support may affect adaptation to stress in which cognitions play a central role. For example, Lazarus, Averill, and Opten's (1974) appraisal model of stress proposes that a stress response is in part a function of individuals' judgments about whether their social resources are sufficient to cope with a situation that is perceived to be threatening. On the other hand, it should be emphasized that perceived support measures tell us little about how these perceptions of support are developed. For example, a positive evaluation of the support network by an 8-year-old child may be the consequence of the recent receipt of appropriate help or of a positive attachment experience in the first 2 years of life.

Enacted Support

This type of measure refers to the frequency of supportive transactions that have taken place. Very few researchers have assessed enacted support among children. Zelkowitz (1984) examined the frequency of the supportive transactions of maintenance, nurturance, and recreation whereas Furman and Buhrmeister (1985) assessed the frequency of several different kinds of support (enhancement of worth, instrumental help, companionship, affection, intimacy, and reliable alliance).

Enacted support measures are unique in that they assess the recent exchanges that have occurred within the network. However, the meaning of different levels of enacted support is complex. Higher levels of enacted support may reflect the presence of greater amounts of stress, because support is more likely to be sought in times of stress. On the other hand, high levels of enacted support at times of low stress may reflect a dependent orientation toward the person's social network.

ASSESSING CHILDREN'S AND ADOLESCENTS' SOCIAL SUPPORT

In this section, we will discuss several inventories for measuring social support among children and school-age adolescents. More specifically, we will summarize the conceptual framework used in defining social support (in the cases where authors have provided this information), the dimensions of social support the inventory assesses, the content and format of the inventory, and information on reliability and validity of these measures. We included inventories for review only if researchers examined the internal consistency or retest reliability of the scale and provided information on the validity of the inventory. We will first discuss scales in which only one social support concept is assessed and then examine those inventories that assess support more broadly.

Using Saunders's (1977) Nurturance Scale, Belle and Longfellow (1983) have operationalized social support as confiding in others. This inventory provides a measure of social embeddedness that is specific to a particular type of supportive transaction: confiding about both negative events (e.g., bad dream, fight with a friend, worries) and positive events (e.g., something really good happens, something nice that you have done at school). Children name the people whom they tell about nine situations, and the total number of situations about which a child confides in a particular person constitutes the score for that supporter.

As shown in Table 13.1, the stability of children's reports of confiding in particular classes of individuals over a 3-month period varied across type of confidant (Belle & Longfellow, 1984). Belle and Longfellow noted that the low agreement may in part be due to the timing of the two interviews. The first interview occurred during the school year and the second during the summer. Thus opportunities to spend time with particular classes of confidants may have changed markedly. The average internal consistency reliability for confiding scores is .68.

Results of two studies of the relations between choice of confidant and children's mental health (Belle & Longfellow, 1983, 1984) provide some evidence of the construct validity of this inventory. In these investigations of children 5–12 years old, the frequency of turning to five categories of confidants (mother, father, sibling, friend, and no one) was significantly correlated with measures of locus of control, self-esteem, loneliness, worries, and parental report of behavioral adjustment. Children who reported more often confiding in their mothers exhibited significantly higher self-esteem, more internal locus of control, and less loneliness. Confiding in friends was significantly associated with less loneliness, while confiding in no one was significantly related to lower self-esteem and a more external locus of control.

Bryant's (1985) conceptualization of support is much more comprehensive than that used by other researchers. She views support as including both experiences of relatedness to others and experiences of autonomy from others. In Bryant's inventory, information about three major categories of support is obtained: others as resources (persons in the peer, parent, and grandparent generation; pets), intrapersonal sources of support (hobbies, fantasies, skill development), and environmental resources (places to get off to by oneself, formal organizations, unsponsored meeting places). Given our view of social support as involving transactions between people, only the subscales that are interpersonal in nature will be considered. There are 10 such social embeddedness measures included in Bryant's inventory. Separate scores are derived for supporters within the peer, parent, and grandparent generation (e.g., num-

TABLE 13.1. Internal Consistency and Test–Retest Coefficients for Social Support Scores

Scale and Authors	Social Embeddedness	Internal Consistency	Test–Retest	Perceived Support	Internal Consistency	Test–Retest	Enacted Support	Internal Consist-ency	Test–Retest
Nurturance Scale (Belle & Longfellow, 1984; Saunders, 1977)	Confiding								
	mother	.61	.35						
	father	.85	.69						
	sibling	.78	.39						
	friend	.65	.14						
	no one	.50	.37						
Neighborhood Walk (Bryant, 1985)	Network size								
	-knowledge & interaction								
	-intimate talks		all scores > .85 (coefficients for each score are not reported)						
	-10 most important individuals								
	(above scores computed separately for peer, parent, and grandparent generations)								
	-special talks with adults								
Zelkowitz's Inventory (1984)									
child's section	Nurturance	.85	.57				Recreation	.70	.76
	Maintenance	.92	.48						
parent's section	Total network size			Closeness of relationship			Recreation	.91	.90
							Occasional maintenance	.94	.83

(continued)

TABLE 13.1. *(continued)*

Scale and Authors	Social Embeddedness	Internal Consistency	Test–Retest	Perceived Support	Internal Consistency	Test–Retest	Enacted Support	Internal Consistency	Test–Retest
							Daily maintenance	.96	.98
							Nurturance	.95	.91
Network Relationship Inventory (Furman & Buhrmeister, 1985)				Satisfaction with relationship	>.60 (exact value is not reported)		Attachment Reliable alliance Enhancement of worth Social integration Guidance Opportunity for nurturance (separate scores computed for: mother, father, grandparent, older brother, younger brother, older sister, younger sister, best friend, teacher)	M = .80 (alpha coefficients for each subscale score are not reported)	
Hirsch & Reischl's Inventory (1985)	Cognitive guidance Emotional support Tangible assistance						Activities with friends	.64	
							Confiding in friends	.69	

	(above scores assessed for family problem and school problem)								
	Boundary density								
	Reciprocity (for friendships only)	.22							
Inventory of Socially Supportive Behaviors (Barrera, Sandler, & Ramsay, 1981)							Frequency of supportive activities	.92 (adolescent sample) .93, .94 (college student sample)	.88 (college student sample)
Arizona Social Support Interview Schedule (Barrera, 1980)	Total network size		.88 (college student sample)	Satisfaction with support	.50 (adolescent sample) .33 (college student sample)	.69 (college student sample)			
	Unconflicted network size								
	Conflicted network size		.54 (college student sample)	Need for support	.70 (adolescent sample) .52 (college student sample)	.80 (college student sample)			
Children's Inventory of Social Support	Total network size -family		.52	Satisfaction with support -family	.52	.77			

(continued)

TABLE 13.1. (continued)

Scale and Authors	Social Embeddedness	Internal Consistency	Test–Retest	Perceived Support	Internal Consistency	Test–Retest	Enacted Support	Internal Consist-ency	Test–Retest
(Wolchik, Sandler, & Braver, 1984)	-nonfamily adults		.65	-nonfamily (peer & adult)	.71	.50			
	-nonfamily peers		.82						
	Conflicted network size			Feeling toward supporter					
	-family		.60	-family		.87			
	-nonfamily adults		.46	-nonfamily adult		.74			
	-nonfamily peers		.61	-peer		.65			
	Total number of support functions								
	-family	.80	.48						
	-nonfamily adult	.80	.45						
	-peer	.77	.85						
	Number of multiplex relationships								
	-family		.42						
	-nonfamily adult		.48						
	-peer		.79						

ber of adults in parents' generation whom the child knows and interacts with; number of times peers named as a resource for intimate talks).

Unlike all other available measures, this inventory is administered while the interviewer and child walk around the child's neighborhood. Bryant selected this method of administration because she believed that the visual and kinesthetic cues could enhance the reliability of children's reports and because this format would not seem like a test. As indicated in Table 13.1, 2-week test–retest reliabilities are highly satisfactory. The high levels of stability are most likely due to the saliency of the visual and kinesthetic cues that occur during administration and the consistent use of follow-up questions about interactions with people mentioned as supporters.

Bryant (1985) has examined the relations between support and several measures of psychological well-being in 7- and 10-year olds. Multiple regression analyses were conducted in which measures of social-emotional functioning (empathy, acceptance of individual differences, attitudes toward competition, attitudes toward individualism, locus of control, and social perspective taking) were regressed on sets of predictor variables consisting of conceptually related support categories. In these analyses, the predictiveness of single support variables, as well as sets of support variables after controlling for the effects of gender, age, family size, gender of sibling, and socioeconomic status, was examined. In addition, whether or not the predictive value of support differed as a function of developmental level and familial context was assessed. The pattern of findings is complex and will not be reviewed in detail here. In general, the results indicate that higher levels of support are associated with better social–emotional functioning and that family size, developmental level, and gender moderate the relations between support and several aspects of psychological functioning. More specifically, Bryant concluded that effective use of support was related to enhanced social–emotional functioning among 10-year-olds but not among 7-year-olds. Also, support from adults in both the parent and grandparent generation was associated with better adjustment for children in large, but not small, families. Depth and breadth of relationships with adults were associated with different developmental correlates for boys and girls. For example, extensive, casual involvement with adults was positively associated with internal locus of control and perspective-taking skill among boys but negatively associated with these variables among girls. However, intensive involvement with adults was associated with stronger internal locus of control in girls and weaker internal locus of control in boys.

In Zelkowitz's (1981) examination of preschoolers' social support processes, support was defined as the gratification of basic needs such as material needs, love, attention, acceptance, and training for social responsibility. In Zelkowitz's measure, both mothers and children report on the children's social support networks. However, the content of these two versions of the inventory differs somewhat (Zelkowitz, 1984).

The maternal version includes measures of social embeddedness, enacted support, and perceived support. Social embeddedness has been assessed as the total network size (Zelkowitz, 1984). Enacted support is assessed using ratings of the frequency with which each network member performs several specific maintenance, nurturant, and recreational activities. Separate scale scores are derived for maintenance (daily and occasional), emotional, and recreational support by first totaling the ratings of the frequency with which each network member performs several specific activities and then taking an average across network members. Perceived quality of support is measured as the average rating of the closeness of the child's relationship with each network member.

Both social embeddedness and enacted support measures can be derived from the children's version. Children answer a series of open-ended questions about who performs several specific maintenance tasks and who provides emotional support in several different situations. Also, children rate the frequency with which they have engaged in several recreational activities with each nonparental network member. Nurturance and maintenance scale scores consist of the average of the total number of supportive activities listed for each person. Recreational support scores are computed in the same manner as maternal scale scores for enacted support measures.

Correlations between maternal and children's reports of support functions performed by network members were .89, .54, and .30 for daily maintenance, nurturance, and recreation, respectively (Zelkowitz, 1984). Zelkowitz suggested that the low correspondence on recreation may be due to differences in the content of items. Test–retest coefficients (over an interval of 1–2 months) for scale scores for maternal and children's reports averaged .90 and .60, respectively. As shown in Table 13.1, alpha coefficients for the scale scores are acceptable.

Although the construct validity of this measure has not yet been examined, Zelkowitz (1981) used scores on a very similar inventory to assess whether support from adults other than mothers was associated with less aggression in preschoolers from low-income families. In this study, support scores were based on interviews with mothers and children and on observational data that were collected during assessments in the subjects' homes. Results indicated that children who received higher levels of support from fathers engaged in significantly less aggressive behavior than did children who received less support. Also, Zelkowitz examined whether support from adults buffered the effect of stress on adjustment. She found that children whose families were living under highly stressful conditions but who received high levels of support from adults were significantly less aggressive than children who experienced high levels of stress and low levels of support.

In Furman and Buhrmeister's (1985) Network Relationship Inventory, both perceived and enacted support are assessed. In developing this inventory, the authors relied extensively on Weiss's (1974) theory of social provisions. Weiss proposed that individuals seek out the following kinds of social support in their interactions with others: attachment, reliable alliance, enhancement of worth, social integration or companionship, guidance, and opportunity for nurturance. Also, Weiss hypothesized that different kinds of provisions are obtained in different relationships.

In addition to tapping the above six support functions, the Network Relationship Inventory assesses the degree of relative power, conflict, and satisfaction in the relationship as well as the importance of each relationship. For each of the 10 subscales, children answer three questions about their relationships with each of the following: mother, father, grandparent, older and younger brother, older and younger sister, best friend, and teacher. Test–retest reliabilities for this inventory have not yet been reported. Internal consistency reliability figures are satisfactory, with the alphas across the 90 subscale scores averaging .80.

Consistent with Weiss's theory, results of a validation study (Furman & Buhrmeister, 1985) indicated that children reported seeking different types of social support from different individuals. Among a sample of children ranging in age from 11 to 13 years old, mothers and fathers were listed as the most frequent sources of affection, enhancement of worth, a sense of reliable alliance, and instrumental aid. After parents, children turned to grandparents most often for enhancement of worth and affection and to teachers for instrumental aid. Friends were the greatest source of companionship. Mothers and friends were given the highest ratings on the intimacy scale.

Hirsch and Reischl (1985) also have employed an inventory in which several specific types of social support are assessed. Respondents list those individuals who have provided cognitive guidance, emotional support, or tangible assistance in relation to the most problematic family and the most problematic school "hassle" that occurred during the past few months. The total numbers of individuals who provide each type of support function comprise the support scores. Two additional measures of social embeddedness are included in this inventory. Boundary density is obtained by asking the respondent how well her or his parents and friends know each other, and reciprocity of relationships with friends is assessed by three questions about initiation of interactions and mutual confiding. Measures of enacted support within friendships are obtained by assessing the frequency of shared activities and confiding. Stress in friendships is assessed with four questions about degree of conflict, problems trusting the friend, infrequent contact, and separation by considerable geographic distance. Alpha coefficients for the scores for reciprocity, confiding, and activities within friendships averaged .52. Test–retest reliabilities have not yet been reported.

Examining the relations between social support and psychological functioning among school-age adolescents with depressed, arthritic, and normal parents, Hirsch and Reischl (1985) found that higher levels of support for problematic situations, stronger friendships, and more parent–friend linkages were associated with *better* adjustment in the normal group but with *poorer* adjustment among the depressed and arthritic groups. The authors suggested that the inverse association between support and adjustment in the high-risk groups may be due to the shame associated with having an ill parent, which leads to increased anxiety about friendships. However, they also cautioned that because of the small sample size (n = 16 in each group) the findings must be interpreted with caution.

Barrera has developed two inventories for assessing social support that reflect his view of support as a multifaceted construct including specific helping transactions, subjective appraisals of the support received, and the social relationships within which support is provided. One of these scales, the Inventory of Socially Supportive Behaviors (ISSB; Barrera et al., 1981), is a 40-item inventory that assesses reports of enacted support. Subjects rate the frequency with which others performed supportive activities (e.g., "gave you over $25"; "helped you understand why you didn't do something well") during the last month using a 5-point Likert scale. Assessment of internal consistency and test–retest reliabilities of ISSB scores among college students have indicated adequate psychometric properties (Barrera et al., 1981) and results of several studies with college students have provided evidence of the construct validity of this inventory. For example, ratings of supportive behaviors provided by family members are positively associated with measures of cohesiveness of the family (Barrera et al., 1981).

The Arizona Social Support Interview Schedule (ASSIS; Barrera, 1980, 1981) was designed to assess structural aspects of social networks and subjects' satisfaction with and need for support. The following support functions are included in the ASSIS: material aid, physical assistance, intimate interaction, guidance, feedback, and social participation. Subjects list individuals who have provided these functions within the last month and, for each type of support function, rate their satisfaction with the support they received and how much that support was needed. Research with college samples has indicated adequate test–retest and internal consistency reliabilities of scores derived from this scale.

Both of these inventories are typically used with adults. However, Barrera (1981) employed these scales in a study of the relations between social support and adjustment among pregnant adolescents in the age range of 15–19 years (M = 17.2 years). The internal consistency reliabilities for scores derived from the ASSIS and ISSB in this sample are shown in Table 13.1. Barrera assessed the direct relations between measures of adjustment and of social embeddedness (total network size, unconflicted network size, conflicted network size), perceived quality of support (need for support, satisfaction with support), and enacted support (ISSB scores). Also, he examined whether social support served to buffer the impact of stressful life events using multiple regression analyses in which the stress by support interaction term was entered after the stress and support terms. Correlation analyses indicated that, whereas support satisfaction was significantly negatively related to several measures of symptomatology, scores for enacted support, support need, and conflicted network size were *positively* related to several indices of symptomatology. Significant interaction effects occurred for total network size and unconflicted network size when depression was the criterion variable. More specifically, the relation between stressful events and depression was smaller for adolescents with larger total and larger unconflicted networks than for adolescents with small total and small unconflicted networks. None of the other indices of social support interacted significantly with stress.

In developing the Children's Inventory of Social Support (CISS), we also conceptualized social support as a multidimensional construct including the social ties that constitute the support network, the exchange of helping transactions with network members, and the individual's evaluation of the help received. The CISS is derived from the Arizona Social Support Inventory Scale (Barrera, 1981). However, we adapted the content and format of the ASSIS to make the scale more appropriate for younger children. On the basis of previous conceptual work on the content of support (Barrera & Ainlay, 1983; Cochran & Brassard, 1979), we included five kinds of support functions: recreation/play, advice/information, goods/services, emotional, and positive feedback. During the interview, each kind of support is defined and children list all the people inside and outside their families who have provided this kind of support during the previous couple of months. In addition, children rate their satisfaction with each kind of support they have received from family and nonfamily members and rate their feelings toward each network member. Children also list individuals who sometimes make them feel "angry, bad, or upset." Children identify family members and nonfamily members who interact with each other when the children are not present and provide information on the age, gender, and relationship (cousin, teacher, etc.) for each supporter.

Several measures of social embeddedness can be derived from the CISS. For example, all of the following scores can be computed: total network size, network size for each of the five support functions, total number of support functions received, number of multiplex relationships (relationships in which more than one function is provided), conflicted network size (supporters who are also sources of serious negative feelings), and boundary density or the degree of linkage between family and nonfamily supporters. Perceived quality of support measures include satisfaction with specific kinds of support and feelings toward supporters. Given results of previous research (Cauce et al., 1982) that indicate that peer and family support are differentially related to adjustment, we computed separate scores for family members, nonfamily adults, and peers.

We have computed alpha coefficients for the following summary scores: number of functions provided by family members, number of functions provided by nonfamily peers, number of functions provided by nonfamily adults, satisfaction with support from family members, and satisfaction with support from nonfamily supporters (peer and nonfamily adults). The scores for number of functions were computed by summing the number of supporters within each specific category (e.g., family) across the five functions of support. Satisfaction scores were computed by averaging the satisfaction ratings for support provided by nonfamily or family supporters across the five kinds of support. With the exception of satisfaction with support from family, the internal consistency of these measures was acceptable. Test–retest reliabilities, which were assessed over a 2-week interval, are shown in Table 13.1.

Examination of the pattern of test–retest correlations for the social embeddedness measures indicates that, in general, the stability of indices of peer support was higher than that of measures of support provided by family and by nonfamily adults. One possible explanation for this finding is that contact with extended family and with nonfamily adult supporters such as mother's boyfriend and father's girlfriend may fluctuate more than contact with peers. Alternatively, the less stable scores for family members and nonfamily adults may reflect differences in accuracy of reporting across assessments. More specifically, recent conflicts with people mentioned in the first interview may lead the child to exclude them as supporters during the second administration. Conflicts with family members and with nonfamily adults may be either more salient (particularly in the context of a transition in family structure) or more frequent than are those with peers, and thus the influence of conflicts on reporting support from family and nonfamily adults may be greater than that on reporting peer support.

We have recently revised the CISS in order to enhance the stability of the scores. Modifications included: identification of a specific time marker (e.g., end of summer vacation), which begins the 3-month interval about which the child reports supportive transactions; frequent reminders about this time interval; and frequent follow-up questions that include use of visual prompts that list the various types of supporters (e.g., brothers, sisters, aunts, etc.).

The construct validity of the CISS has been examined in a sample of children of divorce ranging in age from 8 to 15 years. Higher levels of social competence, as assessed using the Perceived Competence Scale for Children (Harter, 1981), were significantly correlated with higher levels of peer support. More specifically, social competence scores were significantly positively related to the number of multiplex peer relationships ($r\ (136) = .23$; $p < .01$), to the number of supportive functions provided by peers ($r\ (136) = .23$; $p < .01$), and to the score for feelings toward peer supporters ($r\ (136) = .18$; $p < .05$). Also, social competence scores were inversely related to the number of conflicted relationships with peers ($r\ (136) = -.18$; $p < .05$). The weak to moderate relations between indices of children's social competence and social support may in part be due to the lack of differentiation between actively solicited support and support that is passively received. It is possible that actively solicited support is more strongly related to children's social competence than is passive social support.

Correlational and multiple regression analyses of the relations between social support and symptomatology were also used to examine the construct validity of this inventory (Wolchik, Ruehlman, Braver, & Sandler, 1985). In these analyses, factor scores for social support were used. These scores were based on the network size for each of the five support functions. Both parents' and children's reports of children's adjustment served as criterion variables. The total score on the Child Behavior Checklist (Achenbach, 1978; Achenbach & Edelbrock, 1979) was used as the measure of parental report. Summed z-scores for children's reports of depression (Kovacs, 1981), anxiety (Reynolds & Richmond, 1978), hostility (Braver, 1984), and self-esteem (Harter, 1982) were used as the children's measure of adjustment.

Relations between social support and adjustment differed, depending on the source of support. More specifically, higher levels of *family* support were significantly positively related to parental report of children's adjustment whereas support from peers and support from nonfamily adults were nonsignificantly related to adjustment. For children's reports of symptomatology, none of the support scores (family, nonfamily adult, peer) was significantly, directly related to adjustment. However, significant Stress × Support interaction effects occurred for family support and nonfamily adult support but *not* for peer support. Interestingly, the pattern of these interactions was not a prototypical stress-buffering effect (Cohen & Wills, 1985). Under conditions of high stress, children who reported higher levels of support were better adjusted than were children with low support. However, under conditions of low stress, children with high support reported *more* adjustment problems than did children with low support. It may be that children who have extremely helpful networks but few stressors with which to cope interpret the overresponsiveness of their networks as indicative that they must need help and thus perceive themselves as less healthy than children with less helpful networks. Future research in which children's perceptions about the support they receive in situations differing in terms of need for support would be valuable.

Summary

Currently, there are only a few social support inventories whose psychometric properties have been examined. In general, the internal consistency reliabilities of most measures are acceptable. It is, however, difficult to draw definitive conclusions about the adequacy of the test–retest reliabilities of the scores on these inventories. With the exception of Bryant's (1985) inventory, which involves visiting the child's neighborhood, there appears to be little stability of scores on these measures over time. However, for two inventories, the test–retest intervals were lengthy (1–2 months—Zelkowitz, 1984; 3 months—Belle & Longfellow, 1983). It is highly likely that the amount of support children receive *actually* changes over intervals of this length. Thus it is not possible to determine whether the lack of agreement in children's reports over time noted by Zelkowitz (1984) and Belle and Longfellow (1983) is due to problems with the inventories or to true fluctuations in support. The use of shorter intervals of time (e.g., 2–3 days) between assessments should reduce the impact of changes in level of support, and therefore a shorter interval may be more appropriate for assessing test–retest reliability.

Researchers should also consider using other methods to increase the accuracy of children's reports. For example, inclusion of an introductory section in which children identify the individuals with whom they have regular contact might be useful. More specifically, listing the names of nuclear and extended family members, teachers, counselors, clergy, babysitters, and friends might serve to prime the child to recall supportive interactions. For younger children in particular, it may be useful to have parents participate in listing potential supporters. This list could also be employed as a visual prompt after questions about specific types of support functions. The use of follow-up probes that provide concrete structure (Bierman, 1983; Bryant, 1985) may also increase both the reliability and validity of children's reports. Instead of asking open-ended questions such as "Who else tells you good things about yourself?" researchers might ask whether or not each member of the social network has told the child good things about herself or himself and then ask the child to describe these interactions. Clearly, an important issue for future research concerns the development of inventories that yield valid and reliable indices of support and that can be administered efficiently.

The available data on the construct validity of measures of social support indicate weak to moderate relations between social support and adjustment. Further, although most researchers have demonstrated positive relations between social support and adjustment, Hirsch and Reischl (1985) found an inverse relation between support and adjustment for some groups of adolescents, and Wolchik and colleagues (1985) reported a stress buffer effect that was not entirely consistent with the stress-buffering model of social support. The weak relations between social support and adjustment may be due to measurement problems. More specifically, measures with poor reliability will attenuate relations between support and adjustment. Once inventories with highly reliable indices of social support have been developed, we will be in a better position to address the issue of construct validity.

SOCIAL SUPPORT AND ADJUSTMENT

Research investigating the relations between social support and children's adjustment is in the early stages. Because of the correlational, cross-sectional nature of the available data, it is clearly premature to draw causal inferences about social support and adjustment. Further, in general, the associations between support and adjustment have been small or moderate. Although one possible explanation for the small magnitude of these correlations involves measurement problems that were discussed earlier, it is also possible that social support plays only a limited role in children's adjustment. It is important to keep these caveats in mind when examining the data on the relations between social support and adjustment. We have already discussed some of these findings in the previous section. In this section, we will integrate these data with the results of other studies that have used less formally developed social support inventories.

Several researchers have demonstrated that higher levels of social support are associated with better psychological functioning using cross-sectional research designs. Most of this research has examined children in stressful situations. For example, psychological adjustment and social support were significantly positively related among samples of children and adolescents experiencing stressful situations such as parental divorce (Guidubaldi & Cleminshaw, 1983; Santrock & Warshak, 1979; Wolchik et al., 1984; Wolchik et al., 1985), school transitions (Felner, Ginter, & Primavera, 1982), poverty (Cauce et al., 1982; Sandler, 1980; Werner & Smith, 1982), and pregnancy (Barrera, 1981). More recently, Bryant (1985) has shown that social support was positively significantly associated with concurrent levels of psychosocial functioning among children who were not experiencing a major life transition. Several researchers have reported that social support is directly related to adjustment (e.g., Barrera, 1981; Belle & Longfellow, 1984; Wolchik et al., 1985). Also, researchers have suggested that social support may interact with level of stress such that the relations between stress and adjustment are reduced under conditions of high support (Barrera, 1981; Wolchik et al., 1985; Zelkowitz, 1984).

In the studies cited above, a wide variety of approaches have been employed to assess social support. Given the limited amount of research on the relations between social support and children's functioning, this diversity in ways of operationalizing social support can be useful in identifying what aspects of support are most strongly associated with better adjustment. The usefulness of a differentiated approach to studying social support is already evident in the adult literature. For example, Cohen and Wills (1985), in a major review of the literature on the effects of social support on adults' adjustment, concluded that measures of social embeddedness tend to be directly related to better adjustment whereas measures of perceived support interact with measures of stress in predicting adjustment.

At present, there are only a few studies that have examined the relations between symptomatology and social support of children and adolescents using measures with acceptable psychometric properties. Thus we cannot determine whether the relations between measures of social embeddedness, perceived quality of support, and enacted support and adjustment that have been found for adults also occur for children. Identification of which aspects of social support (i.e., social embeddedness, perceived quality of support, enacted support) are most strongly related to adjustment and whether these aspects of support are directly related to adjustment or interact with stress will have important implications for the design of intervention programs.

Several factors appear to influence the relations between social support and adjustment. As noted earlier, Bryant (1985) has observed a moderating effect of family size, as well as the child's gender and age. Studying adolescents, Cauce and colleagues (1982) demonstrated that the strength of relations between social support and self-concept measures varied as a function of adolescents' gender and ethnic background. Another important factor that determines whether social support is significantly related to better adjustment is the source of support. Support provided by family members and by adults outside of the family has been shown consistently to relate to better adjustment (e.g., Bryant, 1985; Guidubaldi & Cleminshaw, 1983; Santrock & Warshak, 1979; Wolchik et al., 1984; Zelkowitz, 1981). In contrast, several researchers have reported nonsignificant relations between peer support and adjustment. For example, in our research with children of divorce, peer support was significantly positively related to measures of social competence but not to measures of symptomatology. Similar results have been reported by Bryant (1985) and Cauce and colleagues (1982). Of the six dependent variables Bryant considered, peer support predicted only one, attitudes toward individualism. Cauce and colleagues found that adolescents who reported higher levels of informal support (support from peers and nonfamily, nonprofessional adult supporters) displayed poorer academic performance and more absenteeism. In contrast to most findings on peer support, Berndt and Hawkins (1984, 1985) observed a positive relation between social support from peers and cognitive, social, and general self-esteem.

There are several possible explanations for these findings on support from peers. First, children and adolescents may be able to provide useful social support only for problems they have actually experienced. More specifically, if children have had an opportunity to experiment with different ways of coping with the adaptive demands posed by the stressor, they may be able to provide understanding as well as specific suggestions for dealing with problems. Peer support may have been associated with better adjustment among children experiencing a transition to a new school (Berndt & Hawkins, 1984, 1985; Felner et al., 1982) because all of these children were facing the same stressor. It is also possible that the lack of a positive relation between peer support and adjustment may be due to the young age of most of the samples in which peer support has been studied. Developmental changes in interpersonal skills such as role-taking and problem-solving abilities as well as in definitions of friendship (cf. Eisenberg & Harris, 1984; Furman & Bierman, 1984; Hunter & Youniss, 1982; Sharabany, Gershoni, & Hofman, 1981) will clearly influence children's abilities to offer support as well as to seek support from their peers. Examination of age-related differences in the relation between peer support and adjustment is an important issue for future research. Another explanation for the absence of a positive relation between peer support and adjustment involves measurement issues. In general, peer support has been indexed by the number of peers who provide specific support functions. The use of measurement approaches that assess qualitative aspects of friendships such as depth, breadth, and duration may reveal a different picture.

One critical question that has not been considered adequately concerns the causal directionality that might be inferred from observed relations between social support and psychological well-being. Although it is usually assumed that social support leads to better adjustment, it is also highly plausible that level of adjustment determines the degree of social support received. More specifically, well-adjusted children may be more likely to cultivate richer social support systems than poorly adjusted children. Alternatively, poor adjustment may lead to distortions in perceptions of the amount of support available or received. For example, depressed children may report that they have received less support than they actually received. With the exception of the study by Berndt and Hawkins (1984, 1985), cross-sectional designs have been used, thus weakening possible inferences about causal relations. Berdnt and Hawkins employed a longitudinal design in their study of the relations between peer social support and adjustment during the transition to junior high school. On the basis of the pattern of zero-order correlations between measures of support and adjustment as assessed on three occasions, Berndt and Hawkins suggest that a bidirectional influence exists between social support and adjustment. The results of causal modeling analyses planned by these authors will be extremely useful in furthering our understanding of the interrelations between social support and adjustment. Critical directions for future research include the use of longitudinal designs and analytic techniques such as path analysis and structural equation modeling, which allow testing of hypothesized causal paths between variables as well as the assessment of whether interventions that result in increases in children's social support lead to improvements in psychological adjustment.

The means by which social support may affect psychological adjustment have been discussed in detail elsewhere (cf. Barrera, in press; Cohen & Wills, 1985; Thoits, 1985), and therefore our discussion of this issue will be brief. Explanations of a positive impact of social support differ depending on which model of social support one adopts: the main effect model or stress-buffering model. The stress-buffering model proposes that support is related to psychological adjustment only for individuals experiencing stress. More specifically, under conditions of high stress, adjustment should be better for those individuals with high levels of support than for those individuals with low levels of support. The main effect model proposes that social support has a beneficial impact regardless of one's level of stress. Within the main effect model, the positive effects of social support may be due to its ability to provide a sense of predictability and stability, to enhance self-esteem, and to generate positive affect (Cohen & Wills, 1985). Social support may also influence psychological adjustment by providing a set of identities that give meaning to life and provide a sense of security (Thoits, 1985). Within a buffering model, support from others may decrease the impact of stress by providing solutions to the problems posed by the stressful situations, by reducing the perceived importance of the problems, and/or by reducing the degree of threat posed by these problems.

RELATIONS BETWEEN CHILDREN'S CHARACTERISTICS AND SOCIAL SUPPORT AMONG CHILDREN OF DIVORCE

Empirical examination of how support networks may differ as a function of children's stable characteristics such as age, birth order, gender, and ethnicity as well as other modifiable characteristics (e.g., level of interpersonal reasoning abilities) has obvious implications for understanding differential reactions to stress situations as well as for developing preventive interventions. For example, girls may adjust better to stress situations such as parental discord (Emery, 1982; Porter & O'Leary, 1980) because of their larger and/or more responsive social networks. It is also possible that children with higher levels of problem-solving skills are more adept at mobilizing supportive behaviors from available supporters than are children with less developed problem-solving skills. Thus enhancement of problem-solving skills may be targeted in prevention programs as a means of increasing support. Nonetheless, despite the theoretical and clinical importance of these research issues, only a few investigators have examined individual and/or environmental factors that are related to characteristics of support networks. In this section, we will discuss our own research on gender and age differences in characteristics of support networks among children of divorce and relate our findings to those of other researchers.

The 139 children who completed the CISS as part of their participation in the Children of Divorce Project had experienced parental separation within the past 2½ years. The sample included approximately equal numbers of girls and boys, who were in the age range of 8–15 ($M = 11.4$ years). Approximately two-thirds of the sample were in maternal custody whereas the remainder of the children were in joint custody arrangements. Subjects were recruited through sampling of court records of requests for marital dissolution and through responses to newspaper articles about the study. Joint custody families were also recruited using the files of Conciliation Court, which reviews all proposed joint custody arrangements. Each of the families listed in the files of this court was sent a letter requesting participation. In families in which there was more than one child in the age range of 8–15 years, we selected only one child to participate to ensure independence of responses. Selection was random with the constraint that our sample consist of approximately equal numbers of boys and girls of each age.

To compare the social support networks across age and gender, 2 (gender) × 2 (age 8–11 and 12–15) multivariate analyses of variance were computed. This age division was made on the basis of past research that has found several differences in the characteristics of relationships of adolescents and those of children in late elementary school (Berndt, 1982; Diaz & Berndt, 1982; Hunter & Youniss, 1982). Three separate multivariate analyses of variance were computed for scores for family, nonfamily adult, and nonfamily peer supporters. Dependent variables included total network size, number of multiplex relationships, total number of support functions, size of conflicted network, and average feeling toward supporters. None of the multivariate effects in the analysis on family support variables was significant. The analysis for nonfamily adult support variables revealed a significant gender effect, multivariate $F(5, 92) = 3.49$; $p < .01$. Similarly, the multivariate effect for gender was significant in the analysis of peer support variables, multivariate $F(5, 129) = 2.80$; $p < .05$. The age effect and age by gender interactions were not significant in the analyses for nonfamily adult or peer variables. The means of these social support variables and level of significance for the univariate follow-up tests across gender are presented in Table 13.2.

As shown in Table 13.2, girls reported having more nonfamily adult supporters than did boys. Girls described more multiplex relationships in both their nonfamily adult and peer networks and reported receiving more support functions from both peers and adults than did boys. Also, girls felt more positively toward their peer and nonfamily adult supporters than did boys.

The absence of significant relations between age and peer support is somewhat surprising given previous research by Belle and Longfellow (1984). Differences in the social support variables examined in the two studies may account for the discrepant results. Whereas the CISS scores used in the present analyses collapsed support across several different categories, Belle and Longfellow examined only one kind of support: confiding in others.

The observed gender differences are consistent with and extend the results reported by other researchers. The present finding that females report more support than do males is consistent with previous literature. For example,

TABLE 13.2. Social Support Scores Across Gender

	Girls (n = 77)	Boys (n = 62)
Family		
Network size	7.4	6.5
Total number of support functions	20.7	16.9
Number of multiplex relationships	5.2	4.1
Conflicted network size	1.1	0.7
Average feeling toward supporter	6.3	6.3
Nonfamily Adult		
Network size****	3.9	2.2
Total number of support functions***	6.9	3.6
Number of multiplex relationships***	1.5	0.8
Conflicted network size	0.1	0.1
Average feeling toward supporter***	6.1	5.3
Nonfamily Peer		
Network size	8.7	8.6
Total number of support functions*	18.7	14.6
Number of multiplex relationships**	4.6	3.2
Conflicted network size	0.9	0.6
Average feeling toward supporter**	5.9	5.7

* p. <.10
** p. <.05
*** p. <.01
**** p. <.001

Bryant (1985) observed that 7- and 10-year-old females reported more intimate talks with peers than did their male counterparts. Gender differences in feelings about support received from peers have also been noted in other samples, with girls reporting greater satisfaction with support (Burke & Wier, 1978) and greater helpfulness of informal sources of support such as friends and nonfamily adults (Cauce et al., 1982).

Gender differences in support processes may be due to different socialization experiences of boys and girls. For example, greater importance is attached to interpersonal relationships for girls (e.g., Douvan & Adelson, 1966), and dependency is reinforced more often in girls than in boys (Fagot, 1978; Serbin, O'Leary, Kent, & Tonick, 1973). These socialization experiences may lead to girls feeling more comfortable than boys about seeking and receiving social support. Moreover, results of a recent study by Belle, Burr, and Cooney (1985) suggest that boys and girls have different ideas about why children confide in others. Whereas girls were more likely to identify seeking practical help as a reason for confiding, boys were significantly more likely than girls to list sharing of factual information and confiding because others ought to be told or would find out anyway as explanations of confiding. Other differential socialization experiences may also set the stage for the development of differences in the support networks of boys and girls. For example, several researchers (e.g., Lever, 1976; Sutton-Smith, Rosenberg, & Morgan, 1963; Tietjen, 1982; Waldrop & Halverson, 1975) have reported that boys are more likely than girls to play in groups of three or more children whereas girls select activities that are dyadic in nature. This difference in play preferences would seem to lead to more opportunities for developing intimate relationships for girls than for boys.

Our data, along with those of other researchers, suggest that gender may play an important role in determining the breadth and depth of children's social support. Not only do boys and girls describe differences in the composition of and attitudes toward their social networks (Bryant, 1985; Cauce et al., 1982; Wolchik et al., 1984), but different types of supportive relationships are differentially predictive of adjustment for boys and girls (Bryant, 1985). We do not yet understand why these gender differences occur. Exploring children's cognitions about support as well as examining the ways in which they mobilize their support networks might increase our understanding. For example, researchers might assess how children select which individuals to approach for assistance, how they request help, and how they feel about themselves when others provide assistance.

The richer and more extensive social relationships of girls may provide some protection against the negative impact of stressful events. Thus the often-noted tendency for boys to show more adverse effects than girls to a variety of stressful events including the birth of a sibling (Dunn, Kendrick, & MacNamee, 1981), parental discord (Block, Block, & Morrison, 1981; Emery, 1982; Porter & O'Leary, 1980), and parental divorce (Guidubaldi, Cleminshaw, Perry &

Mcloughlin, 1983; Hetherington et al., 1981)* may be due in part to differences in characteristics of support networks. Clearly, more research is needed that explores the extent to which social support mediates gender differences in reactions to stressful events.

DIRECTIONS FOR FUTURE RESEARCH

As discussed earlier, the available data on children's social support networks indicate a positive relation between social support and adjustment. The clinical implication that by bolstering support networks we can facilitate children's psychological well-being is exciting. However, there are many research questions that need to be answered before the data base on social support can be useful in the design of intervention programs.

One critical issue for future research concerns the use of prospective research designs. As noted earlier, longitudinal studies are necessary before we can draw causal inferences about the relations between social support and adjustment. Another important issue concerns the factors that influence whether or not social support is positively related to adjustment. Current research indicates that characteristics of the person who provides support (e.g., age) and those of the person who receives support (e.g., gender, age) influence whether or not support is associated with better adjustment. However, we do not understand the means through which these factors influence the relation between support and adjustment. Also, we have identified only a few of the many personal factors that may interact with each other and with support to determine its relation to adjustment. For example, personality characteristics such as control perceptions may influence the relation between support and children's adjustment. Sandler and Lakey (1982) have demonstrated that social support acted as a buffer against the impact of negative life events on adjustment for adults with internal locus of control whereas a protective effect did not occur among adults with external locus of control. Children's cognitions and feelings about the process of receiving help should also affect the relation between social support and adjustment. Illustratively, if children feel that support is being provided for ulterior motives, they may devalue it. Moreover, if children believe that asking for assistance is a sign of weakness, they will hesitate to seek support, or if they do seek support, it may have less beneficial impact than it would for children who make different attributions about

*It should be noted that findings of research on gender differences in children's adjustment to divorce are not entirely consistent. Researchers using relatively young samples have reported gender differences. However, using a sample with a broad age range, Kurdek and his colleagues (Kurdek, Blisk, & Siesky, 1981) did not find significant gender differences. Similarly, in our research with children 8–15 years old, a significant gender effect occurred for only one of five measures of adjustment. It may be that gender differences are more marked for younger children.

needing support. Attention to how beliefs about support may differ as a function of both age and gender would also be useful.

Investigation of whether the relation between particular types of support and adjustment differs across stressful situations is another task for researchers. It is likely that various kinds of support will be differentially related to adjustment depending on the match between the demands or adaptive tasks posed by the stressor and the type of support that is provided (Cohen & McKay, 1984). For example, emotional support may be associated with better adjustment for children who are coping with the death of their parent because a central adaptive task involves grieving. Positive feedback may be more significant than other kinds of support for children whose parents arc severely depressed because their parents tend to use overly critical standards of evaluation. Alternatively, it may be that emotional support is the most beneficial type of support across many different stressful situations. Support from particular sources may also be differentially related to adjustment depending on the stressful situation. For example, support from extended family may be positively related to adjustment among children experiencing parental divorce because issues involving the stability of family ties are particularly salient whereas such support may not be significantly associated with adjustment among children facing a transition in schools. Empirical examination of the importance of a match between adaptive tasks and type or source of support provided will have important implications for intervention programs.

We also need to explore the negative aspects of social relationships and their relation to adjustment. Recent research with adults (e.g., Rook, 1984) has indicated that negative social interactions detract from well-being. Similarly, research has indicated that having supporters who are also sources of negative interactions is positively associated with symptomatology among children and adolescents (Barrera, 1980; Wolchik et al., 1984). Teaching children to decrease negative social interactions as well as to increase positive social interactions may be a critical component of interventions. However, current methods of assessing the negative aspects of children's social relationships are crude. For example, researchers have noted whether supporters are sources of negative interactions, the degree of conflict in relationships, and whether problems with trusting the supporter have occurred. A challenge facing researchers is the development of more sophisticated methods of assessing negative aspects of supportive relationships.

SUMMARY

The study of children's social support processes has suggested that social support has exciting potential as a protective resource. In this chapter, we have summarized our current knowledge and raised many questions for future research. It should be clear that at present there are more questions than answers about the contribution of children's social support to their sense of well-being.

The answers to these questions will have important implications for both theory development and clinical applications. Once we understand what kinds of support facilitate children's adjustment in what situations and how social support may operate to enhance well-being, the next challenge will involve designing programs to help children cope more effectively by enhancing their use of interpersonal resources.

REFERENCES

Achenbach, T. M. (1978). The Child Behavior Profile: I. Boys aged 6–11. *Journal of Consulting & Clinical Psychology, 46,* 478–489.

Achenbach, T. M., & Edelbrock, C. S. (1979). The Child Behavior Profile: II. Boys aged 12–16 and girls aged 6–11 and 12–16. *Journal of Consulting & Clinical Psychology, 47,* 223–233.

Arend, R. A., Gove, F., & Sroufe, L. A. (1979). Continuity of individual adaptation from infancy to kindergarten: A predictive study of ego-resilience and curiosity in preschoolers. *Child Development, 50,* 950–959.

Asher, S. R., & Gottman, J. M. (Eds.). (1981). *The development of children's friendships.* Cambridge: Cambridge University Press.

Barrera, M., Jr. (1980). A method for the assessment of social support networks in community survey research. *Connections, 3,* 8–13.

Barrera, M., Jr. (1981). Social support in the adjustment of pregnant adolescents: Assessment issues. In B. H. Gottlieb (Ed.), *Social networks and social support.* Beverly Hills: Sage.

Barrera, M., Jr. (in press). Distinctions between social support concepts, measures and models. *American Journal of Community Psychology.*

Barrera, M., Jr., & Ainlay, S. L. (1983). The structure of social support: A conceptual and empirical analysis. *Journal of Community Psychology, 11,* 133–143.

Barrera, M., Jr., Sandler, I. N., & Ramsay, T. B. (1981). Preliminary development of a scale of social support: Studies on college students. *American Journal of Community Psychology, 9,* 435–447.

Belle, D., Burr, R., & Cooney, J. (1985, March). *Boys and girls as utilizers of social support.* Paper presented at the annual meeting of the Eastern Psychological Association, Boston.

Belle, D., & Longfellow, C. (1983, April). *Emotional support and children's well-being: An exploratory study of children's confidants.* Paper presented at the biennial meeting of the Society for Research in Child Development, Detroit.

Belle, D., & Longfellow, C. (1984). *Confiding as a coping strategy.* Unpublished manuscript, Boston University.

Berndt, T. J. (1982). The features and effects of friendship in early adolescence. *Child Development, 53,* 1447–1460.

Berndt, T. J., & Hawkins, J. A. (1984, August). *Friendships as social supports for children during school transitions.* Paper presented at annual meeting of the American Psychological Association, Toronto.

Berndt, T. J., & Hawkins, J. A. (1985, April). *The effects of friendships on students' adjustment after the transition to junior high school.* Paper presented at the annual meeting of the American Educational Research Association, Chicago.

Bierman, K. L. (1983). Cognitive development and clinical interviews with children. In B. B. Lahey & A. E. Kazdin (Eds.), *Advances in clinical child psychology* (Vol. 6). New York: Plenum.

Block, J. H., Block, J., & Morrison, A. (1981). Parental agreement–disagreement on child-rearing orientations and gender-related personality correlates in children. *Child Development, 52,* 965–974.

Braver, S. L. (1984). *Development of a hostility scale: The Braver aggression device: BAD.* Unpublished manuscript, Arizona State University.

Bryant, B. (1985). The neighborhood walk: A study of sources of support in middle childhood from the child's perspective. *Society for Research on Child Development Monographs* (Serial No. 210), *50* (3).

Burke, R. J., & Wier, T. (1978). Sex differences in adolescent life stress, social support and well-being. *The Journal of Psychology, 98,* 277–288.

Caplan, G. (1974). *Support systems and community mental health: Lectures on concept development.* New York: Behavioral Publications.

Cauce, A. M., Felner, R. D., Primavera, J., & Ginter, M. A. (1982). Social support in high risk adolescents: Structural components and adaptive impact. *American Journal of Community Psychology, 10,* 417–428.

Cobb, S. (1976). Social support as a moderator of life stress. *Psychosomatic Medicine, 38,* 300–314.

Cochran, M. M., & Brassard, J. A. (1979). Child development and personal social networks. *Child Development, 50,* 601–616.

Cohen, S., & McKay, G. (1984). Social support, stress and the buffering hypothesis: A theoretical analysis. In A. Baum, J. E. Seager, & S. E. Taylor (Eds.), *Handbook of psychology and health: IV. Social psychological aspects of health.* Hillsdale, NJ: Erlbaum.

Cohen, S., & Wills, T. A. (1985). Stress, social support, and the buffering hypothesis. *Psychological Bulletin, 98,* 310–317.

Diaz, R. M., & Berndt, T. J. (1982). Children's knowledge of a best friend: Fact or fancy? *Developmental Psychology, 28,* 787–794.

Douvan, E., & Adelson, J. (1966). *The adolescent experience.* New York: Wiley.

Dunn, J., Kendrick, C., & MacNamee, R. (1981). The reaction of first-born children to the birth of a sibling: Mothers' reports. *Journal of Child Psychology & Psychiatry, 22,* 1–18.

Eisenberg, N., & Harris, J. D. (1984). Social competence: A developmental perspective. *School Psychology Review, 13,* 267–277.

Elder, G. (1974). *Children of the Great Depression.* Chicago: University of Chicago Press.

Emery, R. E. (1982). Interparental conflict and children of discord and divorce. *Psychological Bulletin, 92,* 310–330.

Fagot, B. (1978). The influence of sex of child on parental reactions to toddler children. *Child Development, 49,* 459–465.

Felner, R. D., Farber, S. S., & Primavera, J. (1980). Children of divorce, stressful life events, and life transitions: A framework for preventive efforts. In R. H. Price, R. F. Ketterer, B. C. Bader, & J. Monahan (Eds.), *Prevention in mental health: Research, policy and practice.* Beverly Hills: Sage.

Felner, R. D., Ginter, M., & Primavera, J. (1982). Primary prevention during school transitions: Social support and environmental structure. *American Journal of Community Psychology, 20,* 277–290.

Furman, W., & Buhrmeister, D. (1985). Children's perceptions of the personal relationships in their social networks. *Developmental Psychology, 21,* 1016–1024.

Furman, W., & Bierman, K. L. (1984). Children's conceptions of friendship: A multimethod study of developmental changes. *Developmental Psychology, 20,* 925–931.

Garmezy, N. (1983). Stressors of childhood. In N. Garmezy & M. Rutter (Eds.), *Stress coping and development in children.* New York: McGraw-Hill.

Gottlieb, B. H. (1983). *Social support strategies: Guidelines for mental health practice.* Beverly Hills: Sage.

Guidubaldi, J. (in press). Differences in children's divorce adjustment across grade level and gender: A report from the NASP-Kent nationwide project. In S. A. Wolchik & P. Karoly (Eds.), *Children of divorce: Empirical perspectives on adjustment.* New York: Gardner.

Guidubaldi, J., & Cleminshaw, H. (1983, August). *Impact of family support systems on children's academic and social functioning after parental divorce.* Paper presented at the annual meeting of the American Psychological Association, Anaheim, CA.

Guidubaldi, J., Cleminshaw, H. K., Perry, J. D., & Mcloughlin, C. S. (1983). The impact of parental divorce on children: Report of the nationwide NASP study. *School Psychology Review, 12,* 300–323.

Harter, S. (1982). The Perceived Competence Scale for Children. *Child Development, 53,* 87–97.

Hetherington, E. M., Cox, M., & Cox, R. (1981). Effects of divorce on parents and children. In M. E. Lamb (Ed.), *Nontraditional families: Parenting and child development.* Hillsdale, NJ: Erlbaum.

Hirsch, B. J. (1979). Psychological dimensions of social networks: A multimethod analysis. *American Journal of Community Psychology, 70,* 263–277.

Hirsch, B. J., & Reischl, T. M. (1985). Social networks and developmental psychopathology: A comparison of adolescent children of a depresed, arthritic or normal parents. *Journal of Abnormal Psychology, 94,* 272–281.

House, J. S. (1981). *Work stress and social support.* Reading, MA: Addison-Wesley.

Hunter, F. T., & Youniss, J. (1982). Changes in functions of three relations during adolescence. *Developmental Psychology, 18,* 806–811.

Kessler, R. C., Price, R. H., & Wortman, C. B. (1985). Social factors in psychopathology: Stress, social support, and coping processes. *Annual Review of Psychology, 36,* 531–572.

Kovacs, M. (1981). Rating scales to assess depression in school-aged children. *Acta Paedopsychiatrica, 46,* 305–315.

Kurdek, L. A., Blisk, D., & Siesky, A. E. (1981). Correlates of children's long-term adjustment to their parents' divorce. *Developmental Psychology, 17,* 565–579.

Lazarus, R. S., Averill, J. R., & Opten, E. M., Jr. (1974). The psychology of coping: Issues of research and assessment. In G. V. Coelher, D. H. Hamburg, & J. E. Adams (Eds.), *Coping and adaptation.* New York: Basic.

Lever, J. (1976). Sex differences in the games children play. *Social Problems, 23,* 478–487.

Links, P. (1983). Community surveys of the prevalence of childhood psychiatric disorder: A review. *Child Development, 54,* 531–548.

Maccoby, E. E., & Martin, J. A. (1983). Socialization in the context of the family: Parent–child interaction. In P. H. Mussen (Ed.), *Handbook of child psychology* (Vol. 4). New York: Wiley.

McCubbin, H. I., & Patterson, J. M. (1981). *Systematic assessment of family stress, resources and coping: Tools for research, education, and clinical intervention.* St. Paul, MN: Family Social Science.

Moos, R. H. (1974). *The social climate scales: An overview.* Palo Alto: Consulting Psychologists Press.

Moos, R. H., & Moos, B. S. (1981). *Family environment scale manual.* Palo Alto: Consulting Psychologists Press.

Porter, B., & O'Leary, K. D. (1980). Marital discord and childhood behavior problems. *Journal of Abnormal Child Psychology, 80,* 287–295.

Reynolds, C. R., & Richmond, B. O. (1978). What I think and feel: A revised measure of children's manifest anxiety. *Journal of Abnormal Child Psychology, 6,* 271–280.

Rook, K. S. (1984). The negative side of social interaction: Impact on well-being. *Journal of Personality & Social Psychology, 46,* 1097–1108.

Rook, K. S. (1985). The functions of social bonds: Perspectives from research on social support, loneliness and social isolation. In I. G. Sarason & B. R. Sarason (Eds.), *Social support: Theory, research and applications.* Boston: Martinus Nijhoff.

Rutter, M. (1979). Protective factors in children's responses to stress and disadvantage. In M. W. Kent & J. E. Rolf (Eds.), *Primary prevention of psychopathology: Vol. 3. Social competence in children.* Hanover, NH: University Press of New England.

Sandler, I. N. (1980). Social support, resources, stress, and maladjustment of poor children. *American Journal of Community Psychology, 8,* 41–52.

Sandler, I. N., & Block, M. (1979). Life stress and maladaptation of children. *American Journal of Community Psychology, 7,* 425–440.

Sandler, I. N., & Lakey, B. (1982). Locus of control as a stress moderator: The role of control perceptions and social support. *American Journal of Community Psychology, 10,* 65–80.

Sandler, I. N., Wolchik, S. A., & Braver, S. L. (1985). Social support and children of divorce. In I. G. Sarason & B. R. Sarason (Eds.), *Social support: Theory, research and applications.* Boston: Martinus Nijhoff.

Santrock, J. W., & Warshak, R. A. (1979). Father custody and social development in boys and girls. *Journal of Social Issues, 35,* 112–125.

Saunders, E. B. (1977). *The nurturance scale.* Unpublished report, Stress and Families Project, Harvard University.

Serbin, L. A., O'Leary, K. D., Kent, R. D., & Tonick, I. J. (1973). A comparison of teacher response to the preacademic and problem behavior of boys and girls. *Child Development, 44,* 796–804.

Sharabany, R., Gershoni, R., & Hofman, J. E. (1981). Girlfriend, boyfriend: Age and sex differences in intimate friendship. *Developmental Psychology, 17,* 800–808.

Sutton-Smith, B., Rosenberg, G. G., & Morgan, E. (1963). The development of sex differences in play choices during preadolescence. *Child Development, 34,* 119–126.

Thoits, P. (1985). Social support and psychological well-being: Theoretical possibilities. In I. G. Sarason & B. R. Sarason (Eds.), *Social support: Theory, research and applications.* Boston: Martinus Nijhoff.

Tietjen, A. M. (1982). The social networks of preadolescent children in Sweden. *International Journal of Behavioral Development, 5,* 111–130.

Waldrop, M. F., & Halverson, C. F. (1975). Intensive and extensive peer behavior: Longitudinal and cross-sectional analyses. *Child Development, 46,* 19–26.

Waters, E., Wippman, J., & Sroufe, L. A. (1979). Attachment, positive affect, and competence in the peer group: Two studies in construct validation. *Child Development, 50,* 821–829.

Weiss, R. (1974). The provisions of social relationships. In Z. Rubin (Ed.), *Doing unto others.* Englewood Cliffs, NJ: Prentice-Hall.

Wellman, B. (1981). Applying network analyses to the study of support. In B. H. Gottlieb (Ed.), *Social networks and social support.* Beverly Hills: Sage.

Werner, E., & Smith, R. (1982). *Vulnerable but invincible: A longitudinal study of resilient children and youth.* New York: McGraw-Hill.

Wolchik, S. A., Ruehlman, L., Braver, S. L., & Sandler, I. N. (1985, August). *Social support of children of divorce: Direct and stress buffering effects.* Poster presented at the annual meeting of the American Psychological Association, Los Angeles.

Wolchik, S. A., Sandler, I. N., & Braver, S. L. (1984, August). *The social support networks of children of divorce.* Poster presented at the annual meeting of the American Psychological Association, Toronto.

Youniss, J. (1980). *Parents and peers in social development—A Sullivan-Piaget perspective.* Chicago: University of Chicago Press.

Zelkowitz, P. (1981, August). *Children's support networks: Their role in families under stress.* Paper presented at the biennial meeting of the Society for Research in Child Development, Boston.

Zelkowitz, P. (1984, August). *Comparing maternal and child reports of children's social networks.* Poster presented at the annual meeting of the American Psychological Association, Toronto.

PART SIX

Issues in Life Cycle Development

In most of the chapters in Parts I to V, the authors have focused on development in childhood. However, in recent years, there has been increasing interest among developmental psychologists in change across the life span and in what has been called life span developmental psychology. In the last three chapters in this volume, issues related to development and behavior in the post-childhood years are explored.

In Chapter 14, Laurie Chassin, Clark Presson, and Steven J. Sherman demonstrate how principles from the interface of social and developmental psychology can be used better to understand adolescents' behaviors. In specific, they use concepts related to decision making, motives, cognitive schemes and biases, and the development of cognitive structures to examine adolescents' health-related behaviors. In doing so, they not only provide a useful and provocative perspective on adolescent behavior, but also demonstrate how social psychological principles can be applied to the analysis of a variety of developmental issues.

There are a variety of methods for studying change across the life span. One of the most useful is the longitudinal approach. In Chapter 15, Paul Mussen discusses the advantages of this approach for the study of change and the antecedents thereof. In doing so, he presents examples of findings from the longitudinal studies at the University of California, Berkeley. In addition, Mussen suggests procedures for improving future longitudinal studies. Thus this chapter includes both a wide sampling of the important findings that have resulted from the Berkeley longitudinal studies and a useful analysis of the longitudinal method.

In Chapter 16, the final chapter of this volume, James Birren and Bonnie Hedlund present a very different and innovative approach to the study of development in adulthood, the use of autobiography. Birren first reviews the history and status of the autobiographical method. He then discusses how the guided autobiographical method can be used to study themes or meaning in adult development, life events that cause change (as perceived by the individual), and the consequences of change. Finally, the therapeutic effects of guided autobiography procedures are examined, and useful suggestions for further research with autobiographical procedures are offered.

CHAPTER 14

Applications of Social Developmental Psychology to Adolescent Health Behaviors

LAURIE CHASSIN
CLARK C. PRESSON
STEVEN J. SHERMAN

Adolescence as a developmental stage has received relatively little attention from researchers studying behavioral health, partially because of relatively low mortality and morbidity during the adolescent years (Brown, 1979). However, there are several reasons why adolescence is an important stage for behavioral health interventions. First, adolescence is an age group with rising mortality rates (United States Department of Health, Education, and Welfare, 1979). Second, the major causes of adolescent mortality and morbidity have important behavioral components. These causes include accidents, homicides, suicides, pregnancy, and substance abuse, and are more likely to be influenced by behavioral and life-style modifications than by advances in medical technology. Third, adolescence is a time during which important health-relevant behaviors (e.g., cigarette smoking, alcohol use) are initiated. Although these behaviors may have only subtle short-term implications for health, their long-term impact can be profound.

Thus in terms of health promotion interventions adolescence is a more important developmental stage than its associated mortality and morbidity rates would indicate. Indeed, adolescents are an important target age group for health promotion interventions. However, if successful health promotion interventions are to be directed at adolescents, it becomes important to understand the bases on which adolescents make health-relevant behavioral decisions. Effective interventions are best developed from a thorough empirical understanding of the target behavior to be influenced (Chassin, Presson, & Sherman, 1985).

Preparation of this chapter was supported by NICHD Grant HD13499 and NCI Grant CA37001.

Although adolescents initiate many behaviors that carry important health implications, it may be misleading to think of these as *health behaviors.* Such a term suggests that the behaviors in question are adopted or rejected *because* of their health implications. Karoly (1982) defines health self-regulation as "the ongoing process by which individuals gather, evaluate, and act upon data relevant to their physical health and formulate long term and/or provisional health objectives" (p. 47). By this definition, it is not clear whether or not most adolescents actually engage in health self-regulation. Rather, we know very little about the extent to which health concerns are salient and organizing dimensions of adolescents' behavioral choices. Adolescents may engage in behaviors that have profound health consequences for reasons that have little or nothing to do with physical health concerns. Because little is known about whether health concerns actually underlie adolescents' behavioral decisions, the current chapter will make a distinction between *health behaviors* (adopted or rejected on the basis of health motives) and *health-relevant behaviors* (having health implications but adopted or rejected for a variety of possible motives other than health concerns).

The purpose of the current chapter is to consider possible determinants of adolescents' health-relevant behavioral decisions. We will attempt to embed this discussion of decision making within a wider framework of theory and research in social cognitive development. In order to understand health-relevant decision making, it is necessary to understand the broader context of the development of adolescent decision making in general.*

DECISION MAKING AND COGNITIVE STRUCTURES

From a cognitive social psychological perspective, decision-making processes are guided by relevant knowledge structures and cognitive representations of the behavioral domain. These cognitive structures or schemata consist of organized sets of information within different domains of knowledge (Bobrow & Norman, 1975; Rumelhart, 1980). New information is typically attended to, encoded, and retrieved through such existing structures (Bransford, 1979; Rumelhart, 1984; Wyer, 1980). In other words, schemata direct and often bias our attention to, our interpretation of, and our memory for socially relevant information (Cantor & Mischel, 1977; Markus, 1977). Because judgments and behavioral choices are made on the basis of our interpretation of and memory

*The focus of this chapter will be on the behavioral decision making of healthy adolescents. Thus the chapter considers the adoption of health-relevant behaviors such as diet, exercise, and substance use in terms of the primary prevention of illness. Similar decisions with important health implications are made by adolescents with chronic illnesses (e.g., behaviors reflecting medical compliance or noncompliance). Although these behaviors can be considered within a similar developmental framework, they are beyond the scope of this chapter.

for relevant information, it is clear that schematic processing has major effects on these judgments and behaviors.

For any piece of information, it should be realized that the information can be processed in terms of a number of appropriate and relevant knowledge structures. The particular schema through which a given event is processed can affect the meaning given to that information and thus the subsequent effects of that information on behavior. For example, a target person's kind but dishonest behavior (e.g., helping a friend cheat on a test) can be interpreted and coded primarily in terms of its positive (kind) features or its negative (dishonest) features. Depending on which of these categories has been activated and made accessible, an observer's judgments of the behavior and subsequent reactions to the target person will be quite different (Carlston, 1980).

Given the role of schemata or knowledge structures in influencing information processing and behavioral decisions, it becomes important to understand adolescents' general schematic representations and their health schemata in particular. In addition, it will be important to consider developmental changes in the nature of these cognitive representations. More specifically, the present chapter will be organized around three major issues:

1. What is the nature of the development of knowledge structures from childhood to adolescence? How do cognitive representations of complex social constructs change from childhood to adolescence? What are the implications of these developmental changes for cognitive representations of "health"?
2. What is the relation between these knowledge structures and behavior? Do cognitive representations of health underlie adolescents' behavioral decisions?
3. If health concerns are not the primary determinants of adolescents' health-relevant behavioral decisions, what are other factors that might motivate these behavioral choices?

Unfortunately, it must be noted at the outset that there is only limited empirical and theoretical work on the development of cognitive representations in adolescence. Most of the work on the development of cognitive structures and process has been done with younger children (Mandler, 1983). This relative neglect should not be taken to mean that no important developmental changes in representation occur at adolescence. Certainly recent work in the development of complex social categories (e.g., representations of "self") suggest important changes at adolescence (Damon & Hart, 1982; Harter, 1983b; Selman, 1980). Nevertheless, there remains a lack of available data on developmental trends in adolescents' cognitive representations in general, and there is a similar dearth of information in the health domain. Given the relative lack of available data, the goal of the present chapter will include speculating about the ways in which general developmental trends should influence the nature of adolescents' cognitive representations of health and, in turn, the ways in which these cognitive representations should guide adolescents' health-relevant decision making. In addition, we will suggest several directions for future research that may be useful for understanding adolescents' health-relevant behaviors.

DEVELOPMENTAL CHANGES IN THE NATURE OF COGNITIVE REPRESENTATIONS

Among the general advances in cognitive functioning in adolescence (Inhelder & Piaget, 1958), there are several principles that seem particularly important for understanding the development of representations and how they may influence behavior. First, although the young child is often tied to very concrete aspects of an object or problem, the adolescent's reasoning and understanding of the world become more abstract. The underlying basis for representing conceptual categories shifts during this time from representations based on specific, concrete exemplars to representations based on more abstract qualities and dimensions (Kosslyn & Kagan, 1981). That is, the young child's knowledge structures are often based on concrete, available instances. In contrast, the adolescent's knowledge structures are built up from an integration of information and features across multiple examples. This shift to more general abstract categories helps to organize more coherent, stable categories of thought, and leads to prototypic representations that are complex and abstract enough to integrate increasing numbers of diverse elements. This development marks the beginning of truly schematic, abstract prototypic representations.

The developmental change from exemplar-based to prototype-based representations should have implications of the development of decision making. The decision making of younger children will be based on a consideration of available concrete instances. For example, in considering the health implications of cigarette smoking, young children might consider only the health status of their parent who smokes. By contrast, adolescents may have already developed a schematic representation of a "smoker" in which the health consequences are derived from an integration and weighing of multiple examples. For older adolescents, the ability to draw on schematic representation is added to and coexists with decision making based on available concrete instances.* This suggests that the decision making of younger children and older adolescents would be influenced by different approaches. Young children would be

*The reader may note parallels between these two bases of representation and two decision-making heuristics—the availability heuristic and the representativeness heuristic (see Sherman & Corty, 1984, for a fuller discussion of these heuristics). However, no developmental research has been done concerning the use of these two heuristic principles of judgment.

more influenced by immediate and particular examples. Of course, for young children this influence may be short-lived because it can be superseded by new immediate examples. For older adolescents, influencing decision making should involve changing more complex and integrated belief systems, actually changing the prototypic representation (see Sherman & Corty, 1984). Such change would be gradual and not based on any single event. When new information (or a particular concrete example) is encountered, it would be integrated over multiple events within the existing representation.

Not only does the basis of representation change from concrete instances to more abstract prototypes, but the organization of the representations also changes, becoming more differentiated and integrated. As new information is assimilated to the representation there is increasing complexity, which requires greater integration. General increases in cognitive complexity and differentiation of representations in adolescents have been shown for social categories (e.g., Selman, 1980). Moreover, similar developmental trends have been observed in a health-related domain as well (Schlegel & DiTecco, 1982).

Schlegel and DiTecco (1982) were primarily interested in how the structure of one kind of cognitive representation (evaluative judgments or attitudes) changed with increasing experience with the attitude object. They demonstrated that, with increased behavioral involvement with marijuana, adolescents' representations became more complex, differentiated, and hierarchically organized. Importantly, the same differences in complexity and differentiation of cognitive structure were observed in comparing different age groups (high school vs. college) within a given level of experience. That is, either at earlier stages of marijuana involvement or at younger ages the attitude structures were relatively simple, and tended to consist primarily of unidimensional affective evaluation (good–bad) components. With development and with increased involvement with marijuana, the representations came to include many more diverse, specific beliefs, which required a more elaborated, complex structure that included multiple dimensions to integrate the differentiated elements.

The similarity between the changes in representational organization due to increased experience and those due to developmental level seems quite natural. In fact, observed developmental changes in cognitive representations are likely to result both from age-related increases in cognitive ability in adolescence and from the general increases in behavioral experience that accompany adolescence.

Similar to Schlegel and DiTecco, many other theorists and researchers have noted increases in the complexity of cognitive representations from childhood to adolescence. Inhelder and Piaget (1958) describe children's thinking as limited to perceiving and representing the world in very unidimensional, all-or-none terms. This tendency to center on only a single aspect at a time in a given situation or problem limits the child's cognitive success in complex problem-solving situations. In contrast to the unidimensional thinking of the child, the adolescent is able to consider multiple, even potentially conflicting, dimensions of a behavior or concept at the same time.*

The increased complexity of representation and the ability to consider the multidimensional nature of the world have important implications for adolescents' behavioral decision making. In evaluating a particular behavior, the young child will tend to view it in black-and-white terms along a single dimension. For example, the younger school-age child is often a crusading "anti-smoker" who cannot understand how anyone could possibly want to smoke. The behavior is seen as all bad for all people (Meltzer, Bibace, & Walsh, 1984). At a somewhat later age, when the young adolescent first begins to recognize the multivalent qualities of a behavior, he or she may initially not fully appreciate and integrate the conflicting aspects. At this stage, the young adolescent may demonstrate behavioral ambivalence or inconsistency, flip-flopping among competing evaluations or dimensions on different occasions or situations (Harter, 1983a). For example, the young adolescent will begin to recognize that smoking may well have positive as well as negative aspects. However, a young adolescent exposed to peer smoking may be able to consider only the potential social gains associated with trying a cigarette in the immediate situation. At other times, only the negative health risks will be salient. At an even later stage, the older adolescent will be able to recognize and evaluate the health and possible social costs along with the potential social gains, and recognize that these conflicting qualities coexist.

It is likely that at the time when multiple dimensions of a behavior are initially recognized the adolescent may be most flexible and easy to influence in terms of accepting or rejecting various behavioral alternatives (e.g., whether or not to initiate smoking). As the representation becomes more fully integrated and differentiated in older adolescence, the coexistence of the multivalent qualities may be reunitized within a single, complex representation. Once this reintegration has taken place, the representation may be more difficult to change. This line of thinking is reminiscent of that presented by Hayes-Roth (1977). She suggested that, early in one's cognitive experience with a domain, the units are represented simply and independently. Later on, the relations among units strengthen and the representation is considerably more complex. Finally, with enough experience, the entire set of relations is unitized and a simple representation is again achieved, but one based on large, well-integrated units. As the fully integrated representation is formed, the adolescent's evaluation of the behavior is likely to solidify again and become more like the black-and-white simplistic representation of the young child. However, at this time, the certainty is based on growing amounts of direct expe-

*The first ability to consider multiple aspects of a situation appears in purely cognitive domains and can be demonstrated in the early concrete operational period. However, in social and emotional domains this ability is established somewhat later (Harter, 1983a). The social world is more complex because the situations are more multidimensional and the dimensions themselves are less concrete. Further, the affective state of children often limits their reasoning performance when dealing with social phenomena.

rience and cognitive consistency, rather than the all-or-none thinking of the younger child. In a sense, the evaluations of a young child can be described as "simple-minded," the inexperienced adolescent's as "open-minded," and the more experienced individual's as "close-minded." In terms of the influence process, the period of time in which representations are being formed and elaborated (the "open-minded" period) may offer the most potential for cognitive change.

THE RELATION OF COGNITIVE REPRESENTATIONS OF "HEALTH" TO ADOLESCENTS' BEHAVIORAL DECISIONS

The discussion to this point has attempted to describe some of the general cognitive developmental changes in the nature of cognitive representations from childhood to adolescence. Now we turn more specifically to cognitive representations of "health" and to the question of whether these cognitive representations are related to adolescents' behavioral decisions. Specifically, if adolescents actually make decisions about health-relevant behaviors (e.g., smoking, nutrition, exercise) on the basis of health concerns, several implications follow. First, adolescents must have cognitive representations or knowledge structures of health that include the attributes of health and illness and the behaviors associated with healthy and unhealthy outcomes. Second, these representations or schemata not only must exist but also must be relatively accessible. That is, the health or illness schema must be activated during the time that the relevant behavioral decision is being made. Third, the judgment or decision must actually be filtered through these health-related cognitive structures. That is, health concerns, even if represented in accessible knowledge structures, must be used in preference to other accessible and competing categories that might affect behavioral decisions. In other words, the health schema must be relatively important (as well as accessible) when the decision is made. Fourth, if behaviors are adopted or rejected on the basis of their health implications and if health schemata are general enough to include diverse behaviors, then individuals' behaviors should covary to form clusters or consistent health life-styles. We will now consider the available evidence for each of these four implications. In addition, we will consider possible developmental changes in each and suggest research directions that can reveal the role of health in adolescents' behavioral decision making.

Adolescents' Cognitive Representations of Health

If adolescents "gather, evaluate, and act upon" data relevant to their physical health, then they should have some kind of definition and stable and organized conception of what "health" is (Karoly, 1982, p. 47). If well-developed cognitive schemata of health do not exist for adolescents, it is unlikely that health concerns or the health implications of behavior will enter decisions about whether or not to adopt those behaviors.

A number of researchers have attempted to describe cognitive representations of health among children and adolescents. Most of their studies have relied on interview or questionnaire methods to identify these definitions. They generally have found that adolescents' definitions of health are complex and multifaceted, and that they are considerably broader than traditional notions of physical health.

For example, Natapoff (1978, 1982) interviewed subjects in the first, fourth, and seventh grades. She found that their major definitions of health included feeling good and being able to participate in desired activities. The number of elements in subjects' health definitions increased with age, suggesting that adolescents' health conceptions are more complex than those of younger children. Moreover, 32 percent of the seventh graders (as opposed to 2 percent of the first graders) mentioned mental health as part of their definition. Similarly, Korlath (1981) found that adolescents' concerns included a wide range of psychological and interpersonal problems (depression, family problems, etc.) as well as personal appearance (e.g., acne, body weight). If adolescents' definitions of health are indeed as broad as these studies indicate, then behavioral decisions motivated by interpersonal, social, psychological, and physical appearance concerns could all be considered health-motivated behaviors. However, in this case, the concept of health self-regulation becomes so broad that it may lose its utility.

Methodologically, previous studies of adolescents' health definitions also suffer from another problem. In most of these studies, investigators simply asked individuals in a direct way to define what health means and to list behaviors and characteristics associated with health. This methodology is quite problematic, however, when it comes to establishing the existence of stable cognitive representations of health. Clearly subjects can answer direct questions about what health means or what kinds of behaviors are healthy or unhealthy. Whether the answers to such questions indicate and describe the prior existence of a network of associations or whether the answers are created only at the time of the questions is uncertain. This same criticism has been aimed at much work in the areas of attitudes and social perception. Do expectations, attitudes, impressions, and attributions exist in subjects' heads prior to social psychologists asking about them, or do social psychologists create such expectations and attitudes simply by asking subjects what they think or believe?

A solution to this problem is to employ more indirect means for assessing the existence of and structure of knowledge representations. Recent work has shown that procedures such as priming and the use of measures such as latency in making judgments can be used effectively to assess underlying cognitive structures (Bargh, 1982; Higgins, Rholes, & Jones, 1977; Srull & Wyer, 1979, 1980). For example, it should be possible to prime subjects passively with health-related words or phrases and determine the extent to which such priming affects the interpretation of events or the direction of health-relevant judgments. The priming of a category such as health can be achieved by unobtrusively presenting subjects with health-related words (e.g., *exercise, hospital, disease*) as they do a sentence-construction or color-naming task (as in Higgins et al., 1977; Srull & Wyer, 1979, 1980). Priming can even be achieved by presenting these words subliminally (as in Bargh & Pietromonaco, 1982). If health schemata exist in a strong sense, these priming procedures should cause subjects subsequently to interpret the ambiguous behaviors or characteristics of a target person in health-relevant terms.

Another indirect means for assessing health schemata in adolescents involves the use of a methodology developed by Cantor and Mischel (1977). Cantor and Mischel showed that if person schemata exist (e.g., introverts or extraverts) they can be activated by describing a target person in schema-consistent terms. Once the schema has been activated and is applied to the target, certain biases in memory are evidenced. For example, subjects will wrongly remember having seen traits and behaviors that are consistent with the activated schema but that had not actually been presented. If health and illness schemata exist for adolescents, it should be possible to activate these schemata by the presentation of target individuals who are described as exhibiting a consistent set of healthy or unhealthy traits and behaviors. Activation of such schemata can be assessed by looking for the now-documented memory biases that follow from schema activation.

Recent pilot work by the present authors suggests that this methodology might indeed prove useful for the identification of health schemata in adolescents. College students (n = 308) were presented with descriptions of four target characters, one prototypically healthy, one prototypically unhealthy, and two control targets (one for the healthy character and one for the unhealthy character). Each target was described by 12 sentences presented individually on slides. The order of target presentation was counterbalanced, and the order of sentences within a description was randomized. After reading the characteristics of these targets, subjects were given a recognition memory test. The recognition items consisted of items that actually appeared in the acquisition list, items that were consistent with the healthy and unhealthy prototypes but had not been previously presented, and health-irrelevant items that had not been presented.

If health schemata exist, two hypotheses follow. First, subjects should correctly recognize more of the actually seen items for the healthy and unhealthy prototypic characters than for the two control characters. This hypothesis was tested in a 2 (prototypic vs. control characters) × 2 (healthy vs. unhealthy characters) within-subjects ANOVA with the dependent measure being the percentage of acquisition items that were correctly identified. Results showed a significant main effect of both health status of target and target versus control condition (both p's $< .001$). As predicted, participants had higher hit rates for the words describing the prototypic targets than for control targets, $F(1, 307 = 10.86$; $p < .001$. However, this effect was limited to unhealthy targets (two-way interaction; $p < .001$). For the prototypic unhealthy target, subjects were 86% accurate compared to 76% accuracy for the unhealthy control target.

Second, if health schemata exist, more false recognition of the actually unseen but health-related items should occur for prototypic than for control targets. No such difference should occur for health-irrelevant items. This hypothesis was tested in a 2 (healthy vs. unhealthy characters) × 2 (prototypic vs. control characters) × 2 (health-irrelevant vs. relevant item) within-subjects ANOVA. The dependent measure was the percentage of falsely recognized items. The hypothesis was supported by a significant interaction between the health relevance of the item and the prototypic versus control condition, $F(1, 307) = 44.0; p < .0001$. As predicted, relative to the control targets, when prototypic characters were judged, there was more false recognition of health-relevant items than of health-irrelevant items. For health-relevant items, the prototypic targets showed 8% more intrusion errors than did the control targets. For health-irrelevant items, the difference was less than 1%. This pattern was found for both healthy and unhealthy prototypic characters.

These data are important in demonstrating that health information is processed schematically. When targets were described in primarily healthy or unhealthy terms, memory intrusions consistent with the basic description were made. Thus the health category does operate as a meaningful structure through which to encode information.

These preliminary findings suggest several directions for research. First, this methodology could be applied across age groups to detect developmental differences in the strength of the health schema. As described above, schematic effects should become stronger with age paralleling the shift from exemplar-based to prototype-based representation. Second, these pilot data suggest that the cognitive representation of *unhealthy* is stronger than the representation of *healthy*. This might indicate that people make behavioral decisions more on the basis of avoiding unhealthy outcomes than on the basis of promoting health. Again, developmental differences in the relative strengths of the *healthy* and *unhealthy* prototypes are of interest for future research. Third, this methodology could be used to detect individual differences in the strength of health schemata. Theoretically, schematic versus aschematic individuals should differ in important ways in terms of their behavioral decisions (Markus, 1977). For example, Markus (1977) found that schematic individuals made more confident self-predictions about behavior on schema-relevant dimensions and were also more resistant to counterschematic information. Adolescents who are schematic with respect to health may rely more on health information to make behavioral decisions and may actively seek out such health information. Thus it may be highly schematic adolescents who actually engage in health self-regulation.

THE ACCESSIBILITY OF ADOLESCENTS' HEALTH SCHEMATA

Clearly it is not enough simply to document the existence of cognitive representations of health among adolescents. Work in the area of social cognition has found that only when these representations are accessible do they guide subsequent judgments and behavior. Research in the area of priming (Higgins

& Chaires, 1980; Srull & Wyer, 1979, 1980) indicates that increasing the accessibility of cognitive categories raises the likelihood that these categories will be used in the interpretation of ambiguous behavior or in the solution to behavioral problems (Higgins & Chaires, 1980). Likewise, in studying the relation between attitudes and behavior, Fazio (in press) has shown that the mere existence of an attitude represented in memory is not sufficient to ensure attitude–behavior consistency. Only when the attitude is automatically accessed upon exposure to the attitude object or when it is rendered accessible through experimental manipulation will subsequent behavior be based upon these evaluative considerations.

To date, there has been no empirical work attempting to determine the accessibility of adolescents' cognitive representations of health. However, there has been work attempting to predict adolescents' health behaviors prospectively from cognitive factors using the Health Beliefs Model (Millstein & Irwin, 1982). The Health Beliefs Model (cf. Kirscht, 1983) predicts health behaviors from cognitive factors such as perceptions of vulnerability to disease and disease severity. As was not the case with work based on adult populations, Millstein and Irwin (1982) found that the Health Beliefs Model failed to predict adolescent health behavior. One possibility is that adolescents' health beliefs were not sufficiently accessible to play a guiding role in their subsequent behavioral decisions. Research comparing the accessibility of health beliefs across the life span would be useful in clarifying the role of the health construct in directing behavior among children, adolescents, and adults.

The Relative Importance of Health to Adolescents

Even if a particular knowledge structure is activated, it is possible that other relevant structures are also activated at the time of an important behavioral decision. The degree to which any category or dimension enters into a decision will depend upon the relative importance of that category and the weight that it carries in the judgment process. Adolescents, even if they have accessible and well-developed health schemata, also have cognitive representations concerning social acceptance, physical attractiveness, and so forth. These dimensions might well carry more weight in decisions about health-relevant behaviors.

Research on the perceived importance of health to adolescents generally has relied on direct interview methodologies. Altman (1982) found that children 13–14 years old more often spontaneously mentioned health as "important to their lives" than did younger subjects (21% of children 13–14 years old, 16% of children 11–12 years old, and 9% of children 8–10 years old). This suggests that the importance of health concerns increases from childhood to adolescence. Similarly, Radius, Dillman, Becker, Rosenstock, and Horvath (1980) found that 44% of adolescents reported worrying about their health. These data suggest that health is indeed an important concern for the adolescent age group.

However, it is important to remember that these direct interview methods suffer from social desirability response biases and that they have not contrasted the importance of health motives with other motives. Gochman (1975) used a more indirect methodology in comparing the importance of health and physical appearance motives in a dental health context. Gochman had subjects choose among pictures of mouths varying in attractiveness (straight vs. crooked teeth) and in health (varying numbers of cavities). Using this more indirect procedure, he found that the level of health motivation actually declined with age from third to seventh grade. Only among the youngest subjects was there a preference for health over appearance. These data suggest developmental trends in which physical health motives show a relative decrease from childhood to adolescence at the same time that other competing motives, such as physical attractiveness or social acceptance, may become dominant. However, these developmental trends may not be possible to detect without the use of more unobtrusive methodologies as well as methodologies that directly compare the relative importance of health and social motives underlying health-relevant behaviors.

Do Adolescents Have Consistent Health Life-Styles?

According to Leventhal, Cleary, Safer, and Guttman (1980), a health life-style implies that an individual's diverse behaviors reflect "an underlying self-definition or coherent way of life" (p. 155). If behaviors are adopted or rejected on the basis of their health relevance, then health behaviors would be expected to covary in consistent clusters. Moreover, the existence of coherent health life-styles in adolescents has important intervention implications. If coherent health life-styles exist, then interventions based on general appeals to health should affect a wide range of behaviors, and programs aimed at a particular health behavior might produce wider changes as well. However, if health behaviors do not covary, then interventions must target the most important behaviors (or most modifiable behaviors) individually (Kirscht, 1983).

To date there is only limited information on the extent of clustering of health behaviors. Among adult samples, Mechanic (1979) found no support for a unified health life-style, and Harris and Gluten (1979) found five internally consistent but only modestly related factors: health practices (diet, stress reduction); safety practices; preventive health care (doctors' visits); avoiding environmental hazards (such as pollution); and avoiding hazardous substances (such as cigarettes). Among adolescents, health behaviors have been shown to covary in some ways. For example, many studies have shown that adolescents who regularly drink alcohol are also more likely to smoke tobacco or marijuana as well as to use other drugs (Jessor, Chase, & Donovan, 1980; Rachal et al., 1980). Not only are different adolescent substance use behaviors highly intercorrelated, but they are also associated with other risk-taking problem behaviors (Jessor & Jessor, 1977) such as early sexual activity, delinquency, and aggression, which may themselves have health implications (Jessor, 1984).

Although these negative health behaviors covary, this does not necessarily mean that health concerns are the common link that determines their adoption or rejection. The most extensive theoretical account of this pattern of behavior has been proposed by Jessor and Jessor (1977). Jessor and Jessor describe these adolescent problem behaviors as reflecting experimentation with adult-like status in violation of age-graded norms. According to Jessor and Jessor, the transition-prone adolescents who are most likely to engage in these behaviors are generally unconventional, show greater tolerance for deviant behavior, place more value on independence, have less perceived parent and peer controls, and are exposed to more models for problem behaviors. According to this account, health-relevant behaviors such as smoking, alcohol use, and drug use covary not because of their health implications but because of their common status (along with early sexual activity) as rebellious, problem behaviors.

In contrast to the many studies that have demonstrated high correlations among negative health (problem) behaviors, the covariation of positive health behaviors (i.e., diet, exercise, seat belt use) is unknown. Although there have been limited suggestions of inverse relations between drug use and positive health behaviors such as eating regular meals and exercising regularly (see Jessor, 1984), there is no empirical literature that has addressed the issue of whether a larger health life-style does or does not exist for adolescents. Such research is needed to establish whether or not clustering observed among various health-relevant behaviors reflects a true "health" motive. Moreover, research should be done to identify whether there are individual differences or developmental differences in the internal consistency of health life-styles. Such individual differences are likely to parallel differences in cognitive representations of the health construct.

In short, the above discussion suggests several issues and directions for future research that must be considered in attempting to understand the role of health motives in adolescents' behavioral decisions. These are as follows: (1) whether health schemata exist for adolescents and if so, the nature of their structure; (2) how and when these schemata develop prior to and during adolescence; (3) what is the accessibility of these health-related cognitive knowledge structures; (4) what is the relative importance of health schemata as opposed to other cognitive structures held by adolescents; and (5) whether adolescent health behaviors covary into coherent health life-styles. Only when these issues are clarified will we be able to understand whether health concerns play a role in adolescent behavioral decisions and to specify what this role might be.

ALTERNATIVE BASES OF ADOLESCENT HEALTH BEHAVIORS

The discussion to this point has addressed whether or not health concerns actually motivate adolescents' adoption or rejection of health-relevant behaviors. Applying theoretical principles of social cognitive development, we have considered ways in which cognitive representations of health may change with age and may motivate behavioral decisions among adolescents. We have also made suggestions concerning research strategies that might clarify the role of health concerns in adolescents' behavioral decisions. A further question concerns what factors aside from health might motivate these behavioral choices.

Candidates for other motives underlying adolescent health behaviors can be found by considering some of the unique features of adolescence as a developmental stage. Although adolescence is best viewed as a period of slow and gradual change rather than abrupt discontinuity and turmoil (Dusek & Flaherty, 1981), there are several particular themes that become dominant during this developmental period.

1. Adolescence can be viewed as a time of striving for independence and maturity and of separation from adult control. If so, then behaviors might be adopted as a way of expressing an adultlike status or rebellion against adult values. These motives have already been discussed in the context of Jessor and Jessor's (1977) problem behavior theory.
2. Adolescence can be viewed as a time during which identity concerns become highlighted (Erikson, 1959). Behaviors may be adopted as a way of experimenting with particular identities in that behaviors can express or implement a set of attributes or characteristics. Because of heightened self-awareness at adolescence (Elkind, 1967; Elkind & Bowen, 1979), adolescents may be particularly susceptible to adopting behaviors because of self-image and identity motives.
3. Adolescence can be viewed as a time in which peer relations are especially important (Coleman, 1980). Thus adolescents may adopt behaviors as a way of conveying a particular social image to a peer audience.

A consideration of these facets of adolescent development suggests that self-concept and social motives may be particularly important determinants of behavioral choices in this age group. In particular, adolescents may choose behaviors as a way of expressing a particular identity or self-concept or as a way of protecting their self-concept and coping with threats to the self. We will now review existing evidence concerning these self-concept and social motives as determinants of adolescents' health-relevant behaviors. To date, this evidence has largely been confined to studies of negative behaviors (such as cigarette smoking or alcohol use). Theoretically, most of these social and self-image motives could underlie positive health-relevant behaviors as well. For example, behaviors such as exercise or food choices could certainly be dictated by motives to project a particular social image rather than to attain a state of "health." Several existing health promotion interventions have appealed to these self-image and social image motives in order to enhance positive health-relevant behaviors (e.g., Botvin & Eng, 1980). However, to date, little empirical work has been done to investigate the social bases of adolescents' positive health-relevant behavioral decisions. Therefore, our review will be confined to negative health-relevant behaviors.

Self-Expressive Motives: Social Image Factors in Adolescent Health Behaviors

One reason for adopting a behavior is to use the behavior as a way of implementing a particular social identity. That is, a behavior may convey or express a set of particular attributes or characteristics of the actor. Dressing in a sweat suit, placing bumper stickers on cars, or sporting a Mohawk haircut are all ways in which people can demonstrate their particular social identity. For adolescents, who are particularly concerned with issues of self-definition and role experimentation, health-relevant behaviors may represent ways of implementing these identities in their own eyes. For example, adolescents may chew tobacco as a way of expressing a jock or cowboy image. Having a well-worn ring on one's blue jeans pocket from carrying around a tobacco can may convey membership in this social group.

Some of these identity expressions may seem negative or paradoxical. For example, given the stigma associated with adult cigarette smoking, why would an adolescent wish to express such an image? First, our research has found that some of the associated images are not totally negative, but rather contain both positive and negative characteristics. The image of cigarette smoking carries negative qualities such as foolishness or academic failure, but also conveys positive qualities such as toughness, precocity, and sociability. These positive qualities may be reinforced or created by media influence in which image-oriented advertisements are used to promote negative health behaviors such as smoking and drinking alcohol. A second explanation can be found in the characteristics of adolescents' self-concepts. Adolescent experimentation with social identities tends to be short term rather than long term (Archer, 1982). That is, when adolescents experiment with different social identities they do not necessarily see these identities as long-term commitments. Because most adolescent experimentation with identities tends to be short term, they may be able to view themselves as expressing a "smoker" image without any implication of long-term commitment to adult smoking.

In addition to expressing a set of characteristics in the actor's own eyes, a particular behavior may serve to project that image to a wider peer audience. Thus a behavior might be adopted as a means of impression management, to create a particular image in the eyes of valued peers. Both self-expressive and impression management motives might be expected to be particularly important among adolescents.

Our own research has produced findings consistent with the role of self-expressive motives in certain adolescent health behaviors. As mentioned above, we have found an ambivalent social image associated with cigarette smoking, and we have found particular attributes to be conveyed by chewing tobacco and alcohol use as well. Our data demonstrate that nonsmoking adolescents whose self-definitions and aspirations are consistent with the characteristic smoking "image" are more likely to plan to smoke in the future (Barton, Chassin, Presson, & Sherman, 1982; Chassin, Presson, Sherman, Corty, & Olshavsky, 1981), and that similar self-concept–social image relations can be found for smokeless tobacco and alcohol use as well (Chassin, Presson, Sherman, McLaughlin, & Giola, 1985; Chassin, Tetzloff, & Hershey, 1985).

It is important to note, however, that there may be important stage differences in behavioral motives such that social image factors may be more important in initiating than maintaining health behaviors. For example, Leventhal and Cleary (1980) proposed that there is a preparation stage associated with cigarette smoking in which adolescents perceive and evaluate the social image associated with smoking, and they suggest that this social image is important to beginning smoking. However, once a person becomes a regular smoker, other motives may become more important in maintaining smoking. For example, nicotine addiction or tension reduction may be important at later stages of smoking. Social image factors may be more important for initial adolescent experimentation with health-relevant behaviors than for later adult maintenance or habitual performances of these behaviors.

The notion that health-relevant behaviors may serve self-expressive and impression management functions is an important one from the standpoint of health promotion interventions. For negative health behaviors, interventions might seek to give adolescents alternate ways of expressing valued characteristics and attributes. Several social skills training programs (e.g., Life Skills Training, Botvin & Eng, 1980) take this approach. To promote positive health behaviors, interventions might seek to link these behaviors with a valued social image or identity. To some extent this may be happening naturally as a part of the current emphasis on physical fitness. Advertisements for "light" foods, low-alcohol beverages, and cigarettes with low tar and nicotine feature models posed in exercise clothing and engaging in physical activity. These advertisements reflect the fact that images of positive health are now becoming socially desirable and attractive. Unfortunately, such images are also currently being used to reassure consumers that the new junk food, alcohol, and nicotine products are not *really* dangerous to health. Thus social image factors are being used by advertisers to counter perceived health dangers in their products. However, to date, there is still little empirical evidence concerning the role of social image or self-expressive motivations in adolescents' positive health behaviors.

Self-Protective Motives: Coping with Threats to Self-Esteem

Aside from expressing or conveying a particular self-image, adolescent health behaviors may be adopted as a means of protecting a fragile or threatened self-concept. For example, it has long been proposed that alcohol or other drugs may be used to cope with negative affect or mood states. Hull (1981) suggests that one mechanism underlying such affect regulation involved protection of the self-concept. Hull suggests that alcohol blocks the encoding of self-relevant information and therefore reduces a painful state of self-awareness among individuals who are receiving negative messages about the self. Thus one way that health-relevant behaviors may protect self-esteem is by blocking negative self-relevant information from awareness.

Another self-protective strategy is the somewhat paradoxical use of "self-handicapping" (Berglas & Jones, 1978). Self-handicapping involves behavioral and attributional strategies to protect the self-image from potential threats. In using self-handicapping strategies, an individual arranges the circumstances of performance so that the causes of failure will be externalized and the causes of success will be internalized.

When an individual with a positive but uncertain sense of self-esteem faces the possibility of poor performance on an upcoming task, this task is perceived as a severe threat. In order to guard against this threat, the self-handicapper reaches out for impediments and handicaps to performance so that personal responsibility for failure is minimized. Ironically, however, the handicap increases the actual possibility of failure at the same time that it externalizes responsibility for failure. Berglas and Jones (1978) demonstrated this phenomenon in a laboratory task. Some individuals engaged in a task designed so that they could succeed by using their knowledge and ability to solve a set of problems. Others attempted a series of insoluble problems and were given bogus success feedback after these attempts. This latter group thus experienced success that was not contingent on their performance. Berglas and Jones (1978) hypothesized that these individuals would experience a shaky sense of confidence based on a success that was unaccompanied by feelings of mastery and control. Following this task, all subjects were given a choice of taking a performance-enhancing or performance-impairing drug. Males in the noncontingent success group (but not those in the contingent success group) showed a strong tendency to choose the drug that would impair performance. This was presumably a self-handicapping strategy designed to protect their fragile images of competence from the possibility of failure.

Tucker, Vuchinich, and Sobell (1981) replicated this finding with alcohol use, suggesting that some health-relevant behaviors could serve as self-handicapping strategies. Other health-relevant behaviors such as going without sleep before a big exam or adopting a "sick" role may also serve as self-handicapping strategies. Poor performance is attributed to the impediment, although success (should it happen to occur) is attributed to the individual more than ever—he or she succeeded *despite* an impediment to good performance.

Self-handicapping strategies may represent important motives underlying adolescents' health-relevant behaviors because adolescents are particularly concerned with enhancing their self-image, especially in the eyes of peers. However, to date there have been no studies of self-handicapping in child or adolescent populations and no studies that link self-handicapping to naturally occurring health behaviors in these age groups.

SUMMARY

The goal of this chapter has been to show how health-relevant decision making can be understood in terms of the basic principles of social cognitive development. We have pointed to several important developmental changes that are likely to affect adolescents' knowledge structures that, in turn, affect behavioral decisions. We have also discussed different aspects of these knowledge structures (e.g., their accessibility and relative importance) that influence the extent to which they are actually used in behavioral decision making. In applying principles of social cognition to health decisions, it is clear that little empirical or theoretical work has been done either on the general development of representations in adolescence or on the development of health knowledge structures. It is hoped that one of the outcomes of this chapter will be to encourage researchers to pursue this work. To achieve this goal, we have pointed to several methodologies and directions aimed at clarifying developmental changes in health schemata and at relating health schemata to behavioral decisions.

One important point to be stressed again is that, although adolescents make decisions that have very important implications for health, health concerns may not necessarily be the primary basis on which these decisions are made. As discussed above, a consideration of the characteristics of adolescence as a developmental stage suggests that social and self-concept motives are likely alternative determinants of these decisions. From a practical standpoint, however, what is important is that the determinants of health-relevant behaviors are understood so that programs and interventions can be targeted at these factors. A better understanding of the acquisition of these behaviors will allow for the development of more effective intervention programs (Chassin, Presson, & Sherman, 1985).

Throughout this chapter we have raised specific implications for adolescent health promotion. On a general level, however, what seems clear is that adolescence is a potentially fruitful stage for implementing health interventions. Prior to adolescence, when thinking is likely to be "simple-minded," interventions are likely to produce effects but these may very well be short term and quite easily reversible when new, conflicting information is encountered. Alternatively, subsequent to adolescence, once integrated and stable representations are developed, change may be difficult to achieve. Adolescence may involve a period of relative "open-mindedness" during which new representations are being constructed, abstractions are being made, and differentiation and integration among elements are proceeding. In the self-concept domain, these processes can be seen in experimentation with new roles and new identities. This open-mindedness leads to the potential for change. If positive behavioral changes are incorporated into the consolidation that can occur after such experimentation, such change is more likely to be long-lasting.

However, this period of flexibility and change has the potential for negative outcomes as well as positive ones. Adolescents are likely to adopt new behaviors as short-term experiments without implying commitment to future implications for life-style. This experimentation can unwittingly lead to longer-term effects and commitments as habits and/or "addictions" are formed. If the behaviors adopted are positive (e.g., exercise, good diet), the outcomes are likely to be positive. On the other hand, if the behaviors adopted are negative (e.g., cigarette smoking, poor eating habits, substance use), then unintended unhealthy adult life-styles are likely to follow. Rarely does the adolescent smoker intend to become an adult smoker. Rarely does the adolescent junk-food eater think about adult hypertension or cardiac fitness. However, precursors of unhealthy adult life-styles are likely to be apparent by adolescence. Given the ineffectiveness of treatment programs designed to modify these life-styles later in adult life, primary prevention during adolescence is an important goal for health promotion campaigns.

REFERENCES

Altman, D. (1982). *Understanding health attitudes and conceptions of health and illness developmentally: Implications for health education.* Paper presented at the annual meeting of the American Psychological Association.

Archer, S. L. (1982). The lower age boundaries of identity development. *Child Development, 53,* 1551–1556.

Bargh, J. A. (1982). Attention and automaticity in the processing of self-relevant information. *Journal of Personality & Social Psychology, 43,* 425–436.

Bargh, J. A., & Pietromonaco, B. (1982). Automatic information processing and social perception: The influence of trait information presented outside of conscious awareness on impression formation. *Journal of Personality & Social Psychology, 43,* 437–449.

Barton, J. L., Chassin, L., Presson, C., & Sherman, S. J. (1982). Social image factors as motivators of smoking initiation in early and middle adolescence. *Child Development, 53,* 1499–1511.

Berglas, S., & Jones, E. E. (1978). Drug choice as a self-handicapping strategy in response to noncontingent success. *Journal of Personality & Social Psychology, 36,* 405–417.

Bobrow, D. G., & Norman, D. A. (1975). Some principles of memory schemata. In A. Collins & D. G. Bobrow (Eds.), *Representation and understanding: Studies in cognitive science.* New York: Academic.

Botvin, G., & Eng, A. (1980). A comprehensive school-based smoking prevention program. *Journal of School Health, 50,* 209–213.

Bransford, J. D. (1979). *Human cognition: Learning, understanding, and remembering.* Belmont, CA: Wadsworth.

Brown, S. S. (1979). The health needs of adolescents. In *Healthy people: The Surgeon General's Report on health promotion and disease prevention: Background papers.* USDHEW (PHS) Publication No. 79-55071A.

Cantor, N., & Mischel, W. (1977). Traits as prototypes: Effects on recognition memory. *Journal of Personality & Social Psychology, 35,* 38–48.

Carlston, D. E. (1980). The recall and use of traits and events in social inference processes. *Journal of Experimental Social Psychology, 16,* 303–328.

Chassin, L., Presson, C., & Sherman, S. J. (1985). Stepping backward in order to step forward: An acquisition-oriented approach to primary prevention. *Journal of Consulting & Clinical Psychology, 53,* 612–622.

Chassin, L., Presson, C., Sherman, S. J., Corty, E., & Olshavsky, R. (1981). Self-images and cigarette smoking in adolescence. *Personality & Social Psychology Bulletin, 7,* 670–676.

Chassin, L., Presson, C., Sherman, S. J., McLaughlin, L., & Gioia, D. (1985). Psychosocial correlates of adolescent smokeless tobacco use. *Addictive Behaviors, 10,* 431–435.

Chassin, L., Tetzloff, C., & Hershey, M. (1985). Self-image and social image factors in adolescent alcohol use. *Journal of Studies on Alcohol, 46,* 39–47.

Coleman, J. C. (1980). Friendship and the peer group in adolescence. In J. Adelson (Ed.), *Handbook of Adolescent Psychology,* New York: Wiley.

Damon, W., & Hart, D. (1982). The development of self-understanding from infancy through adolescence. *Child Development, 53,* 841–864.

Dusek, J., & Flaherty, J. (1981). The development of the self-concept during the adolescent years. *Monographs of the Society for Research in Child Development, 46*(4).

Elkind, D. (1967). Egocentrism in adolescence. *Child Development, 38,* 1025–1034.

Elkind, D., & Bowen, D. (1979). Imaginary audience behavior in children and adolescents. *Developmental Psychology, 15,* 38–44.

Erikson, E. (1959). Identity and the life cycle. *Psychological Issues, 1,* 50–100.

Fazio, R. H. (in press). How do attitudes guide behavior? In R. M. Sorrentino & E. T. Higgins (Eds.), *The handbook of motivation and cognition: Foundations of social behavior.* New York: Guilford.

Gochman, D. S. (1975). The measurement and development of dentally relevant motives. *Journal of Public Health Dentistry, 35,* 160–164.

Harris, D. M., & Gluten, S. (1979). Health protective behavior: An exploratory study. *Journal of Health & Social Behavior, 20,* 17–29.

Harter, S. (1983a). Children's understanding of multiple emotions: A cognitive-developmental approach. In W. F. Overton (Ed.), *The relationship between social and cognitive development.* Hillsdale, NJ: Erlbaum.

Harter, S. (1983b). Developmental perspectives on the self-system. In E. M. Hetherington (Ed.), *Handbook of child psychology: Vol. IV. Socialization, personality, and social development.* New York: Wiley.

Hayes-Roth, B. (1977). Evolution of cognitive structure and process. *Psychological Review, 84,* 260–278.

Higgins, E. T., & Chaires, W. M. (1980). Accessibility of intercorrelational constructs: Implications for stimulus encoding and creativity. *Journal of Experimental Social Psychology, 16,* 348–361.

Higgins, E. T., Rholes, W. S., & Jones, C. R. (1977). Category accessibility and impression formation. *Journal of Experimental Social Psychology, 13,* 141–154.

Hull, J. G. (1981). A self-awareness model of the causes and effects of alcohol consumption. *Journal of Abnormal Psychology, 90,* 586–600.

Inhelder, B., & Piaget, J. (1958). *The growth of logical thinking from childhood to adolescence.* New York: Basic.

Jessor, R. (1984). Adolescent development and behavioral health. In J. D. Matarazzo, S. M. Weiss, J. A. Herd, N. E. Miller, & S. M. Weiss (Eds.), *Behavioral health: A handbook of health enhancement and disease prevention.* New York: Wiley.

Jessor, R., Chase, J., & Donovan, J. (1980). Psychosocial correlates of marijuana use and problem drinking in a national sample of adolescents. *American Journal of Public Health, 70,* 604–613.

Jessor, R., & Jessor, S. L. (1977). *Problem behavior and psychosocial development: A longitudinal study of youth.* New York: Academic.

Karoly, P. (1982). Developmental pediatrics: A process-oriented approach to the analysis of health competence. In P. Karoly, J. J. Steffen, & D. O. O'Grady (Eds.), *Child health psychology: Concepts and issues.* New York: Pergamon.

Kirscht, J. P. (1983). Preventive health behavior: A review of research and issues. *Health Psychology, 2,* 277–303.

Korlath, B. (1981). Cited in Blum, R. W., Youth's views of health and services. In *Compendium of resource materials on adolescent health.* DHHS Publication No. (HSA)81-5246.

Kosslyn, S. M., & Kagan, J. (1981). "Concrete thinking" and the development of social cognition. In J. H. Flavell & L. Ross (Eds.), *Social cognitive development.* New York: Cambridge University Press.

Leventhal, H., & Cleary, P. (1980). The smoking problem: A review of research and theory in behavioral risk modification. *Psychological Bulletin, 88,* 370–405.

Leventhal, H., Cleary, P., Safer, M., & Guttman, M. (1980). Cardiovascular risk modification by community-based programs for life style change: Comments on the Stanford study. *Journal of Consulting & Clinical Psychology, 48,* 150–158.

Mandler, J. M. (1983). Representation. In J. H. Flavell & E. M. Markman (Eds.), *Handbook of child psychology: Vol. III.: Cognitive development.* New York: Wiley.

Markus, H. (1977). Self-schemata and processing information about the self. *Journal of Personality & Social Psychology, 35,* 63–78.

Markus, H., & Sentis, K. B. (1982). The self in social information processing. In J. Suls (Ed.), *Psychological perspectives on the self* (Vol. 1). Hillsdale, NJ: Erlbaum.

Mechanic, D. (1979). The stability of health and illness behavior: Results from a 16-year follow-up. *American Journal of Public Health, 69,* 1142–1145.

Meltzer, J., Bibace, R., & Walsh, M. (1984). Children's conceptions of smoking. *Journal of Pediatric Psychology, 9,* 41–56.

Millstein, S. G., & Irwin, C. E. (1982). *Predicting adolescent health behavior: The influence of prior health beliefs.* Paper presented at the annual meeting of the American Psychological Association, Washington, DC.

Natapoff, J. (1978). Children's views of health: A developmental study. *American Journal of Public Health, 68,* 995–1000.

Natapoff, J. (1982). A developmental analysis of children's ideas of health. *Health Education Quarterly, 9,* 130–141.

Rachal, J. V., Guess, L. L., Hubbard, R. L., Maisto, S. A., Cavanaugh, B., Waddell, R., & Benrud, C. (1980). *Adolescent drinking behavior: Vol. I. The extent and nature of adolescent alcohol and drug use: The 1974 and 1978 national sample studies.* Research Triangle Park, NC: Research Triangle Institute.

Radius, S. M., Dillman, T. E., Becker, M. H., Rosenstock, I. M., & Horvath, W. J. (1980). Adolescent perspectives on health and illness. *Adolescence, 15,* 374–384.

Rumelhart, D. E. (1980). Schemata: The building blocks of cognition. In R. J. Spiro, B. C. Bruce, & W. F. Brewer (Eds.), *Theoretical issues in reading comprehension.* Hillsdale, NJ: Erlbaum.

Rumelhart, D. E. (1984). Schemata and the cognitive system. In R. S. Wyer & T. K. Srull (Eds.), *Handbook of social cognition* (Vol. I). Hillsdale, NJ: Erlbaum.

Schlegel, R. P., & DiTecco, D. (1982). Attitudinal structures and the attitude–behavior relation. In M. P. Zanna, E. T. Higgins, & C. P. Herman (Eds.), *Consistency in social behavior: The Ontario Symposium* (Vol. 2). Hillsdale, NJ: Erlbaum.

Selman, R. (1980). *The growth of interpersonal understanding.* New York: Academic.

Sherman, S. J., & Corty, E. (1984). Cognitive heuristics. In R. S. Wyer, Jr., & T. K. Srull (Eds.), *Handbook of social cognition* (Vol. 1). Hillsdale, NJ: Erlbaum.

Srull, T. K., & Wyer, R. S., Jr. (1979). The role of category accessibility in the interpretation of information about persons: Some determinants and implications. *Journal of Personality & Social Psychology, 37,* 1660–1672.

Srull, T. K., & Wyer, R. S., Jr. (1980). Category accessibility and social perception: Some implications for the study of person memory and interpersonal judgments. *Journal of Personality & Social Psychology, 38,* 841–856.

Tucker, J. A., Vuchinich, R. E., & Sobell, M. B. (1981). Alcohol consumption as a self-handicapping strategy. *Journal of Abnormal Psychology, 90,* 220–230.

United States Department of Health, Education, and Welfare. (1979). *Healthy people: The surgeon general's report on health promotion and disease prevention.* PHS Publication No. 79-55071. Washington, DC: U.S. Government Printing Office.

Wyer, R. S. (1980). The acquisition and use of social knowledge: Basic postulates and representative research. *Personality & Social Psychology Bulletin, 6,* 558–573.

CHAPTER 15

Longitudinal Study of the Life Span

PAUL MUSSEN

When psychologists first began to conduct longitudinal studies—about 70 years ago—they were fired with enthusiasm, seeing such studies as potential sources of vital and valid information about how the individual grows and changes in physical, cognitive, social, and emotional ways. The enormous difficulties and inordinate costs of such studies were recognized right from the start, but it was felt that many fundamental questions about human development could never be answered adequately unless individuals were studied systematically over long periods of time.

For many reasons the early enthusiasm about longitudinal studies diminished in a few decades. In the early and mid-1960s, behavioral scientists proposing to do new longitudinal studies, or to extend existing ones, found it very difficult to get funding for their research. Study sections evaluating these proposals seemed to believe that funding more longitudinal research would be "throwing good money after bad."

Happily, longitudinal studies are again in an "up" phase. Although we are more aware of the problems and difficulties of longitudinal research and the limitations on generalization of findings than we were years ago, most behavioral scientists recognize that some critical issues of human development—issues of how individuals become what they are—simply cannot be investigated without using the longitudinal method.

What are these critical issues? In my opinion they can be stated quite succinctly: tracing continuities and discontinuities, stability and change, in human development and attempting to explain individual differences in the course of development; evaluating how biological, social, psychological, and situational or contextual variables affect many aspects of development, and the interrelationships among these; and assessing the impact of early experiences on subsequent behavior, personality, and cognitive functioning. In other words, for understanding real people, living, growing, and changing in the real world, interacting with others and coping with real problems and transitions, there is no satisfactory alternative to the longitudinal method.

At the time that longitudinal studies were initiated, developmental psychology was synonymous with child psychology, so longitudinal studies were originally studies of development in childhood. Some of the major ones eventually expanded their horizons to include data on adult development. Much of contemporary developmental psychology is life span oriented, attempting "to describe, explain and optimize intraindividual change in behavior and intraindividual differences in such change across the lifespan, that is, from conception to death" (Baltes, Reese, & Nesselroade, 1977, p. 4).

THE BERKELEY LONGITUDINAL STUDIES

The Institute of Human Development at the University of California in Berkeley is generally recognized as a world center for longitudinal studies, and it is the site of two prominent long-term intensive and extensive studies. In addition, a number of excellent new longitudinal studies have grown up around the Institute in the last 20 years.

The first major study, known as the Guidance Study, was begun by Jean Macfarlane in 1928 (Macfarlane, 1973). It was designed as a 6-year study to assess the prevalence and severity of behavior problems in a normal sample of children and to investigate the biological and environmental factors related to those problems, as well as the influence of parent counseling. By the end of 6 years, many other, more general questions about personality development intrigued the investigators, so the study was extended to examine the interactions of psychological, social, and biological factors in personality development.

The original sample, 228 participants (every third child born in Berkeley between January 1928 and June 1929), was studied from birth on. Berkeley was primarily a university community, so that the families involved were above average in educational status although below average in incomes; there were very few minority group members in this study.

Height, weight, and health records were kept from birth onward, and parents were interviewed in detail about their own health histories. When the study members were 21 months old extensive data collection at the Institute of Human Development began. Each participant was assessed every 6 months between the ages of 2 and 4 and annually from 5 to 18 by means of medical examinations, health histories, intelligence tests, and intensive interviews with mothers and children. Interview schedules included information on socioeconomic status, interpersonal relations among family members, strains and satisfactions in the home, patterns of discipline, display of affection and anger, and children's appraisals of the personalities of their family members. Follow-ups of the study members were made at ages 30 and 40, approximately, and at the time of the last follow-up, completed only a couple of years ago, participants were approximately 50 years old—truly a life span study (Macfarlane, 1973).

The second major study at the Institute, the Oakland Growth Study, was undertaken in 1931 by Harold E. Jones and Mary Jones in collaboration with

Herbert Stolz, the first director of the Institute of Child Welfare (now called the Institute of Human Development). The 212 participants were 10–12 years old when the study was initiated, and the intention was to study normal adolescent development, psychological maturation, and peer relationships. Although participants were recruited from the fifth and sixth grades of five elementary schools in Oakland, they were all planning to attend the same junior high school. The entire sample was white and 60% were from middle-class families (Macfarlane, 1973).

Participants were tested and interviewed and received medical examinations through the 6 years of junior and senior high school. Observations were made in school and in social situations such as picnics, dances, and athletic events and in a clubhouse established by the study near the school playground. In addition, inventories of adjustment, interests, attitudes, and preferences as well as individual and group intelligence and achievement tests were administered. These participants were also seen when they were approximately 30 and 40 years of age, and at the last follow-up, they were almost 60 years old—this, too, has become a life span longitudinal study.

Given the tremendous amount of data collected, it is not surprising that these studies have been the sources of literally thousands of papers and books. I will briefly summarize a few studies and findings of the two major longitudinal projects that demonstrate the multifaceted nature of the longitudinal method, emphasizing, on the one hand, its power and potential and, on the other, its limitations. Some of the studies involve a life span perspective; others are restricted to particular segments of the life span. After these examples, there are critiques of the longitudinal approach and suggestions for improving longitudinal work, especially in the light of recent advances in methodology and recent assessments of psychology by philosophers of science and behavioral scientists.

My first illustration is a simple one dealing with physical development, specifically, height (Honzik, 1973). If we tried to assess changes in height through group averages based on cross-sectional studies, we would get a false picture of the normal course of development. Examination of longitudinal growth curves of individuals demonstrates that there is great diversity in patterns that is hidden in the averages. Shown in Figure 15.1 are the average heights of a sample of boys and girls from birth to maturity. The curves of growth appear quite smooth, as though there were no real growth spurts. Actually, different individuals have their adolescent growth spurts at different ages, so that spurts are washed out in the averages. Consider, then, the third and fourth curves (Honzik, 1973). The first shows the growth curves of two boys who reached the same terminal height, but with growth spurts at very different ages. One of them had a major growth spurt at 10–12 years and the other at 12–16 years. Individual patterning of growth is lost in averages derived from cross-sectional studies.

But with a longitudinal study we can do more than simply establish large individual differences in growth rates and the occurrence of growth spurts.

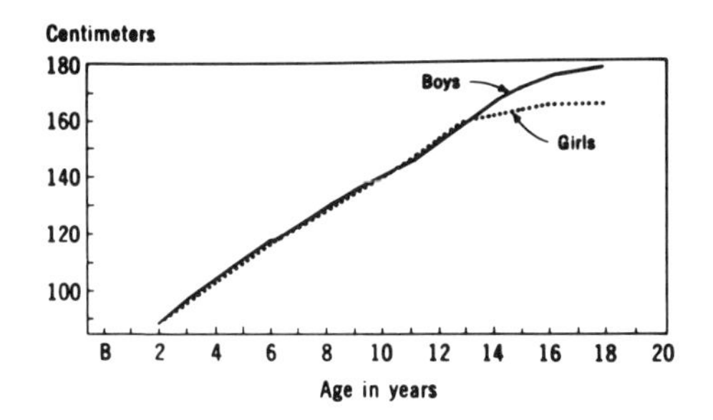

Average heights of a constant sample of boys and girls from birth to maturity. Guidance Study.

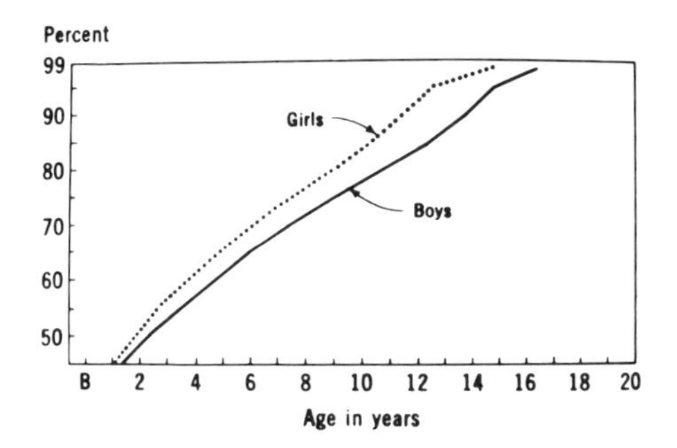

Percent of mature height at successive ages. Guidance Study.

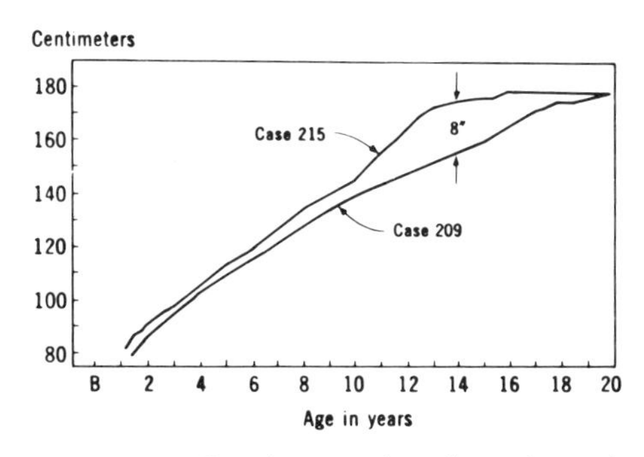

Growth curves of two boys who reach the same terminal height by different routes.

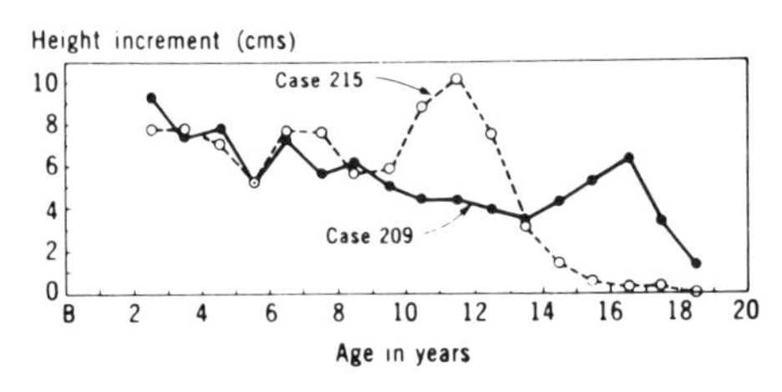

Growth rate in terms of height increments for two boys

Figure 15.1. Height growth curves. (From Honzik, 1973.)

We can also determine whether or not differences in rates of maturation make any differences in the individual's psychological development. The Institute of Human Development studies have included measures of personality and social behavior at many age periods, so we could examine the effects of rate of maturing on personality development during adolescence, and, in addition, because we followed these people longitudinally, we could determine whether any effects endured (Jones & Bayley, 1950; Jones & Mussen, 1958; Mussen, 1961; Mussen & Jones, 1957, 1958).

During adolescence, boys who were late in maturing were rated as less attractive, less well poised, more tense and eager, more attention getting, more restless, and less popular than were those who matured early. They had negative self-concepts and greater feelings of inadequacy, feelings of rejection, and dependency needs. Many of these differences appeared to persist over long periods of time. In a follow-up study of the participants when they were 30 years of age, late maturers were relatively less self-controlled and responsible, more dependent, and more inclined to turn to others for help and support (Mussen, 1961).

Longitudinal studies may also provide a more accurate account of progress in cognitive development than cross-sectional studies do. For example, cross-sectional studies suggest that performance on intelligence tests improves during childhood, adolescence, and into early adulthood but begins to decline around age 30. Longitudinal studies on the other hand have not shown any decline in intellectual performance until age 50 or even 60. These patterns are presented in Figure 15.2 (Baltes et al., 1977).

What accounts for the difference in the decline shown through cross-sectional methods? The best hypothesis is that we are dealing in the cross-

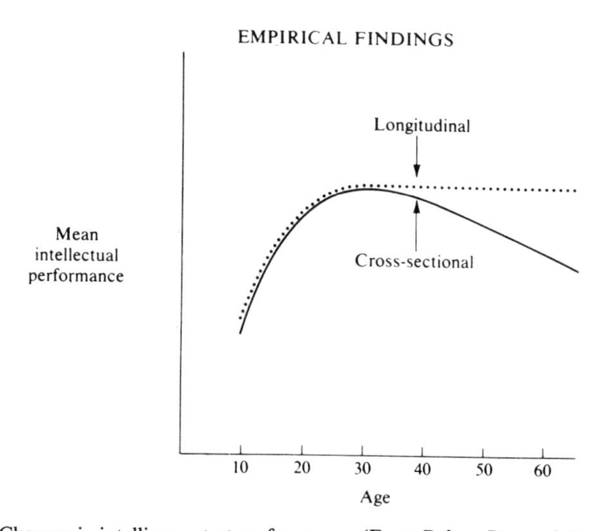

Figure 15.2. Changes in intelligence test performance. (From Baltes, Reese, & Nesselroade, 1977.)

sectional studies with cohort differences, that is, differences between people born at different periods of time. If this study were conducted in 1960, the 60-year-old participants would have been born in 1900, the 40-year-olds in 1920, the 20-year-olds in 1940. Undoubtedly the different age groups would vary on many other relevant dimensions, such as type and average amount of formal schooling, and the recency of their test-taking experience.

Only through longitudinal studies can we assess the stability of intelligence or of intellectual functioning through the life span. Such studies show that tests given to infants under age 2 have little value in predicting future test scores, but the scores of children 4 years old or older are more highly predictive; that is, intelligence after that age tends to be more stable. For example, the correlation between test scores at 7 and at 10 is .78; between 9 and 10, .90. Test scores at ages 8 and 12, and the ages in between, are fairly highly predictive of adult intelligence test performance (correlations above .70). The stability of intelligence test scores is greater for shorter than for longer periods of time (Honzik, Macfarlane, & Allen, 1948).

The correlations are not sufficiently high to preclude the possibility of marked changes in the IQs of individual children, however. In fact, repeated testings of the participants in longitudinal studies show that the IQs of over half the children show a variation of 15 or more points at some time during the school years, and many fluctuate more than 20 points. In other words, even though intelligence test scores seem rather stable at the later ages, the longitudinal data also make clear the need to be cautious in using test scores in predicting the future status of individual children (Honzik, 1973).

The example in Figure 15.3 illustrates this point. Case 534 shows relatively great stability over time, whereas case 567 shows a great many changes in the intelligence test scores, and she is not by any means the most extreme case.

Examination of the case histories of children whose mental test scores fluctuated a great deal showed that these children had many disturbing experiences during their school years. Extremely harsh discipline, divorce in the family, and severe illness were associated with depressed scores, whereas periods of relative tranquility resulted in higher scores.

This example illustrates an important advantage of longitudinal research: its potential for testing stability or continuity in psychological functioning. But we must not be overly impressed or overgeneralize the findings on stability. Even though intelligence test performance is generally stable, the performance of many individuals varies from one age to another. Longitudinal data enable us to look at exceptions to a general rule of stability and to investigate why some individuals' performances fluctuate.

Current debates on continuity or stability versus discontinuity are not centered on physical qualities or intelligence, because both of these presumably have genetic bases; rather they concern the persistence of personality characteristics. Personality ratings of the Guidance Study members, based on interviews, were made annually between the ages of 5 and 16. Bronson (1966) summarized these ratings, dividing them into four age groupings, 5–7, 8–10,

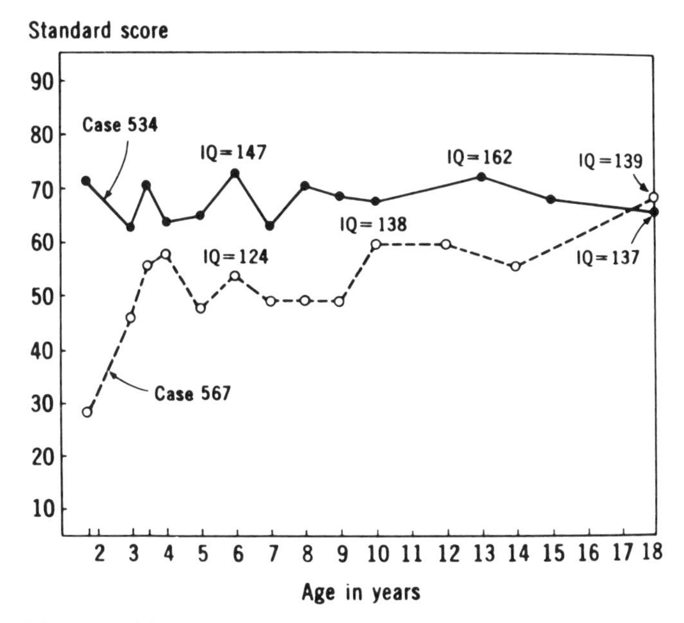

Figure 15.3. Two girls with similar mental test scores at age 18. (From Honzik, 1973.)

11–13, and 14–16. Cluster analyses yielded three major dimensions: expressiveness versus withdrawal, placidity–control versus reactivity, and passivity versus dominance. Expressiveness–withdrawal turned out to be the most stable of these dimensions over the four age periods with a mean correlation of .73 for boys and .65 for girls, high correlations for these kinds of data. The other two dimensions showed moderate stability coefficients, the correlations in the range of .43–.55. These findings are consistent with those of other longitudinal studies, which show long-term stability for active, expressive, extroverted behavior.

When the study members were 30 years old, Bronson interviewed them about their life problems and satisfactions, coding the data by means of a *Q*-sort set devised by Jack Block (1961, 1971). The stability of expressive behavior was impressive. Boys who had been highly expressive as youngsters and adolescents continued to be expressive, gregarious, self-accepting, and productive adults. Expressive girls were as adults outgoing, talkative, and assertive in interpersonal situations, exhibited a rapid personal tempo, and were open about their needs and impulses. In short, for both males and females, expressiveness during childhood and adolescence was related to sociability and lack of reserve in adulthood (Bronson, 1968).

The passive control dimension that Bronson extracted also showed continuity into the adult years. Boys who were highly controlled in childhood were overcontrolled, inhibited, rigid, and humorless in adulthood, and females who were high in the placidity–control dimension as children tended to become calm, self-satisfied, dependable, and comfortably adjusted women. Apparently the control aspect of this dimension was more characteristically continuous in males and the placid component in females persisted (Bronson, 1968).

Probably the most comprehensive of the longitudinal studies on personality development making use of the Institute of Human Development data was that conducted by Jack Block and published under the title *Lives Through Time* (Block, 1971). Block combined data from both the Berkeley Guidance Study and the Oakland Growth Study, assessing patterns of development from early adolescence through middle adulthood. A 90-item *Q*-sort was used to evaluate archival data on the study members for the periods of junior and senior high school, and the extensive interview and test data were collected when the participants were in their mid thirties. Archival data and adult data were evaluated completely independently; that is, the judges who assessed the study members during adolescence—on the basis of the entire pool of data on them—were not the ones who made the adult assessments. This procedure permits the testing of changes in the salience of personality attributes over time, and personality continuity can be measured by correlating *Q*-sort items at different age periods.

Correlational analyses provided convincing evidence in favor of continuity of personality particularly between the junior and senior high school years. Fully 96% of the correlations between junior and senior high items for men and 89% of these correlations for women were significant, and of the correlations between senior high and adulthood, 59% of the men's and 60% of the women's were significant.

From junior high school to senior high school and from senior high school to adulthood, males and females showed stability in maintaining an intellectual, reflective, thoughtful attitude toward themselves and their world. Block's analyses, like Bronson's, showed continuities between junior and senior high school in characteristics such as expressiveness and responsiveness as well as in personal effectiveness and skill and comfort in interpersonal relationships. Boys exhibited stability over the adolescent years in maintaining a positive attitude about themselves and their ability to control their own lives. Between early and middle adolescence females were stable in personal adjustment, social sensitivity, orientation toward others, and sexual interests. From senior high to adulthood, males exhibited great stability with respect to dependability and impulsivity and females over the same period showed evidence of continuity of a passive, conforming, feminine attitude or an expressive, aggressive, autonomy (Block, 1971).

Block's analyses confirmed the common observation that some individuals become stabilized in personality early in life whereas others change considerably over time; some are characterized by stability, others by change. Furthermore, some people change at one period in their lives, others at other periods. To look at change more systematically, Block correlated each individual's *Q*-sorts between junior high school and senior high, and between senior high and adulthood. These correlations are indices of the stability of the individual's composite personality picture across these age periods. The average correlation from junior high to senior high was .75 and from senior high to adulthood .55 with very few sex differences in the correlations. This is strong evidence of general personality consistency with, as usual, higher stability for the shorter interval between the two adolescent assessments than for the longer interval between middle adolescence and adulthood.

Nevertheless Block noted extreme variation among individuals in the degree of personality consistency. The across-time correlations for some individuals were low and for others very high; participants could be classified as stable or changeable in personality, and correlates of stability and change could be examined. In general, those that changed markedly revealed unfavorable qualities of personality: insecurity, dependence, fearfulness, lack of self-confidence. Nonchangers were more self-confident, nonintrospective, adaptable, mature, productive, alert, thoughtful, and fluid. This is just a sampling of the adjectives that characterized these groups (Block, 1971).

There are many other studies of consistency over time and personality based on the IHD data or on other sets of data that are beyond the scope of this chapter. The major overall conclusions drawn from these studies very much favor the notion of consistency and stability of personality rather than the arguments of those who maintain that most personality functioning is situationally determined.

INVESTIGATION OF ANTECEDENT-CONSEQUENT RELATIONSHIPS

Up to this point I have discussed longitudinal studies as the best source of information about continuities and discontinuities, stability and change in physical growth, in cognitive functioning, and in personality. Very little has been said about antecedent conditions or the context in which behavior develops and changes.

Another critically important advantage of the longitudinal method is its great potential for the investigation of the antecedents of psychological developments and the contexts in which development occurs. Unfortunately, only a few longitudinal studies have really concentrated on the contexts of development or, if they have attended to these, they have not analyzed their data in depth. A major exception to this is Diana Baumrind's (1967, 1971) study, which included meticulous observations of children and parents as well as sophisticated analyses of family interactions and the personality characteristics of the study population. Baumrind collected a rich body of data indicating that three distinct patterns of child rearing—authoritarian, authoritative, and permissive—have major differential effects on the personalities of children. Moreover, she has been able to show that the early child-rearing practices have enduring and pervasive effects on the child's personality. She found a marked consistency between many aspects of early and later personality functioning (Baumrind, 1971).

One of the most striking illustrations of the use of longitudinal studies to examine the effects of broad contextual variables—sociohistorical factors in this case—is the work of Glen Elder, a sociologist who analyzed the effects of the Great Depression on the children in the Berkeley study (Elder, 1974). The Great Depression of the early 1930s did not affect all families equally; some suffered severe economic privations, some did not. Elder's design permitted him to compare the stability and change in the psychological development of children in deprived families and in families who did not experience such privation. The differentiation was based on whether family income was reduced more or less than 35%.

Elder noted that greater participation in domestic roles and outside jobs was one of the most salient characteristics of children of the depression. By the time they were teenagers, 90% of the daughters from deprived families were doing domestic chores and 65% of the boys were doing some kind of paid work. These figures are much higher than the figures for peers in nondeprived families. Apparently, the economically deprived children were developing a sense of responsibility quite early in their lives (Elder, 1974, 1981). They were also much more adult oriented than their peers from nondeprived families and were described as seeking adult company, hanging around and identifying with adults. "Economic hardship and jobs increased their desire to associate with adults, to grow up and become adults" (Elder, 1974, p. 82). "Adversity and work experience among those middle class and working class boys served to crystallize their orientation toward work and adult independence. . . . We see no substantial negative effect of this condition or of generalized hardship in the accomplishments and health of these children at middle age" (Elder, 1981, p. 17).

Using the longitudinal data to evaluate the long-term consequences of the Great Depression, Elder found that boys from deprived families, from either the working or middle class, made firmer vocational commitments in late adolescence and were more likely to be judged as mature in vocational interests than were the children of nondeprived parents. In adulthood they entered a stable career line at an early age and developed a more orderly career pattern, generally following the occupation they chose in adolescence. In general, they were high in achievement motivation and the desire to excel. Their economic misfortune, coming in adolescence, seems to have had a salutary effect on their development.

The effect on the girls was different. Those who suffered economic loss seemed to emphasize maternal roles that had been prominently displayed by their mothers during the depression, and a smaller proportion of them entered college. Compared to their peers, they tended to marry early and to stop work at the time of marriage. By the time the depression had its greatest impact, the children in the Oakland sample were old enough to understand the grave difficulties that their families were experiencing and to contribute to coping with them (Elder, 1974).

What happened to younger children who were still psychologically dependent on their parents who were faced with the depression? Elder was able to answer this question by examining the deprived and nondeprived families in the Guidance Study, for the members of this study were very young at the time of the depression. The results contrasted sharply with those derived from the Oakland Growth Study. Whereas the family's financial distress seemed to have an enhancing effect on the life course of the middle-class boys who were adolescents when they experienced the depression, boys who lived through the depression in early childhood showed the opposite effects. For example, in high school the Guidance Study children from deprived families had lower grades and aspirations, lower self-esteem, and were less likely to finish college than their nondeprived peers. They seemed to lack personal meaning, tended to withdraw from adversity and avoid commitments, and generally seemed more self-defeating; they seemed to feel victimized and vulnerable as a result of having suffered in the depression when they were younger (Elder, 1974).

This brief account gives the flavor of Elder's work. Using the available longitudinal data, he was able to examine in detail the broad contexts of development and to examine interaction effects. Specifically, he was able to show how differences in broad social and economic variables affected behavior, differentially at different times and for different sexes and classes. Elder's analyses illuminate the complexity of social influence on the development of behavior. Essentially he made use of a sad experiment of nature, investigating the impact of a highly significant social–economic phenomenon on development.

Although the data gathered in the early years of the Berkeley studies were rich and varied, little information about social attitudes was collected. Later follow-ups included interview questions about sociopolitical opinions. For example, in the 1968–1970 follow-up, when the study numbers were 40–50 years of age, they were asked their opinions about two issues that were polarizing the nation, black demands and the Vietnam War. Each participant also rated himself or herself on a scale from very conservative to radical with regard to each issue. On the basis of their responses and self-ratings, each was categorized as liberal, conservative, or middle of the road. The liberals were those who rated themselves as liberal or liberal radical, believed the Vietnam War was wrong and favored rapid withdrawal, and supported black demands and black militancy. The conservatives were those who rated themselves as strongly conservative, believed the United States must win the war, and were unsympathetic to black demands, believing that the socioeconomic position of most blacks was "their own fault." Using these criteria we were able to classify 73% of the total group; of these 30% were liberals and 70% were conservative (Mussen & Haan, 1981).

Because there were no significant data on early sociopolitical attitudes, we could not explore continuity in this domain. We could, however, examine the developmental histories of study members, who, as middle-aged adults, had different social attitudes; that is, we could determine what kinds of people, judged earlier in their lives, became liberals and conservatives (Mussen & Haan, 1981). The investigation focused on personality characteristics at four time periods, early adolescence (ages 13–14), late adolescence (17–18), early adulthood (the early thirties), and middle adulthood (40–50). Our basic data were 90 *Q*-sort items used to quantify the rich quantitative data at all four time periods (sample items: rebellious; values intellectual matters; is self-dramatizing; seeks reassurance).

Starting with a series of hypotheses based on *The Authoritarian Personality* (Adorno, Frenkel-Brunswik, Levinson, & Sanford, 1950), we confirmed that liberals and conservatives had vastly different personality structures throughout their lives. For example, throughout the prolonged period from early adolescence to middle adulthood (i.e., at all four time periods, extending approximately 35 years), the liberals were significantly more *philosophically concerned* and *rebellious* than conservatives, *valued independence* more and *prided themselves more on objectivity.* Over this long period, conservatives were consistently rated higher than liberals in *submissiveness* and *seeking reassurance.*

The *Q*-sort data also suggest that after adolescence liberals became less moralistic and less conventional and less uncomfortable with uncertainty whereas conservatives maintained consistently high ratings in these variables over the years.

It may be inferred that from early adolescence to middle adulthood liberals are rebellious, more concerned with subjective matters and philosophical issues, show relatively little adherence to conventional values, and value independence highly. These qualities, together with their willingness to acknowledge their own feelings and to regard their own and others' problems with detachment (high ratings in *prides self on objectivity*), are indications of high levels of ego strength. In contrast, from early adolescence onward, conservatives were found to be lacking in independence, relatively insecure, submissive to authority, conventional in their thinking, moralistic, disinclined toward introspection, and uncomfortable with uncertainty (i.e., intolerant of ambiguity). Hence they have strong needs for reassurance (Mussen & Haan, 1981).

The final illustration of the usefulness of longitudinal studies for investigating antecedent–consequent relations is focused on the prediction of life satisfaction in later life from personality structure in early adulthood (Mussen, Honzik, & Eichorn, 1982). This study was based on the mothers and fathers of the Guidance Study population. Infants became study members as soon as they were born and the investigators began to study them when they were 21 months old. At that time, their mothers, who were on the average 30 years old, and their fathers, who were 33, were interviewed twice, once in the home and once at the Institute. On the basis of these interview protocols, clinicians rated the mothers on a series of 21 personality and cognitive characteristics such as amount of energy, satisfaction with life, self-esteem, intelligence, mental alertness, and restlessness. A second kind of evaluation consisted of sixty-three 5-point early family ratings such as health, physical stamina, concern about education, adequacy of income, mother's satisfaction with father's occupation, mother's adjustment to work, amount of leisure time, self-confidence, sexual adjustment, and friendliness of father to mother (Mussen et al., 1982).

Between 38 and 40 years after the first ratings were completed, the surviving parents, 53 mothers and 25 fathers, were again intensively interviewed. At that time the mothers were 69 years old, on the average, and the fathers were 72. The interviewers had not known these parents previously and had no information about them or about how they had been rated 40 years earlier. After each interview was completed, the interviewer and another trained clinician, following standard instructions, independently rated each parent on five characteristics that together comprised the widely used global Life Satisfaction Rating (LSR) standardized by Neugarten, (1961): zest versus apathy; resolution and fortitude; congruence between desired and achieved goals; self-concepts; and mood tone (ranging from happy optimistic attitudes and mood to pessimistic and complaining). Then it was possible to explore the question of what kind of person and what early adulthood experiences were associated with high or low levels of life satisfaction at age 70.

According to the results, mothers who scored high on LSR at 70 had in early adulthood been mentally alert (keenly responsive rather than remote, detached), cheerful, satisfied with their lot; they did not appear fatigued, self-conscious (self-assurance, poise), worrisome, or anxious. In brief, integrating these characteristics into a composite personality picture, we found that the woman who at 70 was well satisfied with her life was, in her early thirties, alert, self-assured, and possessed of a positive, buoyant, and responsive attitude toward life.

Men rated high on life satisfaction at 70 were likely to have been described in their early thirties as healthy but not preoccupied with their health, of good physical stamina, emotionally stable, energetic, self-confident, satisfied with their jobs, and having a strong sense of privacy. Their wives also tended to be healthy (although concerned about their health), self-confident, even tempered, and not tense or worrisome. They and their spouses had little conflict about relatives or the size and management of the family income.

In contrast to the findings for men, only a few of the women's or their husbands' early family ratings were found to be predictive of the women's LSR at 70. As in the case of the men, the women's good health and self-confidence in early adulthood were associated with higher LSR at 70, but most of the significant early predictors involved the home and marital situation: adequacy of income, amount of leisure time, sexual adjustment, marital adjustment ("adjustment to each other"), the friendliness (as opposed to hostility) of the mother toward her husband and child, the friendliness of the husband toward the wife, the closeness of his bond to her (whether friendly or hostile), and husband–wife agreement on expenditures, recreational interests, cultural standards, and discipline of the children. For men, only the friendliness of the wife toward the husband and lack of conflict over the wife's recreation were also significant predictors (Mussen et al., 1982).

Judged from correlations with the early family ratings, particularly after these were reduced to a limited number of dimensions through cluster or component analyses, we concluded that men who were most likely to be highly satisfied with their lives at 70 were, as young adults, relaxed, emotionally stable, and in good physical condition, and, in addition, married women who shared these characteristics. Women's later life satisfaction, on the other hand, seems to be more strongly influenced by qualities of the early marital relationship and other life circumstances, such as adequate income and leisure time. Their own or their husbands' traits were less powerful predictors of their later life satisfactions.

What accounts for these sex differences in the antecedents of life satisfaction at 70? One plausible explanation rests, in large part, on traditional sex differences in the roles, interests, and activities in the parents' generation. For the women, when they were in their early thirties, the roles of wife, mother, and homemaker were primary; if they had other roles outside the home, these were of secondary importance. Consequently, the qualities of early marital and family relationships—and the qualities of personal security, self-esteem, and sense of well-being resulting from these relationships—may be the principal foundations of women's lasting satisfaction with life. The fact that women's later life satisfactions were found to be less predictable than men's may be a result of greater discontinuities over time in their roles and functions.

IMPROVING LONGITUDINAL STUDIES

It must be apparent from these examples that longitudinal studies can be enormously productive and useful in many areas of psychology. From the perspective of developmentalists who believe that the discipline must focus on real people living their real lives and must deal with real problems, it is clear that we must have more and higher-quality longitudinal studies than we have had in the past. Longitudinal studies are extraordinarily expensive and they require inordinate amounts of time, energy, and creativity. What can be done to improve and extend longitudinal studies, to increase their utility and contribution? A few comments on these issues follow, some of them relevant to studies in the behavioral sciences generally.

First, what phenomena should be chosen for study? Clearly we cannot study everything; if we try to—as the early Berkeley studies did—we are likely to come away with less than adequate measurements of many aspects of development and an "omnium gatherum" mess. How then should investigators choose the foci of the study? My own bias is in favor of selecting variables that seem, for theoretical and empirical reasons, to have social relevance, that is, variables that pertain to human welfare and the quality of life. It is not highly socially useful to study longitudinally the development of trivial abilities, skills such as the apposition of the thumb and forefinger. Nor would it seem useful to study longitudinally the development of ability to learn nonsense syllables, unless this ability has proven to be related to abilities such as learning in the classroom or on the job. From what we know or think, it probably is worthwhile to study the long-term effects of variations in child-rearing practices the way Baumrind (1967) is doing. In Baumrind's studies, and in those of Jeanne and Jack Block (Block & Block, 1980), the target behaviors are broadly and carefully defined, socially significant parent and child variables. The Blocks' emphasis is on the development of ego functioning and ego resiliency, tested in many different ways and studied over long periods of time.

It must be acknowledged that what we judge to be feasible and of social utility depends on the culture and historical times in which we live. Not too many decades ago studying the effects of divorce on children's development did not seem nearly as important as it does today because relatively few children experienced divorce in their own families. Problems of drug abuse did not seem highly socially relevant until relatively recently. There are many other examples. It is inevitable that what is judged socially important will vary from period to period.

The zeitgeist or tenor of the times can also inhibit some kinds of studies. For example, until a few decades ago, it would have been difficult or impossible to study sexual behavior longitudinally and in depth. Nowadays, with more open attitudes and greater freedom to talk frankly, we can more readily investigate these issues longitudinally.

Some other recommendations for longitudinal studies are very much interrelated. It seems abundantly clear that behavior and development are joint products of individuals' biological makeups, their personality and abilities, *and* the context in which they live and grow. Longitudinal studies have not been traditionally concerned with the contexts of behavior, emphasizing as they did continuity rather than antecedent–consequent relations. There is an urgent need to include more systematic evaluations of *contexts* in longitudinal studies, as Elder did in the study described earlier (Elder, 1974). But that investigation was done retrospectively; socioeconomic status and the incomes of the families in the longitudinal study had fortunately been collected, so Elder was able to reanalyze the data in terms of economic deprivation or nondeprivation.

In general, however, contexts have not been systematically dealt with in longitudinal research. Thus in evaluating child-rearing practices the Berkeley investigators relied heavily on interviews with parents, hardly adequate data for objective assessment. Baumrind's study (1967, 1971), a more recent one, deals systematically with the child-rearing context, using well-planned, intensive observations of family interactions in the naturalistic home setting. Almost no studies have systematic means of evaluating the school, neighborhood, and peer environments in which the child is developing. We need more input from other disciplines—sociology, anthropology, education, economics—to assist psychologists in making meaningful evaluations of environments and events that affect continuity and change, the contexts that influence stability or modification of behavior.

Closely related to this is the need for more careful and systematic use of *multidimensional, multimethod, interactive* approaches. The psychological phenomena with which developmental psychologists are concerned are inherently complex, almost invariably determined by many factors and interactions among these factors. Again, citing the Elder study, we were able to see the interaction of economic deprivation, socioeconomic status, sex, and age when suffering deprivation on children's behavior. In looking at antecedent-consequent, or cause-effect, sequences we must use multivariate statistical techniques, so that *interactions,* rather than effects of single variables, are highlighted. Until very recently, psychological studies included only minimal biological data, specifically anthropometric measures such as height, weight, and pubertal status. A great deal is now known about the psychological effects of constitutional and endocrinological factors, so it would seem advisable to include more biological assessments in longitudinal studies. Then one could test *interaction* effects of many different kinds of variables, biological, psychological, sociological, historical.

In addition, multiple measures for most psychological and social variables are needed because single measures in the behavioral sciences are not generally adequate. Studies of continuity of intelligence for example would be much more meaningful if they were based on evaluations of several different kinds of thinking and problem solving, rather than on standard intelligence tests exclusively.

Two other aspects of method and assessment in longitudinal study deserve further attention. One is the need for more extensive use of naturalistic methods, including observation of individuals in social relationships in real-life situations. Certainly experimental and laboratory methods are very useful in testing hypotheses, but to understand people in the real world, and to achieve results that we can confidently generalize, we must stress naturalistic observations more than has been done in the past.

Also missing from most longitudinal studies is a phenomenological point of view, in-depth probing of emotions and attitudes, of reactions to crisis situations and life transitions. As part of more naturalistic study, I would advocate more extensive use of self-reports about the meanings and interpretations of events. In brief, longitudinal research is inevitably pluralistic research—pluralistic in aspects of behavior that are studied, in methods, and in analyses of data. To do such research well requires more careful planning and design than most longitudinal studies have had when they were initiated. Many of them started out as fairly straightforward short-term studies that somehow grew simply because investigators became intrigued with new questions and had populations they could continue to study.

Finally, there is the enormous problem of generalizability of the findings of longitudinal studies. A number of prominent investigators such as Baltes and Schaie (1973) maintain that, because different cohorts of participants live in different historical periods, the findings of one longitudinal study, say, a study of people born in 1920, cannot be generalized to another population, say, a population born in 1960. This criticism probably has merit, although these authors may exaggerate the importance of their argument. It is true, however, that we must be very cautious in generalizing findings. Relations discovered in one longitudinal study must be checked out independently in different populations. Consider, for example, the findings from the life satisfactions study of Mussen and colleagues (1982) described above. The most important antecedents of later life satisfaction of women of that generation were their early family life and their relationships with their husbands. But bear in mind that these women grew up in an era with an entirely different zeitgeist from today's. Modern women's satisfaction in later life may be much more dependent on their earlier success or failure in a career, in establishing independence, and in a sense of having controlled their own destinies. Clearly contexts, social and historical events, limit the range of our generalizations. Of course the best test of whether or not the findings can be generalized is to study another population—longitudinally if necessary, if not, taking a cross-section and investigating whether or not the relationships found in one study are replicated in another time period.

This caveat about generalization is important not only in longitudinal studies, but in the empirical work in all behavioral sciences. Almost all findings from studies in economics, sociology, and psychology are of limited generalizability. It seems to me that social scientists in general are—properly—becoming more aware of the need to specify precisely the conditions under which principles or generalizations obtain. Many social scientists and philosophers of science agree that we have not discovered, and may never discover, the kind of general laws that have been found in physics and chemistry. Of course physical scientists are keenly aware of constraints on their findings, but they are usually able to define very precisely the conditions under which generalizations do and do not apply. Unfortunately, although behavioral scientists make sensible guesses and good hypotheses and do the best analyses possible, they cannot measure all the factors that may influence their findings and therefore they cannot be certain about how wide, or how restricted, their generalizations may be.

REFERENCES

Adorno, T. W., Frenkel-Brunswik, E., Levinson, D. J., & Sanford, R. N. (1950). *The authoritarian personality.* New York: Harper.

Baltes, P. B., Reese, H. W., & Nesselroade, J. R. (1977). *Life-span developmental psychology: Introduction to research methods.* Monterey, CA: Brooks/Cole.

Baltes, P. B., & Schaie, K. W. (1973). On life-span developmental research paradigms:

Retrospects and prospects. In P. B. Baltes & K. W. Schaie (Eds.), *Life-span developmental psychology: Personality and socialization.* New York: Academic.

Baumrind, D. (1967). Child care practices anteceding three patterns of the preschool behavior. *Genetic Psychology Monographs, 75,* 43–88.

Baumrind, D. (1971). Current patterns of parental authority. *Developmental Psychology Monographs, 4,* 99–103.

Block, J. (1961). *The Q-sort method in personality assessment and psychiatric research.* Springfield, IL: Charles C. Thomas.

Block, J. (1971). (In collaboration with Haan, N.). *Lives through time.* Berkeley: Bancroft Books.

Block, J. H., & Block, J. (1980). The role of ego-control and ego-resiliency in the organization of behavior. In W. A. Collins (Ed.), *Development of cognition, affect, and social relations.* Minnesota Symposium on Child Psychology (Vol. 13). Hillsdale, NJ: Erlbaum.

Bronson, W. C. (1966). Central orientations: A study of behavior organization from childhood to adolescence. *Child Development, 37,* 125–155.

Bronson, W. C. (1968). Stable patterns of behavior: The significance of enduring orientations for personality development. In J. P. Hill (Ed.), Minnesota Symposia on Child Psychology, II. Minneapolis: University of Minnesota Press.

Elder, G. H., Jr. (1974). *Children of the Great Depression.* Chicago: University of Chicago Press.

Elder, G. H., Jr. (1981). Social history and life experience. In D. H. Eichorn, J. A. Clausen, N. Haan, M. P. Honzik, & P. Mussen (Eds.), *Present and past in middle life.* New York: Academic.

Honzik, M. P. (1973). Perspectives in the longitudinal studies. In M. C. Jones, N. Bayley, J. Macfarlane, & M. P. Honzik (Eds.), *The course of human development.* Waltham, MA: Xerox College Publishing.

Honzik, M. P., Macfarlane, J. W., & Allen, L. (1948). The stability of mental test performance between two and eighteen years. *Journal of Experimental Education, 17,* 309–324.

Jones, M. C., & Bayley, N. (1950). Physical maturing among boys as related to behavior. *Journal of Educational Psychology, 41,* 129–148.

Jones, M. C., & Mussen, P. H. (1958). Self-conceptions, motivations, and interpersonal attitudes of early- and late-maturing girls. *Child Development, 29,* 491–501.

Macfarlane, J. W. (1973). The Berkeley studies: Problems and merits of the longitudinal approach. In M. C. Jones, N. Bayley, J. Macfarlane, & M. P. Honzik (Eds.), *The course of human development.* Waltham, MA: Xerox College Publishing.

Macfarlane, J. W. (1973). Objectives, samples, and procedures. In M. C. Jones, N. Bayley, J. Macfarlane, & M. P. Honzik (Eds.), *The course of human development.* Waltham, MA: Xerox College Publishing.

Mussen, P. H. (1961). Some antecedents and consequents of masculine sex typing in adolescent boys. *Psychological Monographs, 75* (506, Whole No. 9).

Mussen, P., & Eisenberg-Berg, N. (1977). *Roots of caring, sharing, and helping: The development of prosocial behavior.* San Francisco: Freeman.

Mussen, P. H., & Haan, N. (1981). A longitudinal study of patterns of personality and political ideologies. In D. H. Eichorn, J. A. Clausen, N. Haan, M. P. Honzik, & P. Mussen (Eds.), *Present and past in middle life*. New York: Academic.

Mussen, P. H., Honzik, M. P., & Eichorn, D. H. (1982). Early adult antecedents of life satisfaction at age 70. *Journal of Gerontology, 37,* 316–322.

Mussen, P. H., & Jones, M. C. (1957). Self-conceptions, motivations, and interpersonal attitudes of late- and early-maturing boys. *Child Development, 28,* 243–256.

Mussen, P. H., & Jones, M. C. (1958). The behavior-inferred motivations of late- and early-maturing boys. *Child Development, 29,* 61–67.

Neugarten, B. L., Havighurst, R. J., & Tobin, S. S. (1961). Measurement of life satisfaction. *Journal of Gerontology, 16,* 134–143.

Rushton, J. P. (1980). *Altruism, socialization, and society.* Englewood Cliffs, NJ: Prentice-Hall.

Staub, E. (1978). *Positive social behavior and morality: Social and personal influences* (Vol. 1). New York: Academic.

CHAPTER 16

Contributions of Autobiography to Developmental Psychology

JAMES E. BIRREN
BONNIE HEDLUND

The senior author's interest in autobiography was raised while teaching a graduate course on the psychology of aging in Hawaii in 1976. Each day the class was required to write a two-page essay on some aspect of the psychology of the adult life, for example, learning, memory, or motivation. Toward the end of the course the students were required to write an ungraded essay, two pages about their lives as branching trees or rivers, the purpose being to give them a different perspective on development. The following questions were asked: What made their lives flow the way they did? What were the events, people, and circumstances that led to their lives flowing one way rather than another? The answers to these questions addressed many areas. Sometimes a fire burned down the family home and the family had to move, the father took another job in a new city, a mother died, or a wartime draft occurred; such events deflect a life in process into new channels. Sometimes a new teacher can turn on the young student, or a student can form a crush on a teacher leading to important changes in the life course. Fitting the consequences of such experiences into the rubric of a developmental psychology enriches our thoughts about the important processes of life.

Discussions of the class referred to earlier took off in new ways after the two-page essays were presented; it then had the quality of an intellectual "happening" both for the class and for the senior author. Members of the class wanted to keep in touch after the class finished and the author wanted to pursue autobiography in greater depth, to understand what had been uncorked in the single-session exchanges. One of the important features of the autobiographical essays was that class members read them to the group. It was probably the interaction of the group in reaction to the contents of the individual autobiographies that provided the liveliness to the session. Individuals saw parts of themselves in the development of others. Contrasts also developed and the range of individual differences was given detail. Then followed the struggle to form a picture of how most people develop, as well as one of how individuals develop in the same and different ways.

In the year following this class the senior author received a small grant to prepare a course on the topic "Psychological Development Through Autobiography." The funds were used to pay a group of graduate students to prepare papers on the many aspects of autobiography. These papers led to the lecture content of a subsequent course, its reading lists, and the elaboration of the essay topics on which the students of that course were to write. No longer was it to be just a single essay on branching points, but 9 or 10 essays on different topics required over the 10 days of the class meetings.

The development of a course in this area, as well as the senior author's interest, was timely in terms of a trend in the research literature that was beginning to look at biography and autobiography as an important data base. This author's interest in the area was representative of a movement in contemporary psychological literature that has continued to grow over the last decade.

PRESENT STATUS OF BIOGRAPHY

Biography and autobiography have become more popular in recent years, receiving attention in popularly written books as well as in scholarly works. The increase in literature on this subject has been noted in such journals as *The Chronicle of Higher Education* (Paul, 1982) and *Biography,* begun in the last decade as an interdisciplinary quarterly. Scholars in a variety of fields including English, history, and psychology have contributed articles on the topic. For example, Robert Sears, a developmental psychologist, published an article entitled "Mark Twain's Exhibitionism" (Weissbourd & Sears, 1979, 95–117).

The emergence of biography as a major source of contemporary literature and as a psychological focal point is a reflection of the zeitgeist of a changing society. Within psychology itself there is a return to an earlier period when biographical materials, along with overt behaviors, were regarded as useful sources of information about the development of individuals. There is little doubt that behaviorism created a climate within which personal documents were diminished as a useful if not important source of ideas and data about growing up and growing old. For this reason, the publication of B. F. Skinner's autobiography itself may have elicited surprise that the crown prince of behaviorism would take his subjective experiences so seriously as to publish an account of them.

However, with pressures on behaviorism both from the neurosciences and from the humanistic tradition, the brain has again come to be regarded as containing something other than malleable material organized into piles as a function of environmental contingencies. Today, both the "hardware" and the "software" of the nervous system are taken more seriously, as are the statements that individuals make about their development. Here, the basic proposition is that autobiographical materials are important sources of clues concerning the processes of growing up and growing old, clues that might not be readily available otherwise and that may be followed up in designed research.

One example of personal documents as an irreplaceable source of information is the collection of slave testimony that contains two centuries of letters, speeches, interviews, and autobiographies "that reveal the mind of the slave, his private world, the accommodations he worked out with his master, how he survived from day to day, and the configuration of his culture and family life" (Blassingame, 1977, p. xi). Not only is this material of interest to historians trying to recreate the nature of plantation life and slavery as an institution, it also provides the psychologist with information about the development of individuals under incredible social and physical circumstances. The editor of the volume appropriately calls attention to problems of veracity in the accounts of slaves' family lives but notes that "most of the accounts written by the blacks themselves not only have the ring of truth but they can usually be verified by independent sources" (Blassingame, 1977, p. xxxix). His quotation of Roy Pascal is also relevant to the issue of distortion of detail in the quest of a good story: "All autobiographies must, like novels, have a story-structure. But it would be wrong to suppose that this imposes a regrettable limitation on their truthfulness, on their range of truthfulness. It is their mode of presenting truth" (p. xxxviii).

Autobiographies, as oral histories, enable one to reconstruct an historical period. The intent of oral histories is to reconstruct an epoch such as the Great Depression or World War II. A second use of autobiographies is the reconstruction of an institution, such as slavery discussed earlier. For example, the purpose of reconstructing the early stages of the development of a school, church, or business enterprise may be to seek generalizations about the developmental processes of institutions. In a similar manner one can use the autobiography to reconstruct the development of an individual's life and, through the exploration of many individuals, move toward generalization. In autobiography one is dealing with material of significance to the individual, for example, what was important in growing up and growing old and how events were perceived internally rather than externally.

In this regard, the present chapter will review the relevant literature and describe the methodology the authors have used to collect autobiographical data, discuss some of the strengths and limitations of autobiographical data, present some alternative ways of analyzing such data, and introduce some speculations derived from work with autobiography.

REVIEW OF THE LITERATURE

The use of autobiographical information better to understand human behavior dates back to early in this century. G. S. Hall (as cited in Annis, 1967) used diaries and autobiographies as a source of information when developing his theories on adolescence. When behaviorism became a primary focus of American psychology, the autobiography, along with other subjective data sources, was relegated to the fringe areas of psychological research. Since that time, research using autobiographical data has continued, but never as a primary force in psychology.

As in the early case of G. S. Hall, autobiographical data often have been used in theory construction. For example, Murray (1938) used autobiographies along with 28 other assessment techniques to develop his theory of personality. In his book *Explorations in Personality,* he stated that the autobiographies "furnished indispensable data" (p. 420) and suggested that future studies of personality should allow subjects time to develop autobiographical data further. Murray (1938) argued that the basic unit for psychology should be the life cycle of the individual. He pointed out: "The history of the organism is the organism. This proposition calls for biographical studies" (Murray, 1938, p. 39). In Murray's view, only the life span reveals the *themas,* that is, the trends or themes around which behavior is organized; and the life span is marked by periods of assimilation, differentiation, and integration. In development, the individual not only differentiates but also experiences an integration of the self and the development of a unifying life theme that organizes the behavior of individuals and directs further development.

Citing the early proponents of the autobiographical method, in 1942, Allport published his monograph *The Use of Personal Documents in Psychological Science.* In it he made a strong plea for continued use of personal documents in psychological research, of which autobiography is but one possible type. Allport postulated that, given proper controls, personal documents can provide an inner view of the person that may not be accessed through other types of data collection methods. Although Allport's monograph did not result in the movement of research employing personal documents to the forefront of psychology, a small number of investigators have continued to pursue such research.

As mentioned earlier, one use of autobiographical data has been to generate hypotheses and theories. For example, Frenkel, working in conjunction with Buhler, used autobiographies and other life history material to develop a stage theory of development across the life span (Buhler & Massarik, 1968; Frenkel, 1936). White (1952) used material from case studies to develop a theory of personality development; and Buhler & Massarik (1968) constructed a theory of how values develop and are used to guide behavior across the life cycle. Freedman (1974) used autobiographies of schizophrenics to develop hypotheses concerning the perceptual and cognitive disturbances that occur during schizophrenic episodes. And Lowenthal's longitudinal work on coping styles that adults use when facing major transition points in life (Lowenthal, Thurnher, & Chiriboga, 1975) incorporated life history material as one source of information for the study. More recently, Levinson, Darrow, Klein, Levinson, and McKee (1978) used autobiographical reports in their study of men in their middle years and generated a stage theory of adult development.

Counseling psychology, a second area in which autobiographies are an important data source, showed the largest increase of studies utilizing these types of data in the last decades. For example, Shaffer (1954) used autobiography in conjunction with an adjustment inventory to determine the level of adjustment of secondary students. In addition, a number of studies have suggested the value of using autobiographies to assess vocational and personal needs (Cottle & Downie, 1960; Hahn & MacLean, 1955; Riccio, 1958; Tyler, 1953).

A third area that has employed autobiographical materials is that of clinical treatment. Baird (1957) and Tolbert (1959) have used autobiography to increase insight for students in counseling situations. And Butler and Lewis (1982) also see the process of life review as an integral part of old age. They have developed a life review questionnaire for use by professionals who are providing services to older adults. Likewise, Bratter and Tuvman (1980) have incorporated life review into their training program for peer counselors who service elderly persons in the community.

In addition to these movements in psychology, related disciplines such as anthropology, sociology, and history have used autobiography, biography, and related methods as sources of data. For example, one approach used in anthropology is the life history method. Life histories are oral life stories supplemented with biographical information drawn from other sources such as court, medical, or psychological records (Bertaux, 1981). The life history method results in a view of the person's life that is a product of the interaction between the anthropologist and the individual in historical context. For example, Meyerhoff (1978) uses the life history approach in *Number Our Days,* her book about the Jewish community of older adults that live in Venice, California. She presents the lives of a number of individuals and shows how the surrounding community's lack of concern for these older adults is affecting their lives. She also depicts the strong value system that holds this community of older adults together. Using a similar approach, Bohannan (1980) has investigated the nonwelfare poor who live transient lives focused around the center-city hotels in San Diego. The purpose of these anthropological studies is to describe and better understand how these cultural microcosms arise within the larger culture.

Straying from the life history method, Bertaux (1981) has edited a group of articles by sociologists in his book *Biography and Society.* Although these articles are international and cover a variety of topics, their commonality lies in the method used to collect the data. Bertaux calls this methodology *life stories,* and he distinguishes them from life histories on the basis that they incorporate only oral life stories and are not supplemented with other life history documents. The articles in Bertaux's volume examine a variety of topics using life stories, for example, "Social-Life History as Ritualized Oral Exchange," "The Actor and the System: Trajectory of the Brazilian Political Elites," and "Life Histories and the Analysis of Social Change." The use of the term *life history* in these titles points to the confusion that exists within the community of social scientists concerning the best descriptive term for their work. Bertaux is attempting to delineate a clearer separation between these terms, which are often used interchangeably.

A second movement in sociology, that of *ethnomethodology,* also allows for the use of personal documents. Benson and Hughes (1983) define ethnomethodology as being aimed at examining "the ordinary, common-sense, mundane world in which members live and do so in a way that remains faithful to the methods, procedures, practices, etc., that members themselves use in constructing and making sense of this social world" (p. 30). This type of methodology acknowledges as valid any data that illuminate the way individuals understand and experience the society in which they live. Autobiography and other personal documents are often expressions of this experience.

Finally, in yet another discipline, an example of the use of the traditional or published autobiography has been proposed by the historians Cole and Premo (1984). These investigators propose qualitative analysis of autobiographies written by persons over the age of 55 during the last 150 years. The purpose of Cole and Premo's research is better to understand the historical identities of the elderly and to contrast these with the identities of elderly adults in today's society.

The above survey of the literature has illustrated the ways in which autobiography has been used in a variety of disciplines better to understand individuals and society. The use of personal documents, of which autobiography is but one type, has generally been limited to only a small percentage of investigators. However, its application is currently on the rise and is expected to contribute valuable data to future understanding of developmental processes. Still, in order to ensure the effective use of autobiographical materials, we must first take into account the salient methodological issues that arise in the use of this data base.

METHODOLOGICAL ISSUES

Major reasons for the reluctance of psychologists as well as scholars in other disciplines to accept autobiographical data are found in the inherent methodological difficulties in this type of data. Gaston (1980) discusses a major criticism of personal documents such as autobiography under the heading "Problems of Conceptualization of Data." This conceptualization problem has typically taken two forms. First, investigators who look at autobiographical data with a preconceived hypothesis often ignore aspects of the data that do not directly relate to their a priori position. Therefore, alternative explanations of the data are often missed and only those aspects of the data that support that position are considered.

The second form of the criticism is directed toward those studies that use poorly formulated or ambiguous methodologies. The principles applied to the analysis of the data need to be clear and well formulated for it to be understood how the conclusions drawn by the investigator relate. The difficulty regarding the use of any autobiographical data set is in overcoming these problems of data conceptualization without the method of analysis destroying the richness of the material reported by the autobiographer. In this regard, Gaston (1980) suggests two methods that have been developed by sociologists.

One method, *analytic induction,* has been discussed by Denzin (1970) in his book *The Research Act.* In using this methodology the researcher begins with a hypothesis that serves as an explanation of the phenomenon in question. After examining the first case, a decision is made as to whether or not the hypothesis holds for that case. If the hypothesis does not explain the case, it is reformulated so that the information gained from the case is explained. As the analysis progresses, each case is evaluated in regard to the immediate hypothesis. Whenever the data from a given case are not explained by the hypothesis, the hypothesis is corrected to incorporate the new information. The goal of this methodology is to achieve a universal explanation of all data in the sample.

Whereas the method of analytic induction starts with a hypothesis, the other approach suggested by Gaston derives a hypothesis from the data rather than starting with an a priori explanation of the data. In their book *The Discovery of Grounded Theory* Glaser and Strauss (1967) presented the *constant comparative method.* The basic unit of the constant comparative method is the category. Categories are constructed from the data by fitting each piece of information from the data into as many categories as possible. As the analysis progresses, categories become better defined, both in terms of what properties exist within the category and in terms of how that category differs from other categories. Hypotheses are formulated by describing the relationships that emerge among the categories, and a theory is constructed that explains the interconnections of these hypotheses.

The strength of both the method of analytic induction and the constant comparative method is that they tie the results of the analyses to the data that they seek to explain. In addition, both methods consider negative cases and use systematic methodologies; therefore both overcome major objections to the use of autobiographical or, more generally, personal documents as data sources. A problem that exists with these methodologies is one common to research in general: The conclusions are only universal to the extent that cases that invalidate them are not yet identified. A major difference between the two methodologies is that analytic induction requires enough previous research to allow for the formulation of an initial hypothesis. Therefore the constant comparative method is more appropriate for areas of inquiry that have had little or no prior investigation.

A major argument against the use of autobiography as a data source has been that people may not be accurate reporters about their lives. They may consciously or unconsciously withhold or color the information given as with any self-report measure. One study by Shaffer (1954) attempted to assess the extent of this particular problem in autobiographical materials and found it to be minimal. Five hundred student autobiographies were examined for deception and dishonesty. First, an attempt was made to identify gross exaggerations, internal inconsistencies, and improbabilities. Some evidence for deception was found in 3% of the documents. A second approach was to test for honesty by concentrating on objective data contained in the autobiography (e.g., date of birth) that could be verified against other records. The accuracy of reporting was found to be 99% in this analysis. Finally, the material was compared against an independent survey of vocational choices and showed an 85% correspondence between stated vocational goals. Each autobiography was also rated for self-insight. The rating showed a normal distribution and these ratings were significantly positively correlated with an objective measure of adjustment, the Bell Adjustment Inventory.

The issue of unconscious deception is reduced in relevance when studies by cognitive psychologists such as Thomae (1970) and Cohen and Lazarus (1979) are considered. Thomae has developed postulates of human behavior that address this issue. Two in particular support the idea that personal interpretation of immediate experience is a primary factor in how the individual reacts behaviorally as well as emotionally to life events. The first postulate states that "perception of change rather than objective change is related to behavioral change"; the second is that "any change in the situation of the individual is perceived and evaluated in terms of the dominant concerns and expectations of the individual" (1979, p. 7). Likewise, the work of Cohen and Lazarus demonstrates that stress is appraised in terms of threat, loss, or challenge depending on how the individual *perceives* the immediate experience rather than on the objective characteristics of the situation. In other words, research supports the idea that the perception, not the actual occurrence, serves as a stimulus for behavioral change. Since individuals carry the history of past experiences with them continually, it may be more important when doing research on psychological aspects of development to understand the individual's interpretation of his or her experiences than to have objective information about these experiences.

Other issues in the use of autobiographical data include generalizability and the practicality of employing the types of methodologies that yield the most objective analyses. Most autobiographies have been written by well-known or famous people. One purpose of the present research is to obtain autobiographies from people who would be unlikely to write and publish their life stories. Although our sample is skewed in the direction of people who are verbal, highly educated, white, and female, it is a sample that resembles a greater proportion of the general population than that represented in published autobiographical writing. Modifications in methodology could allow this technique to be used in other, more representative samples.

The practicality of using the type of methodologies necessary to do valid research with autobiographical data is an important issue. Methodologies such as the constant comparative method and analytic induction require large amounts of experimenter time. Careful reading and categorization of the material from one author are related to material furnished by other autobiographers. As in all research, sample size becomes an important issue. The number of participants used in a study must be large enough to allow for generalization, but it becomes especially important when working with data sources like autobiography to have a sample size that is manageable.

The above discussion has considered the problems that appear to be inherent in qualitative types of data. The potential of autobiography is that it offers a rich source of data for theory development. Personal documents are of particular value to the psychologist who is interested in the subjective meaning and interpretation of events and experiences in the course of human development. Topics such as childhood memories, experiences with love and hate, concepts of death, experiences of success and failure, and ambitions and goals require the subjective reporting of individuals to be accessible to the psychologist. In this regard, autobiographies have the potential for being a rich source of data for examining the course of human development. Personal documents can be used in the construction of typologies, for example, groups of people who are similar in terms of some aspect of their personal development. Neugarten, Havighurst, and Tobin (1968) as well as Reichard, Livson, and Peterson (1962) demonstrate the usefulness of typologies based on extensive life history material for examining the developmental nature of personality in adulthood. Information emerging from autobiographical research may be used to develop new theories of human development and to generate testable hypotheses about the course of human lives.

Recently, Wrightsman illustrated the need to expand psychological methodology to include autobiographical and other types of personal documents as data sources (Wrightsman, 1980). In his 1980 presidential address to the Society of Personality and Social Psychology, Wrightsman stated that most research in the areas of personality and social psychology uses methodologies and subject selection techniques that place severe constraints upon the ways in which information on adult personality is obtained. Wrightsman quotes the following statistics, which were obtained in a review of 226 articles published in either the *Journal of Personality* or the *Journal of Personality and Social Psychology.* More than 70% of the 226 studies used college students as subjects, more than 50% used experimental manipulations rather than natural settings, and the majority of the studies measured the subjects' performance at only one point in time. Wrightsman suggests that one way to broaden psychology's view of adult development is to increase the use of personal documents in psychological research. Rather than detailing a particular method, Wrightsman proposes that many of the difficulties that arise with the use of personal documents can be overcome by using them in conjunction with other types of data. Convergence among the various types of data can then be used as a measure of reliability.

The primary goal of the authors' research has been to increase our knowledge of the issues in psychological development over the life span by using autobiographical documents as sources of data. By analyzing autobiographical themes, we hope to develop hypotheses about how behavior becomes organized over the life span. It is theorized that the participants' writing can be sorted into themes that will describe normal or typical events in adult development as well as the normal reactions to these occurrences. This process may result in a description of successful aging, an area that is often ignored because of psychologists' tendency to focus on the pathological aspects of development.

GUIDED AUTOBIOGRAPHICAL METHOD

Guided autobiography is a topical approach to the collection of autobiographical data. Using this method, autobiographical statements have been collected from participants in a course entitled "Psychological Development Through Autobiography." As part of the course requirement, participants wrote 9 two-page autobiographical essays, each essay on a different topic. Over the past 8 years, the senior author and an associate, B. J. Hateley, have taught this 10-session course at the University of Southern California. Each session of the course lasts approximately 3 hr and is divided between a lecture and a small group session. The lectures are centered around topics related to developmental psychology and autobiography. The small groups are used to read and discuss each person's autobiographical statement. Groups usually consist of five class members and a facilitator. Topics for each essay are assigned during the preceding class session, and sensitizing questions, designed to help the participants in focusing on the assigned topic, are distributed and discussed when the topic is assigned. Some of the topics that have been used are "Major Life Branching Points," "History of Your Sexual Development," "Career History," "History of Loves and Hates," "History of Health and Body Image," "Money History," and "History of Your Meaning-in-Life Goals."

DATA BASE

Approximately 175 autobiographies have been collected using this methodology. The class participants were adults ranging between the ages of 22 and 85. Women represented 82% of the sample, and 84% of the participants were Caucasian, 11% were black, and 5% were from other ethnic groups. The educational level was skewed toward higher education with 4% of the sample having only a high school education, 13% having some college, 29% having a 4-year degree, 36% a master's degree, and 18% having earned a doctorate. As can be seen from these characteristics, the sample cannot be characterized as representing the general population of adults in the United States.

ANALYSES OF GUIDED AUTOBIOGRAPHICAL DATA

A series of studies has been conducted utilizing these classes in guided autobiography as a data base in one of two ways. First, the autobiographical material collected has been used directly as a data source, most frequently to analyze essays that were written on one or two of the autobiographical topics. These descriptive analyses reflect the preliminary stage of systematic investigation of the data set. A primary goal of these studies has been to develop a content analysis system that can provide not only analyses of an individual's series of essays, but also a method that will be able to make intersubject comparisons in terms of life paths, age differences, and so forth.

Analysis of Mode of Expression

Among the more persistent issues in psychology is the analysis of self-descriptors in relation to other aspects of behavior. For example, Stoddard (1980) made an attempt to differentiate among career women, working women, and housewives on the basis of their verbal behavior. The subjects for Stoddard's study were 11 older women (5 career women, 3 working women, and 3 housewives) who had participated in a course in guided autobiography. All of these women had had some college education. One of the advantages of selecting autobiographical material for these analyses is that the subjects were not checking answers on a multiple-choice form or responding to items on a personality questionnaire. Rather, their verbal behavior was observed, in a sense, without the subjects being aware.

Stoddard's analysis of the verbal content was undertaken by distinguishing those instances when the individual was speaking about other persons and those when she was linking some aspect of herself with someone else. Judgments of the particular words had to do with evaluating the strength and weakness of verbs used in these descriptors. An index of active and strong expressions was developed by taking the ratio of active and strong expressions divided by the total references. A ratio of self-esteem was developed by adding to the numerator the total of all singular and plural self-references in which the subject said something positive about herself, the total of all singular and plural negative references subtracted from the positive score, and the total of singular and plural humorous positive and negative references. The denominator of the fraction consisted of all unassigned units plus the number of positive references. The discomfort–relief quotient was developed by computing a ratio of the total of all items that contained evidence of conflict, discomfort, or unhappiness to the total number of descriptions. Thus the statement "When I was in elementary school, I was the happiest girl in the world" would be scored positively or as relief, whereas "My mother became seriously ill during my adolescence" would be coded as a negative item or one related to discomfort.

The principal finding of this study was that the life roles of the women could be predicted by a discriminant analysis using their scores from the three methods of content analysis. The career women had a higher mean for the activity ratio and the self-esteem ratio, and a lower score on the discomfort ratio. From such results, one might expand the research to include men and the use of different age groups. Certainly, if the current hypothesis holds that people express increasing mastery with age, then one should expect that it would be expressed in the content analysis of autobiographical statements.

The analyses to be reported were based on essays from two classes of the guided autobiography course conducted in 1978. The size of the sample was approximately 46 with an age range of 22–81 and a mean age of 53. There were 8 males and 38 females in the sample, a ratio that is characteristic of the autobiographical data set in general. When follow-up data are presented the sample size drops depending on the particular items being discussed.

Meaning in Life

A sample of 145 autobiographical essays on the topic of meaning in life was analyzed. This sample spanned several years of autobiographical data. The organizing themes, or meanings in life, people express about their lives can change over time as one achieves closure on one part of his or her life or, in many cases, one develops one major thread that ties together his or her entire life. The types of things people choose as meanings in life appear to be finite for the majority of persons. In the present sample, four major categories emerged: altruism or service, 22%; personal growth or a continual desire to expand and learn about oneself, 16%; personal relationships with husbands, children, and close friends, 15%; and either religious or individual belief system, 11%. A miscellaneous category was created for those meanings in life reported by less than 10% of the population. This included work, creativity, hedonistic activities, and learning or discovery. Only 2% of the sample reported that their lives were without meaning in life. A subsample of 50 of the 145 essays was rated by an independent rater. The two raters achieved an 88% agreement. This study suggests that concepts exist in the data and that they can be identified by independent investigators. The areas of meaning in life found in the present study are not unique to this sample. They are similar to those compiled by DeVogler and Ebersole (1980) and Yalom (1980). An additional facet of this population concerning categories of meaning in life was that 11% of the present sample reported a series of life goals that they saw as providing meaning in life even though they were unable to formulate a theme that connected these goals.

Branching Points

The participants' branching points essays were content-analyzed by life event, emotional reaction to that event (positive or negative), and themes, approximately 4 months after the analysis of meaning in life. A branching point was operationally defined as a life event that an individual reports as occurring and having an impact strong enough to cause (in the individual's perception) cognitive, affective, and/or conative change. A theme usually encompassed more than one event. Examples of themes are gaining independence from one's family of origin, establishing a career, helping others, and raising a family. Essays were read in their entirety and general themes were noted. Then the essays were read again and particular events were listed. Whenever possible, the main theme(s) was listed as a way of summarizing the reported life events. The total number of branching points reported were 361 with an average of 8 branching points per person.

Of the participants, 24% reported events related to a family theme; 21% reported school-related events; moving was reported by 13%; work, 1%; death, 9%; and health, 8%. A miscellaneous category was created for events that were reported less frequently than 10 times. This represented 14% of the events reported and topics included were religion, travel, influential others, historical events, retirement, and enlistment in the military service.

A 2-year follow-up of these participants included 25 respondents. The respondents were asked to list the major branching points in their lives, rate the amount of personal choice they felt they had concerning each event (the scale ranged from no personal choice—0—to complete personal choice—3), the age they were when the event occurred, the pleasantness of the event (0—very unpleasant to 4—very pleasant), a description of their emotions at the time of the event, their emotions concerning the event at the present time, and the consequences or how the event influenced their lives. A copy of the original branching point essay was included, but respondents were encouraged to make any changes or additions that they wished.

One analysis compared the branching points listed on the follow-up with the content analysis of the original essays. This analysis was conducted by the junior author. Eighteen (72%) listed branching points that they had not listed in the original essay, but only three (12%) mentioned branching points that occurred since they took the class. All three of these subjects were under the age of 40. This suggests the hypothesis that people stop seeing events as turning points at a certain time; however, due to the small sample size, future follow-up data are necessary to test the hypothesis. Alternative views are that further branching points are not likely to occur in a 2-year time span and that branching points become branching points by reviewing one's life rather than while they are actually occurring.

Thirteen participants (25%) omitted branching points that they had referred to in their original essays. This, along with the participants who added additional branching points, suggests that with the passage of time and/or a different environment while responding, some life events change in their saliency. In terms of actual life events, 47 were added that were not in the original essays and 32 that were in the original essays were omitted in the follow-up data.

The degree of personal choice that participants felt concerning the branching points listed in the original essays was not rated. The self-ratings on the follow-up data showed that 68% of the respondents felt they had no control over branching points that occurred before the age of 12. Control was perceived for events after the age of 12 and, on a 0–3 scale, ranged from 1.29 to 3.0 with a mean of 2.06. The large variance in degree of control among the respondents was evident with a standard deviation of 1.35.

Overall themes that the rater formulated from the events participants saw as branching points were compared with the category(s) that was formulated on their meaning-in-life essays. There was 72% agreement between life events that participants felt were branching points and their statements concerning what made life meaningful to them.

Analysis and Measurement of Change

The second way data from the guided autobiography course were used was in measuring degree of change in those who participated in the autobiographical process. When participants were asked directly about the autobiography course and the effect they felt it had on them, they reported that they felt more centered in themselves, more introspective, more self-confident, more self-accepting, more comfortable about their lives, more able to express themselves, and more open about sharing their values after taking the course. Not all participants gave such glowing reports, but in approximately 90% of the follow-up questionnaires it was reported that the experience had a positive effect on the participants' lives. This figure held not only when questionnaires were administered at the conclusion of the course, but also when responses to follow-ups were solicited up to 2 years after the course was completed. However, these figures are based on the 50% of the questionnaires that were returned. An interesting study would be to follow up those who did not return the questionnaires and determine their present feelings concerning their autobiographical experience.

In an attempt to quantify the change that has been reported by participants, Reedy and Birren (1980) used a battery of tests, which included the Leary Interpersonal Checklist (Nugent, 1978), the Tredway Mood Scale (Tredway, 1978), and the Speilberger State–Trait Anxiety Scale (Speilberger, Gorsuch, & Luchene, 1970). Self-concept was measured in terms of the congruency among real self, ideal self, and social self. Participants were asked to complete the measures on two occasions: once before the class began and once at the conclusion of the class. It was hypothesized that the autobiographical experience would enable individuals to achieve a better-integrated sense of themselves. Integration was measured by the distance between the three aspects of self-concept. If integration occurred, the distance between the real, ideal, and social self would decrease. Of the 45 participants, 60% showed increased integration with the greatest change occurring in the perception of the social self. This suggests that participants' sense of how others perceived them became more like their reported self-perceptions of their real and ideal selves. The most pronounced finding was that at posttest the participants described other people as being more affectionate and generally more like themselves than they had at pretest. In other words, these participants felt that the distance between themselves and others decreased and that it decreased because other people became more similar to themselves. This finding corresponds to reports on the follow-up data. Many participants felt that their attitudes toward other people changed because of the autobiographical process. They reported feeling that other people were more accepting of them, that people were more like each other than they had previously believed, that they were no longer fearful of what others thought about them, and that they felt they were more accepting of the differences between people. These findings suggest that guided autobiography can help people feel more socially connected and thereby can increase the likelihood of interpersonal interaction.

A different measure of change was used with the most recent guided autobiography course. George Kelly's (1955) Repertory Grid Task was given to the class members both prior to and after the class experience. The reason for using this measure was to let the participants be measured by idiosyncratic constructs that they themselves use when evaluating significant people in their lives. Some interesting possibilities were suggested by the results even though a control group was not used. First of all, the major comparison of interest was how they evaluated what they saw as their real or actual selves in relation to the people they would like to be ideally. No change was found in the group data. While trying to understand these data, each individual's premeasure was examined and it was found that the initial difference between the real and ideal self was small. Then, by looking at the difference in scores between pre- and postmeasures for each individual, it was discovered that all subjects except one showed change, but that the direction was divided evenly between negative and positive change. This suggests that change may occur; however, the initial effect may vary in direction for individual participants. Follow-up studies would need to be done to determine whether the direction of change varies over time and which characteristics predict change.

THERAPEUTIC EFFECTS OF GUIDED AUTOBIOGRAPHY

Historically, autobiography has been used by individuals as a method of self-help and/or self-cure. For centuries, autobiography has been used for two important therapeutic goals: as a confessional document to achieve catharsis and as a means to increase self-insight and self-discovery. The earliest known autobiographies, dating back as early as the Sixth Dynasty in Egypt (Misch, 1951), were objective, impersonal, historical memoirs. Beginning with Augustine's confessions in 400 A.D., autobiographies began to be written that were highly introspective and self-revealing. Christianity and the New Testament directed human beings' attention to their inward feelings and the state of their heart and soul, thereby encouraging introspective self-analysis. The popularity of autobiography as a literary form increased dramatically in the seventeenth century. Matthews and Rader (1973) report that, of the 7000 autobiographies written in England up to 1955, 90% were written in the nineteenth and twentieth centuries, about 400 in the eighteenth, 200 in the seventeenth, and only a dozen or so before then. Protestant England in the seventeenth century provided a new religious as well as intellectual atmosphere that was fertile for the growth of autobiography. At that time, confessional and conversion narratives were popular and scientists such as Bacon advocated that the human being's inner world and spirit could be scientifically explored.

More recently, autobiography has been used in therapeutic treatment programs. A number of writers (e.g., Allport, 1942; Butler, 1963; Lauer & Goldfield, 1970; Lickorish, 1975; Murray, 1938) have argued for the usefulness of autobiography as a way to increase self-insight, elevate self-esteem, generate feelings of pride, mastery, and self-actualization, and reduce feelings of loneliness and social isolation. Annis (1967) suggested that autobiography can put individuals in better positions to know themselves and perhaps allow them to solve problems without psychotherapy when the emotional issues are not too great. In this regard, the autobiographical process may have special import for older adults.

A number of theorists have suggested that at each age or stage of life there is unique developmental work to do. According to these theoretical perspectives, the healthy person is one who successfully deals with the key issues or conflicts characteristic of a particular phase of development. A number of contemporary writers, such as Hall (1922), Buhler & Massarik (1968), Erikson (1959), Jung (1962), Butler (1963), and Birren (1964), have suggested that integrating one's experience is one of the important developmental tasks of the later years of life.

For example, Buhler (1967) maintained that fulfillment is the goal of the later years of life. For Buhler, an essentially fulfilled person is able to say that he or she had a good life and that he or she would not want it any different or much different if he or she had to live it all over again. From biographies of over 400 individuals, Frenkel (1936) concluded that the later years of life are a time for drawing up the balance sheet of life and that this is commonly accomplished by the writing of memoirs and autobiographies.

Like Buhler, Butler (1963, 1974) maintains that the unique developmental work of old age is to clarify, deepen, and find meaning in the accumulated experiences of a lifetime. According to Butler, old age is unique in that only then can the individual experience a personal sense of the entire life cycle. Butler argues that the process of life review is a normal developmental task of the later years and is characterized by bringing old memories and experiences to awareness and by resolving and integrating previously unresolved conflicts and traumas from the past. The life review process involves taking stock of one's past and present, deciding what to do with the time left, and coming to a satisfying resolution about the legacy one will leave behind.

Finally, Birren (1964) also has argued that the task for older adults is to integrate their lives as they have been lived in relation to how they might have been lived. The individual must integrate and reconcile his or her past with both past and present life values and goals. Birren notes that certain elements of reconciliation are also seen at other developmental transition points, for example, at the time the mother's last child leaves home or before retirement. Not only does reconciliation provide the opportunity to clarify the past and the meaning of one's life, but it also permits the individual to reconcile the legacy and image he or she will leave behind, to modify future plans, and to reaffirm the past values and goals. It is the belief of the present authors that guided autobiography, by encouraging a life review in a systematic manner, facilitates this process of reconciliation and integration. Reedy and Birren (1980) found that, when older participants in guided autobiography were compared to younger participants, the older group showed greater increases in integration of self-concept. This suggests that the autobiographical process may be especially beneficial for older adults.

Through their work with life histories, Meyerhoff and Tufte (1975) found that society in general does not have a structure for the old to present their life stories and thus facilitate the process of life review. They feel that artificial situations must be created so that such opportunities can be provided. Guided autobiography can provide a setting for a systematic review of the events of one's life. In guided autobiography, individuals relive and remember a wide range of personal experiences such as prosperity and depression, health and illness, births and deaths, failures and successes. Through this process an individual can become aware of the various aspects of his or her life and often achieve a sense that his or her life has been significant.

In addition to providing a forum for the construction of a written record of an individual's life, guided autobiography allows for the sharing of one's experiences with other persons. The social dimension provided by the small groups appears to provide the participants with a sense that their lives have been valid. Other people have heard and acknowledged the individual's life. In a sense, the individual's life becomes exalted and affirmed through interaction with the other group members.

A key feature in writing and exchanging autobiographical experiences in the group is thought to be the process of developmental exchange. *Developmental exchange* refers to the mutual exchange between individuals of personally important historical and emotional events. From our experience with autobiography it appears that individuals who are involved in developmental exchange move from tentatively and guardedly alluding to important features of their lives toward an increasingly open sharing of deeply personal material. In the process of developmental exchange, people implicitly take into account the affective importance of the shared information. Individuals trade personal information equivalent in affective value, though not necessarily similar in content. It is believed that this process of developmental exchange increases self-understanding and self-acceptance, enhances self-esteem, and leads to increased acceptance of other people and an increased willingness to self-disclose with others. Developmental exchange may be the element that leads to the development of affective bonds with others and to a sense of identification with others in the group. This process appears to result in a change in individuals' attitudes toward themselves and others.

Although we have emphasized the value of the autobiographical experience for the older adult, our experience suggests that guided review of autobiography is seen by participants as being of value at any age. A mix of ages appears to add a dimension to the process that might not exist in a group similar in age. Old, young, and middle-aged adults appear to enjoy reflecting on the similarities and differences found among the generations. The younger members of the groups often help older members understand the intergenerational relations that the older people had previously found confusing or hurtful. Older members often become surrogate parents or grandparents for the younger participants. The depth of these relationships is illustrated by the tendency of group members to keep in touch with one another long after the class is over.

It should be noted that writing a guided autobiography and sharing it with others in a group is not the same thing as psychotherapy. It may be that both autobiography and psychotherapy have some processes and outcomes in common. however, guided autobiography is cognitively oriented, involves a directed exploration of specific autobiographical themes generally important in people's lives, and involves an exchange of this autobiographical material with others in a guided discussion group. Psychotherapy, by contrast, is problem centered and seeks to relieve symptoms or limitations in behavior by a variety of psychotherapeutic techniques ranging from insight to behavior modification. Guided autobiography is meant to give individuals the opportunity to explore their past and to gain a greater awareness of their life experiences. It is not meant as a way to solve problems or to deal with specific major difficulties being faced in the present.

SUGGESTIONS FOR RESEARCH

The autobiography instructor and the discussion group leaders were dominantly impressed by the remarkable degree of adaptability in people. Of course, the individuals who engaged in writing these autobiographies were highly selected, and an overriding impression was their history of adapting well to changing environments. The term *coping strategies* does not seem to capture the breadth of adaptability demonstrated. The outcomes in so many instances would seem to defy prediction, as in the case of the little Armenian boy who saw his father and uncles killed in the family compound by Turkish troops. This man had a career in America as a university professor. Another example is that of the Hispanic woman who married a man from Pakistan and went there to live as a young mother in a totally foreign land. Her husband died in Pakistan when her daughter was very small. With that background would you have predicted that she would have become a professor with a doctorate in human development? There are so many examples in our autobiographies of individuals who seem to have transcended their early experience and events to display unique lives.

In this regard, the term *polymorphic adaptability* comes to mind to capture the succession of adaptations seen in lives. This term implies that individuals react to events in ways that show shifts in emotion, changes in goals, and changes in ideas. Here we see the trilogy of Aristotle: affect, cognition, and conation. Adaptation involves all of these in the service of an individual who is assessing the changes in the environment or within the self. Adaptability implies that there is a capacity to deal with environments never seen before, that there is within people a potential for adaptability in concept like that of a small organism that survives antibiotics and becomes a new strain resistant to attempts to control it.

An example of complex adaptation to a circumstance never met before by the individual is that of the physician in Denmark who hid Jews on his tuberculosis ward during World War II so they would escape their Nazi hunters. In this example we see a complex adaptation to a circumstance never met before by the individual. Another example is that of the young educated black woman who married a physician and discovered that he was impotent. After dissolving the marriage she spent her young and mid-adult years abroad educating illiterates in developing countries. The ways in which the crises of emotion, goals in conflict, irrelevant skills and information in the face of demanding events, and even catastrophe are resolved remind one of the organisms who survived evolution's selective pressure by capitalizing on a mutation. To return to the theme expressed here, the histories of lives in autobiography show, above all, humankind's adaptability to circumstances never before met by an individual or culture. Our opinion is that clues to adaptive strength can be gleaned from autobiography, clues that may in part help to reveal the "backbone" of our strength in meeting the highly complex circumstances of life not tested in the laboratory nor gleaned from questionnaires.

As mentioned previously, it has been theorized that review of one's life is an essential part of old age, as well as an activity that might be profitably pursued at various points in the life cycle. In 1922, the developmental psychologist G. S. Hall, best recognized for his work on adolescence, examined the issues of late life. On the point of integration, he said:

> Perhaps the chief suggestion is that every intelligent man, as he reaches the age of senescence, should thus pass his life in review and try to draw his lesson, not only for his own greater mental poise and unity, but for the benefit of his immediate descendants, for whom such a record must be invaluable. Thus the writing of autobiography will sometimes become a fifth hygienic prescription for a well-rounded-out old age. (Hall, 1922, p. 117)

To this we add the idea that written autobiographies may leave a record of how adults grow old, which may increase psychology's knowledge of the issues of adult development.

REFERENCES

Allport, G. W. (1942). *The use of personal documents in psychological science* (*Bull. 49*). Social Science Research Council.

Annis, A. P. (1967). The autobiography: Its uses and value in professional psychology. *Journal of Counseling Psychology, 14(1),* 9–17.

Baird, C. R. (1957). The autobiography. *The Education Digest, 19,* 39–43.

Benson, D., & Hughes, J. A. (1983). *The perspective of ethnomethodology.* New York: Longman.

Bertaux, D. (1981). *Biography and society.* Beverly Hills: Sage.

Birren, J. E. (1964). *The psychology of aging.* Englewood Cliffs, NJ: Prentice-Hall.

Blassingame, J. W. (Ed.). (1977). *Slave testimony.* Baton Rouge: Louisiana State University Press.

Bohannan, P. (1980). Unseen community: The natural history of a research project. In D. Messerschmidt (Ed.), *Anthropologists at home.* New York: Cambridge University Press.

Bratter, T. E. & Tuvman, E. (1980). A peer counseling program in action. In S. Stansfeld Sargent (Ed.). *Nontraditional therapy and counseling with the aged.* New York: Springer.

Buhler, C. (1968). The developmental structure of goal setting in group and individual studies. In C. Buhler & F. Massarik (Eds.), *The course of human life.* New York: Springer.

Buhler, C., & Massarik, F. (1968). *The course of human life.* New York: Springer.

Butler, R. (1974). Successful aging and one role of life review. *Journal of the American Geriatrics Society, 22,* 529–535.

Butler, R. (1963). The life review: An interpretation of reminiscence in the aged. *Psychiatry, 26,* 65–76.

Butler, R. N., & Lewis, M. I. (1982). *Aging and mental health* (3rd. ed.). St. Louis: Mosby.

Cohen, F., & Lazarus, R. (1979). Coping with the stresses of illness. In G. C. Stone, F. Cohen, N. Adler, *Health psychology—A handbook.* San Francisco: Jossey-Bass.

Cole, T. R., & Premo, T. (1984). *Aging in American autobiography: Meaning, identity, and history.* Unpublished manuscript.

Cottle, W. C., & Downie, N. M. (1960). *Procedures and preparation for counseling.* Englewood Cliffs, NJ: Prentice-Hall.

Denzin, N. K. (1970). *The research act.* Chicago: Aldine.

DeVogler, K. L., & Ebersole, P. (1980). Categorization of college students' meaning in life. *Journal of Psychology, 46,* 387–390.

Erikson, E. H. (1963). *Childhood and society.* 2nd ed. New York: Norton.

Erikson, E. (1959). *Identity and the life cycle.* Psychological Issues, Monograph 1. New York: International Universities Press.

Freedman, B. (1974). The subjective experience of perceptual and cognitive disturbances in schizophrenia. *Archives of General Psychiatry, 30,* 333–340.

Frenkel, E. (1936). Studies in biographical psychology. *Character & Personality, 5,* 1–34.

Gaston, C. (1982). *The use of personal documents in the study of adulthood.* Paper presented at a meeting of the American Psychological Association, Washington, DC.

Glaser, B. G., & Strauss, A. L. (1967). *The discovery of grounded theory.* New York: Aldine.

Hahn, M. E., & MacLean, M. S. (1955). *Counseling psychology.* New York: McGraw-Hill.

Hall, G. S. (1922). *Senescence, the last half of life.* New York: Appleton.

Jung, C. (1962). *Modern man in search of a soul.* Translated by W. S. Delland & C. F. Baynes. London: Routledge and Kegan Paul.

Kelly, G. A. (1955). *The psychology of personal constructs.* Volumes 1 and 2.

Lauer, R., & Goldfield, M. (1970). Creative writing in group therapy. *Psychotherapy: Theory, Research & Practice, 7(4),* 248–51.

Levinson, D. J., Darrow, C. W., Klein, E. B., Levinson, M. H., & McKee, B. (1978). *Seasons of a man's life.* New York: Knopf.

Lickorish, J. (1975). The therapeutic use of literature. *Psychotherapy: Theory, Research & Practice. 12(1),* 105–109.

Lowenthal, M. F., Thurnher, M., & Chiriboga, D. (1975). *Four stages of life.* San Francisco: Jossey-Bass.

Matthews, W., & Rader, R. (1973). *Autobiography, biography and the novel.* Los Angeles, CA: UCLA Press.

Meyerhoff, B. G. (1978). *Number our days.* New York: Touchstone.

Meyerhoff, B. G., & Tufte, V. (1975). Life history as integration: personal myth and aging. *The Gerontologist, 15,* 541–543.

Misch, G. (1951). *The history of autobiography in antiquity.* Cambridge: Harvard University Press.

Murray, H. A. (1938). *Explorations in personality.* New York: Oxford.

Neugarten, B. L., Havighurst, R. J., & Tobin, S. S. (1968). Personality and patterns of aging. In B. L. Neugarten (Ed.), *Middle age and aging.* Chicago: University of Chicago Press.

Nugent, M. D. (1978). *Updating Leary's wheel: A new instrument with new uses.* Paper presented at the annual meeting of the California Association of Marriage and Family Counseling, San Diego.

Paul, A. (1982). Biography is one sign of what may be new life in the art of recounting lives. *Chronicle of Higher Education, 24,* 19–25.

Reedy, M. N., & Birren, J. E. (1980). *Life review through autobiography.* Poster presented at the annual meeting of the American Psychological Association, Montreal.

Reichard, S., Livson, F., & Peterson, P. G. (1962). *Aging and personality.* New York: Wiley.

Riccio, A. C. (1958). The status of the autobiography. *Peabody Journal of Education, 36,* 33–36.

Shaffer, E. E. (1954). The autobiography in secondary counseling. *Personnel & Guidance Journal, 32,* 395–398.

Speilberger, C., Gorsuch, R., & Luchene, R. (1970). *State–trait anxiety manual.* Palo Alto: Consulting Psychologists Press.

Stoddard, J. B. (1980). *Content analysis: A study of the implications of differences in verbal behavior in groups of women.* Unpublished master's thesis, University of Southern California.

Thomae, H. (1970). Theory of aging and cognitive theory of personality. *Human Development, 13,* 1–16.

Tolbert, E. L. (1959). *Introduction to counseling.* New York: McGraw-Hill.

Tredway, V. (1978). *Mood effects of exercise programs for older adults.* Unpublished doctoral dissertation, University of Southern California.

Tyler, L. E. (1953). *The work of the counselor.* New York: Appleton, Century, Crofts.

Weissbourd, R., & Sears, R. R. (1979). Mark Twain's exhibitionism. *Biography, 2,* 95–117.

White, R. (1947). Black boy: A value analysis. *Journal of Abnormal & Social Psychology, 42,* 440–461.

White, R. (1952). *Lives in progress.* New York: Holt, Rinehart, & Winston.

Wrightsman, L. S. (1980). *Personal documents as data in conceptualizing adult personality development.* Presidential address to the Society of Personality and Social Psychology, American Psychological Association, Montreal.

Yalom, I. D. (1975). *Existential psychotherapy.* New York: Basic Books.

Author Index

Numbers in *italics* refer to footnotes.

Subject Index